CRITICAL EVIDENCE

Critical Evidence taps into a growing body of scholarship that demonstrates evidence law is fundamentally about power, setting the boundaries of whose voices will be heard and what types of knowledge will be cognizable in courts of law in the United States. The book brings together leading and emerging Critical Evidence scholars to examine the major rules that govern admissibility in court, from relevancy to hearsay to privileges. These scholars show that many such rules are not neutral as constructed or applied, but, in fact, privilege insiders at the expense of outsiders, namely poor people, women, people of color, disabled people, and LGBTQ+ people. Through a close reading of rules and doctrine, *Critical Evidence* shows that evidence law must and should change in order to serve as a system that promotes truth, justice, and fairness for all in the American legal system.

Bennett Capers is the Stanley D. & Nikki Waxberg Professor of Law at Fordham Law School, and has published widely. His co-edited books include *Critical Race Judgments: Rewritten U.S. Court Opinions on Race and Law* (2022) and *Feminist Judgments: Criminal Law* (2022). He has been a visiting professor at Yale Law School, Columbia Law School, Boston University School of Law, and University of Texas Law School.

Jasmine E. Harris is a Professor of Law at the University of Pennsylvania Carey Law School. Her publications appear in prominent law reviews, interdisciplinary journals, and edited book volumes. Harris is a co-editor of *McCormick on Evidence*, one of the leading evidence treatises. A frequent contributor to national public discourse, Harris's commentary appears in media outlets such as the *New York Times*, *Washington Post*, *Bloomberg*, *National Public Radio*, and *TIME Magazine*.

Julia Simon-Kerr is the Evangeline Starr Professor of Law at University of Connecticut School of Law. Her scholarship has been cited by numerous Federal Courts of Appeals and State Supreme Courts and has been discussed in media outlets such as *NPR* and *The Atlantic*. She serves as the Academic Advisor to the Connecticut Code of Evidence Committee and is a co-founder of the Prior Impeachment Reform Coalition. She has been a visiting professor at Yale Law School.

Critical Evidence

Edited by

BENNETT CAPERS

Fordham University School of Law, New York

JASMINE E. HARRIS

University of Pennsylvania Carey Law School

JULIA SIMON-KERR

University of Connecticut School of Law

CAMBRIDGE
UNIVERSITY PRESS

CAMBRIDGE
UNIVERSITY PRESS

Shaftesbury Road, Cambridge CB2 8EA, United Kingdom

One Liberty Plaza, 20th Floor, New York, NY 10006, USA

477 Williamstown Road, Port Melbourne, VIC 3207, Australia

314–321, 3rd Floor, Plot 3, Splendor Forum, Jasola District Centre, New Delhi – 110025, India

Cambridge University Press is part of Cambridge University Press & Assessment, a department of the University of Cambridge.

We share the University's mission to contribute to society through the pursuit of education, learning and research at the highest international levels of excellence.

www.cambridge.org
Information on this title: www.cambridge.org/9781009851558
DOI: 10.1017/9781009851565

When citing this work, please include a reference to the DOI 10.1017/9781009851565

First published 2026

A catalogue record for this publication is available from the British Library

A Cataloging-in-Publication data record for this book is available from the Library of Congress

ISBN 978-1-009-85155-8 Hardback
ISBN 978-1-009-85158-9 Paperback

Contents

* *Excerpted.*

About the Editors

Bennett Capers is the Associate Dean for Research, Stanley D. and Nikki Waxberg Chair, Professor of Law, and Director, Center on Race, Law, and Justice at Fordham Law School.

A former federal prosecutor, his academic interests include the relationship between race, gender, technology, and criminal justice, and Professor Capers is a prolific writer on these topics. His articles and essays have been published or are forthcoming in the *California Law Review*, *Columbia Law Review*, *Cornell Law Review*, *Harvard Law Review*, *Michigan Law Review*, *Minnesota Law Review*, *New York University Law Review*, *UCLA Law Review*, and *Yale Law Journal*, among others. In addition to co-editing *Critical Race Judgments: Rewritten U.S. Court Opinions on Race and Law* (Cambridge University Press) (with Devon Carbado, Robin Lenhardt, and Angela Onwuachi-Willig), *Feminist Judgments: Rewritten Criminal Law Opinions* (Cambridge University Press) (with Corey Rayburn Yung and Sarah Deer), and *Criminal Law: A Critical Approach* (Foundation Press) (with Roger Fairfax and Eric Miller), he also has a forthcoming book about prosecutors, *The Prosecutor's Turn* (Metropolitan Books). His commentary and op-eds have appeared in the *New York Times*, *Washington Post*, *Slate*, and other media. He has been a visiting professor at Columbia Law School, University of Texas Law School, Boston University Law School, and Yale Law School.

Prior to teaching, Professor Capers spent nearly ten years as an Assistant U.S. Attorney in the Southern District of New York. His work trying several federal racketeering cases earned him a nomination for the Department of Justice's Director's Award in 2004. He also practiced with the firms of Cleary, Gottlieb, Steen & Hamilton and Willkie Farr & Gallagher. He clerked for the Hon. John S. Martin, Jr. of the Southern District of New York. He is a graduate of Princeton University, where he graduated *cum laude* and was awarded the Class of 1983 Prize, and of Columbia University School of Law, where he was a Harlan Fiske Stone Scholar.

Prior to joining Fordham Law School, he taught at Brooklyn Law School, where he was the Stanley A. August Professor of Law, and before that at Hofstra University School of Law, where he served as Associate Dean of Faculty Development in 2010–2011, and where he received the 2009 Lawrence A. Stessin Prize for Outstanding Scholarly Publication. He has thrice been voted Teacher of the Year, is an elected member of the American Law Institute, and has served as the Director of Research for the Uniform Laws Commission, a Senior Technology Fellow at the NYU Policing Project, Chair of the AALS Criminal Justice Section, and Chair of the AALS Law and Humanities Section. Governor Cuomo twice appointed him to serve on judicial screening committees, first the New York State Judicial Screening Committee for the New York Court of Claims, and then the New York Judicial Screening Committee for the Second Department. In 2013, he served as Chairperson of the AALS 2013 Conference on Criminal Justice. That same year, Judge Scheindlin appointed him to Chair the Academic Advisory Council to assist in implementing the remedial order in the stop-and-frisk class action *Floyd v. City of New York*. He has also served for several years as a Commissioner on the NYC Civilian Complaint Review Board.

Jasmine E. Harris is a Professor of Law at the University of Pennsylvania Carey Law School.

Jasmine E. Harris is a law and inequality legal scholar with expertise in disability law, anti-discrimination law, and evidence. Her work addresses law's capacity to define and advance social norms of inclusion. Her evidence scholarship explores topics such as the application of critical theories to evidentiary rules, principles, and doctrine and the relationship between evidence and anti-discrimination laws and theories.

Her recent academic articles have or will appear in such leading law reviews and journals as the *Columbia Law Review*, *New York University Law Review*, *UCLA Law Review*, *University of Pennsylvania Law Review*, *Boston University Law Review*, *Yale Law Journal Forum*, among others. Harris also co-edits a preeminent evidence treatise, *McCormick on Evidence*.

Harris also writes frequently about disability and equality law for popular audiences. Her essays have appeared in the *New York Times*, *San Francisco Chronicle*, *Ms. Magazine*, and *Tribune Wire*, in addition to academic blogs such as the American Constitution Society's *Expert Forum* and the Harvard Law School Petrie-Flom Center's *Bill of Health*. She is regularly quoted in media outlets such as the *New York Times*, *Washington Post*, *TIME*, *Forbes*, CNBC, National Public Radio, PBS NewsHour, *Chronicle of Higher Education*, *Guardian*, *Harper's BAZAAR*, and *USA Today*.

A range of federal and state lawmakers and legal advocates regularly seek Harris's opinion on issues of legislative and policy reforms related to disability laws and civil litigation. Harris is a member of the inaugural Steering Committee tasked with developing a National Smithsonian Museum of Disability History and Culture. She also serves on the Board of Directors for two of the largest disability rights organizations in the country: The Arc of the United States and Disability Rights California.

Harris is an elected member of the American Law Institute. Harris was appointed by the United States Chief Judge of the Third Circuit Court of Appeals to serve as Co-Reporter for Third Circuit's Committee on Model Civil Jury Instructions.

Harris is a recipient of the A. Leo Levin Award for Excellence in Teaching at Penn Carey Law and has received recognition for her teaching and mentorship of students at other universities. The Law & Society Association named Harris a co-recipient of the John Hope Franklin Prize for her article, "The Political Economy of Conservatorship," published in the *UCLA Law Review*.

Harris graduated *magna cum laude* from Dartmouth College with a bachelor's degree in Latin American & Caribbean Studies. She received her juris doctorate from Yale Law and clerked for the late Honorable Harold Baer, Jr., United States District Judge for the Southern District of New York. She has worked in both private and public interest law. Harris practiced in the areas of complex commercial litigation, securities, and government investigations as a Senior Associate with WilmerHale. She also worked as a staff attorney at Advancement Project, a national civil rights organization, where she assisted grassroots advocacy campaigns to advance racial justice in education and address the school to prison pipeline through legal, policy, and strategic communications efforts.

Julia Simon-Kerr is the Evangeline Starr Professor of Law at UConn School of Law.

Professor Simon-Kerr is a leading scholar of evidence. Her work on credibility and lying in the law, among other topics, lies at the intersection of evidence theory and critical legal perspectives, while also influencing reform. In her published work on credibility, she has explored how the law reflects dominant historic conceptions of what makes people worthy of being believed, and the implications of this along lines of race and gender. Her research has also highlighted the constitutional dimensions of deeply held evidentiary principles, such as the prohibition on character evidence, and recently she has written about the federal evidence rulemaking process. Her current works in progress explore evidence law and anti-subordination, and law's response to the problem of reason-giving that is indifferent to truth, particularly in the context of generative AI.

Professor Simon-Kerr's scholarship has been cited and relied on by multiple federal courts of appeals and state supreme courts, as well as being discussed in media outlets such as *The Atlantic* and National Public Radio. She is a co-Chair of the Evidence Summer Workshop at Vanderbilt University, a founder and co-Chair of the Prior Conviction Impeachment Reform Coalition, and she serves as the Academic Advisor to the Connecticut Code of Evidence Committee. Professor Simon-Kerr has also written on education law, gender and the law, and law and literature. Her paper "Systemic Lying" was selected for the Harvard/Stanford/Yale Junior Faculty Forum. She is the recipient of the Perry Zirkel '76 Distinguished Teaching Award at UConn Law.

Professor Simon-Kerr received her undergraduate degree at Wesleyan University and her J.D. at Yale Law School. She joined the faculty at UConn after a stint as a Bigelow Fellow and lecturer in law at the University of Chicago Law School. She has been the Maurice R. Greenberg Visiting Professor at Yale Law School. Professor Simon-Kerr clerked for Justice Jaynee LaVecchia of the New Jersey Supreme Court and Judge Kermit V. Lipez of the United States Court of Appeals for the First Circuit.

Contributors

Ronald J. Allen is the John Henry Wigmore Professor of Law at Northwestern University, in Chicago, IL. He is an internationally recognized expert in the fields of evidence, criminal procedure, and constitutional law. He has published seven books and over 100 articles in major law reviews. He has been quoted in national news outlets hundreds of times, and appears regularly on national broadcast media on matters ranging from constitutional law to criminal justice.

Nila Bala is Acting Professor of Law at UC Davis School of Law, where she teaches evidence, criminal law, and children and the law. A former public defender, her research focuses on children's rights and the criminal justice system, as well as emerging technologies. Her recent scholarship has appeared or is forthcoming in the *Yale Law Journal, California Law Review, Michigan Law Review, Washington University Law Review, Boston College Law Review, University of Chicago Law Review Online, Federal Sentencing Reporter*, and the *New York University Review for Law & Social Change*, among other journals.

Valena E. Beety is the Robert H. McKinney Professor of Law at Indiana University's Maurer School of Law, as well as an innocence litigator and a former federal prosecutor. She is a co-editor of *The Wrongful Convictions Reader* (2d ed., Carolina Academic Press 2023), author of *Manifesting Justice: Wrongly Convicted Women Reclaim Their Rights* (Kensington Books 2022), and author of *Pink Crime: Fighting the Criminalization of Motherhood, Pregnancy, and Queer Identity* (The New Press 2026). She is also a co-author of the treatise *Scientific Evidence*.

Jeffrey Bellin is Professor at Vanderbilt University Law School. Professor Bellin is the author of *The Law of Evidence*, a low-cost Evidence casebook, *Mass Incarceration Nation: How the United States Became Addicted to Prisons and Jails and How It Can Recover* (Cambridge University Press 2023), and the Hearsay volume for the "Wright & Miller" treatise.

Asees Bhasin is Visiting Assistant Professor of Law at the University of Maryland Carey School of Law. Her current research lies at the intersections of critical evidence law, race and the law, and reproductive justice. Her scholarship has appeared or is forthcoming in the *California Law Review*, *Yale Law Journal*, and the *Georgetown Immigration Law Journal*, among others.

Kiel Brennan-Marquez is the Wallace Stevens Professor of Law at the University of Connecticut School of Law. Kiel Brennan-Marquez teaches courses in constitutional law, civil and criminal procedure, evidence, and law and technology. His research explores how machine learning and artificial intelligence are transforming our legal institutions – and what, if anything, is lost when human decision-makers are replaced by automated systems.

Bennett Capers is the Associate Dean for Research and the Stanley D. and Nikki Waxberg Professor of Law at Fordham Law School, where he teaches evidence, criminal law, and criminal procedure, and is also the Director of the Center on Race, Law, and Justice. A former federal prosecutor, his academic interests include the relationship between race, gender, technology, and criminal justice, and he is a prolific writer on these topics. His articles and essays have been published or are forthcoming in the *California Law Review*, *Columbia Law Review*, *Cornell Law Review*, *Harvard Law Review*, *Michigan Law Review*, *Minnesota Law Review*, *New York University Law Review*, *UCLA Law Review*, and *Yale Law Journal*, among others.

Alejandra Caraballo is Clinical Instructor at Harvard Law School's Cyberlaw Clinic. Professor Caraballo's professional focus has been on advancing the civil rights of LGBTQ+ people in a variety of civil legal contexts such as health care access, immigration, and family law.

Montré D. Carodine is Professor of Law at the University of Alabama Law School, where she teaches evidence, law & popular culture, critical race feminism, and major race trials. She has published several articles in top law journals, including the *Indiana Law Journal*, the *UC Davis Law Review*, the *William and Mary Law Review*, and the *Maryland Law Review*. She has also published several book chapters.

Edward K. Cheng is the Hess Chair in Law at Vanderbilt Law School where he also serves as Director of the Cecil D. Branstetter Litigation & Dispute Resolution Program. Professor Cheng's research focuses on evidence (especially expert evidence), law and statistics, and remedies. Professor Cheng is a co-author of the five-volume treatise *Modern Scientific Evidence* (Thomson Reuters), is the host of *Excited Utterance*, a long-running podcast focusing on scholarship in evidence and proof, and has hosted the Evidence Summer Workshop annually at Vanderbilt since 2019. His articles have been published in the *Journal of Legal Studies*, *Yale Law Journal*, and *Stanford Law Review*, among other prestigious law journals.

Erin R. Collins is the S. D. Roberts & Sandra Moore Professor of Law at the University of Richmond School of Law where she teaches courses on evidence law, criminal procedure, punishment law, sentencing law, and crimmigration law. Her scholarship critically examines popular criminal system reforms, such as specialized criminal courts, gender-responsive punishment practices, and actuarial sentencing, with a particular focus on how evidence-based, data-driven reforms can replicate systemic inequities and stall decarceration efforts. Her work has appeared in or is forthcoming in the *UCLA Law Review*, *NYU Law Review*, *Georgetown Law Journal*, and *BYU Law Review*, among others.

Caroline L. Davidson is the Norma J. Paulus Professor of Law at Willamette Law School. Professor Davidson's scholarship explores international and comparative criminal law and procedure, transitional justice, and human rights. In particular, it focuses on the relationship and tensions between human rights law and international criminal law, domestic responses to atrocity crimes, and criminal law responses to sexual and gender-based violence. Her work has been published in leading journals, including the *Cardozo Law Review*, *Harvard Journal of Law & Gender*, *Virginia Journal of International Law*, and *Columbia Human Rights Law Review*, among others.

Andrea L. Dennis is the John Byrd Martin Chair of Law at the University of Georgia School of Law, where she has also served as Associate Dean for Academic Affairs. A former assistant Federal Public Defender, she has taught criminal law, evidence, criminal procedure, children and the law, and family law. Her scholarship explores criminal defense lawyering, race and criminal justice, criminal informants and cooperators, youth advocacy, legal socialization of youth and the cradle-to-prison pipeline. She is co-author of the book *Rap on Trial: Race, Lyrics and Guilt in America* (The New Press 2019), which has received international attention and in 2020 won a Hugh M. Hefner First Amendment Award. Practitioners and U.S. courts nationwide have cited her research on rap lyrics as criminal evidence.

George Fisher is the Judge John Crown Professor of Law at Stanford Law School and Faculty Co-Director of the Criminal Prosecution Clinic. Professor Fisher is a former Massachusetts assistant attorney general and assistant district attorney. In his scholarship he explores the history of criminal law and criminal institutions from prisons to juries, from plea bargaining to the regulation of alcohol and drugs. Professor Fisher is a four-time winner of the John Bingham Hurlbut Award for Excellence in Teaching at Stanford Law School.

Michele Gilman is the Venable Professor of Law at the University of Baltimore Law School. She is also the Director of the Saul Ewing Advocacy Clinic, and Co-Director of the Center on Applied Feminism. Professor Gilman's scholarship focuses on how data-centric technologies impact marginalized people and the law's response to those impacts. Her articles have been published in the *California Law Review*, the *Vanderbilt Law Review*, the *Washington University Law Review*, and the *Fordham Law Review*, among many others.

Jasmine B. Gonzales Rose is Professor of Law and Class of 1960 Scholar at the Boston University School of Law and a leading Critical Evidence scholar whose research examines how race, racism, and anti-racism are utilized and considered as sources of proof in litigation, as well as how juror language disenfranchisement systematically limits who can serve as fact finders. Her scholarship has been published or is forthcoming in numerous journals, including the *Yale Law Journal*, *Boston University Law Review*, *Minnesota Law Review*, *Wisconsin Law Review*, *Hastings Law Journal*, *Harvard Civil Rights-Civil Liberties Law Review*, and *New York University Review of Law and Social Change*, as well as in several edited volumes.

Daniel S. Harawa is Professor of Law at NYU School of Law and the Director of the Federal Appellate Clinic, where his work focuses on race and the criminal legal system. Daniel's scholarship has appeared or is forthcoming in the *Harvard Law Review*, *Yale Law Journal Forum*, *California Law Review*, *Georgetown Law Journal*, *Washington University Law Review*, and *Minnesota Law Review*, among other journals.

Jasmine E. Harris is Professor of Law at the University of Pennsylvania Carey Law School. She is a law and inequality legal scholar with expertise in disability law, anti-discrimination law, and evidence. Her work addresses law's capacity to define and advance social norms of inclusion. Her evidence scholarship explores topics such as the epistemic tensions in evidence law and anti-discrimination law. Her recent academic articles have or will appear in such leading law reviews and journals as the *Columbia Law Review*, *New York University Law Review*, *UCLA Law Review*, *University of Pennsylvania Law Review*, *Boston University Law Review*, *Yale Law Journal Forum*, among others.

Alexis Hoag-Fordjour is the David Dinkins '56 Professor of Law and Co-Director of the Center for Criminal Justice at Brooklyn Law School, where she teaches and writes in the areas of criminal law and procedure, evidence, and abolition. Her scholarship focuses on criminal procedure, particularly the right to counsel, and how race and ethnicity have impacted the jurisprudence. Her writing has appeared in the *New York University Law Review* (twice), *Michigan Law Review*, *Fordham Law Review*, *U.C. Davis Law Review*, *Harvard Civil Rights-Civil Liberties Law Review*, and other journals.

Edward J. Imwinkelried is the Edward L. Barrett, Jr. Professor of Law Emeritus at UC Davis School of Law. He has written numerous books and articles on Evidence – his book *Scientific Evidence* is considered a classic in the field – and his work has been cited in over 900 federal and state judicial decisions, including by the U.S. Supreme Court in the groundbreaking case *Daubert v. Merrell Dow Pharmaceuticals*. In 2020, the Evidence Law Section of the American Association of Law Schools honored him with the John Henry Wigmore Award for Lifetime Achievement.

Tom Lininger is the Orlando John and Marian H. Hollis Professor at the University of Oregon School of Law. One of Lininger's research interests is the application of the evidence rules to accusers and defendants in prosecutions of domestic violence and sexual assault. Lininger's latest scholarship has advocated for revisions to ethical and evidentiary codes in order to promote access to justice and ensure fair treatment of indigent parties. His scholarship has appeared in the *Duke Law Journal, Virginia Law Review, Michigan Law Review, Northwestern University Law Review, Cornell Law Review, Texas Law Review*, and *Minnesota Law Review*, among other journals.

G. Alexander Nunn is Associate Professor of Law at Texas A&M School of Law. Professor Nunn has expertise in evidence and proof and evidence and federal courts. He explores how evidentiary rules and the allocation of decision-making authority in the courtroom affect verdict accuracy, efficiency, and legitimacy. His publications have appeared in top law reviews and journals including the *University of Pennsylvania Law Review, Cornell Law Review, Notre Dame Law Review, Emory Law Journal*, and *Northwestern Law Review*, among others.

Ngozi Okidegbe is Associate Professor of Law at Boston University Law School, an Assistant Professor of Computing & Data Sciences, and Michaels Faculty Research Scholar at Boston University. Her research focuses on law and technology, evidence, criminal procedure, and racial justice. Her recent scholarship has appeared or is forthcoming in *Critical Analysis of Law, Connecticut Law Review, Wisconsin Law Review, UCLA Law Review, Cornell Law Review, and Michigan Law Review.*

Jennifer D. Oliva is Professor of Law and Val Nolan Faculty Fellow at Indiana University's Maurer School of Law. Her research and teaching interests include health law and policy, privacy law, evidence, torts, and complex litigation. Her scholarship has been published by or is forthcoming in, among other publications, the *Virginia Law Review, California Law Review, Duke Law Journal, Northwestern University Law Review*, and *UCLA Law Review.*

Aviva A. Orenstein is Professor of Law and the Karen Lake Buttrey and Donald W. Buttrey Chair at the Indiana University's Mauer School of Law. Professor Orenstein writes and teaches in the area of evidence. More specifically, her scholarly interests concern the intersection of evidence law and culture, and she is currently writing about jurors' emotions and how the emotion of regret can justify rules excluding character evidence. Orenstein has authored three books and several articles published in notable publications.

Anna Roberts is Professor of Law at Brooklyn Law School, with articles published in journals that include the *University of Chicago Law Review, Vanderbilt Law Review, Washington University Law Review, Minnesota Law Review, Boston University*

Law Review, *Boston College Law Review*, *Alabama Law Review*, and *U.C. Davis Law Review*, and a book chapter published by Oxford University Press. Roberts's scholarship focuses on the contrast between how criminal records are formed and how they and those who have them are viewed and discussed. She has explored this contrast in topics such as prior conviction impeachment, exclusion of people with criminal records from juries, and criminal system vocabulary.

Gabriela Rodriguez graduated with a Juris Doctor degree from the University of Connecticut School of Law in January of 2026. During Law School, she was a law student representative with UConn's Asylum and Human Rights Clinic. Before attending law school, she acted as a case manager for humanitarian and family-based immigration cases at an immigration law firm.

Franklin D. Rosenblatt is Associate Professor of Law at Mississippi College School of Law. He writes and teaches about constitutional law, evidence, international criminal law, and military law. His main research interest is disciplinary and penal sanctions for members of national armed forces. He is a former U.S. Army JAG officer and current President of the National Institute of Military Justice.

Julia Simon-Kerr is the Evangeline Starr Professor of Law at the University of Connecticut School of Law where she teaches evidence, civil procedure, and a seminar on law & lying. Professor Simon-Kerr is a leading scholar of evidence. Her work on credibility and lying in the law, among other topics, lies at the intersection of evidence theory and critical legal perspectives, while also influencing reform. In her published work on credibility, she has explored how gender influences the types of evidence being used to impeach witnesses, how much of United States' credibility doctrine rests on outmoded proxies for social worthiness, and how the law reflects deeply held societal conceptions of what makes people believable.

Maneka Sinha is Professor Law at the George Washington University School of Law. She was formerly Visiting Professor of Clinical Law at NYU School of Law, where she was the founding Director of the Forensic Defense Clinic. She also previously taught at the University of Maryland Carey Law School, where she directed the Criminal Defense Clinic and taught courses on forensic evidence and technology. She has extensive experience in criminal litigation and is recognized for her expertise in forensic evidence and technology issues. Maneka's research explores the use of forensic evidence and policing technology in the criminal legal system.

David A. Sklansky is the Stanley Morrison Professor of Law at Stanford Law School and Faculty Co-Director, Stanford Criminal Justice Center. Professor Sklansky teaches and writes about policing, prosecution, criminal law, and the law of evidence. His newest book, *Criminal Justice in Divided America: Police, Punishment, and the Future of Our Democracy*, was published by Harvard University Press.

Professor Sklansky is also a faculty affiliate of Stanford's Center for Comparative Studies in Race and Ethnicity.

Deirdre M. Smith is Professor of Law Emerita at the University of Maine Law School. During her time as a full-time member of the faculty, she taught a range of courses, including Evidence, Remedies, Professional Responsibility, Disability Law Seminar, General Practice Clinic, and Lawyering Skills for Clinical Practice. She is highly regarded for her extensive scholarship, which has focused most recently on court systems, judicial ethics, minor guardianship, adoption, and kinship care.

Rebecca Wexler is the Alfred W. Bressler Professor of Law at Columbia Law School. Rebecca Wexler's teaching and research sit at the intersection of law and technology, with a specific focus on privacy and secrecy in the context of the criminal legal system. Her work has explored topics including trade secrets, data privacy, and law enforcement privilege. Wexler's scholarship has appeared in the *Michigan Law Review*, *Harvard Law Review*, *Stanford Law Review*, *The Yale Law Journal Forum*, *NYU Law Review*, *UCLA Law Review*, *Texas Law Review*, *Vanderbilt Law Review*, and *Berkeley Technology Law Journal*, as well as in peer-reviewed computer science publications.

Foreword: An Outsider's Tribute

Edward K. Cheng

I am honored to write the foreword to this pioneering volume on critical approaches to evidence law. I count this volume's editors and contributors among my closest colleagues and friends in the field, scholars whom I have long respected and learned from. More broadly, as someone who cares deeply about building the field of evidence, I am delighted to see the development of new schools of thought, which are essential to our field's vibrancy. An academic field without dissension, controversies, and challengers is ultimately a moribund one. The insights in this volume and the intellectual energy behind them are thus not only important to evidence law today, but to its future as well.

But more than anything, I am honored to write this foreword because I am emphatically *not* a Critical Evidence scholar. I firmly believe that evidence law's primary (if not sole) function should be the pursuit of empirically accurate results. My normative commitments are therefore partly in tension with some of the contributing authors' positions in this book. And yet, the editors have generously and graciously entrusted me with this task, an indication of the special community we have built that values open critique and dialogue with other viewpoints.

* * *

Critical scholarship offers an important lens for all evidence scholars, critical and non-critical alike. For those of us focused on accuracy, the work in this volume uncovers areas in which the evidentiary system – sometimes by accident, sometimes by design – fails to live up to those accuracy goals. We are all the product of our individual backgrounds and experiences, and to the extent that the legal system is run by the privileged and the powerful, it has the tendency to overlook the perspectives of the marginalized. Exposing blind spots and identifying places where legal actors may be ignorant or myopic toward alternative viewpoints are arguably what critical scholarship does best.

Thanks to Jeff Bellin and Julia Simon-Kerr for helpful comments.

Another key contribution of critical scholarship is exposing the uneven distribution of error costs. Proof is not just some abstract plaything for theorists to optimize, but a practical process that invariably makes mistakes. How those mistakes are distributed, and who bears the resulting social fallout, are always important to understand, regardless of one's starting philosophical or ideological commitments. The pursuit of accuracy may be largely objective and neutral, but the distribution of error is not, and it deserves considered political and ethical debate.

That said, critical theory is not beyond reproach, and I want to challenge two threads in Critical Evidence scholarship. Here, I do not wish to tar with too broad a brush, as some will argue that these are only marginal or fringe views, but I do not think that is always the case.

The first thread is the attempt to mix the goal of empirical accuracy with substantive goals. For example, some will argue at times that the evidentiary rules should fight "subordination" or some other social evil. This temptation to deploy the evidentiary rules to serve substantive purposes surfaces in other literatures as well. Law-and-economics scholars, for instance, have argued that evidentiary rules should promote desired primary behavior (as opposed to merely accurately reconstruct the past).[1] As I have argued elsewhere, such mixing is a Faustian bargain.[2] Achieving accuracy itself is already hard. Adding substantive policy goals both complicates and politicizes the task, turning a difficult project into a nearly impossible one.

The second thread is the view in some critical circles that truth itself is relative or dependent on power. To be clear, my critique here is directed not at scholarship showing that evidentiary processes have been distorted by power (and therefore should be reformed), but rather claims that truth is inherently determined or tainted by power. To be sure, questioning an objective reality can be a useful philosophical exercise that helps us probe whether we are being as neutral as we think. But from the standpoint of legal practice, I would argue that there must either be an objective reality, or we must *assume* that there is. Are there borderline cases? Sure. Can we disagree on what to do substantively once the facts are ascertained? Of course. But the very idea of the "rule of law" must assume, even if only axiomatically, that there is an objective reality. After all, the rule of law means little if truth is manipulable.

Up until now, evidence has been a relatively neutral and apolitical project. This is not to say that evidence law itself has always been neutral and apolitical – critical scholarship has shown that not to be the case. But at least, the *goal* of accurate decision-making is one that carries broad consensus. Infusing the evidentiary rules with substantive goals apart from accuracy, or suggesting that objective accuracy does not exist, will almost surely destroy such consensus. And for what gain? Plenty of legal venues exist already for battling out our ideological preferences. It seems to

1 *E.g.*, Richard A. Bierschbach and Alex Stein, *Mediating Rules in Criminal Law*, 93 VA. L. REV. 1197, 1253 (2007); Louis A. Kaplow, *Burden of Proof*, 121 YALE L.J. 738 (2012).

2 Edward K. Cheng, *The Perils of Evidentiary Manipulation*, 93 VA. L. REV. IN BRIEF 207, 208 (2007).

me that we should try to preserve at least one area in which we can all agree on a common objective.

I suspect many Critical Evidence scholars would disagree with me on these two points, including many of the contributors to this volume. The readers of this volume may disagree with my criticisms as well. But again, debate in this case is a positive good. It makes the entire field of evidence more vibrant. Beyond this, neither of these criticisms takes away from my appreciation of this book. One of its goals, after all, is to challenge the status quo and to shake up a field that too often seems staid and old-fashioned. In that respect and others, it succeeds.

* * *

In closing, let me return to my original punchline: Even if you are not a Critical Evidence scholar, this volume is worth your dedicated study. A critical perspective can powerfully reveal the problems and costs of the existing evidentiary rules and structure. The critique may be uncomfortable, it may even provoke your ire, but it jars us out of our complacency with the status quo. On this score, you will find many gems in the chapters that follow. They illuminate the world of evidence with much needed light, and they will make you think differently, just as they have me.

Yet in the long run, it seems to me that Critical Evidence scholars will need to walk a careful line. It is one thing for critical scholarship to tear down in the name of improving accuracy. Exposing when the evidentiary rules have been hijacked to serve powerful interests, or when evidentiary error is unevenly distributed will strengthen our proof system to the betterment of all. But it is quite another thing to tear down accuracy itself. In our polarized world, I worry whenever scholarship has the effect of pushing us further apart, rather than bringing us closer together toward shared goals. For some of the founders of critical theory, politicization was a feature, not a bug, for it helps reformers re-imagine what is possible.[3] I am far less sanguine. If one replaces accuracy with substantive goals, or truth with ideology, nothing guarantees that one's desired replacement will win the ideological free-for-all that follows. Radical reimagination may have the ability to spark new virtuous cycles, but it equally has the ability to spawn vicious ones. It is thus my fervent hope that the new generation of critical scholars embraces the goal of empirical accuracy rather than fosters its demise.

Congratulations again to the editors and contributors of this volume. I am grateful for their insights and their intellectual companionship, and I look forward to the many discussions these papers will surely inspire, as we all grow the field of evidence together.

3 *E.g.*, Roberto Mangabeira Unger, What Should Legal Analysis Become (Verso 1997).

Foreword

Edward J. Imwinkelried

Like Professor Cheng, I am an outsider to Critical Evidence scholarship. Like Professor Cheng, I believe that the primary function of evidence law is the pursuit of accurate outcomes. However, again like Professor Cheng, I think that this volume is a worthwhile read for all Evidence scholars as well as judges, litigators, rulemakers, and legislators.

One of my primary research interests is the law of evidentiary privilege. It is an understatement to say that over the years my views on the topic have evolved. As a law student, I learned the comforting conventional wisdom that the recognition of absolute communications privileges comes cost free. Dean Wigmore's treatise taught that a court or legislature should recognize such a privilege only when the "element of confidentiality [is] essential to the full and satisfactory maintenance of [a] relation" that, in society's opinion, "ought to be sedulously fostered." (8 J. WIGMORE, EVIDENCE § 2285 (McNaughton rev. 1961)). In cases such as *Jaffee v. Redmond*, 518 U.S. 1 (1996) and *Swidler & Berlin v. United States*, 524 U.S. 399 (1998), the Supreme Court endorsed the dean's instrumental theory, presuming that the legal and psychotherapy privileges denied the judicial system little or no relevant evidence because, but for the existence of the privileges, the communications would not have occurred. As Professor Melanie Leslie has written:

> In a perfect [Wigmorean] world, the privilege would shield no evidence. Privilege generates the communication that the privilege protects. Eliminate the privilege, and the communication disappears… . [T]he privilege protects only … statements that would not otherwise have been made.

(Leslie, *The Costs of Confidentiality and the Purpose of Privilege*, 2000 WIS. L. REV. 31, 31.)

However, shortly after the turn of the century, I began work on the first edition of THE NEW WIGMORE: EVIDENTIARY PRIVILEGES. The longer I studied the subject, the more skeptical I became of the claim that absolute privileges come with minimal cost. To begin with, I discovered that previous commentators had raised numerous common sense doubts about assumption that clients and patients would not confide or consult without the assurance of an absolute privilege. Absent that assurance, would a patient who was emotionally *in extremis* refuse to consult the one person who might be able to help them? In addition, I discovered the large number of empirical studies of the legal and psychotherapy privileges, which yielded findings at odds with the assumption. Study after study demonstrated that in many cases, clients and patients are primarily focused on the "here and now" of the immediate problem and are not terrified at the prospect of subsequent compelled judicial disclosure in a lawsuit that might never be filed.

It became evident that there were real, substantial costs to the recognition of absolute privileges. I realized that in many cases, the enforcement of the privilege resulted in the exclusion of relevant, reliable evidence that could easily lead to a miscarriage of justice in either a criminal or civil case. That realization led me to support both a shift to a regime of qualified privileges and increased use of the accused's constitutional to introduce critical, demonstrably reliable evidence to trump privilege claims.

This study of privileges taught me two larger lessons. One is that seemingly sound evidentiary rules often exact significant costs that are sometimes overlooked. The second is that once those costs are acknowledged, the costs might warrant the major revision of the evidentiary rule.

The essays in this volume build on those lessons. Most of the essays follow a common pattern. Initially, the essay describes a current evidentiary rule. The essay next identifies previously ignored social costs of the routine application of the rule. The costs are often burdens imposed on a marginalized segment of American society. Finally, in light of those costs, the author calls for the reform of the rule.

Legislators, rulemakers, judges, attorneys, and scholars outside the Critical Evidence movement should emulate the essayists' search for the hidden costs of evidentiary rules. The evaluation of any evidentiary rule is incomplete without that search, and the incompleteness of the assessment can readily lead to injustice. In some cases I disagree with the essayists' identification of costs, and in other cases I have doubts about their proposed rule reforms. However, in the final analysis, this volume voices a plea for complete, intellectual honest analysis of all the costs of evidentiary rules. By encouraging completer consideration of the burdens imposed by evidentiary rules, the essayists have rendered an important service to the legal profession and all the segments of the society that the profession professes serve.

Acknowledgments

First and foremost, this project is a result of the work and commitment of our contributors, to whom we are extremely grateful! Almost all of the contributions here were workshopped at a colloquium held at Fordham Law School in March 2025. We would like to thank the participants at that colloquium for their generous and enriching participation. We are particularly indebted to Fordham Law School, the University of Connecticut, and the University of Pennsylvania Law Schools for their sponsorship of the event, and our respective deans for supporting the work we do. We also want to thank our students who took our first Critical Evidence seminars at our respective schools. Their enthusiasm for thinking critically about evidence rules and doctrine served as a welcome reminder that we were on to something important and necessary. A note of thanks to Brooke Coleman, Suzette Malveaux, Portia Pedro, and Elizabeth Porter, editors of *A Guide to Civil Procedure: Integrating Critical Legal Perspectives* (NYU Press 2022). Your book project helped inspire this one; thank you for generously sharing your thought process and offering advice as we developed our book.

Our next thank you goes to the team that helped us edit and finalize the book. From Fordham Law School: research assistant Emily Gwydir. From University of Pennsylvania Law School: research assistants Sadie Basila, Aiman Shahab, Dominique Malone Boni, and Penn Carey Law librarian Mary Shelly. We are also grateful to Cambridge University Press and our editor Matt Gallaway for championing this project from the beginning and the editorial team who helped bring this to publication. Finally, we thank our families for their patience, love, and understanding as we worked on this book. From Bennett: my husband Seth Michael Forman. From Jasmine E. Harris: Grant, Lincoln, and Lilyana. From Julia Simon-Kerr: Florian, Clara, and Iris.

Introduction

Bennett Capers, Jasmine E. Harris, and Julia Simon-Kerr

This volume offers the first collection of Critical Evidence scholarship. By using the moniker, "Critical Evidence," we mean to denote a school of thought that is quite broad but shares certain features. First, Critical Evidence scholars maintain that social conditions matter to what an ideal system of evidence will look like. The quality, depth, and breadth of knowledge inputs affect the quality of the knowledge produced through the application of rules in an adjudicative process. Critical Evidence thus questions one fundamental assumption of the rationalist tradition in evidence, namely, that the system generally achieves "rectitude of decision through correct application of valid substantive laws" and "rational weighing of evidence" by an "impartial decisionmaker."[1] Given an unequal society,[2] even rules of apparent neutrality will not necessarily be applied neutrally or produce neutral results. In addition, Critical Evidence shows how certain evidence rules are not as neutral as they seem. Normativity is baked into the evidence system in ways that have been underappreciated in the field. Critical Evidence is also concerned with how evidence law sets boundaries around whose voices will be heard in court (and how) and what types of knowledge will be cognizable there. It surfaces how these boundaries tend to reinforce existing socio-legal hierarchies and power dynamics. Finally, Critical Evidence does not "accept the perspective of the established

[1] WILLIAM TWINING, THEORIES OF EVIDENCE 15–16 (Stanford University Press 1985).

[2] *See, e.g.*, Students for Fair Admissions, Inc. v. President & Fellows of Harvard Coll., 600 U.S. 181, 337 (Sotomayor, J., dissenting) ("Put simply, society remains 'inherently unequal.' Racial inequality runs deep to this very day.") (citation omitted); Catharine A. MacKinnon and Kimberlé W. Crenshaw, *Reconstituting the Future: The Equality Amendment*, 129 YALE L.J. F. 343, 357 (2019) ("[D]espite the focused and determined efforts of committed movements, communities, organizations, lawyers, and some scholars, led by generations of valiant activists, the United States remains a deeply unequal society. Its laws, against formidable interventions for change, have largely operated to maintain that inequality."); Kevin R. Johnson, *Essay: Bringing RaceXGender Equality to the Unequal Profession*, 51 SW. L. REV. 200, 202 (2022) ("[Racial and gender inequities at U.S. law schools] reflect the systemic racial and gender injustice in U.S. society."); R. Richard Banks et al., *Discrimination and Implicit Bias in a Racially Unequal Society*, 94 CAL. L. REV. 1169, 1180 (2006) (discussing the claim of unequal treatment in the context of police shooter bias).

order,"[3] and, instead, looks for perspectives that are missing, suppressed, or erased. Methodologically, the field asks a set of epistemic, relational, and contextual questions to unearth and contend with the operation of power in the construction of facts, drafting, codification, interpretation, and application of rules. At bottom, if, as Bentham observed, the "field of evidence is no other than the field of knowledge,"[4] Critical Evidence scholarship is interested in the ways in which knowledge is shaped by power.

While evidence scholars have only recently adopted the moniker "Critical Evidence," Critical Evidence is not new. At least not entirely. Feminist scholars, in particular, have been writing from a critical perspective about evidence for over forty years. Critical Legal Studies scholars, in the legal realist tradition, have also questioned the presumptive neutrality of evidence rules. What is new is evidence scholars from a variety of perspectives – feminist, Critical Race Theory, disability theory, queer theory, and more – viewing their critiques as belonging under a collective banner.

In many ways, Critical Evidence takes up some of the deepest puzzles in the field. For example, William Twining famously described a paradox in the fact that because knowledge is relative, culture itself can shape relevance.[5] Others, including Ron Allen in the excerpt in this volume, have highlighted as a central conundrum of evidence law that much of the evidence in any trial will consist of what is in the fact finders' minds already. Critical Evidence builds on these insights and considers their systematic impact on marginalized groups. Evidence law regulates the construction of a set of facts to give content to individual and group rights and responsibilities. Legal decision-makers draw on a base of experience and accepted knowledge, but they are limited by their own experiences when they assess the probative value of evidence before them. For example, Jasmine E. Harris, in an excerpt in this volume, has argued that the flawed baseline of common knowledge and experience about disability in society can undermine fact finders' capacity to fairly adjudicate the rights and responsibilities of disabled people.[6] What does it mean when these inevitable contingencies within the system of proof intersect with a deeply unequal society that has socialized both the judges making evidentiary rulings and the jurors bringing knowledge into the courtroom?

Critical Evidence scholars also build on the notion that evidence rules exist to counteract bias. As scholars of evidence have long recognized, evidence doctrine

3 Robert Cover, Justice Accused: Antislavery and the Judicial Process 1 (Yale University Press 1975).

4 Jeremy Bentham, An Introductory View of the Rationale of Evidence, *in* The Complete Works of Jeremy Bentham 5 (John Bowring ed., 1843).

5 William Twining, Rethinking Evidence: Exploratory Essays 121–34 (Cambridge University Press 2006) (1990).

6 Jasmine E. Harris, *(Un)Common Knowledge & Experience*, 105 Boston U. L. Rev. 1113 (2025).

and rules are tools through which law can be used to resist existing hegemonies.[7] Indeed, modern evidence rules, like the prohibition on character evidence, are explicitly intended both to promote truth-seeking, and to counteract the kind of subordinating bias with which Critical Evidence scholars are concerned. After all, at least in theory, evidence rules are where U.S. law makes good on the commitment that "a defendant starts his life afresh when he stands before a jury."[8] Critical Evidence takes seriously this aspiration of evidence law to ensure that trials focus on reliable evidence by taking account of acts related to the conduct at issue in the specific proceeding rather than past character, status, or reputation. Above all, Critical Evidence embraces evidence law's ultimate promise to seek the truth while promoting fairness in adjudication,[9] and it does so by pointing out where evidence law falls short.

The Critical Evidence tradition has a long history of seeking to expose the perceptual and power distortions that can render problematic even the most seemingly rational of evidentiary processes. Consider, again, the feminist critiques. In the early 1990s, feminist evidence scholars in the United States, including Aviva Orenstein, Kit Kinports, and Rosemary Hunter, began positing that rational reasoning may not unlock neutral, value-free knowledge in a world in which historical and geographical context inevitably distorts perception, and in which men have controlled the levers of power in society to the exclusion of women among other groups.[10] In 2000, Mary Childs and Louise Ellison edited the closest cousin to this book, *Feminist Perspectives on Evidence*, which compiled an illustrious cast of international evidence scholars writing in the field. They explained that feminist evidence scholarship was "concerned with past and present social constructions of 'women' and … a commitment to the principle that these social constructions should not lead to inequality or oppression."[11] Black feminist scholars also turned their attention to

7 For example, John Langbein writes that "[f]rom the Middle Ages to our own day, the driving concern animating the Anglo-American law of evidence has been to protect against the shortcomings of trial by jury." *Historical Foundations of the Law of Evidence: A View from the Ryder Sources*, 96 COLUM. L. REV. 1168, 1194 (1996). These shortcomings include the risk of "partiality." *Id.* Arguably, similar concerns are an even older feature of thinking about evidence. Aristotle describes how a judge may reject prejudicial judgments, such as those that might be invoked by excessive appeals to emotion, by focusing on the opposite emotion. ARISTOTLE, NICOMACHEAN ETHICS bk. II, at 111–13 (H. Rackham trans., Harvard University Press 1956) (c. 384 B.C.E.). *See also*, Timothy Barr, *A Rule That Bends: Aristotle on Pathos and Equity*, 54 PHIL. & RHET. 149 (2021) ("If prejudicial *pathe* 'warp' the judge, it is not simply because it inclines them in one direction but because its purpose is to prevent the judge from attending closely to the case and determining what is *orthos* or right.").

8 People v. Zackowitz, 254 N.Y. 192, 197 (1930).

9 FED R. EVID. 102.

10 *See, e.g.*, Aviva Orenstein, *"My God!": A Feminist Critique of the Excited Utterance Exception to the Hearsay Rule*, 85 CAL. L. REV. 159 (1997); Kit Kinports, *Evidence Engendered*, 1991 U. ILL. L. REV. 413 (1991); Rosemary C. Hunter, *Gender in Evidence: Masculine Norms vs. Feminist Reforms*, 19 HARV. WOMEN'S L.J. 127 (1996).

11 MARY CHILDS AND LOUISE ELLISON, FEMINIST PERSPECTIVES ON EVIDENCE 5 (Routledge 2000).

evidence law during this period, highlighting ways in which the evidentiary system failed to account for historical bias against Black women.[12] Disability law scholars also responded to specific doctrinal or policy developments in evidence law, such as the Supreme Court's decision on expert scientific evidence in *Daubert v. Merrell Dow Pharmaceuticals*,[13] to highlight the impact of such developments on disabled people.[14]

Within the next decade, the field of Critical Evidence (absent the title) continued to grow as a new group of scholars, building on what previously were relatively siloed conversations, began exploring how cultural normativity intersects with the evidentiary system to the detriment of historically subordinated groups.[15] For example, in 2017, Jasmine Gonzales Rose offered the first account to explicitly apply a critical race theoretical lens to evidence.[16] In reading each other's work, and in conversations at conferences around the country – at roundtables at the annual Law and Society conference, and at panels organized by the Evidence Section at the annual meetings for the Association of American Law Schools, and at Vanderbilt's annual Evidence Workshop, for example – many of us began to realize how much overlap there was in our interest in how power shapes the evidentiary process, even while our approaches varied. In fall 2022, the editors of the *Vanderbilt Law Review* hosted a symposium on *Reimagining the Rules of Evidence at 50* that brought together evidence scholars, many of them looking at evidence through a critical lens, and resulted in an excellent symposium volume.[17] In January 2024, the *Connecticut Public Interest Journal* at University of Connecticut School of Law hosted a symposium titled *Evidence Through a Critical Lens*. Months later, Jasmine E. Harris and Julia Simon-Kerr designed a Critical Evidence course that they co-taught to students from both their institutions and invited as speakers many of the contributors to this book. (Indeed, the course was such a success, and the students produced such incredible papers, that we included one student's paper in this volume.) Bennett Capers started teaching a Critical Evidence course the following semester and likewise invited

[12] Marilyn Yarbrough and Crystal Bennett, *Cassandra and the "Sistahs": The Peculiar Treatment of African American Women in the Myth of Women as Liars*, 3 J. GENDER RACE & JUST. 625 (2000).

[13] 509 U.S. 579 (1993).

[14] *See, e.g.*, Peter D. Blanck and Heidi M. Berven, *Evidence of Disability after Daubert*, 5 J. PSYCH., PUB. POL'Y & L. 16 (1999); Deirdre M. Smith, *Who Says You're Disabled? The Role of Medical Evidence in the ADA Definition of Disability*, 82 TULANE L. REV. 1 (2007) and *An Uncertain Privilege: Implied Waiver and the Evisceration of the Psychotherapist–Patient Privilege in the Federal Courts*, 58 DEPAUL L. REV. 79 (2008). *See also*, Michael L. Perlin, Astrid Birgden, and Kris Gledhill, *"The Witness Who Saw, /He Left Little Doubt": A Comparative Consideration of Expert Testimony in Mental Disability Law Cases in Common and Civil Law Systems*, 6 J. INVESTIGATIVE PSYCH. OFFENDER PROFILING 59 (2009).

[15] *See, e.g.*, Julia Simon-Kerr, Note, *Unchaste & Incredible: The Use of Gendered Conceptions of Honor in Impeachment*, 117 YALE L.J. 1854 (2008); Bennett Capers, *Real Women, Real Rape*, 60 UCLA L. REV. 826 (2013).

[16] Jasmine Gonzales Rose, *Toward a Critical Race Theory of Evidence*, 101 MINN. L. REV. 2243 (2017).

[17] Symposium, *Reimagining the Rules of Evidence at 50*, 76 VAND. L. REV. 1603 (2023).

many of the contributors to present their work. At some point, Critical Evidence, as a discipline and as an idea for this book, emerged as a project. In March 2025, we co-convened a Colloquium on Critical Evidence at Fordham Law School and invited contributing authors as well as sending out broader calls to ask other evidence law scholars to join us in discussing the book, its goals, and in workshopping the contributing authors' draft chapters. In addition to the authors, several evidence professors, whose work does not necessarily take a critical approach to evidence, attended and contributed to the discussions. This exchange of ideas, good faith engagement, and advancement of evidence law are at the heart of this project.

Contextually, it is perhaps no coincidence that Critical Evidence, as a school of thought, began to take off in this particular time when some political conservatives are waging an attack against Critical Race Theory, feminism, and almost anything different. Indeed, we recognize that some evidence scholars (and perhaps some legal scholars more broadly) will no doubt view Critical Evidence with hostility. As one scholar recently wrote, "an ideologically loaded (Neo-Marxist) and reductionist tool like sex or race is as crude an attempt to explain the law of evidence 'as if a surgeon were to perform his delicate operations with a meat ax.'"[18] Yet another scholar offered perhaps a more representative take, calling one piece of feminist evidence scholarship an "intensely parochial discussion[]."[19] It may be unlikely that this volume – or any collection of critical scholarship – can win over critics who dismiss our very endeavor, and regard the pursuit of universal principles stripped of context as the only true form of evidence theory. Nonetheless, we hope such critics will take the time to read and consider the scholarship in this volume as a route towards future dialogue. We will also channel Martha Minow and observe that one of the deep virtues of taking a critical approach in any field is that it involves "searching … for practical justice, not just more theory."[20]

Critical Evidence is also a highly practical endeavor. When we teach students to recognize and challenge embedded assumptions within the evidentiary system, we are teaching them to be better lawyers and to work to improve the law. Take evidence of flight as an example. The probative value of flight of a criminal defendant from the police has received special consideration in evidence law as highly probative of guilt. But when put into context based on a community's experience with over-policing and police violence, or an individual's experience as a person on the autism spectrum with heightened fight or flight responses, the probative value of the flight is reduced. Recognizing and contesting this, and other similarly

[18] Kyriakos N. Kotsoglou, Book Review, Criminal Law and Criminal Justice Books (June 1, 2022) (reviewing PHILOSOPHICAL FOUNDATIONS OF EVIDENCE LAW (Christian Dahlman, Alex Stein, and Giovanni Tuzet eds., Oxford University Press 2021)).

[19] Paul Roberts, *Theorizing Evidence Law*, 43 OXFORD J. L. STUD. 629 (2023) (reviewing Julia Simon-Kerr, *Relevance Through a Feminist Lens*, in PHILOSOPHICAL FOUNDATIONS OF EVIDENCE LAW (Christian Dahlman, Alex Stein, and Giovanni Tuzet eds., Oxford University Press 2021)).

[20] Martha Minow, *Feminist Reason: Getting It and Losing It*, 38 J. LEGAL EDUC. 47, 48 (1988).

flawed default assumptions, is not only part of the project of Critical Evidence. It is part of the project of evidence law itself. In harmony with the expressed purpose of the Federal Rules of Evidence, Critical Evidence scholars seek to "promote the development of evidence law, to the end of ascertaining the truth and securing a just determination."[21] In fact, in this sense, Critical Evidence is core to the project of legal education: we train students to spot legal issues, identify assumptions, and use those insights to craft persuasive arguments on behalf of their clients. Critical Evidence theorists are also unified in exploring the ways the evidence system – including the rules, the legal actors strategically deploying them, and the gatekeepers interpreting them – is structured to perpetuate advantages for some and disadvantages for others; in short, subordination. This critical lens shows logic, knowledge, and ultimately determinations of truth cannot exist in a vacuum. The social context in which evidence problems are asked and answered will inform where we start and where logic takes us.

Importantly, Critical Evidence also is committed to imagining something better. Consider one of the seminal evidence cases, *Tanner v. United States*, 483 U.S. 107 (1987). When offered an opportunity to change the rules regarding post-verdict review of jury decision-making – jurors admitted to being intoxicated during deliberations – the Supreme Court declined. Writing for the majority, Justice Sandra Day O'Connor famously cautioned: "It is not at all clear … that the jury system could survive such efforts to perfect it." Critical Evidence rejects this fear of change and refusal to imagine something better. It rejects too the concern raised by Justice Jackson in *Michelson v. United States*, 335 U.S. 469 (1948), that to "pull one misshapen stone out of the grotesque structure [of evidence law] is more likely simply to upset its present balance between adverse interests than to establish a rational edifice." From the point of view of Critical Evidence scholars, upsetting the present balance is precisely what is needed, and needed right now. Indeed, probing the structural integrity of our body of evidence law, and imagining and fashioning better rules, may be the best hope to ensure evidence law's longevity and sustainability.

THE BOOK'S STRUCTURE

A word about the structure of the book. Early on, we decided to organize this book around both rules and doctrine in a way that tracks the typical evidence course. But we also wanted to begin with something that is often missing in evidence books and courses: a fuller discussion of the drafters of the Federal Rules of Evidence, and the current committee members who, in effect, "maintain" and "police" the rules. Accordingly, we begin in Part One ("Introduction to the Field and Its Actors") with contributions focused on the decision-makers. It is probably not surprising that the original drafters were all white, and almost all male. To our knowledge, there was

[21] Fed. R. Evid. 102.

no one openly gay, disabled, or working class. Even now, the Committee is largely monolithic and statist, with the Department of Justice in effect having close to a veto power over proposed amendments. Our point here is not that identity is everything. But identity does matter and shapes one's views, a point brought home in the contributions of Julia Simon-Kerr, Ngozi Okidegbe, and Montré Carodine. Indeed, that we are all shaped by our identities and lived experiences leads to the other decision-makers we focus on in Part One: jurors. To be sure, we have become a country of pleas and settlements, and jury trials seem rarer with each passing year. Still, even pleas and settlements take place "in the shadow of trial," with lawyers negotiating dispositions based on how they think jurors will interpret the evidence. For this reason, jurors, even in the absence of jury trials, play an outsized role. We, accordingly, include contributions addressing jurors as decision-makers, and reckoning with their infirmities and biases.

From there, the book turns to the rules themselves, with sections devoted to the most prominent – and sometimes contested – rules. Indeed, in many ways Part Two ("The Rules") is the heart of the book. It begins with a section on Rules 401 and 403, in which contributors explore the race, gender, and class assumptions built into our "common sense" understanding of relevancy and prejudice, and the real-world consequences of these assumptions. For example, Asees Bhasin's contribution, "Relevance, Reconsidered," focuses on an infanticide case to show that assumptions about how pregnant women should behave can fundamentally alter the story told at trial. A trial court judge's biases and cultural perceptions can shape assessments about what is relevant, and what is unfairly prejudicial, and in doing so can expand the impact of carceral laws. From there, the next section turns to contributions on character evidence. As Judge Cardozo stated in *People v. Zackowitz*, a fundamental tenet of evidence law is that "character is never an issue in a criminal prosecution unless the defendant chooses to make it one. In a very real sense a defendant starts his life afresh when he stands before a jury, a prisoner at the bar."[22] Rule 404 codifies this tenet, and yet as the contributions in this section demonstrate, this seemingly neutral rule obscures how much character evidence jurors in fact consider, whether it is the use of rap lyrics evidencing character, evidence of disability, class or dress evidencing character, or any of a hundred other things. The remainder of Part Two continues in a similar vein, with sections and contributions on credibility, especially on how a prior conviction is treated as probative of credibility; on sex trials and the problematic use of Rules 412–15, which govern the exclusion and admission of sexual behavior evidence in cases alleging sexual misconduct; on hearsay, i.e., Rules 801–7, and further limitations imposed by the Sixth Amendment's right to confrontation; on the fraught topic of lay and expert testimony, governed by Rules 702–6; and finally on privileges, governed by Rules 501–2, which insulate

[22] 254 N.Y. 192, 197 (1930).

some communications from disclosure at trial, and, in effect, can privilege some people more than others.

The observant reader will note that some sections are longer than others. This reflects where Critical Evidence scholars are focusing attention today. For example, there are a variety of contributions on expert testimony, and we could have included even more. Other sections are briefer – the section on privileges comes to mind – suggesting areas that are still waiting to be explored, and critiqued, by Critical Evidence scholars. But regardless of the length of each section, there is a throughline. Contributors look at the rules critically, but also provocatively and constructively. For example, Nila Bala's contribution "Parent-Child Privilege as Resistance" not only argues for a parent-child privilege. As the title indicates, she also argues how such a privilege can function as "resistance." Tom Lininger's "Underprivileged: A ClassCrit Perspective on Evidentiary Privileges" takes another tack by showing how class-based our evidentiary privileges are, and charting a path for making privileges more equitable. And Gabriela Rodriguez, in a contribution first written as a seminar paper for Harris and Simon-Kerr's Critical Evidence class, asks whether symmetry in the rules itself entrenches power differentials, using immigration proceedings as a case study.

Finally, the book ends with Part Three ("Expanding Evidence"). We chose this capacious title for this part because of the contributions we received and the excerpts we wanted to include, which seemed to go beyond viewing the rules in isolation to viewing the rules in toto, considering their collective impact, and imagining something completely different. For example, in her contribution "Bending Evidence Rules Towards Decarceration," Erin Collins makes a persuasive argument for just that, bending the rules, but in favor of criminal defendants, to help level the imbalance of power that exists between criminal defendants and the state. And though on the surface Maneka Sinha's contribution "Reimagining *Daubert v. Merrell Dow Pharmaceuticals, Inc.* as a Non-Reformist Reform" might seem to focus solely on expert testimony, her argument goes deeper, and is clearly just one salvo in her larger project of abolition. There is also Montré Carodine's contribution "Race Is Evidence/Evidence Is Race: Flipping the Script on the 'Racial Lens.'" Revisiting some of her earlier work on race as character evidence, Carodine offers a far more ambitious argument here: that thinking through "race" and how we "know" race can help us rethink the very concept of evidence and proof.

There are two more things to say about the contributions to this book. Other than specifying a word limit for each chapter, and sharing our planned structure for the book, our instructions were deliberately minimal. We merely described the book project – to engage with the many ways our system of proof systematically privileges insiders while failing certain groups, in particular people of color, women, people with disabilities, LGBTQ+ people and others who are socially marginalized and sit at the intersections of these marginalized identities. And we added the following: "While this book will offer a critical perspective on evidence, within that umbrella it will be heterogeneous. Different critical scholarly approaches – responsive to legal formalism – can offer a depth to approaching the same evidentiary topics. We welcome contributions incorporating Critical Race Theory, Feminist Theory, Critical Disability, Queer Theory, Class-Crit Theory, Law and Political Economy, and more." That is it. We emphasize these instructions here to explain, and celebrate, the range of the contributions to this book, from the variations in critical approaches to the variation in style and voice.

The second thing to say may seem more mundane but is equally important. In addition to asking scholars to write new essays specifically for this book, we believed a few already published pieces were important to the emerging canon of Critical Evidence and should be included as well. To that end, we sought and secured permission from those authors to include excerpts from some of the seminal published work taking critical perspectives on evidence. These excerpts are mixed in with the original contributions to this volume, but with a difference. To make reading easier – and because of the interwoven nature of law review article footnoting – we elected to include these excerpts but, for the most part, to not reproduce their original footnotes. We encourage readers who want to learn more after reading these excerpts to seek out the full articles. Citations are provided.

Envisioning the future of evidence law requires active listening and robust debate. Perhaps even more than this, it requires courage and creativity. Scholars must have the courage to ask difficult questions, and they must be creative, willing to redefine problems and see new prescriptive pathways. Although these paths may be difficult to bring into focus, we believe they are not impossible to build. We hope this volume will contribute to that enterprise, and we look forward to the continued growth and development of Critical Evidence.

PART I

Introduction to the Field and Its Actors

SECTION 1

The Rulemakers

INTRODUCTION

It is not uncommon for evidence books to begin with the history of the Rules of Evidence. Indeed, to most students of evidence, the story is familiar. As George Fisher relays in his well-known evidence book:

> In 1965, Chief Justice Earl Warren of the Supreme Court appointed an advisory committee of judges, practitioners, and academics, who drafted the original slate of the proposed rules. Guided principally by its reporter, Professor Edward W. Cleary, the advisory committee drew not only from the common law but also from earlier codification efforts, including the Model Code of Evidence in 1942 and the Uniform Rules of Evidence of 1953. The committee delivered its proposed rules to the Supreme Court in November 1972. The Court approved the rules essentially without change and sent them to Congress.[1]

Fisher goes on to say that Congress scrutinized and amended the proposed rules before enacting them in 1975. Given this version of the history of the Rules, one could be forgiven for thinking of the Rules as neutral, objective.

But other than being "judges, practitioners, and academics," who exactly were the Advisory Committee members who fashioned the rules? How many women were on the Committee, or people of color, or other people from traditionally marginalized groups? And what of Congress, which enacted the Rules of Evidence? To be sure, identity isn't everything, but might it explain why the Advisory Committee

1 George Fisher, Evidence 3 (3d ed., Foundation Press 2013).

promulgated, and Congress enacted, a character evidence rule, Rule 404, that permitted defendants accused of rape to introduce evidence of the sexual character of the victim to support a claim of consent, a rule that remained in place until it was amended in 1978 with Rule 412?

Given the usual telling of the history of the rules of evidence, and the fact that the rules so rarely change, one could be forgiven too for not realizing that a Rules Advisory Committee still exists.

In a book skeptical of the rules' neutrality, then, it makes sense to begin by looking critically at the rulemakers. In "Prosecutors and Federal Evidence Rulemaking," Julia Simon-Kerr critiques how federal evidence rulemaking has been structurally captured by prosecutors and former prosecutors, creating a system resistant to reform despite seismic social and scientific changes. This resistance to change is also the focus of the excerpt from Alex Nunn's "The Living Rules of Evidence," in which he argues that, in codifying the Rules of Evidence, the rulemakers also ossified them, making them resistant to addressing modern injustices, such as exonerations, the #MeToo movement, and racial subordination. The other inclusion in this section is Ngozi Okidegbe's "Evidence Rulemaking and Community Participation." Okidegbe foregrounds the anti-democratic nature of evidence rulemaking, and argues we should open ourselves up to "collective and contentious action from socially marginalized communities in evidence rulemaking" to better align evidence law with its stated and laudable purpose, "to administer every proceeding fairly, eliminate unjustifiable expense and delay, and promote the development of evidence law, to the end of ascertaining the truth and securing a just determination."

Prosecutors and Federal Evidence Rulemaking

Julia Simon-Kerr

One of the contributions of critical theory when applied to any area of law is to center questions that might otherwise not be asked. How does power and its absence shape the system? What normative baselines undergird decisions? What perspectives are expressed through law and which are missing? For evidence law, examining power hierarchies, starting assumptions and missing perspectives raises a central question: Who makes the rules?

We do not need to read much beyond the title of Brooke Coleman's article, "#SoWhiteMale: Federal Procedural Rulemaking Committees," to get a basic answer to this question.[1] The evidence rules were drafted in 1965 by a committee of powerful white men who largely codified common law precedent created by equally advantaged white men. The rules were enacted after modification by Congressional committees made up almost entirely of white men of similar privilege. Scholars, myself included, have observed that federal rulemaking omits the knowledge and voices of women, people of color, and others, and suggested ways in which that omission manifests in the rules and policies these committees produce.[2] In this volume and elsewhere, Professor Okidegbe makes a compelling case for diversifying rulemaking by bringing affected communities into the rulemaking process.[3]

What has been less well-documented, however, is the degree to which evidence rulemaking power is concentrated in the hands of prosecutors and former

Many thanks to Ngozi Okidegbe for her inspiring work on rulemaking and our many conversations on the topic. Thanks also to the students in my Fall 2024 Critical Evidence class, to my coteacher, Jasmine E. Harris, and to Bennett Capers and the students in his Spring 2025 Critical Evidence course, all of whom helped this chapter along. And a huge thank you to Anna Janson, for her phenomenal research assistance.

1 Brooke D. Coleman, *#SoWhiteMale: Federal Procedural Rulemaking Committees*, 68 UCLA L. Rev. 370 (2020).

2 Julia Simon-Kerr, *A New Baseline for Character Evidence*, 76 Vand. L. Rev. 1827, 1848–51 (2023).

3 *See* Ngozi Okidegbe, "Evidence Rulemaking and Community Participation," in this volume.

prosecutors.[4] Of the eight members and one Chair on the Federal Rules of Evidence Advisory Committee (Advisory Committee or Committee), six are prosecutors or former prosecutors.[5] Two-thirds of the Committee thus has substantial experience representing the government in criminal matters. In contrast, only one member, the representative from the Federal Public Defender's Office, has spent significant time representing individual defendants in criminal cases. An additional two members of the Committee have or had trial practices centering on defending large corporations.

Rulemaking power is thus concentrated in the hands of lawyers and judges who for the most part have represented parties with more power in contests against those with far less. I will argue below that this power imbalance on the rulemaking committee is significant in the context of the broader landscape of evidence law. At the federal level, evidence law has changed very little – perhaps even to the point of stagnation[6] – since the codification of the Federal Rules in 1975. The Advisory Committee's remarkable commitment to preserving the existing rules in the face of ever-mounting calls for reform is related to the structure and composition of the Committee itself. A committee stacked with prosecutors and former prosecutors has ensured that few proposals ever make it out of the Committee and into the notice and comment phase of rulemaking, and even fewer result in changes to the rules themselves. At least one Chief Justice, at whose pleasure committee members serve, is on record suggesting that changes to evidence rules should be kept to a minimum and that the Committee should not engage in law reform. Per this dictate, committee membership has been able to see to it that little changes. By maintaining the status quo, in turn, the Evidence Advisory Committee has doubled down on rules that, as scholars in this volume and elsewhere have shown, serve to reinforce and reify existing power imbalances. The result is a familiar cycle: those with power making choices that maintain that power.

I. EVIDENCE RULEMAKING AND THE ROLE OF PROSECUTORS

The Advisory Committee has what has been described as a "colorful past."[7] The Committee was first formed in 1965 in order to draft a set of proposed evidence

[4] There has been some commentary on the ideological composition of the Civil Rules Committee. *See, e.g.*, Stephen B. Burbank and Sean Farhang, Rights and Retrenchment: The Counterrevolution Against Federal Litigation 77–82 (Cambridge University Press 2017); Brooke D. Coleman, *One Percent Procedure*, 91 Wash. L. Rev. 1005, 1017 (2016).

[5] The current Committee chair, Judge Jesse Furman, is a former AUSA. In addition, all four judges on the committee are former prosecutors: Valerie Caproni, S.D.N.Y., a former AUSA; Mark Massa, Indiana Supreme Court, a former AUSA; Edmund Sargus Jr., S.D. Ohio, a former U.S. Attorney; Richard Sullivan, 2nd Circuit, a former AUSA. And finally, the Department of Justice has a permanent ex officio seat on the committee.

[6] G. Alexander Nunn, *The Living Rules of Evidence*, 170 U. Penn. L. Rev. 937, 940 (2022).

[7] Coleman, *supra* note 1, at 380.

rules.[8] But Congress was so displeased with the proposed rules on privileges that it decided to eliminate the Committee after the rules were adopted in 1975.[9] For almost twenty years, the rules were then attended to by the Advisory Committee on Criminal Rules with an assist from the Civil Rules Committee. Without a dedicated committee, the Federal Rules of Evidence were amended six times in comparison to over 100 substantive amendments to the Federal Rules of Civil Procedure during the same time period.[10] In 1993, after prominent calls for attention to the flagging Federal Rules of Evidence, Chief Justice Rehnquist reconstituted the Committee.[11]

The Advisory Committee holds public meetings at which it gathers information and considers proposals to amend the rules.[12] These meetings, while open to the public, are not open to public participation.[13] Only invited participants can speak.[14] Those wishing to express a view to the Committee may, however, submit letters or other written materials. The meetings have in recent decades been held in Washington, D.C. and in other hub locations across the country.[15] Only if the Committee proposes a rule revision is there a notice period during which members of the public and others are invited to comment on the rules.[16] Once the Advisory Committee approves a rule change proposal, it reports that proposed change to the Standing Committee.[17] That committee must then approve it before it is sent to the full Judicial Conference for review and then to the Supreme Court for approval.[18] Once the Supreme Court approves a rule change, the proposed rule goes to Congress, which can reject, modify, or ignore the proposal.[19] If Congress

[8] *Id. See also*, A SELF-STUDY OF FEDERAL JUDICIAL RULEMAKING: A REPORT FROM THE SUBCOMMITTEE ON LONG RANGE PLANNING TO THE COMMITTEE ON RULES OF PRACTICE, PROCEDURE AND EVIDENCE OF THE JUDICIAL CONFERENCE OF THE UNITED STATES, 168 F.R.D. 679, 686 (1995) [hereinafter SELF-STUDY].

[9] Coleman, *supra* note 1, at 381.

[10] Edward R. Becker and Aviva A. Orenstein, *The Federal Rules of Evidence After Sixteen Years – The Effect of "Plain Meaning" Jurisprudence, the Need for an Advisory Committee on the Rules of Evidence, and Suggestions for Selective Revision of the Rules*, 60 GEO. WASH. L. REV. 857, 859 (1992).

[11] *Id.* at 861; SELF-STUDY, *supra* note 8, at 686.

[12] *Open Meetings and Hearings of the Rules Committee*, U.S. CTS., www.uscourts.gov/forms-rules/about-rulemaking-process/open-meetings-and-hearings-rules-committee (last visited Mar. 23, 2025).

[13] Advisory Committee on Evidence Rules; Meeting of the Judicial Conference, 89 Fed. Reg. 76870, 76870 (Sept. 19, 2024).

[14] *Id.*

[15] *See, e.g.*, Federal Rules of Evidence Agendas for Committee Meetings (Nov. 8, 2024, New York) (Apr. 19, 2024, Washington) (Oct. 27, 2023, Minneapolis) (Apr. 28, 2023, Washington) (May 6, 2022, Washington) (Nov. 5, 2021, Washington) (Oct. 25, 2019, Nashville).

[16] Symposium, *The Politics of (Evidence) Rulemaking*, 53 HASTINGS L.J. 733, 736 (2002) ("If the Advisory Committee doesn't draft it, a change doesn't go to anybody. Because the rulemaking power has been delegated to such a degree, the Advisory Committee is on the bottom of the totem pole, but it has to start there to go anywhere.").

[17] Paul R. Rice, *Advisory Committee on the Federal Rules of Evidence: Tending to the Past and Pretending for the Future?*, 53 HASTINGS L.J. 817, 819 (2002).

[18] *Id.*

[19] *Id.*

does nothing, the rule becomes effective the December following the date of submission.[20] Congressional inaction has long been the norm.[21]

At eight members plus a Chair, the Evidence Advisory Committee is the smallest federal procedural rulemaking committee.[22] It is also the only such committee with no academic member.[23] It consists of five judges, two attorneys in private practice, a representative from the Office of the Federal Defender, and an ex officio member from the Department of Justice (DOJ).[24] A law professor also serves as the Reporter to the Committee, drafting rules and preparing advisory memoranda as needed.[25] While the DOJ and the Office of the Federal Defender select their representatives for the Committee, the other members are all appointed by the Chief Justice of the Supreme Court.[26]

Committee members' terms are limited to no more than six years,[27] but the Reporter and the DOJ's ex officio member are not subject to these term limits.[28] Professor Dan Capra, the current Reporter, has served in the role since 1996.[29] Elizabeth Shapiro represented the DOJ at Committee meetings from April 2007 through at least November 2025.[30] The Office of the Federal Defender, by contrast and consistent with term limitations, has had six representatives on the Committee since it was reconstituted.[31]

By structuring the Committee in this way, and in particular by creating an ex officio membership for the DOJ while all other members serve three-year terms and are limited to two such terms, Chief Justice Rehnquist all but guaranteed that a prosecutor would be the most long-standing member of the Committee. Unsurprisingly, the DOJ has taken advantage of this structure by consistently sending the same representative to the Evidence Advisory Committee. Elizabeth Shapiro has served on the Committee for almost twenty years, making her an influential voice in a body where, by design, all other members have dramatically less institutional knowledge

20 *Id.*

21 *Id.*

22 Coleman, *supra* note 1, at 392. Technically, the committee has nine members, but the ninth vacancy, for an academic member, has never been filled.

23 *Committee Roster*, U.S. Cts., www.uscourts.gov/file/78432/download (last visited Mar. 23, 2025).

24 *Id.*

25 *Committee Membership Selection*, U.S. Cts., www.uscourts.gov/forms-rules/about-rulemaking-process/committee-membership-selection (last visited Mar. 23, 2025).

26 *About the Judicial Conference of the United States*, U.S. Cts., www.uscourts.gov/about-federal-courts/governance-judicial-conference/about-judicial-conference (last visited Mar. 23, 2025).

27 *Committee Membership Selection*, *supra* note 25.

28 Daniel J. Capra and Liesa L. Richter, *Poetry in Motion: The Federal Rules of Evidence and Forward Progress as an Imperative*, 99 B.U. L. Rev. 1873, 1903 (2019).

29 *Faculty Directory*, Fordham L., www.fordham.edu/school-of-law/faculty/directory/full-time/daniel-capra/ (last visited Mar. 23, 2025).

30 *See* Federal Rules of Evidence Committee Meeting Minutes 1 (Apr. 12–13, 2007); Federal Rules of Evidence Committee Meeting, Nov. 5, 2025.

31 *Past Members of the Rules Committees*, U.S. Cts., www.uscourts.gov/forms-rules/records-rules-committees/past-members-rules-committees (last visited Mar. 23, 2025).

and experience. Only the Reporter has more experience on the Committee, and he has no Committee vote.[32]

Not only is Attorney Shapiro the longest standing member by over a decade, all five judges currently on the Committee are former prosecutors themselves, as is one of the attorneys in private practice.[33] The federal judiciary as a whole is similarly skewed. An analysis in 2021 found that "former courtroom advocates for government (389, 44.20 percent) … outnumber[ed] former advocates for individuals against government (57, 6.47 percent) by nearly seven to one."[34] But, as a recent empirical study of all six Judicial Conference Rules Committees suggests, the predominance of former prosecutors on the Evidence Advisory Committee is not simply a function of their disproportionate presence in the judiciary. That study found that between 1992 and 2022, judges with prosecutorial experience served on federal rules committees at equal or higher rates to their availability in the pool in all but eleven years.[35] In contrast, "prior work experience as a public defender [had] a statistically significant and negative effect on the odds of [rules] committee service."[36]

Although this chapter focuses on the role of prosecutors, it is important not to lose sight of other power dynamics on the Advisory Committee. Even in a group of six federal rules committees that one study puts at 94 percent white, this Advisory Committee stands out.[37] It still has never had a Black member. There is one Latino member at present, who joined the Committee as the representative from the Office of the Federal Public Defender in 2022.[38] The Rules were drafted by a committee of white men before being modified by the House and Senate, again using committees almost entirely comprised of white men.[39] And, the doctrines that served as the foundation for the rules developed over centuries of common law when white men held exclusive access to the

[32] Daniel J. Capra and Liesa L. Richter, *Long Live the Federal Rules of Evidence!*, 31 GEO. MASON L. REV. 1, 11 (2023).

[33] *See supra* note 5. John Siffert, one of the two attorneys on the Advisory Committee, worked as a prosecutor early in his career. Lankler, Siffert, Wohl, John Siffert. *Available at* www.lswlaw.com/lawyers/john-siffert.

[34] Clark Neily, *Are a Disproportionate Number of Federal Judges Former Government Advocates?*, CATO INST. (May 27, 2021), www.cato.org/study/are-disproportionate-number-federal-judges-former-government-advocates#procedure-findings.

[35] Dawn M. Chutkow and Michael Heise, *The Rulemakers: An Empirical Analysis of Chief Justice Appointments to the Judicial Conference Rules Committees*, 74 CASE W. RES. L. REV. 991, 1019 (2024).

[36] *Id.* at 1009.

[37] Coleman, *supra* note 1, at 391.

[38] *Id.* (describing the rules committee as "an all-white committee" in 2020); Federal Rules of Evidence Committee Meeting Minutes (May 6, 2022) (welcoming new member Rene Valladares).

[39] The advisory committee members appointed in 1965 all present outwardly as white and male. They were: Albert E. Jenner, Jr., David Berger, Hicks Epton, Robert S. Erdahl, Judge Joe Ewing Estes, Prof. Thomas F. Green, Jr., Egbert L. Haywood, Assoc. Dean Charles W. Joiner, Frank G. Raichle, Herman F. Selvin, Judge Simon E. Sobeloff, Craig Spangenberg, Judge Robert Van Pelt, Prof. Jack B. Weinstein, Edward Bennett Williams, Prof. Edward W. Cleary (reporter). U.S. CTS., www.uscourts.gov/file/1966pdf (last visited Mar. 23, 2025). The judiciary committees in the House and Senate that

bench and bar, and near-exclusive access to the courtroom itself. At present, out of six appointed positions on the Advisory Committee, only one is held by a woman.[40]

This portrait shows an Evidence Advisory Committee that is dramatically unrepresentative along multiple dimensions. Most saliently for our purposes, the Committee structurally maximizes prosecutorial power. The DOJ holds the most long-standing voting position on the Committee, with its representative serving almost three times as long as any term-limited member. Further, appointments by the Chief Justice have ensured that former prosecutors occupy all of the judicial roles of the Committee. Finally, the two roles for practicing attorneys have been given to men whose experience involves defending powerful corporations from suit, making them most positionally aligned with prosecutors in a power analysis.

Considering a counterfactual emphasizes the significance of the structural and professional imbalances on the Rules Committee. Imagine a committee on which a representative from the federal defenders would serve as long as the defenders liked, gaining experience and status. Their counterpart would be a term-limited member from the DOJ. Former public defenders would occupy the Chair and all four seats for judges. The two attorneys in private practice would have extensive experience steering class action lawsuits alleging consumer fraud by large corporations and suing to vindicate plaintiffs who had suffered government abuses. Also appointed to a voting term might be a Critical Evidence scholar. It is too simplistic to assert that one's career determines one's understanding of the world. Still, this committee would be experienced at seeing certain perspectives, in particular those of defendants in criminal cases and plaintiffs in cases challenging corporate and governmental actions. They would be aware of certain issues and problems by virtue of their work experience while there may be no reason to expect them to be alert to others. It is possible to see how these committee members' backgrounds would influence their decisions once on the Committee through no lack of good will or competence. And the same is true for the actual Committee as currently composed. It is slanted so dramatically toward the experience of prosecutors, and additionally of large corporations, that we should expect these viewpoints to matter for evidence rulemaking outcomes.

II. THE PROSECUTORS AND THE RULES

Evidence is law's epistemology.[41] It establishes what the legal system accepts as proof and forms a central part of how law filters reality. Evidence rules are ostensibly

extensively engaged with and modified the rules had five members who were not white men over the course of working on the rules.

40 *Committee Roster*, *supra* note 23. Historically, the committee has been 85% men. Coleman, *supra* note 1, at 391.

41 Catharine A. MacKinnon, *Mainstreaming Feminism in Legal Education*, 53 J. LEGAL. ED. 199, 209 (2003).

tailored to seeking just and accurate determinations.[42] Yet in facilitating, and at times making decisions about what evidence is admissible or relevant on a given question, the Rules create incentives that can shape reality even as they seek to help fact finders reconstruct it. Furthermore, unlike other procedural rules, that make few to no claims about empirical reality as they set filing deadlines or allocate the number of depositions, evidence rules claim an empirical foundation. The Rules embody beliefs about how people or things work. They use underlying assumptions about incentives, human behavior, or personality traits to tailor what evidence about character or credibility comes into court, which hearsay is deemed reliable, and what evidence should be excluded despite its clear relevance.

If evidence rules claim to translate empirical facts into truth-seeking rules, at least in theory, those evidence rules would need to be updated as we learn more about the world.[43] A lot has changed in the half century since the Federal Rules of Evidence were adopted. Frederick Sanger developed DNA sequencing in 1977, but DNA evidence was not used in a courtroom setting until 1987.[44] As DNA helped exonerate more and more of the wrongfully convicted, those cases helped show that eyewitnesses can be very wrong even as they are very certain of themselves. Two eminent groups of scientists and lawyers have studied what passes for forensic science in our courtrooms and found the majority of it to be unscientific and unreliable, at least as currently practiced.[45] And social scientists have determined that people do not necessarily make more reliable statements under certain conditions as assumed by hearsay rules.[46]

Socially, the country has also changed enormously. Though felony convictions are still stigmatizing, particularly for Black men, the sheer volume of criminal law and the percentage of Americans presently or previously incarcerated means that

42 FED. R. EVID. 102.

43 Not every armchair psychological assumption underlying the FRE is problematic. For a thoughtful discussion of whether it matters that the FRE rely on "'old' understandings of human nature," see Timothy T. Lau, *Reliability of Dying Declaration Hearsay Evidence*, 55 AM. CRIM. L. REV. 373, 405 (2018); Teneille R. Brown, *The Content of Our Character*, 126 PENN. ST. L. REV. 1 (2021).

44 James T. Griffith and Susan L. Leclair, *DNA in the Courtroom: The 21st Century Begins*, 1 U. MASS. L. REV. 62, 80 (2006).

45 COMM. ON IDENTIFYING THE NEEDS OF THE FORENSIC SCI. CMTY., NAT'L RSCH. COUNCIL, STRENGTHENING FORENSIC SCIENCE IN THE UNITED STATES 188 (2009), www.ojp.gov/pdffiles1/nij/grants/228091.pdf [NAS REPORT]; PRESIDENT'S COUNCIL OF ADVISORS ON SCI. & TECH., FORENSIC SCIENCE IN CRIMINAL COURTS 122 (2016), https://obamawhitehouse.archives.gov/sites/default/files/microsites/ostp/PCAST/pcast_forensic_science_report_final.pdf [PCAST Report].

46 This in contrast to FRE 803(2), which allows excited utterances as an exception to hearsay. *See* Steven Baicker-McKee, *The Excited Utterance Paradox*, 41 SEATTLE U. L. REV. 111, 153 (2017) (explaining that "individuals vary in their inclination and ability to lie while under stress, in the types of lies they tell while in an excited state, and in the sorts of conditions under which they are more or less motivated or able to lie"). *See also*, FRE 804(b)(2), which allows dying declarations as an exception to hearsay in prosecutions for homicide. Bryan A. Liang, *Shortcuts to "Truth": The Legal Mythology of Dying Declarations*, 35 AM. CRIM. L. REV. 229, 240 (1998) (describing physiological and psychological data showing likelihood of "impaired cognition" of dying declarants).

many more Americans are likely to know someone with a prior conviction. Other indicia of credibility have changed as well. While maintaining financial standing, having a stellar reputation in the community, or complying with some vision of heterosexual orthodoxy used to be fixed proxies for morality and believability, the elite cultural hegemony that once cemented those ideals has been replaced by more fractured and contested norms of believability.

In the face of new knowledge and social change, federal evidence rules have remained notably fixed. Tellingly, the most significant changes – changes to evidentiary rules in sex crimes cases and the incorporation of the Daubert standard into the rules on expert testimony – came about as a result of Congressional action prompted by specific social movements and Supreme Court precedent.[47] But in so many other areas where federal rulemakers might have acted in light of new information, they have chosen to do nothing. There has been no meaningful change to rules on expert and scientific testimony in response to the NAS or PCAST reports. The hearsay rules continue to embrace ideas about human cognition and truthfulness that are questionable at best.[48] The rules governing credibility and character evidence remain rooted in nineteenth-century conceptions of social worthiness and antiquated ideas about debiasing and character.[49] And specialized relevance rules continue to cling to the outdated behavioral assumption that excluding evidence about insurance will keep jurors in a tort case from factoring the possibility that a party has insurance into their damages calculation.[50] The list could go on.

Many of the inaccuracies described above are substantial and indefensible. Rule 609, for example, which allows impeachment with prior convictions, has no demonstrated benefit to fact-finding and has been shown to contribute to wrongful convictions by silencing defendants with criminal records.[51] As Professors Beety and Oliva discuss in this volume, faulty forensics continue to lead to wrongful convictions even as they prop up the carceral state.[52] Teaching or taking an evidence class is now an exercise in unpacking one foundationless armchair psychological explanation after another. Yet even the most criticized and problematic rules remain virtually unchanged from their 1975 iterations. An attorney who learned the Federal Rules of Evidence in 1975 and spent the next fifty years on a space station would be able to

47 *See, e.g.*, Aviva A. Orenstein, *Deviance, Due Process, and the False Promise of Federal Rules of Evidence 403*, 90 CORNELL L. REV. 1487, 1495–505 (2005); Mark A. Behrens and Andrew J. Trask, *Federal Rule of Evidence 702: A History and Guide to the 2023 Amendments Governing Expert Evidence*, 12 TEX. A&M L. Rev. 43, 44 (2024).

48 *See supra* notes 47–8 and accompanying text.

49 *See, e.g.*, Julia Simon-Kerr, *Credibility by Proxy*, 85 GEO. WASH. 152, 185–92 (2017).

50 Edith Greene, *On Juries and Damage Awards: The Process of Decisionmaking*, 52 L. CONTEMP. PROBS. 225 (1989) (noting empirical evidence that jurors are influenced by insurance in awarding damages even when it is not in evidence).

51 John H. Blume, *The Dilemma of the Criminal Defendant with a Prior Record – Lessons from the Wrongfully Convicted*, 5 J. EMPIRICAL LEGAL STUDS. 477, 488–92 (2008).

52 Valena E. Beety and Jennifer D. Oliva, *Evidence on Fire*, 97 N.C. L. REV. 483, 502 (2019).

use them effectively in a federal courtroom today. While for some, this may look like laudable stability and a sign of success, for those who systematically bear the weight of the rules' failures, it is anything but.

Why the stasis? This is a perennial question, but it has sparked heated scholarly exchange. For example, when Professor Alex Nunn argued that codification and the onerous rulemaking process are at the heart of the problem, Professors Dan Capra and Liesa Richter – who works with Professor Capra as an "Academic Consultant" to the Advisory Committee – raced to defend the process, cataloging amendments to the rules.[53] At the heart of this disagreement, however, is not really a factual claim about whether the rules are largely inert, but rather differing beliefs about the normative desirability of deference to the existing code and a commitment to slow, incremental change.

This chapter posits that one driver of the evidence rules' relative inertia may be more mundane and more sinister. Chief Justice Rehnquist is on record advising Evidence Advisory Committee Chairs that they should not "engage in law reform,"[54] and it is possible that Chief Justice Roberts has done the same. As Professors Chutkow and Heise write in their recent empirical analysis of federal rules committees, "[w]ithin the Judicial Conference structure, historical and anecdotal evidence supports the contention that Chief Justices use appointments strategically to affect substantive outcomes and consolidate power within the judicial bureaucracy, usually by preferencing judges with aligned political or ideological views to serve in key appointive positions."[55] Fixity in the rules has been seen as a positive by those who fear problems with predictability and administrability that might arise in a more fluid evidentiary regime.[56] While the focus on operability is relatively mundane, there is a more problematic dimension to this resistance to reform, one that requires looking at the broader context in which these rules operate. Notwithstanding growing concerns about wrongful convictions, mass incarceration, overcriminalization, and racial disparities in the criminal legal system, and notwithstanding the clear resource imbalances on the civil side that systematically favor large corporate entities, those who hold power over the Advisory Committee are apparently satisfied with the status quo. And one way to ensure the continuation of that status quo is to create a committee that is structurally designed to resist change, even without an explicit charge to avoid reform.

Enter the Prosecutors

Since 1993, the DOJ has had the most powerful seat on the Evidence Rules Advisory Committee in the sense that it is not subject to the term limits of all other members. Further, at present only two members of the Committee have no prosecutorial

53 *See generally*, Nunn, *supra* note 6; Capra and Richter, *supra* note 32.

54 Rice, *supra* note 17, at 829 ("The Chief Justice has made it clear to new chairpersons that he does not want the Committee to engage in law reform ....").

55 Chutkow and Heise, *supra* note 35, at 999.

56 Capra and Richter, *supra* note 28, at 1876.

experience. This matters because, as described above, the positionality of group members will inevitably influence their views of the rules. Research in other contexts has found that "having been a former prosecutor, as well as the length of time that service spans, makes a judge significantly more likely to rule against a motion to suppress."[57] Going further, critical theorists have argued that the predominance of prosecutors on the bench is one root cause of pervasive "counter-majoritarian and antidemocratic judicial decisionmaking."[58]

In the case of the Federal Rules of Evidence, that predominance favors the status quo where the rules have been most contested. Rule 609 is perhaps the most maligned of all the Federal Rules of Evidence. It permits prior convictions to be introduced to impeach the credibility of a witness, including the accused in criminal cases, on the theory that those convictions are relevant to the witness's credibility. Scholars and judges criticized the practice of prior conviction impeachment even before it was codified in the Federal Rules, and the criticism has continued unabated in the years since. Empirical studies have shown that jurors use prior convictions to lower the burden of proof in close cases and that the rule contributes to wrongful convictions by deterring the accused from testifying.[59] Scholars, including this author, have demonstrated the rule's link to antiquated conceptions of which witnesses are worthy of belief and to racist and xenophobic witness incompetency practices of the late nineteenth and early twentieth centuries.[60] Scholars have also shown that the rule currently disadvantages racial minorities who are disproportionately likely to have prior convictions due to racialized policing and charging practices.[61] In addition, scholars have demonstrated that judges often ignore the balancing tests embodied in the rules.[62] And there is no consensus on which crimes are admissible as bearing on truthfulness or untruthfulness.[63]

The Advisory Committee has considered proposals to change Rule 609 seventeen times since it was reconstituted in 1993.[64] During that time, the Reporter has

57 Banks Miller and Brett Curry, *When Advocates Become Adjudicators: Tracing the Effects of Prosecutorial and Public Defense Experience on Judicial Decision Making*, 51 AM. POL. RSCH. 796, 796–804 (2023).

58 Brandon Hasbrouck, *Movement Judges*, 97 N.Y.U. L. REV. 631, 651 (2022).

59 Theodore Eisenberg and Valerie P. Hans, *Taking a Stand on Taking the Stand: The Effect of Prior Criminal Record on the Decision to Testify and on Trial Outcomes*, 94 CORNELL L. REV. 1353, 1358–61 (2009); Blume, *supra* note 51, at 488–92.

60 *See, e.g.*, Simon-Kerr, *supra* note 49, at 185–92.

61 *See, e.g.*, Anna Roberts, *Conviction by Prior Impeachment*, 96 B.U. L. REV. 1977, 2004–5 (2016).

62 *See, e.g.*, Jeffrey Bellin, *Circumventing Congress: How the Federal Courts Opened the Door to Impeaching Criminal Defendants with Prior Convictions*, 42 U.C. DAVIS L. REV. 289, 293 (2008).

63 *See, e.g.*, Simon-Kerr, *supra* note 49, at 185–92.

64 Meetings of the Advisory Committee on Evidence Rules (Nov. 1996, Apr. 1997, Apr. 2015, Oct. 2015, and Apr. 2016, considering a unified notice provision applicable to Rule 609) (Oct. 1998, Nov. 2008, Apr. 2009, and Nov. 2009, proposing or approving technical amendments to Rule 609) (Apr. 2002, Nov. 2003, and Apr. 2004, forming an amendment substituting "character for truthfulness" for "credibility" and changing "if it involves dishonesty or false statement" to "that readily can be determined

consistently advocated for change. Certain academics have been invited to speak to the Advisory Committee about the need for reform. Yet, the only non-technical change to the rule came in 2006 in the form of a small amendment that did not succeed in clarifying which crimes are admissible under a portion of the rule that forces judges to admit prior convictions if they involve "dishonesty or false statement." The Advisory Committee apparently continued to agree, as it did in 1993, that "one should not open a Pandora's box by recommending changes to Rule 609."[65]

In 2023–24, through the work of Professor Capra and an invited presentation by Professor Bellin, the Advisory Committee once again considered a proposal to change the rule. Professor Bellin suggested eliminating the part of the rule that permits impeachment of defendants in criminal cases with their prior convictions.[66] Most agree that that part of the rule is the most problematic as it contributes to the loss of testimony from the accused, offers a huge lever to prosecutors in plea bargaining, causes the fact finder to make forbidden propensity inferences, and can add no probative information over and above the accused's obvious incentives to lie or tell the truth. Prior to the Advisory Committee meeting, in addition to Professor Bellin's presentation, the Coalition for Prior Conviction Impeachment Reform, a group of eleven leading scholars on the issue, wrote in support of the proposal.[67] Both that letter and Professor Bellin's proposal cited empirical evidence showing the silencing of the accused and the effect on the burden of proof.

The Advisory Committee then met in April 2024 to discuss the proposed change. The Committee's discussion was not itself a rule change proposal. Instead, such discussion is the first step in the rule change process and takes place at a meeting open to members of the public.[68] Only if the Committee puts forward an actual proposal for a rule change would the public be invited to contribute comments. Thus, only members and invited speakers could be heard at the April meeting.

At the April meeting, the Committee member from the Office of the Federal Defender, ensured that the Advisory Committee heard a presentation in support of the proposal from a highly experienced Federal Public Defender, including information the office had collected about how often public defenders' clients are silenced or take

to have been a crime of dishonesty or false statement) (Apr. 2014, rejecting the addition of a probative-prejudicial balancing test to Rule 609(a)(2)) (Oct. 2017, Apr. 2018, Oct. 2023, and Apr. 2024, discussing the potential abrogation of Rule 609(a)(1) and other substantive changes).

65 Meetings of the Advisory Committee on Evidence Rules (Sept. 1993).

66 Meeting of the Advisory Committee on Evidence Rules, Presentation by Professor Jeffrey Bellin (Oct. 27, 2023). *See also*, Jeffrey Bellin, *Eliminating Rule 609 to Provide a Fair Opportunity to Defend Against Criminal Charges: A Proposal to the Advisory Committee on the Federal Rules of Evidence*, 92 FORDHAM L. REV. 2471 (2024).

67 Letter from the Coalition for Prior Conviction Impeachment Reform to the Advisory Committee on Evidence Rules (Apr. 11, 2024), www.uscourts.gov/file/78468/download.

68 There seem to be no special efforts to alert the public to the existence of Advisory Committee meetings.

pleas rather than risk being impeached with prior convictions.[69] The presentation also highlighted the racial inequities in a rule that attaches a discrediting collateral consequence to prior convictions, given the racialized reality of the criminal legal system.[70]

The DOJ, in contrast, came to the meeting with a presentation that essentially said, "nothing to see here." Judges can do balancing and exclude prior convictions. According to the DOJ, if some judges admit prior convictions very similar to what has been charged in a given case, those errors are just a mistaken application not a problem with the rules.[71] Although the DOJ did not highlight this in the presentation, Rule 609 offers advantages to prosecutors seeking convictions.[72] Perhaps the largest of those is that accused people would rather take plea bargains than face a trial in which they must stay silent or risk exposing their prior convictions to the jury. Either choice is a bad one for the defendant and a positive for a prosecutor whose goal is a guilty plea or conviction.

Most Advisory Committee members seemed to accept the DOJ's viewpoint. They suggested that in the absence of "data" on how Rule 609 is being used, there was no reason to believe there is any problem with the rule.[73] Essentially, the DOJ was successful in characterizing all existing information on problems with Rule 609 as "anecdotal."[74] There was no discussion of the problem of racial injustice, and no acknowledgment of the other substantive problems with the rule. With the exception of the representative from the public defenders, the Committee simply chose not to engage with the substantial legal scholarship that has provided data – empirical and otherwise – to substantiate the problems with the rule. Nor did it ask that the DOJ provide "data" that might demonstrate the rule's validity, such as by demonstrating a connection between prior convictions and a witness's likelihood of lying on the witness stand. The status quo was taken as presumptively right. In short, it seemed clear that "data" was not really the issue. Rather, the Committee lacked any political will to make a change.

Over objections based on feasibility and necessity from both the Reporter and the representative from the Federal Judicial Center, the Advisory Committee did decide to ask for "data" from the Center on how Rule 609 operates vis-à-vis defendants in criminal cases.[75] It also agreed to meet again to talk about the possibility of

69 Minutes from the Meeting of the Advisory Committee on Evidence Rules 7–8 (Apr. 19, 2024) ("[Federal Public Defender Melody Brannon] closed by explaining that the availability of Rule 609(a)(1) impeachment is preventing criminal defendants from testifying, thus preventing them from going to trial, resulting in guilty pleas even in cases where there is a viable defense.").

70 *Id.* at 7 ("[Ms. Brannon] explained that the prejudice from Rule 609(a)(1) impeachment is enhanced for her clients of color due to their disproportionately higher rates of prior conviction.").

71 *Id.* at 9 (Apr. 19, 2024) ("If trial judges are applying [the balancing test] improperly, Mr. Miller [from the DOJ] suggested that there could be opportunities for judicial education but that a rule amendment was not the correct response.").

72 Of course, as Professor Roberts writes in her chapter, "Teaching Impeachment", in this volume, prosecutors may choose to eschew the opportunity to use Rule 609.

73 Minutes from the Meeting of the Advisory Committee on Evidence Rules at 11 (Apr. 19, 2024).

74 *Id.* at 10.

75 *Id.* at 10–12.

adding the word, "substantially" to the balancing test under which prior convictions are admitted against defendants in criminal cases.[76]

Such a change is small compared to what advocates have been seeking. And it is precisely the kind of adjustment that the Advisory Committee favors. Prior to its May 2025 meeting, the Committee seemed undecided on whether to approve the amendment. The winds shifted once Elizabeth Shapiro, still representing the DOJ, succeeded in introducing certain changes to the Advisory Committee Notes and subsequently announced the DOJ's support for the amendment. As others have observed, "if the DOJ opposes a proposed amendment on any plausible ground, the chances of that proposal progressing to the next stage are very slim indeed."[77] In this case, the DOJ's change of position carried three votes with it, and the amendment passed a Committee vote by 8–1.[78] At the time of writing, the notice and comment period for this proposal is ongoing.

This description of the discussion around Rule 609 is symptomatic of larger dynamics, both on the Federal Advisory Committee and likely on many state rules committees around the country. At the federal level, efforts to revise the rules on character evidence, hearsay, and expert testimony, to name just a few, have all been met with analogous refusals by the Committee to seriously contemplate the substantive problems at the heart of those rules. Instead, the Committee has refused to act or sought compromises that would maintain the evidence code as it exists.[79] At the state level, it is difficult to draw definitive conclusions without more individualized inquiry as the states take differing approaches to evidence rulemaking. Nonetheless, there are lessons that can be drawn. All but three states permit impeachment with prior convictions, and as at the federal level, there has been almost no meaningful change to state rules. Looking to the federal example suggests that homogeneity of interests – and particularly committees dominated by prosecutors or former prosecutors – is a likely contributor.

III. CONCLUSION

In a 1995 self-study of federal judicial rulemaking conducted by the Judicial Conference, one comment stands out. Robert Evans of the American Bar Association wrote that the membership of the Evidence Rules Advisory Committee needs attention. It is important, he argued, that "appointments to the rules committees reflect the demographic diversity of the legal community and that membership also more

76 *Id.*

77 Capra and Richter, *supra* note 28, at 1910–11.

78 This observational account is substantiated by a close reading of the meeting minutes and report to the standing committee. They suggest that the Committee had been deadlocked on the proposal (one member was absent, hence the tie at 4-4) but then voted 8-1 in favor of the change. In the interim, two changes to the proposal, including a revised Advisory Committee Note "as edited by the Department of Justice" meant that the DOJ announced its support for the provision. *Compare* Minutes of the Meeting of November 8, 2024, Evidence Committee Agenda Book, May 2, 2025 *with* Advisory Committee on Evidence Rules Report to the Standing Committee, June 10, 2025.

79 *See* Anya Bernstein and Julia Simon-Kerr, *Keeping Evidence Real*, 111 Iowa L. Rev. 589 (2026).

substantially represent the practicing bar, especially trial lawyers and criminal defense lawyers, and the academy."[80] Thirty years later, this statement is as true as ever.

The Advisory Committee needs demographic diversity and different modes of engaging with sources of knowledge beyond the elite.[81] But the change that might make the greatest immediate difference in the absence of any other structural change would be to term limit the DOJ's representative on the Committee. Further, although prosecutors represent the public and the search for truth, as Professor Roberts reminds us in this volume,[82] representing the diversity of the legal community matters. Former prosecutors on the Committee should be balanced by an equal number of former public defenders.

Whether a simple play for continuity or a more troubling mechanism for perpetuating government control over the rules of evidence, the existing structure has created a legitimacy problem for the rules of evidence. Law students may laugh when they learn the rationale for Rule 411 – the rule excluding evidence about insurance – but they are closer to crying when they try to reconcile the prohibition on propensity evidence with the practice of prior conviction impeachment. What today's students see is a system in which prior conviction impeachment is an end run around the legal system's commitment to judging acts not character and a tool for prosecutors to secure convictions.

Why can't the Advisory Committee grasp what these law students find so intuitively obvious? After decades of good faith efforts at persuasion, the time has come to consider whether this is a committee that is unpersuadable by design. Rule 609 helps secure convictions. Rule 411 is silly but apparently unthreatening to the corporate bar. The hearsay rules are a can of worms best left untouched.[83] This might all be in some way defensible if, in fact, the rules also meaningfully assist the trier of fact in finding the truth. For many of these rules, it is clear that they do not. Rather, it seems, those in power are content with a stasis that maintains it.

Evidence rules should offer consistency and predictability in the trial process. But if we want a system that also promotes truth and justice, the rules must also be responsive to social change and new facts. And rulemakers must be proactive when rules become a source of injustice and antithetical to finding the truth. The thirty-year experiment of prosecutorial control over rulemaking has shown that prosecutors are ill-suited to accomplishing this mandate. If anything, government power has become more entrenched through interpretations of the rules that disfavor marginalized groups and a committee unwilling to make all but the smallest of corrections. Breaking the prosecutorial monopoly on rulemaking power is an obvious and necessary precondition to making any changes to the rules, and it is one that is long overdue.

80 SELF-STUDY, *supra* note 8, at 714 (Comment from Robert D. Evans, Director, Governmental Affairs Office, American Bar Association).

81 *See* Okidegbe, *supra* note 3; Bernstein and Simon-Kerr, *supra* note 79.

82 Anna Roberts, "Teaching Impeachment," in this volume.

83 This is not to say that the Advisory Committee never acts. For example, it has recently been progressing towards a rule intended to address problems with evidence generated by artificial intelligence.

Evidence Rulemaking and Community Participation

Ngozi Okidegbe

In November 2022, Curtis James Jackson, Aubrey Drake Graham, and 100 other hip-hop artists signed an open letter on change.org, "Art on Trial: Protect Black Art," denouncing the use of defendant-authored rap lyrics as evidence in criminal trials.[1] The petition was a direct response to Fulton County District Attorney Fani Willis's public announcement that her office would seek to admit the rap lyrics of Jeffery Lamar Williams (a.k.a. Young Thug) as proof of criminal intent in his RICO prosecution.[2] Mr. Williams's rap lyrics were ultimately found conditionally admissible by Judge Ural Glanville, the then presiding judge in the case.[3] But the target of the petition was broader. It demanded not only a change in prosecutorial practice – a common form of public protest, but a change in the rules of evidence. The petition explained how common it is for prosecutors to introduce rap lyrics as evidence in criminal trials and went on to describe it as a racially targeted practice that "punishes already marginalized communities and their stories of family, struggle, survival, and triumph."[4] Because triers of fact tend to lack the racial

For helpful comments and discussion, I am very grateful to Bennett Capers, Jenny Carroll, Erin Collins, Jasmine Gonzales-Rose, Daniel Harawa, Jasmine E. Harris, Kathryn Miller, Jamelia Morgan, Alex Nunn, Aviva Orenstein, and Julia Simon-Kerr. I also received many useful comments and suggestions at the 2023 Lutie A. Lytle Black Women Law Faculty Workshop, 2023 University of New Mexico School of Law Faculty Workshop, 2025 Critical Evidence Colloquium, and 2025 Law and Society Annual Meeting.

1 Kevin Liles, *Art on Trial: Protect Black Art*, CHANGE.ORG (June 8, 2022), www.change.org/p/art-on-trial-protect-black-art; Warner Music Grp., *Art on Trial: Protect Black Art* (Nov. 1, 2022), www.protectblackart.co/.

2 Tat Bellamy-Walker, *Georgia DA Fani Willis Says Rap Lyrics Will Continue to Be Used in Criminal Cases*, NBC NEWS (Sept. 1, 2022, 3:34 PM), www.nbcnews.com/news/nbcblk/georgia-da-fani-willis-says-rap-lyrics-will-continue-used-criminal-cas-rcna45680; Re-Indictment at 31, 34, 47–8, State v. Williams, No. 22 SC182273 (Ga. Super. Ct. 2022), https://ga-fultoncountysuperiorcourt2.civicplus.com/DocumentCenter/View/1346/REINDICTMENT.

3 Deena Zaru, *Judge Rules Rap Lyrics Can "Conditionally" Be Used as Evidence in Young Thug Trial*, ABC NEWS (Nov. 9, 2023, 1:19 PM), https://abcnews.go.com/US/judge-rules-rap-lyrics-conditionally-evidence-young-thug/story?id=104760646.

4 Warner Music Grp., *supra* note 1.

literacy needed to recognize rap music as art, they are predisposed to treat lyrics as "autobiographical depictions of [a criminally charged person's] lived experiences or personal knowledge."[5] Rather than appreciating that "[r]appers are storytellers, creating entire worlds populated with complex characters who can play both hero and villain," the open letter noted that "more than any other art form, rap lyrics are essentially being used as confessions in an attempt to criminalize Black creativity and artistry."[6] The letter concluded by calling for legislative intervention to limit the use of rap lyrics as evidence.[7]

Reading this letter reoriented me. It was not the first time that I heard an argument against the use of rap lyrics as evidence in criminal trials. In her pathbreaking piece, "Poetic (In)justice? Rap Music Lyrics as Art, Life, and Criminal Evidence," Professor Andrea Dennis surfaces how the use of rap lyrics as evidence is part of an array of practices that fuel mass incarceration and the criminalization as well as discrediting of Black lived experiences and art.[8] In an empirical study on the prevalence of this practice, Professors Dennis, Erik Nielson, and their students found that rap lyrics authored by charged persons were admitted as evidence in at least 700 reported cases.[9] But what struck me about the petition was its audience. Though it demanded change from system insiders, specifically legislators, prosecutors, and trial judges, it was not solely directed to them. Rather, the petition was also directed at empowering the rap industry, the hip-hop community, and the Black and Brown communities subjected to mass criminalization and prosecution.[10] Though drafted and publicized by industry leaders (Kevin Liles is the former president of the Warner Music Group), the petition reflected and had built upon years of grass-root organizing by racially marginalized rappers and community members bringing attention to the race-d and class-ed nature of the evidentiary system and the importance of democratic collective action in contesting it.[11]

The petition provides an opportunity to think about the place of collective and contentious action from socially marginalized communities in evidence rulemaking. What role could such actions have in redressing how evidence law supports social subordination? While rap lyric evidence has garnered significant attention,

5 Ngozi Okidegbe, A *"Bad Rap": R. v. Skeete and the Admissibility of Rap Lyric Evidence*, 66 CRIM. L.Q. 294, 296 (2018).

6 Warner Music Grp., *supra* note 1.

7 *Id.*

8 *See generally*, Andrea L. Dennis, *Poetic (In)Justice? Rap Music Lyrics as Art, Life, and Criminal Evidence*, 31 COLUM. J. L. & ARTS 1, 18, 30 (2007); *see also*, Charis E. Kubrin and Erik Nielson, *Rap on Trial*, 4 RACE & JUST. 185, 197, 201–3 (2014).

9 Erik Nielson and Andrea L. Dennis, *Mapping Rap on Trial*, www.rapontrial.org/ (last visited June 1, 2025). For my part, I have studied the racially targeted practice in the Canadian context – *see generally*, Okidegbe, *supra* note 5.

10 Warner Music Grp., *supra* note 1.

11 *See, e.g., Circling the Elements*, https://circlingtheelements.wixsite.com/hip-hop-conference (last visited June 1, 2025), which was an annual hip hop conference that brought together rap artists and scholars.

the practice is illustrative, rather than aberrative of how the rules of evidence fail socially marginalized criminally charged people, their families, friends, and communities. In theory, the rules operate as a safety valve to screen out untrustworthy evidence that risks undermining trial accuracy, fairness, or efficiency.[12] In practice, this gatekeeping function has done little to protect these interests, especially when it comes to socially marginalized people who encounter the system as criminally charged people.[13] Consider other examples. In most jurisdictions, proof of a charged person's undocumented status is admissible to impeach their credibility, but testimonial or documentary evidence that would contextualize this status is inadmissible collateral character evidence.[14] In most jurisdictions, criminal convictions can be admitted against a testifying charged person or their witnesses for impeachment purposes, but the disciplinary record of a testifying police officer is inadmissible propensity evidence.[15] Professor Bennett Capers explains how a wide array of information that jurors will take into account, such as "style of dress [of a witness or charged person], the presence of family members, [gender presentation] and race" are "rarely treated as evidence by the Rules" and therefore are unregulated by them.[16] And finally, judges routinely qualify police officers as experts on the meaning of admitted rap lyrics, but inversely tend to exclude defendant-proffered experts, such as sociologists, cultural studies scholars, or even rappers under the common knowledge ban under the rules governing expert evidence.[17]

On the surface, these examples might seem too specific to be redressed by a party-driven evidentiary system like ours. After all, the unfair prejudice noted in the above examples arise from a party's choice to introduce relevant evidence that is embedded with harmful social meaning for one group but not for another group. No evidentiary system can redress the unfair prejudice that every specific piece of evidence may pose for the trier of fact. It is the reason why we have the balancing test under Rule 403 to consider issues of unfair prejudice on a case-by-case basis, right? Not exactly. The rules of evidence strive to account for the unfair prejudice that the introduction of certain types of evidence can pose, just not with socially

[12] Bennett Capers, *Evidence Without Rules*, 94 NOTRE DAME L. REV. 867, 869 (2019).

[13] Montré D. Carodine, *Race Is Evidence: (Mis)Characterizing Blackness in the American Civil Rights Story*, *in* CIVIL RIGHTS IN AMERICAN LAW, HISTORY, AND POLITICS, 66, 80–2 (Austin Sarat ed., Cambridge University Press 2014); Jasmine Gonzales Rose, *Toward a Critical Race Theory of Evidence*, 101 MINN. L. REV. 2243, 2259 (2017).

[14] Christian Powell Sundquist, *Presumed Guilty: "Illegal Alien" Evidence and the Rights of Non-Citizen Defendant*, 81 N.Y.U. ANN. SURV. AM. L. 19, 48–51 (2025).

[15] Julia Simon-Kerr provides this example in support of her contention that the rules on character evidence are created for and structurally designed to serve the interests of those racialized white and gendered as male. Julia Simon-Kerr, *A New Baseline for Character Evidence*, 76 VAND. L. REV. 1827, 1832–3, 1840–1 (2023).

[16] Capers, *Evidence Without Rules*, *supra* note 12, at 868.

[17] JACK I. LERNER AND CHARIS E. KUBRIN, RAP ON TRIAL: A LEGAL GUIDE FOR ATTORNEYS 81–2 (2022), https://cpb-us-e2.wpmucdn.com/sites.uci.edu/dist/d/2220/files/2022/08/Rap-on-Trial-Legal-Guide-v1.1.pdf. *See* FED. R. EVID. 702 advisory committee's note on proposed rule.

marginalized communities in mind. Consider, for example, the specialized rules of relevance.[18] These rules are concerned with how triers of fact are prone to misapprehend the probative value of specific categories of evidence in ways that undermine trial accuracy and fairness on the one hand and discourage socially valuable activities on the other. Among the targeted pieces of evidence are subsequent remedial measures, settlement negotiations, offers to pay medical expenses, and liability insurance.[19] One might wonder why the rules of evidence appear more worried about a jury awarding damages in a medical malpractice case on the basis that the doctor is insured (a result detrimental to insurance companies' bottom line) than a jury wrongly convicting a racially marginalized rapper on the basis of racial and class tropes about rap lyrics.

In the last decade, Professors Montré Carodine, Jasmine Gonzales Rose, Bennett Capers, Julia Simon-Kerr, and other Critical Evidence scholars have raised the centrality and complicity of evidence law in upholding how the criminal system subordinates groups on the basis of race, class, gender, sexual orientation, and disability.[20] Many have contributed to this very book. They aim to transform the relationship between evidence law and social hierarchy by showing how evidence law subordinates socially marginalized groups whether by the rules themselves,[21] judicial discretion in interpreting the rules,[22] prosecutorial practice around the rules,[23] or all of the above.[24] It is a project of emancipation and antisubordination. But the project is incomplete. To date, the potential place of collective action by socially marginalized communities in evidence law has been undertheorized. What the number of signatories of the petition reveals is that at least some segment of the marginalized communities most affected by the rules

[18] The author thanks Julia Simon-Kerr for bringing this point to my attention.

[19] Fed. R. Evid. 407, 408, 409, and 411.

[20] *See generally, e.g.*, Carodine, *Race Is Evidence*, *supra* note 13, at 66–8, 80–2; Erin Collins, *Evidence Rules for Decarceration*, 50 Fordham Urban L.J. 353, 353–5 (2022); Capers, *Evidence Without Rules*, *supra* note 12, at 874; Gonzales Rose, *Critical Race Theory*, *supra* note 13, at 2243; Anna Roberts, *Models and Limits of Federal Rule of Evidence 609 Reform*, 76 Vand. L. Rev. 1879, 1880 (2023); Simon-Kerr, A *New Baseline*, *supra* note 15, at 1830; Jasmine B. Gonzales Rose, *Racial Character Evidence in Police Killing Cases*, Wis. L. Rev. 369, 389-91 (2018).

[21] Anna Roberts, *Impeachment by Unreliable Conviction*, 55 B.C. L. Rev. 563, 576 (Mar. 28, 2014) (discussing how "due to uneven distributions of criminal convictions, and because of race-based assumptions of guilt, the rule disproportionately affects people of color").

[22] George Fisher, Evidence 158–9 (4th ed., Foundation Press 2022) (noting how FRE 410 has been interpreted as barring the introduction of a prosecutor's statements during plea negotiations at trial, despite the explicit language of the rule that only charged persons' statements are barred); *See also*, Guerrilla Guides, Guerrilla Guides to Law Teaching No. 5: Evidence (Sept. 5, 2017), https://guerrillaguides.wordpress.com/2017/09/05/no-5-evidence/.

[23] Montré D. Carodine, *The Mis-characterization of the Negro: A Race Critique of the Prior Conviction Impeachment Rule*, 84 Ind. L.J. 521, 536 (2000).

[24] *See* Bennet Capers, *Race, Gatekeeping, Magical Words, and the Rules of Evidence*, 76 Vand. L. Rev. 1855, 1857–61 (2023).

seek to interject their views and be heard. More specifically, they seek to intervene into evidence rulemaking.[25]

Despite this, there is little place for bottom-up movements, contentious politics, and collective action from socially marginalized communities in evidence rulemaking. These communities are unable to stop, shape, or determine the rules themselves or influence how they are interpreted. Legal reform around rap lyrics as evidence stands as an anomaly to this trend. In recent years, a few states have introduced or passed legislation aimed at constraining the admissibility of artistic expression with the implicit motivation to limit the admissibility of rap lyric evidence.[26] These successes are rare and are more the result of the interests of powerful and politically connected constituencies than bottom-up organizing. For example, though the push to redress the unfair treatment of rap music under the rules of evidence started as a bottom-up movement, recent legislative reform has come at the behest of the music industry.[27]

It is this current state of evidence rulemaking that this chapter seeks to push back against. My hope is to show how and why evidence rulemaking should be democratized. By using the term "democratize," I mean to invoke the "demosprudential" vision of democracy developed by Professors Lani Guinier and Gerald Torres, where collective action and contentious politics by ordinary people operating as a social movement influence legal reform.[28] In one sense, evidence rulemaking is democratic. The rules are the product of the judicial branch acting on its own or with final approval from the legislature, meaning that evidence rulemaking is accountable to the demos politically.[29] Yet, in another sense, evidence rulemaking

[25] The chapter uses "evidence rulemaking" to refer to jurisdictions where their highest court is empowered either constitutionally, statutorily, or by inherent power to promulgate most evidentiary rules and oversee the development of rules of evidence for courts: *See generally*, Thomas Ward Frampton and Brandon Charles Osowski, *The End of Batson? Rulemaking, Race, and Criminal Procedure Reform*, 124 COLUM. L. REV. 1, 12–14 (2023) (describing judicial rulemaking and the differences between federal judicial rulemaking and state-level judicial rulemaking in the context of criminal procedure).

[26] *See* Assemb. B. 2799, 2021–2022 Leg., Reg. Sess. (Cal. 2022); CAL. EVID. CODE § 352.2(b)(1)–(3) (West 2023); H.B. 475, 2022–2023 Leg., Reg. Sess. (La. 2023); H.B. 1429, 2023 Reg. Sess. (Md. 2023) (introduced); S.B. 1738, 2023 Legis. Sess. (N.Y. 2023) (introduced); H.B. 990, 2023 Reg. Sess. (Ga. 2023) (introduced); H.B. 353, 102d Gen. Assemb., Reg. Sess. (Mo. 2023) (introduced); H.B. 3420, 103d Gen. Assemb. (Ill. 2023) (introduced).

[27] Kevin Liles started the petition when he was chairman and CEO of Warner Music Group. Warner Music Group has been very involved in the publicity around the petition. *See* Warner Music Grp., *supra* note 1.

[28] Lani Guinier and Gerald Torres, *Changing the Wind: Notes Toward a Demosprudence of Law and Social Movements*, 123 YALE L.J. 2740, 2749, 2757 (2014).

[29] *See, e.g.*, Rules Enabling Act, ch. 651, 48 Stat. 1064 (1934) (codified as amended at 28 U.S.C. § 2072 (2018)) (governing federal evidence rulemaking and indicating that rulemaking is shared between Congress and the judicial branch); ARIZ. CONST. art. 6, § 5(5); ARIZ. REV. STAT. ANN. § 12-109 (2023) (Arizona's Supreme Court exercises rulemaking power that is derived from the constitution); State v. Templeton, 59 P.3d 632, 641 (Wash. 2002) (noting that Washington's rulemaking comes from

is not democratic. Those with the most power to shape the rules are members of a narrow segment of society – lawyers, judges, academics, and legislators.[30] And while these system insiders are not a monolith, and some insiders (prosecutors and former prosecutors) exercise more authority than others (academics and public defenders), rulemakers are part of the system insiders' class.[31] Advisory committees are chaired and staffed with system insiders who control the progression of the evidentiary rules and, unlike in the administrative rulemaking context, are under no obligation to account for how public viewpoints received through notice and comment processes informed their decision to adopt, amend, or reject a rule change.[32] At the same time, notice and comment processes are by and large dominated by practicing attorneys and law academics giving the legal field a de facto right of first refusal over reform.[33] This alongside structural discrimination and distributional inequalities means that the rules and how they are interpreted tend to reflect moral panics, the whims of system insiders, or the needs of powerful political interest groups.

The anti-democratic nature of evidence rulemaking is not a system flaw. Evidence rulemaking is operating as intended.[34] Evidence rulemaking has not been viewed as an appropriate site for democratization. It was not designed to be informed, influenced, or constrained through collective action particularly by the most marginalized members of the demos.[35] In fact, the technical nature of the rules along with their litigation focus points against robust (or potentially contentious) bottom-up collective participation. Socially marginalized communities have an informational

its inherent power). Another argument is that evidence rulemaking is democratic because arguably "it is an exercise in democracy to deprive judges of some of their traditional powers and to place those powers into the hands of lay juries." Otto M. Kaus, *All Power to the Duty – California's Democratic Evidence Code*, 4 LOY. L.A. L. REV. 233, 233 (1971). *But see also*, Ethan J. Leib, *Are the Federal Rules of Evidence Unconstitutional?*, 71 AM. U. L. REV. 911, 911 (2021) (contending that the rules of evidence violate the principle of separation of powers).

30 Kenneth W. Graham Jr., *California's Restatement of Evidence: Some Reflections on Appellate Repair of the Codification Fiasco*, 4 LOY. L.A. L. REV. 279, 286–9 (1971).

31 Julia Simon-Kerr, "Prosecutors and Federal Evidence Rulemaking," in this volume (documenting "the degree to which evidence rulemaking power is concentrated in the hands of prosecutors and former prosecutors").

32 Administrative Procedure Act, 5 U.S.C. §§ 553, 706 (2006). Though this problem affects judicial rulemaking generally, the permutation of this problem in evidence rulemaking has been subjected to less scholarly scrutiny in comparison to rulemaking around criminal procedure and civil procedure: *see, for example*, Brooke D. Coleman, *#SoWhiteMale: Federal Civil Rulemaking*, 113 NW. U. L. REV. 52, 55–8 (2018); *see generally*, Frampton and Osowski *supra* note 25, at 4.

33 Graham, *supra* note 30, at 288 (discussing this problem in the context of California's evidence code). Though not the product of judicial rulemaking, a similar dynamic occurs in judicial rulemaking.

34 Paul Butler makes this point in the context of criminal law reform. Paul Butler, *The System Is Working the Way It Is Supposed to: The Limits of Criminal Justice Reform*, 2019 FREEDOM CTR. J. 75, 81 (2020) (explaining how "many of the problems identified by critics are not actually problems, but are instead integral features of policing and punishment in the United States. [The problems] are how the system is supposed to work.").

35 G. Alexander Nunn, *The Living Rules of Evidence*, 107 U. PA. L. REV. 937, 950–6 (2022) (describing federal evidence law's transition from a creature of common law to judicial rulemaking).

disadvantage that undermines their ability to judge the tradeoffs associated with any specific rule change or any specific change to a rule's interpretation. These factors support keeping evidence rulemaking a technocratic affair. Perhaps, when one considers the value-laden judgments of rulemaking and the need to maintain a functioning system of litigation, we should defer to the expertise of system insiders and not bring in the demos.[36]

Shifting toward a demosprudential approach would invite a different starting point as to who should have a say in evidence rulemaking. Demosprudence stresses that law reform should neither start nor stop with legal elites. While legal elites have a place, law reform should be understood as a dialectic between courts, lawyers, legislatures, and social movements.[37] Democratizing evidence rulemaking under a demosprudential vision is a worthy pursuit.[38] It could provide another mechanism for rulemakers to recognize, consider, and account for the normative values embedded in the current rules of evidence, as well as how those values orient the rules toward the reinforcement of social hierarchies. It could enable rulemakers to scrutinize how the rules interact with the structures of race, gender, class, disability, heteronormativity, cisgenderism, and the intersection thereof to penalize and exert control over marginalized individuals and communities. Moreover, it could provide the basis for recognizing that ordinary people should have a say in the epistemic underpinnings of our evidentiary system and perhaps even power over it. If we engage in a demosprudential approach, we might be able to generate a broader conversation about how to create durable social change from below that would make evidence rulemaking more inclusive, responsive, and democratic.

In the remainder of this chapter, I will describe the state of evidence rulemaking and the current avenues for public participation. I will then conclude by identifying two possible reforms that would provide a path toward a democratic iteration of evidence rulemaking "that inform[s] and [is] informed by the wisdom of the people."[39]

EVIDENCE RULEMAKING AND PUBLIC PARTICIPATION

In order to imagine what a democratic iteration of evidence rulemaking could look like, it is important to first contextualize its current state. As background, evidence rulemaking is but one model of evidence law. Unlike with the Rules of Criminal

[36] Paul H. Robinson, *Democratizing Criminal Law: Feasibility, Utility, and the Challenge of Social Change*, 111 Nw. U. L. Rev. 1565, 1566 (2017) (discussing how the "grand principle [of democratizing criminal law] must give way to practical realities" since "some of the realities … might derail a movement toward democratizing criminal law").

[37] Guinier and Torres, *supra* note 28, at 2749.

[38] In this volume, Michele Gilman's chapter on "The Relevance and Prejudice of Poverty Evidence" touches on the importance of a demosprudential approach for providing judges and defense lawyers with a framework "for bringing the larger social context of poverty into the courtroom."

[39] Lani Guinier, *Foreword: Demosprudence Through Dissent*, 122 Harv. L. Rev. 4, 15–16 (2008).

Procedure and the Rules of Civil Procedure, several jurisdictions do not engage in judicial rulemaking for their rules of evidence. In New York and at least five other states, evidentiary rules remain a product of common law jurisprudence that is occasionally modified by statute.[40] In at least two states, evidentiary rules are controlled by the legislature with the judiciary exerting back-channel influence.[41]

In evidence rulemaking jurisdictions, evidence rulemaking is typically managed by an advisory committee solely focused on the rules of evidence.[42] However, a few jurisdictions have a single committee that manages criminal procedure, civil procedure, and evidence rulemaking.[43] Within evidence rulemaking, there are two models. In the first model, which is the most common, the state supreme court has exclusive authority to promulgate evidentiary rules either from the state constitution, its inherent power, or from statute.[44] Under the second model, the judicial branch and the legislative branch share authority to promulgate rules. This shared authority can take different forms. In Alaska, for example, the Alaskan Supreme Court has the authority to make evidentiary rules, but those rules can be changed by the legislature by a two-thirds vote.[45] Federally, on the other hand, the Supreme Court of the United States promulgates a rule that can only go into effect if Congress chooses not to reject, modify, or delay it.[46]

Notwithstanding these minor differences, the substance of evidence rulemaking remains largely the same. Typically, an advisory committee consisting of system insiders is tasked with periodically reviewing, correcting, and updating the rules. In most jurisdictions, advisory committees consist primarily of judges with a few positions reserved for practicing lawyers and one non-committee position reserved for an academic usually serving as a liaison or reporter.[47] In a few jurisdictions, advisory

40 Fisher, *supra* note 22, at 3.

41 *See, e.g.*, Ga. Code Ann. §§ 24-1-1 to 24-99-3 (2023); Barbara S. Gaal, *Evidence Legislation in California*, 36 Sw. U. L. Rev. 561, 561 (2008) ("Most evidentiary rules in California are statutory and are contained in the Evidence Code.").

42 *See, e.g.*, *Code of Evidence Oversight Committee of the Supreme Court*, Conn. Jud. Branch, www.jud.ct.gov/Committees/code_evidence/ (last visited June 1, 2025).

43 In Maryland, evidence rulemaking is managed by the Maryland Supreme Court Standing Committee on Rules of Practice and Procedure: *Standing Committee on Rules of Practice and Procedure*, Md. Cts., www.mdcourts.gov/rules (last visited July 1, 2025). In Delaware, evidence rulemaking is managed by Delaware Supreme Court Permanent Advisory Committee on Supreme Court Rules, Rules of Civil and Criminal Procedure, and Rules of Evidence. *See Opportunities to Serve: Supreme Court Boards, Commissions and Committees*, Del. Cts. Jud. Branch, https://courts.delaware.gov/supreme/committees.aspx (last visited July 1, 2025).

44 Ariz. Const. art. VI, § 5 ("The Supreme Court shall have the power to make rules relative to all procedural matters in any court.").

45 Alaska Const. art. IV, §15 ("The supreme court shall make and promulgate rules governing the administration of all courts. It shall make and promulgate rules governing practice and procedure in civil and criminal cases in all courts. These rules may be changed by the legislature by two-thirds vote of the members elected to each house.").

46 Rules Enabling Act, ch. 651, 48 Stat. 1064 (1934) (codified as amended at 28 U.S.C. § 2072 (2018)).

47 *See, e.g.*, U.S. Cts., Advisory Committee on Evidence Rules (May 2, 2025), www.uscourts.gov/sites/default/files/document/2025-05_evidence_rules_committee_agenda_book_final.pdf; *Code of Evidence Oversight Committee of the Supreme Court*, *supra* note 42.

committees are a branch of the state bar and therefore consist primarily of lawyers.[48] In either case, advisory committees are typically empowered to propose a new rule or rule change, which is subsequently required to undergo a public notice and comment process.[49] Following the notice and comment process, the proposal is sent to the highest court in the jurisdiction for approval.[50] If it is approved, the proposed rule either comes into effect automatically or only after a specified time of legislative inaction.[51]

With that background, we can turn to the question of the place of participation in evidence rulemaking. Despite the intricacies of each jurisdiction's approach to evidence rulemaking, one commonality shared is the lack of participation by the public, specifically by socially marginalized communities. This democratic exclusion has three dimensions. The first dimension concerns the makeup of advisory committees. Generally speaking, committee members are either judges, practicing attorneys, government officials, and in some cases academics. The exact configuration of committees varies by jurisdiction. In the federal sphere, for example, the Advisory Committee on Evidence Rules is chaired by a United States District Court judge and its membership consists of one United States Court of Appeals judge, two other United States District Court judges, an Indiana Supreme Court judge, two private practice attorneys, one representative from the Office of the Federal Public Defender's, and principal associate Deputy Attorney General (ex officio).[52] In Colorado, on the other hand, committee members consist of eight judges, three private practice attorneys, a representative from Colorado's state public defenders, two professors, a representative from the Colorado Attorney General, and a representative from the Denver District Attorney's office.[53] In Florida, the committee members are all members of the Florida bar.[54] In most jurisdictions, eligibility to serve on the advisory committee is de facto reserved for those in the legal field.[55]

[48] *See, e.g.*, *Code and Rules of Evidence Committee*, THE FLA. BAR [hereinafter Florida Rules of Evidence Committee], www.floridabar.org/about/cmtes/cmte-cm215/ (last visited June 1, 2025).

[49] *See, e.g.*, *How the Rulemaking Process Works*, U.S. CTS., www.uscourts.gov/forms-rules/about-rulemaking-process/how-rulemaking-process-works (last visited June 1, 2025).

[50] *Id.* Note that there are sometimes steps between a proposed amendment going from the advisory committee to the court. For example, when the advisory committee on the rules of evidence in the federal context supports a proposed amendment, they must send it to the judicial conference and standing committee on rules of practice and procedure. If both approve the change, then it is sent to the full Supreme Court.

[51] *See, e.g.*, *Committee on Rules of Practice and Procedure*, IND. JUD. BRANCH, www.in.gov/courts/iocs/committees/rules/ (last visited July 1, 2025); Federal system: *How the Rulemaking Process Works*, *supra* note 49.

[52] *See, e.g.*, ADVISORY COMMITTEE ON EVIDENCE, *supra* note 47, at 7 (this is the makeup as of May 2, 2025).

[53] *Rules of Evidence Committee*, COLO. JUD. BRANCH, www.coloradojudicial.gov/rules-evidence-committee?language=es (last visited June 1, 2025).

[54] Florida Rules of Evidence Committee, *supra* note 48.

[55] *Committee Membership Selection*, U.S. CTS., www.uscourts.gov/forms-rules/about-rulemaking-process/committee-membership-selection (last visited June 1, 2025). In jurisdictions where the advisory committee is a branch of the state bar, only members of the state bar are eligible to

It is rare for a member of the public to serve on an advisory committee, though it is permitted in a few jurisdictions.[56]

The second dimension concerns who can propose a new rule or a rule change. In most jurisdictions, rule changes can only be formally proposed by the advisory committee or by the court itself. The exceptions are Pennsylvania, Washington State, Arizona, and the federal regime, where any individual can file a petition for a rule change to the Court or submit a rule change suggestion to the advisory committee.[57] Even in these contexts, socially marginalized communities still face barriers to effective participation in the rulemaking process, specifically regarding formulating rule suggestions in a register cognizable to rulemakers. In "Knowledge in the People: Rethinking 'Value' in Public Rulemaking Participation," the authors describe how every rulemaking community has epistemic, linguistic, and normative practices that govern which viewpoints will be credited and which ones will be discredited by a rulemaking body.[58] While they identify this problem in the administrative context, the same rings true in evidence rulemaking. Evidence rulemaking practices discourage rulemaking suggestions based upon narrative, storytelling, or personal experience. The epistemic underpinning of evidence rulemaking operates to exclude ways of knowing about the world accessible only to socially marginalized communities.[59] This epistemic exclusion limits the kind of interventions that can influence the rulemaking process with disproportionate effect on socially marginalized communities.

The third dimension concerns notice and comment processes. In theory, notice and comment processes are meant to give the public an opportunity to learn about and give their input into proposed new rules or rule changes.[60] Ideally, they ensure transparency, public accountability, and that rules reflect the public interest or at the very least do not stray far from them.[61] In practice, notice and comment processes in

serve. *Administration of Rules of Evidence Committee*, ST. BAR OF TEX., www.texasbar.com/AM/Template.cfm?Section=Consider_a_State_Bar_Committee&Template=/CM/HTMLDisplay.cfm&ContentID=41398 (last visited June 1, 2025).

56 *But see*, *Advisory Committee on Rules*, N.H. JUD. BRANCH, www.courts.nh.gov/resources/committees/advisory-committee-rules (last visited June 1, 2025).

57 *See, e.g.*, *How to Suggest a Change to Federal Court Rules and Forms*, U.S. CTS., www.uscourts.gov/forms-rules/about-rulemaking-process/how-suggest-a-change-federal-court-rules-and-forms (last visited June 1, 2025); ARIZ. R. SUP. CT. 28 (2019); *Supreme Court Rulemaking*, WASH. CTS., www.courts.wa.gov/court_rules/pdf/GR/GA_GR_09_00_00.pdf (last visited June 1, 2025); 201 PA. CODE r. 103 (2025), www.pacodeandbulletin.gov/Display/pacode?file=/secure/pacode/data/201/chapter1/s103.html&d=reduce.

58 Cynthia R. Farina et al., *Knowledge in the People: Rethinking "Value" in Public Rulemaking Participation*, 47 WAKE FOREST L. REV. 1185, 1188–90, 1193–4 (2012).

59 Russell K. Robinson, *Perceptual Segregation*, 108 COLUM. L. REV. 1093, 1120 (2008) ("In general, [B]lack and [W]hite people obtain information through different informational networks, which results in racialized pools of knowledge.").

60 Beth Simone Noveck, *The Electronic Revolution in Rulemaking*, 53 EMORY L.J., 433, 441–2, 517 (2004) ("Participation in rulemaking is one of the most fundamental, important, and far-reaching of democratic rights.").

61 Richard A. Bierschbach and Stephanos Bibas, *Notice-and-Comment Sentencing*, 97 MINN. L. REV. 1, 5 (2012).

evidence rulemaking do not serve this function. Though this problem plagues notice and comment processes in administrative rulemaking as well, evidence rulemaking is particular in how captured it is by system insiders. In my research on the comments submitted in the federal context, it is incredibly rare to come across a comment that is not from an academic, a public defender, a defense lawyer, a representative from a national civil rights organization, a private practice attorney, or a retired government official. A major reason for this lack of participation comes from how the proposed amendments to the Rules are drafted. If one did not have a clear understanding of the rules of evidence, how they interact with each other, and how they operate in a court setting, it is hard to comment on whether a rule should be adopted as is, modified, or rejected. Consider, for example, the 2024 amendment to Rule 106 of the Federal Rules of Evidence, which came into effect January 1, 2025. The Rule allows a party to introduce a writing that completes an already admitted statement over a hearsay objection. For one to comment on the correctness of this approach, one would need an understanding of the hearsay rule as well as the circumstances in which a party would seek to introduce another part of an already admitted statement. This informational hurdle is further exacerbated by the language of the proposed amendments themselves, which are nearly linguistically impenetrable to those who are not part of the epistemic community that currently controls evidence rulemaking.

A further barrier to public participation is that the notice and comment processes at the state level vary in their accessibility to the public. While in Arizona, notice and comment processes are similar to that available at the federal level, Delaware has no information about if and how its notice and comment processes operate.[62] These dimensions combine to create an iteration of evidence rulemaking that is democratically exclusionary to the public as a whole. However, given the demographic makeup of those on advisory committees, on Supreme Courts, and in the academy, this democratic exclusion is disproportionately experienced by socially marginalized communities, who lack other avenues to have their lived experiences and value preferences considered by rulemakers.[63] We live in an iteration of evidence rulemaking that cannot be shaped by the knowledge, perspectives, values, or needs of the socially marginalized communities.

APPLYING A DEMOSPRUDENTIAL APPROACH TO EVIDENCE RULEMAKING

What is demosprudence? Developed by Professors Lani Guinier and Gerald Torres, demosprudence provides a way "to view lawmaking [and meaning-making]

[62] *Court Rules Forum*, AZCOURTS, www.azcourts.gov/Rules-Forum (last visited June 1, 2025). Delaware has no public information on its website regarding notice and comment in evidence rulemaking; At the state level, participation in the notice and comment processes is noticeably lower than at the federal level.

[63] Coleman, *supra* note 32, at 56, 68 (describing this issue in the context of civil procedure rulemaking).

from the perspective of popular mobilizations."[64] It starts from the position that social change neither starts nor ends with courts, legislatures, or lawyers.[65] Rather, "for legal change to reflect real social change it must take account of, and engage with, alternative or contending sources of power" that emanate from "social movements and other sustained forms of contentious politics and collective action."[66] This point is particularly salient when it comes to securing legal change that has the potential to benefit the lives of political and economic minorities who "cannot simply rely on judicial decisions [or legislative action] as the solution to their problems."[67] Social movements make social change possible by subjecting conventional understandings of current law and legal principles to critique and interrogation, enabling new social meanings connected to "the lived experiences of those on whose behalf they are named" to assume their place.[68] They also make social change durable by operating as "*resources* for the protection" of legal change.[69]

Although the concept of demosprudence originally focused on constitutional rights, principles, and doctrine, its application has not been limited to that sphere.[70] Applying it to evidence rulemaking is warranted given that opening up "space to those previously excluded or marginalized" to participate in rulemaking that affects their lives provides "the necessary conditions for a genuine 'community of consent.'"[71] It would be a recognition that the power to make evidentiary rules should – as is the case with the exercise of other public law powers in other contexts – derive its moral force and legitimacy from the people affected by it.[72] Evidence rulemaking should be understood as a democratic project.

This begs the question of how might we move toward a demosprudential approach to evidence rulemaking? Two caveats are in order. First, such a shift would be radical and not a complete solution. A complete solution lies outside of law, perhaps even in Afrofuturism or the abolition of certain rules.[73] Yet, democratizing evidence rulemaking is worth pursuing, since it has the potential to be part of the multifaceted solution needed to dismantle the complicity of evidence

64 Guinier and Torres, *supra* note 28, at 2745.
65 *Id.*
66 *Id.*
67 *Id.* at 2749.
68 *Id.* at 2759; Jack M. Balkin and Reva B. Siegel, *Principles, Practices, and Social Movements*, 154 U. PA. L. REV. 927, 929 (2006).
69 Guinier and Torres, *supra* note 28, at 2759 (emphasis original).
70 *See generally*, Monica Bell et al., *Toward a Demosprudence of Poverty*, 69 DUKE L.J. 1473, 1507 (2020) (proposing that judges engage in a demosprudential approach to redress the criminalization of poverty).
71 Guinier and Torres, *supra* note 28, at 2749, 2744.
72 *Id.* at 2752.
73 Collins, *supra* note 20, at 373 (noting how "some rules are so unprincipled and/or unjustified that they should be abolished").

rulemaking in social hierarchy. We need only to look at rape shield or at the recent measures to limit the introduction of rap lyrics to see how collective, sustained, and contentious organizing by socially marginalized communities can produce change that surfaces the need to completely rethinking evidence law. Second, Professor Lani Guinier leaves open the role of legal elites in a demosprudential project. While her co-authored piece, "Changing Winds,"[74] was exclusively focused on social movements operating without the aid of traditional legal elites, her sole-authored piece, "Foreword: Demosprudence Through Dissent," contended that legal elites, particularly judges have an important function in ushering in a more democratic iteration of law, doctrine, and principles.[75] For this reason, this section considers two reforms, one based on empowering rulemakers and the other based on empowering socially marginalized communities. With that in mind, it is useful to think about how a demosprudential approach could be operationalized. One modest approach would be to provide rulemakers with the knowledge needed to create rules that take into account the lived realities of socially marginalized communities. This type of proposal has been advanced before. In exploring how judges could sensitize themselves about the role of the current criminal law process in criminalizing poverty, Professor Monica Bell, Stephine Garlock, and Alexander Nabavi-Noor turn to judicial rulemaking.[76] They contend that judges can, in their capacity as rulemakers, "create and revise rules from the perspective of how people *actually live*."[77] They go so far to suggest judges and court staff should "spend[] time in the neighborhoods in their jurisdictions where poor litigants reside."[78] One could imagine adapting this proposal to the evidence rulemaking context. During the rulemaking process, rulemakers could have an affirmative duty to read and take into account empirical research on how the rules of evidence affect socially marginalized communities. Critical empirical work on how the rules affect how socially marginalized charged persons navigate the criminal legal system is an emerging area of evidence law scholarship.[79]

Requiring rulemakers to engage in the lived experience of socially marginalized communities could produce rule changes that recognize the social stratification that the rules indirectly support. Consider, for example, how in 2018, Washington became among the few jurisdictions to make evidence of a witness's immigration status generally inadmissible.[80] The rule change emerged from a petition submitted by Columbia Legal Services, Northwest Immigrant Rights Project, Legal Voice,

74 Guinier and Torres, *supra* note 28.

75 Guinier, *supra* note 39, at 16, 102, 113 (discussing how judicial dissents can take on a demosprudential role).

76 Bell et al., *supra* note 70, at 1520.

77 *Id.* at 1521 (emphasis original).

78 *Id.* at 1522.

79 Jasmine Gonzales Rose et al., *Antiracist Expert Evidence*, 134 Yale L.J. 2362, 2365 (2025).

80 Sundquist, *supra* note 14, at 21, 60–1.

and the Washington Association of Prosecuting Attorneys.[81] The petition explained how failing to restrict the introduction of evidence of a witness's immigration status had been discouraging the testimony of undocumented immigrant victims and witnesses and was a barrier to their access to the justice system.[82] Though the rule change did not mention this petition by name, there is reason to believe that the contextualization of the lived experiences of undocumented people helped push the Washington Supreme Court to approve the rule change. For this reason, requiring rulemakers to consult the work of critical scholars or even hold meetings with socially marginalized communities could broaden rulemakers' knowledge base and equip them with tools to reduce the social harms of the current rules.

To illustrate the importance of such a reform, it is useful to consider how an affirmative duty would apply to this chapter's opening example. Imagine if an advisory committee had an affirmative duty to consider the impact of the current admissibility standard for rap lyric evidence in criminal trials on racially marginalized charged persons and their communities. To accomplish this mandate, one would imagine committee members involving racially marginalized rappers, particularly ones convicted in part due to the admission of their rap lyrics at their criminal trial. They might hold a one-day summit where racially marginalized rappers present evidence, answer questions, and are compensated for their time and labor. They might also review empirical evidence on the prevalence of the practice, such as Professors Erik Nielson and Andrea Dennis's database showing nearly 700 cases of rap lyric evidence. This committee would then have access to a diverse set of knowledge sources from which to decide whether an amendment to the rules of evidence is needed to limit prosecutors' ability to introduce rap lyric evidence given its role in racial subordination. One downside is that this approach is predicated on an active evidence rulemaking process. However, this assumption may not bear resemblance to reality. In "The Living Rules of Evidence," Professor Alexander Nunn makes the point that rulemaking has been frozen in time, at least at the federal level.[83] If that is true, then requiring rulemakers to proactively account for the lived realities of socially marginalized communities may not lead to rule changes. This brings us to the second, and more radical, proposal. One could imagine subjecting the rules of evidence to a periodic citizen audit. Professors K. Sabeel Rahman and Hollie Russon Gilman define audits as "the organized, strategic use of participatory monitoring techniques to hold government actors accountable."[84] In "From Civic Tech to Civic Capacity: The Case of Citizen Audits," Professor Rahman aims to identify and generate the

[81] Columbia Legal Servs., et al., *Proposal to Adopt New Rule of Evidence 413 Concerning Evidence of Immigration Status*, WASH. CTS., www.courts.wa.gov/court_rules/?fa=court_rules.proposedRuleDisplay&ruleId=605 (last visited June 1, 2025).

[82] *Id.*

[83] Nunn, *supra* note 35, at 959, 962.

[84] K. SABEEL RAHMAN AND HOLLIE GILMAN, CIVIC POWER: REBUILDING AMERICAN DEMOCRACY IN AN ERA OF CRISIS 184 (Cambridge University Press 2019).

pressure needed to respond to "fundamental failures of governance and disparities of political power" that reduce life chances and opportunities for marginalized communities.[85] Cop watching is an often-cited example of citizen audits. As Professor Jocelyn Simonson's work explores, mass policed communities audit the police by recording and disseminating videos of routine police violence as part of a larger effort to challenge the idea that the criminal system protects public safety.[86] The question becomes how to institutionalize citizen audits to ensure that they are autonomous and in the hands of socially marginalized communities. Professor Rahman contends that it is possible to build mechanisms within governing bodies themselves that give excluded communities an opportunity to help "define and then monitor outcomes."[87] Using the example of the Community Reinvestment Act of 1977 (CRA), he contends that citizen audits of bank lending have become common due to the design features of the CRA, specifically the fact that the CRA requires the collection and publication of data on bank lending.[88] This feature allowed community groups representing socially marginalized communities to perform their own audits on the data.[89] Another important design feature concerns how the CRA allows citizens to request the agency to investigate banks "that community groups felt were falling short of local needs."[90] This feature put pressure on banks to take into account local needs so as to avoid an investigation that might ultimately lower their CRA score.[91]

Applying this idea to evidence rulemaking, one approach would be to create a unit dedicated to evaluating the social impact of the rules. It could be modeled off the racial equity impact unit housed under the Maryland Department of Legislative Services that evaluates the racial impact of criminal justice legislation.[92] The unit could be required to engage with different community groups to develop working definitions and methods for tracking the disparate impact of the rules. The unit could also set up a process allowing any person to request that a rule or evidentiary practice be assessed for exacerbating or creating social inequities that undermine the rules' gatekeeping function. One could imagine requiring the unit to collect and make public data on the impact of assessed rules, which would allow for socially marginalized communities to conduct their own investigations. Involving these communities both at the policy level and providing them with access to data could empower them to render the rules' impacts more visible. It might also generate the

85 K. Sabeel Rahman, *From Civic Tech to Civic Capacity: The Case of Citizen Audits*, 50 PS: POL. SCI. & POL. 751, 751 (2017).

86 Jocelyn Simonson, *Copwatching*, 104 CAL. L. REV. 391, 398, 401 (2016); Bennett Capers, *Policing, Technology, and Doctrinal Assists*, 69 FLA. L. REV. 723, 724–5 (2017).

87 Rahman, *supra* note 85, at 755.

88 *Id.* at 755.

89 *Id.*

90 *Id.*

91 *Id.*

92 Md. Dep't Legis. Serv., *Racial Equity Impact Notes*, GEN. ASSEMB. MD. DEP'T LEGIS. SERV., https://dls.maryland.gov/about-us/racial-equity-impact-notes (last visited June 1, 2025).

political pressure needed to force the rulemakers to revise rules found to be strongly connected to social hierarchy or even create new rules. The impact could be radical. It could become part of a larger social movement that could orient the rules of evidence toward systemic reform.

CONCLUSION

The rules of evidence support the subordination of socially marginalized communities. The current paradigm governing evidence rulemaking supports this function. Democratizing the paradigm holds a potential path forward. Tapping into demosprudence opens up new possibilities of how to empower socially marginalized communities to incorporate their views and values into a system that democratically excludes them. By transforming evidence rulemaking into a system that can support the contentious and collective actions of socially marginalized communities, the rules of evidence can be reimagined. Perhaps it is possible to dismantle the rules complicity in social hierarchy, but only if its future iteration can be shaped by the viewpoints, values, and real-life experiences of the communities most harmed by the rules. Only then might we move toward a more inclusive and democratic iteration of evidence rulemaking for all.

The Living Rules of Evidence

G. Alexander Nunn[1]

INTRODUCTION

The jurisprudential evolution of evidence law is dead. At least, that's what we're expected to believe. After all, it's been forty-seven years since the common law pedigree of evidence law came to an end in the United States. Ushered in on the wings of a growing positivist movement, the enactment of the Federal Rules of Evidence purported to quell judicial authority over evidence law. Instead, committees, conferences, and members of Congress assumed responsibility for regulating our evidentiary regime, thereby capturing the evolution of evidence law in a single, transparent code. And as with other transitions to positive law, perhaps that shift inherently suggested that the Federal Rules of Evidence are "not a living organism" but simply a "legal document" that "says what it says and doesn't say what it doesn't say."

Of course, a dead evidentiary regime is not inherently anathema. Indeed, there are compelling arguments in favor of taking the lifeforce out of written law. By channeling all legal change through rulemakers and elected officials, controlling evidence law becomes clear and uniform across jurisdictions. Litigants can more readily predict which evidence is admissible and which evidence will be thrown out well before their trial date. Moreover, as a matter of political theory, the effort to codify evidence law ensures that rules regulating the flow of information in the courtroom are the product of careful, deliberate, and politically accountable actors. In the abstract, then, the turn to a codified evidentiary regime seems rather beneficial.

But reality is often unkind to abstract ideals. Frameworks that seem normatively desirable *in vacuo* often see problems emerge in application. And the Federal Rules of Evidence are no exception.

The inherent difficulty accompanying evidence law's transition to an unflinching code stems from the historic turbulence of evidence law itself. Since its relatively recent emergence in the late eighteenth century, evidence law has not been particularly stable. Indeed, for much of its history, evidence law was rather shallow in

[1] Excerpted from G. Alexander Nunn, *The Living Rules of Evidence*, 170 U. Pa. L. Rev. 937 (2022).

substance. In 1806, for example, a judge made the somewhat hyperbolic assertion that "[t]here is but one decided rule in relation to evidence, and that is, that the law requires the best evidence." Hyperbole aside, early evidence law was certainly a different creature than its modern descendant. In the early era, there was no firm exclusionary rule barring hearsay from the courtroom. Character evidence was fair game. Judges frequently advised juries on the merits of cases. Fearing perjury, many states still did not allow defendants to offer sworn testimony in the courtroom as late as 1890 – just eighty-five years before the codification of the Federal Rules of Evidence. As late as 1881, civil parties, too, were disallowed from offering sworn testimony in the courtroom.

Taken as a whole, then, stability in our evidentiary regime has been the exception, not the rule. The changes made to evidence law in just the century or two prior to the codification movement were fundamental in nature. Rather than fine-tuning a relatively stable machine, judges and state legislatures introduced massive reforms that sought to both align evidence law with evolving cultural norms and better ensure that trials achieve their ultimate goal of accurate, legitimate verdicts.

But the codification movement froze evidence law in time. The enactment of the Federal Rules of Evidence in 1975 took the then-existing culmination of a rapidly developing legal doctrine and suspended it at a rather arbitrary point in history.

Of course, evidence law's civil turn need not necessarily have led to substantive torpidity. Rulemakers are certainly capable of evaluating whether evidence law is achieving its normative aims and amending the regime when it's seen to be falling short. Indeed, there are now committees and conferences tasked with assuming the role of the common law judge by proposing beneficial changes. If the codification effort simply transmuted the evolution of evidence law from judicial caselaw to administrative and legislative channels, the effort would rightly be seen as benign – perhaps even desirable.

Codification, though, has bred entrenchment. The arrival of the Federal Rules of Evidence ushered in an anomalous era in evidence law, an era marked by relative stagnation in the doctrinal space. That's not to say that rulemakers have been lazy. Far from it. In the last half century, they have introduced no less than thirty substantive amendments to the Federal Rules and have entertained scores more. But the approved changes have been modest. Unlike the fundamental transformations in evidence law in the era leading up to codification, most of the amendments since the enactment of the Federal Rules of Evidence make only minimal alterations. A 2020 amendment modified the notice requirements for the introduction of prior acts under Rule 404(b). A 2019 amendment clarified the application of the residual hearsay exception under Rule 807. A 2017 amendment provided an easier means of authenticating electronic documents under Rule 902. Missing, though, are the broad structural changes and continual systematic introspection that have historically dominated evidence law.

One might fairly suggest that there's a simple explanation for the relative stability of evidence law under the Federal Rules – perhaps evidence law has reached its optimum. Perhaps the centuries preceding the codification effort were so fundamentally turbulent precisely because evidence law was in its infancy. Structural issues in our evidentiary regime have since been hammered out and, now, only modest fine-tuning is necessary. Thus, rulemakers' avoidance of significant evidentiary reform is merely the product of an absence of calls for any further change.

Were only it so. Although evidence law has stagnated over the last half century, the world around it has continued to evolve. In particular, developments in both the empirical and normative literatures testify to the continuing necessity of broad-scale evidentiary reform. … There has been no effort – nor even a suggestion – to fundamentally reshape evidence law to account for modern understandings. To borrow the words of fellow commentators, rulemakers have instead chosen an "inherently conservative" approach, expressing a simple affinity for the general status quo. …

I. TOWARD A CODIFIED EVIDENTIARY REGIME

Despite its prominent place in the American juridical landscape today, the Federal Rules of Evidence constituted a rather anomalous intervention at the time of their enactment. This is not to say that codification is unique to evidence law, nor even that the Federal Rules of Evidence were at the forefront of the twentieth century's broader codification movement. Rather, it's a recognition that the creation of an affirmative evidentiary code constituted a tectonic shift – a fundamental departure – from the centuries-old process by which courts previously regulated and improved our evidentiary regime.

Historically, evidence law was largely a creature of the judiciary. Common law jurisprudence served as the driving force behind evidentiary progression. Even as a positivist movement began to swell in the country a century ago, evidence law was initially seen as beyond the reach of codification. For instance, despite receiving the formal authority to draft a controlling evidentiary code from the Rules Enabling Act of 1934, stakeholders and the Supreme Court were initially in "no mood to tinker with the law of evidence." Instead, the common law progression of evidence law would continue. But that sentiment, of course, did not hold for long. The initial resistance to the evidence codification movement eventually gave way to ever-increasing calls for a uniform repository of evidence rules. And, indeed, the installation of the Federal Rules of Evidence in 1975 marked the death knell of evidence law's jurisprudential progression.

If the enactment of the Federal Rules of Evidence merely transferred the historic evolution of evidence law from judicial channels to more administrative avenues of change, there would be little reason for complaint. Capturing the progression of our evidentiary regime in a single controlling code can offer material normative gains by improving uniformity and transparency across jurisdictions.

But the turn to a positivist evidentiary regime has given rise to a more insidious consequence. Rather than merely redirecting the channels of evidentiary evolution in the United States, the enactment of the Federal Rules of Evidence has seemingly foreclosed the possibility of material change to our evidentiary regime altogether. In the half century since the federal evidence code emerged, rulemakers have entertained only modest amendments to the Federal Rules, simply fine-tuning the same system installed in the 1970s. Fundamental change to our evidentiary regime, change designed to ensure that evidence law accords with best empirical understandings and evolving standards of decency, has become all but impracticable. …

Despite evidence law's common law roots, historic turbulence, and fundamental constitutive reinventions, a swelling positivist movement in the latter half of the nineteenth century brought with it the winds of change. The political climate of the time increasingly favored legislative and administrative aggregations of power. Commentators have noted, for example, that in "the aftermath of its Watergate battle with the Executive branch, Congress was jealous and assertive of its powers." Across many substantive spaces, statutes and codes began displacing decisionmaking authority previously vested in the judiciary. And evidence law was no exception.

Although stakeholders initially predicted that evidence law would withstand the positivist movement's calls for codification, revolution came amid the sociopolitical turmoil of the 1960s. It was in the early part of that decade when the Judicial Conference and Standing Committee on Rules of Practice and Procedure first assembled a Special Committee on Evidence to expressly consider a reinvention of evidence law as a codified regime. And indeed, the Special Committee encouraged the development and adoption of a uniform code of evidence rules. Soon thereafter, Chief Justice Earl Warren established the first Advisory Committee on the Federal Rules of Evidence. The Advisory Committee, in turn, proposed its first draft evidentiary code in 1970. Following a series of revisions, the Supreme Court sent the draft Federal Rules of Evidence to Congress for approval in 1972. After two years of its own extensive share of negotiations, revisions, and substantive adjustments, Congress voted in favor of the evidence code in 1975. With a signature from President Gerald Ford in 1975, the Federal Rules of Evidence became law.

Without question, the enactment of the Federal Rules of Evidence was a positivist triumph. Contrary to centuries of practice, the code seemed to foreclose longstanding judicial authority to shape and evolve evidence law. Rather, rulemakers would hold the key to any evidentiary change. They became the new gatekeepers. And traversing their new gate is quite the endeavor.

Most (formal) amendments to the Federal Rules of Evidence now find their inception in the Advisory Committee on the Rules of Evidence. The Advisory Committee, which is composed of judges, practitioners, and academics, is charged with "carry[ing] on a continuous study of the operation and effect" of the Federal Rules. If the Advisory Committee supports a particular amendment to the evidentiary code, the game is not yet over – in fact, the labyrinth has just begun. The proposed amendment is sent from the Advisory Committee to the Judicial Conference and Standing Committee on Rules of Practice and Procedure. If it passes muster with the Judicial Conference, it is then sent to the full Supreme Court. Once the Supreme Court approves of a change, the proposed amendment takes a trip across First Street to Congress, where both the House and Senate have an opportunity to review the proposed change, and only once the amendment survives scrutiny from Congress does it take effect.

With that foundational understanding of evidence law's new constitutive form in place, it's worthwhile to take a step back for evaluation. To be sure, in a vacuum, the transition from a common law to a codified evidentiary regime might not seem particularly material. One might fairly question whether labeling the transition "revolutionary" is accurate. And indeed, theoretically, codification of the rules of evidence might be seen not only as substantively inconsequential but also juridically beneficial. After all, a copy of the Federal Rules of Evidence in every courtroom ensures that our evidentiary regime is applied fairly and consistently across jurisdictions.

But problems have emerged in practice. Fifty years of experience has revealed that the civil turn in American evidentiary law has, functionally speaking, resulted in the death of the historic progression of our evidentiary regime. The Federal Rules' cumbersome amendment process has largely foreclosed the possibility of the material change needed to ensure that evidence law continually accords with best empirical and normative understandings. In fact, it has had quite the opposite effect. It channels rulemakers into an "inherently conservative" approach that forgoes significant changes in favor of maintenance of the status quo. For instance, even if rulemakers did deem a particular amendment desirable, the current bureaucratic maze establishes a de facto three-year process to actualize it. Perhaps that long time horizon wouldn't be too detrimental were rulemakers willing to traverse it, but that has not been the case. Scholars have recognized that rulemakers have proven reluctant to tinker with any material aspect of the modern evidentiary code. Instead, likely in recognition of the fact that the code is generally achieving its goal of fostering legitimate adjudication, rulemakers have steered clear of the broad-scale structural reform that previously dominated the evidence landscape in the centuries preceding the Federal Rules' enactment.

Thus, evidence law has become frozen in time. The then-existing culmination of centuries of evidentiary evolution was enshrined in the 1975 code – a relatively arbitrary point in time, substantively speaking – and rulemakers have since demonstrated little appetite for continuing the common law's progressive evolution of our evidentiary regime.

Importantly, recognizing rulemakers' reluctance to broadly reform evidence law is not meant to imply that they have been inactive. Far from it. Rulemakers have pioneered no less than twenty-nine substantive amendments to the evidentiary code in the past half century.

But what close examination of those amendments reveals is that the last half century's changes to evidence law have been modest by historical standards. Those structural changes to our evidentiary regime made even just a century prior to the enactment of the Federal Rules of Evidence have all but disappeared. Recall that just 111 years before the Rules froze evidence law in time, the American trial was an entirely different affair. In many jurisdictions, defendants could not offer sworn testimony on their own behalf. The oath, not cross-examination, was the courtroom's primary truth-seeking tool. Even restrictions on character or propensity bars were relative newcomers. It took broad structural changes to transition away from that outdated form of adjudication.

Consider, too, a modern reference point. Even within the last half century, those small pockets of evidence law still free from rulemakers' grasp have continued to undergo radical reconstitution. Take the Confrontation Clause. Importantly for our purposes, the Confrontation Clause's residence within the Sixth Amendment dictates that its corresponding jurisprudence was largely unaffected by the enactment of the Federal Rules of Evidence. Statutes, of course, cannot supersede constitutional provisions. So, while the codification of the Rules largely froze the majority of our evidentiary regime in place, Confrontation jurisprudence maintained the natural state of judicial fluidity that typifies (portions of) constitutional law. And, perhaps as expected given the historic norm, Confrontation jurisprudence has continued to fundamentally evolve while the rest of evidence law has stood still. In the 1980s, just five years after the enactment of the Federal Rules of Evidence, the Supreme Court's decision in *Ohio v. Roberts* ushered in a jurisprudential era that conceived of the Confrontation Clause as provision primarily rooted in principles of reliability. That is, the *Ohio v. Roberts* Court considered the Confrontation Clause to be a witness-production adjudicatory tool predominantly designed to improve the reliability of evidence. Twenty-four years after *Roberts*, though, the Supreme Court radically reinvented the Confrontation Clause. In accordance with the historic spirit of evidence law, it fundamentally realigned doctrine to square it with (what the Court perceived as) improved understanding. To wit, the Supreme Court's 2004 decision in *Crawford v. Washington* overruled *Ohio v. Roberts*. And notably, the jurisprudential transformation offered by *Crawford* was not a minor recalibration; instead, *Crawford* entirely reimagined the Confrontation Clause as a provision centered around legitimacy and fairness principles rather than reliability. *Crawford* dramatically expanded the exclusionary scope of the Confrontation Clause, significantly changing the playing field of criminal adjudication.

Now compare these broad structural changes to the relatively modest amendments made to the Federal Rules of Evidence. Consider, for example, recent amendments to Federal Rule of Evidence 404. Rule 404 is one of the more controversial evidentiary rules. It allows, in certain situations, character and propensity evidence into the courtroom when that evidence is purportedly offered for a non-propensity rationale. But even when offered for a so-called permissible purpose, the introduction of propensity evidence requires factfinders to engage in nigh-impossible mental gymnastics; it is of course quite difficult to "unring the bell" and disregard information once it's before you. Because improper use of propensity evidence has a disproportionately negative effect on defendants, scholars and activists have long called for a major structural reformation of Rule 404. Yet, despite those calls for material change, rulemakers have steered clear. Instead, amendments to Rule 404 have pursued minor adjustments. For instance, a 2000 amendment introduced a "tit for tat rule," expanding the situations in which prosecutors can introduce character evidence against a defendant. A 2006 amendment clarified that general character evidence (as opposed to specific acts) is inadmissible in civil cases. A more recent 2020 amendment focused on notice requirements, requiring that an intention to introduce past acts is broadcast well before trial.

The amendments outlined above are by no means unimportant. They each offer necessary improvements or clarifications. But they are also demonstrative of an affinity for the status quo. Missing from the list of amendments – and from the list of changes even considered by rulemakers – is any substantial engagement with the underlying structural issues driving evidence law. Missing is continual, persistent self-reflection as to whether our current regime is best serving the normative ideals of accuracy and legitimacy. Missing is any attempt to expressly consider evidence law's role in falsely convicting scores of defendants exonerated by the Innocence Movement; or evidence law's potential to aid victims in the #MeToo era; or evidence law's place in an urgent national reckoning over race and the justice system.

Where does all this currently leave evidence law?

Evidence law is, by and large, frozen in time. Of course, it was by no means a foregone conclusion that the positivist turn culminating in the enactment of the Federal Rules of Evidence would put an end to evidence law's progressive historic evolution. Indeed, one could imagine an active body of rulemakers continually sifting the empirical and normative literatures as part of a perpetual introspective effort to optimize our evidentiary regime. Instead, amendments to the Rules have been rare; structural change has been non-existent.

And so as scientific and cultural understandings evolve, evidence law remains stagnant. The status quo reigns supreme.

SECTION 2

And Jurors

INTRODUCTION

Jurors are arguably the single most important motivator of U.S. evidence law. Fear of juror bias, and the tenet that jurors' knowledge of a case must be limited to facts immediately relevant to what is alleged in a charge or pleading, have shaped the rules since their origination at common law. Although jury trials now form a small part of how legal disputes are actually decided, jurors are still an outsized presence in the evidentiary system as the evidence rules and the possibility of a jury trial shape plea bargaining and settlement. Any comprehensive study of evidence thus must grapple with how the jury's shadow has molded the evidentiary system and the rules. And it also must account for the ways in which real juries are resistant to the type of regulation the rules seek to impose.

This section includes two excerpts from work that is not strictly within the Critical Evidence canon and yet introduces ideas central to the development of the field. George Fisher's "The Jury's Rise as Lie Detector," has been a central pillar of the evidence curriculum since its publication in 1997. In it, he shows that juries were conceived of as doing "lie detection" only relatively late in their use in trials. Further, this framing of the jury's role "followed the force of events," including changes to testimonial incompetency laws for Black witnesses, rather than arising by design or because of any actual ability of jurors to detect lies.

Turning from history to theory, the excerpt from Ron Allen's "Factual Ambiguity and a Theory of Evidence," although also not squarely within the genre, raises a key issue for Critical Evidence scholars in thinking about juries, or any fact finder: jurors come to court with preexisting knowledge and experiences that function *as evidence*. Highlighting and grappling with this baseline knowledge – information that is in some fundamental ways untouchable through evidence regulation because it exists prior to trial – is a central preoccupation for Critical Evidence thinkers.

In the excerpt from her piece, "(Un)Common Knowledge & Experience," Jasmine E. Harris picks up this theme. She conceptualizes the jury as a site of norm infusion into the system and identifies informational touchpoints at which a judge regulates the flow of information to juries. She then asks, "What if the normative baseline is inherently flawed?" at any of those points, taking disability as a potent example of the problems that can arise when jurors bring flawed social norms into the courtroom.

Rounding out this section is Daniel Harawa's critique of the no-impeachment rule and the Supreme Court's response to the problem of juror bias. In his chapter, "*Peña-Rodriguez v. Colorado*: Jury Secrecy and the Performance of Racial Justice," he argues that the Court's precedent in *Peña-Rodriguez v. Colorado*, by requiring proof of "overt" racism in order to impeach jurors, ignores subtler and more pervasive forms of bias that shape verdicts.

Together, these contributions complicate the conception of juries as lie detectors, and they raise questions for evidence law. What are the costs and benefits of a jury system that is essentially one of norm infusion and enforcement, particularly in a deeply unequal society where normativity may be infused with racism, sexism, or with problematic conceptions of disability? How do and should evidence rules respond?

Factual Ambiguity and a Theory of Evidence

Ronald J. Allen[1]

III. THE THEORY OF JUDICIAL EVIDENCE AND THE NATURE OF JURIDICAL AMBIGUITY

... I think it fair to say, at any rate, that we lack consensus over the extent of our knowledge of conventional affairs (some people know, or believe they know, matters that elude others) or in what order aspects of it should be studied (some people regret ambiguity about wine more than ambiguity about truthfulness at trial; others do not). And of course, it is not obvious, outside of legal disputes, what the payoff might be for investing greater resources than we presently do in an organized effort to eliminate conventional ambiguity, which is probably why we invest the resources that we do.

Faced with such wide-ranging and intractable ambiguity, the law must forgo reliance on any formalized theory of evidence and instead locate the decision over what is evidence somewhere and more or less live with the results. Contrary to conventional legal belief, this locus is not the trial judge (unless sitting without a jury); it is instead the fact finder. Virtually all proffered material is admissible at trial; trial judges affect admissibility very little, and the formalities of the rules of evidence even less. The proffered data become evidence if they influence a fact finder. Whether they do is determined by the sum total of that person's experiences at the moment of decision, experiences which will by that time include the advocates' efforts to enlighten the fact finder about the implications of the material produced at trial and all the other observations generated by the trial.

Thus the banality of the theory of juridical evidence. Evidence is not a set of things, as the conventional theory would have it; it is instead the process by which fact finders come to conclusions about the past. It is banal in the sense that it reduces to the proposition that a disinterested fact finder reconstructs the past based on all the observational inputs available at the moment of judging. But with its banality comes genius. The genius of the theory of juridical evidence lies in the twin

[1] Excerpted from Ronald J. Allen, *Factual Ambiguity and a Theory of Evidence*, 88 Nw. U. L. Rev. 604, 627–30 (1994).

recognition that there is no alternative except official orthodoxy on conventional matters and that the probability of gathering the necessary information for an accurate reconstruction of the past increases astronomically with the size of the fact finding body and not just with the size of the evidentiary proffer at trial. Each fact finder is in essence a solitary scientist constantly reducing conventional ambiguity. This type of ambiguity is treated differently from the scientific variant because resources would be wasted by attempting to reach explicit agreement on its contours, and so we do not organize assaults on it. But when a dispute arises involving it, we gather a small set of individuals, from one (a judge) to twelve (an historical jury), to pool its members' knowledge in order to make sense of the evidence adduced. Given the lack of a social justification for organizing conventional knowledge on a scientific model, the law achieves an analogous result by holding a convention of lay scientists and requiring that they deliberate long enough to reach agreement.

This is not to say that juridical fact finding is wholly conventional in the sense that it bears no necessary relationship to reality and thus to the environment. Quite the contrary, for the same reason that most people do not starve in the presence of food or step in front of moving vehicles. Most of us navigate our environment quite effectively largely because we have a good grasp generally of the nature of reality, and more specifically, and more to the point, the conditions of a good explanation are well known even if only intuitively. …

Reason is the organizing force in the mental life of an intelligent creature – the orderer of chaotic events into coherent experience. It is the instrumentality by which mind secures its grasp upon a difficult and unstable world. The rules of reason are "regulative principles" – instructions that keep the conduct of our various affairs on an efficient, effective, and thus intelligent basis. Reason is eminently practical – it wants what works (is efficient and effective). But it pre-eminently also wants what makes sense. The systematic aspect of reason inheres in its drive for intelligibility – in its demand for ways of proceeding whose appropriateness other intelligent agents can in principle perceive. …

There is no *a priori* definition of evidence, nor is there an *a priori* set of rules that determines factual findings, save for the commitment to rationality. Rather, each decision is a unique function of the interaction of the parties' sense of ambiguity with the fact finders' understanding of it that remains rational notwithstanding each decision's uniqueness and our inability to capture the decision process in a set of necessary and sufficient rules. …

Rather than carrying around in our heads tables of relative frequencies or likelihood ratios, we carry around stories, scripts, and scenarios, all more or less robust and all subject to modification in a virtually infinite variety of ways. "Evidence" in the human brain is embedded in these contexts, although fluidly in a way that permits constant cycling back and forth between the data, new and old, and their stories. It is into this bubbling cauldron that the trial "evidence" must enter, and its effect is determined by the interaction of the data with the prior knowledge stored in the related chunks constituting stories. Trial observations instantiate these stories and work modifications of them. This, of course, merely reemphasizes the dynamic nature of evidence and highlights that the data at trial that the conventional theory refers to as evidence is merely the means by which the preexisting stories and scenarios of fact finders are put into play, as it were, in order to fashion an estimate of what actually happened. …

The Jury's Rise as Lie Detector

George Fisher[1]

INTRODUCTION

...This Article tells the long story of the jury's slow coming of age as the system's lie detector at criminal trials. It chronicles the deaths of the old evidence rules that effectively withheld from the jury the task of settling credibility conflicts between sworn witnesses. Like the characters of many good stories, these rules led uneventful lives but suffered noteworthy deaths, touched by the intrigue of treachery and factional strife. I will emphasize two features of the evolutionary process. First, it was astoundingly slow. Despite the jury's attractiveness as a means of resolving credibility conflicts, the system displayed a remarkable resistance to change, an inertia of planetary proportions disturbed only by explosive events. Second, the most important of these explosions were external to the system. As a result, the evolutionary process was not principled, driven by a conviction that the jury can and should resolve credibility conflicts. Instead, the rule changes that most greatly expanded the potential for sworn credibility conflicts at criminal trials were products of political firestorms. In this sense, faith in the jury's powers of lie detection only followed the force of events. ...

The system has become more and more willing over time to declare that the jury – and not the oath – has the job of screening untrustworthy evidence from the decisionmaking process. We see the system's changing declaration of the jury's role in the gradual erosion of those evidence rules that had spared juries the task of deciding which of two competing witnesses lied under oath. As the system gave the jury ever greater authority to resolve conflicts between sworn witnesses, it thereby declared the jury to be the system's lie detector. It did so, I will argue, because it perceived the jury to be an ever more reliable guarantor of the legitimacy of the system's verdicts – and because it perceived the oath to be an ever less reliable guarantor. Whether juries in practice actually did anything different is largely beside the point, except to the extent that what jurors did might have reflected what the system declared they should do.

[1] Excerpted from George Fisher, *The Jury's Rise as Lie Detector*, 107 YALE L.J. 575 (1997).

I. THE ORDEAL AND THE JURY TRIAL: THEORETICAL PRELUDE

Although the jury's origins lie hidden in Dark Ages rituals, we can trace the origins of the sort of jury that concerns us here – the criminal trial jury – with something like pinpoint accuracy: The first true criminal jury trial seems to have taken place at Westminster in 1220. Juries had long acted to resolve various civil disputes, especially claims about land, and they had for decades served as accusing bodies in criminal cases in the manner of modern grand juries. But not before 1220 did a jury sit in judgment of a criminal accused with the discretion either to acquit or to condemn.

The occasion of this sudden birth of trial by jury was the sudden death of trial by ordeal. Before 1215, criminal trials had proceeded by ordeal or by battle. In the ordeal of cold water, the accused was tossed in a pool with a rope tied around his hips. If he sank, he was hauled out an innocent person, for the purity of the water had accepted him; but if the water repelled him and he floated, he was condemned. In the ordeal of hot iron, the accused walked barehanded with a hot iron bar. Three days later, when her bandages were removed, her healing hands revealed her fate: if the wounds were healing cleanly, she was absolved; if corruptly, condemned. In all events, the judgment was God's. But in 1215 the Church forbade priests to officiate at ordeals and suddenly stripped these rituals of their divine imprimatur. English and other European justice systems soon abandoned the ordeal in criminal cases. Though the Church took no action against trial by battle, that form of trial lacked the popular support needed to fill the role of the lost ordeals; too often, combat between accuser and accused ended badly for a worthy but weak litigant. Moreover, it was not always obvious who should do battle for the prosecution. Criminal justice systems throughout Europe, therefore, suddenly sought a new form of trial.

In the familiar history of these events, the English turned to trial by jury, elevating an institution that once had served in lesser roles to be final arbiter of guilt or innocence. At the same time, the countries of the European Continent adopted the "rational" Roman-canon forms of proof, which exalted the probative power of sworn eyewitness testimony and of the accused's confession, often coerced through torture. ...

II. THE RISE OF DEFENSE WITNESSES

...[W]e may safely draw three useful conclusions about sixteenth-century criminal procedure. The first is that the defendant could call no witnesses. There seem to be few explicit statements of this negative proposition, but all the major authorities have accepted it as true. The trial of Nicholas Throckmorton of 1554, contained in the State Trials, supplies the most famous expression of the rule. Throckmorton attempted to call a witness on his behalf, but the witness "was not suffered to speak."

"[W]hy," Throckmorton asked the court, "be ye not so well contented to hear truth for me, as untruth against me?" He pointed out that Queen Mary herself had instructed the court that "notwithstanding the old error amongst you, which did not admit any witness to speak [against the Queen], … her highness's pleasure was, that whatsoever could be brought in the favour of the subject, should be admitted to be heard." The chief justice did not respond to Throckmorton's allegation, but merely told him: "[Y]ou have no cause to complain, for you have been suffered to talk at your pleasure."

A trial at which only one side may present evidence will never in the normal course of events call on the jury to choose between sworn witnesses. Yet, as the chief justice told Throckmorton, defendants were "suffered to talk at [their] pleasure." Hence our second bit of information is that defendants themselves could speak at trial, and juries therefore often must have heard competing versions of events. …

The defendant's inability to take the oath made the jurors' task as lie detectors easier. By choosing simply to credit sworn evidence over unsworn, they could avoid a difficult comparison of credibility. Many small comments in various treatises and trial records, which I will report in time, suggest that juries routinely did just that. Although some juries no doubt chose to credit the defendant's unsworn tale over the prosecution's sworn testimony, the system never put juries in capital cases to the task of weighing competing oaths. And it never put juries in a position where, in order to condemn the defendant, they would have to reject sworn testimony. …

III. COPING WITH CREDIBILITY CONFLICTS

…In the 100 or 150 years before Parliament gave defendants the right to call sworn witnesses, several broad competency rules had evolved to control who could and who could not give sworn evidence in civil and criminal courts. These rules barred from the witness stand all parties to the proceeding – both plaintiff and defendant in a civil suit and all criminal defendants. The rules excluded spouses of parties, persons with financial interest in the case, convicted felons, irreligious persons, and various other classes of people. In effect, this panoply of competency rules preempted the jury's lie-detecting function by declaring certain witnesses to be likely liars as a matter of law. Exactly when the rules evolved is unclear. Wigmore traced the rule barring civil parties to the sixteenth century and that barring all other interested persons to the mid-seventeenth century. But it seems that these dates merely mark the earliest references Wigmore could find; the rules may well have been older. Barbara Shapiro notes that the rules bear a close, if simplified, resemblance to the testimonial disqualifications that prevailed in the Roman-canon law of the Continent.

There is no doubt as to the rules' rationale. All sources agree that they sought to keep from the witness stand anyone whose temptation or inclination to lie was greater than average. …

IV. THE RISE OF DEFENDANT TESTIMONY

...Cracks [began] to show in the complex of competency rules that had served to keep the most probably perjurious witnesses from taking the stand. In a much-quoted passage from 1786, Lord Mansfield remarked that "of late years the Courts have endeavoured, as far as possible, consistent with [the old] authorities, to let the objection go to the credit, rather than to the competency, of a witness." That is, some courts had begun to construe competency rules narrowly, permitting challenged witnesses to testify and letting the jury judge their credibility. By the first years of the nineteenth century, Leonard MacNally could begin a general treatise on evidence in criminal cases with the bold claim that a jury could reject the testimony even of a sworn, positive witness if the jury was suspicious of the witness's "excess of warmth" or his "solicitous reserve" or even his "affectation of candor."...

By resorting to this contrivance of competency rules to protect the oath's role as a guarantor of truth, the system betrayed its persistent doubt about the jury's capacity to spy out and disregard a perjured witness. Greenleaf admonished in his 1842 treatise, "If no means were employed totally to exclude any contaminating influences from the fountains of justice," the jury would "constantly" give "the testimony of a witness, unworthy of credit, ... as much consideration as that of one, worthy of the fullest confidence." And yet this cardhouse of competency rules collapsed. One by one, first in the civil context and then in the criminal, both in England and in America, the rules came down. Although I will speculate below on some forces that might have sped the rules' demise, I cannot pretend to have found the moving force behind each step in this progress toward modernity. Instead I will focus on the last, most dramatic, and (in the criminal context) by far most important step: the downfall of the rule that forbade criminal defendants to testify under oath.

Maine led the common law world when it gave accused felons the right to the oath in 1864. Many states quickly followed, almost all of them Northern. Seeking an explanation for this North-first movement to permit defendant testimony will require us first to explore another North-first phenomenon, for it turns out that competency rules barring civil parties from testifying also came down in the North before the South. I will argue that in both cases the North acted first because of the distorting influence of a related but quite different issue – the right of nonwhites to give evidence in Southern courts. ...

The earliest hint that the South's refusal to let nonwhites testify might have something to do with the North's seemingly disconnected decision to let criminal defendants testify appears in the appendix to John Appleton's 1860 Treatise on the Law of Evidence. Appleton had, as I have said, merely gathered together in this treatise essays he had published separately many years earlier. To these, he now added a largely unrelated appendix on the exclusion of nonwhite witnesses, which he condemned as "disastrous" and "enormous." It is revealing that the arguments Appleton mounted against racial exclusion laws sounded much like the arguments he made over and over again in the body of the treatise attacking, in succession, all of the old competency rules: As civilization progresses, "It is seen that the credit of witnesses can be more satisfactorily determined after than before a hearing. All are received as witnesses, and the various corroborating and discrediting circumstances are weighed and considered." So intent was Appleton to stake his opposition to racial competency rules on general principles that he made it a point to preface his argument with the concession that the rightfulness of slavery "may ... be fully admitted."

The inability of African Americans to testify in Southern law courts would shortly become one of the preeminent political issues of the day. Only the questions of black suffrage and of slavery itself generated more tension between North and South during the closing years of the Civil War and the first several years of the Reconstruction era. The strategy at which Appleton hinted in his appendix – to attack racial competency rules on the same terms as all other competency rules – soon found favor in the North. It is unclear why Northerners shunned the more obvious strategy of attacking the Southern racial exclusions as racist. Perhaps Northern politicians feared offending those border and Northern states that still maintained such laws. Or perhaps Northerners had their own doubts, founded in their own well-documented racism, about whether nonwhite witnesses were fully as credible as whites. In any event, they argued that, like all other once-disfavored classes of witnesses (interested persons, felons, atheists), nonwhites should be permitted to testify, and juries should be permitted to assess their credibility one by one.

But that argument pointed North as well as South. By staking the case against racial exclusion laws on general principles, Northerners exposed themselves to the countercharge of hypocrisy should they be caught harboring any of the old competency rules. The North proved to be intensely sensitive to the charge of hypocrisy, whether made by Southern forces or, as was often the case, from within its own ranks. It chose to abandon the last of its old competency rules rather than to bear the risk of that accusation. In the pages ahead, as I trace the course of the Northern attack on Southern racial exclusion rules, I will pay particular attention to this dynamic of charge and countercharge. The North-South battle over the issue of black testimony laws was waged in three major campaigns: in 1862, 1864, and 1866. We will see that the countercharge of hypocrisy was made at almost the earliest opportunity. ...

The defendant testimony laws of the late nineteenth century removed the last great barrier shielding juries from full frontal credibility conflicts of the sort they face so routinely today. In 1882, not even twenty years after Maine first let accused criminals take the oath in their own defense, one observer declared that the direst predictions of the opponents of the new laws had come true:

> Experience has, beyond all question, proved [the defendant's option to testify] to be the most powerful and the most fruitful incentive to perjury ever devised by the legislator. In total disregard of that ever-present and irresistible instinct of self-preservation, which is "nature's first law," it holds out to the man guilty of crime

> the overpowering temptation of denying his guilt under oath, in the delusive hope that he will be believed, thus adding perjury to his other crime.

The jury now faced the most demanding lie-detecting task it had yet encountered: In criminal cases, where the standard of proof was beyond a reasonable doubt and the stakes were the life or liberty of the defendant, the jury would have to listen to the prosecution's sworn accusation and the defendant's sworn denial and label one of them truth and the other lie.

Yet the system did not, as I hope I have made clear, invest the jury with this new lie-detecting role because of a conviction that the jury had grown equal to the task. It is true that over the preceding centuries the system had slowly complicated the jury's lie-detecting work in criminal cases, first by permitting the defendant to call witnesses, then by permitting those witnesses to be sworn. It is true that Bethel's rule and the other common law evidence rules that sought to guide juries when they confronted apparent conflicts of oaths had slowly eroded. And it is true that in the decades before Maine and other Northern states tore down this last great barrier to conflicts between oaths, many jurisdictions had begun to dismantle the system of competency rules that sought to keep the most likely liars from reaching the witness stand. There is no doubt that the bar against sworn defendant testimony would have fallen in due time – this was surely one of those battles between past and future that the future was destined to win. Still, the epochal conflict between North and South brought change before its time. The system perhaps had to struggle to summon the confidence in its juries that its laws now proclaimed. …

It hardly seems likely, however, that a series of widely spaced and seemingly disconnected social forces – the Glorious Revolution of 1688, the American Civil War of the 1860s, the feminist revolution of the 1970s – could account fully for the jury's growing role as the system's lie detector. Such a historical account, implausible on its face, would grow ungainly and ridiculous if it tried to account for all the other moments and trends that in great ways and small have increased the factfinding autonomy of the jury. Some of these I have mentioned already: The newly found right of criminal defendants in the middle of the sixteenth century to call unsworn witnesses, which I can attribute to no particular historical event except perhaps the anecdotal and unexplained largesse of Queen Mary; the slow deaths of Bethel's rule, the principle of numerology, and the rule of falsus in uno; and the demise of competency rules in civil cases in the mid-nineteenth century, which Jeremy Bentham or Andrew Jackson may or may not have inspired.

It would be foolish to argue that each of these trends and events traces to a political or social controversy that operated outside the justice system. I make no such claim here. On the contrary, when all of these historical transformations are lined up alongside one another, they permit one broad and inescapable historical generalization: At least over the last several centuries and arguably since its founding, the criminal trial jury has consistently increased its lie-detecting role, while the role of the oath in assuring the accuracy of evidence at trial has steadily diminished. Perhaps, as I have argued here, specific events external to the justice system triggered the most notable transformations along this road. Something internal to the system, however, must have made those transformations so welcome and enduring – otherwise, we would expect to see some reversals along the road. Yet, the jury's role as the system's lie detector has only grown and has never, for a sustained time, diminished.

I suggest that the most substantial force behind this enormous historical trend has been the system's concern with its own apparent legitimacy. In Part I, I argued that this concern drove the system to embrace the oath as a channel to divine wisdom after the abolition of the ordeal had removed the divine sanction from criminal verdicts. Yet, the oath, for reasons that are perhaps already too clear, was an inherently unstable source of systemic legitimacy. Its illusory power to assure truthful outcomes depended on a contorted scheme of feints and screens. Because obvious perjury would have exposed the oath's incapacity to guarantee truthful testimony, the system did not undertake to punish perjury. Because contradictory oaths would have exposed the oath as a failure, the system forbade contradictory oaths. When the system finally relented and began to permit defense witnesses to contradict the oaths of prosecution witnesses, it forbade them to do so under oath. When it later permitted defense witnesses to be sworn, it did what it could to prevent head-to-head credibility conflicts that would have exposed one witness as a liar. A bevy of competency rules sought to keep the likeliest liars from the witness stand, and Bethel's rule helped juries to evade the conclusion that oaths were in conflict.

As we now know, these contorted maneuverings to protect the system's legitimacy actually eroded that legitimacy. Bentham aimed his most withering ridicule at the old system of competency rules, which he said purported to guard the truth but in fact merely hid from the jury many potential sources of truth. But long before Bentham and long before the Enlightenment or the Scientific Revolution, ordinary people must have shaken their heads in wonderment at a system designed to find truth that permitted only one party to the cause to present any sworn evidence at all.

The jury, in contrast, promised a remarkably reliable source of systemic legitimacy. Its usually private and inarticulate decisionmaking protected it from the sort of embarrassing public failures that so regularly threatened the oath. Although two oaths all too easily could conflict, the jury's verdict stood alone and, at least within the system's formal bounds, was almost immune from contradiction. Moreover, whether by tradition or conscious design, the jury's verdict has been largely impenetrable. There never has been a mechanism by which the defendant or anyone outside the system could command the jury to reveal its decisionmaking processes. The jury's secrecy is an aid to legitimacy, for the privacy of the jury box shrouds the shortcomings of its methods. …

We could perhaps regard the wonderful convenience of jury lie detecting with more equanimity if there were any sound evidence that juries are good at this task.

But most of the evidence we have suggests that juries have no particular talent for spotting lies. Not only do experimental subjects rarely perform much better than chance at distinguishing truth from falsehood, but they think they are better lie detectors than they are. And we could perhaps feel more complacent about where this long history has brought us if we knew that we had reached at last a stopping point where we could pause to assess the state of affairs. But the jury's lie-detecting role is still growing. …

(Un)Common Knowledge & Experience

Jasmine E. Harris[1]

INTRODUCTION

Our current system of dispute resolution presumes that lay fact finders enter the courtroom with a common base of knowledge and experience to adjudicate facts fairly and apply the law as instructed by the court. What happens when this assumption is incorrect or incomplete?

Debates about a "post-truth" society, the nature of expertise, and the malleability of facts that are unfolding in public spaces outside of legal institutions raise two related questions about the administration of justice. First, if knowledge and experience are politicized, what information is reasonably within a jury's baseline, particularly in highly normative areas of law, such as antidiscrimination? And, second, if knowledge and experiential baselines are deficient, do current institutional mechanisms, education, media, political debate, law and legal procedures and rules have ways of remedying or mitigating harm to litigants? Institutional devices such as the regulation of jury pools, the use of expert testimony, judicial notice, and jury instructions designed to mitigate biases and educate a jury to carry out its charge may fall short in the context of certain kinds of information, social norms, and experiences. …

I. THE ORIGINS AND EVOLUTION OF (UN)COMMON KNOWLEDGE AND EXPERIENCE

… The use of the jury was integral to first English, then American trial systems (and by extension, political governance). Early models of dispute resolution focused on the local expertise of community members who presumably had knowledge of the facts in question in a case (for example, proper title to land). As such, they could be active investigators and apply their shared local knowledge and experience, under oath, to efficiently resolve disputes. In fact, by the twelfth century in England, those assembled for trial by jury first swore under oath that they did have facts to share and

1 Excerpted from Jasmine E. Harris, *(Un)Common Knowledge & Experience*, 105 B.U.L. Rev. 1113 (2025).

resolve the matter before them. If someone did not have relevant facts, they were dismissed and replaced. The substantive "knowledge required of [the jury] is their own perception, or what their fathers have told them, or what they may trust as fully as their own knowledge." However, by the fifteenth century, "judicial experience and expertise replaced community knowledge as the center of litigation authority." Reliance on lay fact finders led to the introduction of rules to regulate the admission of probative evidence and mitigate prejudice to the fact-finding process. …

Over time, the function of fact-finding became distinct from any personal role in the matter before the court. Today, personal knowledge of the facts, actors, or even general experience with the nature of the case is often disqualifying and may subject a potential juror to a preemptory strike for cause. Juries went from "active knowers" to relatively "passive receivers of evidence" provided to them by courts; incidentally, courts also assumed a greater role in the regulation of proof in service of jury objectivity. The once-localized jury became more anonymized and distant from the facts of a particular case, yet jurors were still expected to resolve the matter before them based on the information provided during the trial, funneled through a presumed common base of knowledge and experience (albeit much broader and less connected). The jury also serves an expressive function as a democratic institution where laypeople participate in the administration of justice and check judicial expertise in dispute resolution.

Court-based adjudication focuses on a single case before the court; however, in order for fact finders to decide among disputed facts and accounts of an event, grievance, or claim, they must decide which accounts become legal facts. They do this based on the evidence presented and rely on their common base of knowledge and experience to assess credibility and assign probative weight to real and testimonial evidence.

Legal fact finders have encountered information deficits when faced with increasingly complex legal, policy, and social challenges. That is, greater industry specialization and professionalization combined with increased diversity along multiple axes (for example, racial, ethnic, religious, gender, and socioeconomic) has produced jury pools charged with resolving complex disputes outside of their own knowledge and experience. Courts have addressed resulting information deficits through the increased use of expert evidence and exclusionary rules of evidence empowering judges to regulate the flow of information (and the quality of that information) to the jury.

Figure 1 … offers an overview of different informational touchpoints to consider how courts use different procedures and rules to regulate the flow of information deemed relevant to carry out the fact finder's responsibilities. Our legal system assumes jurors bring knowledge and experience to the courtroom for limited purposes such as assessing credibility (and the court instructs them accordingly). The bulk of the jury's receipt of information and instruction takes place in T1 through T3 through the court and the presentation of evidence. Jurors are generally instructed to

FIGURE 1 Informational touchpoints
T0 Pre-jury Summons: Potential jurors with a set of individual values, norms, or experiences which may vary geographically (locally, regionally, urban, rural) or demographically (race, gender, socioeconomic status, educational attainment, employment status, etc.) are summoned; eligibility for jury service varies as does the information available to the court system (treatment of felony convictions, conservatorship, disabilities, home address); society exists with a set of values and norms (nationally, may vary temporally).
T1 Jury Summons and Voir Dire: Jurors bring individual knowledge and experiential baselines to court and enter jury box; voir dire court and lawyers give potential jurors information about the case, and instructions on voir dire process, during which lawyers' questions test biases and baseline, and some jurors are screened out or excused from service.
T2 Preliminary Instructions and Trial: Jurors receive information from court (opening jury instructions), lawyers (opening and closing remarks), sensory engagement with witnesses (lay and expert), physical evidence, and character and reputation evidence; they make observations to determine facts by assessing credibility and probative weight; they are sometimes allowed to take notes or ask questions.
T3 Jury Charges: Judge instructs and charges the jury.
T4 Jury Deliberations: Jurors use their common base of knowledge and experience to assess information received in T2 and T3.
T5 Verdict and Post-verdict Interventions: Jury reaches verdict; parties may file post-trial motions, such as Judgment as a Matter of Law or Judgment Notwithstanding the Verdict, and formal appeals.

be recipients of information presented during the trial; the common base of knowledge and experience will be that which develops within the four corners of the case. Their prior baseline of knowledge and experience from T0 comes in as a method of evaluation and engagement with the evidence presented in the case. Consider a model jury instruction from the Third Circuit Court of Appeals:

> You should use your common sense in weighing the evidence. Consider it in light of your everyday experience with people and events, and give it whatever weight you believe it deserves. If your experience tells you that certain evidence reasonably leads to a conclusion, you are free to reach that conclusion.

During T1 through T3, knowledge accumulation is regulated by rules of procedure and evidence. Judges sit as evidentiary gatekeepers pretrial and during trial to ensure evidence passes a low threshold for relevance (has legal and logical relevance); where the proffered evidence raises the potential for confusion, distraction and delay, or for bias for or against one of the parties, judges decide whether to exclude on those grounds or impose other proscriptions. Where a matter is beyond the juror's common base of knowledge and experience at T0, the parties account for information deficits through the presentation of lay opinion, expert testimony, or scientific evidence. In addition to content, juries receive instructions on the decision-making process itself and how to evaluate what they have heard, seen, and experienced during the trial. Studies suggest that the court's regulatory exercise in containment and directing jurors to compartmentalize the information provided, using certain pieces for one purpose but not another, may be challenging if not futile in some instances.

Yet the work of the jury is highly normative. This is true for some areas of law more than others most notably criminal law and torts despite general prohibitions on jurors using known facts from their experience rather than the information presented to them in the court. According to Valerie Hans, "[c]onventional wisdom holds that juries are the purest method for incorporating social norms and cultural understandings into the civil justice system." Hans and other scholars such as Peter Schuck have argued for examining this claim in the context of tort law because "[t]he master ideas that drive tort law doctrine reasonableness, duty of care, and proximate cause are as loose-jointed, context-sensitive, and openly relativistic as any principles to be found in law."

Hans describes jury deliberations as an opportunity for contestation of different conceptions of social norms and values while moving towards one objective vision of quintessentially porous concepts such as "reasonableness" in torts. What makes this norm infusion possible, however, is the presence of either a cohesive single baseline to start (as early English juries were white men of status) or alternatively, one or more competing conceptions that must be resolved through debate and exchange.

But what if the normative baseline is inherently flawed and lacks factually correct information in T0 (before jury service), T2 or T3 (at the start of the trial or during trial), and T4 (at the onset of deliberations), such that the information deficits are never cured or never even have the possibility of being cured? What if no alternative views are presented during trial (by the judge or the parties), and no one in the jury room has a different set of experiences to draw from?

Interestingly, tort law is not only highly normative but also an area of law where the use of expert evidence to manage knowledge deficits is frequent and widespread. In civil trials, experts testified most frequently in tort cases, accounting for approximately 45% of such cases (primarily personal injury and medical malpractice cases), followed by civil rights cases, for which experts testified in 23% of cases. With respect to the qualifications and substantive knowledge of experts, medical and mental health experts were the most common. Some scholars argue that juries lack competence for resolving tort claims precisely because they lack the normative frameworks for proper resolution, which may help explain the proliferation of legal experts in these cases. ...

We now have lay juries with perhaps fewer points of common knowledge and experience entering (at least on the civil side) highly specialized spaces. Courts charge juries with deciding highly normative questions based on expert evidence and their own experiential baselines. Before a jury can hear expert evidence, however, judges must distinguish between matters within the jury's competence and those where specialized knowledge would be "helpful" or even "necessary."

II. DISABILITY AS (UN)COMMON KNOWLEDGE

...

A. *Disability Law as Normative*

Disability rights laws, like other civil rights laws, are deeply tied to collective moral and ethical principles about equality, justice, and human dignity. Law reflects a set of mandatory rules of behavior for a community; its interpretation and application to a set of facts will implicate social values, norms, and practices.

Congress found that "the Nation's proper goals regarding individuals with disabilities are to assure equality of opportunity, full participation, independent living, and economic self-sufficiency for such individuals." The Americans with Disabilities Act ("ADA") intended to "provide [that] clear and comprehensive national mandate for the elimination of discrimination against individuals with disabilities." Interpretation of the ADA requires adjudicators (court and jury alike) to confront the meaning of disability discrimination as distinct from the look (and, at times, feel) of formal equality in the context of other civil rights statutes. In the context of disability antidiscrimination laws, equality means differential treatment at times, whereas the push for civil rights often required equal treatment to advance equal opportunity.

Beyond the general intent expressed in the preamble, interpretation of key legal concepts and factual determinations requires engagement with community values, personal knowledge and experience to balance competing interests. The core of the ADA's remedial requirement to provide "reasonable accommodations," like the "reasonable person" or "reasonableness" standards in tort law, relies on individual and collective knowledge and experience to give it meaning. Title I of the Americans with Disabilities Act, for instance, prohibits discrimination on the basis of disability against a "qualified individual," defined as "an individual who, with or without reasonable accommodation, can perform the essential functions of the employment position that such individual holds or desires." Failure to provide a reasonable accommodation to an otherwise qualified individual with a disability constitutes discrimination under Title I of the ADA. The statutory modifier of "reasonableness" qualifies the provision of accommodations; for example, "undue hardship," an affirmative defense in the employment context, reduces the reasonableness of the requested accommodation. To make this determination, after hearing testimony from fact and perhaps expert witnesses, jurors will receive instructions from the court that characterize or describe an accommodation to help mitigate information deficits from T0 and, perhaps, remaining even after the trial in T2. The Third Circuit's Model Instruction describes "accommodation" in the following way and allows for the parties to negotiate the language needed to tailor the instructions to the specific case:

> [In deciding whether [plaintiff] was denied a reasonable accommodation, you must keep in mind that [defendant] is not obligated to provide a specific accommodation simply because it was requested by [plaintiff]. [Plaintiff] may not insist on a particular accommodation if another reasonable accommodation was offered. The question is whether [defendant] failed to provide any reasonable accommodation of [plaintiff's] disability.]
>
> In general, an accommodation is a change in the work environment or in the way things are customarily done that enables an individual with a disability to enjoy equal employment opportunities.
>
> ...

Regarding a defendant's affirmative defense of "undue hardship," which could mitigate the degree of reasonableness of the accommodation, the model instructions state: ...

> Under the ADA, [defendant] does not need to accommodate [plaintiff] if it would cause an "undue hardship" to its business. Defendant must prove to you by a preponderance of the evidence that [describe accommodation] would be an "undue hardship." The term "undue hardship" means an action requiring significant difficulty or expense, when considered in light of the following factors [list all of the factors set out below that are relevant in light of the evidence] ....

An expert in a Title I disability employment discrimination case, such as a qualified ADA compliance consultant, might further assist the jury in its service by testifying, for example, that the disabled plaintiff's request for a sit-stand desk and five minutes of stretch time every three hours is a common request for people with carpal tunnel syndrome, costs $2,000, and would help the disabled employee perform the essential functions of their position as a data analyst. The jury may hear from the employer's expert, also an ADA compliance consultant, who may say that the requested accommodation poses an undue hardship because it modifies the uniform aesthetic of the office (all other employees have built-in, uniform desks designed as part of the company's brand).

The jury's job would be to use this information, as well as testimony from fact witnesses and their common base of knowledge and experience, to evaluate the evidence and decide whether plaintiff's requested accommodation was "reasonable." Other judgments include, also in the employment context, whether the individual is otherwise "qualified" (meaning they could perform the "essential functions" of their job "with or without reasonable accommodation"). Defenses such as "direct threat" challenge the individual's qualification, while "undue hardship" and "fundamental alteration" defenses challenge the "reasonableness" of the accommodation requested.

Disability law, then, is not just about enforcing rules but about shaping society's values, protecting marginalized communities, and continuously negotiating what fairness and inclusion mean in different contexts, all of which is a highly normative exercise. …

B *Information Deficits and Flawed Social Norms of Disability*

One in four adults in the United States (over 70 million people) has one or more disabilities, according to the United States Centers for Disease Control ("CDC"). Though the prevalence is high (even if not widely understood as such), the public visibility is low because of a number of factors, some of which I address in previous work. …

How do we know that information deficits about disability exist and the nature of the deficits? First, Congress said we have a problem through the promulgation of the Americans with Disabilities Act itself. The rich legislative history, notably the contributions of disability advocates Justin and Yoshiko Dart, document the experiences of disabled people across the United States with deeply flawed assumptions about their capacity and lives. …

Second, empirical studies not only confirm that some disability norms are flawed, but also offer insights as to which ones may be problematic. For example, one recent study captured the attitudes of healthcare professionals with respect to disability. In a national survey of 714 practicing U.S. physicians, "82.4 percent of participants reported that people with significant disability have worse quality of life than people without disability." Furthermore,

> [o]nly 40.7 percent of physicians were very confident about their ability to provide the same quality of care to patients with disability, just 56.5 percent strongly agreed that they welcomed patients with disability into their practices, and 18.1 percent strongly agreed that the health care system often treats these patients unfairly.

Interestingly, research on the "disability paradox" paints a more complicated picture of quality of life than captured in this study. "The apparent paradox is: Why do many people with serious and persistent disabilities report that they experience a good or excellent quality of life when to most external observers these people seem to live an undesirable daily existence?" "In practice, the anomaly is that patients' perceptions of personal health, well-being and life satisfaction are often discordant with their objective health status and disability." These findings demonstrate the potential informational deficits that jurors may experience, deficits that, this Essay argues, may not be sufficiently addressed through the current methods of knowledge accumulation for fact finders. This may affect jurors' knowledge base but also shapes the nature and quality of expert opinion evidence meant to fill those informational gaps, as Part III will address.

Relatedly, a recent poll ("The Arc Poll") was conducted by The Harris Poll on behalf of The Arc of the United States, the largest national disability rights organization serving people with intellectual and developmental disabilities. The Arc Poll offers additional support for the existence of a flawed base of common knowledge and experience with respect to people with intellectual and developmental disabilities ("ID/D"). For context, estimates vary with respect to the exact percentage of people with ID/D in the United States, but one CDC summary reported that 3% to 5% of the U.S. population, or approximately one in twenty people, has an intellectual or developmental disability. …

Examples of information deficits and faulty norms uncovered by the study include general information about people with ID/D such as the following:

45% agreed with or weren't sure about the statement, "All people with autism are good at math."
80% agreed with or weren't sure about the statement, "Individuals can grow out of certain disabilities."

Perhaps most relevant to the finding of facts and application of disability rights law, The Arc Poll found that the general population continued to associate people with ID/D with dependency:

50% agreed with or weren't sure about the statement, "Individuals with IDD are dependent and always need help."
26% disagreed with or weren't sure about the statement, "People with IDD can contribute to society."
35% said that when they picture someone with IDD, they picture a child.
59% agreed "strongly" or "somewhat" agreed with the statement, "People often think that individuals with IDD are a burden on society."

The vast majority of the general population agree that disability rights are human rights (95% strongly or somewhat agree), though approximately half qualify this by saying that "[t]he rights of individuals with IDD can depend on their abilities" (52% strongly or somewhat agreed).

Other significant findings include those about the general public's views of independent living and decision-making, which are core parts of current and historic disability rights movements and are critical for matters related to community integration and conservatorship or guardianship. …

While most of the respondents from the general population acknowledged that society has a responsibility to provide needed supports for people with ID/D, "[m]any vastly underestimate the lack of supports for the IDD community." For example: …

Finally, the general population's self-assessment of their own knowledge about contemporary disability reflects confidence in their knowledge base. On a scale from 1 (not at all informed) to 7 (very informed), the highest percentage of survey respondents among the general population rated their knowledge as informed (roughly "4"): …

We might understand the information deficits discussed in this Section as a part of To, jurors' baseline common knowledge about and experience with disability. In what kinds of cases might information deficits or misinformation arise? Imagine a jury awarding suboptimal damages because of assumptions about whether a person with an intellectual or developmental disability could secure employment or whether, in a tort action, a defendant's actions truly resulted in a compensable loss of community participation for a disabled person. Consider cases where the defendants are individuals with ID/D and a jury may rule against them because, for example, jurors doubt the person has an intellectual disability given that they can do such things as cook a meal or drive a car, which jurors erroneously believe to be beyond the ability of someone legitimately with that diagnosis. Or in the context of criminal sexual assault cases or family law cases about the termination of parental rights, jurors may lack knowledge or experience or have misconceptions about a disabled person's sexual capacity (from inability to provide consent to asexuality or hypersexuality) or their capacity to be a parent.

III. EXISTING METHODS OF REGULATING INFORMATION DEFICITS

… Several procedural and evidentiary rules seek to mitigate the lack of a common base of knowledge and experience and to remedy certain informational and decisional errors as well as biases.

A. *Expert Evidence*

Although expert evidence offers a path to supplement information deficits or address misinformation, the content and quality of evidence that can successfully pass through these evidentiary hurdles may not sufficiently address existing information deficits or may do so in ways that privilege one party over another. Lawyers must first decide to introduce the evidence, and judges must make a threshold determination regarding its reliability and utility. Lawyers rely on expert witnesses to address issues beyond the jury's competence (that is, beyond their baseline knowledge and experience), while judges determine the admissibility of that expert testimony, in part, by distinguishing between matters within the common base of knowledge and experience of the jury and those matters beyond the base that require (or might benefit from) expertise. This line drawing between expert testimony and the jury's competency illustrates what courts perceive to be the content of jurors' baseline knowledge and experience and the types of information deficits at work. Judges regulate the admission of relevant evidence in the first instance by asking whether the proffered evidence makes a fact of consequence (determined by the substantive law at issue) more or less likely. If the court believes that a jury lacks the knowledge and experience to find a particular fact, it may be more inclined to value the introduction of expert testimony. …

Consider another Third Circuit case, *Diaz v. Saucon Valley Manor Inc.* Appellees claimed that Diaz was required to offer expert evidence or other sufficient evidence that her alcoholism constituted a disability under the ADA. In response, the Third Circuit affirmed the district court's rationale as proof of jurors' common knowledge and experience with alcoholism. The court held that alcoholism, although a diagnostic category, was one where there is a firmly rooted common base of knowledge and experience:

> We are not talking about evidence of some medical condition involving the central nervous system and nobody can pronounce the word and we don't know what it means where we need an expert. Alcoholism is a commonly encountered form of substance abuse in our society, and I think you look at the jury voir dire how many hands went up when they said there was alcohol abuse in the family. There was a significant amount.

Even this discussion of alcoholism, however, ignores the normativity embedded in the experience of alcoholism. What about even less-understood diagnostic categories of disability such as intellectual or developmental? The Arc Poll showed areas where the knowledge base was weaker. Normative judgments about a disabled person's decisional capacity could impact factual findings in disability cases where a person with ID/D's capacity is at issue (such as in guardianship, civil commitment, or criminal cases). Will the introduction of expert evidence help in some cases? It depends on the content of that information and what the parties see as the actual informational deficits at work. ...

Death penalty cases offer another context for examination of the high-stakes impact of information deficits on substantive case outcomes. Here, jurors are charged to determine whether a criminal defendant has an "intellectual disability" that can mitigate punishment under *Atkins v. Virginia* and related cases. "[W]hen lay jurors arbitrate intellectual disability claims, they tend to believe that only persons with extreme impairments are intellectually disabled." Scholars have explored the ability of experts to "cure" misinformation about intellectual disability in the capital context and have discussed the ways in which psychological processing, such as "motivated cognition" unconscious bias similar in operation to confirmation bias when there is some bias in support of preexisting preferences or mixed evidence to support those preferences works against the ability of expert evidence to remedy information deficits.

B. *Jury Pool Representativeness*

Some may argue that the jury's representativeness and pooling from a broad cross[ ] section of society can bring different perspectives together to contest problematic baseline norms during deliberations (T3), a time when jurors reconcile the evidence presented and the court's instructions with their individual knowledge and experiential baselines. However, in the context of disability, legal rules and procedures sometimes screen out people with visible disabilities who might bring greater experiential knowledge. Such is the case of Colorado attorney, Spencer Kontnik. In July 2021, Denver County summoned Kontnik, who is deaf, for jury duty. Kontnik arranged for an interpreter with Communication Access Realtime Translation ("CART") with the court, something he had done on countless occasions as a practicing attorney in the same courthouse. People who are deaf or hard of hearing use CART, similar to a closed captioning system, to communicate effectively and accurately. Before allowing the prospective jurors to come into the courtroom, the presiding judge discussed Kontnik's potential service without hearing from him or asking him any questions. The transcript provided in Kontnik's complaint included the following statement by the court:

> All right. So, an issue's come up with a juror who is hearing impaired and under the ADA we have a Court Interpreter who's here and present and all set up to help him.
>
> But the parties have approached and stipulated to allowing him to be excused just on the grounds that things might be tough for him and also the court would be required to have [an] alternate just in the event there's ... issues with the interpretation or with the juror's ability to serve.
>
> So, just based on that and given that this will likely be a one-day trial I'll agree with the stipulation and allow for that juror to be excused.
>
> And I want to say thank you so much to the Interpreter for being here.

Kontnik's suit survived a motion to dismiss, but the court ultimately granted summary judgment to the defendant, finding that Kontnik was not entitled to relief despite the court's violation of the antidiscrimination act at issue. ...

Moreover, knowledge and experience are typically grounds for juror dismissal (for cause or preemptory challenges) under our jury selection processes. Lawyers under the current system claim to value jurors who can be "blank slates" and receive the information required to fairly resolve a dispute before the court. The reality may be that all agree biases exist and, instead, seek to identify positive biases for their client (or the state) as a strategic lawyering matter. Another model could be to accept that biases are rampant and difficult to capture during voir dire. Rather than invest in smoking out and dismissing jurors with relevant experience or knowledge, another approach could embrace knowledge and experience as valuable, seek to limit discretionary dismissals, and redesign the voir dire process and trial processes that follow to manage that knowledge and experience in ways that could improve jury deliberations.

C. *Post-verdict Processes*

Post-verdict processes (T5) may allow parties and courts to correct the use of impermissible information in the jury's decision-making but only in narrow circumstances when issues become known. As a result, such processes may not reach the type of structural deficits described here. …

Some challenges to the verdict, however, may affect constitutional rights, at least in criminal cases. For example, the Supreme Court confronted racial bias in jury deliberations in *Peña-Rodriguez v. Colorado*. More specifically, the Court considered whether the default "no impeachment rule" which prevents jurors from testifying about what happened during deliberations to protect juror competency and the finality of the verdict could be pierced when it conflicted with a criminal defendant's constitutional rights. The defendant, Miguel Peña-Rodriguez, was convicted of sexual assault in Colorado. After the trial, two jurors informed Peña-Rodriguez's attorney that another juror had made racially biased remarks about Peña-Rodriguez and his Mexican heritage during deliberations: specifically, that Peña-Rodriguez was guilty because "Mexican men take whatever they want" and that he did not trust Mexican men. Peña-Rodriguez moved for a new trial, arguing that the verdict was tainted by racial bias. In a five-to-three decision, the U.S. Supreme Court held that the Sixth Amendment guarantees a criminal defendant a right to an impartial jury and that racial bias in jury deliberations violates that right, thus carving out an exception to the otherwise impenetrable no-impeachment rule.

However, it is unclear whether a court hearing a similar case where racial bias was replaced with disability bias would similarly pierce the no-impeachment rule based on competing constitutional considerations. Unlike state action based on race which receives the highest level of constitutional scrutiny (strict scrutiny) and lowest level of judicial deference, courts apply the lowest tier of constitutional scrutiny (rational basis review) to state action based on disability with the greatest deference to states. In addition to the status of disability in this constitutional pecking order (or perhaps related to this status), law and society have framed disability bias and discrimination as less animus driven, more rational, and more likely a product of misguided benevolence. Imagine, for example, a sexual assault case where the defendant has an intellectual disability. The jury returns a guilty verdict. Post-verdict jury interviews by defense counsel reveal that one juror said on a number of occasions that he knew that men with intellectual disabilities are innately sexually aggressive and "can be predators." The juror interviewed said that he and others found this very convincing, and it helped him (and others) reach the verdict. This hypothetical is similar to *Peña-Rodriguez*, but as a matter of law and culture, it might produce a different result, though the bias is no less harmful.

Thus, although procedural and substantive mechanisms exist to identify and remedy jurors' informational and experiential deficits with respect to disability, Part III demonstrates the limitations of these devices. At best, the mechanisms discussed offer opportunities for the circulation of additional information that could mitigate existing information deficits; at worst, these mechanisms block the flow of relevant and potentially curative information.

IV. THINKING OUTSIDE THE BOX

... There are few opportunities for self-correction of factual inaccuracies, or the development of equality norms related to disability. In fact, there are deliberate barriers to information flows that cabin what information people can discuss and a lack of safety nets in place for when this information is disclosed and discussed but misused as a ground for discrimination and exclusion.

A. *Other Informational Touchpoints*

1. Pre-jury Summons (T0)

Prescriptions for flawed social norms include investment in antidiscrimination enforcement and education outside of the context of dispute resolution. Here, consider The Arc Poll responses and how some, such as the responses on people with autism being good at math or those with Down syndrome being happy all the time signal a real disconnect between the everyday life experiences of the general population in the United States with disabled people. Are there opportunities for meaningful contacts of the sort that may produce norm changes, or will the existing forms of interactions reinforce stereotypes? For example, the Individuals with Disabilities Education Act, in theory, establishes a legal default for integrated education where nondisabled and disabled students might interact meaningfully in schools; however, have the desired norm shifts been stunted by factors such as the design or implementation of the law or negative aesthetic and affective responses to disability in integrated settings? Enforcement of disability antidiscrimination laws may create the conditions for norm shifts by reducing architectural, programmatic, and practical barriers to the meaningful participation of disabled people in all facets of society, from employment and education to marriage and parenting. The interpretation of legal rights and responsibilities, as this Essay has shown, depends on the content of existing norms and frameworks used to decide the law and apply it to a set of facts.

2. Jury Summons and Voir Dire (T1)

During jury selection in cases involving disability (either disability laws or a party with a disability), a special juror selection questionnaire could operate as an opportunity for the court and the parties to understand the knowledge and

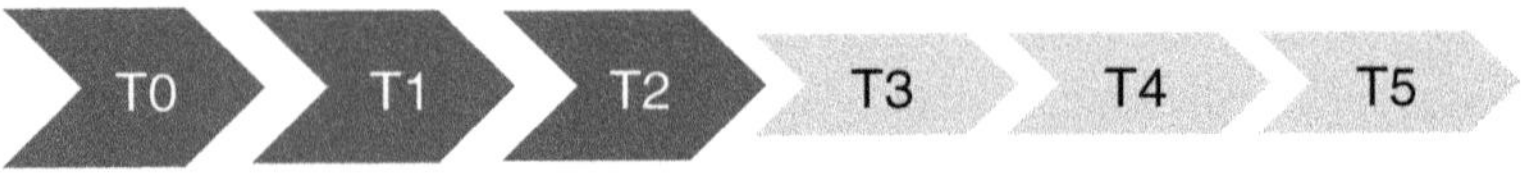

FIGURE 2 Other informational touchpoints

experiential baselines of the jurors with respect to disability. This would be more than a general question during voir dire about whether the person has anyone with a disability in their orbit. The questions may be more direct and reflect the structural norms of disability that would operate in the background and inform jury deliberations.

This could be an intervention that disrupts the ordinary adversarial process in civil cases where the parties can manipulate informational imbalances as part of their strategy (such information may have value for settlement or plea-bargaining purposes as well). However, given how sticky disability norms are and the existing information deficits, an intervention like this may be warranted. …

B. *Open Questions and Considerations*

This final Section raises a set of challenges and questions for further development.

In terms of curing information deficits, does the nature of the information matter? Can the information deficit be easily remedied through the transfer of (some, better, different) information and received by jurors within the current adjudicative framework? For example, the literature on management leadership distinguishes between "technical" and "adaptive" challenges:

> While technical problems may be very complex and critically important (like replacing a faulty heart valve during cardiac surgery) they have known solutions that can be implemented by current know-how. They can be resolved through the application of authoritative expertise and through the organization's current structures, procedures, and ways of doing things. Adaptive challenges can only be addressed through changes in people's priorities, beliefs, habits, and loyalties. Making progress requires going beyond any authoritative expertise to mobilize discovery, shedding certain entrenched ways, tolerating losses, and generating the new capacity to thrive anew.

Arguably, the challenge of information deficits in the case of disability presented in this Essay is mixed but may lean heavily on the adaptive side. That is, having an expert testify that more people with ID/D attend college than people know may solve a technical challenge, but having the same expert testify that people with intellectual disabilities have the necessary capabilities to be parents may present a more stubborn adaptive challenge.

Another question here concerns the tension (apparent or actual) between two empirical facts: that disability is pervasive (70 million adults) and yet there are pervasive information deficits about it. If one in four people has a disability, then why are there not more people with disabilities in jury pools and selected as jurors? Spencer Kontnik's case helps explain that even when disabled people are present in the pools, they may be intentionally dismissed. But this raises an important question as well: Would a jury of all disabled people cure the representativeness problem? The answer is that it might create relatively better conditions to bridge the knowledge and information deficits but would not be fully prescriptive because disability is not a monolith *and* because the problem is not limited to one's identity alone. …

CONCLUSION

… Although this Essay focused on the disability case study, disability could be the canary in the coal mine, offering a useful lens for thinking about information deficits in other contexts. Epistemic injustices are intimately tied to power. In this sense, and putting aside the one-dimensional examination of disability thus far, the problem of information deficits, misinformation, and biases extends to other subordinated identities that should be examined together, independently and intersectionally.

Peña-Rodriguez v. Colorado, Jury Secrecy, and the Performance of Racial Justice

Daniel S. Harawa

The secrecy of jury deliberations is foundational to our entire jury system … or so we are told. In theory, the secrecy allows jurors to speak their minds and vote their consciences. These upsides of jury secrecy are so important that it is broadly believed, as one court put it, that opening the door to deliberations would "destroy the jury system itself."[1] It is no surprise, then, that every state and the federal government has an evidentiary rule that prevents the piercing of deliberations.

But in a fledgling multiracial democracy that has yet to fully reckon with its racist roots, including how that racism still manifests today, is jury secrecy truly a good thing? What about if the very same secrecy that allows people to speak their minds also allows them to voice their bigotry? And if that bigotry comes to light, what are we to do about it if probing deliberations is akin to "destroy[ing] the jury system itself"?[2] The Supreme Court was supposed to tackle some of these questions in *Peña-Rodriguez v. Colorado*.[3] The decision had the potential to be a blockbuster exploration of race and the jury system. Yet the answers the Court provided were far from satisfying.

***

The history of juries deliberating in secret can be traced back to medieval England. And while societies and legal systems have obviously evolved since then, the purported reasons for why juries deliberate in private have not. According to the Supreme Court, jury secrecy has four "public policy" purposes.[4] It prevents harassment.[5] It protects freedom of debate.[6] It promotes public confidence in the jury system.[7] And it preserves the finality of verdicts.[8]

1 United States v. Thomas, 116 F.3d 606, 623 (2d Cir. 1997).
2 *Id.*
3 580 U.S. 206 (2017).
4 McDonald v. Pless, 238 U.S. 264, 267–8 (1915).
5 Clark v. United States, 289 U.S. 1, 13 (1933).
6 Tanner v. United States, 483 U.S. 107, 120 (1987).
7 *Id.* at 121.
8 Warger v. Shauers, 574 U.S. 40, 45 (2014).

The secrecy of jury deliberations is protected by the evidence rules of every state and the federal government. Referred to as "no-impeachment" rules, they generally provide that "[d]uring the inquiry into the validity of a verdict or indictment, a juror may not testify about any statement made or incident that occurred during the jury's deliberations; the effect of anything on that juror's or another juror's vote; or any juror's mental processes concerning the verdict or indictment."[9] Subject to a few very limited exceptions, these no-impeachment rules expressly prohibit courts from "receiv[ing] a juror's affidavit or evidence of a juror's statement on these matters."[10]

Throughout history, the Supreme Court has jealously guarded the secrecy of jury deliberations, even in the face of flagrant juror misconduct. Take, for example, a criminal case predating the codification of the rules of evidence, *Hyde v. United States*.[11] That case involved four defendants, and there was evidence that the jury convicted two of the defendants and acquitted the other two as part "of a bargain."[12] The Court held that even if this were the case, the trial court was prohibited from hearing "testimony of jurors" about "matters which essentially inhere in the verdict itself."[13]

Or consider *Tanner v. United States*, where there was evidence that jurors were drunk and high during the defendant's trial – one juror described the jury room as "one big party."[14] There, the Court held that evidence of the jurors' inebriation was inadmissible under the federal no-impeachment rule.[15] In so holding, the Court emphasized that "long-recognized and very substantial concerns support the protection of jury deliberations from intrusive inquiry."[16] And to the Court, these concerns trumped the countervailing constitutional concerns implicated by jurors deciding one's fate while under the influence.

While the Supreme Court has repeatedly trumpeted the importance of jury secrecy and the no-impeachment rule, a question started percolating in the lower courts: What if there was evidence that a juror reached a verdict for racist reasons? Must the no-impeachment rule still stand? It was this question that the Court was called to answer in *Peña-Rodriguez v. Colorado*,[17] a case with watershed potential.

Peña-Rodriguez involved what Justice Elena Kagan called at oral argument "the best smoking-gun evidence you're ever going to see about race bias in the jury room."[18] She was right.

9 Fed. R. Evid. 606(b).
10 *Id.*
11 225 U.S. 347 (1912).
12 *Id.* at 381.
13 *Id.* at 384.
14 483 U.S. 107, 115 (1987).
15 *Id.* at 116–17.
16 *Id.* at 127.
17 580 U.S. 206 (2017).
18 Oral Argument at 45:20, Peña-Rodriguez v. Colorado, 580 U.S. 206 (2017) (No. 15-606), www.oyez.org/cases/2016/15-606.

Miguel Peña-Rodriguez faced trial for charges related to sexual harassment and assault.[19] Post-trial affidavits revealed that during deliberations, one of the jurors, who was also an ex-law enforcement officer, made several racist statements, including that he believed Mr. Peña-Rodriguez was guilty because "in [his] experience as an ex-law enforcement officer, Mexican men had a bravado that caused them to believe they could do whatever they wanted with women."[20] He also said Mr. Peña-Rodriguez was likely guilty because "he's Mexican and Mexican men take whatever they want," and that "nine times out of ten Mexican men were guilty of being aggressive toward women and young girls."[21] This juror further told his fellow jurors that he did not believe Mr. Peña-Rodriguez's alibi witness because he was "an illegal" (in fact, the witness was a lawful resident).[22] Despite this rank racism, the Colorado courts, applying the state's no-impeachment rule, held that they could not consider this evidence and therefore they upheld the jury's guilty verdict.

In the face of unmistakable evidence of racial bias infiltrating the jury's deliberations, the Supreme Court had a choice: hold that the no-impeachment rule stands strong even in the face of racism, or craft some kind of racial-bias exception to the no-impeachment rule. The Court chose the latter path, making a self-congratulatory show of doing so along the way.

In an opinion long on rhetoric, the Court declared that it is "imperative to purge racial prejudice from the administration of justice."[23] In the Court's idealized world, the jury functions as "a criminal defendant's fundamental 'protection of life and liberty against race or color prejudice,'" and thus, "[p]ermitting racial prejudice in the jury system damages 'both the fact and the perception' of the jury's role as 'a vital check against the wrongful exercise of power by the State.'"[24] In light of this important imperative, the Court held "that where a juror makes a clear statement that indicates he or she relied on racial stereotypes or animus to convict a criminal defendant, the Sixth Amendment requires that the no-impeachment rule give way."[25]

For the first time, the Supreme Court recognized a constitutional exception to the centuries-old no-impeachment rule. And in so doing, many thought that the opinion marked an important step forward in the efforts to combat racial bias in the administration of criminal law.[26] Nevertheless, a look under the hood of *Peña-Rodriguez* should temper all expectations. Because while the Court's grand pronouncements sounded

[19] Peña-Rodriguez, 580 U.S. at 211.
[20] *Id.* at 212.
[21] *Id.* at 213.
[22] *Id.*
[23] *Id.* at 221.
[24] *Id.* at 223 (quoting Powers v. Ohio, 499 U.S. 400, 411 (1991)).
[25] *Id.* at 225.
[26] *See* Daniel S. Harawa, *The False Promise of Peña-Rodriguez*, 109 CALIF. L. REV. 2121, 2123 and n.13 (2021) (collecting reactions to decision).

good, where the rubber would meet the road is in the standard the Court would set to go about "purg[ing] racial prejudice from the administration of justice."[27] When exactly does the no-impeachment rule have to "give way" in the face of racial animus?

The standard the Court set has two parts. To fall within the racial-bias exception to the no-impeachment rule, the bias must be "overt."[28] But even "overt" bias (more on this later) is not enough to satisfy the new exception because a defendant must also show that the "racial animus was a significant motivating factor in the juror's vote to convict."[29] And even then, a defendant is not guaranteed a new trial; all that they are guaranteed is that a court will hear evidence of the racial bias espoused in the jury room. It is up to that court to decide what to do next.[30]

Applying a critical lens to *Peña-Rodriguez* and the standard that the Court set to overcome the no-impeachment rule, the Court's claimed commitment to purging racial bias from the jury system was, at best, shallow. And time has shown that perhaps *Peña-Rodriguez* has had the opposite effect from its claimed intent. Now, under this new standard, it is arguably *harder* to purge everything but the most egregious forms of racial bias from the jury room.

THE FAULTY PREMISE OF "OVERT" RACIAL BIAS

The Supreme Court held that to overcome the no-impeachment rule, a criminal defendant must first show that the racial bias was "overt." But "overt" is hardly what the most spewed forms of racism look like today. As leading critical race scholars have long explained, gone are the days where racism manifested itself in slurs and epithets, though that is not to say that slurs are not hurled. The "once pervasive use of epithets has morphed into the coded transmission of racial messages through references to culture, behavior, and class."[31] "Now, when racial bias is expressed, it is often in the form of coded language and dog whistles."[32] Counter to this reality, the Supreme Court required evidence of "overt" racial bias to overcome the no-impeachment rule, when much of racism today is *covert*. And it was not as if this fact was lost on the Court. In 1979, when Jim Crow was still the recent past, the Court recognized that "discrimination takes a form more subtle than before."[33]

Because it is now largely socially unacceptable to be outwardly racist, scholars have noted that jurors are reluctant to express any racist ideologies during the jury

27 Peña-Rodriguez, 580 U.S. at 221.

28 *Id.* at 225.

29 *Id.* at 225–6.

30 *See id.* at 228 ("The Court also does not decide the appropriate standard for determining when evidence of racial bias is sufficient to require that the verdict be set aside and a new trial be granted.").

31 Ian Haney López, Dog Whistle Politics: How Coded Racial Appeals Have Reinvented Racism & Wrecked the Middle Class 129 (Oxford University Press 2015).

32 Harawa, *supra* note 26, at 2134.

33 Rose v. Mitchell, 443 U.S. 545, 559 (1979).

selection process. As Professor Anna Roberts cogently explained: "While potential jurors may harbor bias of which they are aware, taboos are likely to prohibit its disclosure, however skillful the questioning. Jurors will often give the answer that seems acceptable."[34] Yet, still, the Supreme Court adopted an "overt" racial-bias requirement, designing a standard that would elide all but the most egregious expressions of racial animus.

Since *Peña-Rodriguez*, shocking instances of racial bias have been held by courts not to be "overt" enough to get past the no-impeachment rule. Take, for instance, the United States Court of Appeals for the Sixth Circuit's decision in *United States v. Robinson*.[35] There, three Black men were on trial for fraud.[36] During deliberations, two Black women jurors expressed doubt about their guilt. In response, the white woman foreperson told those jurors that she "found it strange that the *colored* women [were] the only two that can't see that the defendants were guilty," and accused the jurors of trying to protect their "[B]lack brothers."[37]

Despite the foreperson referring to the Black women as "colored," and despite the foreperson expressing clear hostility toward what she perceived as those jurors acting out of racial solidarity, the court held that the *Peña-Rodriguez* "overt" bias requirement was not met.[38] The court reasoned that "none of the foreperson's remarks [came] close to the *Peña-Rodriguez* juror's level of stereotyping or animus, and the foreperson's remarks were not directed against [the defendants] in the same way that the *Peña-Rodriguez* juror's remarks were directed against the defendant in that case."[39] Thus, this type of behavior – which raises real questions about the impartiality of the jury – was left untouched by the *Peña-Rodriguez* standard. By setting a standard that does not capture this type of casual racism, the Court tacitly held that this type of bias during deliberations is acceptable, directly undercutting the Court's claimed "imperative to purge racial prejudice from the administration of justice."[40]

THE NONSENSICAL SIGNIFICANT MOTIVE TO CONVICT REQUIREMENT

But the overt-racial-animus requirement is not the only problem with the *Peña-Rodriguez* standard. The *Peña-Rodriguez* Court also required criminal defendants to show that the overt racial bias was a "significant motivating factor in the juror's vote

34 Anna Roberts, *(Re)forming the Jury: Detection and Disinfection of Implicit Juror Bias*, 44 CONN. L. REV. 827, 844 (2012).
35 United States v. Robinson, 872 F.3d 760 (6th Cir. 2017).
36 *Id.* at 766–7.
37 *Id.* at 768, 771 (emphasis added).
38 *See id.* at 770–1.
39 *Id.* at 771.
40 Peña-Rodriguez, 580 U.S. at 221.

to convict."[41] This aspect of the standard flies in the face of what we know about how racism works, especially our evolving understanding of implicit racial bias.

Let us begin with implicit bias. "Implicit bias is a preference for, aversion to, attitude toward, or stereotype about a group or a person based on group membership that is outside the realm of conscious awareness and not subject to direct introspection."[42] Everyone has implicit biases that operate along various forms of identity. However, over the past two decades, much research has been done about the negative implicit biases people hold towards Black people and people with darker skin, including that they are "more likely to be viewed as violent, hostile, and aggressive."[43] And these biases, which affect our thoughts and actions in imperceptible ways, are both "powerful and pervasive."[44]

Long before *Peña-Rodriguez* was decided, legal scholars and judges were discussing the problem of implicit bias and the jury system. As one judge explained, because the jury selection process is so focused on identifying explicit bias, voir dire may actually "allow implicit bias to flourish."[45] Considering the way jury selection is conducted in most courtrooms in America, there is no real effort to surface potential jurors' implicit bias. As such, current jury selection processes risk "sanitizing or providing cover for" the inclusion of jurors whose implicit biases may have a real effect on how they view a case.[46] In an effort to combat this very real problem, scholars have proposed, and jurisdictions are experimenting with, ways to capture and remediate implicit bias in the jury selection process.[47]

Given what we know about implicit biases and how they affect our decision-making process, the idea that after a juror expresses *explicit* bias, a defendant must still show how their bias motivated their vote to convict makes little sense. Recall that the racial-bias exception to the no-impeachment rule only kicks in after a defendant learns that a juror expressed "overt" racial animus. And this juror would have had to express this overt racial animus in a social context where, more likely than not, it is viewed as

41 *Id.* at 225–6.

42 Goodwin Liu, *Implicit Bias, Structural Bias, and Implications for Law and Policy*, 25 U. Pa. J. Const. L. 1280, 1283–4 (2023).

43 Roberts, *supra* note 34, at 833.

44 Judge Mark W. Bennett, *Unraveling the Gordian Knot of Implicit Bias in Jury Selection: The Problems of Judge-Dominated Voir Dire, the Failed Promise of Batson, and Proposed Solutions*, 4 Harv. L. & Pol'y Rev. 149, 150 (2010).

45 *Id.* at 158.

46 *Id.*

47 *See, e.g., id.* at 165–70; Roberts, *supra* note 34, at 863–5; Cynthia Lee, A *New Approach to Voir Dire on Racial Bias*, 5 U.C. Irvine L. Rev. 843, 866–9 (2015); Dale Larson, A *Fair and Implicitly Impartial Jury: An Argument for Administering the Implicit Association Test During Voir Dire*, 3 DePaul J. for Soc. Just. 139, 158–9 (2010); Colin Miller, *The Constitutional Right to an Implicit Bias Jury Instruction*, 59 Am. Crim. L. Rev. 349, 354–61 (2022); *see also*, Beth Shwartzapfel, A *Growing Number of State Courts Are Confronting Unconscious Racism in Jury Selection*, Marshall Project, May 11, 2020, www.themarshallproject.org/2020/05/11/a-growing-number-of-state-courts-are-confronting-unconscious-racism-in-jury-selection (discussing the various efforts to address implicit bias).

widely unacceptable to be overtly racist. If a juror feels free enough to openly espouse racist ideas, then it is only logical to think that, in addition to their overt bias, that juror also harbors similar unconscious biases. And because these unconscious biases affect decision-making in imperceptible ways, requiring a defendant to concretely tie the juror's bias to their vote again flies in the face of how we know racism works.

What is more, if, as the Supreme Court explained, the *expression* of overt racial bias "damages both the fact and the perception of the jury's role as a vital check against the wrongful exercise of power by the State,"[48] once the racism escapes the juror's mouth, the damage is done. At that point, there is no reason to believe that the juror was fair or that they based their vote on the evidence. Ponder the facts of the following case and ask yourself whether an outsider looking in would be convinced that racial bias had nothing to do with the outcome.

Williams v. Price involved a Black man on trial for first-degree murder.[49] When a white woman juror expressed sympathy for the Black defendant, multiple jurors hurled slurs and insults at her, including a fellow juror calling her a "n[*****] lover."[50] A juror also told her that "I hope your daughter marries one of them,"[51] "them" being Black men. And on top of this, a defense witness heard one of the jurors say in the courthouse lobby, "All n[******] do is cause trouble."[52]

Despite the jurors' unabashed racism, a Pennsylvania district court held that the *Peña-Rodriguez* racial-bias exception to the no-impeachment rule was not satisfied. As that court saw it, the exception was not met because the "slur was directed to [the juror], not to [the defendant]."[53] And because the "reprehensible and abhorrent" slurs were directed at the juror (even though they were referencing the defendant), the court held that they "do not show that racial animus was a significant motivating factor in the vote to convict."[54] The court therefore concluded that this evidence was insufficient to allow piercing the jury's deliberations.

One can count the ways in which the jurors in *Williams* expressed their racial bias. Most obviously, they used the n-word, which is "perhaps the most offensive and inflammatory racial slur in English, … a word expressive of racial hatred and bigotry."[55] Then, the jurors openly expressed anti-miscegenation beliefs, themselves borne from the racist trope of protecting white women from "oversexed and obsessed"

48 Peña-Rodriguez, 580 U.S. at 223 (quotation marks omitted).

49 Williams v. Price, No. 98cv1320, 2017 WL 6729978 (W.D. Pa. Dec. 29, 2017).

50 *Id.* at *7.

51 Williams v. Price, 343 F.3d 223, 227 (3d Cir. 2003).

52 *Id.* at 227.

53 Williams v. Price, No. 2:98CV1320, 2017 WL 6729978, at *9 (W.D. Pa. Dec. 29, 2017).

54 *Id.*

55 Swinton v. Potomac Corp., 270 F.3d 794, 817 (9th Cir. 2001) (quotation marks omitted); *see also*, Ayissi-Etoh v. Fannie Mae, 712 F.3d 572, 580 (D.C. Cir. 2013) (Kavanaugh, J., concurring) (describing the n-word as "probably the most offensive word in English" because "[n]o other word in the English language so powerfully or instantly calls to mind our country's long and brutal struggle to overcome racism and discrimination against African-Americans").

Black men.[56] And finally, the jurors made clear that these views were not limited to this one Black defendant, but that *all* Black people were troublemakers. Yet despite this potpourri of anti-Black racism, the court in *Williams*, out of the belief that it was dutifully following what the Supreme Court said in *Peña-Rodriguez*, held that this was not enough. If the Supreme Court's goal in *Peña-Rodriguez* was truly "to eliminate racial bias in the jury system"[57] – which, after reading *Williams*, seems debatable, at best – its decision and the standard it set fell gloriously short.

THE MISTAKE OF NOT SAYING WHAT HAPPENS NEXT

The shortcomings of *Peña-Rodriguez* go beyond the ineffectual standard that the Court announced. One must also consider what the Court *did not* say. Let's say that a juror does express "overt" racial animus. And let's say that the juror tied that animus to their decision to convict. While a defendant making this showing allows for inquiry into the substance of the deliberations, it does not necessarily mean that the defendant will be granted a new trial, because what happens next is a question that the Court did not feel compelled to "address."[58] As such, some courts still require a defendant to prove harm, i.e., that the racist statement affected the verdict in some substantive way in order to get any relief.[59] And in the face of the Supreme Court's silence, courts have found that the *Peña-Rodriguez* standard was satisfied and yet have still decided a defendant was not entitled to relief. A decision out of California provides a striking example.

In *People v. Hernandez-Delgado*, a Salvadoran defendant was convicted of first-degree murder.[60] After trial, a defense investigator interviewed one of the jurors, who revealed that she "'still had doubts' when she 'voted guilty.'"[61] This juror also disclosed that another juror "'mentioned the fact that [the] defendant was from El Salvador,' which 'made [that juror] feel he was more guilty' because 'so many murderers come from El Salvador.'"[62] The juror reported that in response to that comment, someone told the juror, "'You can't use that.'"[63]

The defendant moved for a new trial based on juror racial bias, which the trial court denied.[64] In affirming, the California appeals court assumed that the statement

56 Robin A. Lenhardt, *Beyond Analogy: Perez v. Sharp, Antimiscegenation Law, and the Fight for Same-Sex Marriage*, 96 CALIF. L. REV. 839, 874 (2008).

57 Peña-Rodriguez, 580 U.S. at 223.

58 *Id.* at 228.

59 *See* Harawa, *supra* note 26, at 2164; *see also, e.g.*, Shillcutt v. Gagnon, 827 F.2d 1155, 1159 (7th Cir. 1987) (requiring a defendant to show that "there is a substantial probability that the alleged racial slur made a difference in the outcome of the trial").

60 People v. Hernandez-Delgado, No. H043755, 2018 WL 6503340, at *1 (Cal. Ct. App. Dec. 11, 2018).

61 *Id.* at *16.

62 *Id.* (brackets omitted).

63 *Id.*

64 *Id.* at *15.

satisfied the racial-bias exception to the no-impeachment rule articulated in *Peña-Rodriguez*.[65] But the court nevertheless held a new trial was not required because there was no proof that the defendant "suffered actual harm."[66] The court reached this conclusion by pointing out that the racist comment was "brief"; the juror who made the comment "was immediately reprimanded" by a fellow juror; and the juror who revealed the racist comment also "indicated that lengthy deliberations followed that focused on the legal concepts of reasonable doubt and circumstantial evidence."[67] This was all enough to assure the court that the juror's "improper" comment did not have any harmful effect.[68] *Peña-Rodriguez*'s silence permits this type of decision.

The *Peña-Rodriguez* Court should have explained that there is no harm requirement once the racial-bias exception to the no-impeachment rule is satisfied, precisely to avoid an outcome like the one above, which dangerously underappreciates the influence of racism. First, requiring a defendant to prove harm, i.e., that the racism tainted their verdict, ignores the fact that just the *expression* of racism is harmful to the adjudicative process and to the jury system more broadly. Even Justice Alito, who *dissented* from the Court's decision in *Peña-Rodriguez*, understood "that even a tincture of racial bias can inflict great damage on [the jury] system, which is dependent on the public's trust."[69] "Once a juror's racial bias is exposed, the damage to the legitimacy of that jury is already done."[70] Second, once a juror expresses racial bias, there is no way to know for sure how that bias affected their thought processes – people do not say everything aloud. Put another way, just because a juror did not say anything else that is biased does not mean they did not have any other biased thoughts. Third, and just as importantly, there is no way of knowing whether that juror's racial bias affected *other* jurors' thought processes.[71] For all we know, a juror could have heard the juror's statements about people from El Salvador and indexed that information, using it later in their calculus for their vote to convict.

By leaving open what happens after the racial-bias exception to the no-impeachment rule is satisfied, the Court created a world where egregious racial bias towards a criminal defendant can come to light and yet their conviction still stands. If the Court in *Peña-Rodriguez* was seeking to fulfill its "duty to confront racial animus in the justice system,"[72] it failed its mission.

* * *

65 *Id.* at *17.
66 *Id.* at *18 (quotation marks omitted).
67 *Id.*
68 *Id.*
69 Peña-Rodriguez, 580 U.S. at 237 (Alito, J., dissenting).
70 Harawa, *supra* note 26, at 2165.
71 *Id.*
72 Peña-Rodriguez, 580 U.S. at 222.

So why didn't the Court's decision in *Peña-Rodriguez* live up to its promise? One reason is that the Court has a cramped view of racism and what forms of animus offend the Constitution. As Professor Khiara Bridges has explained when surveying the Roberts Court's race jurisprudence, the Roberts Court has an "impoverished conceptualization of what 'counts' as racism against people of color," such that the Court's "racial common sense is that racism against people of color is what racism looked like during the pre-Civil Rights Era – in the bad old days."[73] Thus, in *Peña-Rodriguez*, the Court took a case that features old-school-styled racism and set a standard tailored to the facts of that case. In the process, it ensured that much of the racism and racial bias that people of color experience today would go uncaptured and thus be allowed to flourish. And whether unintentional or by design, by advancing racial justice narratives while only remediating the most grotesque examples of racial bias, decisions like *Peña-Rodriguez* risk a "pacification effect,"[74] lulling people into believing that the case represents racial progress when post-decision case law proves that narrative demonstrably false. Thus, the real beneficiary of the decision is not the average defendant of color, but the Court itself – the decision makes it look as if it opposes racism, when what the Court *really* opposes is the overt racism that makes the judicial system look bad.

Perhaps another way to view *Peña-Rodriguez* is as the canary in the coal mine. Professors Lani Guinier and Gerald Torres explained that "[r]ace ... is like a miner's canary."[75] Back in the day, when miners entered the mines, they brought a canary with them.[76] Because the canary had a more fragile respiratory system, it would get sick if there were any toxic gases in the mine.[77] The canary's condition would warn the miners of the dangerous environment and alert them to leave.[78] As Guinier and Torres's thesis goes, racism and racial bias operate similarly, warning of broader social ills that will eventually affect everyone.[79]

From that perch, *Peña-Rodriguez* exposed how egregious forms of racial bias can infiltrate the trial process. But there is no reason to think this will stop at race. Indeed, we have already seen how other forms of bias – gender, sexual orientation, religious, ethnic, etc. – can distort trials and their outcomes.[80] Bias is not limited to

73 Khiara M. Bridges, *Foreword: Race in the Roberts Court*, 136 Harv. L. Rev. 23, 24–5 (2022).

74 Paul Butler, *The System Is Working the Way It Is Supposed to: The Limits of Criminal Justice Reform*, 104 Geo. L.J. 1419, 1467 (2016).

75 Lani Guinier and Gerald Torres, The Miner's Canary: Enlisting Race, Resisting Power, Transforming Democracy 11 (Harvard University Press 2003).

76 *Id.*

77 *Id.*

78 *Id.*

79 *Id.*

80 *See, e.g.*, Rhines v. Young, No. 5:00-CV-05020-KES, 2018 WL 2390130, at *3, *6 (D.S.D. May 25, 2018), aff'd, 899 F.3d 482 (8th Cir. 2018), cert. denied, 139 S. Ct. 1567 (2019) (where jurors expressed homophobia in a case involving a gay defendant); United States v. Benally, 546 F.3d 1230, 1231 (10th Cir. 2008) (where jurors expressed bias about Native people in the case where the defendant was

race. When we can see clearly how racial bias affects jury deliberations, we can start to more vividly imagine how other biases, especially those that target the most marginalized, can also affect trials. Viewing *Peña-Rodriguez* as the canary underscores the need to heed how biases break down the jury process for marginalized defendants, and to consider what that means for the institution as a whole. As Guinier and Torres conclude: The distress of those who are racially marginalized "is the first sign of a danger that threatens us all."[81]

Which brings us back to a question that opened the chapter: Do secret jury deliberations further justice in a society that has deeply ingrained racial biases? Because we have secret deliberations, there's no real data about how often explicit or "overt" bias is uttered in the jury room. And we have not even begun to wrap our heads around how often implicit bias affects deliberations. All this makes trial in front of one's peers a dicey proposition, particularly for people of color, and *especially* for Black people. Thus, rather than viewing the decision as a racial justice "win," *Peña-Rodriguez* should be seen as a call to critically reassess the jury system itself, including whether it is truly capable of producing just outcomes for all, equally.

a member of the Ute Mountain Ute tribe); United States v. Shalhout, 280 F.R.D. 223, 230 (D.V.I. 2012), aff'd, 507 F. App'x 201 (3d Cir. 2012) (where jurors expressed anti-Arab racism); United States v. Heller, 785 F.2d 1524, 1526 (11th Cir. 1986) (where jurors expressed antisemitic views); *see also*, State v. Martinez, 476 P.3d 189, 192 (Wash. 2020) (acknowledging that jurors may have biases based on gendered stereotypes).

81 Guinier and Torres, *supra* note 75, at 11.

PART II

The Rules

SECTION 1

Relevance and Prejudice

INTRODUCTION

If there are two rules that dominate all of evidence law, those two rules would have to be Rule 401 of the Federal Rules of Evidence, which defines whether evidence is "relevant," and Rule 403, which provides that a court may exclude otherwise relevant evidence "if its probative value is substantially outweighed" by the danger of "unfair prejudice, confusing the issues, misleading the jury, undue delay, wasting time, or needless presenting cumulative evidence." Given these two rules, judges are constantly conducting a balancing test, weighing the probative value of a piece of evidence against the risk of unfair prejudice or the like. Beyond this, Rules 401 and 403 undergird the more specialized relevancy rules that govern the rest of the Article IV rules, from Rule 404 (governing the admissibility of character evidence) to Rule 411 (governing the admissibility of liability insurance) to Rules 412–15 (governing the admissibility of prior sexual conduct in sexual assault cases).

Rule 401 seems simple enough. Evidence is relevant if "it has any tendency to make a fact more or less probable than it would be without the evidence; and the fact is of consequence in determining the action." As Asees Bhasin writes in her chapter, "The question of whether evidence is relevant forms one of the court's first inquiries when considering its admissibility." But how does a court determine relevancy? It is sometimes said that common sense and the common knowledge of the community are essential in assessing relevancy and probative value. But as Critical Evidence scholars increasingly ask, Whose common sense? And doesn't this standard benefit some communities at the expense of others?

The three chapters in this section show that Rules 401 and 403 are anything but neutral. In "Relevance, Reconsidered," Asees Bhasin observes that judges' assessment of relevancy and prejudice are heavily informed by their "priors," i.e., their individual experiences, backgrounds, and of course biases. To illustrate this, Bhasin offers a case study from the pregnancy criminalization context. And she shows "how a seemingly neutral and innocuous Rule 401 determination creates social meaning and knowledge and expands the scope of criminal laws." In "The Relevance and Prejudice of Poverty Evidence," Michele Gilman brings a class critique to relevancy. She explores how poverty can be used as a sword, including, for example, to explain a person's motive to commit a crime. But poverty also may operate as a shield, excluded when it might expose the state's failure to provide a safety net or address inequality. This section ends with an excerpt from "Toward a Critical Race Theory of Evidence," in which Jasmine Gonzales Rose argues that the Rules of Evidence are slanted in favor of racial insiders, and invites the reader to consider how normative assumptions based on the experience of those with racial privilege in society play a role in relevancy determinations. She does so through the example of flight evidence.

Relevance, Reconsidered

Asees Bhasin

INTRODUCTION

The concept of relevance is considered the cornerstone of evidence law. The question of whether evidence is relevant forms one of the court's first inquiries when considering its admissibility. As per Federal Rule of Evidence 401 ("Rule 401"), which has been adopted widely across states, not only must the piece of evidence have "any tendency" to make the proposition it is offered for more or less probable, but such evidence must be material to the case or the substantive legal issue at hand.[1] As per Federal Rule of Evidence 402, irrelevant evidence is inadmissible in court.[2] Judges determine whether evidence is relevant, and in making this assessment, wield a significant amount of power in deciding which fact matters to the case at hand. In dictating these terms, judges shape how litigants can tell their stories at trial, and what information they can use to bring or refute claims.

Whether certain evidence meets the relevance threshold is not meant to be an esoteric inquiry for polymaths. Instead, in opting for "logical relevance,"[3] the drafters of the rules of evidence ensured that relevance would be assessed by commonsense reasoning and by using one's experiences to glean whether the evidence is logically probative and material in a case.[4] This standard imposes a far lower threshold than the alternate, heightened "legal relevance" standard, proposed by John Henry Wigmore, that requires evidence to have a "plus value" to be admissible.[5] Not only is computing relevance a seemingly simplistic task, but the burden imposed by the standard is ostensibly minimal. Courts have overwhelmingly agreed that the rule governing relevance establishes "a low bar."[6]

1 FED. R. EVID. 401.
2 FED. R. EVID. 402.
3 George F. James, *Relevancy, Probability and the Law*, 29 CALIF. L. REV. 689 (1941).
4 JAMES BRADLEY THAYER, A PRELIMINARY TREATISE ON EVIDENCE AT THE COMMON LAW 256 (Boston, Little, Brown & Co. 1898).
5 1 WIGMORE, EVIDENCE § 28 (3d ed. 1940); JOHN HENRY WIGMORE, EVIDENCE IN TRIALS AT COMMON LAW (P. Tillers ed., 3d ed., Little, Brown and Co. 1983).
6 Dmitry Karshtedt, *Nonobviousness: Before and After*, 106 IOWA L. REV. 1609, 1663 (2021).

Philosopher and jurist Jeremy Bentham wrote extensively on evidence law and posited that procedural law aimed to accomplish "a rectitude of decision" by correctly applying the law to true facts based on reasoning using relevant evidence.[7] To this date, judges continue to evoke this similar sentiment of rationality and objectivity in their evidentiary findings, including that of relevance. A close observation, however, exposes a wide variance in how Rule 401 is applied, shattering this myth of objectivity and consistency across contexts.

One of the causes underlying the variance in interpreting Rule 401 is the role of the individual judges themselves. Given that relevance is to be assessed through commonsense generalizations, the knowledge and standpoints of the individual judges heavily inform how evidence is assessed. Such assessments are also heavily impacted by the biases the judges hold and by the norms and stereotypes that exist within the culture. As this chapter will demonstrate, evidence steeped in biases and stereotypes, therefore, gains relevance and is admitted at trial. In admitting such evidence, judges often rely on the "low bar of relevance" to rationalize their decisions. In fact, at the lower court levels, the widely cited language of the low bar helps circumvent a meaningful and searching application of Rule 401.

The next section consists of a case study from the pregnancy criminalization context to show how relevance determinations can fundamentally alter the story told at trial. It shows the role that a trial court judge's biases and cultural perceptions can play in shaping such assessments, and how this act of cultural translation can expand the scope of criminal laws. It also underscores how a seemingly neutral and innocuous Rule 401 determination creates social meaning and knowledge and expands the scope of criminal laws.

CASE STUDY: *AKERS V. MARYLAND*

In *Akers v. State of Maryland*, the state sought to prosecute Ms. Moira Akers for second-degree murder and first-degree child abuse, arguing that she suffocated her newborn by placing it in a plastic zip bag.[8] Moira Akers denied the charge, arguing instead that she experienced a stillbirth while at her home.[9] The prosecution sought to introduce two pieces of evidence: first, evidence in the form of her own statements that she did not seek prenatal care for this pregnancy despite having sought prenatal care for two previous pregnancies; and second, her internet search history regarding terminating a pregnancy at home.[10] In particular, the

7 William Twining, *Bentham's Theory of Evidence: Setting a Context*, 18 J. BENTHAM STUD. 20, 27 (2019).

8 Akers v. State, No. C-13-CR-19-000367, 2024 WL 338958, *1 (Md. App. Ct. Jan. 30, 2024), *rev'd*, 331 A.3d 853 (Md. 2025).

9 *Id.* at *2.

10 *Id.* at *6.

internet searches of the following terms: "rue tea for abortion;" "over-the-counter pills that cause miscarriage;" and "how to end an ectopic pregnancy."[11] She had also navigated to a website titled "woman resort to over-the-counter remedies to end pregnancy."[12]

The *Akers* case provides us with the opportunity to analyze several different approaches adopted in interpreting Rule 5-401, Maryland's version of Rule 401. In this case, courts reached different outcomes and proffered differing reasons. First, the trial court admitted both pieces of evidence after a cursory analysis of Rule 401.[13] Upon review, the Appellate Court of Maryland (ACM) upheld the lower court's determination.[14] In justifying their decision, the judges at the ACM level discussed the low bar of relevance and stated that alternative theories for why Moira Akers did not seek prenatal care would not materially alter the relevance determination.[15] Similarly, on the abortion searches, the appellate court found that this evidence was relevant to understanding her intent. Again, here, while acknowledging the prejudicial nature of this evidence, the court found it to be sufficiently probative. Ultimately, the Supreme Court of Maryland reversed, with two judges dissenting.[16]

The sections below focus on the reasoning adopted by the majority and the dissent at the Supreme Court of Maryland. They discuss the variance in the approaches adopted and highlight how Rule 401 is a subjective inquiry influenced by factors such as the methodology utilized and prevailing dominant norms and stereotypes.

The Role of Methodology and Baseline Questions

The trial and appellate courts engaged in a common pattern that is noticeable in Rule 401 reasoning. The legal analysis was cursory and relied on commonsense reasoning to mask greater contestation. The courts did not adequately engage with the question of how the evidence made the proposition more or less probative, whether statistically or through a discussion of human nature and conduct. While it is true that lower court judges have a limited amount of time they can spend on explaining procedural decisions, the lack of robust reasoning pertaining to an evidentiary decision with serious public policy ramifications is regrettable. Finally, the Supreme Court of Maryland reversed, holding that both pieces of evidence should have been excluded as irrelevant.[17] This decision, however, was not unanimous.

The majority at the Supreme Court of Maryland took issue with the reasoning put forth by the prosecutor, finding that the state "fail[ed] to establish a logical connection

[11] *Id.*
[12] *Id.*
[13] *Id.*
[14] *Id.* at *18.
[15] *Id.*
[16] *Id.* at *16.
[17] Akers v. State, 331 A.3d 853, 882 (Md. 2025).

between Ms. Akers' early consideration of her reproductive right to terminate a pregnancy and the absence of 'a plan if the baby was born alive.'"[18] The judges reached this conclusion due to the absence of proof of the underlying premise that "it is more probable for a woman who contemplates abortion in the early stages of her pregnancy to harm a live child or to not have a plan for the child upon delivery."[19] In this way, the majority at the Supreme Court of Maryland disagreed that there was any probabilistic connection between the evidence offered and the conclusion drawn.

The dissent, in turn, turned to McCormick's insights on the two ways of thinking about probative value. The first way to glean probative value is by posing the question, "[d]oes learning of this evidence make it either more or less likely that the disputed fact is true?"[20] The dissent argued that the majority erroneously followed this approach. The second way is to consider the probability of the evidence *given* the hypothesis. The dissent, in adopting this approach and following a different formula for computing relevance, focused on the proposition that "[e]vidence that is more likely to arise when the hypothesis is true than when it is not true supports the hypothesis; whereas, evidence that is less likely to arise under the hypothesis than not-H supports not-H."[21] The dissent applied this second approach, beginning from the premise that the hypothesis was true, which was that Moira Akers had killed her baby. The dissent justified the adoption of the second starting point as the correct one, arguing that the hypothesis here was one that the jury at the lower levels had already found to be true. In applying this method, the dissent asked, "whether a mother who immediately kills her baby upon its birth is more likely to have a stronger and more consistent desire not to have another child than a woman who does not kill her child."[22] Answering this question affirmatively, it found the evidence of the abortion searches to be relevant.

This case presents two very different approaches to the relevance inquiry. Not only do the baseline questions differ, but the values imbued within those questions differ as well. While the majority started carte blanche, the dissent started from the assumption of guilt. The latter approach seems particularly improper given that the only evidence supporting the assumption that the child had been murdered was the result of a heavily contested, and highly unreliable "Floating Lung Test" that determined that the baby had taken a breath.[23] Akers consistently held that the baby was not born alive and further stated that she had not felt her baby move in weeks. The starting point, then, of the dissent's relevance inquiry was skewed towards the prosecution's version of the truth. As such, in this case, the choice of methodology dictated the finding of relevance.

18 *Id.* at 876.

19 *Id.*

20 *See* Akers, 331 A.3d at 887 (Gould, J., dissenting).

21 *Id.*

22 *Id.* at 892.

23 *See* Aziza Ahmed, *Floating Lungs: Forensic Science in Self-Induced Abortion Prosecutions*, 100 B.U. L. Rev. 1111 (2020).

The Influence of Dominant Norms and Stereotypes

The reasoning adopted at the ACM, and by the dissenting judges of the Supreme Court of Maryland, shows how bias and stereotypes infect relevance determinations. In particular, their reasoning when analyzed reflects dominant cultural expectations of pregnant persons, and deep-seated stereotypes about "bad mothers" that constructed the probative value.

Consider why the dissent found that Akers' internet searches were probative. These searches, they argued, were probative of whether Akers had a strong and consistent desire not to have another child, which, in turn, was probative of whether she had a motive to kill her baby upon its birth.[24] While such reasoning can be critiqued on many levels, an immediate question that arises is why a desire to avoid having future children is associated with infanticide. In fact, the prosecution did not offer any evidence to prove this association. In the absence of such evidence to prove this link, it is unclear why the dissenting judges so "clearly" believed that a woman who kills her baby upon birth is more likely to have a consistent desire not to have another child than a woman who does not kill her baby. One reason for this may be due to the dissenting judges' beliefs about how pregnant people should behave and react.

In her article "Punishing Maternal Ambivalence," Elizabeth Kukura highlights how the feeling of maternal ambivalence marks a deviation from cultural narratives around parenthood and is greeted with deep stigma from society.[25] Because the dominant narrative of pregnancy involves overjoyed reactions, any other reaction or behavior may be viewed as suspicious and, as in this case, criminal.[26] Judges and prosecutors are not impervious to such dominant rhetoric that upholds good motherhood norms and vilifies maternal ambivalence. It is no surprise, then, that they import such suspicion into relevance determinations and associate factors such as ambivalence with violence. The relevance inquiry, then, reifies norms about ideal behavior around mothering.

The judges were persuaded to accept these generalizations by the prosecutors, who purposefully conflated maternal ambivalence with violence, thereby capturing and weaponizing a cultural norm that had been violated. The prosecution's own words, during the closing statement, bring visibility to this association. The prosecutor said:

> Perfect, beautiful Baby Boy Akers was born and died on November 1st, 2018. He lived only a few moments, taking a few breaths, before his mother, the defendant, snuffed out his life. Why? Because she didn't want another child. She wanted to terminate this pregnancy and when she chose not to, she took matters into her own hands upon his birth that afternoon[,] at around 3:30 on November 1st of 2018.[27]

[24] *See Akers*, 331 A.3d at 896 (Gould, J., dissenting).
[25] *See* Elizabeth Kukura, *Punishing Maternal Ambivalence*, 90 Fordham L. Rev. 2909, 2910 (2022).
[26] *Id.*
[27] *See Akers*, 331 A.3d at 865.

The "bad mother" or "irresponsible mother" stereotype casts a dark shadow on the trial, and the evidence in this case primed this stereotype, and was considered relevant by the judges at the trial and appellate levels, as well as the dissent of the Supreme Court of Maryland.

The Expansion of the Scope of Criminal Laws

While the relevance inquiry is considered a procedural one with case-specific implications, the impact of evidentiary decisions can transcend individual cases and have larger societal implications. For example, in *Akers*, the defendant's undesirable conduct (contemplating abortion) and the abstention from desirable conduct (receiving prenatal care) while pregnant were used to deduce her post-birth intent, beliefs, and mental state. In doing so, the lower courts and the dissent made large inferential leaps.

Firstly, the ACM and Supreme Court dissent assumed, based on abortion searches made very early in her pregnancy, that Akers remained ambivalent through the course of her pregnancy. Secondly, and more importantly, even if that were true, these judges assumed that her pre-birth feelings and emotions towards her fetus would remain consistent towards her newborn child. In setting up this inferential web, the prosecutor offered no evidence in this case that Akers considered a fetus to share the same status as a child or would feel the same way towards a fetus as she would a child.

In the absence of any evidence showing that attitude towards a fetus or a newborn child is unchanging, giving credence to this line of reasoning affirms harmful fetal personhood logic espoused by anti-abortion advocates who advocate that a fetus must have the same rights and require the same treatment. Using similar patterns of reasoning, many different types of evidence could be admissible against an individual being prosecuted for harming their newborn. This may include the ingestion of sushi for dinner, consistently drinking three cups of coffee a day, or considering putting one's newborn up for adoption. The decision in *Akers*, then, creates a dangerous precedent and expands the scope of criminal laws by treating benign and mundane conduct as suspicious, thereby changing its status to that of "relevant evidence" that prosecutors can use to criminalize innocent conduct that goes against their notions of a "good mother."

THE NEED FOR A REINVIGORATED RELEVANCE INQUIRY

The discussion above highlights how relevance is a highly subjective inquiry influenced by, among other things, the approaches and methodologies adopted by individual judges and the biases and stereotypes they may hold. This case is just one out of multiple cases within the pregnancy criminalization context where such patterns in relevance reasoning are notable.

This discussion of the *Akers* case adds to the existing literature on how dominant norms inform probative value. Professor Jasmine Gonzales Rose has detailed how white normativity informs how evidence of flight from the police becomes relevant.[28] She argues that flight evidence would only be admissible or probative if it were atypical or abnormal, but judges often do not require attorneys to prove these elements.[29] In unpacking these assumptions that are informed by white dominant norms, judges may be able to understand flight as a justified and normal response to over-policing, racial profiling, police violence, and mass incarceration.[30]

Legal scholars have also observed the role stereotypes have played in informing probative value. For instance, in the eighteenth century, stereotypes around chastity and sexuality informed decisions that a woman's sexual history was relevant to whether she could be raped or not.[31] Gendered stereotypes and tropes that cast women as evil and promiscuous continues to infect evidentiary decisions. For example, consider the hyper-sexualization of Brenda Andrews, who was sentenced to death for the capital murder of her husband alongside her co-defendant and boyfriend James Pavatt.[32] At trial, the prosecutor referenced Ms. Andrew's relationship with the co-defendant, and displayed her thong to the jury, stating: "The grieving widow packs this to run off with her boyfriend. The grieving widow packs this to go sleep in a hotel room with her children and boyfriend. The grieving widow packs this in her appropriate act of grief. Going to the beach … Going to the beach a lot."[33] Overruling relevance related objections from the defense attorney, the trial court allowed the statements. The Oklahoma Court of Criminal Appeals upheld this decision, arguing that this evidence "show[ed] the extent and the nature of the relationship between Pavatt and Appellant, and their intentions in fleeing to Mexico – not as a grieving widow, but as a free fugitive living large on a Mexico beach."[34] The United States Supreme Court eventually found that the admission of this evidence led to a violation of Ms. Andrew's constitutional right to due process.[35]

Additionally, the *Akers* case, as well as the different examples above, show that the issue of biases and stereotypes infecting the relevance inquiry is not a one-of-a-kind circumstance or a context-specific issue. Prosecutors have similarly introduced irrelevant evidence that primes stereotypes of Arabs as terrorists,[36] and immigrants

28 *See* Jasmine Gonzales Rose, *Toward a Critical Race Theory of Evidence*, 101 MINN. L. REV. 2243, 2253 (2017).

29 *Id.* at 2285.

30 *See id.* at 2269.

31 Julia Simon-Kerr, *Unchaste and Incredible: The Use of Gendered Conceptions of Honor in Impeachment*, 117 YALE L.J. 1854, 1856–7 (2008).

32 Andrew v. White, 145 S. Ct. 75, 78 (2025) (per curiam).

33 Brief of Former Federal Judge et al. as Amici Curiae Supporting Petitioners at 13, Andrew v. White, 145 S. Ct. 75 (2025) (No. 23-6573), www.supremecourt.gov/DocketPDF/23/236573/301162/20240222144232127_Andrew%20Amicus%20Brief.pdf.

34 *See* Andrew v. State, 164 P.3d 176, 192 (Okla. Crim. App. 2007).

35 Andrew v. White, 604 US 86, 92 (2025).

36 *See, e.g.*, *Salim v. Mitchell – Lawsuit Against Psychologists Behind CIA Torture Program*, ACLU (Aug. 17, 2017), www.aclu.org/cases/salim-v-mitchell-lawsuit-against-psychologists-behind-cia-torture-program.

as liars or criminals.[37] As you read through this volume, you may even consider the probative value of rap lyrics often offered to impeach defendants found problematic by Andrea Dennis,[38] as well as the evidence of poverty offered to show the motive of criminal defendants, as discussed by Michele Gilman.[39] Thus, there appears to be a systemic issue with how Rule 401 is incorrectly interpreted, warranting intervention and rectification.

Before addressing how judges can apply Rule 401 critically, first, there ought to be a discussion of what the purpose of focusing on Rule 401 is, when Federal Rule of Evidence 403 (Rule 403) exists and allows judges to exclude relevant evidence if its probative value is substantially outweighed by the danger of unfair prejudice.[40] The Advisory Committee of the Rules of Evidence describes "unfair prejudice" to mean an "undue tendency to suggest decision on an improper basis, commonly, though not necessarily, an emotional one."[41] It is no secret that judges overwhelmingly rely on Rule 403 for the exclusion of prejudicial evidence, particularly evidence that implicates politically polarizing subjects.

Yet, there are both theoretical and practical considerations that flow from relying on Rule 403 instead of Rule 401 to deal with evidence based in bias. First, under Rule 403, the judge relies on their own understanding of the psychology of jurors and seeks to predict how they would process certain evidence or information.[42] In invoking Rule 403, the implicit message is not that the evidence itself lacks veritistic value, but rather that the hypothetical juror lacks the ability to give the evidence the appropriate weight it deserves. This, in turn, implies that the evidence deserves some weight, just not a disproportionate amount. Consider the evidence related to the abortion searches that the prosecution attempted to use in the *Akers* case. Courts have acknowledged that abortion-related evidence may be excluded due to the "fierce emotional reaction that is engendered in many people when the subject of abortion surfaces in any manner,"[43] and have held that the issue of abortion is prejudicial. That said, if the *Akers* court were to solely exclude the evidence of the abortion internet searches because it would inflame the jurors, it would signal that the evidence has *some* probative value. This allows the court to create new scientific facts and legitimize associations between ambivalence and infanticide. In doing so, the court risks preserving, or even increasing, the stigma around maternal

37 *See* Christian Powell Sundquist, *Presumed Guilty: "Illegal Alien" Evidence and the Rights of Non-Citizen Defendants*, 81 N.Y.U. ANN. SURV. AM. L. 19 (2025).

38 *See* Andrea Dennis, "Character (Evidence) Assassination," in this volume.

39 *See* Michele Gilman, "The Relevance and Prejudice of Poverty Evidence," in this volume.

40 FED. R. EVID. 403.

41 FED. R. EVID. 403 advisory committee note.

42 Edward J. Imwinkelried, *The Meaning of Probative Value and Prejudice in Federal Rule of Evidence 403: Can Rule 403 Be Used to Resurrect the Common Law of Evidence?*, 41 VAND. L. REV. 879, 906 (1988).

43 Nickerson v. G.D. Searle & Co., 900 F.2d 412, 418 (1st Cir. 1990).

ambivalence and abortion contemplation, contributing to it being perceived with suspicion. By shirking away from explicitly exposing the cultural biases implicated in inference-drawing through a robust Rule 401 analysis, courts allow such faulty and unreliable evidence to run rampant within the legal system, thereby compromising on values of accuracy and fairness that the evidentiary system seeks to champion.

There may be a few other practical benefits of a robust Rule 401 analysis. Finding certain types of evidence irrelevant may preclude prosecutors from collecting and introducing certain types of evidence. This may be outcome-altering in cases, such as within the pregnancy criminalization realm, where prosecutors bring lawsuits guided by their political beliefs and feelings on what constitutes permissible conduct or not, without adequate evidence to back up their cases. Additionally, relying on Rule 401 has implications for the standard of review used on appeal. Since Rule 403 determinations are discretionary, they are reviewed for abuse of discretion and seldom reversed on appeal, with the court often finding the error to be harmless.[44] By contrast, there is a case to be made that Rule 401 determinations should be reviewed under the de novo standard of review because it is a question of law, allowing appellate courts to have a second look. Using Rule 401 instead of Rule 403 can facilitate this second look. Finally, a robust Rule 401 analysis ensures that judges apply Rule 403 more carefully as well, and adequately weigh the probative value aspect, as opposed to just accounting for the prejudicial effect of certain evidence.

Having demonstrated why Rule 401 is the appropriate rule to apply when confronted with biased evidence, the following analysis now focuses on how judges can, in practice, interpret Rule 401 when dealing with this type of evidence. As an important starting point, judges must uncover the hidden or coded meanings that underlie inferences and identify how stereotypes and dominant norms inform those inferences. Next, instead of using their common sense to dictate their reasoning, judges should be mindful of whether their commonsense understandings rely on broad generalizations or stereotypes. Judges should also question whether there is any evidence – social, scientific, or otherwise – that explains the inference. If not, judges should be aware of how the inferences put forth are based on folk wisdom. That said, the existence of data on an issue may not always be reliable or accurate, given the rapid politicization of expertise. Judges should, instead, as Professor Julia Simon-Kerr has suggested, assess not just the probabilistic connection but also the underlying "belief system that connects two propositions."[45] In doing so, judges should become aware of how biases trickle down into research design.

In addition to probabilistically analyzing the strength of the inferences, judges should assess whether the inferences are too speculative or remote, so as to be

[44] *See* Old Chief v. United States, 519 U.S. 172, 183 n.7 (1997); Peter Nichols, *De Novo Review in Deferential Robes?: A Deconstruction of the Standard of Review of Evidentiary Errors in the Federal System*, 54 SYRACUSE L. REV. 531, 533 (2004).

[45] *See* Simon-Kerr, *supra* note 31, at 17.

relevant, because too many inferences would be required on the part of the jurors to assess the true probative value of the evidence, thereby allowing bias to run amok. Furthermore, in cases where the relevance of a piece of evidence depends on whether another fact exists, judges may choose to rely on the rule of conditional relevance, which requires that the party proffering the evidence must show sufficient proof that the fact exists.[46] For example, in the *Akers* case, the evidence of the internet abortion searches would be relevant only if the prosecution were able to prove that ambivalence before birth was associated with the unwillingness to keep the child alive after birth. Judges may find that evidence of the abortion searches is only conditionally relevant and requires the prosecution to prove the missing fact in order to be admissible.

It would not be surprising if there were resistance to the idea that judges should utilize Rule 401 to exclude evidence that prima facie seems probative. Critics of this approach may argue that the bar of relevance is low and that the hurdle imposed by Rule 401 is so insignificant that any evidence under this standard is relevant. For instance, Professor Donald Crump has argued that even witness testimony that would be a reading of all the names in a Los Angeles telephone book may be technically relevant under the standard because it may include names, several that are identical to the defendant's, which would, to some degree, however minute, advance the proposition that the defendant was misidentified.[47]

While the evidentiary culture around the rule of relevance continuously emphasizes the low bar, the reality is that courts routinely find evidence to be irrelevant, debunking any notion that Rule 401 poses no hurdle. Importantly, courts exclude evidence of structural racism and discrimination as irrelevant to the case at hand.[48] Similarly, in wrongful conviction cases, the evidence of the inadequacy of police investigations has been deemed irrelevant.[49] These examples reveal a concerning pattern. On the one hand, evidence that exposes the existence of inequity and bias within the system is considered irrelevant due to its lack of case specificity and because it is not "of consequence" to the case at hand. On the other hand, evidence based in stereotypes and generalizations is considered relevant and admissible at trial. This exposes a double standard within the system and demonstrates the shape-shifting nature of the bar of relevance. It also debunks the myth that there is a neutral, objective, low bar of relevance. Judges must be aware of how interpretations of Rule 401 exacerbate inequality and should strive to apply it critically in a way that helps reduce the role played by individual and cultural biases.

46 FED. R. EVID. 104.

47 David Crump, *On the Uses of Irrelevant Evidence*, 34 HOUS. L. REV. 1, 2 (1997).

48 *See* Rose, *supra* note 28, at 2245, 2284–5; Alex Nunn, *The Living Rules of Evidence*, 170 U. PA. L. REV. 937, 987 (2022).

49 *See* Ethan Singer, *When Police Mess Up: The Lack of a Defense to Inadequate Police Investigations*, 54 COLUM. HUM. RTS. L. REV. 1168, 1209–10 (2023).

The discussion above has identified some ways in which judges can exclude evidence based in bias on relevance grounds. One persisting issue observable in the current evidentiary system and exemplified by the trial court and appellate courts' approach in the *Akers* case is that judges gloss over Rule 401 determinations, often failing to provide detailed reasoning. In applying Rule 401, judges should be encouraged to provide their reasoning, particularly in cases where the evidence's relevance is contested and implicates matters of social and cultural importance. Enhanced judicial transparency will provide litigants with a clearer understanding of the judges' rationales and whether it is influenced by bias. It would also allow appellate judges to review such reasoning, and, given its wide impact on the public at large, allow legislators and rules committee members to step in, if needed.

In addition to the role judges can play, attorneys, particularly defense counsel, should raise Rule 401 objections and identify how the evidence offered primes stereotypes and lacks both probative value and materiality in the given case. Counsel may choose to introduce expert testimony to call into question the truth of the inferences being made by the opposing counsel. Even when objecting on Rule 403 grounds, counsel should consider focusing on the probative value prong adequately.

CONCLUSION

This chapter has sought to advance the discussion around how interpretations of Rule 401 lack objectivity and neutrality, and instead, can reflect and entrench existing biases and stereotypes. It has done so using the *Akers v. State of Maryland* case as an example where the determination of relevance was shaped by the judges' methodology, and prevailing stereotypes and dominant norms surrounding pregnancy and motherhood. It has advocated for a critical application of Rule 401, wherein judges are aware of how inferences connecting the evidence to the purpose for which it is offered are informed by stereotypes by biases. It has been argued that the language of the "low bar" of relevance should not be used to mask contestation, and rather that greater judicial transparency is needed to understand how judges interpret relevance.

The Relevance and Prejudice of Poverty Evidence

Michele Gilman

Persistent poverty and economic inequality are features of American society. In turn, they shape people's engagement with the legal system. People experiencing poverty end up in housing court facing evictions, in criminal court facing charges for crimes of desperation, in small claims court facing debt collection, and in family court facing removal of their children. Yet the rules of evidence generally erase the facts of poverty and social class in trials. Sometimes this is salutary by removing the prejudice a party can face simply for being poor in a supposed meritocracy. Yet it is impossible to "erase" the bias poor people can face in court because their social class is obvious through other cues. Moreover, the relevance rules exacerbate the effects of poverty by masking economic injustice and thereby dampening calls for collective action. At the same time, the lack of substantive rights for poor people and resources to meet their legal needs is putting pressure on the rules of evidence to contend with financial disparities, which is arguably outside their underlying purposes. A Critical Evidence approach requires us to chart a path forward for bringing the larger social context of poverty into the courtroom. Accordingly, this chapter discusses how the evidentiary rules governing relevance inside the courtroom relate to and impact the economic realities outside the courtroom.

Under Federal Rule of Evidence 401 and its state analogs, evidence is relevant if: (a) it has any tendency to make a fact more or less probable than it would be without the evidence; and (b) the fact is of consequence in determining the action. Under Federal Rule of Evidence 403 and its state analogs, relevant evidence may be excluded "if its probative value is substantially outweighed by a danger of one or more of the following: unfair prejudice, confusing the issues, misleading the jury, undue delay, wasting time, or needlessly presenting cumulative evidence." Both rules play a role in determining the admissibility of evidence about poverty in court.

PRESSURE FROM POVERTY

In 2023, the official poverty rate in the United States was 11.1 percent, constituting 36.8 million people.[1] Certain groups suffer higher poverty rates due to this nation's history of discrimination and subordination. The 2023 poverty rates were 17.9 percent for Black Americans; 16.9 percent for Hispanic Americans; and 21.2 percent for Native American and Alaska Natives.[2] Forty percent of Americans report that they lack the funds to handle a $400 emergency.[3] At the same time, the rich are getting richer. The income share of the top one percent of Americans has gone from 10 percent in 1980 to 19 percent in 2020.[4] The top 0.1 percent of Americans hold 13.5 percent of all wealth,[5] while the bottom 50 percent of Americans hold only 2.5 percent.[6] Wealth inequality is exacerbated for people of color; white families have six times the average wealth of Black and Hispanic families.[7]

Poverty is directly correlated with higher odds of finding oneself in court. Living in poverty "creates an abrasive interface with society; poor people are always bumping into sharp legal things."[8] While the vast majority of poor people do not violate the law, most criminal offenders are from poor backgrounds.[9] Further, policing policies that target low-income neighborhoods funnel many low-income people into the court system. The criminalization of poverty also feeds criminal dockets. For instance, cities across America make the daily tasks of living for the homeless a crime, with laws that forbid sleeping, eating, begging, or sitting in public spaces. In 2024, the Supreme Court upheld these practices.[10] At the same time, states are charging criminal defendants an array of fines and fees to fund the criminal legal system, which in turn is creating a new form of debtors' prison as poor people cannot

1 Emily A. Shrider, U.S. Census Bureau, P60-283, Poverty in the United States: 2023 (2024).
2 *Id.*
3 Bd. of Governors of the Fed. Rsrv. Sys., Report on the Economic Well-Being of U.S. Households in 2017, 21 (2018), www.federalreserve.gov/publications/files/2017-report-economic-well-being-us-households-201805.pdf.
4 *Distribution of Household Wealth in the U.S. Since 1989*, The Fed (Sept. 20, 2024), www.federalreserve.gov/releases/z1/dataviz/dfa/distribute/table/#quarter:137;series:Net%20worth;demographic:race;population:all;units:shares;range:1989.3,2023.4.
5 *Share of Net Worth Held by the Top 0.1% (99.9th to 100th Wealth Percentiles) (WFRBSTP1300)* (Mar. 21, 2025, at 13:48 CDT), Federal Reserve Bank of St. Louis: FRED, https://fred.stlouisfed.org/series/WFRBSTP1300.
6 *Share of Net Worth Held by the Bottom 50% (1st to 50th Wealth Percentiles) (WFRBSB50215)* (Mar. 21, 2025, at 13:48 CDT), Federal Reserve Bank of St. Louis: FRED, https://fred.stlouisfed.org/series/WFRBSB50215.
7 *Nine Charts about Wealth Inequality in America*, Urban Institute (Apr. 25, 2024), https://apps.urban.org/features/wealth-inequality-charts/.
8 Stephen Wexler, *Practicing Law for Poor People*, 79 Yale L.J. 1049, 1050 (1969–1970).
9 *See* Erica J. Hashimoto, *Class Matters*, 101 J. Crim. L. & Criminology 31, 32 (2011).
10 City of Grants Pass, Oregon v. Johnson, 603 U.S. 520 (2024).

pay these costs and face incarceration as a result.[11] The collateral consequences of a criminal record further compound poverty by limiting the ability of people to obtain jobs, housing, public benefits, and more. Poverty is not only a predictor of involvement in the criminal legal system, but also an outcome.[12]

On the civil side of the docket, cases involving people experiencing poverty dominate the 20 million civil cases heard each year in state courts.[13] As "other branches of government have failed to respond to growing inequality," state courts are left dealing with the fallout.[14] Family courts each year remove 200,000 children from their homes and place them into foster care on the basis of abuse and neglect charges. Most of these cases involve alleged neglect, which is often a proxy for poverty. Neglect charges arise from greater state surveillance of people living in poverty, stress from living in economic turmoil, lack of social supports, and "[h]istorical trauma and structural and systemic racism."[15] On civil court dockets, consumer debt collection cases dominate.[16] Most of these cases involve a corporate creditor represented by counsel suing a pro se plaintiff. In housing court, about 3.9 million people a year receive an eviction judgment; they are mostly poor as well as disproportionately Black and female.[17] Together, housing and debt collection cases make up more than half of civil court dockets.

More than 70 percent of low-income people face civil legal disputes in a given year, yet 80 percent of them lack legal counsel.[18] The rules of evidence are one of many barriers pro se litigants must navigate in the legal system.[19] While most court cases involve low-income people, the vast majority of resources within the legal system flow to wealthy individuals and corporations.[20] These resources include lawyers

11 Devah Pager, Rebecca Goldstein, and Bruce Western, *Criminalizing Poverty: The Consequences of Court Fees in a Randomized Experiment*, 87 AM. SOC. REV. 529 (2022).

12 *See* Judge Lisa Foster, *Injustice under Law: Perpetuating and Criminalizing Poverty Through the Courts*, 33 GA. ST. U. L. REV. 695, 714 (2017).

13 *See* Colleen F. Shanahan and Anna E. Carpenter, *Simplified Courts Can't Solve Inequality*, 148 DAEDALUS 128, 129 (2019).

14 *Id.* at 129.

15 CHILDREN'S BUREAU, U.S. DEP'T OF HEALTH & HUMAN SERVS., SEPARATING POVERTY FROM NEGLECT IN CHILD WELFARE (2023), www.govinfo.gov/content/pkg/GOVPUB-HE23_1200-PURL-gpo195170/pdf/GOVPUB-HE23_1200-PURL-gpo195170.pdf.

16 Casey Chiapetta, *Debt Collection Cases Continued to Dominate Civil Dockets During Pandemic*, PEW (Sept. 18, 2023), www.pewtrusts.org/en/research-and-analysis/articles/2023/09/18/debt-collection-cases-continued-to-dominate-civil-dockets-during-pandemic.

17 *See* Nick Graetz et al., *Who Is Evicted in America*, EVICTION LAB (Oct. 3, 2023), https://evictionlab.org/who-is-evicted-in-america/.

18 LEGAL SERVS. CORP., THE JUSTICE GAP: MEASURING THE UNMET CIVIL LEGAL NEEDS OF LOW-INCOME AMERICANS (2017), https://lsc-live.app.box.com/s/6x4wbh5d2gqxwy0v094os1x2k6a39q74.

19 *See generally*, Andrew C. Budzinski, *Overhauling Rules of Evidence in Pro Se Courts*, 56 U. RICH. L. REV. 1075 (2022).

20 *See* Robert W. Gordon, *Lawyers, the Legal Profession & Access to Justice in the United States: A Brief History*, DAEDALUS 177, 178 (Winter 2019); Robert Rubinson, *A Theory of Access to Justice*, 29 J. LEGAL PROF. 89, 90–1 (2005).

and the actors they work with to serve clients, such as paralegals and experts, as well as the resources that pay for decision-makers and the adjudicative apparatus that supports them, such as clerks and bailiffs.[21] Trials involving poor people can take mere minutes, while trials involving wealthier people and entities are afforded all the time necessary to present a case. It remains true that "[p]roviding equal justice for poor and rich, weak and powerful alike, is an age-old problem."[22]

HOW EVIDENCE LAW RESPONDS

Challenges to poverty evidence on the grounds of relevance and unfair prejudice often arise when it is introduced to explain or impugn a low-income litigant's motive or character. On the flip side, the issue of poverty may be raised by a low-income litigant who is prejudiced by a lack of resources to generate exhibits or expert evidence to support their claim or defense. This section considers how courts have applied the relevance and prejudice rules in responding to both these scenarios.

The Relevance of Poverty Evidence

America is a country of haves and have-nots, and poor people are disproportionately entangled in the legal system – but these realities are suppressed in trials. The black-letter law is that the financial condition of the parties is not relevant in a trial, as well as unfairly prejudicial. The Tennessee Supreme Court aptly summarized this principle: "The rights and liabilities of the parties should be adjudged on the basis of their past conduct and legal relationship rather than their financial conditions. Evidence of a party's financial condition is usually not admissible because it may create a risk that a fact finder will ground its decision on prejudice or sympathy and not on the merits of the case."[23] It is unlikely, however, that suppressing the introduction of poverty-related evidence effectively takes the issue off the table, as the fact finder will perceive a witness's social class through other cues, such as speech or dress. Moreover, by deeming poverty irrelevant, courts can ignore the political, social, and economic context that brings people to court, which in turn allows the perpetuation of injustice.

In criminal cases, the issue of poverty can arise when the state argues that a person's impoverished state provided them with a motive to commit a crime. In *United States v. Mitchell*, the Ninth Circuit rejected this motive theory in a case involving a defendant charged with bank robbery.[24] In the case, there was conflicting evidence

[21] Rubinson, *supra* note 20, at 90–1.
[22] Griffin v. Illinois, 351 U.S. 12, 16 (1956).
[23] In re Estate of Smallman, 398 S.W.3d 134, 151 (Tenn. 2013).
[24] United States v. Mitchell, 172 F.3d 1104, 1108–9 (9th Cir. 1999).

as to whether the defendant was the robber. On the one hand, an eyewitness who was outside the bank picked him out of a lineup; on the other hand, the bank tellers gave varied descriptions of the robber, several of which did not fit the defendant. The government thus leaned heavily into the theory that the defendant had the motive to rob the bank because he was poor. The trial court admitted testimony from the defendant's landlord that he paid rent in cash the day after the robbery; from his former boss who said that he had fired the defendant; from his father to show that he could not support himself or his wife and children; and from an FBI agent who said that he was overdrawn at his bank before the robbery. During closing argument, the prosecutor pulled this testimony together to emphasize the defendant's lack of money and thus, his motive to rob a bank. The defendant was convicted.

The defendant appealed, and the Ninth Circuit reversed on the grounds that the trial court erred by allowing the poverty evidence. On appeal, the government argued that the poverty evidence was relevant under Federal Rule of Evidence 404(b), to establish the defendant's motive, to which the Ninth Circuit responded, "Being poor is not a crime, wrong, or act," rendering 404(b) inapplicable. As to relevance and prejudice, the Ninth Circuit noted "it is necessary to consider the facts of the particular case." The court then reasoned:

> Poverty as proof of motive has in many cases little tendency to make theft more probable. Lack of money gives a person an interest in having more. But so does desire for money, without poverty. A rich man's greed is as much a motive to steal as a poor man's poverty. Proof of either, without more, is likely to amount to a great deal of unfair prejudice with little probative value.[25]

As the *Mitchell* court pointed out, there are exceptions to the principle of poverty's irrelevance, such as when a defendant obtains sudden wealth after committing a lucrative crime or when the defendant was in financial straits and owed substantial sums. However, the evidence in *Mitchell* did not show "more than the mere fact that the defendant is poor."[26] For instance, although the defendant paid his rent in cash following the alleged crime, he had always paid his rent in cash previously during his tenancy.[27]

This blackletter principle that poverty, without more, is irrelevant and prejudicial serves justice in cases like *Mitchell* by blunting the effect of stereotypes about the poor. Poor people have long faced stigma and discrimination in the United States. The prevailing explanation for poverty in the United States is that people are poor due to behavioral choices. Under this "culture of poverty" theory, the poor make bad choices that trap them in poverty. This theory aligns with the American myth of meritocracy, which holds that anyone can pull themselves up by their bootstraps

[25] *Id.* at 1108–9.
[26] *Id.* at 1109 (quoting United States v. Jackson, 882 F.2d 1444, 1449 (9th Cir. 1989)).
[27] *Id.* at 1110.

with hard work and determination.[28] In turn, this myth implies that failure to thrive in a capitalist economy is tied to moral failure. By limiting evidence about the financial status of the parties, courts can limit this pervasive anti-poor bias. Nevertheless, a person's financial status can be evident to the judge and jury through a party's appearance, speech, attire, and profession, which are markers of social class. Indeed, there is evidence that many judges have an implicit bias against the poor (among other characteristics), even when evidence of poverty is not expressly introduced in court.[29] Thus, it is doubtful that making poverty officially "irrelevant" takes that factor entirely out of the equation.

Moreover, denying the relevance of poverty in court can mask the ways in which our substantive laws and policies abandon or punish the poor. Consider that poverty is not a defense to a crime. In 1971, Judge David Bazelon of the United States Court of Appeals for the District of Columbia famously challenged this assumption, arguing, in dissent to a decision upholding a murder conviction, that juries should be allowed to consider a defendant's "rotten social background" (RSB); that is, how growing up under circumstances of severe environmental deprivation can subsequently influence a criminal defendant's mental state and actions.[30] Judge Bazelon argued that permitting the RSB defense would force society to examine the causes of crime and to consider "whether income redistribution and social reconstruction are indispensable first steps toward solving the problem of violent crime ...."[31] In the years since Bazelon proposed the RSB defense, there has been extensive psychological and social science research about how poverty influences child development and people's behavior in ways that can increase crime – all of which supports the rationale for an RSB defense.[32] Nevertheless, there is little appetite for recognizing an RSB defense,[33] due to its perceived undermining of individual responsibility and threat to public safety.

Judge Bazelon's call for courts to confront the empirical realities of poverty aligns with James Macleod's theory for broadening the aims of evidence law.[34] He argues that judges should interpret the rules to combat systemic racial and economic injustice rather than focusing solely on the narrow goal of ensuring the jury reaches an accurate verdict.[35] This broad view is "more cognizant of the trial's place within a broader system and broader set of justice-related considerations."[36] In the broad

[28] *See generally*, STEPHEN J. MCNAMEE AND ROBERT K. MILLER, JR., THE MERITOCRACY MYTH 1–2 (2d ed., Rowman & Littlefield 2009); Mark R. Rank, *Toward a New Understanding of American Poverty*, 20 WASH. U. J.L. & POL'Y 17, 25 (2006).

[29] *See generally*, Michele Benedetto Neitz, *Socioeconomic Bias in the Judiciary*, 61 CLEV. ST. L. REV. 137 (2013).

[30] United States v. Alexander, 471 F.2d 923, 926 (D.C. Cir. 1973) (Bazelon, C.J., dissenting).

[31] *Id.* at 965.

[32] *See* Michele Gilman, *The Poverty Defense*, 47 U. RICH. L. REV. 495, 542–3 (2013).

[33] *Id.* at 504–6.

[34] James Macleod, *Evidence Law's Blind Spots*, 109 IOWA L. REV. 189, 229 (2023).

[35] *Id.*

[36] *Id.* at 230.

view, a court might consider some forms of "prejudice" as particularly unfair, such as disparate resources between the parties or racial bias.[37] MacLeod supports his broad vision by pointing to a variety of contexts in which the Rules focus on values other than accuracy, such as the rules on privilege and the rules barring evidence of statements made during settlement and plea negotiations.[38]

This interpretive method resonates with me as a civil poverty lawyer given that judges typically will not allow me to refer to my client's poverty to explain the larger social context of their legal problem. For instance, in representing a tenant facing eviction for failure to pay rent, it is irrelevant – in court, at least – that the client lacks rent money because she lost her job or had to take off work to care for a disabled child or did not get this month's child support check. I cannot discuss the unstable low-wage workforce, the lack of a living wage, or the inadequate childcare system. Everyone in the courtroom pretends these conditions do not exist.

Similarly, Vicki Lens conducted an ethnographic study of family court child maltreatment proceedings, finding that the parents, almost exclusively low-income Black and Hispanic women, were effectively silenced in court.[39] Lens reflected, "Narratives are ... shaped by what is left out. While poverty was a constant undertone, it was rarely brought to the surface. Neither was the larger structural context within which parents lived their lives or the confounding variables of race and discrimination."[40] Lens acknowledges that "a court's purview is the micro, not the macro," yet "the failure to acknowledge structural obstacles reinforced narratives of personal irresponsibility."[41]

Poverty is also invisible to the Constitution and anti-discrimination statutes. The Constitution does not provide affirmative rights to public support, such as a right to housing, food, or health care.[42] Further, American law does not protect people from discrimination based on their socioeconomic status. The Supreme Court has ruled that poverty is not an immutable characteristic and thus does not deserve heightened constitutional protection. As a statutory matter, federal and state civil rights laws protect against discrimination based on race, gender, disability, age, national origin, religion, sexual orientation, and genetic history – but they do not protect the poor.

Further, much Supreme Court doctrine reinforces economic inequality.[43] The Court defers to laws and policies that harm the economic interests of the 99 percent,

37 *Id.* at 230. As an example, he points to the case of Commonwealth v. Serge, 896 A.2d 1170, 1183 (2006), discussed *infra*.

38 *Id.* at 236.

39 Vicki Lens, *Judge the Other: The Intersection of Race, Gender, and Class in Family Court*, 57 FAM. CT. REV. 72 (2019).

40 *Id.* at 79.

41 *Id.*

42 *See* Mario L. Barnes and Erwin Chemerinsky, *The Disparate Treatment of Race and Class in Constitutional Jurisprudence*, 72 L. & CONTEMP. PROBS. 109, 111 (2009).

43 *See* Michele Gilman, *A Court for the One Percent: How the Supreme Court Contributes to Economic Inequality*, 2014 UTAH L. REV. 389 (2014).

while rejecting legislative attempts to redistribute societal benefits. For instance, the Court has rejected government attempts to voluntarily desegregate schools, while deferring to laws that result in unequal financing for rich and poor school districts. As a result, poor children receive subpar educations, dooming many of them to the bottom of the economic ladder. Similarly, the Court overturned Congress's attempt to rein in campaign financing, while upholding state voter identification laws that suppress the votes of the poor. These rulings reinforce economic inequality and uphold an economy that drives poor people into the legal system, where they typically confront a more powerful opponent, such as a prosecutor seeking to convict them for a crime, a child welfare agency removing their child, a landlord trying to evict them, or a creditor collecting on a debt.

Poverty and Lack of Evidence

Once a low-income person is entangled with the legal system, principles of due process and equal protection remove some hurdles to access to justice, but do not come close to equalizing the playing field. The Supreme Court has struck down filing fees and costs in certain cases involving fundamental rights, such as criminal appeals,[44] divorce cases,[45] and parental termination of rights cases,[46] while upholding these types of fees in bankruptcy cases[47] and appeals of public benefits denials[48] – deeming financial stability less than fundamental. With regard to access to counsel, poor defendants in criminal cases have a right to lawyer,[49] but public defender systems struggle under the weight of massive dockets, and thus legal representation is often lacking in quality.[50] Meanwhile, there is no "civil Gideon" right,[51] although some jurisdictions provide counsel in cases involving termination of parental rights and a handful of states and cities have recently created rights to counsel in housing cases. Without a lawyer, navigating the legal system, including the rules of evidence, is essentially hopeless, and indeed, pro se litigants suffer worse outcomes than represented parties.[52] As Gene Nichol writes, "We have … assured that [the court system is] hugely complicated, cumbersome, mysterious, professionally technical, adversarial, and expensive … It is as far beyond the kin [sic] of most citizens as brain

44 Griffin v. Illinois, 351 U.S. 12 (1956).
45 Boddie v. Connecticut, 401 U.S. 371 (1971).
46 M.L.B. v. S.L.J, 519 U.S. 102 (1996).
47 United States v. Kras, 409 U.S. 434 (1973).
48 Ortwein v. Schwab, 410 U.S. 656 (1973).
49 Gideon v. Wainwright, 372 U.S. 335 (1963).
50 *See generally*, Erwin Chemerinsky, *Lessons from Gideon*, 122 YALE L.J. 2676 (2013).
51 Lassiter v. Department of Social Services, 452 U.S. 18 (1981).
52 *See* Victor D. Quintanilla, Rachel A. Allen, and Edward R. Hirt, *The Signaling Effect of Pro Se Status*, 42 L. & SOC. INQUIRY 1091, 1093 (2017) ("This meta-analysis demonstrated that in fields of average complexity in trial courts, pro se claimants are on average 6.5 times more likely to lose than counseled claimants.").

surgery is to me. That means, of course, that, without counsel, the door we have theoretically opened is, in practice, closed shut."[53]

Even with a lawyer, many cases require expert witnesses to explain scientific and technical concepts; however, poor people cannot afford to pay them. In *Ake v. Oklahoma*, the Supreme Court held that states must pay for psychiatric experts in capital, criminal cases where the defendant's sanity is at issue.[54] However, "the implementation of *Ake* falls far short of what is needed," since it is limited to psychiatric experts, and "the courts have applied *Ake* restrictively and routinely denied defense motions for expert appointments even when it is clear that expert services would be highly beneficial to the accused."[55] And, *Ake* does not apply to civil cases. Although Rule 706 allows courts to appoint experts, courts rarely deploy the rule. When used, it is for the purpose of providing a "neutral" assessment for the fact finder on particularly complex issues, not to expand expert assistance to low-income litigants.[56] Moreover, the parties in civil cases must pay for such experts, and in criminal cases, the available funds are limited, thus undermining any potential of Rule 706 to equalize the playing field.[57] To be sure, courts and legislatures have expanded the right to experts somewhat to cover other needed experts in a wider range of criminal cases, but coverage is still spotty and inconsistent.

The Constitution is not doing the work of providing poor people with meaningful access to the legal system, and legislators are not funding adequate legal services for the poor. In turn, this is putting downward pressure on the Rules of Evidence to equalize the scales of justice. Can they handle this function? In *Commonwealth v. Serge*, the Justices on Pennsylvania's highest court grappled with the economic disparity between a criminal defendant and the state.[58] In that case, the defendant was charged with murdering his wife. At trial, the state offered, and the trial court admitted, a computer-generated animation (CGA) reflecting its experts' theory of the shooting. The CGA cost between $10,000 and $20,000.[59] The defendant was unable to afford a CGA of his own; indeed, $10,000 was the entire cost of his publicly funded defense.[60] On appeal, he argued that the state's CGA should have been excluded under Rule 403 because its probative value was substantially

53 Gene R. Nichol, *Judicial Abdication and Equal Access to the Civil Justice System*, 60 CASE W. RES. L. REV. 325, 348 (2010).

54 470 U.S. 68 (1986).

55 Edward J. Imwinkelried, *Impoverishing the Trier of Fact: Excluding the Proponent's Expert Testimony Due to the Opponent's Inability to Afford Rebuttal Evidence*, 40 CONN. L. REV. 317, 323–4 (2007).

56 Hannah Jacobs Wiseman, *Pro Bono Publico: The Growing Need for Expert Aid*, 60 S.C. L. REV. 493, 517 (2008).

57 3 FEDERAL EVIDENCE § 7:25 (4th ed.) (Background and purpose).

58 896 A.2d 1170, 1183 (2006).

59 *Id.* at 1183.

60 *Id.*

outweighed by the unfair prejudice to him, particularly given the economic disparity between the parties.[61]

The majority held that although there is "no obligation to provide the defendant the finances necessary to create a CGA of his or her own," the monetary disparity between the parties was a relevant factor with regard to the CGA's admissibility.[62] "[T]he trial court sitting with all facts before it, including the monetary disparity of the parties, must determine if the potentially powerful effect of the CGA and the inability of a defendant to counter with his or her own CGA should lead to its preclusion."[63] Ultimately, the court upheld the admission of the CGA in that case, ruling that it was not emotionally charged, and moreover, that the trial judge gave the jury extensive cautionary instructions before playing the CGA, informing the jury that the CGA simply illustrated the expert testimony, but was not itself fact. This ruling rightly recognizes that Rule 403 has the flexibility to promote goals of economic justice within and outside the narrow facts of a specific case.

Three concurrences shared differing views on the issue of economic disparity. In the first concurrence, the justice agreed with the majority that monetary disparity was a relevant factor in conducting a 403 balancing but went further to argue that due to unfair prejudice, "[i]n many cases this will require the trial court to give money to the defense to procure a CGA."[64] In the second concurrence, the justice agreed that the interests of justice "may require providing an indigent defendant with the funds necessary to respond to a CGA produced by the Commonwealth." However, this justice criticized the "substantial" cost of the CGA, remaining "[un]convinced that the cost was worth the expenditure of scarce public financial resources." This led the justice to conclude in some cases, the wiser course of action may be to exclude the state's CGA altogether.[65]

The third concurrence took an entirely different tack. The justice stated: "Admissibility of evidence is not a function of finances of the parties. If one side chooses to develop evidence, of this or any type, its admissibility cannot rest on a determination of the relative resources of the other party. Relevance, not money, is what makes something admissible." Instead of turning to the rules of evidence, courts should consider any entitlement to resources "under existing principles," such as the due process clause. Of course, as noted above, a poor defendants' entitlement to resources for litigation is almost nil. This is a constrained vision of Rule 403 that is disconnected from the evidence rules' purpose to secure justice, as articulated in Rule 102.

[61] Appellant waived the argument by not raising it before the trial court, but the Pennsylvania Supreme Court addressed the argument regardless. *Id.* at 1184.

[62] *Id.* at 1185.

[63] *Id.*

[64] *Id.* at 1188.

[65] *Id.* at 1189–90.

In his reflection on the case, Edward Imwinkelried agreed with the third concurrence that wealth should not be a factor in Rule 403 balancing, as "[t]here is no evidence whatsoever that the drafters of Rule 403 entertained an egalitarian goal of leveling the evidentiary playing field."[66] Of course, the drafters did not envision many evidentiary scenarios that judges must resolve. Imwinkelried acknowledges there may be extreme cases in which a trial judge should bar expert testimony under Rule 403. Such cases arise when "the proponent's expert has impressive credentials, the expert's methodology does not involve an objective decisional criterion, there is no available data as to the methodology's error margin, and the tools at the judge's disposal in the case are inadequate to alleviate the danger of jury overvaluation of the testimony."[67] In these cases, it is not poverty that is a Rule 403 factor, but rather the inability to afford a rebuttal witness, which in turn "heightens the risk of jury overvaluation. That risk is a legitimate factor in the Rule 403 calculus."[68]

While the cost and complexity of creating CGAs and similar digital evidence is decreasing with the advent of generative AI, litigants will still need experts to provide the underlying theory for a digitally created exhibit. They will also suffer prejudice if they lack the necessary expertise to challenge an opponent's exhibit. In a footnote, the *Serge* decision acknowledged that prejudice may be heightened when dealing with expert technologies that generate results, as opposed to those that simply depict expert testimony.[69] In such cases, the court stated, Rule 403 may justify excluding the evidence or providing necessary funds to a defendant.[70] Judges committed to a broader, justice-oriented view of evidence law may find that Rule 403 provides a way to consider economic justice, although this approach is rare.[71]

Courts Without Evidence Rules

Any discussion of Rules 401 and 403 would be incomplete without acknowledging that there is a large swath of litigation involving poor people where the rules of evidence do not apply at all. In small claims cases involving low-dollar litigation and in administrative cases (where access to health care, housing, and public benefits are adjudicated), there are typically no rules of evidence governing the proceedings. This is by design, given that most low-income litigants in these forums are unrepresented. On the one hand, this makes it easier for poor people to represent themselves unencumbered by the complexities of the rules of evidence. On the other hand, it means that their more powerful opponents can introduce and prevail on unreliable,

66 Imwinkelried, *supra* note 55, at 338.
67 *Id.* at 354.
68 *Id.* at 353–4.
69 896 A.2d at 1178–79 n.11.
70 *Id.*
71 Macleod, *supra* note 34, at 232–3.

irrelevant, and prejudicial evidence. Further, in a rule-less courtroom, judges have more power to silence litigants and are "given unreviewable discretion to weigh the evidence, risking that judges who engage in flawed, biased, or mercurial decision-making will reach those decisions behind the closed curtain of unreviewable standards ...."[72] With or without rules of evidence, pro se litigants will struggle to obtain justice in an adversarial system. They will either flail or be steamrolled.

TOWARD A DEMOSPRUDENCE OF EVIDENCE LAW

In sum, caselaw reveals two strands when it comes to the evidentiary relevance of poverty in court. First, a person's wealth is irrelevant to most legal disputes. On the one hand, this limits the prejudice that poor people face in American society. On the other hand, this principle allows the judicial system to avoid confronting the structural and systemic forces that push poor people into court. Second, a financial disparity between the parties may be relevant in determining the admissibility of expensive, expert evidence, although this is hardly a consensus view, and courts are wary of spending judicial resources to equalize the playing field. Thus, under both relevancy approaches, the reality outside the courtroom is not acknowledged inside the courtroom.

The theory of demosprudence, or "the study of the dynamic equilibrium of power between lawmaking and social movements,"[73] provides a way to use the rules of evidence to confront poverty.[74] Lani Guinier and Gerald Torres developed this theory to make space for "those previously excluded or marginalized and enable[] them to participate more fully in helping to make decisions that affect their lives."[75] Further developing this theory, Monica Bell, Stephanie Garlock, and Alexander Nabavi-Noori applied demosprudence to challenge criminal legal debt, articulating ways that judges can engage in a "conversation between the public and the courts."[76] These authors are concerned that due process claims are the primary mode of challenging criminal legal debt; for instance, defense attorneys will argue that criminal defendants should have individualized hearings to assess their ability to pay bail.[77] This focus on process addresses procedural protections once a case is in court, but it does not encompass the reasons that people appear before court in the first place.[78] In other words, the due process lens allows courts to elide the substantive ways

[72] Budzinski, *supra* note 19, at 1116.

[73] Lani Guinier and Gerald Torres, *Changing the Wind: Notes Toward a Demosprudence of Law and Social Movements*, 123 YALE L.J. 2740, 2749 (2014).

[74] In this volume, Ngozi Okidegbe's chapter "Evidence Rulemaking and Community Participation," turns to demosprudence to advance a vision of community participation in evidence rulemaking that would be responsive to the interests of socially marginalized people.

[75] Guinier and Torres, *supra* note 73, at 2749–50.

[76] Monica Bell, et al., *Toward a Demosprudence of Poverty*, 69 DUKE L.J. 1473, 1478 (2020).

[77] *Id.* at 1502–5.

[78] *Id.* at 1501.

that poverty is criminalized.[79] It emphasizes "individualized liberty over collective equality ...."[80] Accordingly, the authors sketch a vision of demosprudence in which judges will "observe and address the realities of poverty even when traditional doctrine truncates the possibility of legal intervention."[81]

To engage in demosprudence, judges must have an expansive view of their role: "Judging is not merely the rendering of decisions based on preexisting legal rules; it can also encompass the articulation of legal values, the management of courtrooms, the making of rules about broader judicial operation, and the representation of the ethical principles of the legal system."[82] Under the authors' recommendations, judges should address the context of poverty in rendering opinions; develop testimony about social context to ensure it appears in trial transcripts; undertake rulemaking to establish ethical standards for the bench to reduce socioeconomic biases; educate themselves and their staff about the context of poor people's daily lives; deploy "active judging," which involves ensuring that pro se litigants claims are fully developed; and proactively engage with the communities in which they sit. In addition, society should build a more diverse judiciary and courthouse staff, including those from disadvantaged backgrounds.

This vision of demosprudence provides a touchstone for considering how judges might use the relevancy rules to broaden the story of poverty that is told in court. Judges could expand notions of relevance to give litigants and their advocates space to explain the underlying causes and social context that led them to court. This would be consistent with a broad reading of Rule 102's command to construe the rules of evidence to secure "just determination[s]."[83] In areas such as character evidence and impeachment, the evidence rules are applied differently for criminal defendants given the stakes of their cases and the bundle of constitutional rights afforded to them. Thus, it is within the spirit of the rules to recognize that certain populations require expansive interpretations of the rules to achieve justice.

Judges can also opine when substantive law is mismatched to the realities faced by marginalized populations. In so doing, they create a public record that serves as a basis for legal and policy reform by social movements and legislators. Through an expanded notion of relevance, judges can acknowledge the dignity and autonomy of the people who appear before the bench by demonstrating empathy through active listening. Particularly where there are interpretive issues and statutory ambiguities, judges can take social context into account as an interpretive tool. At the same time, judges can continue to exclude evidence of socioeconomic status as prejudicial when it aligns with inaccurate assumptions, stereotypes, and myths about poverty.

79 *Id.* at 1506.
80 *Id.* at 1500.
81 *Id.* at 1507.
82 *Id.*
83 Macleod, *supra* note 34, at 196.

In considering financial disparity, they can continue to fact-find around inequality and articulate the ways in which available tools and resources fail to equalize the scales of justice. To better parse the line between beneficial and prejudicial uses of poverty evidence, judges should receive training in understanding the causes and consequences of poverty and engage with qualitative studies about poverty.

Lawyers also have an important role in demosprudence. Poverty lawyers, criminal defense attorneys, and progressive prosecutors can make arguments that limit the prejudicial harms of poverty evidence while advocating for the relevance of social context evidence that underlies a poor litigant's appearance in court. Lawyers must vigorously advocate for interpretations of the relevance and unfair prejudice rules that serve the goals of economic justice.

The *Mitchell* and *Serge* opinions discussed above share some hallmarks of a demosprudential vision. The judges in those cases forthrightly dealt with the issue of poverty and financial disparity, recognizing the ways that poverty can skew the aims of justice. Their nuanced reasoning lays a foundation for thinking more fully about how to absorb the expansive realities of poverty within the constrained universe of the courtroom. In acknowledging the relevance of poverty, they give the rules of evidence a role in alleviating it.

Toward a Critical Race Theory of Evidence

Jasmine B. Gonzales Rose[1]

INTRODUCTION

It's not what you know, it's what you can prove in court!

This oft-used movie line shows how even Hollywood recognizes the importance of evidence law. At trial, the facts are not determined through an independent investigation of the truth but by how the rules of evidence are employed to admit or exclude evidence. Attorneys use evidence rules to establish the story that the finder of fact, be it a judge or jury, considers in rendering its findings or verdicts. It is often taken for granted that evidence law applies equally to all persons and provides everyone an equal voice in the courtroom, irrespective of race. This Article challenges these assumptions and reveals how evidence law and practice structurally disadvantages people of color.

In courtrooms across the United States, certain evidence receives racially disparate admissibility treatment. Evidence of the "racialized reality" – the lived experience of racial differentiation and hierarchy – of white people is too often submitted to juries with little to no evidentiary scrutiny, while the racialized reality of people of color is routinely excluded, even when supported by evidence-based social science. When the racialized reality of minorities is admitted into evidence, it often comes in only through expert witnesses' white or "insider" voices. This amounts to a dual-race evidentiary system reminiscent of antiquated laws that allowed whites to testify against anyone but barred people of color from testifying against whites. However, unlike these outdated race-based witness competency rules, today's evidentiary racial disparities appear race-neutral.

This Article applies – and, more importantly, calls for increased application of – Critical Race Theory (CRT) to the law of evidence. Critical race evidentiary inquiry is valuable because it exposes how the law of evidence can insidiously operate to

[1] Excerpted from Jasmine B. Gonzales Rose, *Toward a Critical Race Theory of Evidence*, 101 MINN. L. REV. 2243 (2017).

perpetuate racial subordination. Though scholars have applied CRT to other fields of law, including tax, contracts, and property, too few have applied it to evidence law. Antidiscrimination scholarship on the intersection of evidence law and race is sparse and often overlooks the institutionalized manner in which evidence law replicates and perpetuates societal discrimination in the courtroom. Evidentiary rulings ultimately determine substantive outcomes. Thus, those concerned about justice in the legal process should pause to consider how the application of evidence law might subordinate racial minorities and could undergo reform to increase fairness. …

I. RACE AND RACISM IN THE LAW OF EVIDENCE

Before evaluating the contemporary racial landscape of evidence law and proposing reforms, it is prudent to pause for retrospection on the law of evidence and supply a framework for its critique. Section A explores eighteenth and nineteenth century race-based witness competency rules. …

A. *Looking Back: Race-Based Witness Competency Rules*

Today, evidence rules, doctrines, and policies appear race-neutral, but this was not always the case. In the eighteenth through mid-to-late nineteenth centuries, laws barred people of color from testifying in court, especially if the case involved a white person. For instance, the California Crimes and Punishments Act of 1850 provided that "no black or mulatto person, or Indian, shall be permitted to give evidence in favor of or against any white person." Its civil equivalent similarly directed that "[n]o Indian or Negro shall be allowed to testify as a witness in any action in which a White person is a party." These racial restrictions were not limited to Native and black Americans; they applied to other populations of color as well.

Most famously, in the 1854 case of *People v. Hall*, the California Supreme Court held that its witness competency statute barred testimony of witnesses of Chinese descent and all persons who were not white. In *Hall*, a white man had been convicted of murdering a Chinese miner on the basis of testimony by Chinese witnesses. The defendant appealed, claiming that the state's racial evidentiary bar prohibiting testimony by blacks, mulattoes, and Indians against whites should be extended to bar the testimony of Chinese people. The Supreme Court of California agreed, finding that the statute's reference to "black persons" "must be taken as contradistinguished from White, and necessarily excludes all races other than the Caucasian." Accordingly, the court held that the Chinese witnesses' testimony should have been excluded at trial and reversed the conviction.

Motivated by white supremacy, the court in *Hall* recognized the fundamental connection between people's ability to testify in court and their status as full citizens, observing:

> The same rule which would admit [non-white people] to testify, would admit them to all the equal rights of citizenship, and we might soon see them at the polls, in the jury box, upon the bench, and in our legislative halls.
>
> This is not a speculation which exists in the excited and overheated imagination of the patriot and statesman, but it is an actual and present danger.

It is not surprising that three years later, a San Francisco court denied a Mexican American man the right to testify at trial. Manuel Domínguez was one of California's most distinguished and affluent citizens and served on the Los Angeles County Board of Supervisors. Despite his vast landholdings and social and political prominence, he was dismissed as a witness after plaintiff's counsel argued that his Indian blood made him incompetent to testify. As mestizos, individuals with a mix of Spanish and American Indian descent, Mexican Americans were barred from testifying on the basis of their race.

California was not the only state imposing race-based witness competency requirements in the nineteenth century. Throughout most of the country, statutes and judicial decrees prohibited blacks and other people of color from testifying in cases in which white people were parties. In slave-holding states, as well as several western and midwestern states, this bar was usually based explicitly on race. In some northern states, the restrictions focused more on slave status, though being black carried a presumption of slave status and thus witness incompetency. In some states, such as Delaware, black witnesses were allowed to testify on behalf of a white party against a black party, but the opposing black party could not call a black witness to testify against the white party. Irrespective of their articulation, these rules "withdrew the substance of the protection of the laws in many cases and left only the shadow." When people of color were deprived of the ability to testify, whites could abuse, rob, and kill them with near impunity.

Official race-based witness competency rules were eradicated over 150 years ago. Today, evidence laws do not overtly name any race for favored or disfavored treatment. Traditionalists might argue that this means racism has been eliminated entirely from the rules of evidence and that we now have a racially unitary and unbiased evidence system. Viewed through colorblind optics, it appears that racial equality has been achieved in evidence law. However, applying CRT to the law of evidence reveals something different: a dual-race evidentiary system still exists in the United States. ...

C. *The Function of a Critical Evidentiary Analysis*

The function of a critical race evidentiary analysis is twofold. First, application of CRT to evidentiary issues brings to light overlooked racial inequalities under evidence law. Second, an evidentiary analysis of these racial inequalities reveals racial disparities in the parties' relative ability to enter or prevent the admission of evidence. Thus, a critical race evidentiary inquiry does not stop with the application of CRT principles to evidentiary matters. It also applies an evidence analysis to the racial justice problem itself. It explores how conventional treatment of evidentiary issues poses both racial justice and evidence concerns. This often exposes how evidence that supports white privilege and dominance or reflects white norms is treated more favorably than evidence which is probative of structural racism or reflects minority perspectives. The rules of evidence themselves might not have been crafted with a racially discriminatory purpose or otherwise be inherently discriminatory, but their unequal or incomplete application produces a racially subordinating effect.

To make this framework more concrete, an example might be helpful. …

II. A CRITICAL RACE ANALYSIS OF EVIDENCE LAW

…

B. *Flight and Racialized Reality Evidence*

1. Doctrine of Flight

It is a common scene in movies and evidence law casebooks: A burglar alarm sounds or shots ring out. A police officer sees a man near the scene. The man takes one look at the officer and runs. At trial, the prosecutor introduces evidence of the man's flight to prove his guilt for the burglary or shooting. The government's reasoning that evidence of the man's flight is relevant is as old as the Bible: "The wicked flee when no man pursueth."

At first glance, the argument supporting the admission of flight evidence appears simple: only the guilty run. The defendant ran from the police or scene, so the prosecution offers his flight as circumstantial evidence of his guilt. A closer look, however, reveals that flight is often a complex evidentiary issue. Where people of color flee from police, a critical race inquiry reveals structural racial bias entrenched in the evidentiary doctrine of flight. "Black or brown flight" from police is frequently a product of systemic racism. People of color, particularly men, often avoid interaction with police officers because they fear being racially profiled, brutalized, or even killed. However, defendants of color face significant evidentiary barriers to introducing evidence of the systemic racism that motivated their flight and would demonstrate that their retreat does not indicate guilt.

Courts have determined that many kinds of conduct constitute flight from a law enforcement officer, like walking away from an officer or pulling away when an officer puts his or her hand on one's shoulder. The probative value of flight "as circumstantial evidence of guilt depends upon the degree of confidence [that] four inferences can be drawn: '(1) from the defendant's behavior to flight; (2) from flight to consciousness of guilt; (3) from consciousness of guilt to consciousness of guilt concerning the crime charged; and (4) from consciousness of guilt concerning the crime charged to actual guilt of the crime charged.'"

This chain of inferences can be broken at any of the four steps. At the first step, the defendant's conduct might not have actually been flight at all. For instance, the defendant might have just been jogging at the wrong place at the wrong time. Under step two – inferring flight to indicate consciousness of guilt – a person may indeed flee from police but for innocent reasons. The defendant may have been afraid of being falsely accused or asked to be a witness, or he or she may want to avoid a dangerous or potentially time-consuming situation. Others may not want to be seen with a police officer for fear that they may be perceived as complicit with law enforcement, or want to clear the way for police to focus their efforts on finding the true offender. Many courts find that "[w]here the defendant possesses an innocent explanation that does not risk prejudicing the jury against him, it would be expected that the defendant would present his purported reasons for his flight to the jury."

However, there are times when the explanation for flight is not so innocuous. Step three – inferring that consciousness of guilt indicates consciousness of guilt for the crime charged – is often the most problematic and is where evidentiary inquiry usually focuses. Some people may be innocent of the criminal activity afoot but may flee because they are guilty of a separate offense, such as public intoxication or possessing an illegal drug. Individuals who flee because they are guilty of a different offense are prejudiced because they must testify or otherwise supply evidence of their less-than-innocent ulterior motive for flight. In these circumstances, depending upon the nature of the explanation, the probative value of their flight might be substantially outweighed by a danger of unfair prejudice, in which case it may be excluded at the trial judge's discretion. …

2. Racial Implications of Flight

… An issue not yet explored is the unfairness of putting defendants of color in the position of having to testify to explain their reasons for flight from authorities when the motivation to run was related to systemic racism. Philando Castile's experience illustrates the reasons many men of color fear and take every effort, including flight, to avoid contact with the police. Castile was a thirty-two-year-old black man living and working in the Minneapolis-St. Paul metro area. In the last thirteen years of his life, he was stopped by police *forty-nine times*, ostensibly for minor traffic violations. At times, he did not have car insurance. This led to the revocation of his driver's license, which in turn led to fines for driving without a valid license – a cycle of citations and fines that many low-income people of color experience. On July 6, 2016, while he was driving with his girlfriend and her preschool-aged daughter, police stopped him, allegedly for a cracked taillight. As Castile reached for his identification – as instructed – the officer shot him dead. Castile's girlfriend streamed a video of the aftermath on social media that sparked #BlackLivesMatter protests across the nation against racially targeted police violence.

In addition to heightened domestic awareness, there has been increased awareness internationally about United States police violence against racial minorities. Two days after Castile's death, the Ministry of Foreign Affairs of the Bahamas issued a travel advisory to its citizens, who are predominately of Afro-Bahamian descent, concerning the "shootings of young black males by police officers" and advised all Bahamians, especially young males, to exercise "extreme caution" in their interaction with police in the United States. Other countries, including the United Arab Emirates, Bahrain, and New Zealand, issued similar warnings about travel to the United States. While consciousness of police violence against racial minorities might be new to some Americans, Americans of color have long recognized the dangers posed by interacting with the police.

Racially targeted police violence is far from a new phenomenon. As former Seattle Police Chief Norm Stamper noted, police brutality in this country originated with slave patrols. President Barack Obama acknowledged that the roots of racially motivated police shootings "date back not just decades" but "centuries." Not long ago, police enforced discriminatory slave codes and Jim Crow laws and turned a blind eye to mob violence and lynchings against blacks, all of which contribute to racial minorities' history of distrusting the police. Today, African Americans are 3.6 times more likely to be subject to use-of-force by police and 2.5 times more likely to be shot and killed by police than are whites. Similarly, Latinos are killed by police in disproportionate numbers. And, although often overlooked by the media, Native Americans are the group most likely to be killed by police, as they are 3.1 times more likely to be killed by police than whites.

African Americans, Latinos, and Native Americans are often stopped and searched by police simply because of their race. A stop and frisk can easily lead to arrest. An arrest record comes with serious consequences, as it may negatively impact efforts to obtain housing and employment, since both landlords and employers increasingly check criminal backgrounds. In addition to the tangible effects of arrest is the serious risk of harming the person's dignity. People are demeaned when they are wrongfully assumed to be guilty of a crime, stopped, and searched because of their race.

Commentators have described black and Latino communities as de facto police states where heavy police presence and intrusion pervade[] and criminalize[] many aspects of daily life. Behaviors and activities that would not be subject to police intervention in white communities are targeted in black and Latino neighborhoods. For instance, people of color are more likely than whites to be arrested for low-level offenses for which greater police discretion is accorded, such as loitering, being in a public park after closing, or drinking alcohol in public. Further, people of color are often lower income and less able to pay fines or miss work to appear in court. This results in a disproportionate number of people of color being on probation or having warrants pending for low-level offenses. Having an outstanding warrant for something as harmless as unpaid parking tickets can motivate a person to avoid the police. Additionally, people of color and those living in poverty are less likely to possess government-issued identification, making it more likely that they will be cited, taken into custody, or, in the case of some immigrant Latinos, accused of living undocumented.

For many Latinos, the threat of immigration enforcement is an additional looming layer of police presence that may motivate them to run even when innocent of any crime. The Latino experience of "brown flight" is akin to that of the black experience, as Latinos are similarly fearful of police because of over-policing, racial profiling, and police violence. While the media reports on their experiences less frequently, Latinos, like African Americans, are brutalized and killed by police at a higher rate than whites. Latinos, however, are uniquely disadvantaged. They must also combat issues of perceived foreignness in policing, irrespective of whether they are native-born Americans or immigrants.

After the enactment of the Support Our Law Enforcement and Safe Neighborhoods Act – better known as S.B. 1070 in Arizona in 2010 and similar laws in other states – some local police are required to attempt to ascertain the immigration status of anyone detained if "reasonable suspicion exists that the person is an alien and is unlawfully present in the United States." In practice, "reasonable suspicion" usually means "Mexican appearance." Such "show-me-your-papers" laws invite racial profiling despite official prohibitions to the contrary. Latinos are targeted for being "illegal" based on their race, Spanish-language usage, or Hispanic accent, notwithstanding that one-third of the United States' land mass used to be Mexico and that the United States is currently the world's second largest Spanish-speaking country. Also, undocumented immigrants are not the only Latinos who may have reason to avoid law enforcement. United States citizens, legal permanent residents, and other lawfully present Latinos are frequently detained simply because they are perceived to be undocumented immigrants. Additionally, because some Latinos may come from mixed-immigration status families or friendship circles, they may avoid police in an effort to protect their loved ones.

History and social science suggest black and brown flight is often more likely to stem from fear and self-preservation than from guilt. Because of high levels of racial profiling, as well as racially targeted police harassment and brutality, flight from police by people of color is often rational. Fleeing from the police in many African American, Latino, and Native American communities has arguably become the norm in some communities. For many people of color, flight is a reflexive response to a police encounter on the street. History and experience have taught people of color that the police cannot be trusted and that avoiding them is usually the best option. Parents of color teach their children about "safe" behavior around police, which may include "keep[ing] their hands visible[,] … ask[ing] permission to make any move with hands or body," and, most salient here, running from them.

3. Disparate Admissibility of Racialized Reality Evidence

In determining whether a defendant of color's flight is probative of his or her guilt, a key assumption is often overlooked. It is presupposed that innocent people do not run from the police but instead voluntarily and readily submit to police questioning and detention. However, flight from authorities is probative of consciousness of guilt only if fleeing is abnormal. In other words, flight is relevant to prove guilt only if it deviates from the typical behavior of normal, reasonable people in the community. As explained above, in many African American, Latino, and Native American communities, flight is standard custom. Assuming that black and brown flight is atypical and thus deviant is not merely erroneous; it raises significant racial justice and evidentiary concerns.

The assumption that innocent people do not actively avoid or outright flee from the police and immigration authorities is based on white beliefs and norms. For multiple reasons, it is unsurprising that white society holds this belief. First, whites trust the police more than other racial groups. This makes sense; whites are the group least likely to be racially profiled or otherwise targeted because of their race. Moreover, because police are over-representatively white in proportion to the general population, whites are more likely to share the same racial background as the police than any other group. Most importantly, whites enjoy more preferential treatment from police officers than other racial groups; for instance, they are less likely to be victims of force by the police or to be arrested for offenses even when they are statistically more likely to engage in the underlying prohibited conduct. Because whites generally trust, identify with, and receive preferential treatment from the police, it is clear why white experiences, norms, and beliefs signal and conclude that people do not run from the police unless they are guilty.

It is important to recognize that in determining the admissibility of flight evidence, the presupposition that only the guilty run from law enforcement is not commonsense reasoning. It is a fact that must be proved by admissible evidence. In most cases, this would require a qualified expert or lay witness who could testify that flight from police is abnormal in the pertinent community. However, it is not the practice of trial judges to require this type of evidence because the assumption that flight is abnormal is white "racialized reality evidence." Customarily, white racialized reality evidence receives "implicit judicial notice." It is automatically admitted at trial without evidentiary scrutiny.

The conceptualization of racialized reality evidence is significant because it identifies a type of persuasive evidence that receives racially disparate admissibility treatment but is habitually overlooked by jurists and lawyers. By racialized reality evidence, I mean evidence of the lived experience of a person that is directly shaped by the racially stratified system in which he or she lives. Racialized reality is how one experiences our nation's current racial caste system as a benefit or detriment. Racialization is not simply something experienced by racial minorities, with the racial majority living a raceless existence. As racism has a purpose of conferring a benefit on the privileged group or groups, racial privilege is always the corollary of racial subordination. And because racial differentiation and racism permeate every aspect of daily life, there is rarely a race-neutral reality. Rather, people's perception of the world around them depends largely on the position they occupy in society's racial hierarchy. This is true equally for racially subordinated and racially privileged people. …

CONCLUSION

Litigation is often compared to battle. At trial, evidence rules and doctrines are the metaphorical swords that allow evidence to be entered into the record and the shields that exclude evidence. The manner in which evidence law is applied determines the facts that are considered in deciding who wins and loses. For trials to be fair, it is imperative that evidence law applies equally to everyone irrespective of their race. Historically and presently, evidence law has been applied in ways that structurally disadvantage people of color and advantage whites. Continuing legal education on implicit racial bias and preferences – particularly on recognizing white normativity and transparency; proper objections; and increased evidentiary pathways for expert witnesses and people of color to share their experiences of minority racialized reality and systemic racism – would increase racial equity in the courtroom.

But racism will still persist in our evidence law. Structural racism is an unremitting impediment to full justice that requires continual resistance. Fortunately, we have an intellectual armory at our fingertips: the work of generations of CRT scholars waiting to be applied to the law of evidence.

The ideas and examples I provide in this Article are merely a starting point. I hope they inspire a new and robust critical race theory of evidence.

SECTION 2

Character Evidence

INTRODUCTION

"Evidence of a person's character or character trait is not admissible to prove that on a particular occasion the person acted in accordance with the character or trait." Thus begins Rule 404, one of the most litigated rules of evidence. Most of the litigation – through *in limine* motions, and appeals – is about the proper application of Rule 404(b), which states that evidence of a person's other crimes, acts, or wrongs may be admissible if offered for a non-character purpose, such as proving motive, opportunity, intent, preparation, plan, or so on. For example, for a defendant charged with bank robbery, Rule 404 would preclude evidence that the defendant has a prior conviction for bank robbery, if that evidence were offered solely to establish that the defendant has the character of a bank robber and likely robbed this bank. However, if it were offered for some non-character and material purpose – such as to show the defendant has a particular knowledge, for example, how to get past a complicated alarm system shared by the current bank and the earlier bank, then evidence relating to his prior bank robbery may be admissible to show his knowledge, but not his propensity.

Setting aside whether jurors properly parse how they can use such evidence when admitted, the rule may seem straightforward. But in many ways, it raises questions. For starters, does the rule even make sense? In cases like the criminal prosecutions of Bill Cosby and Harvey Weinstein for sexual assault, does it really make sense to say that testimony from other victims should be inadmissible to prove character or propensity. (These particular questions are taken up in Section 4, Sex Trials.)

But more fundamentally, what is character evidence? How does it intersect with demeanor evidence? And when we exclude character evidence – or at least claim to exclude it – doesn't that mean that jurors bring their own biases and priors to deliberations, using them to imprint character onto witnesses and parties based on other things, such as their skin color, or mode of dress?

The chapters in this section explore these and other questions. It opens with Andrea Dennis's "Character (Evidence) Assassination," which pushes back against the admissibility of rap evidence at trial and argues that such evidence amounts to racialized character evidence. Next, in "Disability as a Character Chameleon," Jasmine E. Harris examines the many ways disability itself comes in as character evidence. As she puts it, "disability's profound ties to disqualification make it an extremely effective character chameleon, shifting form to operate as shorthand for a host of undesirable traits." For his contribution, Frank Rosenblatt shifts the focus to the use of character evidence in courts-martial. Specifically, his "Different Spanks for Different Ranks: A Critical Appraisal of Character Evidence in Courts-Martial" examines how the military's "good soldier defense" allows defendants to present evidence of good military character even when it is irrelevant to the charged offense. While this defense may seem neutral and unobjectionable, Rosenblatt shows that it shields high-status servicemembers (often white males) from accountability, and especially undermines sexual assault prosecutions. The two final chapters, both excerpts, turn to evidence that is rarely even recognized as character evidence at all, whether it is things like race or mode of dress (Bennett Capers's "Evidence Without Rules") or demeanor (Kiel Brennan-Marquez's and Julia Simon-Kerr's "Judging Demeanor"). The authors show how the routine admission of such evidence entrenches inequality.

Character (Evidence) Assassination

Andrea L. Dennis

"[C]haracter assassination: the slandering of a person usually with the intention of destroying public confidence in that person." Synonyms: "maligning," "blackening."

Merriam-Webster[1]

Since at least 1989, prosecutors have sought to use rap music evidence to convict defendants.[2] To date, 800-plus cases involving this practice have been identified from commercial databases, media reports, and word-of-mouth.[3] Cases exist in virtually every state and in both federal and state courts. Over time, "rap music evidence" has evolved to include not just lyrics and songs handwritten on paper but also recorded songs, videos, photographs, hand signs, and fashion choices. As technology has advanced, evidence now may be found online or offline.[4]

Police and prosecutors make use of rap music evidence throughout the criminal legal process from investigation through adjudication and sentencing, and even post-sentencing.[5] The evidence has been used to prove a range of charges, including, but not limited to, homicide; gang activity; drug distribution; firearms

1 *Character assassination*, MERRIAM-WEBSTER DICTIONARY, www.merriam-webster.com/dictionary/character%20assassination (last visited July 22, 2025).

2 In 1989, sixteen-year-old Efren Paredes Jr, was convicted as an adult of first-degree murder and sentenced to life without parole. During his trial, prosecutors introduced into evidence rap lyrics that Paredes had written in a school notebook. Paredes v. Vasbinder, No. 03-74826 DT, 2006 WL 1851253, at *6 (E.D. Mich. June 30, 2006).

3 MAPPING RAP ON TRIAL, www.rapontrial.org/. These cases likely represent a miniscule number of the actual number of cases involving rap music evidence.

4 *Id.*

5 *E.g.*, United States v. Johnson, No. 22-2845, 2024 U.S. App. LEXIS 3436, at *1 (3d Cir. Feb. 14, 2024) (trial); United States v. Donald, No. 3:21-cr-8, 2023 U.S. Dist. LEXIS 188828, at *58–86 (D. Conn. Oct. 20, 2023) (trial); United States v. Williams, 663 F. Supp. 3d 1085, 1095–6 (D. Ariz. 2022) (trial); United States v. West, No. 18-249, 2019 U.S. Dist. LEXIS 183007, at *6 (E.D. Pa. Oct. 22, 2019) (investigation); Batiste v. State, No. AP-76,600, 2013 WL 2424134, at *9–10 (Tex. Crim. App. June 5, 2013) (capital sentencing); Steve Hochman, *Rap Artist Is Jailed over Anti-Police Lyrics*, L.A. TIMES (Mar. 4, 1998) www.latimes.com/archives/la-xpm-1998-mar-04-mn-25431-story.html (parole violation). *See also*, ERIK NIELSON AND ANDREA L. DENNIS, RAP ON TRIAL: RACE, LYRICS AND GUILT IN AMERICA (The

possession; threats; assault and sexual assault; prostitution; fraud and identity theft.[6] Common arguments for the usefulness of the evidence are that the evidence is an incriminating statement or full-blown confession; proof of an individual's motive, knowledge or intent to engage in criminal activity; evidence of gang affiliation and activity; or proof of future dangerousness and unlikelihood of rehabilitation.[7]

This chapter explores the almost forty-year battle between rap music evidence and evidence rules to demonstrate that traditional evidence rules are ill-suited for assessing the utility of Black American musical artistry and oral traditions in the criminal legal process. Due to the incompetence of the rules, decision-makers are empowered to overemphasize the value of rap music evidence and leverage racialized and character-propensity arguments. These maneuvers occur even while the system of evidence rules deems these tactics unfairly prejudicial and purports to discourage this type of reasoning. In light of these concerns, this chapter proposes rulemakers categorically declare that, as a social policy, rap music evidence is inadmissible.

THE ESSENTIAL CHARACTER OF RAP MUSIC EVIDENCE

Rapping and rap music are part of the Black American oral tradition and diverse lineage of musical artistry, both of which reject dominant understandings and usages of American English – spoken and written – and music.[8] As a creative art form combining verbal wordplay, poetic devices, and a musical backdrop, rap music should not be analyzed through the interpretive prisms applied to everyday, ordinary spoken and written word.

In the late 1970s, hip-hop culture emerged from the socio-economically devastated streets of the South Bronx, New York. At the time, the South Bronx was literally burning. Widespread fires had destroyed many residential buildings and even entire neighborhoods, displacing large numbers of residents. More than 100 street gangs controlled the area. The city had left its mostly poor, Black and Latino residents without access to many public services, including firefighters, health workers, and law enforcement.[9] From this chaos arose hip-hop, a cultural movement comprised of a number of artistic elements: graffiti art, break dancing, DJing

New Press 2019); Andrea L. Dennis, *Poetic (In)Justice? Rap Music Lyrics as Art, Life, and Criminal Evidence*, 31 COLUM. J.L. & ARTS 1 (2007).

6 NIELSON AND DENNIS, *supra* note 5.

7 *Id.* To a lesser extent, rap music evidence is itself alleged to be criminal, such as when the government alleges an individual made a threat in the form of rap lyrics or the lyrics support or benefit criminal activity.

8 For explanations of rap music's connection to the Black American oral tradition, *see* NIELSON AND DENNIS, *supra* note5. For a timeline of Black American music and descriptions of its ancestry and evolution, *see* Portia K. Maultsby, *The Timeline of African American Music*, CARNEGIE HALL, https://timeline.carnegiehall.org/genres/rap-hip-hop (last visited July 22, 2025).

9 DECADE OF FIRE (Vivian Vàzquez Irizarry and Gretchen Hildrebran, 2018), https://decadeoffire.com/; Martin Tolchin, *Gangs Spread Terror in the South Bronx*, N.Y. TIMES, Jan. 17, 1973, at A1.

(playing pre-recorded music for an audience), and MCing (performing as master of ceremonies). Hip-hop was a unique form of creative self-expression that at times prevented actual physical violence, whether because it served as a coping mechanism, an emotional outlet, or form of ritualized combat.[10]

DJing and MCing quickly evolved into what is today understood as rap music. The DJ creates the music and the MC is the rapper. At its most basic level, rap music is defined as "a form of rhymed storytelling accompanied by highly rhythmic, electronically based music."[11] A nuanced appreciation of the art form reveals that rappers and rap songs adhere to a multitude of formal and informal rules that dictate what a rapper can and cannot do and when rules can be broken. This system of rules is rooted in Black American oral and musical traditions.

Rappers must rhyme while keeping time with a musical beat and layering their voice on top of that beat in a manner that is sonically pleasing to the listener. Rhymes tend to occur on the midpoint or endpoint of a line (a/k/a bar), but not exclusively. Not every word in every song has to rhyme and the same rhyme scheme does not have to be maintained for an entire song. Sophisticated wordplay, dense slang, coded references, phonetic bending, intentional mispronunciations, repetition, and sometimes blazing-fast delivery help rappers rhyme on beat. At times, however, rappers may break these rules. In the end, though, it is not rap if it does not rhyme and if the words and rhymes are not rapped in a way that comfortably blends or meshes with the beat.[12]

Beyond the foundational aspects of beats and rhymes, rappers and rap music rely on many of the same tools deployed by poets and other creative writers. Rappers build characters, tell stories, and rely on symbolism, metaphor, and hyperbole. They create songs using the first-person or third-person perspective and draw from personal, communal, and societal experiences. Much like artists of other genres, many rappers adopt pen names, pseudonyms, or larger-than-life personas distinct from their own. Often, but not always, these alter egos are signaled by a stage name.[13] In these ways, reality, realism, and imagination are woven together to entertain and create a social-emotional experience that resonates with the listener.

Finally, rapping and rap music are rooted in and connected to Black American oral traditions. Self-aggrandizement ("boasting") and self-praise ("toasting") are acceptable, even expected. Competitive banter ("signifying") and insults ("playing the dozens") are unsurprising and welcomed. When performed, hand gestures and other bodily movements are used to non-verbally emphasize or de-emphasize

10 *Cf.* Sally Banes, *Physical Graffiti: Breaking is Hard to Do*, The Village Voice (Apr. 22, 1981), www.villagevoice.com/physical-graffiti-breaking-is-hard-to-do/#google_vignette.

11 Tricia Rose, Black Noise: Rap Music and Black Culture in Contemporary America 2 (Wesleyan University Press 2004).

12 *See* Mickey Factz and Chilla Jones, Ink: A Lexicon of Elite Rap Techniques (Pendulum Ink 2023).

13 *Id.*

words, rhythms and beats, or the musical experience. These ways of communicating can be used for entertainment as well as social and political commentary.[14]

MISCHARACTERIZING THE RELEVANCE OF RAP MUSIC EVIDENCE

Regardless of the layers of complexity and context involved in the creation and performance of rap music, some of which are discussed above, the relevance rules encourage police and prosecutors to offer simplistic, formalistic, and uncritical assessments of the relevance of rap music evidence.

A fundamental rule of evidence – Rule 402 – is that only relevant evidence is admissible.[15] Relevant evidence is defined by Rule 401 as evidence that "(a) has any tendency to make a fact more or less probable than it would be without the evidence; and (b) the fact is of consequence in determining the action."[16] "The standard of probability under the [relevance] rule is 'more … probable than it would be without the evidence.' Any more stringent requirement is unworkable and unrealistic."[17] Hence, it is axiomatic that the relevance threshold is quite low and that the rule favors admissibility.

Ordinary, everyday statements, conversations, and writings, including those made by defendants, are a common form of evidence. The default presumption of evidence rules is that an individual's statements are assumed to be truthful, or at least reliable, until demonstrated otherwise.[18] Additionally, by default, words and their meaning are analyzed through a prism of standard American English.[19]

When viewed through these defaults, rap music evidence is characterized as accurate, direct, and probative evidence of true-life personal experiences, knowledge, and mindset, and devoid of artistic, creative, or expressive context or meaning. For example, the prosecutor in MacKinley "Mac" Phipps' homicide trial argued to the jury: "This defendant who did this is the same defendant whose message is, 'Murder murder, kill, kill, you fuck with me you get a bullet in your brain,'" and "You don't have to be a genius to figure out that one plus one equals two." The prosecutor's arguments were based on lyrics from the song "Shell Shocked" on Mac's

14 Nielson and Dennis, *supra* note 5.

15 Fed. R. Evid. 402. On the flipside, not all relevant evidence is admissible. Fed. R. Evid. 402 advisory committee's notes.

16 Fed. R. Evid. 401.

17 Fed. R. Evid. 401 advisory committee's notes.

18 *See* Fed. R. Evid. 801–7 (Hearsay), 901–3 (Authentication and Identification), 1001–8 (Contents of Writings, Recordings, Photographs).

19 *See, e.g.*, State v. Demesme, 228 So.3d 1206 (La. 2017) (Louisiana Supreme Court rejects claim defendant properly invoked *Miranda*); Erik de la Garza, *Louisiana Court Finds Suspect's 'Lawyer Dog' Request Falls Short*, Courthouse News (Nov. 1, 2017), www.courthousenews.com/louisiana-court-finds-suspects-lawyer-dog-request-falls-short/. *See also*, L. Alexander Walker III, *Black English for Lawyers: A Primer*, 113 Cal. L. Rev. 81, 84 (2025).

studio album that were quoted during the trial: "Big Mac, that's my daddy, rotten dirty straight up soldier … Ya fuck with me, he'll give you a bullet in yo brain." However, the jury never heard that Mac was not rapping about his personal experiences but had instead crafted the lyrics drawing on his father's experience serving in the military during the Vietnam war.[20]

More bluntly, when the head of the gang unit that investigated Antwain Steward for homicide was asked if he considered the fictional or artistic elements of the music videos he and his officers spent hours watching, he responded: "We are not dealing with the brightest guys," and "It's much easier to write about something than to think of something."[21]

But these perspectives and modes of interpretation are insufficient means for assessing the relevance, reliability, and trustworthiness of a Black American poetic, musical, spoken art form that, as earlier described, simultaneously embraces and ignores dominant oral and artistic norms. A rapper's words – individually or collectively – and stories cannot be literally translated into standard English and understood straightforwardly. In rap, meaning is especially fluid across time, space, speaker, listener, and context, and tends to defy common interpretation and understanding. So too, truth and fiction are often enmeshed and indiscernible, even if seemingly apparent.[22]

Be that as it may, the relevance standard is wholly unconcerned by evidence or information that may rightly be considered inherently reliable given its intrinsic characteristics.[23] As a consequence, superficial arguments by police and prosecutors allow rap music evidence to clear the relevance bar and subsequently create a pathway for prosecutors to take advantages that the rules signal should be impermissible.

THE BLACKENING EFFECTS OF RAP MUSIC EVIDENCE

The admission of rap music evidence reminds that evidence rules fail to eliminate reliance on negative racial stereotypes, tropes, and characterizations in the criminal legal process. Rap music evidence proffered by police and prosecutors tends to have violent words and imagery as well as content describing criminal activity. The songs are then labeled for jurors as "gangsta rap,"[24] which carries negative connotations.

[20] David Lohr, *Witnesses: DA Bullied Testimony That Put Rapper Away for 30 Years*, HUFFINGTON POST, www.huffpost.com/entry/mckinley-mac-phipps-wrongful-conviction_n_6612074 (last updated July 10, 2020).

[21] Andreas Ross, *Killer Poetry in Court*, FRANKFURTER ALLGEMEINE (May 21, 2014), www.faz.net/aktuell/gesellschaft/kriminalitaet/ganster-rapper-twain-gotti-wegen-mordes-angeklagt-12944842.html.

[22] *See* FACTZ AND JONES, *supra* note 12; NIELSON AND DENNIS, *supra* note 5.

[23] FED. R. EVID. 401 advisory committee notes ("Relevancy is not an inherent characteristic of any item of evidence but exists only as a relation between an item of evidence and a matter properly provable in the case.").

[24] *E.g.*, United States v. Williams, 663 F.Supp.3d 1085 (D. Ariz. 2023); Bacon v. Klee, No. 2:13-cv-10016, 2015 US Dist LEXIS 143428, at *21 (6th Cir. 2015).

Not too long after hip-hop and then rap music developed on the east coast, the perfect storm of police and prosecution policies birthed a new rap genre on the west coast, Los Angeles, California, to be specific. In the late 1980s and early 1990s, the federal government ramped up efforts to combat drug abuse and gangs. Federal money flowed into states and localities to provide training, equipment, and financial resources to bolster the policing and prosecution of drug and gang-related crimes. Aggressive, military-style policing practices and stringent prosecution policies became the norm. Hyper-policing and police brutality became prominent features of this approach to crime control and several notorious instances unfolded publicly in Los Angeles.[25]

Artists from this disaffected community drew inspiration from these socio-legal events, as well as works by the author Iceberg Slim and blaxploitation films, both of which featured pimps, hustlers, and drug dealers to create what would become known as "gangsta rap." In a short time, west coast gangsta rappers and gangsta rap became mainstream, exposing listeners to the socially, economically, and politically complicated west coast urban underworld of gangs, crack cocaine, and savage policing. In the words of literary theorists, however, "[gangsta rap's] origins as a complex poetic form with deep roots in a variety of literary and ritual traditions have, for the most part, been neglected or obscured."[26]

Eventually, police and prosecutors actively searched for rap music evidence to support their work and were transparent in their belief that the evidence is helpful in blackening the character of defendants. In 2004, a gang prosecution training manual included:

> *Will the Real Defendant Please Stand Up?*
>
> Perhaps the most crucial element of a successful prosecution is introducing the jury to the *real* defendant. Invariably, by the time the jury sees the defendant at trial, his hair has grown out to a normal length, his clothes are nicely tailored, and he will have taken on the aura of an altar boy. But the real defendant is a criminal wearing a do-rag and throwing a gang sign. Gang evidence can take a prosecutor a long way toward introducing that jury to that person. Through photographs, letters, notes, and even music lyrics, prosecutors can invade and exploit the defendant's true personality. Gang investigators should focus on these items of evidence during search warrants and arrests.[27]

25 *See* Kay L. Levine, Joshua C. Hinkle, and Elizabeth Griffiths, *Making Deflection the New Diversion for Drug Offenders*, 19 Ohio St. J. Crim. L. 75, 82 (2021); Nielson and Dennis, *supra* note 5.

26 Nielson and Dennis, *supra* note 5; Ralph M. Rosen and Donald R. Marks, *Comedies of Transgression in Gangsta Rap and Ancient Classical Poetry*, 30 New Literary History 897, 897 (1999).

27 Alan Jackson and Am. Prosecutors Res. Inst., Prosecuting Gang Cases: What Local Prosecutors Need To Know 15–16 (2004) (emphasis in original). At the time of publication, Jackson was Deputy District Attorney, Los Angeles County District Attorney's Office.

Two years later, a gang-policing training manual instructed: "In today's society, many gang members compose and put their true-life experiences into lyrical form … It is equally important to recognize that the lyrics demonstrate that the gangster lifestyle has become mainstream. It is now popular to be a 'gangsta,' the contemporary idiom for gangster."[28]

It further offered: "Many gang members compose hip-hop lyrics that reflect true-life experiences. Search warrants of homes and jail cells often net such writings. The contents of these writings frequently reflect the author's gang mentality and, in some cases, result in solid investigative leads. Occasionally, the writings can be used as evidence."[29]

Notwithstanding these stated positions, courts have rejected defense arguments that rap music evidence is character evidence which should be excluded, even if deemed relevant. Rather, courts embrace government arguments that rap music evidence is admissible non-character, other acts evidence such as a confession or circumstantial evidence of motive, intent, knowledge, or identity.[30]

This outcome is predetermined given the absence of definitions of character and character evidence in the rules, as well as the lack of judicial interpretations of the meaning of character evidence and scope of character evidence regulated by the rules.[31] Both deficiencies contribute to the conclusion that evidence law excludes character evidence only in its narrowest sense and in many instances does not preclude the admission of circumstantial evidence of character.

Rule 404, the chief rule restricting the admissibility of evidence of character, does not define "character" or "evidence of character."[32] Neither do the related Advisory Committee Notes, though the notes do offer some illustrations of character evidence: chastity, driving competency, violent disposition, and honesty.[33]

Relatedly, Rule 405, which sets out methods for proof of character – when character evidence is allowed under Rule 404 – dictates that character testimony must take the form of individual opinion or community reputation and must not include evidence of specific acts or behaviors.[34] Rule 405's Advisory Committee

[28] Donald Lydanne, *Understanding Gangs and Gang Mentality: Acquiring Evidence of the Gang Conspiracy*, GANGS, May 2006, at 1, 1, www.justice.gov/archive/olp/pdf/gangs.pdf. At the time, Lydanne was an FBI intelligence analyst.

[29] *Id.*

[30] *E.g.*, United States v. Stuckey, 253 Fed. Appx. 468, 483 (6th Cir. 2007); *see also*, NIELSON AND DENNIS, *supra* note 5. That being said, more recent, vigorously defended cases have reached the opposite conclusion, *e.g.*, United States v. Williams, 663 F.Supp.3d 1085, 1155 (D. Ariz. 2022).

[31] Traditional statutory construction methodologies are used to interpret evidence rules. Beech Aircraft Corp. v. Rainey, 488 U.S. 153, 163 (1988).

[32] FED. R. EVID. 404.

[33] FED. R. EVID. 404 advisory committee notes.

[34] FED. R. EVID. 405 ("[E]vidence of specific instances of conduct is the most convincing. At the same time it possesses the greatest capacity to arouse prejudice, to confuse, to surprise, and to consume time.").

Notes add: "Traditionally character has been regarded primarily in moral overtones of good and bad: chaste, peaceable, truthful, honest. Nevertheless, on occasion nonmoral considerations crop up, … [Also, character may be] defined as the kind of person one is."[35] The first statement reflects a quite direct and cramped understanding of character evidence. The last sentence seems no more informative than the notion that one knows obscenity when one sees it.[36]

Reference to rules regulating specific types of character evidence is equally unhelpful. Like Rule 404, Rule 608 pertaining to a proof of a witness's character for truthfulness or untruthfulness does not define "character."[37] And like Rule 405, Rule 608 permits evidence in the form of reputation and opinion testimony but excludes specific instances with some exception. However, the Advisory Committee Notes to Rule 608 offer more insight, mandating exclusion of testimony about conduct that allows a fact finder to infer character for untruthfulness. In other words, a litigant cannot offer specific instances of conduct only to attack a witness's character for truthfulness or untruthfulness, except under Rule 609 governing impeachment of credibility by conviction.[38]

Despite the unhelpfulness of these various character evidence rules, examination of a rule not labeled a character evidence rule – though designed to eliminate assumptions about an individual's character – is instructive.

Specifically, Rule 412 – commonly called the rape shield rule – embraces a broad-based, strict, specialized approach for avoiding undesirable characterizations and stereotyping of victim participants in the criminal legal process. Rule 412 was drafted expressly to avoid sexual stereotyping of victims, presumably vulnerable female victims.[39] The rule applies in all cases, excludes evidence whether offered as substantive evidence or for impeachment, and excludes evidence even if admissible under other rules.[40] Sexually related conduct (sexual intercourse, contact), behavior that implies sexually related conduct (use of contraceptive), and behaviors of the mind (such as sexual fantasies) are all excluded.[41] And it does not stop there. Rule 412 protects against admission of evidence that might lead a fact finder to engage in

35 Fed. R. Evid. 405 advisory committee notes.

36 *See* Jacobellis v. Ohio, 378 U.S. 184, 197 (1964) (Stewart, J., concurring) (referring to obscenity, Justice Potter stated "I know it when I see it.").

37 Fed. R. Evid. 608.

38 Fed. R. Evid. 608 advisory committee notes.

39 Fed. R. Evid. 412 advisory committee notes ("The rule aims to safeguard the alleged victim against the invasion of privacy, potential embarrassment and sexual stereotyping that is associated with public disclosure of intimate sexual details and the infusion of sexual innuendo into the factfinding process."). To the contrary, stereotyping of those accused of sexual assault crimes is encouraged. Fed. R. Evid. 413–15. But that's a conversation for another day.

40 Fed. R. Evid. 412(b) advisory committee notes.

41 Fed. R. Evid. 412 advisory committee notes ("Past sexual behavior connotes all activities that involve actual physical conduct, i.e. sexual intercourse and sexual contact, or that imply sexual intercourse or sexual contact. [citations omitted] In addition, the word 'behavior' should be construed to include activities of the mind, such as fantasies or dreams. [citation omitted].").

"stereotypical thinking" such as "dress, speech, or life-style."[42] In criminal cases, admission of evidence covered by the rule is allowed in extremely limited situations invoked by the accused.[43]

Quite openly, Rule 412 aims to eliminate direct evidence of a sexual assault victim's character as well as circumstantial, other acts evidence of a sexual assault victim's character. From this it might be reasonable to conclude that rap music evidence could receive the same type of treatment in courts. However, this has not happened.

Moving outside of the rules themselves, consulting non-legal and legal sources might offer a means of clarifying how the rules do or should understand and regulate character and character evidence.

According to the first definitions offered by *Merriam-Webster's Dictionary*, "character" means: "one of the attributes ... or features that make up and distinguish an individual"; "a feature used to separate distinguishable things into categories"; "the aggregate of distinctive qualities characteristic of a breed, strain, or type"; "the detectable expression of the action of a gene or group of genes"; "the complex of mental and ethical traits marking and often individualizing a person, group, or nation"; and "main or essential nature especially as strongly marked and serving to distinguish."[44]

Black's Law Dictionary offers:

> character n. (17c) 1. A sign, mark, or symbol of any type. 2. A stamp, brand, or graphic symbol placed on something to indicate origin, ownership, etc. 3. An attribute or quality that serves as an indicium of the intrinsic or essential nature of something or someone. 4. The sum of traits that confer distinctiveness. 5. A person's station in life; rank, position, or capacity. 6. The traits or qualities that combine to make an individual human being distinctive from others, esp. as regards morality and behavior; the disposition, reputation, or collective personality traits of someone as they might be gathered from close observation of that person's pattern of behavior <something in his character disallowed him to make the request>.[45]

Evidence luminaries and treatise writers Wigmore and McCormick respectively write: "[Character is] the actual moral or psychical disposition, or sum of traits ... ."[46] and "[ch]aracter is a generalized description of one's disposition, or of one's disposition in respect to a general trait, such as honesty, temperance, or peacefulness."[47]

While these dictionary and legal treatise definitions are more informative than the lack of guidance provided by the evidence rules, none of these interpretations

42 *Id.*

43 FED. R. EVID. 412(b).

44 *Character*, MERRIAM-WEBSTER DICTIONARY, www.merriam-webster.com/dictionary/character.

45 *Evidence*, BLACK'S LAW DICTIONARY (12th ed. 2024).

46 1 JOHN HENRY WIGMORE, A TREATISE ON THE SYSTEM OF EVIDENCE IN TRIALS AT COMMON LAW § 52, at 121 (1904).

47 CHARLES T. MCCORMICK, MCCORMICK'S HANDBOOK OF THE LAW OF EVIDENCE § 195 462 (E. Cleary ed., 2d ed., West Publishing Company 1972) (footnote omitted).

appear to have been grafted onto the rules. Model jury instructions and caselaw seem to have done little in the way of further defining character.[48] In the end, even legal scholars have struggled to define the concept.[49]

Unsurprisingly, in light of an indeterminate understanding of the concept of "character," and hence "character evidence," defense attorneys lose the battle to exclude rap music evidence as impermissible negative character evidence. Instead, a formalist analytical approach to interpreting and applying existing rules on character evidence dictates that because the crafting or enjoyment of rap music evidence constitutes a behavior or act, rather than a personality trait or quality, then it is not evidence of character.

THE UNFAIR ADVANTAGES OF RAP MUSIC EVIDENCE

Judicial tendencies to admit rap music evidence allow prosecutors to exploit the rules and create unfair advantages contrary to the spirit of the rules and intent of the rule drafters. Rule 403 offers judges the discretionary, back-stop option to exclude unfairly prejudicial evidence, such as that which invokes undesirable character-propensity-based reasoning and that which is inflammatory or racially biasing – even if that evidence is relevant.[50] Yet when courts reject Rule 403 objections to rap music evidence, as they do, jurors can and likely do use the evidence impermissibly, as circumstantial evidence that the defendant is violent or criminal.[51]

Indeed, years after the jury's guilty verdict in the homicide case against McKinley "Mac" Phipps, the jury foreman explained to a reporter:

> "The music – the lyrics – they played all that s**t [in court]," Hammell said. "I don't listen to that s**t, but the music might have been the problem. The rap got his mind all messed up. He was living a life that he thought he was a gangsta. He was making it big time with the gold chains and all that s**t that went with it. To shoot somebody in a public place on the dance floor, you gotta think you're a bad son of a b***h."[52]

48 Steven Goode, *It's Time to Put Character Back into the Character-Evidence Rule*, 104 Marq. L. Rev. 709, 773 (2021) ("As has been observed, courts … have devoted surprisingly little effort to defining character."); Jennifer S. Hunt, *The Cost of Character*, 28 U. Fla. J.L. & Pub. Pol'y 241, 289 (2017) (analyzing state and federal pattern jury instructions concerning character evidence).

49 Barrett J. Anderson, *Recognizing Character: A New Perspective on Character Evidence*, 121 Yale L.J. 1912, 1919 (2012).

50 Fed. R. Evid. 403.

51 Jennifer S. Hunt, *The Cost of Character*, 28 U. Fla. J.L. & Pub. Pol'y 241, 253 (2017) ("jurors are likely to make character inferences based on evidence about the defendant's past behaviors that are admitted for ostensibly non-character purposes"); Kerri L. Pickel, *Inducing Jurors to Disregard Inadmissible Evidence: A Legal Explanation Does Not Help*, 19 L. & Hum. Behav. 407 (1995) (juror bias induced by character evidence is not solved by limiting instructions).

52 David Lohr, *Prosecutor Used Hip-Hop as a Weapon to Convict Mac Phipps*, Huffington Post (Mar. 24, 2015), www.huffpost.com/entry/mckinley-mac-phipps-rapper-lyrics_n_6863326.

The perspective of that jury foreman, however, is not merely anecdotal. Psychology elucidates the foreman's perspective, demonstrating that (potential) jurors will hold a similar viewpoint and more problematically, draw on racialized constructions of Blacks as dangerous, violent, and in need of criminal justice control.[53]

For example, in 1999, Stuart Fischoff – the pioneer of media psychology[54] – conducted an experiment to determine the impact violent rap lyrics might have on potential jurors. He presented study participants with basic biographical information about a hypothetical eighteen-year-old African American male. Some participants were shown a set of violent, sexually explicit rap lyrics that the eighteen-year-old had written (the lyrics were actually evidence in a 1995 murder trial), and then asked their perceptions regarding the teen's personality (for example, whether he was caring or uncaring; likable or unlikable; capable of murder or incapable of murder). Fischoff found that the lyrics exerted "a significant prejudicial impact" on his subjects: those who read the lyrics were significantly more likely to think the teen was capable of committing murder. More striking, he found that "exposure to the lyrics evoked a negative reaction in participants that was more intense than the[ir] reaction to being told that the young man was on trial for murder."[55]

Also, in a 1999 experimental study, social psychologist Carrie Fried presented two groups of people with an identical set of violent lyrics but removed any information identifying the source of the lyrics. One group was told the lyrics came from a country song, while the other was told they came from a rap song. Fried found that respondents characterized the lyrics as significantly more threatening and dangerous when labeled as rap rather than country. In other words, rap "primes the negative culturally held stereotype of urban Blacks."[56] In 2016, Adam Dunbar replicated Fried's work. In his study, participants "deemed the exact same lyrics to be more offensive, in greater need of regulation, and more literal and autobiographical when characterized as rap compared with country."[57]

In 2003, Fried compared stereotypes about fans of rap music and heavy metal music. She asked test-subjects to describe either the prototypical rap or heavy metal

53 For discussions of race as evidence outside the context of rap music evidence, *see, e.g.*, Bennett Capers, *Race, Gatekeeping, Magical Words, and the Rules of Evidence*, 76 Vanderbilt L. Rev. 1855, 1855 (2023); Bennett Capers, *Evidence Without Rules*, 94 Notre Dame L. Rev. 867 (2019); Jasmine B. Gonzales Rose, *Toward a Critical Race Theory of Evidence*, 101 Minn. L. Rev. 2243, 2244 (2017); Montre D. Carodine, *Contemporary Issues in Critical Race Theory: The Implications of Race as Character Evidence in Recent High-Profile Cases*, 75 U. Pitt. L. Rev. 679, 679, 681 (2014).

54 Stuart Fischoff, *Media Psychology: A Personal Essay in Definition and Purview*, www.apadivisions.org/division-46/about/fischoff-media-psychology.pdf (last visited July 23, 2025).

55 Stuart P. Fischoff, *Gangsta' Rap and a Murder in Bakersfield*, 29 J. Applied Soc. Psych. 795 (1999).

56 Carrie Fried, *Who's Afraid of Rap? Differential Reactions to Music Lyrics*, 29 J. Applied Soc. Psychol. 705 (1999).

57 Adam Dunbar et al., *The Threatening Nature of "Rap" Music*, 22 Psych., Pub. Pol'y & L. 280, 288 (2016).

fan. She found that fans of heavy metal are viewed as more self-destructive while fans of rap are seen as more threatening to the community.[58] Her work replicated that of Binder, who ten years earlier found that people perceive that those who listen to rap music are more likely to hurt others and that those who listen to rock music are more likely to hurt themselves.[59]

The work of Fischoff, Fried, and others dovetails with studies showing that rap music also activates stereotypes related to race. Scientists have demonstrated that exposure to rap music increases an individual's likelihood of associating Black people with adjectives such hostile, violent, and sexist, as well as making less empathetic judgments toward Black victims.[60] Other studies have found that participants who listened to violent rap music (compared to non-violent rap or no music at all) were likely to view the Black man presented to them in the experiment as more inherently violent and less intelligent.[61]

For their part, some prosecutors have reinforced inappropriate juror decision-making by wielding rap music evidence to depict defendants as loathsome characters or tropes in a crime drama, or caricaturize or stereotype them as criminal-minded. The prosecutor in Taquan Neblett's capital case, for instance, asked the Kentucky trial court to admit rap lyrics purportedly written by Neblett on the day of his arrest yet weeks after the killing. He argued to the court that the graphic and violent nature of the lyrics was a "reflection" of Neblett's "soul" and should be admitted to prove Neblett's guilt. The court rejected the evidence during the guilt phase, but the jury was allowed to hear similar argument during sentencing.[62]

More than thirty years of social science reveals that many people have visceral responses to rap music, that those responses are connected to negative impressions and stereotypes (especially about young men of color), and that those reactions inform people's perceptions when making decisions in the criminal legal setting. Consequently, defendants argue that this (minimally) relevant evidence should be excluded as unfairly prejudicial pursuant to Rule 403. Far too often, though,

58 Carrie Fried, *Stereotypes of Music Fans: Are Rap and Heavy Metal Fans a Danger to Themselves or Others?*, 8 J. MEDIA PSYCH., No. 3, 2–27 (2003). *See also*, Peter J. Rentfrow and Samuel D. Gosling, *The Content and Validity of Music-Genre Stereotypes among College Students*, 35 PSYCH. MUSIC 306, 315–18 (2007).

59 Amy Binder, *Constructing Racial Rhetoric: Media Depictions of Harm in Heavy Metal and Rap Music*, 58 AMER. SOCIO. REV. 753, 753–67 (Dec. 1993).

60 Laurie A. Rudman and Matthew R. Lee, *Implicit and Explicit Consequences of Exposure to Violent and Misogynous Rap Music*, 5 GROUP PROCESSES & INTERGROUP RELATIONS 133, 146 (2002); James D. Johnson, Brad J. Bushman, and John F. Dovidio, *Support for Harmful Treatment and Reduction of Empathy Toward Blacks: "Remnants" of Stereotype Activation among Hurricane Katrina and "Lil' Kim,"* 44 J. EXPERIMENTAL SOC. PSYCH. 1506, 1506 (2008).

61 James D. Johnson, Sophie Trawalter, and John F. Dovidio, *Converging Interracial Consequences of Exposure to Violent Rap Music on Stereotypical Attributions of Blacks*, 36 J. EXPERIMENTAL SOC. PSYCH. 233, 245–7 (2000).

62 NIELSON AND DENNIS, *supra* note 5, at 11–12.

the arguments are unavailing, allowing prosecutors to use rap music evidence to make inflammatory and biasing arguments.[63]

In Tommy Canady's homicide case, at the pretrial motion hearing on the admissibility of lyrics written by Canady, the Wisconsin trial court recognized that the government's introduction of rap lyrics to be listened to and considered by a musically uneducated jury might lead jurors to "think this must be some bad guy." Yet the trial judge accepted the prosecutor's argument that the lyrics were probative because they mentioned the victim and referred to his killing. Further, the judge concluded that the probative value of the evidence was not substantially outweighed by unfair prejudice. The prosecutor later used the lyrics during closing argument to the jury to emphasize Canady's bad character, first stating, "I think it's best described as really a tale of two Tommy Canadys," and then "The defendant described it best in his own words. 'I'm handsome and wealthy, with a monster in me.'"[64]

Similarly, the trial judge allowed the prosecutor in Morgan Baker's homicide case to admit a rap music video in which Baker appeared to prove that Baker was part of the artist's entourage and present on the scene around the time of the shooting, to "complete the story of the crime," and to show Baker had access to guns. The Georgia Supreme Court reversed Baker's conviction, concluding that "the rap music video was highly prejudicial. It allowed the state to introduce impermissible propensity evidence by portraying Baker as a threatening gunman, and the prosecutor severely exacerbated the video's prejudicial impact by emphasizing that it showed Baker's predisposition to gun violence."[65] The court further characterized the prosecutor's statements during closing argument as a "pointed argument that reinforced to the jury Baker's alleged violent character."[66]

Baker was fortunate that the appellate court reversed the lower court decision. Canady was not and many more defendants face a similar outcome.

RESPECTING THE EXCEPTIONAL CHARACTER OF RAP MUSIC EVIDENCE

In recent years, federal and state lawmakers nationwide have tried to erect barriers to the admission of rap music evidence and more broadly "creative expression"; yet, only efforts in California, Louisiana, and Maryland succeeded.[67] Commonly, the proposals and enacted rules aim to raise the bar for admissibility as well as set forth a

63 Tennessee v. Britton, No. M2023-01779-CCA-R3-CD, at *19–20 (Tenn. Crim. App. 2024); People v. Venable, 88 Cal. App. 5th 445, 454 (Cal. Ct. App. 2023); Bumphus v. Commonwealth, No. 2017-CA-000989-MR, 2018 WL 3699754, at *8 (Ky. Ct. App. 2018).

64 Jaeah Lee, *This Rap Song Helped Sentence a 17-Year-Old to Prison for Life*, N.Y. Times, Mar. 30, 2022. Canady's appeal was denied. State v. Canady, 405 Wis. 2d 554 (Ct. App. 2022).

65 Baker v. State, 318 Ga. 431, 448 (2024).

66 *Id.* at 449.

67 Current Legislation, www.rapontrial.org/current-legislation; PACE Act, 2026 Md. Laws. ch. 517.

clear standard for judicial review. The expressed policy rationale underlying most of the approaches is rooted in First Amendment constitutional protections for artistic works and creation. Evidentiary concerns regarding relevance, character evidence, and unfair prejudice are also at play.[68]

But decades of opportunity to observe police, prosecutor, judicial, and juror treatment of rap music evidence in the face of increasingly zealous defense advocacy seeking to exclude or rebut the same evidence, suggests only minimal gains can be made by working to reinforce or reform the current system of rules.

Instead, a state-of-the-art technique for eliminating the harms rap music evidence poses to defendants in the criminal legal process must be imagined. A modest proposal carves rap music evidence out of the scope of evidence rules by reference to norms undergirding the Fourteenth Amendment to the U.S. Constitution.[69] In this way, the proposal leverages an important, existing limit on the admission of relevant evidence, namely Rule 402, which provides that relevant evidence must be excluded if the United States Constitution precludes its admission.[70] Moreover, this strategy mirrors the protections offered by rape shield rules, discussed earlier, and for now avoids a bolder effort to take-down character evidence rules completely in the hope of eliminating the problems generated by the use of direct and indirect character evidence to obtain convictions.

Viewing the discussion in this chapter through the Fourteenth Amendment's Equal Protection lens warrants wholesale exclusion of rap music evidence to prevent discrimination by the state on the basis of race, especially when it concerns Black defendants. Properly contextualized, the use of rap music evidence falls within the long history of racist and racial language, imagery, and tropes used against Black people subject to the criminal legal process.[71] Relatedly, its use ignores the inability of evidence rules and the criminal legal process to reliably assess Black American oral traditions, language, spoken word, and artistry. An Equal Protection rationale also serves to eliminate the asymmetrical disparity of treatment that exists regarding the admissibility of rap music evidence (unregulated by existing rules and primarily concerning Black male defendants) and evidence of sexual predisposition (prevented by rape shield rules and primarily concerning female victims).

[68] As MacKinley "Mac" Phipps, well-known Louisiana rapper and inspiration for Louisiana's bill, explained, "I want to make sure this art can't be used to judge your character." Jake Clapp, *Louisiana Prosecutors Won't Be Able to Use Rap Lyrics as Evidence of Character under New Law*, Gambit (Aug. 11, 2023), www.nola.com/gambit/music/louisiana-prosecutors-won-t-be-able-to-use-lyrics-as-evidence-of-character-under-new/article_40e7ec90-388c-11ee-a290-e361b7e09f7d.html.

[69] U.S. Const. amend. XIV. For similar efforts to eliminate racial evidence, *see* Racial Justice Act, Assemb. B. 2542, 2019–2020 Leg., Reg. Sess. (Cal. 2020), https://leginfo.legislature.ca.gov/faces/billNavClient.xhtml?bill_id=201920200AB2542; Jody D. Armour, *Race Ipsa Loquitur: Of Reasonable Racists, Intelligent Bayesians, and Involuntary Negrophobes*, 46 Stan. L. Rev. 781 (1994); Sheri L. Johnson, *Racial Imagery in Criminal Cases*, 67 Tul. L. Rev. 1739, 1797–803 (1993).

[70] Fed. R. Evid. 402

[71] Nielson and Dennis, *supra* note 5.

Applying a Fourteenth Amendment Due Process filter also justifies a categorical prohibition. As revealed, rap music evidence is artistic evidence that is innately and highly unreliable, though not excluded by relevance standards. Also as demonstrated, both anecdotally and systematically, the true relevance of rap music evidence is its ability to play on decision-makers' tendencies to rely on character-propensity reasoning as well as conscious and unconscious racial biases to impose criminal consequences. Viewing rap music evidence through these prisms, Due Process justifies outright exclusion of rap music evidence to avoid convictions of the factually innocent on the basis of unreliable evidence and unfairly inflammatory and racially biasing thinking.[72]

[72] *See* Johnson, *supra* note 69.

Disability as a Character Chameleon

Jasmine E. Harris

Character evidence rules regulate the admission of a person's character or relevant trait solely to prove they acted consistently with that character or trait in a specific instance. Simply put, the rules intend to exclude general, predictive character evidence to prove an individual's specific behavior. Outside the courtroom, however, law and culture frequently use disability as a form of predictive propensity evidence to regulate access to employment, benefits, and civic life. Although evidence of disability is relevant and admissible in myriad cases central to the adjudication of rights and responsibilities, its strong cultural meaning allows legal actors to fuse concepts like "character" and "fitness," often unknowingly, causing this practice to evade consistent judicial regulation. Indeed, disability's profound ties to disqualification make it an extremely effective *character chameleon*, shifting form to operate as shorthand for a host of undesirable traits and serving as unregulated, circumstantial evidence of non-normativity.

Why does disability remain a character chameleon when courts and scholars have increasingly recognized the character creep that occurs with other protected identities, such as race or gender? This chapter argues the persistence stems from several factors: the complexity of disability as both a cultural and legal concept; its immense breadth; its dual role as medical diagnosis and political identity; and, perhaps most crucially, its deep association with the notion of an objective, measurable, medical impairment. The idea that a diagnostic category encompasses a set of shared characteristics makes it appear predictive of outcomes and establishes its probative value as evidence. This conceals how disability operates as character evidence, which, in turn, allows the practice to more easily escape consistent identification and legal oversight from courts.

This chapter examines the operation of disability as character evidence in courts. Its principal contribution is demonstrating how disability functions as an unrecognized lever of disqualification – one that is functionally identical to character evidence – and explaining why courts consistently fail to identify its prohibited use even when it is operating as such.

Why does it matter whether disability is or is not framed as character evidence? The rules of evidence restrict the use of character evidence precisely because it risks unfair prejudice, encouraging the system to adjudicate a specific act rather than a person's general character or past conduct. Impermissible inferences based on disability include the suggestion that a person with a psychiatric disability is unreliable or dangerous, that a person with an intellectual disability is naïve, or that a wheelchair user is inherently less capable. However, even seemingly benign inferences that highlight vulnerability (and offer greater protection) still rely on propensity reasoning and may pose similar dangers as those concerning violence or dangerousness. Traits associated with human vulnerability (such as dependency or naivety) are also disfavored and disqualifying, albeit in a different manner – for example, by associating the individual with a lack of social or political agency. A party can thus rely on disability to perform inferential, character-based work that would be impermissible in other contexts. This is due to the persistent cultural notion that disability is a legitimate, neutral, and objective category with higher probative value than it truly warrants.

The chapter proceeds in three main parts: The first section briefly outlines the rules regulating character evidence. The second section argues that law and society have established a fraught relationship between disability and character, providing historical and contemporary examples of this association with unfitness. The third section provides examples of disability's use – both as character evidence and otherwise – and analyzes how courts identify (or fail to identify) propensity reasoning. The chapter concludes by offering initial thoughts on how to better regulate disability as character evidence.

THE PROBATIVE VALUE AND DANGERS OF CHARACTER EVIDENCE

The Federal Rules of Evidence adopt an expansive view of relevance. Rule 401 states that evidence is relevant if it has any tendency to make a fact more or less probable (a matter of logical relevance) and if the fact is of consequence in determining the action (a matter of legal relevance).[1]

Although Rule 401 is generally permissive and favors liberal admission, the rule-makers recognized that certain types of evidence pose a greater risk of harm than their probative value warrants. As a matter of policy, Article IV of the Federal Rules of Evidence addresses these categories – such as evidence of character, subsequent remedial measures, and sexual history – because they increase the danger of prejudice, wasted time, or confusion of the issues.[2]

Federal Rules of Evidence 404 and 405 specifically regulate character evidence. The reason for this is simple: a person ought to be judged solely on the actions

[1] Fed. R. Evid. 401.

[2] Respectively, Fed. R. Evid. 404, 405, 407, 411, 412–15.

at issue in the case, not on their general reputation, disposition, or past acts.[3] Consequently, there is a default prohibition against using character evidence to show propensity – the forbidden inference that because a person has a character trait "X" (established by past behavior), they are more likely to have committed act "Y" on the specific occasion before the court.[4]

Notably, the rules themselves do not define "character" despite its ambiguity. However, courts and legal academics have added content over time. For example, legal scholars Mueller, Kirkpatrick, and Richter assert that "character" means "a person's disposition or propensity to engage or not engage in various forms of conduct."[5] They note that character is not a unitary concept and that everyone has multiple character traits, such as a propensity to be truthful or dishonest, or to drive safely or recklessly.[6] Ultimately, the rule drafters determined that the risks of unfair prejudice, confusion, or wasted time associated with propensity evidence generally outweigh its probative value.[7] Therefore, they established a default exclusionary rule – rather than a case-by-case analysis – allowing propensity evidence only in a narrow set of exceptional circumstances.

The Suturing of Disability and Character in Law and Society[8]

Both disability and character are highly normative concepts that often resist strict definition, a feature that makes them highly effective tools for regulation. This inherent normativity is often masked by attempts to ground both concepts in individual bodies and minds, primarily through a medical lens.

More specifically, our character evidence rules developed from common law practices that viewed character as biologically imprinted and, historically, immutable.[9]

3 For a summary of the main policy reasons for the exclusion of character evidence, *see, e.g.*, Roger C. Park, *Character at the Crossroads*, 49 HASTINGS L.J. 717, 720–54 (1998).

4 FED. R. EVID. 404(a)(1) ("Evidence of a person's character or character trait is not admissible to prove that on a particular occasion the person acted in accordance with the character or trait."). In those narrow instances when character is admissible, it can only come in as reputation or opinion evidence about a person's relevant character or character traits; evidence of specific acts is inadmissible for propensity purposes. *See* FED. R. EVID. 405.

5 CHRISTOPHER B. MUELLER, LAIRD C. KIRKPATRICK, AND LIESA L. RICHTER, EVIDENCE, § 4.11, at 188 (6th ed., Aspen Opco 2018).

6 *Id.*

7 *See* Michelson v. United States, 335 U.S. 469, 475–6 (1948) (explaining that "[character evidence] is [not] rejected because character is irrelevant; on the contrary, it is said to weigh too much with the jury and to so overpersuade them as to prejudge one with a bad general record and deny him a fair opportunity to defend against a particular charge").

8 George Yancy's work on the aesthetics of "un-suturing" in the context of race are particularly influential in my use of the term "suturing" here. *See, e.g.*, George Yancy, *White Embodied Gazing, the Black Body as Disgust, and the Aesthetics of Un- Suturing, in* BODY AESTHETICS (Sherri Irvin, ed., Oxford University Press 2016).

9 *See, e.g.*, 1 JOHN HENRY WIGMORE, A TREATISE ON THE SYSTEM OF EVIDENCE IN TRIALS AT COMMON LAW § 52, at 121 (1904) ("Character, then, is to be considered, for the purposes of

This biological framing is why character was once widely accepted as probative (or useful) of conduct. Similarly, disability has long been understood (and often continues to be understood) as a biological or physiological phenomenon that may also be deemed immutable.

Disability as a "Master Trope of Human Disqualification"

The professionalization of medicine and the medicalization of disability enabled the delineation, description, and attribution of disability traits, making them transferable to minoritized and subordinated groups. For instance, historian Douglas Baynton describes the pathologization of women: "[o]pponents of political and social equality for women cited their supposed physical, intellectual, and psychological flaws, deficits, and deviations from the male norm. These flaws – irrationality, excessive emotionality, physical weakness – are in essence mental, emotional, and physical disabilities, although they are rarely discussed or examined as such."[10] Disability studies scholars, David Mitchell and Sharon Snyder, describe the deployment of disability as "a master trope of human disqualification."[11] In the context of race, this trope "prefaces an understanding of inassimilable racial and ethnic differences by providing an empirical designation for 'unfit' bodies [and] disqualifying bodily traits that jettison certain people from inclusion in the continuum of acceptable human variations."[12]

As this master trope, disability has become a socially legitimate proxy for disfavored character traits, unfitness for employment, and a predictor of non-normative conduct. The association between disability and disqualification appears normal and rational. Because disability sometimes involves an actual physiological, behavioral, or functional difference, its discriminatory roots are often invisible and rarely questioned.

relevancy, as the actual moral or psychical [sic] disposition, or sum of traits"); Peter Tillers, *What Is Wrong with Character Evidence?*, 49 HASTINGS L.J. 781, 818 n. 58 (1998) (describing sources tracing the roots of the character evidence rule). The early common law approach to character evidence reflected insights of personality theorists and "trait theory" in psychology that posited the stability of disposition and character, and, thus, offered support for character's probative value. *See* Miguel A. Méndez, *The Law of Evidence and the Search for a Stable Personality*, 45 EMORY L.J. 221, 226–38 (1996) and *Character Evidence Reconsidered: "People Do Not Seem To Be Predictable Characters"* 49 HASTINGS L.J. 871, 877–81 (1998) (describing early "trait theory" and its impact on character evidence debates); GORDON W. ALLPORT, PERSONALITY: A PSYCHOLOGICAL INTERPRETATION 521 (Constable & Co. 1937).

10 Douglas C. Baynton, *Disability and the Justification of Inequality in American History*, *in* THE DISABILITY STUDIES READER 17 (Lennard J. Davis, ed., 5th ed., Routledge 2016).

11 DAVID T. MITCHELL AND SHARON L. SNYDER, NARRATIVE PROSTHESIS: DISABILITY AND THE DEPENDENCIES OF DISCOURSE 125 (University of Michigan Press 2000).

12 SHARON L. SNYDER AND DAVID T. MITCHELL, CULTURAL LOCATIONS OF DISABILITY 135–6 (University of Chicago Press 2006).

Historical Disqualification

Historically, disability disqualification has manifested as categorical denials of citizenship rights, including voting, marriage, family, and jury service.[13] This was based on the belief that disability signaled not only functional incapacity but also a moral deficit inconsistent with civic participation. Legal historian, Rabia Belt, highlights the connection between character and the early disenfranchisement of paupers and those labeled "lunatics" and "idiots."[14] After the American Revolution, some state constitutional delegates advanced a model of political citizenship prioritizing "interlocking qualities of independence, moral virtue, and mental capacity."[15] People labeled "lunatics" and "idiots" were categorically judged to "not pass muster" against these required character traits.[16]

In this regard, disability does not operate separately from other forms of bias like race or gender. Instead, the labels of disability have been used as purportedly objective evidence to disqualify individuals and groups based on other categories, such as race or gender. Legal scholar and sociologist, Dorothy Roberts, notes that the construction of race is an invented political grouping disguised as a biological one.[17] Justifications for slavery, for example, often hinged on the "disability argument" that Black Americans "lacked sufficient intelligence to compete equally with white Americans."[18] This alleged deficit was supported by "neutral" scientific evidence claiming biological inferiority and inherent dependency.[19] Anti-suffragists, aiming to disenfranchise women, also focused on purportedly neutral evidence of sex differences, labeling them "universal female disabilities" to justify political exclusion.[20]

13 *See, e.g.*, T. P. v. Superior Ct. of Fresno County., F040765, 2002 Cal. App. LEXIS 9085 at *4 (Cal. Ct. App. Sep. 26, 2002) (ordering removal of child for parental unfitness based on "cognitive deficits and personality characteristics such as passivity, lack of initiative and assertiveness and co-dependency").

14 Rabia S. Belt, *Mental Disability and the Right to Vote* 74 (2015) (Ph.D. dissertation, University of Michigan) (on file with author).

15 *Id.* at 43.

16 *Id.*

17 Dorothy Roberts, Fatal Invention: How Science, Politics, and Big Business Re-Create Race in the Twenty-First Century 4 (The New Press 2011) ("Like citizenship is a political system that governs people by sorting them into social groupings based on invented biological demarcations. Race is not only interpreted according to invented rules, but, more important, race *itself* is an invented political grouping … that has been disguised as a biological one." (emphasis added)).

18 Baynton, *supra* note 10, at 20 (For example, "the New Orleans Medical and Surgical Journal helpfully explained, 'It is this defective hematosis, or atmospherization of the blood, conjoined with a deficiency of cerebral matter in the cranium, and an excess of nervous matter distributed to the organs of sensation and assimilation, that is the true cause of that debasement of mind, which has rendered the people of Africa unable to take care of themselves.'") (internal citation omitted).

19 *Id.*

20 Yvonne Pitts, *Disability, Scientific Authority, and Women's Political Participation at the Turn of the Twentieth-Century United States*, 24 J. Women's Hist. 37, 38 (2012).

Contemporary Use in Law and Society

Both law and society continue to use disability as evidence of disfavored character traits, unfitness, and disqualification today. This is perhaps most notable regarding substance use disorders, psychiatric, psychosocial, intellectual, and developmental disabilities. Immigration law has historically used disability as evidence of bad character in admissions and naturalization. Alcohol and drug addiction, for instance, are considered legal "character flaws" justifying exclusion.[21]

The long-standing "public charge" exclusion, which bans any person likely to become a public charge from entry to the U.S., can be understood as a character ban based on disability as evidence of bad character.[22] The flawed inferential chain at work is as follows:

1. Admission requires evidence of good moral character, which is marked by independence and self-reliance.
2. Disabled people, as a group, possess the character trait of dependency due to disproportionate reliance on public supports.
3. Therefore, a disabled person or one with a record of disability may be excluded from the U.S. because the presence of disability makes them more likely to become a public charge (such as relying on Medicaid) in the future.

This chain of inferences relies more on eugenic thinking than empirical evidence,[23] yet it demonstrates how the law equates disability with future conduct of dependence, showing that disability and character are often inseparable in law and society.

Disability has also been used as a measure of character and fitness for disqualification across various professions, including law (attorneys and judges), health care, national security, and even parental fitness.[24] Until relatively recently, state requirements for attorney admission used disability as a relevant indicator of character and fitness. The Louisiana Supreme Court, until 2014, required applicants to demonstrate "sound mind, good moral character and fitness to practice law."[25]

[21] Rebecca Sharpless, *Addiction-Informed Immigration Reform*, 94 WASH. L. REV. 1891, 1896 (2019).

[22] 8 U.S.C. § 1182(a)(4)(A) (2025) ("Any alien who, in the opinion of the consular officer at the time of application for a visa, or in the opinion of the Attorney General at the time of application for admission or adjustment of status, is likely at any time to become a public charge is inadmissible.").

[23] *See* Samuel R. Bagenstos, *The New Eugenics*, 71 SYRACUSE L. REV. 751, 753–7 (2021).

[24] *See, e.g.*, Jasmine E. Harris, *Disability and the Dignity of Service*, 71 WAYNE L. REV. 149, 153–65 (2025) (discussing exclusion of people with certain disabilities from positions with Peace Corps and AmeriCorps); Robyn M. Powell et al., *The Americans with Disabilities Act and Termination of Parental Rights Cases: An Examination of Appellate Decisions Involving Disabled Mothers*, 39 YALE L. & POL'Y REV. 157, 164–6 (2020) (discussing the use of disability as evidence of disqualifying to parenting).

[25] Letter from Jocelyn Samuels, Acting Assistant Attorney General, United States Department of Justice to Chief Justice, The Honorable Bernette J. Johnson, Louisiana Supreme Court, et al. re: The United States' Investigation of the Louisiana Attorney Licensure System Pursuant to the Americans with Disabilities Act (DJ No. 204-32M-60, 204-32-88, 204-32-89) 3–4 (Feb. 5, 2014) (internal citation omitted).

The application's "Character Report" included questions on a broad range of mental health disabilities and treatment, which triggered additional investigation if answered affirmatively.[26] In 2014, the U.S. Department of Justice (DOJ) reached a settlement agreement with the Louisiana Supreme Court.[27] The final consent decree eliminated broad questions about disability diagnoses and treatment that "did not effectively predict future misconduct as an attorney."[28]

WHY DISABILITY REMAINS A CHARACTER CHAMELEON

The use of disability as a relevant indicator of character and fitness is increasingly challenged by anti-discrimination efforts (like the DOJ's action in Louisiana), yet disentangling disability and character remains complex. Part of this complexity may stem from the fact that disability rights are younger than other civil rights protections like those based on race or gender (the Americans with Disabilities Act was signed in 1990). However, recency alone does not fully explain it.

Disability persists as a character chameleon for at least three interconnected reasons:

Perception of Objective Stability

Disability is widely understood as an inherently stable, somewhat immutable, and legitimate category with objective ties to medical science and individual pathology. This medicalized view makes disability diagnostic categories seem relevant, probative, and admissible for purposes beyond character, such as assessing conduct and risk. These features allow disability to rely on character-based reasoning and bias, which masks the subjectivity inherent in the diagnostic process itself.[29] For example, psychiatric diagnoses often have lower inter-rater reliability (meaning different professionals are less likely to reach the same diagnosis) and lack the traditional, objective biomarkers or tests available for physical impairments.[30] Research suggests that inter-rater reliability is lower for diagnoses like psychosis or schizophrenia[31] – two mental disabilities that appear in thousands of published court cases.[32]

[26] *Id.* at 4.

[27] Settlement Agreement between the United States of America and the Louisiana Supreme Court under the Americans with Disabilities Act (Aug. 14, 2014).

[28] *Id.*

[29] Debates exist about the degree of subjectivity in psychiatric diagnosis, for example. The Diagnostic and Statistical Manual (DSM) itself reflects shifting theories of behavior and mental illness. Prior versions of the DSM pathologized "homosexuality" itself as a mark of deviance and labeled it a disease; the American Psychiatric Association removed the diagnosis of "homosexuality" from the DSM-II in 1973. Jack Drescher, *Out of DSM: Depathologizing Homosexuality*, 5 BEHAV. SCI. 565 (2015).

[30] Jeremy Matuszak and Melissa Piasecki, *Inter-Rater Reliability in Psychiatric Diagnosis*, 29 PSYCHIATRIC TIMES, Oct. 5, 2012, www.psychiatrictimes.com/view/inter-rater-reliability-psychiatric-diagnosis.

[31] *Id.*

[32] For example, a LexisNexis search in all cases for psychosis or schizophrenia since January 1, 2023 to October 2, 2025 yielded 5,717 case results.

Furthermore, even for those seeking to use disability evidence to prove propensity (like showing a person is inherently untrustworthy or dangerous), research challenges the actual predictive value of such diagnoses.[33]

The Paradox of Remedial Admission

There are times when evidence of disability must be admissible to mitigate systemic or structural inequities. For instance, while a person's race or gender is typically an impermissible factor in judging their qualification, failing to consider evidence of disability (such as the need for an accommodation) may itself constitute discrimination.[34] In this context, differential treatment is considered discrimination for race and gender but, in some instances, remedial for disability.[35] Normally, character evidence is prohibited because it risks unfair prejudice and stereotyping. However, evidence of disability, if framed as part of a person's lived experience rather than a negative character trait, can counter structural inequities and make the legal process more equitable. Defendants with intellectual or psychiatric disabilities are disproportionately represented in the criminal justice system, often because non-disabled perceptions fail to account for non-normative behavior.[36] Evidence of a criminal defendant's Autism Spectrum Disorder (ASD), for instance, may be relevant to explain why they fled due to the sensory overload of police sirens and shouting. The risk lies in using that same diagnosis to argue that their ASD also made them more generally impulsive and combative, making it more likely they were impulsive and combative on the day of the crime (prohibited propensity use).

33 *See, e.g.*, Tori DeAngelis, *Mental Illness and Violence: Debunking Myths, Addressing Realities*, 52 AMA Monitor on Psychology 31 (2021) ("[P]eople often believe that people with mental illness are largely responsible for incidents of mass violence and that people with mental illness are responsible for a large share of community violence. Yet both views have been roundly debunked by research.").

34 Compare Title VII of the Civil Rights Act, 42 U.S. Code § 2000d ("No person in the United States shall, on the ground of race, color, or national origin, be excluded from participation in, be denied the benefits of, or be subjected to discrimination …"), with Title I of the Americans with Disabilities Act (42 U.S. Code § 12112 (a)–(b) ("No covered entity shall discriminate against a qualified individual on the basis of disability [which includes] not making reasonable accommodations to the known physical or mental limitations of an otherwise qualified individual with a disability who is an applicant or employee …").

35 Pregnancy is one example of differential treatment in the context of gender and sometimes falls within the disability framework when there is a specific physical or mental impairment associated with it. There are likely other exceptions.

36 *See, e.g.*, Jasmine E. Harris, *The Aesthetics of Disability*, 119 Colum. L. Rev. 895, 945–6 (2019) (explaining the operation of "the aesthetics of disability" in the context of policing); Judge David L. Bazelon Center for Mental Health Law, *Reducing the Arrest and Jailing of People with Mental Health Disabilities, Including Those with Intersectional Identities* 4 (2025), https://safetyandjusticechallenge.org/resources/reducing-arrest-and-jailing-of-people-with-mental-health-disabilities-including-those-with-intersectional-identities/ ("Over two million people with serious mental illness are still booked into jail each year, and once in jail, can remain incarcerated considerably longer than others.") (internal citation omitted).

Disability may sometimes show a person's relative vulnerability, which can trigger special legal protection in a courtroom (a desirable outcome) but still can function as a disqualifier in broader society. Vulnerability, when treated as a character trait, is a proxy for disqualification because it is antithetical to Western norms of strength, independence, and fierce individualism.[37] This use of disability as character may also rely on propensity reasoning that can undermine agency, particularly concerning sexual consent.[38] An inferential chain suggests that people with intellectual disabilities (IDs) are innately overly trusting and naïve, making them as a diagnostic group, vulnerable to abuse. In a sexual assault case, this leads to the inference that a victim with ID, because of their ID, was more likely to be overly trusting and therefore less likely to have consented. The danger lies in using the existence of ID alone as proof of incapacity to consent rather than showing how ID manifested in the individual. In the extreme, the assumption that all people with ID are over-trusting may be used to suggest that people with ID lack the fundamental capacity to consent to sex. The goal here is not to categorically exclude this evidence, but to recognize the complexity and high stakes of using categorical assumptions, even when they seem to benefit an individual. Addressing this issue may ultimately require a rule change or legislative solution to admit such evidence while managing its underlying propensity reasoning.

The Enduring Power of the Broad, Aggregate Label of Disqualification

Finally, disability retains its power as a character chameleon precisely because it is a broad label designed to capture disfavored human variations. Historically, it has been applied categorically to groups who later fought to distinguish themselves from the disfavored traits (e.g., white women who mobilized after being lumped together with criminals and "mentally disabled" people). Yet, the general label persists. The fact that some class of people could be disenfranchised based on disability as a mark of bad character was not the target of suffragists' advocacy; they simply focused on separating themselves from the label.[39]

37 *See, e.g.*, Martha Albertson Fineman, *The Vulnerable Subject: Anchoring Equality in the Human Condition*, 20 YALE J.L. & FEMINISM 1, 10–11 (2008) (contrasting vulnerability with "universal human subject defined in the liberal tradition" of independence).

38 Jasmine E. Harris, *Sexual Consent and Disability*, 93 N.Y.U. L. REV. 480, 493 (2018) ("One key cautionary lesson for broader sexual assault discussions is to recognize that the risk-averse approach – one that resolves the inherent uncertainties of consent determinations in favor of victim protection over individual agency – may unnecessarily constrain agency and, long-term, may create greater vulnerability to sexual violence.").

39 Pitts, *supra* note 20, at 38 ("Women's rights advocates confronted this politically charged appropriation of medical research by developing new refutations of these associations with disabled, inferior bodies. Their strategies affirmed that disabled bodies did not deserve political authority while simultaneously separating women from the category of disabled.").

Disability continues to be treated as a viable legal and social category for permissible exclusion associated with incapacity, even as the people, behaviors, and traits related to the labels shift over time. Because disability remains a basis for exclusion in this way, disability justice theories recognize the necessary attention to disability in any movement for social change and equality.[40]

EXAMPLES OF DISABILITY AS CHARACTER IN COURTS

Regulating character evidence in courts is highly challenging due to the fraught relationship between disability and character that exists outside the courtroom (as discussed in the previous section). Courts frequently struggle to identify when disability is operating as character evidence. Judges sometimes admit the difficulty of distinguishing character from other permissible uses, and the resulting lines drawn are not always clear or logical.

This failure to recognize disability as character evidence is problematic because disability then becomes a proxy for disqualifying traits like impulsiveness or dangerousness, or a shorthand for stereotypical traits like naivety – even when used to draw a positive inference. Whether operating to prove misconduct or to establish vulnerability, these uses of disability may rely on propensity reasoning, which undermines the dignity and agency of disabled people. This is particularly true when general categories of disability, rather than a person's individual, lived experience, drive judicial reasoning.

Reasoning from a disability diagnosis is inherently probabilistic (propensity reasoning), regardless of whether it is used to show character or credibility. Some courts accept this, while others go to great lengths to distinguish disability from classic forms of character evidence (often while acknowledging the dangers of its character use). Still others articulate the probative value of disability evidence, deny its character nature, and pivot to other permissible uses, such as impeachment.

Unlike race or gender, where it would be difficult to justify admitting evidence of either as predictive of a character trait or for credibility purposes, we might imagine times when disability evidence could be remedial or dignity-enhancing. The central question becomes: Is this beneficial use sufficient to justify its admission even if it violates the propensity ban? And, is disability further proof of the disjointed character rule and doctrine, justifying its re-imagination?

This section of the chapter identifies four primary categories where courts contend with disability as character:

[40] *See, e.g.*, Mia Mingus, *Changing the Framework: Disability Justice: How Our Communities Can Move Beyond Access to Wholeness*, Leaving Evidence (Feb. 12, 2011), https://leavingevidence.wordpress.com/2011/02/12/changing-the-framework-disability-justice/#:~:text=Disability%20justice%20activists%20are%20engaged,bisexual%20and%20queer;%20and%20more (considering the utility of disability justice as a framework for social change).

1. Not Character: Courts determine disability evidence is not evidence of character.
2. Background Fact: Courts treat disability as a useful background fact about a person, not character.
3. Impeachment: Courts allow parties to use disability for credibility or impeachment purposes (character by another name).
4. Permissible Character: Courts permit parties to use disability as relevant character evidence for mitigation purposes, such as during sentencing.

Each category offers insights into the dangers and utility of failing to recognize the propensity reasoning underwriting the court's rationale.

Disability Is Not Character Evidence

Courts often attempt to distinguish between character and non-character uses for disability, but with difficulty and in analytically unsound ways. *Rodriguez v. Schweiger*, a civil rights case against police where the plaintiff was shot during an arrest, is a key example.[41] The plaintiff wanted to use the officer's diagnosis of agoraphobia (an anxiety disorder) to argue that people with this condition are anxious and unstable under stress.[42] The desired inference – that the officer's disability made him more likely to use excessive force – is a classic use of disability as character. However, the plaintiff argued it was not inadmissible character evidence, but evidence of a "condition … which [bore] on the likelihood that a person could or would do something."[43] Is this merely a distinction without a difference? The plaintiff's reasoning still requires propensity reasoning.

The judge ultimately excluded the evidence, finding its limited probative value was outweighed by the danger of confusion and prejudice.[44] Critically, the court's reasoning relied on a different, but equally propensity-based, argument: expert testimony suggested that if the officer with agoraphobia faced such stress, he was more likely to have experienced a panic attack that "disabled him from acting" than to have shot the wounded man.[45] The court simply found one propensity argument more compelling than the other.

This failure to recognize that propensity reasoning drove both sides of the argument is significant. The rules of evidence aim to advance fairness and a coherent theory of application; these goals are undermined when courts fail to engage with inconsistencies related to using disability as character evidence.[46]

41 Rodriguez v. Schweiger, No. 78-C-2295, 1984 U.S. Dist. LEXIS 17564 (N.D. Il. 1984).
42 *Id.* at *5.
43 *Id.*
44 *Id.* at *5–6.
45 *Id.* at *7.
46 *See, e.g.*, FED. R. EVID. 102 ("These rules should be construed so as to administer every proceeding fairly, eliminate unjustifiable expense and delay, and promote the development of evidence law, to the end of ascertaining the truth and securing a just determination.").

Disability Not as Character but as Useful Background Information

Other courts acknowledge the difficult line between disability as character and other uses, reasoning that disability is not character when it offers background information about a party, victim, or defendant. In *Commonwealth v. Bonds*, the Massachusetts Supreme Court found a mother's testimony that her intellectually disabled daughter (the victim of sexual assault) was "too trusting" was not a generalized description of disposition (character), but an "inescapable part of [her daughter's] disorder" that simply "gave the jury a clear picture who the victim was."[47]

This raises a fundamental question: What is the difference between a "character trait" and a "permanent condition," especially when character is often defined as a relatively stable or immutable disposition?[48] The court recognized this muddiness, noting that there is persuasive authority suggesting such evidence is character evidence.[49] While the court cautioned that evidence close to the line could be used improperly (e.g., to evoke sympathy),[50] it relied on the trial judge's discretion to balance probative value against prejudice.[51]

Disability as Character by a Different Name: Impeachment

Another line courts attempt to draw is between disability as inadmissible character evidence and disability as admissible evidence of credibility (impeachment). An impressive body of legal scholarship has shown how credibility rules (like those governing the use of prior convictions) often create a sizable exception to the propensity ban.[52] These rules effectively use a person's status (e.g., as a felon) as a proxy for credibility.[53]

Disability status operates similarly as a backdoor for otherwise inadmissible propensity evidence. In *United States v. Deel* (an interstate theft conspiracy involving veterans with disabilities), the court allowed a testifying defendant to offer a brief recitation of his life history, including disability, "simply as background evidence for the jury's benefit to judge his credibility."[54] Setting aside that using background for credibility arguably violates Federal Rule 608(a), the distinction between character as background and character for credibility is weak. The assumption that a jury can compartmentalize information about disability to

[47] 445 Mass. 821, 830 (Mass. 2006).
[48] *See* Teneille R. Brown, *Bad Habits: Character Evidence by Another Name*, 66 HOWARD L.J. 139 (2022).
[49] Commonwealth v. Bonds, 445 Mass. at 822.
[50] *Id.* at 830–1.
[51] *Id.*
[52] Julia Simon-Kerr, *Credibility by Proxy*, 85 GEO. WASH. L. REV. 152, 154–5 (2017) (arguing that the law has a "deep and enduring commitment to status as a proxy for credibility").
[53] *Id.* at 155.
[54] No. 1:09-CR-00022, 2010 U.S. Dist. LEXIS 12074, at *3 (W.D. Va. Feb. 11, 2010).

infer only credibility, and not infer good or bad character, is highly questionable and can serve as pretext for the backdoor admission of character evidence.

Other courts recognize the danger of using disability for impeachment in the context of sexual assault:

> If used to suggest that a mentally impaired witness is inherently untruthful, character evidence is particularly troubling. It is well recognized that some people with mental disabilities may be especially vulnerable to physical and sexual abuse by virtue of their reliance upon others to meet their daily needs. Their reports of abuse should not be discounted merely because they have a mental disability unconnected to their capacity to perceive, remember, and articulate events.[55]

This court, while cautioning against using disability for propensity purposes, relies on the assumption that mental disability is an immutable condition.[56] This biomedical framing – that mental disabilities are static and unchanging[57] – is notable because the fields of psychology and psychiatry increasingly refute the immutability of mental illness, emphasizing the importance of context and shifting diagnostic theories.[58] Framing mental disability as immutable makes it harder to contest the probative and predictive value of the evidence in court.

Disability as Relevant Character Evidence: Sentencing

Disability also appears as a probative metric of character during the sentencing phase, where the propensity bans that operate during the culpability phase are lifted.

Lawmakers and courts recognize that some defendants, due to a disability, have diminished capacity and should receive leniency in sentencing. Here, evidence of disability is used to argue for mitigation and differential treatment, even if it is character-esque. Some state laws explicitly define certain disabilities, like intellectual disability, as direct evidence of "the character of the offender."[59] Eighth Amendment death penalty jurisprudence, particularly *Atkins v. Virginia*, grants criminal defendants relief from capital punishment based on intellectual disability, in part because it is understood to be a lifelong, permanent condition.[60]

55 Commonwealth v. Despres, 70 Mass. App. Ct. 645, 650–1 (Mass. App. Ct. 2007).

56 *Id.*

57 This is not to suggest the absence of physical or biological impairment; rather, my comment reflects the normativity of the DSM and diagnostic process as to how to interpret and define impairment and variances.

58 *See, e.g.*, Iris Berent and Melanie Platt, *Essentialist Biases Toward Psychiatric Disorders: Brain Disorders Are Presumed Innate*, 45 Cognitive Sci. 1 (2021) (discussing the essentialist, medicalized view of psychiatric disorders that has affected public attitudes about its immutability and concluding, in part, that "people spontaneously essentialize psychiatric conditions that are linked to the brain, even when the brain probe offers no additional diagnostic or genetic information").

59 Ind. Appellate Rule 7(B).

60 536 U.S. 304, 321 (2002) (sentencing a person with an intellectual disability to death is "excessive" in violation of the Eighth Amendment of the U.S. Constitution).

While intellectual impairment may persist over a person's life, it does not mean the person has a fixed disposition. Intellectual disability has two components – intellectual and adaptive functioning – and adaptive functioning can and does shift.[61] People with IDs can and should enjoy full equal status in society. It is not inconsistent to say that for purposes of meting out criminal punishment, considering intellectual disability as a mitigating factor is normatively defensible. Similarly, non-character uses of disability in the culpability stage may be desirable to offer a more complete understanding of the facts.

The ultimate goal is not to ban the use of disability in adjudication, but to surface the inconsistencies and assumptions in its deployment and develop a reasoned, fair framework for its regulation, and to question the viability not of evidence of disability per se, but of the character rule itself.[62] For example, under Indiana Appellate Rule 7(B), judges have discretion to review a sentence based on the "nature of the offense and the character of the offender."[63] In *Shoun v. State*, the defendant argued his intellectual disability should mitigate his life-without-parole sentence. The court rejected the appeal, not because it found intellectual disability was an inappropriate character consideration, but because it lacked direct evidence of the disability and had a record of his "other evidence" of bad character (an extensive criminal record) and the gruesome facts of the case.[64]

While these sentencing and vulnerability cases sometimes advance dignity by recognizing a victim's vulnerability or a defendant's diminished capacity, they still demonstrate a slippery slope. Using disability as proof of vulnerability still leaves open the possibility of reasoning that certain disabilities or diagnoses are acceptable proxies of harm or risk, potentially solidifying the association between disability and incapacity or unfitness (such as incapacity to consent to sex). The aim is to draw attention to the risks to individual dignity and agency that should also be part of the discussion.

CONCLUSION

This chapter has argued that disability functions as a "character chameleon," a socially and legally legitimate proxy for disfavored character traits, unfitness, and non-normative behavior. Though evidence rules prohibit using general character evidence to prove specific conduct (propensity reasoning), disability can evade this regulation. This evasion occurs because disability is widely perceived as an

[61] *See, e.g.*, American Association of Intellectual and Developmental Disabilities, Defining Criteria for Intellectual Disability, www.aaidd.org/intellectual-disability/definition ("Adaptive behavior is the collection of conceptual, social, and practical skills that are learned and performed by people in their everyday lives.") (last visited Oct. 9, 2025).

[62] The development of prescriptive criteria and a framework for analysis is beyond the scope of this chapter, though part of a larger research agenda.

[63] Ind. Appellate Rule 7(B).

[64] Shoun v. State, 67 N.E.3d 635, 642 (2017).

objective, immutable, and measurable medical impairment, giving it a seemingly high probative value that masks its operation as prohibited character evidence.

While specific solutions are beyond the scope of this chapter, the findings point toward several necessary steps. The history of disability's deep ties to propensity reasoning and disqualification necessitates a broader review of how courts regulate its relevance in civil and criminal cases. Character regulation is only one part of this analysis.

The ease with which flaws in legal reasoning go unnoticed, combined with research showing that the knowledge base of legal actors regarding disability is often flawed,[65] suggests that deference to judicial discretion alone is insufficient. Relying solely on Federal Rule of Evidence 403 (which balances probative value against prejudice) may fail to protect individual interests in a fair process.

Potential interventions range from simple accountability measures to detailed legal mandates such as:

- Require Written Judicial Reasoning: One measure is requiring judges to provide clear, written, and publicly available reasoning when ruling on disability evidence. This would create accountability and may combat the replication of societal biases.
- Establish a Special Relevance Rule: A more robust solution could be a special relevance rule governing the admissibility of disability evidence. Such a rule, similar to Federal Rules of Evidence 412–15 (which regulate sexual propensity evidence), would not be limited to character but would directly address the consistent imbalance between disability's probative value and its risk of prejudice across all cases.

Any new rule must inevitably contend with the complexity of disability as a master trope of disqualification. It must distinguish between harmful uses – like excluding evidence of a mental disability used to show a propensity for violence – and potentially beneficial uses, such as proffering evidence of intellectual disability to show a relative vulnerability.

Attention to these asymmetries in crafting any new rule will be paramount. Where lawmakers have found evidence of disability as character critical for mitigation or other purposes (like sentencing), they have already created specific exceptions. This chapter, therefore, begins the necessary, long-term agenda of developing a framework to regulate disability evidence in adjudication and limit its unchecked operation as a character chameleon.

65 Jasmine E. Harris, *(Un)Common Knowledge & Experience*, 105 B.U. L. Rev. 1113, 1125–36 (2025).

Different Spanks for Different Ranks

A Critical Appraisal of Character Evidence in Courts-Martial

Franklin D. Rosenblatt

INTRODUCTION

This chapter explores character evidence in the U.S. military's court-martial system. Courts-martial, unlike civilian criminal trials, permit defendants to present evidence of their own good character even when the character trait is not pertinent to the charged offenses. This derogation has been cheered by some as giving military defendants an extra tool to fight back in a system that may be stacked against them. But concerns about expansive use of character evidence soon became apparent: it tends to distort and confuse the issues in trial, and disproportionately benefits only high-status defendants. For all its good intentions, liberalized military character evidence became a tool of impunity for the powerful and a contributing factor to a sexual assault epidemic in the ranks.

The second section provides a basic overview of the U.S. court-martial system. The third section describes the military's character evidence rules, including the novel "good soldier defense" which erased the usual limitation that defendants are only allowed to raise "pertinent" character traits. After some troubling results of defendants wielding the "good soldier defense," Congress eventually attempted to reign it in, but seems to have merely driven it underground. Regardless of what the character evidence rules say, courts-martial also heavily involve unofficial and unregulated character evidence. The fourth section uses three examples of this – a scene from *A Few Good Men* and two real courts-martial – to show how unofficial character evidence such as military rank and decorations can shape court-martial outcomes in ways that evade formal evidentiary gatekeeping.

A "SEPARATE SOCIETY": HOW THE U.S. MILITARY PROSECUTES CRIME IN THE RANKS

Among the American legal doctrines studied in law schools and debated by scholars, military justice is a sleepy backwater.[1] That obscurity reflects the military itself, which clusters on large bases in mostly rural parts of the United States and on deployments overseas. While many Americans may amorphously support the troops, fewer, especially those who live in large cities, are likely to encounter the military on a daily basis. Because military justice is an obscure topic and different in some ways from civilian justice, this section briefly recounts its basic features.

The U.S. military justice system predates the country itself. When the American colonies agitated for independence from Great Britain, the Americans viewed the British articles of war and naval regulations favorably and adopted them almost out of whole cloth.[2] A decade later, still fresh from war, the drafters of the U.S. Constitution were mindful to preserve these traditions and exempt them from other constitutional commands. So the Fifth Amendment, for example, excepts cases "arising in the land or naval forces" from the grand jury requirement.[3] Congress was conferred the power to "make Rules" for the military,[4] a provision understood to authorize a separate court-martial system.[5] The military and its justice system exist within the Executive Branch, under the President as Commander in Chief.[6]

Insulated from many of the pronouncements of individual rights and procedural developments in civilian courts, American military justice for most of the country's history could be fairly criticized as a "rough form of justice."[7] Critics contended that military justice was too arbitrary and subject to the whims of commanding officers. These contentions boiled over following the Second World War, a time when millions of Americans from all walks of life observed the military justice system's

1 *See, e.g.*, Eugene R. Fidell, *Military Justice Instruction in Civilian Law Schools*, 60 J. Legal Educ. 472, 472 (2011) ("Any law student today will graduate with an understanding of federal or state criminal law and procedure; few will graduate with an appreciation of the military alternatives"); Steven Vladeck, *Why Military Justice Doesn't Get Enough Academic Attention*, Jotwell (Aug. 14, 2018), https://courtslaw.jotwell.com/why-militaryjustice-doesnt-get-enough-academic-attention/ ("The military justice system receives embarrassingly little attention from the legal academy in general and from legal scholarship in particular.").

2 Lawrence Morris, Military Justice: A Guide to the Issues at 2 (Praeger 2010).

3 U.S. Const. amend. V.

4 U.S. Const. art. I § 8, cl. 14.

5 Burns v. Wilson, 346 U.S. 137, 140 (1954) ("Military law… is a jurisprudence which exists separate and apart from the law which governs in our federal judicial establishment.").

6 U.S. Const. art. I § 2.

7 Reid v. Covert, 354 U.S. 1, 35–6 (1957). Popular criticisms of the military justice system persisted, especially during the Vietnam War. *See, e.g.*, *U.S. Military Justice on Trial*, Newsweek, Aug. 31, 1970 at 18 ("Across the political spectrum, critics accuse the military of stacking its juries, muzzling defense attorneys, trying defendants under vague, catchall regulations, trampling on their constitutional rights and, above all, allowing commanding officers to exert improper influence over the proceedings.").

harsh and unflattering dimensions. This collective discontent begot the Uniform Code of Military Justice (UCMJ)[8] in 1951, which is the military justice statute still used today. The UCMJ reflects a compromise: Military commanders retained important roles in selecting which cases to prosecute and other concessions to claims of military necessity, while reformers won efforts to partially civilianize courts-martial, adopting best practices of procedure, party presentation, and an elevated role of lawyers.[9]

Thanks in large part to the UCMJ, an observer watching a court-martial today might mistake it for any other criminal trial in a local or federal courthouse. A defendant (the "accused") sits with counsel, opposite the prosecution, in a modern courtroom (except perhaps on the rare occasion that the court-martial occurs in a more austere setting on a ship at sea or a combat deployment). A military judge wearing a black robe presides. The parties adhere to established procedural rules, call witnesses, marshal evidence, and argue, either before the judge alone or to a military jury ("panel"). As with civilian courts, many proceedings are abbreviated when defendants enter plea bargains with the prosecution. After trial, servicemembers who fare well might return to their military duties, while those sentenced to confinement are sent to a military confinement facility to serve their time and may also be discharged from the service.

There are important differences between military and civilian courts. The military participants in courts-martial wear their military uniforms showing their rank and decorations, which can convey messages about status and military standing to others in the court-martial.[10] Some of the substantive offenses from the UCMJ are familiar, such as murder and rape, while others have no counterpart in civilian life, such as disrespecting superiors, disobeying orders, absence from work, and vaguer offenses such as conduct unbecoming an officer and conduct prejudicial to good order and discipline. The UCMJ covers both local offenses and those committed overseas on military deployments.[11]

Once wary, the U.S. Supreme Court now views military justice favorably. In the 1980s the Court instructed federal courts to give "extreme deference" to military personnel decisions.[12] The Court trusted military justice enough to reverse itself and condone expansive court-martial jurisdiction over crimes committed by off-duty military members with no connection to their service.[13] The liberal lion

8 10 U.S.C. § 801 *et seq.*

9 *See generally*, William T. Generous, Jr., Swords and Scales: The Development of the Uniform Code of Military Justice (Assoc. Faculty Press 1973) (describing the formulation of the UCMJ as the settlement of a clash between reformers such as Harvard Law School Professor Edward Morgan and Pentagon stalwarts such as Frederick Bernays Wiener).

10 *See infra.*

11 Court-martial jurisdiction over military members is worldwide. 10 U.S.C. § 805 ("This chapter applies in all places.").

12 *See* Rostker v. Goldberg, 453 U.S. 57, 64–72 (1981).

13 *See* Solorio v. United States, 483 U.S. 435 (1987).

herself, Ruth Bader Ginsburg, proclaimed military justice to now be "notably more sensitive to due process concerns" than in the past.[14] In deference to the needs of military discipline, the Court became more willing to affirm military convictions that would otherwise be void for vagueness or suffer constitutional defects.[15] The Supreme Court now grants very few petitions for certiorari from military defendants, leaving the military justice system largely free to develop according to its own devices. Thanks to a siloed military appellate system and limits on military defendants seeking collateral review in federal court,[16] the military and its justice system remain a *separate society*, largely unforced to change in response to legal developments in the civilian world.

The military is forced to change, however, when lawmakers in Congress, concerned about unfairness in military justice, exercise their "make Rules" authority and amend the UCMJ. That happened in response to the military justice system's handling of character evidence. The next section describes the military's unique approach to character evidence and why it proved so controversial.

CHARACTER EVIDENCE IN COURTS-MARTIAL

The Propensity Prohibition

The Federal Rules of Evidence and most state evidence codes carefully circumscribe the use of character evidence. They do so not because such evidence does not matter in persuasion and proof, but precisely because it does. Powerfully. Common sense and life experience teach us that what a person has done before tells us much about who they are: their *character*. Using character helps us predict how they will act on a given occasion: their *propensity*. The special potency of propensity reasoning is that factfinders will decide cases based on what someone has done before rather than the actual facts of the case. "Once a thief, always a thief," etc. The federal rulemakers enacted a propensity prohibition in Rule 404 meant to be so strong that it is stated twice: both Rule 404(a) and (b) disallow evidence "to prove a person's character in order to show that on a particular occasion the person acted in accordance" with their character. It is a central tenet of American evidence law that courts should decide cases using actual proof and not propensity.

[14] *See* Weiss v. United States, 510 U.S. 163, 194 (1994) (Ginsburg, J., concurring).

[15] *See, e.g.*, Parker v. Levy, 417 U.S. 733 (1974) (Dr. Levy was an Army doctor who urged racial minorities to not deploy to Vietnam. He was convicted at court-martial of conduct unbecoming an officer and conduct prejudicial to good order and discipline. He challenged his conviction as void for vagueness and a violation of his First Amendment rights. The Supreme Court rejected the challenges, ruling that "[b]ecause of the factors differentiating military from civilian society, Congress is permitted to legislate with greater breadth and flexibility when prescribing rules … ").

[16] 5 U.S.C. § 551(1)(F) and (G) (excluding certain military actions including courts-martial from Administrative Procedure Act review in federal court); Schlesinger v. Councilman, 420 U.S. 738 (1975) (articulating criteria for collateral challenges of courts-martial in federal district courts).

In criminal cases, the federal rules permit a narrow exception to the propensity prohibition: Defendants or victims may offer evidence of character, but only when the character trait at issue is "pertinent."[17] This is easily understood. It makes sense that a defendant in a murder case would be permitted to introduce evidence of his character for peacefulness. There, the trait is pertinent: If believed, it is less likely that he committed such a violent act. On the other hand, it would not make sense for the defendant to introduce evidence that he could not have committed the murder because he was good at his job and had earned many workplace accolades. The character trait of being a good employee is not pertinent to murder. Such evidence is not relevant and tends to confuse the issues.

Except in the U.S. military. There, until recently, military defendants could raise the "good soldier defense" as a defense to any charge. And not just in criminal sentencing, where good deeds or solid workplace performance might be a valid reason for a more lenient sentence, but during the guilt or innocence phase. In courts-martial, evidence of good military character is almost always considered pertinent. The next section explores the origins and partial demise of this unique regime of character evidence.

The "Good Soldier Defense"

The seeds of modern military character evidence doctrine were planted during the adoption of the Military Rules of Evidence in 1980. The Military Rules Advisory Committee, a group comprised exclusively of military officers, wrote Military Rule 404 as a carbon copy of Federal Rule 404. While the wording was the same, the military drafters inserted a proviso in the non-binding commentary to the rule: "It is the intention of the Committee, however, to allow the defense to introduce evidence of a good military character when that specific trait is pertinent. Evidence of good military character would be admissible, for example, in a prosecution for disobedience of orders."[18]

Why did the military drafters follow the federal rule to the letter but insert a comment that threatened to weaken it? On the one hand, the military in the late 1970s was eager to do all it could to bolster public confidence in military justice following torrid criticisms of the system's performance and fairness in the Vietnam era.[19] The adoption of independent military judges and military defense counsel was part of this legitimation. So too was adopting the federal rules, which had been promulgated by respected civilian jurists just a few years earlier in 1975. The military could now boast that its justice system deserved respect by pointing to evidence rules that closely resembled the rules for trials in federal district courts.

17 Fed. R. Evid. 404(a)(2).

18 Mil. R. Evid. 404(a) cmt (1980).

19 *See, e.g.*, Robert Sherrill, Military Justice Is to Justice as Military Music Is to Music (HarperCollins 1970).

While wanting to mimic the federal rules, the military was also keen to continue a long tradition of liberal use of military character evidence in courts-martial. Proponents of more liberal use of military character evidence argued that because military life is different from civilian life, the character trait of being a good soldier is always pertinent. "A soldier is a soldier twenty-four hours a day. Soldierly values are important. Soldiers do not have a job, they are 'in the service.'"[20] Military manuals predating the adoption of the Military Rules of Evidence treated military character evidence permissively. Significantly, the dean of American evidence law himself, John Wigmore, weighed in on military character during his service in the Army in the First World War. He wrote that a certificate of honorable military service should be liberally construed as importing general good character and morality.[21] Wigmore's passage was cited with approval by military judges in bending Rule 404's propensity prohibition, while critics contended that Wigmore's sentiments about wartime service did not amount to an endorsement of deviating from ordinary character rules during the merits phase of courts-martial.[22]

Practitioners in courts-martial noticed the door-slightly-ajar approach to good military character, and swung it all the way open. Military judges were happy to accede and continue the time-honored tradition of what became known as the "good soldier defense." In a 1986 case, the highest military appellate court further loosened the standard by endorsing the efforts of an Air Force defendant who presented merits evidence that he could not have stolen a television because he was an "honest and trustworthy person."[23] By the 1990s, military appellate courts had bent the language of Rule 404[24] and rendered the word "pertinent" meaningless by permitting the defense of good military character "in almost any conceivable trial by court-martial."[25] Military courts allowed this character evidence to support the inference that a military defendant was too professional at his or her military duties to engage in conduct (such as crimes) that would have adverse military consequences.[26] Good soldiers habitually do what they are supposed to do, so the character trait of being a good soldier can be a pertinent defense to any charge.

[20] Paul A. Capofari, *Military Rule of Evidence 404 and Good Military Character*, 130 Mil. L. Rev. 171, 188 (1990).

[21] Elizabeth Lutes Hillman, *The "Good Soldier" Defense: Character Evidence and Military Rank at Courts-Martial*, 108 Yale L.J. 879, 891 (1999).

[22] *Id.* at 891–2.

[23] United States v. Elliott, 23 M.J. 1, 5 (C.M.A. 1986).

[24] *See* Edward K. Cheng, G. Alexander Nunn, and Julia Simon-Kerr, *Bending the Rules of Evidence*, 118 Nw. U. L. Rev. 295 (2023).

[25] Robinson O. Everett, *Military Rules of Evidence Symposium: An Introduction*, 130 Mil. L. Rev. 1, 3 (1990). *See also* Major Lawrence J. Morris, *Keystones of the Military Justice System: A Primer for Chiefs of Justice*, Army Law., Oct. 1994 at 15, 22 (summarizing recent military appellate opinions that expanded the "good military character" defense and allowed it to be presented in any court-martial).

[26] *See* United States v. Wilson, 28 M.J. 48, 49 n. 1 (C.M.A. 1989).

Is the "good soldier defense" a good thing? After all, military members volunteered to serve their country, so a provision of lenity in a system historically viewed as harsh against defendants hardly shocks the conscience. Since racial disparities in military justice persist, including a recent finding that Black and Hispanic service members are twice as likely to face criminal investigation and prosecution than their white peers,[27] lenity might be thought even more sensible. Further, because the military can prosecute a broader range of offenses, including conduct such as disobedience and absence from work that would not be criminalized in civilian life, it might make sense that defendants have more tools to fight back.

The reality is that the "good soldier defense" does not benefit all in the military equally. For one, good military character may be undefinable. Does a soldier who wields a knife in a bar fight demonstrate a commendable warrior spirit (a good soldier) or a disregard for law and poor self-control (a bad soldier)? With character in the eye of the beholder, less privileged and connected military members will fare poorly when charged with the same conduct as their more popular peers.

Moreover, not all military members can wield this potent evidence equally. Junior military members will not have accumulated many accolades and commendations in their brief service. Testimony from their low-ranking military peers will probably carry very little weight. On the other hand, senior military members are more likely to have accreted long lists of military accolades, (possibly inflated) performance reports,[28] and rosters of high-ranking friends who can vouch for their character.[29] This means that the "good soldier defense" can constructively serve as an immunity shield for high-ranking servicemembers (a population that is predominantly white and male)[30] from criminal convictions.

Professor Elizabeth Lutes Hillman was the first to write about this problem in analyzing a 1998 court-martial of the Army's top enlisted soldier.[31] When Sergeant

[27] U.S. Dep't Def., *Internal Review Team on Racial Disparities in the Investigative and Military Justice Systems* 1 (2022), https://media.defense.gov/2023/Jun/08/2003238260/-1/-1/1/IRT-REPORT.PDF (finding that "[s]ignificant racial disparities exist across the investigative and military justice functions"; and that Black and other racial minorities were more than twice as likely to be subjected to adverse action in the military justice system).

[28] Courts-martial permit performance reports to be entered as evidence of good military character. *See* MIL. R. EVID. 405(c) (allowing proof of character by affidavit in addition to reputation and opinion); United States v. Vandelinder, 20 M.J. 41, 42 (C.M.A. 1985). As for the possibility of exaggerated performance evaluations, I recall my service as an officer in the U.S. Army where receiving an annual evaluation of "top 10% officer" was thought to put the officer at risk of not being promoted. The going rate for good officers was "top 1%" even though such a rating should technically only be afforded to only one out of every 100 officers.

[29] Evidence of a pertinent character trait can be proved by opinion or reputation. *See* FED. R. EVID. 405(a), MIL. R. EVID. 405(a).

[30] *Demographics of the U.S. Military*, COUNCIL ON FOREIGN RELATIONS (July 13, 2020, 9:00 AM), www.cfr.org/backgrounder/demographics-us-military ("[W]omen and racial and ethnic minorities remain underrepresented in parts of the military, particularly at the highest levels of leadership.").

[31] *See* Hillman, *supra* note 21, at 881 ("Cloaked in the mantle of long-standing court-martial tradition, justified by doctrines of questionable salience, and preserved by judges resistant to the Military Rules

Major of the Army Gene McKinney was prosecuted for sexual misconduct, the evidence against him included powerful testimony from six of his female subordinates about his harassment. In his defense, McKinney did not focus on the allegations themselves. Instead he paraded a series of witnesses to talk about his military accomplishments and soldierly behavior. This mix of relevant evidence (the prosecution witnesses) and seemingly irrelevant evidence (the defense's character witnesses) effectively muddied the waters, and McKinney was acquitted on all counts except one charge of obstruction of justice. He was sentenced to only a minor reduction in rank that did not affect his retirement pay.

McKinney was not an aberration. The 2010s saw increased public attention on the problem of sexual assault in the military.[32] The most noteworthy case came when Lieutenant Colonel James Wilkerson, an elite Air Force F-16 fighter pilot, was court-martialed and convicted of raping a civilian woman at his home in Aviano Air Base in Italy. In a wrinkle of the military justice system at the time, the military jury's verdict was not the final word; the commanding general still needed to ratify it. That officer, Lieutenant General Craig Franklin, was a member of the same tight-knit F-16 pilot fraternity as Wilkerson. In addition to the trial transcript, Franklin reviewed additional evidence of Wilkerson's military character, including emails sent to him from other F-16 pilots saying that Wilkerson's "integrity is airtight" and his "character is unshakeable."[33] Those submissions must have made a powerful impression, because Franklin chose to toss out the jury's verdict entirely.[34] Franklin then emailed his staff to try to get Wilkerson back into a flying assignment and promoted as soon as possible.[35]

The *Wilkerson* case validated Professor Hillman's criticism that the "good soldier defense" was in reality a tool of impunity for high-status defendants. The case caught the attention of Congress, which quickly ironed out the wrinkle that had allowed commanding generals such as Franklin to toss out rape convictions. Congress then set their sights on character evidence. As one of a series of military justice reforms championed by Representative Jackie Speier and Senators Kirsten Gillibrand and Claire McCaskill, Congress sought to constrain what it felt were improper uses of military character evidence. Congress required the military to amend Military Rule of Evidence 404 to prevent defendants from using good

of Evidence's limitations on character evidence, the good soldier defense advances the perception that one of the privileges of high rank and long service is immunity from prosecution at court-martial.").

32 *See, e.g.*, *The Invisible War* (Docurama Films 2012).

33 The Air Force's FOIA reading room that once contained the *Wilkerson* court-martial documents has been taken down. The once-public documents from Wilkerson's clemency submission are summarized in James Garrett, Max Maxwell, Matthew Calarco, and Franklin Rosenblatt, *Lawful Command Emphasis: Talk Offense, Not Offender; Talk Process, Not Results*, Army Law., Aug. 2014, at 4, 14, n. 96.

34 *Id.*

35 *Id.*

military character unless it is directly relevant to an element of the crime.[36] It also barred admission of military character evidence "for the purpose of showing the probability of innocence of the accused" for a number of offenses.[37]

Despite Congress's efforts to kill it, the "good soldier defense" might have suffered a mere flesh wound. For one, Congress did not categorically restrict military character evidence: it focused mainly on rape and sexual assault, leaving defendants free to attempt to admit expansive character evidence in other cases.[38] Importantly, it seems that the military's legal culture continues to embrace a liberal approach to military character evidence despite Congress's command: "Irrespective of Congressional action or intent, many judges and practitioners will continue to believe that 'good, honorable, and decent service to [the] country is always important and relevant evidence for the triers of fact to consider.'"[39]

EVIDENCE WITHOUT RULES

The saga of the "good soldier defense" tells only part of the story of character evidence in courts-martial. Unofficial character evidence has just as much potential to influence court-martial outcomes.

Every court case, military or civilian, involves hundreds or thousands of facts not entered into evidence.[40] When a witness describes driving a car, the jury accepts without further proof or instruction that this was an automobile, not a railroad car. Jurors bring their life experience with them. A category of non-evidence facts based on life experience includes biases. A juror may believe that a defendant is more likely to have committed a crime because he is a racial minority, for example, or a witness is not as credible because she testifies with upspeak. "Evidence" such as modes of dress, demeanor, speech, and race is often important

36 National Defense Authorization Act for Fiscal Year 2015, Pub. L. No. 113-291, § 536, 128 Stat. 3292 (2014).

37 *Id.* The military amended Rule 404(a)(2)(A) in response to this legislation. The rule now states (with descriptions of the articles added in brackets): (A) The accused may offer evidence of the accused's pertinent trait and, if the evidence is admitted, the prosecution may offer evidence to rebut it. General military character is not a pertinent trait for the purposes of showing the probability of innocence of the accused for the following offenses under the UCMJ: (i) Article 105 [forgery]; (ii) Articles 120–2 [rape and sexual assault; larceny; robbery]; (iii) Articles 123a–124 [bad checks; frauds]; (iv) Articles 126–7 [arson; extorsion]; (v) Articles 129–31 [burglary; stalking; perjury]; (vi) Any other offense in which evidence of general military character of the accused is not relevant to any element of an offense for which the accused has been charged; or (vii) An attempt or conspiracy to commit one of the above offenses.

38 *See id.*

39 Captain Rory T. Thibault, "*The Good Soldier Defense is Dead. Long Live the Good Soldier Defense.*" *The Challenge of Eliminating Military Character Evidence in Courts-Martial*, ARMY LAW., Sept. 2015 at 19, 32 (quoting United States v. Court, 24 M.J. 11, 13 (C.M.A. 1987) (Cox, J., concurring in part and dissenting in part)).

40 FED. R. EVID. 201 advisory committee's note.

to factfinders but goes unchecked by evidentiary gatekeeping. Professor Bennett Capers refers to this as "Evidence Without Rules."[41]

Just like in the civilian world, defendants and witnesses at courts-martial will be judged based on their race, manner of speech, demeanor, and appearance in ways that will usually go unstated. The military, though, takes "evidence without rules" one step further. Military members wear uniforms that convey their military status and achievements. It is no exaggeration to say that every military participant in courts-martial wears his or her resume on her chest. This unregulated and unremarked upon evidence often turns out to be enormously important. This part considers three examples to show the importance of unofficial character evidence.

A Few Good Men

The military courtroom thriller *A Few Good Men* illustrates how unofficial character evidence matters just as much as gatekept evidence. During an early scene at a basketball court, the defense counsel and prosecutor discuss a possible pretrial agreement. The core disputed issue is whether the defendants assaulted a fellow Marine on their own or were ordered to do so by their platoon commander, a Lieutenant. The negotiation comes down to whether the defendants or Lieutenant will be more credible in a swearing contest. The prosecutor argues that he holds the stronger hand because the Lieutenant will deny giving the order and has "four letters of commendation."[42] The defense counters that another officer, Markinson, will inculpate the Lieutenant. The prosecutor retorts, "You know what Markinson did for the first seventeen of his twenty-six years in the Corps? Counterintelligence. Markinson's gone. There is no Markinson."[43] The prosecutor's cold math reveals that in courts-martial, those with high military status such as the Lieutenant will be considered more credible than lower status witnesses, even when their military status has nothing to do with the content of their testimony.[44]

The Lieutenant continued to reap benefits from his elite military status when he testified. During the defense counsel's questioning about whether the Lieutenant ordered a hazing ritual called a Code Red, the military judge interrupts counsel: "I would remind you that you are now questioning a Marine officer with an

[41] *See* I. Bennett Capers, *Evidence Without Rules*, 94 Notre Dame L. Rev. 867, 895 (2018) ("Prosecutors and defense lawyers know that other evidence – whether it is dress or demeanor, an accent or upspeak, or race or gender – matters. They know, too, that there is no need to marshal arguments to get this evidence admitted. This other evidence will simply pass by the evidentiary gatekeepers, unchecked and unremarked upon.").

[42] *A Few Good Men* (Castle Rock Entertainment 1992), Amazon Prime Video time mark 49:48.

[43] *Id.* at 49:58.

[44] *See also*, John Lancaster, *In Military Harassment Cases, His Word Often Outranks Hers*, Wash. Post, Nov. 15, 1992, www.washingtonpost.com/archive/politics/1992/11/15/in-military-sex-harassment-cases-his-word-often-outranks-hers/b0fb4012-fcef-481f-b6f5-f163a3d0fa61/.

impeccable service record."[45] Here we see unofficial character evidence emerge from the shadows to the forefront. Unstated in the judge's admonition is that the Lieutenant is unlikely to have ordered a Code Red because he has a track record of exemplary service, and for defense counsel to even ask about improprieties that would be out of character for a good Marine is an affront to the court. In a civilian trial, it is difficult to imagine a judge chastising a counsel's impeachment of a witness because the witness excels at their work as a barista, teacher, or accountant. In *A Few Good Men*, though, the military judge is not the villain. The movie's narrative arc pushes the audience to accept the judge's intervention as reasonable, with defense counsel seeming like a disrespectful renegade for ignoring customs about kowtowing to military elites. In the military, high status affords many privileges, including the right to be believed in court.

A note on the Lieutenant's appearance and demeanor. Before he testifies, we see that he (played by Kiefer Sutherland) is a white man with an athletic build in a military uniform.[46] He wears an oversized ring signifying from a distance that he attended the elite United States Naval Academy. He wears the crossed rifles insignia of an expert marksman and numerous decorations. He is a commander in the infantry, an elite Marine subspecialty that at the time was foreclosed to women[47] and had few racial minorities.[48] His buzzcut hairstyle could indicate an embrace of a warrior ethos or a rejection of civilian professional appearance norms, or perhaps both. He glowers. When he testifies, he evades a question about whether he had reported an instance of misconduct, and instead launches into a nonresponsive jeremiad about Marine values.[49] He twice shouts in anger in response to other questions.[50]

Any other witness whose professional standing did not matter might be deemed not credible for such evasions and eruptions. This Lieutenant, though, conveys to the military jurors that he is a *high-status* Marine whose impatience is understandable so that he can return to unstated but pressing *national security* matters of the day. The trial transcript would capture very little of this dynamic, and the episode entirely

45 *A Few Good Men*, *supra* note 42, at 1:34:10.

46 *Id.*

47 *See* Hope Hedge Seck, *Marines Continue to Make Female Infantry Officers, with Little Fanfare*, MarineTimes, Oct. 28, 2024, www.marinecorpstimes.com/news/your-marine-corps/2024/10/28/marines-continue-to-make-female-infantry-officers-with-little-fanfare/ (chronicling the first women who joined the ranks of Marine infantry officers in 2020).

48 *See* Hope Hedge Seck, *Behind Closed Doors, Marines Struggle with a Glaring Diversity Problem*, Wash. Post (Oct. 16, 2023), www.washingtonpost.com/national-security/2023/10/16/marines-black-fighter-pilots/ (describing how the elite Marine subspecialties of aviation and infantry are still predominantly white).

49 *A Few Good Men*, *supra* note 42, at 1:32:30 ("I have two books at my bedside, Lieutenant: the Marine Corps Code of Conduct and the King James Bible. The only proper authorities I am aware of are my commanding officer Colonel Nathan R. Jessup and the Lord our God.").

50 *Id.*

circumvents the gatekeeping of the rules of evidence. Yet this unofficial character evidence is essential in understanding what is really happening in the court-martial. The Lieutenant literally gets away with murder.

Chief Eddie Gallagher

Military character evidence without rules is not just Hollywood's imagining. Real courts-martial reveal that military status, whether spoken or unspoken, is often persuasive and potent "evidence." One of the most high-profile courts-martial in recent years was the 2019 Navy court-martial of Navy SEAL Eddie Gallagher for allegedly committing unlawful killings in Iraq. As in civilian trials, counsel in courts-martial use opening statements to preview the most important evidence to come. Gallagher's defense counsel used his opening statement to talk about his client's military status and career achievements as a member of the elite SEALs. The lawyer "strode across the court, stood next to Eddie, and asked him to stand. He listed Eddie's past accomplishments: eight combat deployments, two Bronze Stars for valor, number one lead petty officer, number one chief, sailor of the year."[51]

The available record does not indicate why this vouching was relevant or permitted. Having a track record of military excellence might be pertinent to some offenses. For example, a record of combat distinction might be pertinent to fend off a charge of cowardice before the enemy. Here, though, the connection was not obvious. It seems that Gallagher relied on general character: that he could not have committed the charged offenses because he is an elite SEAL with an impressive service record. Gallagher's defense that he should enjoy impunity because of his elite military status is proof that unregulated military character evidence is as potent as official evidence.

It is not just the defendant's military status that matters. Gallagher benefited from a military jury where the members had experiences and backgrounds similar to his.

> All of them were either enlisted Marines or prior-enlisted warrant officers. On their chests, the vast majority wore the same service ribbons as Eddie: the Iraq Campaign Ribbon, the Afghanistan Campaign Ribbon, and the distinctive Combat Action Ribbon, which signified that they had personally engaged with the enemy. A few had on aluminum bracelets in memory of comrades killed in battle. They were, overwhelmingly, a group of ground-pounding, battle-hardened grunts just like Eddie.[52]

With such jurors, it is easy to see how Gallagher was eventually acquitted for the most serious charges he faced. Their backgrounds and professional achievements, as advertised by what they wore on their chests and arms, revealed common experiences

[51] David Phillips, Alpha: Eddie Gallagher and the War for the Soul of the Navy SEALS 301 (Crown Publishing 2021).

[52] *Id.* at 297.

with Gallagher that would give them a proclivity to see the case in a light more favorable to him. Unofficial character evidence rang powerfully in *Gallagher*.

Sergeant Bowe Bergdahl

Military character evidence without rules was also at play during the highly publicized court-martial of U.S. Army Sergeant Bowe Bergdahl. Bergdahl walked off his base in Afghanistan in 2009, was captured and held by the Taliban-affiliated Haqqani network in Pakistan for five years, then returned to the United States in a prisoner exchange.[53] The exchange presented President Obama's political opponents with an opportunity to attack his national security judgment, and the public mood towards Bergdahl soon soured after years of benign support during his captivity.[54] The Army responded by charging Bergdahl with two offenses under the UCMJ: desertion and misbehavior before the enemy, both for the same act of walking away from his post.

Bergdahl's military uniform was an early point of contention. He arrived to his arraignment at Fort Bragg in his Army dress uniform with all of the badges he was then authorized. These included the Combat Action Badge, the combat service identification badge for the 25th Infantry Division, the three chevrons of rank of a Sergeant (Bergdahl went to Afghanistan as a Private but was promoted to Sergeant administratively while in captivity), and ten overseas service bars on his right sleeve, each indicating six months of service in a combat zone.[55] To a civilian, Bergdahl's badges would mean little other than indicating that he was in the Army. But in the Army, these were respected badges that conveyed warrior credentials – credentials that might matter greatly given the hero-or-traitor nature of his case.

To some who were not sympathetic to him, Bergdahl's wearing of Sergeant rank and coveted badges was an outrage. To Bergdahl's defense team, the uniform was still incomplete. Bergdahl was arguably entitled to wear other military decorations such as the POW Medal (for military members who are held captive by the enemy), Purple Heart (for military members who are wounded in combat), and two other medals, but the issuance of these decorations was put on hold as the criminal case against Bergdahl proceeded. The POW and Purple Heart medals are respected and relatively rare in the Army. Not having these was highly prejudicial to Bergdahl, his counsel argued during a pretrial hearing, because he would be judged based on an incomplete resume in a culture where people are quickly

[53] *See generally*, MATT FARWELL AND MICHAEL AMES, AMERICAN CIPHER: BOWE BERGDAHL AND THE U.S. TRAGEDY IN AFGHANISTAN (Penguin 2019).

[54] *Id.* at 258–60.

[55] Sergeant Bergdahl's uniform and the badges on it was important enough for the Serial podcast to prepare an extensive interactive online display with his uniform and descriptions of his authorized decorations. *See* Mike McQuade, *Deconstructive Bergdahl's Uniform* [interactive map], SERIAL, https://serialpodcast.org/maps/deconstructing-bergdahls-uniform.

sized up based on the badges they wear.[56] Given the prospect of a contested trial, a military jury seeing Bergdahl's wearing of decorations such as a POW ribbon and Purple Heart would be powerful "evidence" that his actions were not motivated by cowardice or treachery. (The Army never awarded these additional medals.)

The anticipated character showdown never happened. Instead, Bergdahl pleaded guilty in 2017 without the benefit of a plea deal. During a two-week long sentencing hearing, the government presented evidence of other military members who were hurt looking for him, and the defense presented evidence of Bergdahl's psychiatric conditions and the torture he endured in captivity. A military judge sentenced Bergdahl to a dishonorable discharge, reduction to the lowest enlisted grade, and a $10,000 forfeiture, but no confinement despite the prosecution's request for a fourteen-year sentence. Though there was never a character clash governed by evidence rules, the *Bergdahl* pretrial hearings showed the central importance of unofficial character evidence.

CONCLUSION

"The power of character evidence cannot be underestimated."[57] The military's experimentation with the novel "good soldier defense" shows both the power and peril of character evidence. On the one hand, having more evidence can sometimes be helpful to the factfinder and aid in achieving just results. But when the admission of character evidence is unfettered, as with the military's evisceration of the requirement that only "pertinent" character traits be considered, the system bears a greater risk of harmful distortions. The military's experimentation helped obscure the criminal liability of powerful and privileged actors, thwarting the proper balance of rights among the participants in criminal trials.

Military justice also demonstrates how pervasive character evidence is. It is naïve to assume that character can be neatly pigeonholed to the testimony of witnesses and formal evidence regulated by evidence rules. Parties can and do find ways to use unregulated character evidence to their side's advantage. The military's experience, where rank and decorations communicate status and shape outcomes, suggests that "evidence without rules" is pervasive, potent, and deserving of further study.

56 The author was Sergeant Bergdahl's military counsel who made these arguments. *See* Dan Lamothe, *Does Bowe Bergdahl Deserve a POW Medal and Purple Heart? His Lawyers Think So*, Wash. Post (Jan. 12, 2016), www.washingtonpost.com/news/checkpoint/wp/2016/01/12/does-bowe-bergdahl-deserve-a-pow-medal-and-purple-heart-his-lawyers-think-so/.

57 United States v. Gagan, 43 M.J. 200, 202–3 (C.A.A.F. 2005) (citing Michelson v. United States, 335 U.S. 469, 476 (1948)).

Evidence Without Rules

Bennett Capers[1]

INTRODUCTION

Imagine walking through a busy courthouse. In Courtroom One, a sexual assault case is in progress. The Assistant District Attorney has just called the victim as a witness. As the victim approaches the stand, you notice that she is modestly dressed, and instantly begin to think of her as credible. Perhaps the jurors, who are nodding, are thinking the same thing. In Courtroom Two, the judge is conducting a *voir dire* as the lawyers begin the process of selecting a jury in an insurance fraud case. Although the jury pool nearly fills the courtroom gallery, you notice a young woman and three small children sitting apart from everyone else. You assume they are the defendant's family, and cannot help but wonder if a guilty verdict will separate the family. Will the jurors wonder this as well? Courtroom Three is almost the opposite, the gallery is completely empty but for you, the only spectator. The defense lawyer is cross-examining a uniformed police officer who claims he observed the defendant throw away a gun as the defendant was running from the officer. Even though jurors are rarely told anything about a defendant's criminal history, you wonder if the defendant, who is black, has a criminal record. You glance at the jurors, who seem bored. Perhaps they are assuming the same thing, and are wondering whether they can simply vote guilty already.

On the surface, these three cases – a sexual assault case, an insurance fraud case, a gun possession case – are different. Yet in one important respect they share something in common: in all of these cases, fact finders will likely rely on "evidence" – a style of dress, the presence of family members, and race – that is rarely treated as evidence by the Rules of Evidence. Indeed, in some instances, the fact finders will rely on "evidence" that runs directly *counter* to evidentiary rules. Most troubling of all, because this evidence is rarely recognized as evidence in the formal sense, it typically enters unnoticed. It typically goes unremarked upon.

[1] Excerpted from Bennett Capers, *Evidence Without Rules*, 94 NOTRE DAME L. REV. 867 (2018).

The first goal of this Article is to call attention to this other evidence. For too long scholars and jurists have proclaimed and insisted that the Rules of Evidence serve as a powerful, all-seeing gatekeeper, culling evidence brought before juries for relevance and trustworthiness. In fact, there is a panoply of evidence that, because it is rarely recognized as such, routinely passes evidentiary gatekeepers unobserved and unchecked. Calling attention to this evidence, indeed exposing it as evidence too, is the first goal of this Article.

The second goal of this Article is to demonstrate that such unregulated evidence matters. Consider the courtroom examples again. It is axiomatic among prosecutors that presenting a rape victim in more modest dress increases the chances of securing a conviction, just as defense lawyers know that having family members and friends in the gallery can increase jury sympathy and the likelihood of an acquittal. Turning to the gun possession case in Courtroom Three, litigators know that quite possibly the most powerful evidence in the case will be the defendant's race. In a very real sense, "race itself is evidence."

All of this has consequences for victims of crime. For example, to the extent that punishment serves the purpose of facilitating victim vindication, it should strike us as a design flaw that such vindication could turn on whether a prosecutor remembers to tell a rape victim to dress conservatively in court. This also has consequences for defendants: the very issue of guilt may turn on whether family members, his or his victim's, are sitting in the courtroom. Even in cases that do not go to trial – the overwhelming majority – this unregulated evidence has outsized consequences, since these cases are negotiated and settled with prospective jurors in mind and in the "shadow of trial." And all of this has consequences for our entire judicial system, especially our criminal justice system. It certainly belies what we tell ourselves about the way justice works, that it is based on the "rule of law." The truth is far less comforting. The determination of outcomes, notwithstanding the Rules of Evidence, is often rule-less. ...

II. EVIDENCE WITHOUT RULES

If the goal of evidence law is "that truth may be ascertained and proceedings justly determined," then that objective is frustrated when outputs turn on improper and unchecked inputs. To demonstrate and show the implications of this point, this part focuses on three types of "offstage" evidence that are frequently considered by jurors, and yet almost always pass unscrutinized by evidentiary gatekeepers. The first two types of evidence may at first glance seem minor – modes of dress and demeanor evidence – but in fact their impact is substantial. The significance of the third type of evidence should be obvious, and yet also passes by largely unchecked by evidentiary rules: race, or what a Critical Race Theorist might call the "sticky tar baby of race." To be clear, these three examples of unregulated evidence are simply that: examples. They do not begin to exhaust the many types of other evidence that come before jurors. However, these three examples do illustrate that what we tell ourselves about evidence law's gatekeeping function is all wrong.

A. *Modes of Dress*

The beginning of all Wisdom is to look fixedly on Clothes, or even with armed eyesight, till they become transparent.

Thomas Carlyle

We felt she asked for it the way she was dressed.

Juror following not guilty verdict in a rape trial

Clothing is rarely the focus of legal scholarship, at least not scholarship about evidence or fact finding, trials or juries. This omission in evidence scholarship is surprising, given evidence law's focus on policing hearsay. This policing of hearsay, after all, governs not only verbal communications, but also non-verbal communications. A nod of the head receives the same scrutiny as a verbal "yes." And yet clothing routinely escapes evidentiary notice. Why is this strange? Because clothing itself is communicative. As Roland Barthes noted half a century ago, "[D]ress itself is a kind of writing." We certainly use it to communicate "status, rank, grade, tribe, milieu, beliefs, values, etc."

And we certainly use dress to communicate ideas to jurors. The *Law Insider* puts the matter of dress front and center: How "the judge or jury perceives you is one of the many factors that will influence a final decision. We can argue all day about whether as a society we should form opinions about people based upon appearance, but that's not going to change the fact that we do." The *Jury Expert* gives similar advice: "While witnesses' verbal and non-verbal behaviors affect their credibility, another factor in jurors' perceptions of them is their appearance." Indeed, in all likelihood, it is the first thing considered by jurors.

Consider the role dress plays during a sexual assault case. Notwithstanding rape shield protections that a victim's style of dress is normally inadmissible, defense lawyers will often offer into evidence the clothes the victim was wearing at the time of the alleged assault. For example, in the trial against William Kennedy Smith on charges that he sexually assaulted a woman, the judge permitted the defense to introduce the victim's "Ann Taylor dress, high heels, black and blue bra and Victoria's secret panties and panty," ostensibly to support the defense theory that the victim did not struggle. But separate and apart from what the victim was wearing at the time of the assault – this clothing after all is at least subjected to evidentiary rules and gatekeeping – there is also the matter of what clothing the victim wears to trial. This latter clothing is not subjected to evidentiary rules. The smart prosecutor will instruct the victim to dress modestly at trial in order to present the victim as a "good girl." By doing so, and without uttering a word, the prosecutor is introducing evidence of the victim's character.

Nor is the strategic use of dress to communicate ideas limited to sexual assault cases. Indeed, dress is, in a certain sense, used strategically in almost every criminal case. Prosecutors ensure that law enforcement witnesses, even officers who exclusively work in plain clothes, dress in uniform during trial; lay witnesses and expert witnesses are similarly groomed for trial. Even witnesses who have pleaded guilty to their role in the offense and are now testifying as cooperating witnesses in exchange for leniency are dressed by prosecutors, usually in prison garb to communicate to the jury that the cooperating witnesses, unlike the defendant, have accepted responsibility for their role in the offense, and are now being truthful. In all of these instances, the prosecutor is using clothing to communicate ideas. In all of these instances, the prosecutor is using clothing as evidence.

Defense lawyers deploy dress as well. Almost every defense lawyer will instruct her male client to wear a suit to directly communicate respect for the court and authority, and indirectly communicate law-abidingness. They ensure that their clients' regular style of dress – for example, a muscle shirt or baggy jeans – does not become "Exhibit A for the prosecution." Public defender offices even keep suits available for indigent defendants. There is sometimes more individualized sartorial management. Consider a handful of well-known cases. A defense lawyer said of Amy Fisher, the "Long Island Lolita" who shot and severely wounded her married lover's wife, "I would have put her in a French schoolgirl dress with a big collar, a dark color, ribbon in her hair, no makeup … . Make her look as young and innocent as possible." Regarding boxing champion Mike Tyson, who was convicted of rape in 1992, the lawyer would have ordered him to wear looser clothing to play down his size, and pastels to soften his appearance. When Patty Hearst, the granddaughter of publishing magnate William Randolph Hearst, was tried on armed bank robbery charges, her lawyer instructed her to wear clothes a couple of sizes too small to give the appearance that she was also a victim. Eric and Lyle Menendez, the wealthy teenagers who were tried for killing their parents, abandoned the suits they wore during pretrial appearances to wear collegiate V-neck sweaters at trial. In the Enron trial, the defense team made sure their clients didn't wear their $10,000 Rolex watches in front of the jury. More recently, the defense team representing Casey Anthony, who faced capital murder charges in connection with the death of her two-year old daughter, instructed her to wear preppy clothing and soft colors to project an image of child-like innocence.

Consider too the advice given by jury consultants. A jury consultant notes that savvy lawyers should spray a defendant's glasses with PAM cooking spray so that the jury cannot see the person's eyes, at least when the lawyer fears the defendant might come across as "shifty-eyed." Lawyers should also direct clients accused of violent crimes to wear glasses, in effect offering what has been characterized as a "nerd defense," since this might increase the chances of an acquittal. Lawyers representing clients accused of white collar crimes should do the opposite – advise their clients not to wear glasses – since glasses may make them look more culpable. Indeed, at least two consultants have described glasses as "one of the most important artifacts used in the courtroom." …

The goal of this section is not to exhaust all of the ways dress is used to communicate ideas to the jury. Rather, the goal is to argue that we should be troubled by a system of justice that turns on whether a prosecutor reminds a rape victim to dress conservatively for trial – in short, to dress like a "good girl." Similarly, we should be troubled by a justice system where guilt or innocence turns on whether a defendant can afford a proper suit, or whether a law enforcement officer wears a uniform when he testifies, or whether the defendant wears glasses, or how an attorney dresses.

The goal too is to call attention to the dissonance between what we tell ourselves about the Rules of Evidence – that they screen all information that juries may hear or see – and the reality: that ideas communicated through dress are routinely considered by jurors without any evidentiary gatekeeping checks at all. To be sure, courts have policed clothing in a handful of circumstances when it rises to the level of a constitutional claim. For example, the Supreme Court has read the due process clause, and its implied presumption of innocence, to impose a bar on compelling a defendant to be tried in prison garb. Courts have also held that a defendant has a First Amendment right to wear a uniform or even religious symbol. But beyond these limited circumstances, the Constitution, and more specifically the Rules of Evidence, are rarely invoked to screen this mode of dress for probative value or unfair prejudice, to say nothing of trustworthiness. Indeed, even the exception for prison garb begs the question: If we recognize the influence prison garb may play in influencing jurors, why are the evidentiary rules so blind to other types of dress? …

C. *Race*

This case has "nothing to do with race."

Lawyer for officer who shot an unarmed black man, Philando Castille

This case has nothing to do with race.

Police official, speaking of the arrest of Harvard Professor Henry Louis Gates for disorderly conduct when police suspected him of breaking into his own home

This case has nothing to do with race.

Prosecutor in case involving white officer's shooting of an undercover black officer

This case has never been about race.

Prosecutor speaking to the press following the acquittal of George Zimmerman for the death of unarmed black teenager Trayvon Martin

Race matters.

Cornel West

Of the three examples of evidence considered by jurors and yet unchecked by the Rules of Evidence, race is the most troubling, especially given our aspiration of equal justice before the law. Indeed, it is arguable that this goal of equality, and indeed color-blindness, prompts us to elide race at trial, at least officially. We tend to think saying nothing is the best policy. Indeed, as the novelist Toni Morrison has observed, "the habit of ignoring race is understood to be a graceful, even generous, liberal gesture."

But what happens when we acknowledge that for jurors, "[r]ace is evidence," even when race is unsaid. An illustration of this can be found in *People v. Goetz*. The case is known for its facts and its national media attention – Goetz, a white man, was acquitted after he shot four black youths on a New York City subway claiming that he reasonably feared deadly force after one or two of the youths asked him for five dollars. The case is also a staple of criminal law casebooks and the discussion of the "reasonable person" standard in self-defense cases. As Professor Jody Armour famously asked, should a "reasonable racist" be able to kill because he "reasonably" fears black men as dangerous and successfully claim self-defense? But there is another aspect of the case that illustrates, in particularly stark terms, how lawyers use race as evidence. At trial, the defense lawyer insisted that the path of the bullets Goetz fired was material to the case, and demanded that he be allowed to re-enact the shooting in court so that the jurors could see the path of the bullets. The defense lawyer then brought in four "volunteers" to show where the victims were standing vis-à-vis Goetz. The four "volunteers," which the defense claimed he needed simply to show the path of the bullets, were large black men. In the words of Professor George Fletcher, the Columbia Law professor who sat in on the trial and later wrote about it, the choice of large black men was patently strategic, designed "to reek with danger." Without saying a word, the defense lawyer put race front and center, and made race evidence.

It would be easy to argue that this back-door race-ing of the four black youths in *People v. Goetz* is atypical. The reality is the exact opposite: that jurors, often with the complicity of lawyers, use race as evidence all of the time, and do so in ways that usually go unchecked by the Rules of Evidence.

Consider again one of the courtrooms visited in the Introduction. In Courtroom Three, a patrol officer was testifying about observing the defendant throw away a gun as the defendant ran from the officer. The officer eventually caught up with the defendant, apprehended him, recovered the gun from where it had been thrown, and arrested the defendant on gun possession charges. Although race was not mentioned in the case – the case is *United States v. Whitmore* – it would be foolhardy to think that race was absent. Race, even when unsaid, is still seen. Race, even when unacknowledged, is still present. Indeed, the defendant's race will likely be the first thing the jurors learn about a defendant, even before they learn his name. Before the first witness is called to the stand, before any opening statements, even before jury selection starts, jurors will see the race of the defendant sitting at the defense table, and will be unable to not see race. And jurors, even the most well-meaning, will likely use that race as evidence.

This has obvious implications for cases involving black or Latino defendants. Social cognition research demonstrates that implicit biases about race – those assumptions and associations we have even when we believe we are "race-blind" – are practically universal. In particular, research suggests a tendency to implicitly associate dark skin with criminality. In death penalty litigation, "the perceived blackness of a defendant is related to sentencing: the more black the more death-worthy." Moreover, this use of race as evidence tends to function automatically, including in ways that the person would not endorse as appropriate if he or she did have conscious awareness. Although this association has been demonstrated in numerous ways, from Harvard's standard implicit association tests ("IAT") to Joshua Correll's shooter bias studies, one study deserves particular discussion. Interested in adapting the standard IAT to something directly applicable to the legal setting, Professor Justin Levinson and others created a Guilty/Not Guilty IAT to test whether people implicitly associate blacks not just with criminality but specifically with guilt. They also tested to see whether their results would predict how mock jurors responded to ambiguous evidence. Their results are revealing: participants displayed a significant association between blacks and guilt (as compared to whites and guilt). A regression model further demonstrated that the association of blacks with guilt also predicted judgments about what weight to give certain evidence. Those with strong associations of blacks and guilt were more likely to judge ambiguous evidence as indicative of guilt in cases involving black defendants. …

There are at least three other ways jurors treat race as evidence. The first has to do with our long history of tying race to credibility, beginning with laws and customs that prohibited nonwhites, including Latinos and Asians, from testifying against whites. Even after race-based competency rules were eradicated, race continued to be tied to credibility. North Carolina, for example, required that "whenever a person of color shall be examined as a witness, the court shall warn the witness to tell the truth." The Oregon Supreme Court twice ruled that Chinese witnesses must be viewed with special scrutiny, stating in one case that "experience convinces every one that the testimony of Chinese witnesses is very unreliable." The point here is not just that this history is important. It is that we have not yet untethered ourselves from history. Social-science literature makes clear that race is still a factor in credibility determinations. Another scholar puts the matter more bluntly: "In an instant, at first sight and without formally entering evidence or investing resources, the party calling the white witness [is] able to bolster the witness's credibility for truthfulness. Conversely, a witness of color is automatically considered less credible." All of this contributes to what the philosopher Miranda Fricker calls "testimonial injustice," which occurs "when prejudice results in the speaker's receiving more credibility than she otherwise would have – a *credibility excess* – or it results in her receiving less credibility than she otherwise would have – a *credibility deficit*." Professor Fricker goes on to note that who receives a credibility excess and who receives a credibility deficit often turns on the race of the speaker.

The second way race is treated as evidence relates to prior convictions and other bad acts. Although evidentiary rules normally bar evidence of a defendant's prior criminal record or other bad acts, jurors likely assume past criminality for black defendants. Again, this is consistent with numerous IAT studies showing that most Americans implicitly associate dark skin with criminality. But it is also consistent with research from another field entirely, Harvard sociologist Devah Pager's research on employment opportunities. Using testers for entry-level jobs advertised in newspapers, Pager found that employers were less likely to pursue black applicants compared to white applicants with identical resumes and interview preparation. Her conclusion: racial discrimination in hiring, at least for low-level jobs, is very real. But her research also lead to a second finding that is less well-known: callback rates still favored white applicants even when white applicants, and white applicants alone, disclosed on their applications that they had a prior conviction. In other words, employers treated white applicants who disclosed having a criminal record as effectively equivalent to black applicants. The most plausible explanation is many employers assumed a history of criminality for black applicants. A recent paper from the National Bureau of Economic Research made similar findings. Again, assuming juror unexceptionalism, this suggests jurors are more likely to treat black defendants as if they had prior convictions, which in turn is likely to contribute to a finding of guilty. As Kimani Paul-Emile has recently written, in this and other ways blackness itself "functions as a disabling condition."

Before moving to the third point, there is one more thing to be said about race as evidence. Not only do we have biases that disfavor racial minorities. We also have biases that favor whites. In particular, we have implicit biases that link whiteness with truth-telling and innocence. In Pager's employment studies, employers assumed white applicants had a "clean slate" unless the white applicant disclosed a prior arrest or conviction. In Joseph Correll's shooter bias, the results showed not only that participants were more likely to mistakenly believe a black individual had a gun, i.e., a false positive. It also found that participants were more likely to wrongly assume a white person did not, i.e., a false negative. Similarly, Justin Levinson's narrative study, which found participants invented aggressiveness when the actor was black, found that participants actually failed to remember evidence of aggressiveness when the actor was white. In short, it is not only in cases involving minority defendants where race matters. Race also matters in cases involving white defendants, whom jurors are more likely to view as presumptively innocent, and cases involving white witnesses, whom jurors deem presumptively credible.

The third point about race as evidence is this: Jurors, most likely without realizing it, appear to use race as a measure of value and worth. Perhaps nowhere is this use of race more challenging and stark than in the death penalty context. The most well-known study is the Baldus study, which became of the subject of the Court's decision in *McCleskey v. Kemp*. The statistical study examined murder cases in Georgia to see what role if any race played in capital punishment determinations. The study concluded that far more important than the race of the defendant was the race of the victim. Even after taking into account 39 nonracial variables, the study concluded that defendants charged with killing white victims were 4.3 times as likely to receive a death sentence as defendants charged with killing black victims. Subsequent studies have reached similar results. Brandon Garrett's recent study of death penalty cases nationwide during the last twenty-five years also supports the argument that decision makers use race as a measure of value and worth. Even though the number of death sentences has steeply declined, for the death sentences that are still imposed, the race of the victim still seems to matter in the counties that impose death. Garrett calls this the "white lives matter" effect. In short, all other things being equal, jurors appear to use race as a proxy for measuring worth (of the victim) and harm (to the community). All of this is using race as evidence. ...

D. *Other Examples*

... Other examples abound. There is evidence to suggest that jurors consider attractiveness – of the defendant and the victim – in determining their verdicts, and that male jurors are significantly more likely to judge overweight women guilty, using their weight to impute character traits of greediness, selfishness, and lack of impulse control. Similarly, there is evidence that jurors consider the fact that a defendant is listening to the trial through an interpreter as a negative, and give less credibility to witnesses who speak with an "outsider" accent while giving extra credibility to those witnesses who speak with an "insider" or even British accent. Or the existence of a tattoo or a natural hairstyle like cornrows as evidence. Even "jury notice" evidence – the idea that jurors are permitted to use "facts within the common knowledge of the community" – could be put into this category of other evidence. Again, all of this matters.

Judging Demeanor

Kiel Brennan-Marquez and Julia Simon-Kerr[1]

INTRODUCTION

Carlos Ruiz and Yaritza Delacruz are tried jointly for heroin trafficking based on evidence from an apartment they shared as romantic partners. Neither testifies. During deliberations, the jury sends out the following note: "Can we take the defendants['] body language into consideration? As evidence?" To which the judge responds: "While not evidence, the jury is entitled to consider any observations you made of the defendants' demeanor during the trial." An hour later, the jury convicts Ruiz but acquits Delacruz. Ruiz appeals, arguing that his conviction was based, in part, on the jury's perception that he looked like a criminal. In other words, Ruiz argues that he failed, while sitting silently at the defendants' table, to *appear* innocent to a group of strangers – strangers who came to court, as anyone would, with acculturated views and biases about how law-abiding people self-present – and that a conviction on this basis violated his constitutional rights.

Will Ruiz win? In many jurisdictions, including Ruiz's own, the answer is no. More than that, in fact: The law allows prosecutors to frame closing arguments around defendant demeanor, and jury instructions often celebrate its probative value. Furthermore, when judges are asked to clarify the case-specific status of demeanor evidence, they tend – as in *Commonwealth v. Ruiz* – to explicitly bless its consideration.

The reflexive use of demeanor evidence at trial is deeply troubling. It provides legal cover for propensity-based reasoning; it invites juries to convict based on whether a defendant seems like "a person who breaks the law," rather than the actual facts of the case. By its nature, this opens the door to bias, stereotyping, and cultural chauvinism, subverting the "basic premise," in the recent words of

[1] Excerpted from Kiel Brennan-Marquez and Julia Simon-Kerr, *Judging Demeanor*, 109 MINN. L. REV. 1503 (2025).

Chief Justice Roberts, that "[o]ur law punishes people for what they do, not who they are." This would be troubling under any circumstances. But it is *especially* troubling when combined with research suggesting that jurors (like all of us) are incapable of extracting useful information about who someone really is from self-presentation, especially across cultural and racial lines. In practice, this turns defendant demeanor into a site of judgment that perpetuates and intensifies many familiar pathologies of our criminal legal system. It becomes a tool by which members of dominant groups – consciously or not – penalize members of non-dominant groups for failing to appear innocent or credible. …

II. REFRAMING THE PROBLEM: DEMEANOR AS PROPENSITY EVIDENCE

B. *The Risk of Unfair Prejudice*

… The problem with demeanor evidence is simple, and very familiar to evidence law: It invites jurors to authorize punishment based on the *kind of person* a defendant appears to be. Or, put a little more technically: the risk is that jurors will (1) infer – rightly or wrongly – that the defendant has a generalized propensity toward criminal conduct, and (2) convict the defendant partly (or entirely) on *that* basis, rather than the actual facts of the case.

To bring this risk alive, consider how defendant demeanor operates as an evidential input. The function of demeanor evidence is to signal characteristics to an observer. Those characteristics may be physical: variables like skin color, gender presentation, and size. Or they may be psychical: variables like identity, personality, and ideational patterns. For demeanor to convey useful information about these latter characteristics, observers must be able to draw meaningful inferences about interiority from outward appearance. This requires generalization. The way demeanor provides "access" to character is by enabling an observer (1) to see (or assume) the presence of physical attributes that (2) suggest the presence of psychical characteristics based on preexisting assumptions about relevant correlations.

This analytic operation poses an inherent risk of prejudice, because it opens the door, by its nature, to generalized inferences of "bad character." Of course, not all inferences drawn from demeanor operate at this high a level of generality; it is possible to infer more specific psychical characteristics, positive or negative, from physical attributes. But that is just the point: The *risk* associated with inferences drawn from demeanor is that they will operate at a misleadingly high level of generality, leading observers to believe they have learned something about a person's *general* inclinations, such as whether the observed person is "good" or "bad" writ large, and to draw adverse conclusions about specific cases on that basis.

Consider the example discussed above: credibility. In everyday life, we often believe ourselves to be capable of assessing the trustworthiness of people based on physical attributes. Cognitive science suggests this experience is largely illusory; humans, as we said, turn out to be terrible honesty detectors, especially across cultural lines. Here, however, the point is about the *form* of inference at work. Whatever the scientific merits or demerits of inferring, based on physical attributes, that someone has a propensity for truthfulness (or the opposite), that inference is more granular than an inference of generalized propensity for wrongdoing. In other words, an observer may be right or wrong – and empirically, they are probably wrong – in their assessment of someone's propensity for truthfulness. But either way, that assessment is more specific, and more susceptible of falsification, than a general assessment of "bad character."

But it gets worse. In this particular setting, general assessments of "bad character," in addition to being epistemically fraught, are closely indexed to cultural hierarchy. The evaluation of demeanor invites observers from dominant cultural backgrounds to penalize people from non-dominant backgrounds. The risk of a demeanor-based penalty is particularly acute along racial lines, but it is not limited to that context. Demeanor penalties can also operate along other dimensions of cultural signification, such as gender, class, religion, and disability. Not only is this intrinsically unfair, it also tends to exacerbate existing pathologies and inequalities in the criminal legal system.

Critical race theorists have long argued that this creates penalties for Black witnesses in the courtroom. As these and other scholars have shown, legal spaces, and particularly courtrooms, still adopt as neutral the white, male baseline. Codes of dress and decorum, a judiciary that still skews white and male, and the hierarchical and tradition-bound nature of legal practice itself all help to subtly reinforce this norm. Legal proceedings also may reward appearances and methods of communicating that are closest to this white male norm.

Scholars have described this as a "demeanor gap" along lines of race and also gender. The demeanor gap incorporates stereotypes about Black people, such as that they are less intelligent or honest, or have a propensity for violence. In this sense, a judge who tells jurors to pay careful attention to a witness's demeanor as an aid to fact-finding is not offering a neutral instruction. Instead, the judge is instructing jurors to use their own acculturation to assess how a witness's demeanor lines up with what they are hearing about the witness's conduct or the likelihood that they are telling the truth. And in a society in which racial and other stereotypes are still pervasive, aspects of the witness's outward appearance, such as the color of their skin or their natural hair, may influence whether a fact finder believes that person's narrative. Indeed, there is evidence that even as an aid in finding the most neutral of facts, such as a person's height, race plays a problematic role. For example, research has found that "people perceive young Black men as taller, heavier, more muscular, more physically formidable and more capable of physical harm than young White men of the same actual size."

To return to Ruiz's case, it seems likely that something about Ruiz as he sat in the courtroom suggested to the jury that he was more likely to have been selling drugs than Delacruz. It is not difficult to identify a pervasive stereotype that could have triggered that conclusion, even as Ruiz sat silently in the courtroom. At the time of Ruiz's trial, Donald Trump was busy promulgating the stereotype of Latino men as illegal immigrants here to commit crimes from the platform of the presidency of the United States. Beyond race and gender, demeanor can convey other stigmatizing information, such as a defendant's social class or apparent disability.

What is more, the link between demeanor and cultural stereotyping is very difficult to guard against, even for observers who actively wish to do so. Many of the "already-biased" aspects of demeanor come back to ineluctable features of how human cognition works. As Professor Teneille Brown puts it, "we cannot *not* make character inferences." This is not a bad thing, per se. From an evolutionary perspective, for example, the human inclination to "database" strangers via character inferences makes a lot of sense; it is likely related to most people's reflexive ability to recognize and remember faces. This process helps us form complex societies as we can both recognize our friends and acquaintances and make accurate predictions about their behavior.

Whatever its neurological origins, however, our impulse toward propensity-based reasoning also encourages the false assumption that character is stable and that people we know will inevitably behave in a particular way consistent with our impression of who they are. It may also lead to fundamental attribution errors whereby we falsely assume that behavior is driven by character and that future behavior will correspond to character. Accordingly, even when we have accurate information about the behavior of others, we may falsely believe that the behavior signifies a character trait rather than a situationally motivated behavior and make wrong assumptions about a person's future conduct based on those character-based conclusions. Indeed, Professor Brown argues that this is the scientific basis for the lay intuition that provided the motivation for character-propensity prohibition.

Particularly when we seek to assess people about whom we know very little, human cognition presents even more barriers to accurate fact-finding. Our brains work to make connections between appearance and character when we form impressions of strangers, but the data that we rely on is often spurious in these situations. We will be inclined to attribute character traits of a friend to a stranger who looks like that friend. We are more benevolent towards faces that look like members of our tribe. Because of these cognitive processes, how we react to the faces of strangers "mainly reflect[s] our [own] circumstances: cultural upbringing, wealth, social class, peer groups, and aspirations." In other words, we inevitably think by using "crude proxies" for actual information about other people. As Professor Brown writes, we use a person's "race, dress, accent and facial features to predict their personalities [and] infer whether [they are] threatening, kind, intelligent or trustworthy" all without realizing we are doing so.

But it gets even worse, at least in the criminal context. Not only do humans readily, often unconsciously, draw inferences about someone's personality, intelligence, trustworthiness, and other characteristics on the basis of superficial features; we also move quickly from these kinds of inferences to *even more general* assumptions about how predisposed someone is to "break the law." And it is this mode of reasoning, we will see below, that existing doctrine has specifically sought to guard against.

C. *The Constitutional Law of "Inferential Risk"*

Even assuming that consideration of defendant demeanor poses all the risks outlined above, it does not follow that demeanor evidence should be subject, by category, to heightened regulation during the trial process, let alone that it should be barred outright. After all, the problem of evidential prejudice is old, persistent, and well-trod. And law's general approach to managing that problem is via some combination of (1) limiting instructions, crafted to discourage juries from indulging in forbidden lines of reasoning, or (2) case-specific challenges, typically framed in the language of Rule 403. The general approach to evidential prejudice, in other words, is *not* to regulate a type of evidence by category. It is to identify specific risks of prejudice case-by-case, and to require the party seeking to keep the evidence out, here the defendant, to explain why the risk is sufficiently great to outweigh the countervailing probative value.

Case-specific demonstrations of prejudice are, indeed, the default paradigm. But the paradigm meets with a number of important exceptions. With respect to some categories of evidence, the Supreme Court has made clear that case-specific balancing, beginning from a presumption of admissibility, is *not* a sufficient answer to the problem of evidential prejudice. Instead, it has recognized a heightened risk of unfairness to criminal defendants across the board, and it has adopted a more prophylactic approach to the regulation of evidence. We believe demeanor fits this pattern.

A cornerstone of our legal system is that criminal law "punishes people for what they do, not who they are." Echoing centuries of common law, FRE 404(a) flatly prohibits adducing a defendant's general propensity for criminal conduct to prove they were more likely, "on a[ny] particular occasion," to have committed a crime. Unlike other areas of the "character evidence" regime, such as witness credibility, this prohibition is categorical. In some circumstances, a defendant may voluntarily open the door to discussion and evaluation of their own character. But there are no true exceptions here – and with good reason. The state simply may not premise its case-in-chief, in whole or part, on a defendant's general propensity to break the law.

This principle is not limited to the FRE. It also animates the Supreme Court's doctrine on fundamental fairness in criminal enforcement. To begin with, direct criminalization of character is *per se* unconstitutional. This is among the only substantive limits on police power that derives from general principles of criminal procedure – in this case, the bar on cruel and unusual punishment – rather than specific countervailing rights (like the First or Second Amendments). Conceptually, the prohibition rests on a distinction between character and conduct. Although the functional boundary between those two categories is not always sharp, the distinction remains foundational. For example, criminalizing the possession of small quantities of a narcotic drug is similar to criminalizing addiction to the same substance; likewise, criminalizing the solicitation of minors is similar to criminalizing pedophilia. In both cases, however, direct punishment of the underlying propensity, whatever its functional similarity, is forbidden. It would represent a step too far by category – the mark of an illiberal legal order.

The same logic extends, furthermore, to punishment *based on* a jury's assessment of defendant character, even where the formal predicate of the criminal act is discrete conduct. There are four settings in which the Court has voiced concern about, and adopted prophylactic rules in response to, the risk that certain kinds of evidence will divert the jury's attention away from the actual facts of the case, toward a defendant's general propensity for wrongdoing. The first two are governed by blanket prohibitions: the state may never adduce a defendant's (1) race or (2) criminal history to show that the defendant had a higher-than-average propensity to commit the underlying crime. The third and fourth settings, by contrast, are governed not by blanket prohibitions, but balancing tests: The government is presumptively forbidden from requiring defendants either (1) to wear shackles and prison garb or (2) to ingest psychotropic medication during trial. This is a presumption rather than an outright ban because the doctrine makes room for countervailing state interests; the question is whether the prosecution can demonstrate a sufficient, case-specific need for physical or pharmacological restraint.

All four variables – race, criminal history, sartorial presentation, and psychiatric status – relate to how a defendant "looks" or "presents" to the jury. And each variable is different; they trigger distinct, if sometimes overlapping, varieties of historical, epistemic, and aesthetic concern. For our purposes, however, the more important thing is what all four variables have in common. With respect to each, the Supreme Court has declined to require a showing of case-specific prejudice as a precondition of post-trial remedy. If any of the forgoing variables are mistakenly introduced into the trial process, that suffices, by itself, to infect the entire proceeding and warrant remedy – typically, a new trial. To secure post-trial relief, in other words, defendants do *not* have to demonstrate the jury likely succumbed to the forbidden form of propensity-based reasoning. The mere risk is enough.

In the abstract, particularly to readers outside the "criminal procedure world," this may not sound momentous. But it stands in marked contrast to the general thrust of the Court's jurisprudence in this area, particularly from the last three decades, which almost universally puts the onus on defendants to demonstrate that errors in the trial process were not "harmless" – that the errors likely impacted the bottom-line result. With respect to propensity-based reasoning, by contrast, the Court has explicitly taken a more prophylactic approach, focused on inferential risk. The question is not whether the jury *actually did* infer guilt from propensity; nor is the question whether it seems, based on the full record, that the jury *plausibly might have* inferred guilt from propensity. The question is whether the risk existed. If it did, that suffices to establish a prima facie concern, as well as a legal presumption, that defendant's trial process rights were infringed.

SECTION 3

Credibility

INTRODUCTION

Credibility – its definition, assessment process, scope, and content – is foundational to legal fact-finding. The American justice system hinges entirely on the ability of the fact finder (judge or jury) to make judgments about whether to believe testimonial and real evidence.

This section examines the normative assumptions underlying the legal regulation of credibility assessments. An excerpt from Julia Simon-Kerr's article, "Law's Credibility Problem," argues that U.S. law treats credibility as if it were a clear, truth-oriented concept. Instead, Simon-Kerr contends that credibility is an incoherent construct rooted in social stereotypes. The Supreme Court, for example, has used credibility as a vague shorthand for distinct concepts such as persuasiveness, demeanor, honesty, and truth. Without clarity on its precise meaning, credibility becomes a catchall for propensity evidence and a tool to reinforce harmful social stereotypes. Simon-Kerr calls on courts to separate credibility into its distinct components and consciously address its deeply normative underpinnings.

Anna Roberts's chapter, "Teaching Impeachment," directly addresses this "credibility problem" within the context of Federal Rule of Evidence 609, which governs the use of a witness's prior criminal convictions for impeachment. There have been many critiques of Rule 609 and its logic and racial impact, including from Roberts herself. Her focus here, however, is slightly different, and turns to how Rule 609 transfers the discretion to use qualifying prior convictions from the court to the prosecutor. While judges ordinarily act as the gatekeepers of admissibility, under certain provisions of Rule 609, once a prosecutor demonstrates that a prior conviction meets the rule's criteria, the judge has no discretion to exclude it. The stakes for criminal defendants are high, as the use of prior convictions is often dispositive in securing a conviction. Roberts offers a pedagogical path forward that recognizes the competing interests of prosecutors and criminal defendants, allowing students to more readily identify the profound choices inherent in the exercise of prosecutorial discretion.

Law's Credibility Problem

Julia Simon-Kerr[1]

INTRODUCTION

... In a country where facts and truth are deeply contested, it would be surprising if we agreed on what makes a person worthy of belief. The premise that there is such a consensus, however, is at the heart of how credibility is conceptualized in the law. Credibility jurisprudence is centered around the fiction that there is a societal understanding of what (and who) is believable.

American law's credibility problem is not only this fiction but the doctrinal and conceptual neglect that perpetuates it. Although facets of credibility jurisprudence are much-maligned in evidence scholarship, to this point there is no generally accepted definition or operative theory of credibility in our legal system. Even as it is largely taken for granted, credibility has long been a source of confusion and consternation within the law. We lack an understanding of how credibility operates within adjudication. Moreover, the justifications offered for evidentiary rules and practices relating to credibility are conflicting and incoherent. Every year, thousands of cases are resolved on credibility grounds – many with life-altering consequences – despite the confusion at the core of the legal concept.

Recently, the Supreme Court had two occasions to address this confusion. ...

When it agreed to hear [*Dai* and *Patel*], the Court seemed poised to determine what "credibility" and its presumption entail. And sure enough, at oral argument, the Justices engaged at length with essential questions like whether there is a difference between being persuasive and credible; how the story being told by an [asylum] applicant relates to a credibility finding; and how reviewing courts might be able to tell when an immigration judge has made a credibility finding if that finding is not explicit. In its eventual unanimous opinion, however, the Court largely avoided discussing credibility. And what little it did say raised more questions than it answered. Writing for the Court, Justice Gorsuch offered two definitions of credibility: that it means both truthfulness *and* "worth[iness] of belief." As

[1] Excerpted from Julia Simon-Kerr, *Law's Credibility Problem*, 98 WASH. L. REV. 179 (2023).

this Article will show, this definition conjoins two distinct understandings of the term while failing to clarify any of the central definitional concerns.

Six months later, the Court ... once again ... ignored central questions about credibility ... such as whether credibility judgments are inherent in all fact-finding, and if so, whether that means any factual determination "requires the exercise of some discretion ... ." Instead of resolving these central conceptual issues, the Court chose instead to use credibility instrumentally in holding a factual judgment nonreviewable.

These recent cases show a Supreme Court unable or unwilling to decide what a credibility finding looks like, what it signifies, or how such determinations operate in the context of other judicial fact-finding. Still, as they discussed credibility and its many forms during oral argument in *Dai*, the Justices sketched an outline of credibility's legal terrain. This Essay finishes that sketch, undertaking work the Court left undone to reveal a taxonomy of credibility. First, credibility is often used interchangeably with persuasiveness. Second, credibility is commonly defined as worthiness of belief. Third, credibility may refer to anything that relates to whether a witness is being honest. Finally, and more obliquely, comes the claim that credibility is a measure of a witness's *propensity* to lie.

This systemization allows us to see with clarity the ways in which credible *is* different from true. Credibility may depend on how persuasive a witness's story is and how that witness looks when telling it. Or it may reflect whether the other evidence in the case suggests a witness is being honest. Yet finding that a witness tells a persuasive story is not the same as finding that her demeanor makes her believable. Finding that the evidence is consistent with a witness's testimony is not the same as holding that we can infer from her tone of voice that she is worthy of belief. Evidence discussed under the banner of credibility may or may not have to do with truth itself. If a witness looks away when testifying, for example, we may decide she lacks credibility, but her averted gaze has no bearing on her actual propensity for untruth. In short, it is only when we can assess what is going into a credibility judgment that we can recognize constraints on what we can expect to get out of that judgment. Even as credibility judgments may represent a composite of impressions of a witness in the context of other evidence, we can and should understand the inputs to credibility as distinct categories.

It is not clear what consequences Justice Breyer feared [at oral argument] if the Court were to announce that "'credible' is different than 'true.'" This Article contends that the consequences of failing to do so, or to acknowledge the many faces of legal credibility, are profound. First, this willful inattention obscures credibility's all-powerful role in legal analysis and case outcomes, as illustrated in microcosm in *Dai* and *Patel*. Moreover, what findings are captured under "credibility" will determine their reviewability on appeal. Taking a broader view, the very foundation of legal credibility – a big picture agreement about what gives a person the capacity to be believed – may no longer hold. We can only see why this is the case if we do the analytic work that the Court refused to undertake. Without mapping credibility in the law and exposing its component parts, we cannot recognize that its role in our system of law centers on stereotypes of believability. In addition, absent greater conceptual clarity, credibility's amorphousness functions to empower ad hoc decision-making and then shield it from review.

Perhaps most importantly, the taxonomy reveals that under the status quo, credibility will inevitably turn our gaze, in one form or another, to answering one question alone, which is whether a witness is conforming with social expectation. Did she meet the fact-finder's preconceptions of how someone believable should look, sound, or behave? Was her past free of errors that matter in credibility judgments? Did her story resonate with the life experience of the judge? In this way, credibility creates and reinforces social norms; its legal instantiation has become a force for regressive social reproduction over time; and it has become a site of fixed racial bias within the system. Credibility insinuates conceptual value judgments into law that are then treated as findings of fact.

Our current credibility regime is not only unjustified, it is also unjustifiable. The privileged few who wrote the rules might once have agreed about the basic qualities that should contribute to credibility and the price that should be paid by those unable to meet its requirements. That notion has endured even as decades of social upheaval and cultural change have begun to upend the power structures credibility jurisprudence so tenaciously reproduces. These fractures silently underlie the analytic difficulties surfaced by the Supreme Court in *Dai* and *Patel*. They raise questions that the legal community can no longer ignore. …

III. SYSTEMATIZING CREDIBILITY

[This] Article has explored four ways of conceptualizing credibility. It has suggested that they are distinct, and that the variations between them matter. It has also argued that confusion surrounding credibility is both deeply embedded within the law and problematic. This final Part makes a modest proposal. Legal actors can and should be clear what we mean when we talk about credibility. [W]ithout such effort, credibility assessments reduce to intuitions about which witnesses seem worthy of being believed. …

There are four primary referents for credibility. First, credibility may refer to the persuasiveness of a witness's narrative. Second, credibility may reflect our perceptions of the witness's worthiness of being believed based on demeanor or other information about the witness. Third, credibility may be understood as a metric of honesty that indicates whether the other evidence in the case suggests a witness is being honest as opposed to deceptive. And finally, credibility is often used as a synonym for truth in the sense that once we have decided evidence goes to credibility, we suggest that it also has a bearing on truth itself.

One way of grouping these concepts is by using the matrix below. We can think of credibility evidence in terms of whether the information offered is specific to

	Truth Unfocused	Truth Focused
Case Unspecific	• Worthiness of Belief (prior convictions, demeanor)	
Case Specific	• Worthiness of Belief (demeanor) • Persuasiveness (matching fact-finder's assumptions)	• Evidence in the case • Persuasiveness (matching realworld observation)

FIGURE 1 Credibility matrix

the case as opposed to being more broadly about the witness's characteristics. Put another way, we can distinguish evidence focused on whether the witness is untruthful in the moment (case specific) from evidence that might show the witness is generally untrustworthy (case unspecific). Separately, we can ask whether the inputs are, in fact, helpful in identifying true statements in the courtroom (truth focused) or whether they are instead truth unfocused in that they employ unproved or disproved social signifiers of believability.

This matrix illustrates graphically the error in the pervasive claim that all inputs to credibility have a bearing on truth. Simply labeling a piece of evidence relevant to credibility does not render it truth-focused. Whether a piece of evidence is tailored to truth or agnostic to it instead requires careful analysis. As the credibility matrix shows, some concepts may fit into multiple categories, depending on what type of evidence is being adduced and how the fact-finder is using it. If a fact-finder believes that because a witness looked away while testifying, she was telling a lie, that is case-specific but also truth-unfocused in the sense that scientific studies have found there are no reliable demeanor-based indicators of lying. If a fact-finder believes the witness looks untrustworthy, that is case-unspecific as well as truth-unfocused. Similarly, witnesses' prior convictions are both case-unfocused in terms of what they reveal about possible lying on the witness stand and truth-unfocused in the sense that we lack any evidence that those with prior convictions are more likely to lie as witnesses. Of course, these forms of credibility evidence do track preconceptions about what makes a witness worthy of belief.

Persuasiveness requires a similarly nuanced analysis. If a fact-finder is unpersuaded by a witness's story because in his mind someone who had the experience the witness describes would have behaved differently, that is case-specific but may also be truth-unfocused. An example of such a scenario is fact-finders who disbelieve testimony about a sexual assault that involved delayed reporting because of the widespread myth that victims of sexual assault will report immediately. By contrast, if the witness tells a story about a UFO landing in her yard and the fact-finder finds that unpersuasive, that is both case-specific and truth-focused. Finally, it is worth noting that although the intersection of case unspecific and truth focused evidence is empty in the matrix, in previous work I have argued that a limited category of information would fit in that box, at least at present: evidence that the witness has lied on the witness stand previously.

Referring to so many disparate forms of evidence under the umbrella of credibility perpetuates the fiction of a functional, truth-oriented legal construct. It is thus worth a brief thought experiment to ask whether the word "credibility" itself has a useful function in the law. Could we not simply talk instead about narrative persuasiveness, honesty, evidence related to truth and worthiness of belief? The answer is that we could. There is no reason that we must use credibility to represent these concepts. Yet, bringing clarity to this area is not as easy as simply removing a shape-shifting word. As the Supreme Court has ably demonstrated, the concepts that inform legal understandings of credibility are difficult to explicate. Much of credibility jurisprudence treats the whole topic of credibility as a matter of lay intuition or common sense that needs no analysis. Concepts that are understood as related to credibility also interact in complex ways with distinct questions like the difference between questions of fact and questions of law. In the absence of the credibility label, rather than offer clarity on the reasons for disbelieving a witness, courts might simply substitute some other word, like truthfulness, for the disparate package that now falls under the banner of credibility. Perhaps more importantly, any argument that we should eliminate credibility is likely a non-starter within a legal system in which the term is both foundational and taken for granted.

Even without a drastic change in verbiage, however, the system offered here would enable courts, commentators and lawyers themselves to achieve greater clarity about what they mean when they talk about credibility. …

[And a] credibility schema could change the incentives that surround adjudication itself. At present, participants in the system have every incentive to discredit opponents through avenues that sound in worthiness. They are well advised to play on stereotypes of disreputability and weaponize minor yet damning prior convictions. Success in such endeavors may not only provide victory but also largely insulate the victory from meaningful appellate review.

CONCLUSION

Some might object that credibility assessments are rarely so simple as the vignettes offered in the preceding Part. A witness may appear untrustworthy while also offering testimony that is internally inconsistent or doesn't align with the other evidence. If credibility assessment is partly intuition, how is a judge to know which factor mattered most in her assessment of the witness's credibility? Credibility judgments made by jurors are even more opaque. Perhaps disentangling the distinct conceptions of credibility is a fool's errand in a system that has incentivized reasoning as little as possible about credibility. The answer to this objection is that the status quo does have a place in the taxonomy. When a judge is unable or unwilling to articulate why a witness has a credibility deficit, that amounts to a worthiness finding. Without categorizing its origins, the judge is acting on a sense that a particular witness lacks the capacity to be believed.

It is precisely because the status quo contains so many visions of credibility that at present, we must bow to Justice Alito and his dictionaries. Credibility is best understood as something that the law uses to encapsulate "worthiness of belief." As Justice Roberts points out, it is highly subjective. Judges may care about different metrics and care to different degrees when they assess it. It is not independently measurable because each judge may view it differently. And so it is critical that credibility not be mistaken for a measure of truthfulness, reliability, or honesty. Rather, it tells us something about the witness's performance on the stand and possibly about her status in society.

In this time of social dissensus, particularly around truth, it matters that worthiness is our de facto credibility metric. To see this, it is helpful to recognize that credibility judgments are a daily part of civil society. They allow us to entrust people we have never met before with fixing our cars or our bodies and to make other decisions that depend on interpersonal contact with strangers. Attempting to comply with the dictates of a credibility-based society itself creates and reinforces norms. We shape our behavior in ways that we hope will make us seem credible. These performances, in turn, reflect and reinforce norms relating to credibility.

Credibility within the law is also a potent vehicle for reinforcing norms. But because it has been doctrinally centered around certain metrics of worthiness, in particular demeanor and prior convictions, it has served to reproduce outmoded or even problematic social values. Dressing conservatively, speaking in the tones expected, and telling the right story all help a witness be seen as credible in the courtroom. At one time, jurors and judges might have largely agreed on what attributes would give a witness the capacity to be believed. And most legal actors may have accepted until recently that respectful attire and certain speech patterns connoted a truthful witness. But these are no longer defensible claims. Turning to other metrics of credibility is no solution. Even as the carceral state invaded communities of color in unprecedented ways towards the end of the last century and into the current one, the law continues to single out prior convictions as crucial indicators of the propensity for lying. In this way, in addition to reinforcing outdated behavioral norms that are often unreachable by those who are least privileged, credibility has become an unyielding avenue for racial bias within the system.

The law's approach to credibility is, simply put, unjustifiable. The white men who once ruled this country and its courts almost exclusively may once have had a uniform vision of credibility. Indeed, defining the behavior that would accord financial and social credit was a self-conscious project of the founders, who saw in such an enterprise a mechanism for stable and productive business relations. Credibility jurisprudence has not strayed far from these values in the subsequent centuries. We still code crimes of violence as less related to credibility because honor norms once suggested as much, we still impeach women with evidence of prostitution convictions because at one time a dishonorable woman could not have credibility, and we still embrace the notion that one's reputation in the community for truth or falsity is both distillable and worth discussing in a court of law. More broadly, the notion that there is such a status as being worthy of belief was once the foundation of laws that prohibited witnesses from testifying on the basis of race. This certainty that worthiness should form the essence of credibility within the law has been untouched even as the power structures that created it, and that it serves to reproduce, have begun to crack. Credibility jurisprudence is built on this crumbling foundation. That is a painful truth that we ignore at our peril.

It may be easy to insist that all of the evidence in a case that has to do with honesty has to do with credibility. It may be convenient to fold persuasiveness and all its amorphous content into the idea of credibility. It may be helpful to the Court – and the legal world more broadly – to accept the fiction that by inputting measures of a witness's worthiness of belief, we can learn her propensity for truthfulness. But neither the convenience of these false equivalences, nor their durability within our system of law can make them true.

Perhaps now, at long last, in a country facing dissensus about basic concepts like facts and truth, it might be possible to see the attenuated place of credibility in law. If we ever did, we can no longer claim a unitary vision of what gives a person the capacity to be believed. In such a world, it is debatable what the concept of credibility can offer our system of adjudication. At best, it is a useful excuse for judgments in hard cases. At worst, it is a tool for jurists, honestly or not, to skirt the truth.

Teaching Impeachment

Anna Roberts

INTRODUCTION

Recent years have brought exciting new scholarship exposing ways in which conventional law teaching may sanitize and strengthen the carceral state and suggesting that alterations to what we do may bring change far beyond the classroom. Alice Ristroph led the way with "The Curriculum of the Carceral State,"[1] which focused on criminal law teaching. Others, including Daniel Harawa,[2] have explored similar themes in criminal procedure, and Shaun Ossei-Owusu has discussed the importance of similar ideas in evidence law teaching.[3]

This chapter continues the conversation, pairing Ristroph's focus on the need to resist the conventional erasure of the governmental actors whose discretionary decision-making controls people with Ossei-Owusu's suggestion that we ought to scrutinize our evidence law teaching. It examines how our teaching might shape the ways in which prosecutors act and are viewed.

Federal Rule of Evidence 609 and its state law analogs (collectively, "Rule 609") – the rules permitting the impeachment of witnesses with their prior convictions – provide a particularly interesting setting for this examination, in part because various efforts to change or remove them have failed, and thus perhaps changing the ways in which they are used becomes an interesting Plan B. In addition, the federal prosecutorial machine has been a powerful force in resisting change to Federal Rule of Evidence 609 (FRE 609).[4] Finally, while of course the role of lawyers is crucial as regards all evidentiary rules,[5] FRE 609 and many of its state law

1 Alice Ristroph, *The Curriculum of the Carceral State*, 120 Colum. L. Rev. 1631 (2020).

2 Daniel Harawa, *Whitewashing the Fourth Amendment*, 111 Geo. L.J. 923 (2023).

3 Shaun Ossei-Owusu, *Criminal Legal Education*, 58 Am. Crim. L. Rev. 413 (2021).

4 *See, e.g.*, U.S. Dep't of Just., Letter to Fed. Advisory Comm. (Apr. 12, 2024), www.uscourts.gov/sites/default/files/24-ev-d_suggestion_from_doj_-_rule_609.pdf.

5 *See* Washington v. Vaile, No. 37943-III, 2023 WL 3371574, at *2 (Wash. Ct. App. May 11, 2023) ("[O]ur justice system is based on the principle of party presentation, in which the courts, as neutral arbiters, generally decide only the issues raised by the parties.").

analogs include provisions that – uniquely in the federal system at least – omit a judicial oversight role.[6] If a prosecutor proffers a qualifying conviction under one of these provisions, the provisions offer zero judicial ability to keep it out.

While casebooks include many critiques of FRE 609, this chapter will argue that in ways analogous to those suggested by these earlier authors, some forms of critique risk reinforcing harmful aspects of the status quo. This chapter identifies such risks and offers pedagogical suggestions to combat them. The classroom offers exciting possibilities for getting students not just to talk about, but to experience, a range of ways of exercising or ceding the prosecutorial power that pervades the operation and continued existence of these rules.

Section I summarizes some of the main themes of recent literature urging scrutiny of ways in which our teaching may further the carceral state and explains the choice to apply them to prior conviction impeachment. Section II consists of the application of these critiques to prior conviction impeachment. Section III suggests teaching possibilities responsive to these critiques, and Section IV discusses possible objections.

I. RELEVANT LITERATURE

In "The Curriculum of the Carceral State," Ristroph suggested that conventional treatments of criminal law bolster the carceral state. They sanitize the system and emphasize its importance and unique procedural protections. They suggest, for example, that our criminal system and its protections are best represented by the trial, rather than by the daily leveraging of threats and promises that brings about guilty pleas. In their focus on the theories of punishment, these conventional treatments bolster the system and obscure the reality of what is done and why. They erase the individual governmental actors whose discretionary decisions bring rules to life and send people to prison. Among other problems, these treatments leave our students with an inaccurate view of the system.

Ristroph connects what happens in the classroom to what happens beyond it, once our students become prosecutors, judges, and lawmakers. She expresses hope that changes in the classroom may lessen the state of carceral dependency in which we find ourselves.

Others, including Harawa and Ossei-Owusu, have extended Ristroph's critiques to criminal procedure. And Ossei-Owusu has discussed their application to evidence law, mentioning the ways in which conventional treatments of that subject fail in areas that include race, poverty, and gender.

This chapter builds on these works, applying this kind of analysis to the teaching of FRE 609 and its state analogs. These rules potentially allow parties of all sorts to

6 *See* Anna Roberts, *Benched Judges*, 100 Ind. L.J. 535 (2025) (discussing jurisdictions that provide for mandatory admission of convictions).

use – or threaten to use – a witness's convictions against them if they testify, with the purported purpose of attacking their "character for truthfulness." One can argue, however, that their use and threatened use are most devastating when leveled by prosecutors against those facing criminal charges. This is in part because the stakes for that category of witness – a possible criminal conviction, sentence, and numerous other consequences – are generally thought of as the highest. And in part because the impact is harshest, since it is only with this kind of witness that jurors can – and some say are intended to[7] – engage in the kind of forbidden reasoning that involves a journey from "you were convicted of X in the past" to "I want you convicted now."

Prosecutorial power is central to the deployment and continuation of these rules: Prosecutors have the power to decide whether to proffer these convictions; the rules may give judges no power to exclude them once proffered;[8] and prosecutors lobby vigorously against their repeal or reform.[9] Thus erasure or obscuration of the prosecutor's role is a risk worth heeding in our teaching. If we focus on judicial decisions about the appropriateness of admitting proffered convictions, the decision to proffer may escape scrutiny.[10] If we focus on the thinking of rulemakers in enacting these rules, the prosecutorial choice to lobby for them and against their reform may escape scrutiny. If we focus on trial litigation and appeals from trial convictions, the prosecutorial choices to leverage the threat of such impeachment to bring about guilty pleas may escape scrutiny.

Ristroph encourages us to care about erasure and inaccuracy not just because accurate portrayal of the system is a worthy pedagogical goal, but also because a more accurate portrayal might play a part in bringing about change. Change is widely agreed to be necessary in the prior conviction impeachment context.[11] Rule 609 and its implementation have been criticized for, among other things, their incompatibility with relevant social science findings on truthfulness,[12] the

7 *See, e.g.*, Jeffrey Bellin, *Circumventing Congress: How the Federal Courts Opened the Door to Impeaching Criminal Defendants with Prior Convictions*, 42 U.C. DAVIS L. REV. 289, 296 (2008).

8 *See* Roberts, *supra* note 6, at 554.

9 *See, e.g.*, ADVISORY COMM. ON RULES OF EVIDENCE, AGENDA BOOK 117 (Apr. 21, 2017), www.uscourts.gov/sites/default/files/advisory_committee_on_rules_of_evidence_-_spring_2017_meeting_materials.pdf ("The proposal to amend Rule 609, in 2006, was originally designed to limit automatic admissibility of prior convictions for impeachment purposes to those convictions in which false statement was an element of the crime. But eventually (because of DOJ objections) the proposal was narrowed to allow automatic impeachment if it could be 'readily determined' that a finding was made that the witness had lied in committing the crime.").

10 Note, for example, that Fisher says, as regards FRE 609(a)(2), that "because such impeachment evidence is to be 'automatically admitted,' the all-important question is which convictions the rule covers." GEORGE FISHER, EVIDENCE 316 (4th ed., Foundation Press 2022). Another all-important question is whether the prosecutor is going to invoke it.

11 In recognition of the need for change, eleven scholars formed the Coalition for Prior Conviction Impeachment Reform. *See The Coalition*, REFORMING-PCI.ORG, www.reforming-pci.org/the-coalition (last visited Aug. 11, 2025).

12 *See* Julia Simon-Kerr, *Credibility by Proxy*, 85 GEO. WASH. L. REV. 152, 212 (2017).

racial injustices that they perpetrate,[13] and the failure of jury instructions to prevent the unavoidable jury misuse to which the evidence is put.[14] Despite these and other objections, reform has been elusive. The states that most recently made significant changes to their practice did so decades ago,[15] and currently the best chance at reform of the much-maligned federal version is the possibility that the word "substantially" be added to its central balancing test:[16] a balancing test that is applied to convictions that in the views of many should be categorically inadmissible. Given that this is an area where change seems crucial but things seem stuck, the Ristroph idea of furthering change by careful attention to what the next generation of decision-makers is learning seems particularly important.

II. RISKS IN TEACHING RULE 609

This section analyzes risks that we might usefully guard against in our teaching of Rule 609. It also identifies moments of opportunity for guarding against those risks. In identifying moments of opportunity, it uses as an example the casebook that I have adopted – Fisher's *Evidence* – which, among its many strengths, includes materials that provide a useful springboard for the kind of approach suggested here.

Obscuring the Role(s) of Prosecutors

A teaching approach that focuses on judicial opinions and rules may set students up more naturally for discussions of the behavior of judges and rulemakers than for discussions of the behavior of prosecutors.[17] A judicial opinion tends to focus the

13 *See, e.g.*, Montré Carodine, *"The Mis-Characterization of the Negro": A Race Critique of the Prior Conviction Impeachment Rule*, 84 IND. L.J. 521 (2009).

14 *See* Theodore Eisenberg and Valerie P. Hans, *Taking a Stand on Taking the Stand: The Effect of a Prior Conviction on the Decision to Testify and on Trial Outcomes*, 94 CORNELL L. REV. 1353 (2009).

15 *See* Anna Roberts, *Conviction by Prior Impeachment*, 96 B.U. L. REV. 1977 (2016) (describing Hawai'i, Kansas, and Montana, which enacted their reforms in the 1960s and 1970s).

16 This activity began with a proposal by Jeffrey Bellin to abrogate FRE 609, then shrunk to consideration of abrogation of 609(a)(1), and then shrunk again to the current proposal, which is to add a "substantially" to 609(a)(1)(B), just before "outweighs." ADVISORY COMM. ON RULES OF EVIDENCE, AGENDA BOOK 103–36 (Nov. 8, 2024), www.uscourts.gov/sites/default/files/2024-11_evidence_rules_committee_meeting_agenda_book_final_10-24.pdf.

17 While a full exploration of other evidence teaching materials is beyond this chapter's scope, note that Jeffrey Bellin's casebook includes materials that fit very nicely with the ideas expressed in this chapter. *See, e.g.*, JEFFREY BELLIN, THE LAW OF EVIDENCE 200 (2d ed. 2025) (introducing readers to ethical rules applicable to prosecutors and asking whether prosecutors "in a jurisdiction where courts seem to be incorrectly interpreting controlling authority, such as Rule 404(b) or Rule 609, to the detriment of criminal defendants" have "an obligation to take advantage of such caselaw or to refrain from invoking it"); *id.* at 192–4 (mentioning the Advisory Committee's 2024 consideration of a proposal to eliminate Rule 609(a)(1) and including an extract from the Department of Justice's letter,

mind more on the judge's reasoning about the evidentiary rule, its soundness, and its application, than on the choices to proffer that may have led to the opinion.[18] Examination of an evidentiary rule may lead more readily to consideration of its soundness than to consideration of the lobbying that helped to bring it about or to obstruct its reform. Fisher lays the groundwork for consideration of the powerful role of the Department of Justice (DOJ) in shaping rules of evidence. In discussing some of the process that led to Federal Rules of Evidence 413, 414, and 415, he includes a quoted passage noting that "the only supporters of the Rules were representatives of the Department of Justice … ."[19] One could usefully build on that reference in the context of Rule 609.

Teaching approaches that are silent regarding the role(s) of prosecutors may leave out important information about who has power and how they use it. Without prosecutorial choices to proffer, the impeachment of those facing criminal charges could not occur. And without the DOJ's interventions at the federal level, FRE 609 would look different;[20] the same may be true of prosecutors at the state level.[21] Teaching approaches that are silent about litigation choices may leave students with the impression that of course the prosecutorial role is to push for the admission of every possible conviction – it goes without saying. Teaching approaches that are silent about prosecutorial lobbying may leave students with the impression that neutral rules get crafted in the clouds and then drop down from the sky, leaving prosecutors with the task of adapting to them.

Preparing Students for Only One Prosecutorial Approach

The prosecutor is said to have an ethical and constitutional "duty to do justice," which is something distinct from figuring out how to "tack as many skins of victims as possible to the wall."[22] It may be true that only a course on, say, prosecutorial ethics, or prosecutorial practice, can delve into the nuances of this concept. But

before advising readers that "[t]he DOJ's arguments won out with the Committee, which backed off the effort"); *id.* at 74 (including a Problem that asks students whether it is unethical for litigators, including prosecutors, to introduce evidence that a judge allows but that is likely to be used by jurors for improper purposes).

18 This may be a particular risk in evidence law, given the emphasis on the judicial role as being one of focusing on questions that the parties bring to the court.

19 FISHER, *supra* note 10, at 245. For details on the role of a DOJ employee in "writing and promoting [Rules 413 and 414], and scripting comments for the legislative sponsors," *see* Aviva Orenstein, *Deviance, Due Process, and the False Promise of Federal Rule of Evidence 403*, 90 CORNELL L. REV. 1487, 1504 n. 60 (2005).

20 *See* ADVISORY COMM., *supra* note 9, at 117 (revealing one example of DOJ as limitation on reform).

21 *See* Richard Lempert, *The Economic Analysis of Evidence Law: Common Sense on Stilts*, 87 VA. L. REV. 1619, 1627 (2001) ("[I]s it politically feasible to ban felony impeachment? In most jurisdictions, no. Prosecutors would scream too loudly, for convictions would be harder to achieve. When prosecutors scream loudly, they are usually heard by legislators.").

22 Donnelly v. DeChristoforo, 416 U.S. 637, 648–69 (1974) (Douglas, J., dissenting).

if one's teaching says nothing about the prosecutorial duty to do justice, one may wonder how easy it is for budding prosecutors to learn of it, and incorporate it into their every decision, at a later stage. Fisher includes material about the distinct role of government attorneys.[23] One can usefully build on it by discussing the prosecutorial duty to do justice.

Fisher also offers introductory material at the start of the book. Things that are not strictly evidence but that provide context so that students will be oriented to the evidentiary work ahead. One might usefully supplement it with an introduction to prosecutorial ethics – a topic that students may not have encountered in earlier courses, as Ristroph's work suggests. One could include in this discussion something about prosecutorial discretion to proffer or to refrain from proffering, lest that set of choices by that set of decision-makers be erased.

Inclusion of this kind of consideration will enrich discussion of Problems that instruct students to lay out "the best arguments on each side." Once students have a sense that the best prosecutorial argument may mean something other than the argument most likely to achieve or protect a conviction, the conversation may become more interesting and useful. Without that kind of information, there may be nothing to counteract the kinds of assumptions that students may have brought with them: that the job of the prosecutor is to "win," and winning is to get a conviction, and that in service of that goal they must argue for the admission of their desired evidence, and oppose whatever gets said by the defense, even if their own is the weaker argument, and indeed may not even pass the laugh test. Without that kind of information, our work on Problems may merely help our students develop stronger and stronger argumentative muscles; we may get them more and more comfortable with pressing the weaker argument, and with finding a way to crush Goliath, even if he tries weapon after weapon, each stronger than the last. If they hear arguments from the other side that are persuasive, our students might otherwise conclude, attorneys of all types must simply work harder to rebut them.

One of Fisher's Problems, in which students dive into the phenomenon of prosecutors proffering rap lyrics,[24] offers a useful springboard for this kind of discussion. The students are asked for the best arguments "for and against admission."[25] This phrasing usefully diverts from asking about the best arguments "on both sides." It thus refuses to merge best prosecutorial argument with best argument for admission. This offers a nice opportunity for professors to distinguish on the one hand what the prosecutor might say in support of admission – the Teacher's

[23] *See* FISHER, *supra* note 10, at 1035–40 (including judicial opinion that explores ways in which a government attorney's duties differ from those of a private attorney, in the context of attorney–client privilege).

[24] *Id.* at 189.

[25] *Id.*

Manual mentions an argument that rather than being pure propensity evidence the rap lyrics shed light on "motive and intent" – and on the other hand what the prosecution *ought* to say, which might be that they concede the evidence's inadmissibility. If we miss this pedagogical opportunity, our students might assume that the "best" prosecutorial argument about this evidence would necessarily be that it goes to "motive or intent," even though such an argument is meritless.[26]

Thus, this is a good moment at which to flag the prosecutorial duty to do justice, rather than simply eliciting the best arguments for and against admission and then moving on. If we merely praise those who came up with the prosecutorial argument invoking "motive or intent," we encourage the flexing and strengthening of muscles that press on toward conviction along routes that are forbidden. We praise the refusal to be swayed by arguments on the other side, arguments that might invoke the chilling of free expression; the denigration of rap as something less than art; or the compounding of racial disparities and stereotypes.[27] In his Teacher's Manual, when discussing other topics, Fisher offers prompts such as "at this point, you might remind the students about X … " Similarly, at this juncture, we might usefully remind our students of the duty to do justice, and ask them how, if at all, it might affect prosecutorial approaches to this evidence. Such a prompt might open up discussion of whether there are defense arguments that could persuade prosecutors and budding prosecutors to alter their thinking and stance. The more that we strengthen our students' muscles of automatic combat, train them to treat what they hear as things to be rebutted rather than weighed, and encourage them to hone their stance as crusaders for conviction, regardless of whether their argument has a firm foundation, the harder it may become for budding prosecutors to step back, and consider conceding.

Law schools train not only future prosecutors but also future legal scholars. If it is true that evidence classrooms tend not to delve into the question of how the duty to do justice shapes evidentiary choices, whether at the trial or appellate level, perhaps it becomes less surprising that there is relatively little legal scholarship on that kind of question. If as teachers we fail to dive into the applicability of these questions to the Rule 609 context, perhaps it becomes less surprising that legal scholars tend to describe Rule 609 as a "windfall" for prosecutors,[28] and something that makes prosecutors' jobs easier,[29] apparently neglecting the question of whether doing justice, and thus doing their jobs well, might not sometimes be separable from achieving convictions.

[26] George Fisher, Teacher's Manual for Evidence 119 (4th ed. 2024) ("Saying his violent character reveals the defendant's motive or intent to kill is pure propensity reasoning").

[27] Fisher's casebook usefully includes materials that provide fodder for these kinds of arguments.

[28] *See* Gene R. Nichol, Jr., *Prior Crime Impeachment of Criminal Defendants: A Constitutional Analysis of Rule 609*, 82 W. Va. L. Rev. 391, 421 (1980).

[29] *See* Robert D. Dodson, *What Went Wrong with FRE Rule 609: A Look at How Jurors Really Misuse Prior Conviction Evidence*, 48 Drake L. Rev. 1, 44 (1999).

Obscuring the Use of Impeachment as a Threat

One of the forms of sanitization of the criminal system that Ristroph identifies in criminal law teaching is an obscuring of the dominance of the plea and a misleading emphasis on the trial and its attendant standard of proof beyond a reasonable doubt. We are at risk of doing the same in our Rule 609 teaching, and in evidence law more generally, if our materials present evidentiary questions as being addressed solely at the trial, and the post-trial appeal, stage. Arguably, Rule 609 has most impact when used by prosecutors to get people to waive testimony and trial, and yet when we read appellate opinions we might get the sense that everyone goes to trial despite their convictions and everyone testifies. That sense might be strengthened when we learn that in the federal system and many of our states, you have to testify if you want to appeal an adverse prior conviction impeachment ruling. Rule 609 can shape plea discussions as much as it shapes trial, and yet teaching approaches that focus on appeals from a trial outcome may not devote any time, let alone any practical exercises, to this issue.

III. TEACHING POSSIBILITIES

Ristroph has done important work in urging us to strive for accuracy in our classrooms. But perhaps there is room too for some aspiration – for some striving toward, or experimenting with, models of prosecutorial behavior that are responsive to reality, to defense arguments, and to the deep questions surrounding what a duty to do justice might require or permit. In that spirit, and motivated by a desire to combat the risks mentioned above, this section suggests some teaching exercises that one might try. The idea would not be to do them all, but to see if any of them appeal, either as written, or with one's own variations. To prompt some thinking about differing approaches, and to emphasize the exploratory nature of the suggestions, some exercises include bullet pointed variations.

Prosecutor as Adherent of the Duty To Do Justice at the Trial Stage

One simulation exercise could, instead of putting students in adversarial roles, with "the best arguments" understood as those most likely to defeat the other side, put them all in role as prosecutors working together to prepare for trial, so that perhaps they have a stronger chance of figuring out the best arguments. The students could be told something about the existence of "the duty to do justice," and could be asked to think through how to approach the fact that the person on trial may testify and has convictions that might qualify under Rule 609. They are to discuss whether to proffer the convictions. One or more of the following additional details could be added:

- Prosecution witness(es) who have qualifying convictions.
- A jurisdiction where the judge lacks discretion to exclude proffered convictions.

- Prosecutors on notice of social science data suggesting that jury instructions do not cure the risk of unfair prejudice caused by prior conviction impeachment.
- Prosecutors on notice of the lack of social science support for the concept of a "character for truthfulness."
- Indications that the previous convictions may have been the product of racially motivated traffic stops.[30]
- Bosses who reward convictions.
- Bosses who ran on a "progressive" platform.

Prosecutor as Thoughtful Wielder of Power in Negotiation

This kind of exercise would put students in role as negotiators, discussing as prosecutors and defenders choices that the prosecutor will have to make, such as whether to proffer the convictions of the person on trial. Depending on professor preference, the defense might hold the view that if the convictions are admitted, it may make no sense for their client to testify or perhaps even to go to trial. Both sides would have been taught the basics of their ethical and constitutional duties. Perhaps both sides would have been given Federal Rule of Evidence 102 as a source that might be relevant (a rule that espouses values that include fairness, truth, and justice).[31]

Prosecutor as Adherent of Duty To Do Justice at the Appellate Stage

This kind of exercise would put the students in an appellate stance. The students might be briefed on a trial in which the prosecution behavior could be said to reek of "overkill."[32] The students might be assigned the role of appellate prosecutors and told the basics of their ethical and constitutional duties. They would then be asked to prepare their stance, vis-à-vis both whether error occurred and whether, if so, it was harmless. A real-life case, in which convictions that were admitted threatened unfair prejudice, could provide source material.[33] The students might also be given an amicus brief providing information on arguments about the lack of legitimate probative value and the risks (such as unfair prejudice) that attend such impeachment.[34]

30 For inspiration, *see* United States v. Leviner, 31 F.Supp.2d 23, 33 (D. Mass. 1998).

31 Fed. R. Evid. 102 ("These rules should be construed so as to administer every proceeding fairly, eliminate unjustifiable expense and delay, and promote the development of evidence law, to the end of ascertaining the truth and securing a just determination.").

32 *See* People v. Castro, 186 Cal. App. 3d 1211, 1216 (1986) (conceding that "it is conceivable that the use of five prior burglary convictions to impeach a defendant in a new trial for a new burglary offense could be termed 'prosecutorial overkill' and an abuse of judicial discretion").

33 *See, e.g.*, State v. Aranda, 372 Or. 363, 366–8 (2024) (mentioning that Mr. Aranda's two first-degree sexual abuse convictions had been admitted for impeachment at his first-degree rape trial).

34 *See, e.g.*, Brief of Amici Curiae Coalition for Prior Conviction Impeachment Reform, et al., State v. Aranda, 2023 WL 1966904 (Or. 2023) (No. S069641).

Prosecutor as Thoughtful Crafter of Office Policy

Budding prosecutors may overestimate the extent to which they, when starting out, possess discretion on issues that matter to them. It might be useful to include a simulation that focuses on policy making by those heading the office. In role as policy makers, the students could discuss what stances the office ought to take regarding prior conviction impeachment: e.g. maximization, maintenance, quiet desuetude, active lobbying for abolition, etc. As in the first exercise, freeing them from an adversarial stance may create more space to analyze what justice might require or permit in this area. Perhaps the prompt tells them that if they do not feel equipped to decide, they could put together a set of questions that they would want answers to before deciding, or the values or goals that should guide them. Some of the following ingredients could be included:

- They work in an office sometimes termed "progressive," and they have come across Steven Zeidman's article urging that "progressive prosecutors" should abandon prior conviction impeachment.[35]
- They have heard of a sister office that abandoned peremptory challenges,[36] a practice arguably sharing many of the same controversial features.[37]
- An intern went rogue and gave them a dossier of things they really "had to read," including one or more of the following: data on the inability of jury instructions to cure the unfair prejudice, statistics on racial disparities compounded by this practice, John Blume's study on the silencing of innocent people (exonerated after conviction) who faced the threat of prior conviction impeachment if they testified,[38] Justin Murray's article urging that prosecutors be color-conscious,[39] and Jasmine Gonzales Rose's work suggesting that "unfair prejudice" should be read as encompassing "racial prejudice."[40]

[35] Steven Zeidman, *Some Modest Proposals for a Progressive Prosecutor*, 5 UCLA Crim. Just. L. Rev. 23, 43 (2021).

[36] *See* Nicole Rinconeno et al., Striking Peremptory Challenges in Jury Trials: Costs, Benefits, and the Restoration of Rts, https://dcjusticelab.org/wp-content/uploads/2022/09/Striking-Peremptory-Challenges-in-Jury-Trials.pdf (highlighting Arlington example).

[37] *See* Anna Roberts, *Defense Counsel's Cross Purposes: Prior Conviction Impeachment of Prosecution Witnesses*, 87 Brook. L. Rev. 1225, 1238 (2022) (stating that peremptory challenges are "known to be used for prohibited purposes and in a way that endorses stereotypes and compounds racial bias").

[38] John H. Blume, *The Dilemma of the Criminal Defendant with a Prior Record: Lessons from the Wrongfully Convicted*, 5 J. Empirical Legal Stud. 477, 491 (2008).

[39] Justin Murray, *Reimagining Criminal Prosecution: Toward a Color-Conscious Professional Ethic*, 49 Am. Crim. L. Rev. 1541 (2012).

[40] Jasmine Gonzales Rose, *Toward a Critical Race Theory of Evidence*, 101 Minn. L. Rev. 2243, 2257 (2017).

Prosecutor as Thoughtful Policy Shaper Beyond the Office

As suggested above, one risks sanitizing or obscuring the nature of the system if one holds back from mentioning the DOJ's role in shaping – and resisting reform to – the Federal Rules of Evidence. Perhaps also if one fails to raise the possibility that evidence law is often shaped to facilitate criminal convictions (the "rationale behind the rationale," as described in one of Fisher's cases[41]). To address this, one could place the students in role as DOJ lawyers amidst the most recent debate about what to do with FRE 609.[42] Perhaps they are to read the submissions suggesting reform and debate how to respond.[43] And again, if they are uncertain, they could be asked to collate the questions that they would need answered in order to be able to form a position, or the values or goals that should guide them. Perhaps instead they are given the DOJ's actual response and told that a colleague drafted it and asked them for their feedback.[44]

IV. DISCUSSION OF POSSIBLE OBJECTIONS

Distraction

One could object that this kind of exercise takes time away from the core project in the typical evidence course, namely teaching one's students the Federal Rules of Evidence. That these questions are more appropriately explored in a prosecutorial clinic or professional responsibility class. That they will not help with the Bar Exam. That one lacks time to muddy the project of learning the rules by considering things like the duty to do justice, because one has to do the real work.

One could respond by asking what the real work is, with things as currently arranged. Building the kinds of muscles that arguably have helped build the carceral state? One could also respond that it is easy to find examples of casebook authors who choose to include context. Fisher introduces us to state cases, for example, when addressing Federal Rules of Evidence 413 to 415, and thus shows us the possibility of different regimes and sheds some light on how we got to where we are. So too the exercises mentioned here would add important context, help explain how we got here, and spur consideration of the existence and possible merits of other approaches. Fisher's treatment of Federal Rules of Evidence 413 to 415 also lays groundwork

41 Fisher, *supra* note 10, at 235 (*quoting* Lannan v. State, 600 N.E. 2d 1334, 1337 (Ind. 1992)).

42 For information on the debate *see supra* note 16.

43 *See, e.g.*, Coalition for Prior Conviction Impeachment Reform Letter to Fed. Advisory Comm. (Apr. 11, 2024), www.uscourts.gov/sites/default/files/24-ev-b_suggestion_from_coalition_for_prior_conviction_impeachment_reform_-_rule_609.pdf.

44 *See* U.S. Dep't of Justice Letter to Fed. Advisory Comm. (Apr. 12, 2024), www.uscourts.gov/sites/default/files/24-ev-d_suggestion_from_doj_-_rule_609.pdf.

for the question of when prosecutors should lobby for or against evidence rules or rule changes. In teaching Rule 609, one can make that question explicit.

One could also respond that these exercises are designed to take students right into the heart of the live issues relating to Rule 609 – when, if ever, it should be used, and why; and whether it should be repealed or reformed and, if so, in favor of what. Prosecutors hold enormous power on all these big questions, and thus getting our students talking about prosecutorial decisions highlights all the major potential areas of change.

Sanitization

One might object that some or all of this work – even while it attempts to push back against forms of sanitization of the system – performs its own sanitizing. If, as Paul Butler claims, the duty to do justice is just "words on paper,"[45] perhaps one sanitizes by having one's students think and act as if it is a real, robust motivator, and indeed one that motivates prosecutors (including line prosecutors!) to take the time to learn about scholarly writings on racial disparities, the meaning of character, or exonerees. Perhaps if one walks into a typical prosecutor's office one finds tacked to the wall not the works of John Blume or Jasmine Gonzales Rose but rather just a collection of skins and one should not attempt to cover it up.

There are a few ways to respond. As suggested above, conjuring bosses who really do just want convictions might do something to guard against an overly rosy presentation of the prosecutor's office, and to remind aspiring prosecutors that the line of a prosecutor's discretion may be very limited. Again, as suggested above, one might also respond that it is valuable to pair the goal of showing the system as it is with some inclusion of aspirational moments and activities, as long as they come with appropriate caveats. Practice in striving toward aspirational goals may make it easier to do the same in the workplace.

An additional sanitization concern would be that through emphasizing the duty to do justice and suggesting that evidentiary decisions can fulfill that duty one is bolstering the idea that our contemporary U.S. systems of prosecution are equipped to bring justice. For those who see the racist and classist history of our criminal system casting a shadow over – or vibrantly alive and infusing – that system, the idea may not pass the laugh test, and its reinforcement may seem a gross derogation of ethical and pedagogical responsibilities. These concerns may merit at the least a caveat, and a discussion of what justice might mean, or be limited to, in this context. Just as one should perhaps speak, in the criminal system, only of *relative* leniency,[46] perhaps here too one should speak only of relative justice, in an

[45] Paul Butler, *Gideon's Muted Trumpet*, N.Y. TIMES (Mar. 17, 2013), www.nytimes.com/2013/03/18/opinion/gideons-muted-trumpet.html (last accessed March 13, 2026).

[46] *See* Anna Roberts, *Criminal Terms*, 107 MINN. L. REV. 1495, 1528 (2023).

acknowledgment that neither continuation nor suspension of criminal prosecution could represent the fuller version for which one might long.

Bias

One might level a variety of bias-related objections against the kinds of exercises mentioned above. One might be that all this focus on prosecution mirrors a disparity that one may find reflected elsewhere in law school.

A possible response is that even while prosecutors' multiple roles create uniquely interesting, important, and unexplored opportunities for debate, one could construct analogous exercises for defense counsel. As regards defense counsel too it would be good if an evidence casebook told us the basics upfront about what it means for the defense to make "the best arguments." That might help lay a foundation for a discussion when we get to Rule 609 of why the answer may not always be obvious. In prior work, I hinted at one potential issue on which such exercises or discussions could focus, when I wrote about the potential dilemma faced by the progressive defense attorney whose duty to advocate vigorously for their client might get complicated if it means deploying convictions against a complaining witness in ways that might have regressive consequences.[47]

Manipulation

One might argue that when in the classroom one has duties to one's students that trump what one might view as duties, desires, or commitments to help those beyond its walls. Such an argument might assert that if part of what is suggested above involves efforts to care not solely about one's students but about those who might be locked up by one's students the professor has violated their pedagogical duties and is now not serving their students but manipulating them in service of societal goals. Perhaps one responds that if one is helping prosecutors understand the law and do their jobs well, that must encompass an understanding of the duty to do justice, and that the doing of justice necessarily encompasses an understanding of, and caring about, those affected.

Frustration

A related objection might be that frustration at all the blocked avenues of change might be leading those intrigued by these exercises to do to the students what they are unable to do to others. That whereas judges, prosecutors, defense attorneys, rulemakers, and policy advocates are free to walk away or ignore, students represent a somewhat captive audience on which to vent one's frustration and at which to

[47] *See* Roberts, *supra* note 37, at 1242–3.

launch one's diatribes. That as if they were puppets, one can assign them roles and moves and that one might be drawn to do this because one cannot do it to those who currently hold the power. Even when through one's scholarship and advocacy one has made multi-pronged arguments that strike their authors as persuasive, judges and prosecutors can punt to the legislature,[48] and DOJ officials can rebut one's arguments in a document that betrays misunderstandings of the law,[49] and there is no easy remedy. But with students, one can offer correction, control the dialogue, frame the issue, declare the takeaways, establish the criteria for success, and one may race to do all this, rather than engaging in other perhaps more fruitful pedagogical enterprises, because one is frustrated elsewhere.

One response is that all the exercises mentioned above are squarely compatible with – and indeed should demand – discussion of all relevant viewpoints, and that ideally the professor is trying to help everyone in the classroom to understand all the potentially persuasive arguments on various sides, adding to the conventional debate rather than seeking to narrow it.

Backfire

A final objection might be that it is unrealistic to hope that one can achieve any sort of desirable change through this kind of teaching technique. Perhaps all of this just gives future prosecutors a whole range of better ways to overpower the defense at trial, on appeal, and in negotiation. A whole new range of areas in which they become adept at developing winning arguments, whether on the limitations of social science, the vulnerabilities of "wrongful convictions" data, or the intractability of racial disparities. That the mindset potentially in place before law school even begins – that litigation is about arguing against the other side, even if you have nothing good to work with – is by the time of this upper-level class too thoroughly honed to be unsettled.

A possible response is that the arguments in favor of trying this approach strengthen when one observes just how blocked other possible areas of ameliorative change seem to be: Advocacy and scholarly efforts to persuade judges, prosecutors, and rulemakers have not worked, at least for the last few decades. In that context perhaps one can make a stronger claim for the necessity and validity of trying to inspire critical engagement among the next generation.

A final possible response is that risk should not be a bar to this or some other kind of critical approach. If one teaches Rule 609 uncritically – if one presents the

48 This happened in both the government's oral argument and the majority opinion in *State v. Aranda*. State v. Aranda, 372 Or. 363, 386-7 (2024).

49 *See* U.S. Dep't of Just., Letter to Fed. Advisory Comm., *supra* note 4. The first misunderstanding is contained in the assertion that "a jury is entitled to hear relevant evidence, see FRE 401." The second is the letter's mentioning with approval a case proffered as an example of prior conviction impeachment, when it appears instead to have involved impeachment by contradiction.

rule and its justifications, and the cases and their approaches, uncritically – one risks quietly endorsing a huge range of harmful and unsupported assumptions, whose adoption by anyone in that classroom could encourage and bolster harmful practices and beliefs affecting the entire span of the criminal system and all those affected by it. Those beliefs include that there are people who are inherently and predictably untruthful, and that convictions will help reveal them, because some convictions reveal people to be liars, and some reveal them as having willfully flouted the rules of society and as possessing a propensity to do so. That convictions – of course! – mean crime commission, and that a lack of convictions means none. Believe all that and you might well want our criminal system as it is, because of its accuracy and its ability to save us – the innocent and truthful – from the willful law breakers and from the liars.

CONCLUSION

It is tempting to partition our lives as academics into the three portions on which we are (separately) evaluated: scholarship, teaching, and service (understood as embracing advocacy). Indeed, some professors making radical proposals in their advocacy may, it turns out, be "stuck" in rather regressive teaching patterns, and perhaps even writing about the carceral state in unwittingly regressive ways.[50] But if what we send out into the world as scholarship and service is failing to achieve what seem like crucial goals, it may be worth considering the extent to which the teaching done by us and our colleagues may be a promising area to examine. It is not a pedagogical distraction to include in our teaching a focus on the crucial decision-points faced by prosecutors with respect to such evidentiary rules as Rule 609. Arguably this rule (like others) sets prosecutors up for trial victory, and they may lack incentives to step back from that launching pad and examine the extent to which victory, narrowly defined, is consistent with their ethical and constitutional duties. They may lack incentives to participate in, or lead, efforts at reforming or repealing those rules. Offering encouragement and practice in the classroom may help create those kinds of incentives, that muscle memory, or at least that openness to talking and listening before launching.

50 *See* Roberts, *supra* note 46.

SECTION 4

Sex Trials

INTRODUCTION

This section addresses the regulation of sexual propensity evidence in sex trials, examining its two contrasting rules:

- The Shield (Federal Rule of Evidence 412), which protects the alleged victim.
- The Sword (Federal Rules of Evidence 413–15), which is wielded against the defendant.

The Shield (Federal Rule of Evidence 412)

One of the earliest reforms to the newly enacted Federal Rules of Evidence concerned the treatment of evidence regarding sexual propensity. Federal Rule 412, often referred to as the Rape Shield Law, was promulgated in 1978 (just three years after the Federal Rules of Evidence were codified). The rule was a direct response to the feminist movements of the 1960s and 1970s.

Before Rule 412, under common law, defendants in sexual assault and rape cases could (and often would) introduce propensity evidence of a victim's sexual history (either past behavior or reputation for being "unchaste"). This evidence was used to argue that the victim likely consented to sex or to impeach the victim's credibility. This practice was based on highly gendered, discriminatory norms of chastity that often placed the victim's character on trial rather than the defendant's actions.

Rule 412 established a general prohibition on admitting evidence of an alleged victim's sexual behavior or predisposition, subject only to a few narrow exceptions (e.g., evidence proving that someone other than the defendant was the source of physical evidence, or specific instances of sexual behavior with the accused to prove consent). Policy goals included protecting victims from embarrassment, harassment, and sexual stereotyping during the trial process and removing barriers to reporting and prosecuting sex crimes.

Two excerpts challenge the extent to which these policy goals have been met. First, Bennett Capers in "Real Women, Real Rape" argues that rape shield laws unintentionally reinforce biased assumptions and the "chastity" requirement they were meant to abolish. By suppressing sexual history evidence, the rules may subtly communicate to jurors that only "good girls" deserve protection. This can turn complainants into "cardboard cutouts," benefiting only those who fit the ideal rape script (young, white, chaste women). Meanwhile, women of color and others outside this mold suffer from "expressive message failure," as jurors fall back on preexisting racist and sexist stereotypes.

Second, Julia Simon-Kerr in "Unchaste and Incredible: The Use of Gendered Conceptions of Honor in Impeachment" traces how American evidence law historically tied women's credibility to their sexual chastity, regularly allowing female witnesses to be impeached with their sexual history based on the cultural belief that "unchaste" women were also untruthful. She demonstrates that even after the rape shield laws were passed, remnants of this logic persist, showing the deep entrenchment of gendered notions of honor in evidence law.

The Sword (Federal Rules of Evidence 413–15)

Moving from the shield to the sword, Caroline Davidson's chapter, "Feminist Take(s) on Other (Sexual) Bad Acts," examines Rules 413, 414, and 415, which were introduced later as part of the Violent Crime Control and Law Enforcement Act of 1994. These rules created a special exception, exclusively for sex crimes, to the general ban on character/propensity evidence (Rule 404). Rule 413 allows evidence of a defendant's commission of another sexual assault offense in a current sexual assault case; Rule 414 applies the same exception to evidence of prior child molestation in a current child molestation case; and Rule 415 extends Rules 413 and 414 to civil cases where they are based on the defendant's alleged commission of sexual assault or child molestation.

Davidson argues that the policy justifications for these rules are shaky when analyzed through a feminist lens. While the rules were a political response to public accounts of high recidivism rates and the need to protect people from "serial rapists and child molesters," they lack support on a feminist foundation. Davidson contends that these rules, for instance, perpetuate gendered stereotypes of "bad men" and "good women," exacerbate racialized and class disparities, and risk wrongful convictions by encouraging juries to convict based on a person's history rather than on proof beyond a reasonable doubt for the crime charged.

Real Women, Real Rape

Bennett Capers[1]

INTRODUCTION

There are several reasons to find rape shield laws troubling. From the point of view of many defense attorneys and civil libertarians, rape shield laws, by curtailing a defendant's ability to offer evidence of a victim's prior sexual conduct, unfairly circumscribe a defendant's Sixth Amendment right to confront witnesses and present relevant evidence in his defense. To make matters worse, many jurisdictions have now coupled rape shield laws with what amounts to rape sword laws – laws that specifically allow the prosecution to introduce evidence of a defendant's sexual history as proof of his character or propensity. Defense attorneys and civil libertarians would argue that these rules not only tip the scales against innocence. They also frustrate the truth-finding process, undermine the notion of innocent until proven guilty, and result in miscarriages of justice.

For entirely different reasons, rape shield proponents have also found rape shield laws wanting. Despite the best intentions of feminist scholars, victim rights advocates, and prosecutors, rape shield laws have failed to protect the privacy of women, put an end to what historically amounted to a chastity requirement, and level the playing field at trial. From their perspective, the rape shield laws are so riddled with exceptions that they amount to sieves.

Nearly thirty-five years after passage of the federal rape shield law and a host of state cognates, these problems alone should be enough to raise questions about the continuing viability of rape shield laws. This Article calls attention to two other problems. Though the issues raised here can be traced to the very enactment of rape shield laws, for the most part they have remained hidden, unnoticed, and unremarked on. The first problem concerns the expressive message communicated by rape shield laws. Though rarely made explicit, the message to jurors sitting on rape trials is that they should assume that the complainant is a virgin, or if not a virgin, at least notionally a good girl, and thus deserving of the law's protection. Because

1 Excerpted from Bennett Capers, *Real Women, Real Rape*, 60 UCLA L. Rev. 826 (2013).

of our rape shield laws, any suggestion that women may lead healthy sexual lives is quietly pushed to the side and corseted. More problematic, any suggestion that all women deserve the law's protection, including women who are sexually active, is suppressed. Instead, women are conscripted as idealized women – as cardboard cutout women – chaste and pure and simple. As such, the first problem is not that rape shields do not work. The first problem is the effects that attend rape shields when they succeed.

The second problem with rape shield laws stems from the first but, because it results from what I call expressive message failure, tugs in a different direction. While the normative message of rape shield laws is that rape victims are good girls and thus deserving of the law's protection, this message can fail if it conflicts with preexisting rape scripts: those assumptions we hold about what rapists look like, what constitutes rape, and most important here, what rape victims look like. If the supposedly ideal rapist remains a male stranger who jumps out of the bushes, preferably black and wielding a knife, there is also a supposedly ideal rape victim: young, attractive, white, female, and chaste. In practice, this means that while some women might ostensibly benefit from rape shield law's expressive message, this advantage does not extend to other women who, because of race or class or some other trait, do not fit the ideal victim script. In these cases, when a rape shield law conceals evidence of a complainant's sexual history, jurors may fall back on default assumptions diametrically at odds with the rape shield law's expressive message. In short, if the question is, "Are rape shields good for all women?" the answer seems to be a resounding no. …

III. REAL VICTIMS

The problems discussed so far, while consequential, are at bottom problems at the margins. Far more troubling are two other problems. The first concerns the expressive message Rule 412 communicates, which is one that privileges, of all things, chastity. The second concerns what happens when rape victims do not fit the traditional rape script, that set of ideas we have about what rape looks like, what rapists look like, and most importantly here, what rape victims look like. In other words, what happens when there is expressive message failure. Both these concerns are addressed below.

A. *The Rape Shield's Expressive Message*

The first problem with rape shield laws has existed since these laws were enacted but has gone unnoticed and unremarked on: In pushing for rape shield laws, rape shield proponents have in fact reinscribed the very chastity requirement they hoped to abolish. This becomes readily apparent when one considers the expressive message communicated by rape shield laws.

Scholars have long stressed the importance of attending to law's expressive message. As Lawrence Lessig observed more than a decade ago, laws are anything but value neutral. They prescribe what behavior is inappropriate, what behavior is orthodox, and what behavior should be rewarded. More importantly, law informs and shapes social mores in ways that are often subtle. This is especially true when it comes to criminal laws. As I have noted in another context:

> The criminal law expressively communicates which homes are appropriate. Stable, monogamous, heterosexual, married homes exist not outside of the criminal law, but under the aegis of it. The criminal law shapes norms. It marks illicit conduct of which it disapproves. It also indirectly marks other conduct as licit. For example, a law that criminalizes same-sex sex almost by definition gives its imprimatur to heterosexual sex, contributing to what Adrienne Rich long ago termed "compulsory heterosexuality." A law that penalizes adultery not only condemns sex outside of marriage, but concomitantly privileges sexual fidelity within marriage. A rule that protects marital communications and insulates spouses from compelled testimony in criminal cases by definition deems other intimate relationships as less worthy of societal protection. In short, the criminal law has always played favorites, both outside of the home and inside the home.

Let me add that while laws, especially those relating to criminal law, are necessarily expressive and value laden, the social meaning expressed by any particular law is not necessarily static.

Now consider two expressive messages communicated by rape shield laws. On one level, rape shield laws communicate that a complainant's sexual history with other individuals is irrelevant to the issue presented in a standard rape trial – that is, whether she consented on this occasion. On this level, rape shield laws communicate that sex does not matter, a sentiment that many advocates of rape shield laws would support. But rape shield laws also communicate the opposite. At the same time that rape shield laws purport to communicate that sexual history does not matter, such laws also communicate that sexual history does matter. In fact, rape shield laws communicate that sexual history matters so much that it must be concealed, corseted, and locked away. Put differently, removing sexual history from the courtroom does more than simply render sexual history irrelevant. It privileges chastity, or something like chastity. Indeed, by pushing for rape shield laws, feminists have inadvertently legitimized the very chastity requirement they found so troubling.

To be clear, my concern is not with the expressive message communicated to defendants, or to prosecutors and defenses lawyers, or even to victims, though how they receive this message is important. Rather, my more pressing concern is with the expressive message sent to jurors. The message to jurors sitting on rape trials is that they should assume that the complainant is a virgin, or if not a virgin, at least a good girl deserving of the law's protection.

To make my point clearer, a thought exercise may be useful. Imagine a jury in a sexual assault case. Imagine too that the complainant is a young, attractive, white woman. She is solidly middle class, well educated, and articulate. In short, she is presentable to the jury. During the course of the trial, the jurors will be inundated with information and, when the complainant testifies, they will likely learn her approximate age, whether she attended college, what she does for a living, and other background information. By virtue of the rape shield, however, there will be no mention of her sexual experience, whether that experience is nil, includes one partner, or includes hundreds. In the absence of this information, the jury is likely to assume that this apparently ideal victim is, sexually speaking, a good girl. Indeed, jurors may even contrast her with other rape victims they have heard about on the news who seem sexually immoderate and whose accusations did not result in convictions. They may contrast her with someone who is not middle class or who is supposedly less presentable. In other words, when jurors are told nothing, they do not assume "nothing." Instead, they use the information they are provided, as well as the surface appearance of the complainant – does she look like a good girl or a bad girl? – to fill in the blank.

All this comes with a perverse result. Rather than disrupting the chastity requirement, rape shield laws in fact codify the requirement, entrenching it further, and without any diminution in the costs. All this plays into antiquated notions that a woman who is not a virgin or who has had sex outside of marriage is damaged goods and is less worthy of the law's protection. Rape shield law's contribution to the feminist agenda is not the subversion of the law's preference for good girls but rather a sleight of hand that unilaterally transforms all women, in theory at least, into virgins (or at least good girls). The complainant, by virtue of the rape shield laws, becomes a woman without a sexual past – a virtual virgin, a virgin anew, or at least a good girl anew.

Put differently, prior to the widespread passage of rape shield laws in the late 1970s, a combination of substantive law requirements and evidentiary rules effectively limited rape law's protection to women who were demonstrably good. As such, only a subset of women was protected. Rather than challenging this privileging of chastity, the primary effect of rape shield laws has been to allow more women to pass as good women. Instead of women being divided into good women and bad women, the rape shield laws allow all women, at least in theory, to seem facially good and thus deserving of the law's protection.

But this shift is not cost free. Even assuming that concealing sexual history benefits rape victims in toto – an assumption I call into question below – feminists should be deeply troubled by a message that, in effect if not intent, reinscribes the chastity requirement. As Anita Allen observed in critiquing traditional expectations about appropriate female behavior, "Conventions of female chastity and modesty have shielded women in a mantle of privacy at a high cost to sexual choice and self-expression." If the goal is gender equality and sexual autonomy, then we must recognize that rape shield laws have the perverse effect of frustrating this goal by indirectly privileging female chastity. We must recognize too that rather than furthering sexual liberty, rape shield laws, through their expressive message and concealment of consensual sex, contribute to what scholars have identified as a "sex-negative" regulatory regime. …

That is one problem. Another is the loss of real women. Instead of trials with real women, rape shield rules dictate trials with cardboard cutouts of women – trials in which women are in effect required to hide their sexual selves and don a cloak of chastity, or something like it. None of this can be good for those of us who care about female agency or about articulating the subject position of women. And none of this can be good for addressing the real problem of rape.

B. *Expressive Message Failure*

There is a related problem with rape shield laws. However, this problem tugs in the opposite direction and occurs when there is expressive message failure. Put differently, the problem here is when jurors reject the good girl message communicated by rape shield laws. While one normative message of rape shield laws is that all rape victims should be treated as good girls and thus deserving of the law's protection, jurors are likely to reject this message if it conflicts with our implicit biases and preexisting rape scripts. To better understand this point, some discussion of narrative theory in juror decisionmaking in general, and rape trials in particular, is useful. Also useful is some discussion of how black women have historically fitted, or rather not fitted, into the general rape script …

1. Narrative Theory and Rape Scripts

While the general view is that jurors and other factfinders decide what really happened by considering all the evidence, engaging in deductive reasoning, and making probability assessments, more recent scholarship makes clear that this rationalist perspective of factfinding is incomplete. In fact, experiential research makes clear that factfinders only partially weigh probabilities when deciding what really happened. Even more critical to factfinders is whether the information they are provided can be assembled into a plausible, teleological narrative. In Andrew Taslitz's discussion of narratives in the courtroom, he observed:

> [J]ury reasoning is story-based. Juries convert evidence into familiar stories, filling in gaps in the evidence where needed to craft a coherent tale. Whom jurors believe turns on the consistency of each witness's testimony with the plausible stories that juries create based upon their preexisting stock. These stock stories come from experience and culture, tales learned from the Bible, children's tales, television, radio, books, magazines, and movies. Stories create our world of meaning; they are the lens through which we view all of life's events.

For example, it is a fundamental precept of playwriting, courtesy of Anton Chekhov, that if a gun appears in Act One, it must be fired by Act Three to satisfy theater-goers' expectations. Similar expectations exist at trial. Indeed, the Supreme Court acknowledged this very point in the seminal evidence case *Old Chief v. United States*. Using an example that recalls Chekhov's admonishment, the Court stated the following:

> [T]here lies the need for evidence in all its particularity to satisfy the jurors' expectations about what proper proof should be. Some such demands they bring with them to the courthouse, assuming, for example that a charge of using a firearm to commit an offense will be proven by introducing a gun in evidence. A prosecutor who fails to produce one, or some good reason for his failure, has something to be concerned about.

This linkage between trials and storytelling, particularly in the form of theater, is not a new one. And indeed it makes sense. To a large extent, the witnesses, the judge, and the lawyers are all performers in the drama. Corey Rayburn Yung has observed that witnesses in particular must perform, even if the range of prewritten cultural scripts available to them is limited. It also makes sense to view jurors in particular as a type of audience. How they receive the performance is important, but they judge it based on how they relate to it. Did they believe the witness's performance? Did they judge the witness's story plausible? How do the stories told by the various witnesses cohere?

Narrative theory has particular salience for rape cases. For starters, often the only witnesses to the actual event are the accuser and the accused, allowing jurors more leeway to view the testimony against their preconceived scripts. As Kalven and Zeisel observed nearly half a century ago in their oft-cited *The American Jury*, it is precisely in the hard cases with ambiguous evidence that jurors feel "liberated" from the constraints of evidence. Indeed, studies show that jurors rely on rape scripts in assessing witness credibility and determining "the truth," and that jurors converge "on whatever stereotypic-consistent imagery and information is available to them." This happens even in the face of jury instructions to consider only the admitted evidence. "Even when the court fully shields the jury from particular evidence that the victim is 'loose' or lying, stereotypes and heuristics continue to operate. Looking at it hermeneutically, the rape trial proceeds on a backdrop of narratives surrounding all the players involved – from police, to defendants, to victims."

Narrative theory also has salience precisely because it explains why rapes that fail to fit the perceived real-rape script remain difficult to prosecute, notwithstanding the numerous reforms to rape law. Patriarchal stories continue to inform "when and why [rape] happens, and to and by whom." For example, because of this country's particular racialized history, in which black men were stereotyped as perpetual sexual threats to white women, the imagined ideal rapist continues to be black, and the ideal rape victim is white and demure. Factfinders are much more likely to find that a rape occurred when this particular black-white dyad is present, even when controlling for all other variables. …

Most importantly, preexisting scripts about what rape victims look like may conflict with rape shield messages and thus result in factfinders applying a different default assumption in cases involving victims who do not fit the script. While young, demure, white women may fit easily into the stock type of the victim, the damsel in distress, or the good girl, and thus receive some benefit from rape shield's protections, women who do not fit this description are likely to find jurors applying different default assumptions. In short, the stock characters are different. While this is true for a variety of women – jurors in a case involving an Asian complainant may view her as "exotically sexual [and] willingly submissive," while jurors in a case involving a Hispanic woman may view her as hot blooded, "wanton and promiscuous" – I discuss black women at length because our law's history of treating black women as negligible is so long. There is another reason why the situation of black women merits particular discussion. Notwithstanding their near invisibility in public imagination about rape, black women in fact face higher rape victimization rates than white women.

2. Rape Scripts, Black Women

The association of black women with sexual accessibility has a long history, from the assumption of twelfth-century travelers to Africa that nakedness signified concupiscence to the legally sanctioned accessibility to black women during American slavery, to the ostensibly scientific belief common during the 1800s that black women possessed a primitive sexual appetite and primitive genitalia. In short, black women were marked as naturally promiscuous, having less need or desire for foreplay than white women, and generally less discriminating in their choice of sexual partners. All this has had consequences when it comes to the sexual victimization of black women. Notwithstanding the black letter law that, after the Reconstruction Amendments, notionally treated all rape victims equally, a type of "white letter law of rape" remained that categorized black women as presumptively unchaste. Thus, in 1918, the Florida Supreme Court could remark with confidence that

> [w]hat has been said by some courts about an unchaste female … being a comparatively rare exception is no doubt true where the population is composed largely of the Caucasian race, but we would blind ourselves to actual conditions if we adopted this rule where another race that is largely unmoral constitutes an appreciable part of the population.

Since lack of chastity also signified untrustworthiness, black women were also deemed less credible than white women. As a result, black women were often viewed as "unrapeable" or responsible for their own rapes.

While much more empirical work needs to be done on the continuing salience of these assumptions, the studies that do exist suggest that stereotypes about black women and their sexuality continue to affect juror decisionmaking. Consider Gary LaFree's oft-cited study of juror attitudes. Controlling for other factors, LaFree concluded that jurors were less likely to render a guilty verdict when the accuser was a black woman. Discussing the results, LaFree speculated that perhaps "jurors were influenced by stereotypes of black women as more likely to consent to sex or as more sexually experienced and, hence, less harmed by an assault." As a juror in one case put it, a "girl her age from 'that kind of neighborhood' probably wasn't a virgin anyway." Other studies have found similar results.

A survey taken in response to the case of Joan Little, a black female prisoner who was prosecuted for killing her jailer, is likewise informative. Little claimed that she killed the jailer to defend herself from rape. In connection with her defense, social scientists conducted a survey of racial and gender attitudes in the county where she was scheduled to be tried. In an attempt to gauge how jurors would respond to her rape allegation, the survey asked, "Do you believe that black women have lower morals than white women?" Sixty-three percent of the individuals surveyed answered yes. …

Again, a thought exercise may be useful. Imagine a jury in a sexual assault case. This complainant, however, is a black woman. During the course of the trial, the jurors will be inundated with information, and they will likely learn where she lives (which, statistically speaking, is likely to be a majority black neighborhood), whether she attended college (which, statistically speaking, is unlikely), and what she does for a living (which, statistically speaking, is likely to be a low-wage job). By virtue of the rape shield, jurors will learn nothing about her sexual experience. But again, jurors who are told nothing do not assume nothing. Instead, jurors are more apt to conclude that the complainant is sexually active and that she may even be a bad girl (sexually indiscriminate and sexually immoderate). Indeed, because of the continued salience of race in this country, jurors may reach this conclusion even when presented with a black complainant who is solidly middle-class, articulate, and fully presentable to the jury.

All this should suggest that the push for rape shield laws in the 1970s warrants further scrutiny. Agitators for change were largely monolithic, and they achieved a result that disproportionately benefits white women. Moreover, there is nothing in the history to suggest that reformers gave any consideration to how rape shield laws might or might not benefit women of color. Rather, the push for rape shield laws, and indeed rape reform in general, betrays what Adrienne Rich refers to as "white solipsism" – that tendency to see whiteness as the norm. The same year feminists agitated for rape shield laws, a study of rape attitudes of thirty-eight judges in Philadelphia revealed that several judges equated the category of "vindictive women" with black women. Another judge stated, "With the Negro community, you really have to redefine the term rape. You never know about them." It is likely that none of this factored into the push for rape shield laws. The result was rape shield laws that, in hindsight at least, are racially contingent in effect.

Indeed, when one considers expressive message failure, the inadequacy of rape shield laws becomes inescapable. In theory, the effect of rape shield laws has been to allow all female rape victims, rather than just a small subset of victims, to present themselves as good. If, as Kimberlé Crenshaw argues, accusers are pigeonholed into a limited number of categories such as "the whore, the tease, the vengeful liar, the mentally or emotionally unstable, or … the madonna," rape shield laws, by shielding sexual history, in theory allow all rape victims to don the guise of the madonna.

But in reality, the transformation is aspirational at best. Conceptually, and despite the rise in nontraditional casting, it is still difficult to envision a black madonna (or for that matter an Asian or Hispanic one). It does not comport with our stock types. The virginal black woman – who in theory should be a deserving victim – is instead assumed to be a Jezebel. …

But here is the larger issue. While my focus has been black women vis-à-vis white women, in fact the expressive message of rape shield laws is likely ineffective when it comes to other victims as well: older women, single women, overweight women, poor women, working women, unattractive women, gay or transgender women, and even male victims. For example, when confronted with an older victim, jurors may fall back on the default stock character of the "disappointed old maid" who secretly wanted sex. When confronted with a homely woman, jurors may apply a different default assumption, casting her as a vindictive, spurned woman. In short, rape shield laws might be good for cardboard cutout women, ideal women, imaginary women, and women who can play the part, but not for the rest of us. In short, rape shield laws are not good for other, real victims of rape.

Unchaste and Incredible

The Use of Gendered Conceptions of Honor in Impeachment

Julia Simon-Kerr[1]

INTRODUCTION

Our legal system hinges on evaluations of credibility. Whom do we expect to tell the truth? When will they tell it? And how do we know they are telling it? These questions must arise, consciously or not, in the mind of any judge or juror who is asked to evaluate witness testimony. The need to judge credibility has been discussed by legal scholars and practitioners and addressed in evidentiary rules dealing with the use of character evidence at trial to impeach witnesses. Missing from this dialogue, however, has been an understanding that the answers to these basic questions about truthfulness have differed on gender lines.

… [A]s American courts developed rules for determining what could and could not be asked in order to impeach the credibility of witnesses, they did so against a cultural background that connected women's truthfulness to their chastity. A woman's "honor," or her culturally recognized moral integrity, so depended on her sexual virtue that her credibility suffered from any real or perceived failings of that virtue. [F]or men, while honor, credibility, and a reputation for truthfulness were fairly interchangeable in the popular imagination of the eighteenth century, the story for women was quite different. For women, honor and credibility depended on chastity and on the reputation for sexual virtue. Because female honor emphasized women's reputation for sexual purity and not their reputation for truth telling, truth itself was prescribed differently for women and men. Women were supposed to appear chaste, so they experienced social pressure to dissemble rather than present the appearance of impropriety. Men, to the contrary, were praised most when they were true to their word.

… [T]his gender difference resonated in early evidence cases as courts struggled to regulate the impeachment of female witnesses. While many courts questioned the rationality of using evidence of unchastity to prove untruthfulness, particularly just

[1] Excerpted from Julia Simon-Kerr, Note, *Unchaste and Incredible: The Use of Gendered Conceptions of Honor in Impeachment*, 117 Yale L.J. 1854 (2008).

for one sex, others seemed to accept as a given the probative value of such chastity evidence. Even beyond the question of relevance, the unique importance of reputation for women's honor resonated in decisions on the type of proof to be allowed in character impeachment – whether to allow evidence of reputation or specific acts. Early courts' inability to reach a consensus on the relevance of a woman's sexual virtue to her credibility – and, if so, how unchastity evidence should be adduced – illustrates the resilience of the gendered notion of honor. At the same time, that most jurisdictions ultimately prohibited lawyers from impeaching female witnesses with sexual history evidence marks a triumph of legal principle over a pervasive cultural norm. Unfortunately, this rationalist triumph did not extend to rape law.

That women who pressed rape charges were typically forced to respond to sexual history evidence will not surprise readers familiar with the history of rape law. Modern rape scholarship has effectively documented the gender biases that permeated the law of rape, biases that included routine permission to explore the victim's sexual history and thus to undermine her credibility. This Note contributes the simple but important point that the link between female honor and chastity did not arise from the law of rape, but rather predated and informed rape law's development. Far from originating in rape trials and the confusing interplay between questions of consent, credibility, and sexual history, the idea that a woman's chastity informs her credibility so permeated American culture that attorneys in cases involving claims as diverse as title to land, assault, arson, and wrongful death routinely attempted to impeach female witnesses by invoking their sexual histories. While early courts sometimes claimed to admit or exclude this chastity-related evidence depending on its purported relevance to the subject matter of the case at hand, they did not do so consistently.

Three points emerge from [a] review of early law in this area. First, America's vision of the truthful woman incorporated ideas about her sexual purity and these ideas informed perceptions of the female witness. Second, the idea that an unchaste woman was also a lying woman arose in early impeachment jurisprudence even in cases where the female witnesses were not the victims of sexual crimes. Third, early courts more often than not thought independently and carefully enough to reject a sexual double standard for testing credibility, at least in cases not involving rape.

... [W]hat seemed like a progressive retreat from the unchaste/incredible equation halted when the issue was rape. In rape cases, unchaste and incredible became unchaste and consenting, a development that might be viewed as a form of "preservation through transformation." If legal logic had enabled many courts to reject the idea that chastity had a bearing on female credibility, the idea resurfaced when the question was posed as one of consent. Although the impossibility of drawing a bright line between evidence admitted to prove consent as opposed to credibility of the victim in a rape case seems obvious and has been well-documented, courts often insisted that sexual history was admissible to prove consent in a rape trial, although not credibility.

Both before the passage of the rape shield laws in the 1970s and more recently in criticizing those laws, legal scholars and others have pointed out an inherent illogic and sexism in the law's approach to rape. The very definition of the crime as the "carnal knowledge of a female forcibly and against her will" meant that courts often required proof of sufficient "resistance" on the part of the woman. Further, corroboration requirements and mandatory jury instructions advising that the rape complainant's "testimony be scrutinized with caution" spoke to the enduring stereotype that "[r]ape [was] … an accusation easily to be made, and hard to be proved, and harder to be defended by the party accused, tho never so innocent." Scholars have generally understood this bias to come from the "long-standing suspicion of rape victims" that developed under the "purview of ancient masculine codes" centered around controlling women, often through the use of violence. That discourse has been powerful within its sphere, but it has not fully accounted for the proposition that, for women, "promiscuity imports dishonesty." [E]arly rape jurisprudence was formed by the culturally entrenched equation of unchaste and incredible.

While our cultural definition of sexual virtue has shifted drastically since the eighteenth century and even since the initial enactment of the rape shield statutes, the idea that a woman's sexual virtue bears upon her credibility is still present today. [M]odern courts admit evidence of prostitution as a crime bearing on credibility. Although prostitution is no longer defined in gendered terms, women are still far more likely to be prosecuted for prostitution-related offenses. That evidence of prostitution can still be admitted to impeach the female witness shows the continuing vitality of the chastity/credibility equation. Even now, at the beginning of the twenty-first century, courts decide whether or not to believe women based on perceptions of their sexual purity.

Feminist Take(s) on Other (Sexual) Bad Acts

Caroline L. Davidson

Some thirty years ago,[1] in the face of strong opposition, including from the National Organization for Women (NOW),[2] Congress amended the Federal Rules of Evidence to add Rules 413–15. A significant number of states have followed.[3] Contrary to the "cardinal" rule of precluding admission of prior bad acts evidence to prove a person's propensity to commit such an act,[4] Rules 413 to 415 explicitly permit admission of evidence of prior sexual assault (413 and 415) and child molestation (414 and 415) for the propensity inference.[5]

This chapter examines these rules through a feminist lens or, perhaps more accurately, feminist lenses, and argues that these exceptional rules, which purport to help women, find little support in contemporary feminist thought. The

1 Christopher B. Mueller and Laird C. Kirkpatrick, 2 Federal Evidence § 4:83 (4th ed., Aspen Law 2023) ("These Rules were controversial and provoked strenuous opposition" and noting the "highly unusual unanimity of the members of the Standing and Advisory Committees, composed of over 40 judges, practicing lawyers, and academicians, in opposing the proposed new Rules" and the opposition of the ABA House of Delegates.).

2 Bennett Capers, *Real Women, Real Rape*, 60 UCLA L. Rev. 826, 845, n. 94 (2013) (noting NOW's opposition to the rules based on "concern that it would diminish basic safeguards accorded criminal defendants").

3 Claire Fahy, *In Sex Crimes Cases, New York Weighs Allowing Evidence of Prior Bad Acts*, N.Y. Times (May 9, 2024), www.nytimes.com/2024/05/09/nyregion/weinstein-testimony-victims.html (discussing a New York bill introducing similar legislation and citing an assemblywoman for the proposition that "sixteen states have adopted the federal rule"). *See also*, Aviva Orenstein, *Deviance, Due Process, and the False Promise of Federal Rule of Evidence* 403, 90 Corn. L. Rev. 1487, 1497 and n. 31 (2005) (noting states that had passed legislation akin to FRE 413–15 or were considering as of 2005).

4 Fed. R. Evid. 404(b)(1) ("Evidence of any other crime, wrong, or act is not admissible to prove a person's character in order to show that on a particular occasion the person acted in accordance with the character."). Victor J. Gold, 23 Federal Practice and Procedure § 5382 (2d ed., Wright & Miller 2026) ("It has been said that one of the cardinal tenets of 'Anglo-Saxon jurisprudence' and due process is that the prosecution must prove that the defendant has committed a crime, not that he is a 'bad person.'").

5 Rules 413 and 414 address the use of evidence of prior sexual assault and child molestation, respectively, in a criminal case. Rule 415 addresses the use of evidence of prior sexual assault and child molestation in a civil case.

rules lack a defensible justification, short of simply making it easier to convict someone accused of sexual wrongs, and are likely to disproportionately affect poor and minority defendants and contribute to the conviction of innocent people. I argue that prior sexual assaults ought to be treated like other prior bad acts and admitted only where there is an argument for their relevance other than the defendant's bad character.[6]

Although space constraints preclude a detailed treatment, in order to contemplate feminist reactions to Rules 413–15, a very brief sketch of strands of feminist theory is warranted. Feminist movements are often described in "waves," and each wave contains several currents. After a first wave of feminism concerned with voting and property rights in the late nineteenth and early twentieth centuries, came a disparate second wave in the second half of the twentieth century. Among the various strands of feminism that emerged in the second wave was liberal feminism, which sought equality for women under the law through facial neutrality in the law.[7] Also among the second wave feminists were the structural or "radical" feminists, a strand "most associated" with Catharine MacKinnon.[8] Structural feminists found liberal feminists' efforts at facial equality under the law to be woefully inadequate given the historic and persistent structural inequality between men and women. Liberal and purportedly neutral laws would merely perpetuate these structures of inequality. Turning to violence against women (VAW), structural feminists tended to see sexual violence as "a manifestation of patriarchy."[9] At the same time, "Third World Approaches to International Law" or TWAIL feminists and feminists

6 *See* Katharine K. Baker, *Once a Rapist? Motivational Evidence and Relevancy in Rape Law*, 110 HARV. L. REV. 563, 578–83, 594–5, 613 (1997) (arguing against Rule 413 based on, among other things, its incorrect premise that people who commit sexual assaults are more likely to recidivate).

7 C. Quince Hopkins et al., *Applying Restorative Justice to Ongoing Intimate Violence: Problems and Possibilities*, 23 ST. LOUIS U. PUB. L. REV. 289, 296–7 (2004) ("Liberal feminists, also referred to as 'sameness' or 'rule equality' feminists, argue that formal equal treatment of men and women will result in formal and functional equality between the sexes."). *See also*, Nicola Lacey, *Feminist Legal Theory and the Rights of Women*, *in* GENDER AND HUMAN RIGHTS 13, 20 (Karen Knop ed., Oxford University Press 2006) ("Liberal feminism is simply the idea that those liberal ideals of equality and rights or liberties apply to women. In this sense, it is not so much a distinctively feminist theory as liberalism applied to women … A key limitation of liberalism from a feminist point of view has been argued to be its individualism.").

8 *See* Julie Simon-Kerr, *Relevance Through a Feminist Lens*, *in* PHILOSOPHICAL FOUNDATIONS OF EVIDENCE LAW 365 (Christian Dahlman, Alex Stein, and Giovanni Tuznet, eds., Oxford University Press 2021). *See also*, Lacey, *supra* note 7, at 23 (associating MacKinnon with radical feminism and attempting to characterize the theory by saying that "radical feminists see sexual difference as having a certain priority in social life; they see sex difference as more 'radical' or basic than, say class difference, or racial, or ethnic difference").

9 Rebecca Jane Hall, *Feminist Strategies to End Violence Against Women*, *in* OXFORD HANDBOOK OF TRANSNATIONAL FEMINIST MOVEMENTS 3 (Rawwida Baksh and Wendy Harcourt eds., Oxford University Press 2015) ("[T]his focus on patriarchal violence divorced from an understanding of race, sexuality, and relations of production created a rift in the contemporary women's movement and helped contribute to the depoliticization of responses to violence against women.").

of color in the U.S. criticized the liberal and radical feminists alike for centering the perspective of affluent, educated, white women in the developed world.[10]

"Third wave feminism" emerged in the 1990s as both an outgrowth and a backlash to the second wave. The third wave is more disparate than even the second, but core elements of the third wave appear to be a rejection of the salience of the category of "woman,"[11] an embrace of sex positivity (in juxtaposition to the perceived prudishness of the second wave), and recognition that gender is but one aspect of a person's identity and of the importance of other vectors of identity, like race, economic status, and the like.[12] Finally, some have identified a post-#MeToo, post-first Trump Administration fourth wave of feminism, which "focuses on reducing sexual violence" and is "deeply intersectional, and emphasizes the experiences of women of color, trans women, and sex workers."[13]

Over the years, feminists have engaged with VAW and sexual violence in different ways. Departing from the model of early anti-establishment shelter movements, which largely eschewed reliance on the police and the criminal justice system, there emerged in the last decades of the twentieth century a feminist coalition that largely embraced the criminal justice system as the remedy for sexual violence and VAW, generally.[14] Aya Gruber has dubbed this groups of feminists

[10] *See, e.g.*, Jennifer C. Nash, *'Home Truths' on Intersectionality*, 23 YALE J. L. & FEMINISM 445, 452 (2011) ("Black feminists' interest in revealing black women's subordinate social, political, as well as *economic* position made analyses of capitalism's injuries central to their critique of white-dominated patriarchy." (emphasis original)); Vasuki Nesiah, *The Ground Beneath Her Feet: 'Third World' Feminisms*, 4 J. INT'L WOMEN'S STUD. 30, 30–1, 33 (2003) (critiquing the colonial lens of mainstream feminist human rights scholarship, particularly for its lack of nuance, problematic narratives of victimhood, and failure to consider the possibility that women in other places may have other priorities).

[11] R. Claire Snyder, *What Is Third-Wave Feminism? A New Directions Essay*, 34 SIGNS 175, 187 (2008) ("Not assuming a unified category of women, most third-wavers take an anti-essentialist stance.").

[12] *Id.* at 183 ("Third-wave feminism presents a tactical response to three major theoretical challenges to second-wave feminism: the 'category of women' debates (initiated by feminists of color) that shattered the idea of a shared women's experience or identity; the end of grand narratives through the decline of Marxism and the rise of poststructuralism, deconstruction, and postmodernism within the academy; and the sex wars that fractured the unified political stand of feminism on many important feminist issues."). *See also*, Barbara Ann White, *Traversing 2nd and 3rd Waves: Feminist Legal Theory Moving Forward*, 39 U. BALT. L. F. I, iii (2008) (identifying a "broad array of possible 3rd wave characteristics: the 'next generation' feminism, the 'anti-"victim" feminism,' the 'socio-cultural-media-focused' feminism, the 'anti-essentialist' feminism, the 'empowering, sexually liberating' feminism, the feminism of 'autobiography' or perhaps instead, the 'narcissistic' feminism, the 'retrogressive' feminism, the 'disintegrative' feminism and conceivably, in an unkind cut, a different, yet still, 'middle-class' feminism, which moreover continues to foster 'western, liberal feminist imperialism' in other parts of the world as well as at home").

[13] Taylor Comerford, Note, *Pornography Isn't the Problem: A Feminist Theoretical Perspective on the War Against Pornhub*, 63 B.C. L. REV. 1177, 1191–2 (2022).

[14] AYA GRUBER, THE FEMINIST WAR ON CRIME: THE UNEXPECTED ROLE OF WOMEN'S LIBERATION IN MASS INCARCERATION 42–4 (University of California Press 2020) ("By the 1980s, experts regularly identified the proarrest, proprosecution position as a distinctly feminist position … Today, second-wave feminism is remembered – fondly or regretfully –for its contributions to policing, prosecution, and punishment.").

"the legal feminists."[15] The antidote to treating VAW as a neglected, private matter,[16] it seemed, was getting the criminal justice system involved. Speaking largely of the same philosophies, others have given this strand of feminist activism the more loaded label of "carceral feminists."[17]

Increasingly, though not uniformly, feminists have questioned the now long-standing feminist alliance with the carceral state. Beginning decades ago, "Black feminists and women of colour in particular … challenged criminalization strategies, arguing for greater understanding of the differential impacts on individuals and groups based on the 'intersections' of race, ethnicity, class, gender and other social categories."[18] This work has continued to the present and evolved into abolitionist feminism.[19]

Along the same vein, Aya Gruber, has argued for a "'neofeminist' – as opposed to post- or non-feminist – approach to gender harm and violence," which acknowledges "sexual misconduct and battering constitute pressing social problems that reflect and reinforce women's subordination and concedes that offender impunity exacts a social price" while at the same time recognizing the costs of the carceral response.[20] Gruber asserts that this neofeminism is intersectional[21] and also "acutely conscious that criminal law causes real injuries and views feminist participation in the penal system with a jaundiced eye," in light of the reality of "a world of racialized overpolicing and overimprisonment."[22] Gruber thus "propose[s] the following as a basic tenet of modern feminist thought: Criminal law is a last, not first, resort."[23]

The explosion of anti-carceral feminist scholarship in recent years indicates that Gruber is not alone in questioning the choice of feminists to ally with the state and the

15 *Id.* at 44 ("Legal feminists were civil rights lawyers and victims' advocates, and they analyzed the problem of battering as a failure of the law, specifically the ineffectuality of criminal law.").

16 Gruber argues that this prevailing narrative is inaccurate. GRUBER, *supra* note 14, at 19 (arguing that "rape law's past is one of selective enforcement, including overenforcement, depending on the gender, marital status, class, and race of those involved in the sexual encounter").

17 Clare McGlynn, *Challenging Anti-carceral Feminism: Criminalisation, Justice and Continuum Thinking*, 93 WOMEN'S STUD. INT'L F. 1, 2 (2022) (describing Elizabeth Bernstein's introduction of the term "carceral feminism" in the sex trafficking context and its evolution to describe "pro-criminalization feminist social movement strategies" or "reliance on state-sanctioned punitive justice as a corrective to sexual violence").

18 *Id.* at 1–2.

19 *See generally*, ANGELA Y. DAVIS ET AL., ABOLITION. FEMINISM. NOW. 69–70 (Hamish Hamilton 2022) (tracing the origins of abolitionist feminism and explaining that the movement "explicitly rejects state attempts to mobilize vulnerability and difference for the purpose of expanding carcerality and instead works to highlight the role of the state in perpetuating violence demanding engagement from people who are most affected and address the root causes of incarceration – poverty, white supremacy, misogyny").

20 GRUBER, *supra* note 14, at 16–17.

21 *Id.* ("It is also mindful that gender is on of multiple intersecting sites of hierarchy, along with class, race, and economic status.").

22 *Id.*

23 *Id.*

criminal justice/legal system to address VAW and sexual violence.[24] Indeed, Karen Engle has argued that abolitionist ideas have even "gained some traction among a broader group of feminist activists who have not always identified as abolitionist."[25]

Now, back to the rules. Rule 413 to 415, which one of the editors of this book has dubbed, "the rape sword rules,"[26] are exceptional evidentiary rules for sexual violence. They explicitly treat prior acts of sexual assault and child molestation differently from other prior bad acts,[27] which are normally excluded, at least if they are being offered for the inference that the defendant has a propensity to commit such acts. The explanation for Rule 404(b)'s typical exclusion of prior bad acts is not that it is irrelevant, but rather that the jury will find it too persuasive and judge the person based on their prior acts and not the facts of the case at hand.[28] This risk seems even greater with societally reviled crimes such as sexual assault and molestation.[29]

Notwithstanding this risk (or perhaps because of it), Rules 413–15 explicitly and intentionally allow admission of prior acts of sexual assault or molestation for "any" relevant matter, which includes the propensity inference.[30] They are quite

[24] At the time of writing a search using the term "anti carceral feminist scholarship" in Google Scholar, for example, yields 18,700 results.

[25] Karen Engle, Toward an Abolitionist Human Rights Court: Rethinking Responses to Gendered and Racialized Violence 28 (Cambridge University Press 2025) (noting however that "[g]aining traction is, of course, far from shifting the mainstream; a number of the signers, particularly those from mainstream shelters in conservative states, faced significant backlash for joining the letter.") (citing Davis, *supra* note 19, at 503–780, 1725–79).

[26] Capers, *supra* note 2, at 831.

[27] David P. Leonard, *The Federal Rules of Evidence and the Political Process*, 22 Fordham Urb. L.J. 305, 306 (1995) (arguing that (then) proposed Rules 413 to 415 "challenged one of the key assumptions underlying the Federal Rules: that the evidence rules, for the most part, should apply the same way in different kinds of cases and treat different types of litigants similarly").

[28] Mueller and Kirkpatrick, *supra* note 1, at § 4:83 ("The longstanding bar against proving criminal misconduct by means of character evidence was never premised on the view that such evidence lacks probative value. Rather, … propensity evidence has been historically rejected *despite its relevance* because 'it is said to weigh too much with the jury and to so overpersuade them as to prejudice on with a bad general record and deny him a fair opportunity to defend against a particular charge.'" (emphasis original)). *See also*, People v. Weinstein, 42 N.Y.3d 439, 475 (2024) (Singas, J., dissenting) ("'[E]vidence of uncharged crimes and prior bad acts may be admitted to prove the specific crime charged when it tends to establish' a defendant's 'intent' … 'Admission of such proof-where intent cannot be inferred from the act or where [the] defendant claims [they] acted innocently – is founded on the law of probabilities. The theory is that the more often the act constituting the crime has been done, the less the likelihood that it could have been done innocently, as if by chance … It is the duplication of the inculpatory conduct which makes the innocent explanation improbable'") (first quoting People v. Cass, 18 N.Y.3d 553, 560 (2012); and then quoting People v. Ingram, 71 N.Y.2d 474, 476, 479–80 (1988)).

[29] Jason L. McCandless, *Prior Bad Acts and Two Bad Rules: The Fundamental Unfairness of Federal Rules of Evidence 413 and 414*, 5 Wm. & Mary Bill Rts. J. 689, 714 (1997) ("The risk of jury misdecision seems to be particularly acute when a court admits evidence of sexual misconduct or child molestation.").

[30] Fed. R. Evid. 413 provides: "In a criminal case in which a defendant is accused of a sexual assault, the court may admit evidence that the defendant committed any other sexual assault. The evidence may be considered on *any matter to which it is relevant*." (emphasis added).

transparently designed to make proving sexual assault and molestation charges easier.[31] Proponents of the rules justified them on three bases: "(1) the need to win convictions in difficult-to-prosecute sex-offense cases; (2) the probative value of sexual-offense evidence;[32] and (3) the need for consistency in judicial decision-making with regard to uncharged-sexual-offense evidence."[33]

It is worth pausing over another argument for the rules. That argument is that, since the evidence may come in anyway under 404(b) exceptions, "a more honest, direct, and predictable approach [is] to make a specific exception for propensity in those types of crimes."[34]

In the New York prosecution of Harvey Weinstein, for example, the trial court admitted evidence from three witnesses who testified about Weinstein's prior sexual assaults against them, to prove intent, by way of the doctrine of chances, and lack of consent.[35] (New York does not have a "rape sword" rule akin to Rule 413.) The trial court instructed the jury that it was not to consider this evidence "for the purpose of proving that the defendant had a propensity or predisposition to commit the crimes charged."[36]

However, admission of similar sexual act evidence under a 404(b) exception remains fraught, since the line between evidence admitted for a legitimate "other" purpose and evidence showing propensity can be very fine. Illustrating this fine line, in *People v. Weinstein*, the New York Court of Appeals reversed Weinstein's conviction, finding the trial court's decision to admit evidence of prior sexual assaults constituted reversible error.[37] Making clear that it believed the prohibition on using other bad acts for the propensity inference as an outgrowth of the presumption of innocence, the majority began its opinion with the sentence: "Every person accused of a crime is constitutionally presumed innocent and entitled to a fair trial and the

[31] *See* McCandless, *supra* note 29, at 691 (discussing Rules 413 and 414, the two rules relating to criminal cases, and stating that "[t]he policy goal of the new rules was to make it easier to prosecute sexual assault and child molestation cases").

[32] Orenstein notes that this argument for the probative values of such evidence stems from three separate arguments: the "credibility gap" faced by women and children, claims that "sex offenders are notoriously recidivistic," and the claim that, with sex crimes, "the sexual aggressiveness and proclivities of the defendants are unique." Orenstein, *supra* note 3, at 1498–9.

[33] Jeffrey G. Pickett, *The Presumption of Innocence Imperiled: The New Federal Rules of Evidence 413–415 and the Use of Other Sexual Offense Evidence in Washington*, 70 WASH. L. REV. 883, 895 (1995); Orenstein, *supra* note 3, at 1502–3 (making the arguments for and against the rules and arguing for changes to them).

[34] Orenstein, *supra* note 3, at 1502–3.

[35] People v. Weinstein, 170 N.Y.S.3d 33, 40 (N.Y. App. Div. 2022) ("[C]omplainants' behavior before and after the sexual encounters risked masking the fact that the alleged assaults were nonconsensual, and that the *Molineux* witnesses placed the incidents in a more accurate context."). *See also*, People v. Weinstein, 42 N.Y.3d 439, 471, 475 (N.Y. 2024) (explaining that using other bad acts to prove intent under *Molineux* relies on the "law of probabilities:" "the more often the act constituting the crime has been done, the less the likelihood that it could have been done innocently, as if by chance").

[36] Weinstein, 42 N.Y.3d at 450.

[37] *Id.* at 444.

opportunity to present a defense."[38] It reasoned that New York caselaw "begin[s] with the premise that uncharged crimes are inadmissible" and "carve[s] out exceptions" from that principle, but only where the evidence is "logically connected to some specific material issue in the case" and is "directly relevant" to it.[39] The majority held that the evidence did not clarify intent, as the evidence on consent was not "equivocal" – the complainants had testified about forcible attacks.[40] According to the majority, either the jury believed the complainants' version of a forcible attack or the defendant's version of a consensual, albeit possibly transactional, encounter.[41]

Further, the Court pushed back on the dissent's argument that evidence of the prior uncharged sexual assaults was necessary to counter "rape myths." It argued that expert testimony to dispel rape myths served that aim without jeopardizing the defendant's right to a fair trial and that the risk of "rape myths" impairing jury fact-finding was diminished in this case since it was not a case with a single complainant.[42] The decision elicited two strongly worded dissents, which discussed at length the role of "rape myths" in prosecutions for sexual assaults in general and in this case specifically, and the utility of evidence of prior sexual assaults to help counter these myths and to prove a lack of consent and the defendant's intent.[43]

Of course, almost all of the uncertainty about the admissibility of other sexual acts evidence would have disappeared if New York had a rule like Rule 413. In fact, a month after the reversal of Weinstein's conviction, legislation was introduced to incorporate Rule 413 into New York state law.[44]

So, what is a feminist to make of rules like Federal Rules of Evidence 413 to 415 that circumvent this thorny "other purpose" analysis seen in *Weinstein*, which may lead to exclusion of the evidence, in favor of clear but extraordinary rules allowing prior sexual assault in for the propensity inference? Given the variety in feminist beliefs described above, it likely depends on your feminist. Some feminists, tracking the dissent in *Weinstein*, may consider these rules a useful corrective to an unfair society and legal system, and continue to place faith in the criminal justice system as the best, or at least a viable, way to combat VAW (and children),

38 *Id.* at 443–4.

39 *Id.* at 457 (quoting People v. Resek, 3 N.Y.3d 385, 390 (N.Y. 2004) and People v. Cass, 18 N.Y.3d 553, 559–60 (N.Y. 2012)).

40 *Id.* at 459.

41 *Id.* at 464.

42 *Id.* at 462.

43 *Id.* at 472–82 (Singas, J., dissenting) (arguing that "consent was at the heart of the case" and that "[b]y ignoring the legal and practical realities of proving a lack of consent, the majority has crafted a naive narrative: that within the most fraught and intimate settings, intent is readily apparent, and issues of consent easily ascertained."); *id.* at 488 (Cannataro, J., dissenting) (calling the majority's decision "an unfortunate step backwards from recent advances in our understanding of how sex crimes are perpetrated and why victims sometimes respond in seemingly counterintuitive ways, endangering decades of progress in this incredibly complex and nuanced area of law").

44 S.B. 9276, 2023–2024 Leg., Reg. Sess. (N.Y. 2024), https://legiscan.com/NY/bill/S09276/2023 (last visited April 1, 2026).

including sexual violence. However, a good number of the camps described above, like this author, would join the many voices that oppose the rules.

Rules 413 to 415 purport to be feminist rules, at least in the very basic sense that proponents of the admission of prior bad sexual acts evidence claim the rules to be good for women. Per Bennett Capers: "The rape shield and rape sword rules … were created *to benefit women*."[45] Likewise, one of the dissents in the *Weinstein* appeal plants a feminist (again, in the sense of looking out for what is good for women) flagpole in disagreeing with the majority's exclusion of the prior sexual assault evidence: "Because New York's women deserve better, I dissent."[46]

Gruber's *Feminist War on Crime* makes a compelling case, however, that this distributive calculus of "what is good for women" is not always clear. It also makes the case that carceral rules that are supposedly good for women – like mandatory charging policies in domestic violence cases or, as here, evidence rules that make proving sexual violence easier – may not in fact be good for women in the real world of American mass, racialized incarceration.[47] As Aviva Orenstein argued some twenty-five years ago, "not all the currently proposed character-based solutions for gaining increased rape convictions are moral, feminist, or even good for women in the long run."[48]

Indeed, an even slightly more nuanced take than the "what's good for women" one starts to make the rules seem less obviously feminist. On the one hand, various strands of feminism – from the radical feminists to the legal feminists to the new fourth wave – are concerned about sexual violence. Arguably, viewed through a radical feminist lens, the Rules are corrective to a criminal justice system, with its purportedly neutral rules of evidence, where the deck is stacked against victims of sexual violence, most often women.[49] As Julia Simon-Kerr has noted, "A central claim of feminist accounts of evidence is that, contrary to accepted wisdom, this system of procedural rules is neither neutral nor value-free."[50] At least one post-#MeToo law review article, has argued for analogously exceptional rules altering evidence rules relating to impeachment of victim witnesses to counter "society's discount[ing] the testimony of women."[51]

45 Capers, *supra* note 2, at 832 n. 17 (2013) (questioning whether they are *in fact* good for women) (emphasis added).

46 People v. Weinstein, 42 N.Y.3d 439, 473 (2024) (Singas, J., dissenting).

47 Gruber, *supra* note 14, at 16–17.

48 Aviva Orenstein, *No Bad Men!: A Feminist Analysis of Character Evidence in Rape Trials*, 49 Hastings L.J. 663, 667 (1998) ("Reject[ing] the [then] new Rule 413 and other attempts to admit evidence of prior bad acts by the accused, which rest on anti-feminist principles and stereotypes about rapists.").

49 *Id.* at 689 ("Whether from the perspective of 'dominance' or 'difference' feminism, Rule 413 thus confronts the essential feminist concern that women are not heard in the courtroom.").

50 Simon-Kerr, *supra* note 8, at 365.

51 Aníbal Rosario-Lebrón, *Evidence's #MeToo Moment*, 74 U. Mia. L. Rev. 1, 1–2, 21 (2019) ("[T]he impeachment of SGBV victims' character for truthfulness is a subtler and perhaps more pernicious patriarchal vestige as it shields itself behind the neutral façade of character for untruthfulness evidence.").

Taking a feminist crack at the concept of "relevance," Simon-Kerr has made a compelling case that our notions of relevance are socially contingent and may be gendered in ways that do not meet the eye.[52] So too may our notions of persuasiveness. Recall: the rationale for the exclusion of prior bad acts propensity evidence is that it is too persuasive.[53] This "too persuasiveness" argument, like relevance, rests on assumptions about what the average finder of fact is likely to find persuasive. We need to know more about this "average" finder of fact and what they find persuasive and should assess Rules 413–15 in light of the beliefs they really hold and not the beliefs they are supposed to hold. If they entertain "false beliefs about sexual assault,"[54] often referred to as "rape myths"[55] and use a woman's chastity as a proxy for her truthfulness[56] (and race as a proxy for both)[57] and the like, there is a credible feminist argument to be made that, at least in some cases, evidence of prior bad acts is not too persuasive, but rather just the right amount persuasive to counter these other highly persuasive, if also problematic, internalized beliefs.[58]

Indeed, this scale-tipping logic is precisely the rationale offered by the proponents of Rules 413–15. The rule's proponent, Representative Susan Molinari "argued that because adult-victim sexual assault cases often turn on credibility determinations, informing jurors of a defendant's past sexual conduct could be critical in 'accurately deciding cases that would otherwise become unresolvable swearing matches.'"[59] Thus, a feminist, and particularly a radical one, may be open to questioning where the persuasiveness scale sits at the point in which the prior bad

[52] Julia Simon-Kerr, *Unchaste and Incredible: The Use of Gendered Conceptions of Honor in Impeachment*, 117 YALE L.J. 1854, 1860–1 (2008).

[53] *See* discussion at *supra* notes 28–29.

[54] Brandon T. Hunley, William O'Donohue, and Monica K. Miller, *Expert Testimony Regarding Typical or Counterintuitive Adult Sexual Assault Behavior: A Review*, 57 U. ILL. CHI. L. REV. 1, 3, 15 (2023) (pushing back on the mythology of "rape myths" by finding that these "misconceptions are not so widely held by jurors that jurors would likely rely on them in their decision making").

[55] *See* Morrison Torrey, *When Will We Be Believed? Rape Myths and the Idea of a Fair Trial in Rape Prosecutions*, 24 U.C. DAVIS L. REV. 1013, 1014 (1991) ("The legal treatment of rape seems to be structured to make it as difficult as possible to establish that any given man has raped any given woman.").

[56] Simon-Kerr, *supra* note 52, at 1860–1, 1870.

[57] Capers, *supra* note 2, at 865–6 ("[B]lack women were marked as naturally promiscuous … Since lack of chastity also signified untrustworthiness, black women were also deemed less credible than white women.").

[58] *Cf.* Victoria Nourse, *The Common Law's Resistance to Gender Violence*, 110 IOWA L. REV. 167, 214 (2024) (defending special propensity rules for prior sexual assaults, at least in the civil context, on the basis that "[j]uries treat women claiming to have experienced sexual assault with heightened skepticism" and "[p]ropensity exceptions for sexual misconduct seek to level the playing field already tilted by a long history of bias against plaintiffs rather than give sexual misconduct plaintiffs any special advantage").

[59] *But see* Capers, *supra* note 2, at 845 and n. 94 (stating that "[n]ot all feminists supported the passage of Rule 413," noting NOW's opposition to the rule, and explaining that "the push for Rule 413 by Rep. Susan Molinari and Sen. Bob Dole, both Republicans, was viewed by some feminists as politically motivated: By supporting Rule 413, the Republican Party could position themselves as committed to women's issues.").

sexual acts evidence might be introduced.[60] As one commentator has argued, Rule 413 is especially useful in cases in "consent-defense acquaintance rape cases."[61]

Even a radical feminist may be concerned, however, about the crudeness of this corrective tool – countering problematic evidence (stereotyping women) with more problematic evidence (pre-judging (mostly) men) based on possible[62] prior bad sex acts. Moreover, this tipping of the scale risks becoming something of a modern corroboration requirement and contributing to pernicious and "anti-feminist" narratives about mendacious women.[63] As Aviva Orenstein and Katharine Baker have noted, Rules 413 to 415 also rest on an anti-feminist narrative that real men do not rape, i.e. rape is rare, and rapists are deviants.[64]

Further, the rules seem to push up against core concerns of the remaining strands of feminist thought. Liberal feminists, and third and fourth generation feminists, are likely to have reservations, albeit for different reasons. Although I am sympathetic to radical feminist concerns that neutral rules can conceal a great deal of inequality, absent compelling evidence that an exceptional rule in fact helps women and that the benefits of the rule outweigh the costs, the liberal feminist fight for equal treatment of women under the law retains appeal. Examining these rules through this lens, Rules 413–15 are equal and also not equal. On their face, they are sex and gender neutral, though in reality most defendants will be men, and most complaining witnesses, women or children.[65] Nevertheless a liberal feminist, concerned with treating women equally under the law and committed to liberal principles generally,

60 Capers notes, however, that the scales have already been tipped once through the rape shield laws keeping out evidence about a woman's sexual history or predisposition. *Id.* at 853.

61 Roger C. Park, *Character at the Crossroads*, 49 Hastings L.J. 717, 741, 764, 774 (1998) (arguing that "character attributions" will happen with or without prior bad act evidence and excluding it "merely means that the character attributions will be based on trivial and misleading data," including demeanor or "stereotypical thinking").

62 These evidence rules do not demand a conviction. *See* McCandless, *supra* note 29, at 699.

63 Orenstein, *supra* note 48, at 695 ("Rule 413 is an inelegant, wrongheaded, and not particularly valiant attempt to even the scales of credibility by piling more women on to one side of the scale. If enough women tell the same story, the logic goes, it must be true. The unfortunate consequence of the Rule's policies and premises is that rape myths are further entrenched, and belief in women will be increasingly tied to corroboration by others.").

64 *Id.* at 692 ("Feminists would reject the notion that only a small, discrete cadre of miscreants and the criminally insane are responsible for rapes … Because, as a feminist, I resist the initial assumption that rape is a rarity perpetrated by a discrete group of sick individuals, I must, as an evidence scholar, question the logic of using prior similar acts to prove rape occurred in a principal case, even in cases of consent."). *See also*, Baker, *supra* note 6, at 576–7, 582 (criticizing the rule for promoting the false narrative that rape and rapists are exceptional).

65 According to the National Sexual Violence Resource Center, "91% of the victims of rape and sexual assault are female, and 9% are male." National Sexual Violence Resource Center, Statistics about Sexual Violence 1 (2015), www.nsvrc.org/sites/default/files/publications_nsvrc_factsheet_media-packet_statistics-about-sexual-violence_0.pdf. According to the United States Sentencing Commission, in 2021, "93.6% of sexual abuse offenders were men." United States Sentencing Commission, Quick Facts – Sexual Abuse Offenders 1 (2021), www.ussc.gov/sites/default/files/pdf/research-and-publications/quick-facts/Sexual_Abuse_FY21.pdf.

is likely to be at least somewhat suspicious of a special rule embracing otherwise problematically over-persuasive evidence in one narrow context only, particularly in the absence of proof that this evidence is any more compelling in that context.[66]

Inspired at least in part by a liberal feminist fight for equality under the law and yet accepting that there may be times where prior sexual assaults are relevant for something other than the propensity inference, such as motive or lack of accident, I would prefer the route of making a litigant fit the prior sexual assault or molestation evidence into the general rule, Rule 404(b)(2)'s other permissible purpose.[67] In other words, the court would have to find that the evidence is relevant for a purpose other than the "he's done it before, so he's done it again" propensity inference. This approach avoids the exceptional treatment for prior acts of sexual assault and molestation, but concededly does not obviate other feminist concerns about introduction of this evidence. In criminal cases, a classic 404(b) other relevant purposes analysis also makes the relevance of the evidence hinge on prosecutorial framing of charges and even has the potential to distort prosecutorial charging decisions, but this concern is, of course, not unique to sexual assault or molestation charges.[68]

Beyond liberal feminists' concerns about the equality of women before the law, Rules 413–15 run squarely into compelling third and fourth generation feminist concerns about the carceral implications of legal rules and the likelihood that they will be applied disproportionately to minority groups.[69] This concern is more than theoretical. As Orenstein has noted, due to the idiosyncrasies of federal jurisdiction, these rules have and will be applied disproportionately to defendants in Indian Country and in the military, where minorities make up a larger share than in the general population.[70] Moreover, Gruber (and many others) have made the

[66] Many critics of the rule have noted that recidivism rates for sexual assaults and child molestation are in fact lower than for other offenses. MUELLER AND KIRKPATRICK, *supra* note 1 ("On the matter of recidivism, many studies conducted to date indicate that rates for persons who commit sexual assaults are actually *lower* rather than *higher* than recidivism rates for persons who commit other crimes." (emphasis original)). *See also*, Erin Collins, *Evidence Rules for Decarceration*, 50 FORDHAM URB. L.J. 353, 361 (2023) ("[I]f proponents of these rules were truly motived by a concern that 404 blocks truthful and reliable evidence of guilt, they would have targeted all crimes with high recidivism rates."). But *see* Park, *supra* note 62, at 759–60 (arguing that bare recidivism rates are the wrong metric and that we should instead be looking at "comparative propensity").

[67] Thanks to Professor Carrie Leonetti for a useful airport chat on this very issue.

[68] For example, if a prosecutor wants to bring in prior bad acts using Rule 404(b), they could choose a charge that requires proving of a pattern. This element provides a theory for the admissibility of the other bad act evidence, which in turn may help to convince the jury that the charged conduct occurred, possibly due to the jury using the evidence for the propensity inference even if instructed not to do so.

[69] Rule 415 applies to civil cases and thus does not carry the same carceral implications. Nevertheless, third and fourth generation feminists would likely want to interrogate whether particular communities are burdened by this rule even in the civil context and the degree to which the rule contributes to problematic narratives.

[70] Aviva Orenstein, *Propensity or Stereotype?: A Bad Evidence Experiment in Indian Country*, 19 CORN. J.L. & PUB. POL'Y 173 (2009) (arguing that these rules contribute to negative stereotypes about

case that the carceral cost to people of color and other historically marginalized communities indirectly imposes a cost on quite a lot of women. Rape sword rules may seem appealing in cases of powerful, serial predators, like Weinstein,[71] but the rules are not restricted to those cases.

Specifically addressing the rape shield and rape sword laws, Capers has argued that these laws have an expressive cost of making trials about imagined good women and bad men and not "real women."[72] The rules also exact a practical one – potentially, acquittal of guilty defendants – when the jury does not buy this imagined narrative because it does not align with jurors' preexisting biases and beliefs.[73] One need not subscribe to a full abolitionist stance (of seeking to end the criminal legal system), feminist or otherwise, to conclude that these rules do more harm than good.

In sum, notwithstanding a long-standing and valid feminist interest in combating sexual violence, it would be a stretch to call these prior (sexual) bad act rules "feminist." Though it may often be difficult for courts to sort out whether prior sexual bad acts are relevant for non-propensity reasons, such as to show motive, intent, or lack of mistake, the blanket admission of evidence of prior sexual assaults in direct contradiction to the long-standing rule against propensity evidence is misguided. The National Organization for Women opposed these rules at the time of their passage in 1994,[74] and, since then, we have come a long way. Modern strands of feminist thought are more attentive to other aspects of identity beyond sex (or gender), to the negative collateral consequences of rules designed to "protect women," and to examining the "anti-feminist" narratives to which purportedly pro-women rules might unwittingly contribute. In short, today's feminists are even less likely to support these rules than the feminists of thirty years ago.

Native Americans and the fact that they are used mostly against Native Americans has likely increased their acceptance). Of course, the more the rape sword laws are incorporated into state law, the less prevalent this disparity.

71 *See* Kate Levine, *The Progressive Love Affair with the Carceral State*, 120 MICH. L. REV. 1225, 1226 (2022) (book review) (calling Harvey Weinstein "the progressive left's perfect villain" and his trial and sentence, pre-appeal "something of a crowning glory for neoliberal feminism's most recent pas de deux with the carceral state" but cautioning progressives to avoid reliance on the criminal legal system not only for violence against women but also for other pressing progressive concerns like police violence and hate crimes).

72 Capers, *supra* note 2, at 859; *cf.* Orenstein, *supra* note 48, at 667 ("Evidentiary mechanisms that reinforce cultural paradigms or somehow capitalize on them because the survivor just happens to fit the stereotype of the 'innocent' victim, are undesirable and ultimately counterproductive from a feminist perspective.").

73 Capers, *supra* note 2, at 859, 869 ("Conceptually, and despite the rise in nontraditional casting, it is still difficult to envision a black madonna (or for that matter an Asian or Hispanic one). It does not comport with our stock types.").

74 *See id.* 826, 845, n. 94.

SECTION 5

Hearsay and Confrontation

INTRODUCTION

When it comes to fame – and also fear – no other evidence rule can rival the rule against hearsay. Law students may easily memorize the basic rule, that out-of-court statements cannot be introduced in legal proceedings to prove the truth of what they assert, but learning to apply it is a different challenge. Adding further complexity, the Confrontation Clause, which for a time traveled in tandem with hearsay, now targets only a subset. It excludes testimonial out-of-court statements offered against defendants in criminal cases but does not reach non-testimonial hearsay. The intuition behind excluding hearsay is straightforward: to protect against judgments based on out-of-court statements relayed secondhand. Relatedly, the Confrontation Clause seeks to protect defendants in criminal cases from being tried by affidavit, constitutionalizing their right to confront the witnesses against them. Scholars, though, have questioned how the hearsay prohibition and the Confrontation right have been justified and operationalized in practice. For example, one prominent critique suggests that the many exceptions to the hearsay prohibition coupled with judicial discretion has led to an overly complex, far from intuitive patchwork that almost certainly does not work as intended.

This chapter begins with two pieces that step away from the doctrinal nuts and bolts and ask a historical question. What does slavery have to do with the origins of the hearsay rule? In the excerpt from David Sklansky's article, he argues that a previously-overlooked case, *Queen v. Hepburn*, should rightly be at the epicenter of the hearsay curriculum and of our thinking about the hearsay rule as it now exists. Sklansky contends that it was this case, in which the Supreme Court rejected an enslaved woman's evidence of her freedom on the grounds that it was hearsay, that firmly established the hearsay rule as a strict prohibition rather than a more flexible principle. Jeff Bellin's chapter pushes back against this conclusion, using the historical record to argue that the *Queen* case was a less significant addition to a preexisting jurisprudential trend towards a fixed prohibition against hearsay. Together, these contributions raise questions about how, in a country whose legal system originated during slavery, we grapple with that history as it relates to modern doctrine.

The remaining two chapters take up hearsay from two additional perspectives. Aviva Orenstein explores how the Confrontation doctrine and the rule against hearsay and its exceptions devalue the kind of indirect or delayed communication that may be used by women and others with less social power, particularly in cases involving sexual or domestic violence. Gabriela Rodriguez turns to the use of hearsay in immigration proceedings, where it is unconstrained by evidentiary strictures. While focused on hearsay, her piece asks a more universal question: What does it mean, in a deeply unequal world, that evidence rules are almost always party-neutral? In many ways, this echoes questions raised by Sklansky and Bellin's exchange. In the context of slavery, oppression, or intense disparities in power, how do "neutral" rules of inflexible application mitigate or exacerbate those disparities?

The Neglected Origins of the Hearsay Rule in American Slavery

Recovering *Queen v. Hepburn*

David A. Sklansky[1]

Queen v. Hepburn is the most important hearsay case in American history, but law students almost never learn about it. Decided by the Supreme Court in 1813, with a majority opinion by Chief Justice John Marshall, *Queen v. Hepburn* is the ruling that, more than any other, marked the transformation of the hearsay rule in the United States from a loose, haphazardly applied principle of preference for live testimony, into more or less what it is today: a strict rule of evidentiary exclusion, subject only to a bounded series of exceptions, and applicable even when better proof is unavailable. *Queen v. Hepburn* also had sweeping, and brutal, practical consequences. It buttressed the institution of slavery by closing off one of the few legal avenues through which people in bondage could seek their freedom. Seldom has a judicial decision about the laws of proof been so consequential.

Nonetheless, *Queen v. Hepburn* does not appear in any of the widely used evidence casebooks. …

I understand why most evidence instructors do not assign *Queen v. Hepburn*, even if they have heard of it, because I made the same choice myself. But that decision now seems to me mistaken, and one purpose of this article is to explain why. …

I.

In January 1810 a woman named Mina Queen filed a petition in the Circuit Court of the District of Columbia charging that she and her daughter, Louisa Queen, were being held in slavery illegally by a man named John Hepburn. The basis for the petition was Mina Queen's claim that her great grandmother, Mary Queen, had come to the American colonies as a free woman and an indentured servant, not a slave. Hepburn was summoned into court, and a jury trial was held five months

[1] Excerpted from David A. Sklansky, *The Neglected Origins of the Hearsay Rule in American Slavery: Recovering* Queen v. Hepburn, 2022 Sup. Ct. Rev. 413 (2022).

later. The Queens were represented by Francis Scott Key, the young lawyer and amateur poet who four years later would write "The Star-Spangled Banner."

We know much less about Mina and Louisa Queen than about their lawyer, but recent historical work has filled in some of the blanks. Between the 1780s and the outbreak of the Civil War, thousands of enslaved people sued for their freedom in American courts, and a good number of these suits were successful. Prominent lawyers like Key often represented these litigants, while in many instances continuing to own slaves themselves. Key, for example, argued more than a hundred freedom petitions between 1807 and 1840, but he was himself a slaveholder and far from an abolitionist. …

Many of the freedom suits, like Mina Queen's, were rooted in claims of genealogy, with the petitioners arguing that they were descended from free women, or from women who had lived free until they were themselves illegally enslaved. The specific nature of the claims varied: in Virginia, for example, the plaintiffs usually argued that they were descended from Native Americans; in Maryland, in contrast, the typical freedom plaintiff argued that he or she was descended from a white woman, or from a woman who had come to the United States unenslaved. Years before Mina Queen filed her petition, some two dozen of her relatives had won their freedom in Maryland courts, based on the same claim later advanced by Mina Queen: that their common ancestor, Mary Queen, had come to America in indentured servitude, not in bondage. The Maryland plaintiffs, enslaved on a plantation owned by the Jesuits who founded Georgetown College in 1789, had proven their cases with depositions taken from people who reported hearing that Mary Queen had come from South America by way of England, not from Africa, that she had dressed like a free woman, and that by rights she should have been free. Her geographic origins were important in part because Lord Mansfield's 1772 decision in *Somerset v. Stewart* had provided grounds for arguing that no one who had passed through England could lawfully be enslaved.

When Mina Queen's freedom petition came for trial, however, the Circuit Court of the District of Columbia excluded crucial portions of the evidence that her relatives in Maryland had introduced. Some deposition testimony was kept out of evidence because the witnesses failed to specify the sources of their information. The critical parts of other depositions were excluded because they recounted what today would be called "double hearsay": for example, what a witness's mother had heard from the witness's grandfather. …

Key also tried to introduce new evidence, not available when the Maryland cases had been tried: a deposition from a man named Fredus Ryland, who recalled having spoken directly with Mary Queen. According to Ryland, Mary Queen said that she had been born free in Guayaquil, a port city in what is now Ecuador, and that she had afterward lived in London … . Ryland's deposition was ruled inadmissible as well, apparently on the ground that since an enslaved person could not testify against a white litigant, her hearsay statements were also inadmissible.

The Ryland deposition had also been excluded several days earlier in the trial of a separate, contemporaneous freedom petition that Key had filed in the District of Columbia on behalf of Priscilla Queen, who may have been Mina's first cousin, against Priscilla's enslaver Francis Neale, a Jesuit priest who was later president of Georgetown College. In that case, the judges explained that "[t]he declarations of an ancestor, while held as a slave, cannot be given in evidence." They nonetheless allowed Key to introduce the deposition of a separate witness, John Jiams, who recalled hearing other people, now deceased, describe Mary Queen as a free woman. In Mina Queen's case, though, the judges instructed the jury to disregard the Jiams' deposition unless they concluded he had been speaking from his own firsthand knowledge, rather than repeating information he had obtained from unnamed others.

The Maryland and District of Columbia courts thus reached different decisions about the admissibility of the depositions offered to prove that Mary Queen had been free. Nonetheless the courts appeared to share an important, underlying assumption: that there was no across-the-board prohibition of hearsay evidence, either in general or with regard to the freedom of a litigant's ancestor. That was partly, as we will see, because both in Maryland and in the District of Columbia the courts were operating within a legal universe in which the rule against hearsay, as a rigid, categorical ban, was still in the process of solidifying.

With little admissible evidence to support Mina Queen's claims about her great-grandmother, the jury rejected her petition for freedom. Key appealed the case to the Supreme Court, where he argued it two years later …

… Key told the Justices that the issue in the case was relatively narrow: whether the fact that Mary Queen had been a free woman could be proved by "hearsay of hearsay." If it could not, he argued, "it will be impossible to prove any ancient fact." Hepburn's lawyers argued for affirmance …, urging that the use of hearsay evidence should be limited to proving "prescription, custom, and pedigree." And in this case, they contended, the hearsay in question had not been offered to prove ancestry, custom, or common usage, but "to prove that a certain ancestor came from England."

In essence, Hepburn's lawyers were arguing that the ban on hearsay should be understood as a rigid, categorical rule, not just a general principle to be balanced against other equities, and not a rule with a fluid, evolving set of exceptions. If they were right, and if hearsay was flatly inadmissible to prove that an enslaved plaintiff's ancestor had been free, it would mean not only that the Maryland courts had been wrong when they freed Mina Queen's relatives, but that the Circuit Court of the District of Columbia had also been wrong in Priscilla Queen's case, when they ruled the deposition by John Jiams fully admissible. In his reply for the appellants, James Morsell argued against the idea that hearsay was automatically inadmissible. Instead, he said, "[t]he general rule of evidence" was that the best available proof should be admitted: "if the evidence offered be the best which the nature of the case admits, and leaves no presumption that there is better behind, it is admissible." And with regard to whether Mary Queen had been free or enslaved, "[a]fter a lapse of 100 years better evidence than this cannot be expected."

The Supreme Court, though, fully embraced the broad ground for affirmance that had been urged by Hepburn's lawyers. Hearsay, Chief Justice Marshall explained for the Court, "is in its own nature inadmissible," even when testimony from a live witness was impossible. There were narrow exceptions to the hearsay ban, for "cases of *pedigree*, of *prescription*, of *custom*, and in some cases of *boundary*." In addition, Marshall said, "[t]here are also matters of general and public history which may be received without that full proof which is necessary for the establishment of a private fact." Beyond that, though, "[t]he danger of admitting hearsay evidence is sufficient to admonish Courts of justice against lightly yielding to the introduction of fresh exceptions to an old and well established rule." Indeed, given the great importance of the hearsay rule, the Supreme Court was "not inclined to extend the exceptions further than they have already been carried."

The reason for excluding hearsay, Marshall explained, is not just that "some better testimony … might be adduced." Even when no better evidence is available, the "intrinsic weakness" of hearsay, "its incompetency to satisfy the mind of the existence of the fact, and the frauds which might be practiced under its cover, combine to support the rule that hearsay evidence is totally inadmissible." Marshall therefore rejected the notion that hearsay should ever be admitted "to prove a *specific fact*, because the eye witnesses to that fact are dead." If, on the contrary, "the circumstance that the eye witnesses of any fact be dead should justify the introduction of testimony to establish that fact from hearsay," then "no man could feel safe in any property, a claim to which might be supported by proof so easily obtained."

The fact that the "property" in this case consisted of human beings did not, in Marshall's view, alter the analysis. "However the feelings of the individual may be interested on the part of a person claiming freedom," he explained, "the Court cannot perceive any legal distinction between the assertion of this and of any other right."

The sole dissenter in the case was Justice Gabriel Duvall. …

Duvall noted in his dissent that Maryland courts had allowed hearsay evidence to prove the freedom of an ancestor who had been dead for so long that live testimony could not be obtained. That was the only sensible result, Duvall argued. Hearsay should be admissible in such cases for the same reason that it was admissible to prove custom, pedigree, or the boundaries of land: it was necessary. "From the antiquity of the transactions to which these subjects may have reference" he explained, "it is impossible to produce living testimony"; therefore "to exclude hearsay in such cases, would leave the party interested without remedy."

Like Key, Duvall was himself a slaveowner – as was John Marshall, on a considerably larger scale. But it was obvious to Duvall that the arguments for admitting hearsay in support of a freedom petition were far weightier than in cases about land boundaries. "It will be universally admitted," he wrote, "that the right to freedom is more important than the right of property. And people of color from their helpless condition under the uncontrolled authority of a master, are entitled to all reasonable protection." Duvall warned that the decision in *Queen v. Hepburn* would slam the door on any freedom petition based on claims of an ancestor's freedom. "A decision that hearsay evidence in such cases shall not be admitted," he said, "cuts up by the roots all claims of the kind, and puts a final end to them, unless the claim should arise from a fact of recent date, and such a case will seldom, perhaps never, occur."

Duvall's admonition proved prophetic. As we will see, the Supreme Court's decision in *Queen v. Hepburn* helped to close off a key legal channel through which enslaved people in the late eighteenth and early nineteenth century sought their freedom. It also did more than any other single case to turn the hearsay ban into what it is today: a categorical, often unforgiving rule of exclusion, not a flexible, intermittently applied principle of preference. *Queen v. Hepburn* did not by itself create the modern hearsay rule, but it was a landmark in the rule's development. …

III.

Although *Queen v. Hepburn* was tried under Maryland law, which governed at the time in the portion of the District of Columbia north of the Potomac River, the Supreme Court treated the hearsay question as a matter of "general law," to be decided according to principles not limited to any particular jurisdiction. Either way, however, judges outside Maryland would follow the holding only if they believed that Chief Justice Marshall had set forth principles that should govern the common law of every American jurisdiction. Moreover, as Farah Peterson has pointed out, most lawyers and judges in the early nineteenth century did not view the United States Supreme Court as the nation's preeminent expositor of the law: they were more likely to look for guidance to eminent state-court jurists – including Spencer Roane, James Kent, and Zephaniah Swift – than to John Marshall. Even Maryland judges might not apply the reasoning of *Queen v. Hepburn* in later cases if they found it unconvincing.

Nonetheless, the decision proved enormously influential. The Supreme Court itself reaffirmed the decision three years later, in *Davis v. Wood*, ruling that a freedom plaintiff could not introduce hearsay evidence, from people who were now dead, that the plaintiff's ancestor was a white woman who had been born in England. Chief Justice Marshall again wrote for the Court, and he rejected out of hand the suggestion that *Queen v. Hepburn* should be revisited. *Queen v. Hepburn* and *Davis v. Wood* all but eliminated the practice of enslaved people suing for liberty based on the free status of their maternal ancestors. Without the possibility of relying on hearsay, such suits were hopeless. And while not every state court followed the *Queen* and *Davis* decisions in rejecting hearsay proof an ancestor's race or status, most did, including the high courts of Maryland and Virginia, jurisdictions that produced a disproportionate share of freedom cases. Freedom cases did not disappear, but, as Jason Gillmer has noted, their focus shifted away from claims of ancestry and toward other claims, including, in many cases, that the plaintiff was white. *Queen v. Hepburn* thus contributed to a process already underway when it was decided: the repositioning of slavery within an increasingly rigid, increasingly explicit, and increasingly binary system of racial caste.

The Supreme Court's decision in *Queen v. Hepburn* also played an important role in transforming the hearsay rule from a loose preference for in-court testimony, with a flexible and open-ended series of exceptions, to a flat prohibition, with only a fixed and limited set of carveouts. John Marshall himself, sitting as Circuit Justice, cited *Queen v. Hepburn* and *Davis v. Wood* in 1825 for the proposition that exceptions to the hearsay rule would not be extended "further than they have been already carried." Writing for the Supreme Court in 1836, Justice Joseph Story took *Queen v. Hepburn* to establish that hearsay was admissible only to prove "pedigree" – i.e., ancestry – or, in the form of reputation evidence, to prove land boundaries and other "claims of a public nature" obtained by long usage. In particular, Story read *Queen v. Hepburn*, along with *Davis v. Wood*, to make clear that "hearsay evidence was not admissible to prove a specific fact, although the witnesses to the fact were dead." Echoing Marshall's reasoning in *Queen v. Hepburn*, Story wrote that hearsay was excluded not just because "it often supposes better evidence behind," but because "it is not upon oath," because there was "no opportunity of cross-examination," because "it is peculiarly liable to be obtained by fraudulent contrivances," and "above all" because "it is exceedingly infirm, unsatisfactory and intrinsically weak in its very nature and character." Consequently, Story explained, the admission of hearsay evidence in any situation was "somewhat of an anomaly."

This view of hearsay had become conventional in the United States by 1836, in large part because of *Queen v. Hepburn*. That same year, Connecticut's highest court declared it "a general principle of the law of evidence" that "mere declarations of third persons as to any fact, or what is commonly called *hearsay* evidence, is inadmissible to establish that fact," because it was "too vague and unsubstantial to afford any reasonable test of its truth." The "few exceptions" to this rule, the court explained, should be "strictly construed," and neither "favored nor extended." The authority for this sweeping rule was *Queen v. Hepburn*. …

… For American courts, *Queen v. Hepburn* was a critical step in the transition of the hearsay rule from a loose preference for sworn, in-court testimony, to a categorical ban on out-of-court statements offered to prove the truth of what they asserted, even when no better evidence was available.

The Supreme Court might conceivably have reached the same decision in *Queen v. Hepburn* even if the case had not concerned an enslaved plaintiff's petition for freedom. The principal force driving the development of the hearsay rule, in the United States as in Britain, was not slavery but the rise of the legal profession, the expanding role that lawyers played in civil and criminal trials, and the increasing control that lawyers, along with judges, asserted over the factfinding process. …

Strictly speaking, moreover, *Queen v. Hepburn* was not a case about slavery; it was a case about procedure. Chief Justice Marshall's opinion for the Supreme Court in *Queen v. Hepburn* stressed that the ban on hearsay evidence was a "general rule," which operated the same regardless of the nature of the substantive right at issue. This was in keeping with the usual practice of nineteenth-century courts to treat enslaved people as just another form of property, to be governed by the same rules. Furthermore, slaveholders sometimes introduced hearsay evidence of their own to disprove a plaintiff's claim that an ancestor had been free, or illegally enslaved. This happened at the trial in *Queen v. Hepburn* itself: John Hepburn's lawyers introduced a deposition by Gabriel Duvall's great-uncle, Benjamin Duvall, relaying hearsay about the origins and legal status of Mina Queen's ancestor, Mary Queen. Therefore, *Queen v. Hepburn* may have helped some freedom plaintiffs by barring evidence that otherwise might have been introduced against them.

There is no doubt, though, that the decision hurt freedom plaintiffs much more than it helped them. Slaveholders might or might not have access to documentary proof, but enslaved plaintiffs almost never could introduce any evidence other than hearsay regarding the race or status of their ancestors. This is a general feature of the hearsay rule: it tends to pose a bigger problem for disempowered litigants, who have less access to admissible written records and are less able to track down live witnesses and bring them to court. Furthermore, in the absence of other proof, courts in slave states often applied a presumption that individuals who appeared to be of African ancestry were lawfully in bondage. Justice Duvall understood that the ruling in *Queen v. Hepburn* would all but shut off an important legal avenue through which enslaved people had sued for freedom; that was why he dissented so strongly. And notwithstanding Chief Justice Marshall's protestations, the slavery context of *Queen v. Hepburn* may have mattered to him as well. Marshall was a major, not a minor, slaveholder. As Paul Finkelman has noted, "[s]laves were a constant factor in his personal life, his economic success, and his children's future." Marshall's lifelong membership in the American Colonization Society reflected, in part, his deep and unrelenting hostility to idea of Black people living free in the United States. He wrote the opinion in seven cases involving enslaved people seeking their freedom; each time, the plaintiff lost. The role that a stronger hearsay rule would play in shutting down freedom suits – and in blocking in Mina Queen's suit in particular – may not have been incidental to Marshall.

IV.

The hearsay rule was not invented in *Queen v. Hepburn*, and courts did not start banning hearsay just to keep African Americans in bondage. Many other legal tools, alas, existed to accomplish that odious end. But *Queen v. Hepburn* did mark a significant point of transition: more than any other single decision, at least in the United States, it turned hearsay from a loose principle of preference for in-court testimony into a rigid rule of evidentiary exclusion. The consequence of applying this new, stricter version of the hearsay doctrine in *Queen v. Hepburn* was to deny Mina Queen the opportunity to challenge her enslavement, and the enslavement of her daughter, by introducing the only evidence available to them of their ancestor's freedom. And the precedent set by *Queen v. Hepburn* had the same consequence for many other freedom plaintiffs and would-be plaintiffs. By strengthening the hearsay rule in *Queen v. Hepburn*, the Supreme Court helped to shut down one of the few legal channels through which enslaved people could seek their own liberty. That may not have been an unintended result; on the contrary, it may have helped to motivate the decision, at least for its author. The hearsay rule, as a genuine rule as opposed to a flexible principle, has its origins, in significant part, in American slavery. …

There was a time when *Queen v. Hepburn* was widely cited, unabashedly, as the principal authority for the inadmissibility of hearsay in the United States. It counts as progress, however slow and partial, that the case eventually became something of an embarrassment and that citations to it grew sparser. Ignoring *Queen v. Hepburn* was better than celebrating it, but it would be better still to remember the decision, to hold it up to the light, and to try to learn from it. The American hearsay rule took its modern form in a decision that kept a woman and her daughter enslaved by suppressing what was known about one of their ancestors. The implications of this fact for how the hearsay rule should be understood and applied today are debatable, but there is little to be said for avoiding the debate – for matching suppression of family history with suppression of legal history. There is little to recommend keeping law students ignorant about the role the hearsay rule played in supporting American slavery and, conversely, about the role American slavery played in the development of the hearsay rule.

Examining the American Hearsay Prohibition's Roots in Slavery

Jeffrey Bellin

INTRODUCTION

John Henry Wigmore described the hearsay prohibition as "a rule which may be esteemed, next to jury-trial, the greatest contribution" of the common law "to the world's jurisprudence of procedure."[1] Like most of Wigmore's pronouncements the praise is overblown, but it fits the traditional view of hearsay regulation as a noble, if imperfect, enterprise. That view is changing, however. David Sklansky recently argued: "The hearsay rule, as a genuine rule as opposed to a flexible principle, has its origins, in significant part, in American slavery."[2] Others agree, explaining that "the rigidness of hearsay rules – the bane of many a law student – owes much to the [Supreme] Court's discomfort with permitting enslaved people to petition for their freedom."[3]

These authors are careful to acknowledge that a desire to protect the institution of slavery was not the *sole* force behind the American hearsay prohibition. Sklansky, for example, notes: "The principal force driving the development of the hearsay rule, in the United States as in Britain, was not slavery but the rise of the legal profession, the expanding role that lawyers played in civil and criminal trials, and the increasing control that lawyers, along with judges, asserted over the factfinding process."[4] But given the unique evil represented by American slavery

Thanks to David Sklansky whose article initiated this important conversation and for his comments on an early draft of this chapter. And thanks to Bennett Capers, Jasmine E. Harris, and Julia Simon-Kerr for inviting me to contribute to this project and for comments on this chapter.

1 *See* John H. Wigmore, *The History of the Hearsay Rule*, 17 Harv. L. Rev. 437, 458 (1904); 1 John Henry Wigmore, Treatise on the System of Evidence in Trials at Common Law § 1365 (1904) (same).

2 David A. Sklansky, *The Neglected Origins of the Hearsay Rule in American Slavery: Recovering* Queen v. Hepburn, 2022 Sup. Ct. Rev. 413, 443 (2022).

3 Bennett Capers, *Race, Gatekeeping, Magical Words, and the Rules of Evidence*, 76 Vand. L. Rev. 1855, 1862 (2023); *see also*, Charles W. Tyler, *Genealogy in Constitutional Law*, 77 Vand. L. Rev. 1713, 1721 (2024) ("The hearsay rule originated as a means of insulating slaveholders from the threat of their slaves' petitions for freedom.").

4 Sklansky, *supra* note 2, at 440.

and the ongoing salience of race, it is important to assess the degree to which the American hearsay rule originated in slavery – and the subsequent implications (if any) for modern evidence law.

The traditional esteem for the hearsay rule stems from its accuracy-enhancing function. No matter how lax a forum's evidentiary standards there must be some limits to the evidence that can be considered. An obvious limit is the degree to which witnesses can testify not to what they know, but to what they heard from someone else. At some point, rumor and gossip become too flimsy a form of evidence to rely on in serious disputes. As Sklansky observes, "The hearsay rule plainly has protected, and continues to protect, against many injustices."[5]

The hearsay rule also has deep roots. It appears in places and eras far removed from American slavery. Scholars trace hearsay prohibitions at least as far back as the 1100s.[6] And the sentiments underlying the rule can be found even earlier. For example, the Bible instructs readers to credit the accounts of "eyewitnesses" over "cleverly devised stories" and emphasizes the importance of face-to-face accusations.[7]

Today, courts in the United States regulate the admission of out-of-court statements with a precise "hearsay" definition, a general prohibition, and numerous exceptions. But this is a modern development.[8] The hearsay prohibition, like all American and English evidence law, was once remarkably porous. Stephan Landsman's study of proceedings in London's Old Bailey courts is illustrative. Landsman explains that in the 1680s, "few rules appear to have restricted the introduction of evidence … Counsel was virtually never present … and there was virtually no recourse to appellate review."[9] Over time, "courts gradually grew more circumspect about hearsay. A common refrain of trial judges, from the middle of the [eighteenth] century on, was that the witnesses should limit themselves to what they knew personally."[10] With lawyers regularly appearing in trials by the end of the eighteenth century, the proceedings reflect "the eventual development of a rather strict rule of exclusion."[11]

5 *Id.* at 444.

6 *See* Jeremy A. Blumenthal, *Shedding Some Light on Calls for Hearsay Reform: Civil Law Hearsay Rules in Historical and Modern Perspective*, 13 PACE INT'L L. REV. 93, 103 (2001) ("[B]y the twelfth century, a rule against hearsay – a rule explicitly requiring witnesses to testify solely from their first-hand knowledge to ensure reliability – was entrenched in the dominant procedural system.").

7 2 Peter 1:16 ("For we did not follow cleverly devised stories when we told you about the coming of our Lord Jesus Christ in power, but we were eyewitnesses of his majesty."); Acts 25:16 ("I told them that it is not the Roman custom to hand over anyone before they have faced their accusers and have had an opportunity to defend themselves against the charges.").

8 *See* Jeffrey Bellin, *Murder on the Hearsay Trail*, 12 TEX. A&M L. REV. 77, 95–102 (2024).

9 Stephan Landsman, *The Rise of the Contentious Spirit: Adversary Procedure in Eighteenth Century England*, 75 CORNELL L. REV. 497 505–6 (1990).

10 *Id.* at 569.

11 *Id.* at 572. Legal historians T. P. Gallanis and John Langbein, drawing on other historical sources, support Landsman's account. *See* T. P. Gallanis, *The Rise of Modern Evidence Law*, 84 IOWA L. REV. 499, 503, 533, 536 (1999) ("Until the 1780s, the courts rarely discussed the hearsay rule," but the "rule against hearsay began to mature into its modern form during the late eighteenth century."); John H. Langbein, *Historical Foundations of the Law of Evidence: A View from the Ryder Sources*, 96

It is this transition, from a mild disfavor for hearsay evidence to a more concrete prohibition that Sklansky and others highlight. And that is the subject of this chapter, exploring whether the modern American hearsay rule is (1) a repurposed tool of enslavers that should be viewed with suspicion; (2) a generic limit on fact-finding that, like any procedural rule, can be used for good or evil; or (3) something in between.

THE INFLUENCE OF *QUEEN V. HEPBURN*

The argument that the American hearsay rule is a vestige of slavery arises from its application in an 1813 Supreme Court opinion, *Queen v. Hepburn*, which affirmed the exclusion of evidence that would have bolstered an enslaved person's legal case for freedom.[12] Chief Justice Marshall, at that time "an active purchaser of slaves on his way to owning hundreds of human beings,"[13] delivered the opinion which Sklansky argues, did "more than any other single case to turn the hearsay ban into what it is today."[14]

There is a facial logic to tracing the genesis of the American hearsay rule to the country's original sin. *Queen v. Hepburn* offers a clear, early pronouncement by the nation's highest court endorsing a strict hearsay prohibition. The opinion also had a powerful pro-slavery impact, hobbling "freedom lawsuits" where individual plaintiffs sought to show that they were unlawfully enslaved.[15] An increasingly inflexible hearsay prohibition "privileged the kinds of evidence slaveholders could control (documentary records and direct testimony) at the expense of the kinds of evidence the enslaved persons could produce (old depositions and family lore)."[16]

COLUM. L. REV. 1168, 1197, 1201 (1996) (explaining that "Evidentiary concerns such as hearsay that had remained within judicial discretion when the judge still dominated the trial were reformulated at the end of the eighteenth century and across the nineteenth century into rules of admissibility and exclusion"; and identifying "a reasonably likely cause: the rise of adversary criminal procedure, that is, counsel's capture of the previously lawyer-free criminal trial").

12 *See* Queen v. Hepburn, 11 U.S. 290, 295–6 (1813); Sklansky, *supra* note 2, at 414; WILLIAM G. THOMAS III, A QUESTION OF FREEDOM: THE FAMILIES WHO CHALLENGED SLAVERY FROM THE NATION'S FOUNDING TO THE CIVIL WAR 171–2 (Yale University Press 2020) ("The rule of evidence against hearsay had taken shape in American courts only in the 1780s … [h]owever, over several decades, lawyers began to invoke the rule to exclude out-of-court statements, and judges began to apply it more strictly.").

13 PAUL FINKELMAN, SUPREME INJUSTICE: SLAVERY IN THE NATION'S HIGHEST COURT 36–48, 64 (Harvard University Press 2018).

14 Sklansky, *supra* note 2, at 424.

15 *See* Jason A. Gillmer, *Suing for Freedom: Interracial Sex, Slave Law, and Racial Identity in the Post-Revolutionary and Antebellum South*, 82 N.C. L. REV. 535, 585 (2004) ("Chief Justice Marshall's opinions in John Davis's cases and in Mima Queen proved tremendously influential, effectively ending suits for freedom of this type.").

16 THOMAS III, *supra* note 12, at 5; *cf.* Jackson ex dem. Bogart v. King, 1825 WL 1813 (N.Y. Sup. Ct. 1825) ("[T]he register of births, marriages and burials is competent evidence."); *see also*, Jasmine B. Gonzales Rose, *Toward a Critical Race Theory of Evidence*, 101 MINN. L. REV. 2243, 2311 (2017) ("[E]vidence law has been applied in ways that structurally disadvantage people of color and advantage whites.").

The effort to explain the American hearsay prohibition as a product of slavery has significant weaknesses, however. It is admittedly difficult to determine with certainty which cases and factors altered the flow of the common law of evidence. But the Supreme Court's opinion in *Queen v. Hepburn* seems best characterized as an illustration of the era's changing hearsay rules – not a cause.

As explained below, the trial court rulings upheld in *Queen* did not apply a strict prohibition. Those rulings admitted a great deal of hearsay, excluding primarily "hearsay of hearsay." In upholding the rulings, the Supreme Court did make a series of general pronouncements about the inadmissibility of hearsay, but those pronouncements tracked existing authorities, adding little to existing legal commentary. In fact, Marshall made a similar pronouncement in an earlier case with no connection to slavery. Further, it is difficult to credit Marshall's statements with shaping American hearsay law. Marshall's generic pronouncements – such as, that hearsay was "totally inadmissible" – vastly overstated the strictness of the hearsay prohibition that would subsequently take hold in England and America.

The limited influence of *Queen v. Hepburn* should be no surprise. The Supreme Court's impact on evidence law in 1813 depended on the Justices' persuasiveness. And that diminished the reach of superficial analysis offered by a court struggling to find its place in the common law landscape. In the early 1800s, English courts and commentators had greater influence over the common law of evidence. And, as Landsman and other historians show, they were well on their way to the same conclusions about the admissibility of hearsay without the influence of American slavery or Marshall's opinion in *Queen v. Hepburn*.

THE TRIAL COURT RULINGS: NO EXCEPTION FOR "HEARSAY OF HEARSAY"

Because *Queen v. Hepburn* itself concerned a barbaric practice whose legality was accepted by the judges without comment, the case report is difficult to read and harder to analyze. Modern readers naturally resist the procedural rulings affirmed in *Queen* not only because those rulings are flawed but because they are beside the point. Mina Queen, the plaintiff in *Queen v. Hepburn*, should have been free regardless of her ancestry. Judges of the era, infected with racism and other prejudices, did not feel the same way. Consequently, the moral failings of the judges in the case seem far more meaningful than the legal ones.

Indeed, the horrific reality of American slavery seeps through the pages of the case report. The case's caption is: *Mima Queen and Child v. Hepburn*. It was a civil suit brought by Mina[17] Queen to deliver herself *and her daughter*

[17] The official caption misspells her name. Sklansky, *supra* note 2, at n. 4. The opinion also appears to misspell the name of a witness, Fredus Ryland, as "Freeders Ryland." These errors suggest that the case report was created by someone observing, rather than involved in, the proceedings. *See* Craig Joyce, *The Rise of the Supreme Court Reporter: An Institutional Perspective on Marshall Court*

Louisa from bondage. In the underlying litigation, a jury and a series of American judges, including the Justices of the Supreme Court, considered whether to grant this relief based on the most arbitrary of facts – the birthplace of Mina Queen's great grandmother, Mary Queen.

Legally speaking, the case illustrates the importance of hearsay to freedom lawsuits. The birth of Mary Queen and her passage to America were long past events. No witness could testify to those facts directly. Consequently, Mina Queen's lawyer, Francis Scott Key, relied on depositions from people who related what others had said about Mary Queen.

The trial court admitted much of the evidence. As explained by historian George Thomas, there were two approaches to hearsay in freedom lawsuits in Maryland at the time, and neither involved a strict hearsay prohibition:

(1) "In several instances, judges had gone so far as to allow in their entirety secondhand statements about what the declarant heard others say about the status of an ancestor."
(2) "Other judges tried to make a distinction in out-of-court statements between hearsay based on direct knowledge and what some called 'hearsay of hearsay,' a secondhand account of what someone heard another person say."[18]

The trial court in *Queen* took the second approach. As Supreme Court Justice Duvall summarized in dissent: "The Court below admitted hearsay evidence to prove the freedom of the ancestor from whom the petitioners claim, but refused to admit hearsay of hearsay."

The trial court's approach is apparent in the rulings challenged on appeal. In addition to the exclusion of a deposition discussed in a separate section below, Queen challenged the exclusion of:

- "part of the deposition of Caleb Clarke, who deposed to a fact respecting the ancestor of petitioners which he had heard his mother say she had frequently heard from her father"[19]

Queen also challenged the trial court's cautionary instruction to the jury concerning its admission of the following evidence:

- "the deposition of Richard Disney, who deposed that he had heard a great deal of talk about Mary Queen, the ancestor of the Plaintiffs, and has heard divers[e] persons say that Captain Larkin brought her into this country, and that she had a great many fine clothes"[20]

Ascendancy, 83 MICH. L. REV. 1291, 1298 n. 6, 1312 (1985) (describing "glaring deficiencies" in the reporting process and explaining that: "It was not until 1834 that the Court ordered the filing with the Clerk of such opinions as *were* written." (emphasis original)).

[18] THOMAS III, *supra* note 12, at 169.

[19] Queen, 11 U.S. at 294.

[20] *Id.*

- "the deposition of Thomas Warfield, who deposed that John Jiams, an inspector of tobaeco, told him that Mary the ancestor of the Plaintiffs was free and was brought into this country by Captain Larkin, and was sold for seven years"[21]

The trial court instructed the jury that it should only consider this evidence if the witnesses relating the statements heard them firsthand, and to disregard the evidence if the statements were "communicated to [the witnesses] respecting the existence of such a report and noise many years after …, without its appearing by whom or in what manner the same was communicated."[22]

This instruction is the closest thing to a hearsay rule that appears in the proceedings. It suggests that hearsay was admissible, so long as this indulgence was not taken too far.

Equally important, the legal question the litigants presented on appeal was not whether there should be a hearsay regime like the one recognized today: a general hearsay prohibition subject to a variety of exceptions. That seemed assumed by all the judges and counsel involved in the case, save one. The question was whether there should be an especially permissive hearsay *exception* that allowed even "hearsay of hearsay" in a case like Queen's.[23]

Francis Scott Key led off the argument for Queen by stating, "The principal exception is to the opinion of the [trial] Court that in tracing a pedigree, the hearsay of hearsay is not admissible."[24] Opposing counsel, John Law, responded: "Hearsay of hearsay is analogous to a copy of a copy. The witness ought at least to state from whom he heard the report."[25] Another opposing lawyer added, "The admission of hearsay is an exception to the general rule of evidence, and therefore must be confined strictly to" the recognized exceptions.[26] The outlier was James Morsell who argued for Queen, in rebuttal: "The general rule of evidence is that if the evidence offered be the best which the nature of the case admits, and leaves no presumption that there is better behind, it is admissible."[27] (Morrell's position is the one that Sklansky argues might have achieved more prominence if not for the resulting opinion.[28])

21 *Id.*
22 *Id.* at 291.
23 *Cf.* R. Kent Newmyer, John Marshall and the Heroic Age of the Supreme Court 428 (LSU Press 2001) (criticizing Marshall for suggesting that "the admission of hearsay evidence in personal liberty cases could not be distinguished from the general rules").
24 Queen, 11 U.S. at 291–2. The case report available from Hein Online labels the respective statements of counsel while the report available on Westlaw does not.
25 *Id.* at 292.
26 *Id.*
27 *Id.* at 298.
28 Sklansky, *supra* note 2, at 425. Sklansky points to American authorities who stressed this "best evidence" principle. But for the reasons discussed above, this vague principle, even if endorsed by the Court, was destined to become a guidepost for crafting categorical exceptions (see, e.g., Federal Rules of Evidence 804, 807), not a substitute for a categorical approach.

Chief Justice Marshall's opinion for the Court similarly framed the case as turning on the hearsay exceptions, concluding: "The general rule comprehends the case, and the case is not within any exception heretofore recognized. This Court is not inclined to extend the exceptions further than they have already been carried." Thus, while Marshall's opinion acknowledged that there were "some exceptions" to the hearsay prohibition, he declared they did not apply. His opinion is short on details but suggests that the "pedigree" exception only applied to statements about Mary Queen's legal status, not to "specific facts" like where she was born or the details of her passage to America.[29] Justice Duvall, in dissent, similarly appears to have viewed the case as turning on the applicability of a situation-specific exception, concluding: "[O]n a petition for freedom where the petitioner claims from an ancestor who has been dead for a great length of time, the issue may be proved by hearsay evidence, if the fact is of such antiquity that living testimony cannot be procured."[30]

Parsing the opinion is challenging because, as both Duvall and Marshall recognized, the common law was fluid. The Supreme Court had limitless options to grant Queen relief, including extending the hearsay exceptions beyond existing boundaries or changing the existing approach altogether. Marshall declined, purportedly on grounds of uniformity. The majority opinion (disingenuously) argued: "the rule ... which the Court shall establish in this cause will not, in its application, be confined to cases of this particular description, but will be extended to others where rights may depend on facts which happened many years past."[31]

[29] *See also*, Gregory v. Baugh, 29 Va. 665, 670 (1831) ("It is an established exception to the general rule which excludes hearsay evidence, general reputation, or tradition, that it is admissible to prove pedigree; but it is not admissible to prove the national character, the quality or the rights, of the ancestor from whom the pedigree is derived, or any other specific fact."); Davis v. Wood, 14 U.S. 6, 8 (1816) ("Evidence by hearsay and general reputation is admissible only as to pedigree, but not to establish the freedom of the petitioner's ancestor, and thence to deduce his or her own."); Ariela Gross and Alejandro de la Fuente, *Slaves, Free Blacks, and Race in the Legal Regimes of Cuba, Louisiana, and Virginia: A Comparison*, 91 N.C. L. Rev. 1699, 1748–9 (2013) ("Community members might testify as to their understanding of a person's race, and the jury could rule on that race accordingly. To determine slave status, however, the jury would require firsthand evidence, documentation, or something more persuasive than hearsay."); Jason A. Gillmer, *Suing for Freedom: Interracial Sex, Slave Law, and Racial Identity in the Post-Revolutionary and Antebellum South*, 82 N.C. L. Rev. 535, 572–3 (2004) ("Nor did the exception for pedigree apply in this instance. That exception was limited to declarations of family members about a person's lineage.").

[30] Queen, 11 U.S. at 298; *cf.* Jason A. Gillmer, *Suing for Freedom: Interracial Sex, Slave Law, and Racial Identity in the Post-Revolutionary and Antebellum South*, 82 N.C. L. Rev. 535, 575 (2004) ("Judge St. George Tucker, a known antislavery advocate, later expounded on the practical reasons for relaxing the rules of hearsay in suits for freedom. As he explained, there is no record for 'births for any but white persons, and those Registers are either all lost, or of all records probably the most imperfect.' Therefore, '[i]n a claim for freedom ... the plaintiff may well be permitted to make out his case on the trial according to the evidence.' Hearsay evidence was admissible, in other words, because that often was the only evidence available."); *cf.* Finkelman, *supra* note 13, at 64 ("Marshall could easily have found an exception to hearsay rules in freedom suits, because they were special kinds of cases.").

[31] Queen, 11 U.S. at 295.

The Justices' complicity in slavery surely reduced their willingness to take the most direct approach to helping Queen: broadly applying the hearsay exception for "pedigree."[32] But their narrow application of the exception does not appear, in retrospect, to be a key moment in the evolution of American hearsay doctrine. A broader exception would have had great significance for freedom lawsuits but little significance for evidence law. The evolving common law hearsay framework would likely have remained on track, gradually solidifying into a general hearsay prohibition with numerous exceptions.

SWEEPING DICTA ON HEARSAY'S TOTAL INADMISSIBILITY

The Supreme Court's opinion in *Queen v. Hepburn* did more than simply affirm the trial court. The Court also made sweeping general pronouncements about hearsay. These pronouncements could have been influential since they articulated legal principles beyond the narrow contours of the trial court's evidentiary rulings. It seems unlikely, however, that these pronouncements changed the course of hearsay law because they either echoed existing legal authorities or failed to permeate the common law.

The primary chance that the *Queen* opinion had to influence hearsay law was the "one general principle" that Marshall framed as the key to the case. Marshall wrote:

> These several opinions of the Court depend on one general principle. The decision of which determines them all. It is this. *That hearsay evidence is incompetent to establish any specific fact, which fact is in its nature susceptible of being proved by witnesses who speak from their own knowledge.*

Marshall likely anticipated that this line would be the case's legacy. The case reporter pulled the line out as one of two used to summarize the evidence rulings in the case. And it appears in Simon Greenleaf's 1843 treatise on Evidence.[33] But modern readers will be excused if the line rings no bells. For it seems to have had no lasting impact on the law of evidence.

We can only speculate about why Marshall's general principle did not stand the test of time. Most likely, no one could puzzle out what Marshall meant. The distinction Marshall draws between "specific facts" that are, and are not, susceptible to proof from a witness with knowledge requires further explanation.[34] All facts at

[32] *See* FINKELMAN, *supra* note 13, at 52 (documenting Marshall's pro-slavery rulings).

[33] SIMON GREENLEAF, TREATISE ON THE LAW OF EVIDENCE 112 (1842).

[34] Greenleaf repeats Marshall's discussion without elaboration before moving onto a comprehensive explanation of the legal principles involved that relies on *Wright v. Tatham. Id.* Sklansky suggests that Marshall was distinguishing prohibited hearsay from testimony about "custom" and "general reputation" – i.e., "that hearsay should be allowed to prove what people generally thought and said, but not what a particular person, who could not be examined in court, reported having observed."

least arguably fit that description. Was this a reference to witness unavailability? And how did this principle fit with the "some exceptions" to the hearsay rule that Marshall acknowledged but declined to list? As discussed above, Marshall seemed to suggest that his "one general principle" limited even the hearsay *exceptions*. But that was never the law. The most well-established common law hearsay exception was an exception for dying declarations.[35] That exception's sole purpose was to admit out-of-court statements from absent witnesses to prove *specific facts*, like who struck the fatal blow.[36]

Marshall's opinion also proclaimed that (1) the hearsay rule did not depend on the existence of "some better testimony which might be adduced in the particular case,"[37] and (2) "hearsay evidence is totally inadmissible" due to "its incompetency to satisfy the mind of the existence of the fact, and the frauds which might be practiced under its cover."[38] These pronouncements ring more familiar. But that is not because of Marshall's influence. It is because they echo other, more influential, authorities. For example, "the period's leading treatise,"[39] *Gilbert on Evidence* first published in 1754 states:

> Hearsay is no Evidence ... though a Person Testify what he hath heard upon Oath, yet the Person who spake it was not upon Oath; ... if the first Speech was without Oath, an Oath that there was such a Speech makes it no more than a bare speaking, and so of no Value in a Court of Justice, where all Things were determined under the Solemnities of an Oath ...[40]

Sklansky, *supra* note 2, at 428. That makes sense but further reveals the opinion's insignificance as it bears little resemblance to the hearsay framework that subsequently developed. The reference also seems to draw on the related but distinct requirement that a witness have personal knowledge. *See* Fed. R. Ev. 602; Charles T. McCormick, Handbook of the Law of Evidence § 10 (1954) ("The same requirement, in general, is imposed upon declarations coming in under exceptions to the hearsay rule, that is, the declarant must so far as appears have had an opportunity to observe the fact declared.").

35 *See* Crawford v. Washington, 541 U.S. 36, 56 n. 6 (2004) ("The existence of that exception as a general rule of criminal hearsay law cannot be disputed."); Mattox v. United States, 156 U.S. 237, 243–4 (1895) ("from time immemorial they have been treated as competent testimony, and no one would have the hardihood at this day to question their admissibility"); King v. Woodcock, 168 Eng. Rep. 352, 353–4 (1789) (recognizing admissibility of "the dying declaration of a person who has received a fatal blow"); State v. Moody, 3 N.C. 31, 31 (N.C. Super. L. & Eq. 1798) ("Declarations of the deceased have sometimes been received.").

36 *See* Mattox v. United States, 146 U.S. 140, 151 (1892) ("Dying declarations are admissible on a trial for murder, as to the fact of the homicide and the person by whom it was committed, in favor of the defendant as well as against him."); Mattox v. United States, 156 U.S. 237, 243 (1895) ("[F]rom time immemorial they have been treated as competent testimony.").

37 Mattox, 156 U.S. at 295–6.

38 Queen, 11 U.S. at 296. Although the historical record is unclear, it is likely that the Court's ruling left Mina Queen enslaved. Thomas III, *supra* note 12, at 189.

39 Gallanis, *supra* note 11, at 503; Langbein, *supra* note 11, at 1172 ("Gilbert's became the most influential eighteenth-century book on evidence.").

40 Geoffrey Gilbert, The Law of Evidence (1754).

Blackstone's 1771 *Commentaries on the Laws of England* similarly state, "no evidence of a discourse with another will be admitted, but the man himself must be produced."[41] A prominent American treatise published in 1803 contains a comment by Edward Christian that tracks one of Marshall's points precisely: "[I]n general the want of better evidence can never justify the admission of hearsay."[42]

Marshall could also claim consistency with himself. Presiding over the treason trial of Aaron Burr six years earlier, Marshall excluded an out-of-court statement, explaining:

> The rule of evidence which rejects mere hearsay testimony, *which excludes from trials of a criminal or civil nature the declarations of any other individual than of him against whom the proceedings are instituted*, has been generally deemed by all essential to the correct administration of justice.[43]

In sum, general denouncements of hearsay like those in *Queen* were nothing new.

Perhaps the strongest indicia of *Queen*'s negligible impact on American hearsay law, however, is that the opinion dramatically overstates the inadmissibility of hearsay in the common law both in the decades after *Queen* and today. In the wake of *Queen*, the common law developed bushels of exceptions and continued a tradition of permitting courts to craft ad hoc exceptions as the need arose, something the Supreme Court could have done in *Queen* itself. Today, the legacy of that common law history is over thirty codified hearsay exceptions and a residual exception for situations when hearsay should be admitted even when it does not fit within a codified exception. Almost all these exceptions permit proof of "specific facts," contrary to Marshall's "one general principle." The sheer quantity of hearsay exceptions, and their routine application in violation of Marshall's "general principle," make it difficult to view modern American hearsay law as a product of *Queen v. Hepburn* and its insistence that hearsay is "totally inadmissible."

Finally, as already indicated, the English common law progressed independently toward a relatively strict hearsay prohibition and that evolution proved more influential in shaping American hearsay doctrine than America's Supreme Court. Soon after *Queen* in 1837, the English courts decided *Wright v. Tatham*,

41 *Queen* cited King v. Eriswell, 3 T. R. 707, 816, 818 (1790) (J. Grose for a divided court) ("[I]t is a general rule that such evidence is not admissible, except in some few particular cases where the exception (for aught we know) is as ancient as the rule"); *see also*, Claiborne v. Parrish, 2 Va. 146, 147 (1795) ("The general rule is, that hearsay evidence is inadmissible."); 4 William Blackstone and St. George Tucker, Blackstone's Commentaries: With Notes of Reference, to the Constitution and Laws, of the Federal Government of the United States; and of the Commonwealth of Virginia 368 (1803) ("[I]n general the want of better evidence can never justify the admission of hearsay.") (comment by Edward Christian); Thomas III, *supra* note 12, at 171–2; Edmund Morgan, *Hearsay Dangers and the Application of the Hearsay Concept*, 62 Harv. L. Rev. 177 (1948) (offering examples from the late 1600s).

42 4 Blackstone, Commentaries, *supra* note 41.

43 United States v. Burr, 25 F. Cas. 187 (C.C.D. Va. 1807).

a canonical case that excluded hearsay evidence (not just "hearsay of hearsay") even when it was the best evidence available.[44] The respected English judges' lengthy opinions offer insightful legal analysis, including analogies and examples that are still taught in American law school classrooms.[45] "*Wright v. Tatham* assumed a generative lead role in the law of evidence" in England and America.[46] The case applied an unflinching prohibition of hearsay – subject, of course, to recognized exceptions – even when live witness testimony was unavailable.[47] And it reached these conclusions without the influence of American slavery and without citation or reference to *Queen v. Hepburn*.[48]

AN ODIOUS EVIDENCE RULE: WITNESS COMPETENCY

While Marshall appears to have tried to obscure this fact in his opinion, the trial court in *Queen v. Hepburn* applied another evidence rule that, unlike the hearsay rule, was unequivocally a product of slavery. The contrast is instructive.

While most of the evidence limited by the trial court in *Queen* fit the "hearsay of hearsay" category, one deposition did not meet that description. As noted in the case report, the trial court excluded:

> part of the deposition of Freeders Ryland, which stated what he had heard Mary, the ancestor of the Plaintiffs, say respecting her own place of birth and residence.[49]

Specifically, Ryland testified that he had heard Mary Queen state where she had been born – a key question in the case.[50] Why was the Ryland deposition excluded? The answer appears to be a 1717 Maryland statute that would have barred Mary Queen from testifying had she appeared as a witness. Specifically, the statute stated:

44 Wright v. Tatham, (1837) 112 Eng. Rep. 488, 515 (K.B.) (Parke, B.) (excluding letters written by deceased witnesses and referring to "the established principles of the law of evidence [that require] all such facts as have not been admitted by the party against whom they are offered" "ought to be proved under the sanction of an oath" and recognizing that "[t]o this rule certain exceptions have been recognized" including one for "pedigrees").

45 *See* JEFFREY BELLIN, THE LAW OF EVIDENCE 282 (2d ed. 2025) ("Guided Problem 6–2: The Captain").

46 Stoddard v. State, 157 Md. App. 247, 251 (2004), *reversed by* Stoddard v. State, 389 Md. 681 (2005).

47 State v. Dullard, 668 N.W.2d 585, 591 (Iowa 2003) (explaining that *Wright v. Tatham* "became the prevailing common law view"); United States v. Zenni, 492 F. Supp. 464, 466 (E.D. Ky. 1980) ("The classic case, which is discussed in virtually every textbook on evidence."); James L. Kainen and Carrie A. Tendler, *The Case for a Constitutional Definition of Hearsay: Requiring Confrontation of Testimonial, Nonassertive Conduct and Statements Admitted to Explain an Unchallenged Investigation*, 93 MARQ. L. REV. 1415, 1424 (2010) ("*Wright v. Tatham* … pronounced the authoritative view of the common law on the subject."); Charles T. McCormick, *The Borderland of Hearsay*, 39 YALE L.J. 489, 502 (1930) (summarizing influence).

48 Sklansky, *supra* note 3, at 439 ("the decision does not appear to have had a significant influence on courts or commentators" in England).

49 Queen, 11 U.S. at 291.

50 *Cf.* State v. Rackich, 66 Wash. 390, 390–1 (1911) ("[W]e think a person, competent otherwise to be a witness, may testify as to his parentage.").

> no negro or mulatto slave, free negro, or mulatto born of a white woman, during his time of servitude by law, or any Indian slave, or free Indian, native of this or the neighboring provinces, [could] be admitted and received as good and valid evidence in law, in any matter or thing whatsoever, depending before any court of record, wherein any Christian white person is concerned.[51]

The judge in a companion case to *Queen* excluded the same Ryland deposition on the grounds that it was barred by the Maryland statute, explaining: "The declaration of the ancestor, while held as a slave, cannot be given in evidence, to prove that the ancestor came from England."[52]

The Maryland statute is never referenced in the report of the Supreme Court's opinion. We can only speculate about the reason. Perhaps Marshall foresaw the point discussed here: that unlike the hearsay rule, the competency statute was indefensible and would be reviled by future (and even contemporary) readers. Instead, Marshall's opinion justifies the exclusion of the Ryland deposition solely through the opinion's overstatement that hearsay was "totally inadmissible" when offered to prove any "specific fact."

Marshall's strained effort to uphold the exclusion of the Ryland deposition without reference to the Maryland competency statute served its purpose of denying Queen's claim. But modern readers should not let Marshall's obfuscation hide the stark contrast between a witness competency rule that was unequivocally a product of slavery, and the evolving common law hearsay prohibition that was not. Witness competency rules track the power structures of their eras. This leaves them irreversibly tainted by their association with oppression.[53] We should look suspiciously at any remnants of such rules.[54] But the same is not true for the hearsay prohibition.

CONCLUSION

A critical lens reveals weaknesses in the important and provocative claim that the American hearsay rule has its origins in slavery. It may be true that, in *Queen v. Hepburn*, "Chief Justice John Marshall used the hearsay rule as a bright-line

[51] United States v. Mullany, 27 F. Cas. 20, 20 (C.C.D.D.C. 1808) (quoting Maryland statute); Whitehurst v. Pettipher, 87 N.C. 179, 181 (1882) ("If the witness cannot testify, neither can what he said be shown after his decease, for this would be to exclude sworn and admit unsworn statements from the same party to establish an existing fact.").

[52] Queen v. Neale, 20 F. Cas. 130 (C.C.D.D.C. 1810). *See* Thomas III, *supra* note 12, at 5; Sklansky, *supra* note 2 (citing Thomas: "that since an enslaved person could not testify against a white litigant, her hearsay statements were also inadmissible").

[53] *See* Julia Simon-Kerr, *Credibility by Proxy*, 85 Geo. Wash. L. Rev. 152, 165 (2017).

[54] *See, e.g.*, Jeffrey Bellin, *Eliminating Rule 609 to Provide a Fair Opportunity to Defend Against Criminal Charges: A Proposal to the Advisory Committee on the Federal Rules of Evidence*, 92 Fordham L. Rev. 2471, 2472 (2024); Montre D. Carodine, *"The Mis-Characterization of the Negro": A Race Critique of the Prior Conviction Impeachment Rule*, 84 Ind. L.J. 521, 537 (2009) (tracing evolution of the witness competency rules to Rule 609).

standard ... to arrest the procedural unraveling of slavery."[55] But that opinion appears to be a reflection of the gradual solidification of evidence rules in England and America, not its cause. This distinction matters because it suggests that the American hearsay rule, unlike a witness competency rule also applied in that case, is not a product of slavery.

Tracing the roots of the American hearsay rule to origins beyond slavery is important because it supports the intuition that hearsay exclusions are as likely to be used for justice as injustice. For example, in the same era as *Queen*, abolitionists attacked the Fugitive Slave Act for permitting hearsay declarations, rather than live testimony, to establish a person's status as formerly enslaved.[56] As both examples illustrate, the evidence rules can be wielded as tools of oppression. But typically, the fault lies not in those rules but in the underlying substantive law and the judges applying it.

[55] *See* THOMAS III, *supra* note 12, at 5.

[56] *See* Evan D. Bernick, *Fourteenth Amendment Confrontation*, 51 HOFSTRA L. REV. 1, 36 (2022) (describing anti-slavery pamphlet that "condemned the Fugitive Slave Act of 1793 on the ground that it empowered 'the slave holder ... himself ... [to] drag [a slave] before any Justice of the Peace ... and if he can satisfy this judge of his own choice, by oral testimony or affidavit'").

Hearsay and Confrontation from a Feminist Gaze

Aviva A. Orenstein

A FEMINIST PROJECT IN LAW

The feminist enterprise in law focuses on power imbalances related to gender and on unacknowledged, unrepresentative assumptions about what is reasonable and normal. On the hunch that the legally postulated "reasonable man" may not represent every reasonable person, feminist jurisprudence seeks out false (whether naïve or disingenuous) assertions of objectivity and neutrality in law and questions their premises. It rejects the retro-epistemology[1] of evidentiary thinking, that is, the belief that there is an objective reality capable of discovery through neutral principles, logic, and clear thinking. Instead, feminist jurisprudence focuses on how language, emotion, and politics all can subtly influence law.[2] Although such analysis can be intensely theoretical, legal feminist critiques of law arise from and honor women's actual experiences. Feminist jurisprudence interrogates the mismatch between those experiences and the law as written and enforced.

In this chapter, I outline a feminist critique of one corner of evidence law: hearsay and confrontation. Other parts of evidence law also invite feminist critiques, particularly rules focused on women, such as the rape shield rule and the exceptions to the character ban for those accused of sex crimes. Additionally, the rules of impeachment historically permitted sexist assumptions (such as the belief that a promiscuous woman could not be trusted to tell the truth on the witness stand), another subject for feminist attention. The focus for this short piece however, is to demonstrate some of the many ways, subtle and overt, that law's

Thanks to the late Sylvia Orenstein, Kayla Behforouz, and Rachel Durbin for their excellent research and editorial help and to John Bunck for his kind and helpful editorial support. Thanks also to Bennett Capers, Jasmine E. Harris, and Julia Simon-Kerr for organizing this volume with enthusiasm, creativity, and rigor.

1 Aviva Orenstein, *Evidence in a Different Voice: Some Thoughts on Professor Jonakait's Critique of a Feminist Approach*, 4 Wm. & Mary J. Women & L. 295, 299 (1997) (coining the term retro-epistemology).

2 *See* Andrew E. Taslitz, *What Feminism Has to Offer Evidence Law*, 28 Sw. U. L. Rev. 171, 174 (1999).

treatment of out-of-court statements represent untested and unthinking notions of universality that can have a distinct gendered effect. The discussion of hearsay and confrontation demonstrates how courts fail to notice, let alone grapple with, issues of gender and power. It also highlights one area of hearsay and confrontation – forfeiture by wrongdoing – in which courts have been somewhat sensitive to the dynamic of domestic violence and have incorporated such knowledge into the legal doctrine of hearsay and confrontation.

Below, I begin with a quick review of hearsay and confrontation doctrine. Next, I briefly consider how the hearsay ban and its exceptions may privilege certain types of communication and communicators. Then, I analyze three discrete areas of evidence law through a feminist lens: the excited utterance exception to the hearsay rule; the definition of "testimonial statements" in Confrontation Clause jurisprudence; and the understanding of forfeiture by wrongdoing in cases of domestic violence.

I. A QUICK REFRESHER ON HEARSAY AND CONFRONTATION

Traditionally, evidence law has reflected skepticism of secondhand evidence and instead has favored in-court testimony based on firsthand knowledge. Out-of-court statements, even those made under oath, are considered hearsay if offered for the truth of those statements. (There are entire categories of out-of-court statements *not* offered for their truth, such as defamatory statements or statements offered for the effect on the listener to show the listener's state of mind, which are not considered here.) Unless a hearsay statement falls within an exemption or exception (of which there are many), it is inadmissible.

Evidence law's distrust of out-of-court statements stems from concerns about the accuracy of the underlying assertions in out-of-court statements, which are usually unsworn and cannot be meaningfully questioned if the declarant (the one who made the statement) is not present in court. Cross-examination of the declarant is considered key to accuracy because it can display the witness's inconsistency, mendacity, bias, or poor memory. Arguably, too, fact finders will make better determinations if they can assess the witness's demeanor.[3]

In criminal cases, defendants also have a Sixth Amendment right to confront their accusers – a constitutional right to look their accusers in the eye as they question the witnesses against them. Addressing due process and dignitary concerns, the constitutional command of confrontation applies even to out-of-court statements, indeed even when the out-of-court statement is sworn or otherwise highly reliable.[4] That said, for

3 But *see* Olin Guy Wellborn III, *Demeanor*, 76 CORNELL L. REV. 1075 (1991) (arguing that people overvalue their ability to discern truthfulness from demeanor).

4 Crawford v. Washington, 541 U.S. 36 (2004) (finding that a tape-recorded statement by an unavailable declarant to police violated the defendant's confrontation right because there was no opportunity to cross-examine the declarant).

many years, courts interpreted the confrontation right as coextensive with the hearsay rules: If a statement was admissible under the myriad of hearsay exceptions, it, by definition, also satisfied the Sixth Amendment confrontation command. However, since the Supreme Court's 2004 decision in *Crawford v. Washington*, the confrontation right has been untethered from hearsay practice. That landmark case established that for out-of-court *testimonial* statements to be admitted against the defendant in a criminal case – more on what counts as testimonial later – the declarant must either (1) be available for in-court confrontation; or (2) the declarant must be proven unavailable, and the statement must have been subject to cross-examination earlier.

II. DOES THE HEARSAY RULE ITSELF PRIVILEGE CERTAIN TYPES OF COMMUNICATION?

Evidence law's traditional hostility to hearsay stems from many important values, such as dedication to accuracy, fair play, and accountability. If hearsay were unlimited, powerful actors could generate many out-of-court statements, reinforcing their financial and political power. But the ban on hearsay also reflects other values, such as a respect for formality, formalism, hierarchy, and guild-like protection of knowledge – values that prompt feminist interest and concern. Functionally, the hearsay ban and preference for in-court testimony recognizes and rewards those who feel powerful and sufficiently entitled to speak in formal settings. Traditionally, not all declarants felt so entitled and some had little access to courts in which to formally relate their experiences and observations. At various points in Anglo-American jurisprudence, non-Christian, non-white, non-male witnesses were treated as unworthy of trust and incompetent.[5] This historical exclusion from the gold standard of evidence – in-court sworn testimony from a witness with knowledge – raises questions about full participation and accessibility today.

From a strictly legal perspective, de jure discrimination against socially disfavored declarants is forbidden. But psychologists have observed that social status and confidence directly affect the perception of a witness's credibility. Therefore, though evidence law is now facially neutral, biases and consequent de facto discrimination

5 *See* Amy P. Walters, *Note, Gender and the Role of Expert Witnesses in the Federal Courts*, 83 Geo. L.J. 635, 636 (1994) ("Historically, women have been excluded from participation in the courts based on the notion that they lacked the necessary physical fortitude or discerning intellect and would 'skew the otherwise reliable factfinding process.'") (citations omitted); Albert W. Alschuler and Andrew G. Deiss, *A Brief History of the Criminal Jury in the United States*, 61 U. Chi. L. Rev. 867, 868 (1994) ("Unpropertied white men, initially excluded from jury service, became jurors fairly rapidly. African-American men, members of other minority groups, and women were included only after long struggles."); *id.* at 885 n. 96 (noting that before the Civil War, many jurisdictions prohibited black men from testifying if a party was white); Ronald P. Formisano and Stephen Pickering, *The Christian Nation Debate and Witness Competency*, 29 J. Early Republic 219, 226 (2009) (noting that up until the 1820s, courts prohibited any witnesses who did not believe in God or punishment in this life or the afterlife).

still infect the courtroom, affecting who feels comfortable testifying, how they choose to express themselves, and how their voices will be heard. Psychologists tell us that even when no formal competency strictures bar testimony, finders of fact may credit women and people of color less than they do their white, male counterparts. A study in 2014 found that while women witnesses smiled more and were perceived as more likable, mock jurors found women to be less credible.[6]

This distrust of women is exacerbated by the formal hearsay rules that sometimes conflict with the way women have traditionally communicated because they were less socially and politically powerful. Those people who are historically disentitled and oppressed are to this day not as fully respected or believed in the courtroom. They are justifiably concerned about being unable to express themselves, and hence unable to be heard or believed.[7] For instance, a woman who experienced a rape may feel that it is difficult to find the words to describe the violation. The victim's means of expression may lead a skeptical, victim-blaming fact finder to disbelieve her. The victim may not behave according to jurors' expectations of victims and, therefore, come across as less credible. Jurors are encouraged to use their common sense, but that very instinct may be polluted with misogyny and false rape myths.[8] The jurors' reluctance to believe the victim reinforces stereotypes about women as liars and inhibits other victims from coming forward.

Those whose voices were literally excluded from public domains and centers of power generally engage in less formal methods of communication. Traditionally, subjugated people transmit information less directly, less confrontationally, and less forcefully, reflecting practical exclusion from formal channels of proof and assumptions about their capacity and credibility.[9] Coded language, tentative

[6] Jacklyn E. Nagle, Stanley L. Brodsky, and Kaycee Weeter, *Gender, Smiling, and Witness Credibility in Actual Trials*, 32 BEHAV. SCIS. & L. 195 (2014). But *cf.* Tess M. S. Neal, *Women as Expert Witnesses: A Review of the Literature*, 32 BEHAV. SCIS. & L. 164 (2014) (finding that the perceived credibility of women as expert witnesses was complicated and can vary with the context of the case).

[7] *See* Jennifer Hornsby, *Disempowered Speech*, 23 PHIL. TOPICS 127, 134–6 (1995) (discussing "ineffability" and "inaudibility" and applying it to sexual attack).

[8] *See* Deborah Tuerkheimer, *Victim, Reconstructed: Sex Crimes Experts and the New Rape Paradigm*, 2024 U. ILL. L. REV. 55, 57 (2024) ("common sense routinely fails when it comes to sexual violence").

[9] A great example of this phenomenon is portrayed in *James*, a novel by Percival Everett (1st ed. Picador 2024), recounting the story of *Huckleberry Finn* from the vantagepoint of the slave, Jim. Jim instructs the slave children on how to address their white oppressors:

> "OK, let's imagine it's a grease fire. She's left bacon unattended on the stove. Mrs. Holiday is about to throw water on it. What do you say, Rachel?"
> Rachel, paused. "Missums, that water gone make it wurs!"
> "Of course, that's true, but what's the problem with that?
> Virgil said, "You're telling her she's doing the wrong thing."
> I nodded. "So what should you say?"
> Lizzie looked at the ceiling and spoke while thinking it through. "Would you like for me to get some sand?"
> "Correct approach, but you didn't translate it."
> She nodded. "Oh, Lawd, missums ma'am, you wan for me to gets some sand?"

assertions, and informal gossip mark the speech of disempowered people, particularly women.[10] Such speech differs markedly from formal sworn in-court testimony followed by cross-examination, which is the gold standard of evidence law. Yet, for less powerful groups, gossip, indirect, and informal transmission of information may be more comfortable, accurate, and fair.

In summary, before we can even address the Rules of Evidence and their limitations on hearsay, we must acknowledge that not all witnesses come before the fact finders with equal presumptions of credibility and reliability; our courtrooms perforce reflect our culture with all its incorporation of stereotypes and biases. People from less powerful groups may not feel entitled to speak or may feel they lack the language and presentation skills that will encourage jurors to listen to them and take them seriously. Modes of outsider speech are devalued, and the strict constrictions of the hearsay rule may serve to silence less privileged, comfortable, or entitled speakers. At the very least, whatever disadvantages women experience in the courtroom begin with sexist presumptions and then are reinforced and intensified by our traditional evidence rules.

With that background in mind, the next section addresses individual aspects of hearsay and confrontation and how they appear from a feminist gaze.

III. THE EXCITED UTTERANCE HEARSAY EXCEPTION IGNORES HOW WOMEN COMMUNICATE, PARTICULARLY AFTER EXPERIENCING SEXUAL ATTACKS

A. *The Excited Utterance*

The excited utterance exception to the hearsay rule provides that out-of-court statements made under the influence of an "exciting" event and made while the speaker is still in a state of nervous agitation or stress may be admitted for the truth of the matters they assert.[11] The theory is that the stress of a startling or provoking event diminishes the declarant's ability to confabulate. As Jack Weinstein and Margaret Berger, the great treatise writers on the Federal Rules of Evidence, explained, "[t]he assumption underlying this exception is that a person under the sway of excitement precipitated by an external startling event will not have the

[10] *See* Karen C. Adkins, *The Real Dirt: Gossip and Feminist Epistemology*, 16 Soc. Epistemology 215, 216 (2002) ("Gossip is a rich subject for feminist analysis: first, because of its historical and negative association with women, but second, because it is such a fecund example of the kind of subjugated discourse of the outsider that is ignored in mainstream academic writing."); Niko Besnier, Gossip and the Everyday Production of Politics 12 (University of Hawaii Press 2009) (focusing on gossip "enables us to understand politics 'from below,' particularly from the perspective of those whose voice is rarely heard in public or from perspectives that are deemed 'not to matter'").

[11] Fed R. Evid. 803(2) allows admission of "[a] statement relating to a startling event or condition made while the declarant was under the stress of excitement caused by the event or condition" whether or not the declarant is available.

reflective capacity essential for fabrication and that, consequently, any utterance will be spontaneous and trustworthy."[12]

Psychologists and evidence scholars have found plenty to criticize in this ancient doctrine.[13] Whatever credibility is gained by the declarant's sincerity and lack of wherewithal to lie is arguably significantly outweighed by memory and perception problems, often caused by the chaos, fear, or violence of the startling event.[14]

Such well-founded criticisms aside, feminist jurisprudence also can offer a critique of the excited utterance exception, particularly in how it privileges speech by those who feel entitled to complain and expect to be heard. When such a style of entitled speech is validated and assumed to be the normal reaction to a startling event, women, who might react differently, particularly after a sexual attack, will be subject to biased and false expectations.

B. *Feminist Concern with the Excited Utterance and Its Application to Sexual Attack*

Feminists are obviously concerned about the legal treatment of women who suffer sexual attacks. Therefore, harms inflicted on women and the focus on sex, power, and gender identity are key subjects of feminist analysis. Relatedly, there is a vast scholarship on why women are not believed when they report sexual attacks, including the just-world hypothesis,[15] presumptions about how "real" victims and perpetrators behave, and plain old misogyny that results in unwillingness to protect women who engage in incautious behavior.[16]

[12] 4 Jack B. Weinstein and Margaret A. Berger, Weinstein's Evidence ¶ 803(2)[01] (1996).

[13] The doctrine is traceable back to the seventeenth century case of Thompson v. Trevanion, 1693 Skin L.R. 402. Scholars propose all sorts of remedies for the perceived unreliability of the excited utterance from a corroboration requirement, *see* Alan G. Williams, *Abolishing the Excited Utterance Exception to the Rule Against Hearsay*, 63 U. Kan. L. Rev. 717, 758 (2015), to a trustworthiness requirement, *see* Lisa L. Richter, *Goldilocks and the Rule 803 Hearsay Exceptions*, 59 Wm. & Mary L. Rev. 897 (2018), to outright abolition, *see* Steven Baicker-McKee, *The Excited Utterance Paradox*, 41 Seattle U. L. Rev. 111 (2017).

[14] *See, e.g.*, John Hohmeier, *Comment: The Excited Utterance and Cortisol: Reality, Justice, and That Bumpy Road on the Search for Truth*, 27 T.M. Cooley L. Rev. 647 (2010) (discussing the role of cortisol in fogging up memory after a high stress event); *see also*, United States v. Boyce, 742 F.3d 792, 801 (7th Cir. 2014) ("And even if a person is so excited by something that he loses the capacity for reflection (which doubtless does happen), how can there be any confidence that his unreflective utterance, provoked by excitement, is reliable?") (Posner, J., concurring).

[15] *See generally*, Melvin J. Lerner, The Belief in a Just World: A Fundamental Delusion (Springer 1980) (coining the terms and explaining how people use the just-world hypothesis to explain and justify many of the positive and negative outcomes, suggesting a logical and moral connection between those outcomes and people's actions; therefore, if someone is attacked, under a just-world theory, the victim did something to deserve the attack).

[16] *See generally*, Deborah Tuerkheimer, Credible: Why We Doubt Accusers and Protect Abusers 10 (Harper 2021) ("When a woman comes forward with an allegation of abuse, … gender, power, sexual entitlement, cultural mythology, and legal protections collide.").

Unsurprisingly, these factors also affect the excited utterance exception. For sure, the excited utterance does not demand that women under the stress of a sexual attack make excited utterances. But the substantive law of rape implicitly does, often operating with the expectation (though not technically requiring) that at the very least, the victim verbally resisted and complained promptly. The excited utterance privileges such excited statements, admitting for their truth such outcries made immediately after or during the stress of sexual attack.[17] False assumptions about rape victims produce the expectations that victims will resist, cry out, or exhibit intense emotion. Indeed, the firm belief that truthful women would immediately denounce their attack and attacker led to the prompt complaint rule in the common law, whereby women claiming they were sexually attacked would only be believed if they reported the attack right after it happened.[18]

Deborah Tuerkheimer argues that "common sense" notions of how women will react to sexual attack do not jibe with how many people actually respond to trauma, which is often to go numb or silent.[19] Such behavior is not a "syndrome" but an observable, regular reaction of fight, flight, or freeze.[20] Society has unrealistic and indeed counterfactual expectations of what makes a genuine victim. Tuerkheimer notes that "[i]f an accuser fails to meet these benchmarks, however unfettered from reality, she doesn't seem like a victim, and her allegation is dismissed."[21]

By contrast, a quiet, calm, and perhaps numb out-of-court statement to a friend a week or two after the attack could be dismissed as inadmissible hearsay.[22] Courts must consider how women's reactions to sexual attacks might vary considerably from the excited utterance's tacit expectation that women will react with outrage and outcry.[23] Essentially, the construction of this excited utterance hearsay exception favors our fantasy of how an honest women would react to a sexual attack and

17 Tuerkheimer, *supra* note 8, at 64–8.

18 *See* Dawn M. Dubois, *Note, A Matter of Time: Evidence of a Victim's Prompt Complaint in New York*, 53 Brook. L. Rev. 1087 (1988).

19 Tuerkheimer, *supra* note 8, at 83–4.

20 *See* Roslyn Myers, *Science "Proves" What Women Have Been Saying for Generations*, 16 Fam. & Intimate Partner Violence Q. 59 (2024) (discussing reactions to stressful attacks and noting that while "fight or flight" are well known, freeze, which applies to rape victims, is an understudied but normal and important reaction to a threatening sexual attack).

21 Tuerkheimer, *supra* note 8, at 63–4.

22 *See* Aviva Orenstein, *"My God!": A Feminist Critique of the Excited Utterance Exception to the Hearsay Rule*, 85 Calif. L. Rev. 159 (1997).

23 When I first wrote about the mismatch between the excited utterance and the actual experience of rape victims, *see id.*, I focused on the then-emerging theory of "rape trauma syndrome" (RTS), which was admitted by some courts to "dispel misconceptions" about how women react to being raped. *See* Tuerkheimer, *supra* note 8, at 60. However, the RTS description was underinclusive of women's experiences, the scientific evidence for RTS was weak, and some were wary of pathologizing reactions to rape by calling it a "syndrome." Courts were appropriately wary of using RTS to prove the absence of consent. *Id.* at 63–4. Although I do not now rely on RTS to critique the operation of the excited utterance exception, the essential points about the mismatch still hold.

not how actual victims often do. Although sexual assault has been presented as the example, one can imagine other circumstances, such as witnesses to crime or other stressful events, where the excited utterance exception rewards assertive male voices at the expense of non-assertive female voices.

IV. THE INTERSECTION OF CONFRONTATION JURISPRUDENCE WITH DOMESTIC VIOLENCE

A feminist analysis of evidence is also illuminating when examining recent Supreme Court jurisprudence in confrontation. The Confrontation Clause jurisprudence addresses various cases of domestic violence, including when the violence results in death.[24] It is hard to ignore the fact that all the first major modern confrontation cases (excepting those dealing with lab reports) involved some form of violence against women. The case, *Crawford v. Washington*,[25] in which Justice Scalia redefined and reinvigorated (some might say resuscitated) the confrontation right, involved an attempted rape.[26] Two years after *Crawford*, in 2006, the Court addressed a pair of domestic violence cases, and in 2008, the Court addressed forfeiture of the confrontation right in a case of domestic violence resulting in the victim's death.

The experiences of women trapped in dangerous, violent, and oppressive relationships, which often reflect traditional gender dynamics run amuck, is of obvious interest to feminists. As with the hearsay analysis above, one important question is whether the doctrine acknowledges and reflects the voices, experiences, and safety of women. As I discuss below, the results are mixed regarding confrontation. One line of cases, those defining "testimonial statements," exhibits ignorance and callousness to women's experience with domestic violence. However, another line of cases involving forfeiture, despite some serious feminist-baiting on the part of Justice Scalia, reflects a more nuanced and sophisticated understanding of the experience of women experiencing domestic violence.

A. *Defining "Testimonial Statements" in the Domestic Violence Context*

Crawford held that for the Confrontation Clause to apply, the challenged out-of-court statement must be "testimonial." To decide whether a statement is testimonial under the Confrontation Clause, the Supreme Court adopted a stark and ultimately unhelpful dichotomy between cases where (1) the woman was reporting

24 Domestic violence is not exclusively perpetrated against women, nor is it solely a feminist concern, but victims are disproportionally wives and girlfriends, and the interest in women's experiences with the law and their safety is an obvious area of feminist concern.

25 541 U.S. 36 (2004).

26 Mr. Crawford, the accused, allegedly tried to avenge the victim's attempted rape of Sylvia Crawford, his wife. *Id.* at 38.

a crime to the police, which rendered her statements testimonial; and (2) where the woman was crying out for help, which rendered her statements non-testimonial, hence not covered by the Confrontation Clause.

Davis v. Washington[27] involved a victim who called 911, stating that her ex-boyfriend, Davis, had just run out the door after hitting her. Because the victim did not appear at Davis's trial (despite the prosecution's attempt to secure her in-court testimony), the state's only live, in-court witnesses were the two responding officers, neither of whom had witnessed the violent incident. Over Davis's objection, the trial court admitted the recording of the 911 call and convicted Davis of a felony violation of a domestic no-contact order.

Hammon v. Indiana,[28] the companion case, involved statements made to law enforcement personnel who responded to a call from neighbors regarding a domestic disturbance. When the officers arrived, they separated the victim and the accused (her husband), but the accused attempted to interrupt the victim's report to police. Ms. Hammon eventually described the violent incident, completing and signing a battery affidavit. Ms. Hammon did not appear at trial and, in fact, wrote to the judge that she did not wish to press charges.[29] The state, over the accused's objections, called the officer who questioned Ms. Hammon to describe what she told him.

In these companion cases, Justice Scalia, writing for the majority, strove to differentiate the "non-testimonial" statements in *Davis* from the "testimonial" statements in *Hammon*. (As noted above, this distinction is consequential because only testimonial statements trigger the Confrontation Clause). According to the Court, non-testimonial statements are "made in the course of police interrogation under circumstances objectively indicating that the primary purpose of the interrogation is to enable police assistance to meet an ongoing emergency."[30] Statements are testimonial, however, "when the circumstances objectively indicate that there is no such ongoing emergency, and that the primary purpose of the interrogation is to establish or prove past events potentially relevant to later criminal prosecution."[31]

Applying this standard to the victims' statements in *Davis* and *Hammon*, the Court concluded that the victim in *Davis* was "speaking about events as they were actually happening, rather than 'describ[ing] past events.'"[32] According to Justice Scalia's majority opinion, the victim in *Davis* (as opposed to Ms. Hammon) was plainly making "a call for help against a bona fide physical threat."[33] The circumstances of the interrogation in *Davis* therefore "objectively indicate its primary purpose

27 547 U.S. 813 (2006).
28 *Id.*
29 *Id.* at 820.
30 *Id.* at 822.
31 *Id.*
32 *Id.* at 827.
33 *Id.*

was to enable police assistance to meet an ongoing emergency."[34] Consequently, the Court held that the victim's initial statements on the 911 call in Davis were non-testimonial and therefore, admissible.

In *Hammon*, by contrast, the Court found "no emergency in progress."[35] The Court explained that the officer questioning Amy Hammon "was not seeking to determine (as in Davis) 'what is happening,' but rather 'what happened.'"[36] The victim's statements in *Hammon*, "were neither a cry for help nor the provision of information enabling officers immediately to end a threatening situation."[37] Therefore, the Court ruled that Ms. Hammon's statements about her abuse were inadmissible.

Essentially, the Court attempted to draw a bright line between women who immediately cry for help and women who are reporting abuse. In doing so, the Supreme Court exhibited cluelessness regarding women's experience of domestic violence, concocting an unworkable distinction between seeking help and reporting harm. Its argument was predicated on an "objective" viewpoint, which as discussed below, can itself be gendered by assuming a male archetype. As noted above, women do not necessarily cry out for help loudly or immediately, even when they are in danger. This may be especially true for women who are further marginalized because of race, immigration status, or other outsider identity. Conversely, summoning police to assure safety in an ongoing relationship, even long after a violent eruption, may be a way of seeking safety.

Justice Thomas, in dissent, argued that the line the majority tried to draw between emergencies and reports of past events, relying on primary motives, is blurry and impossible to apply. He made a persuasive case that Amy Hammon was in as much (if not more) danger when she made her declaration as was the victim in *Davis*.[38]

I find myself in agreement with Justice Thomas, a rare occurrence. The Court's confrontation standard divides victims' statements into neat but useless categories of "testimonial/action is over" versus "emergency-based/event is ongoing." A critique of this dualism holds true for reports of every type of violent crime, where elimination of danger and prosecution of wrongdoers may be twin motivations of both the victims and the police. The line is particularly hard to draw, however, in domestic violence cases, and the Court demonstrates its ignorance and insensitivity to the experiences of domestic violence victims, especially where there is a sustained pattern of violence, so that the victim may live in constant fear. A woman who reports to the police may feel genuinely fearful as she does so. Indeed, reporting may place her in significantly greater danger. Therefore, the distinction between reporting out

[34] *Id.* at 828.
[35] *Id.* at 829.
[36] *Id.* at 830.
[37] *Id.* at 832.
[38] *Id.* at 841 (Thomas, J., concurring in the judgment in part and dissenting in part).

of fear "to enable police assistance to meet an ongoing emergency" and reporting to instigate a legal response "to establish or prove past events" makes little psychological or practical sense. For poor women, especially poor women with children, economic concerns may make leaving their partners or reporting them seem precarious or impossible. The ethics and practicalities of reporting to police become increasingly complicated for women of color, who may rightfully fear the racism of the police, whether it is directed against them (being dismissed as loud and disorderly) or their assaulters, who may be endangered by police brutality.

Commentators have demonstrated and bemoaned the mismatch between the Supreme Court's approach to confrontation and the realities of prosecuting domestic violence. As Professor Deborah Tuerkheimer explains, for women who experience domestic violence, the line between past and present violence is not a bright or distinct one. In talking to police, victims are indeed addressing an emergency, even if they employ past events to describe the history of continuing violence or to explain their fear. Therefore, "a domestic violence victim's safety may be wholly contingent on her communication with police; her 'narration of events' linked inexorably to resolving – however temporarily – the danger posed by her batterer."[39] Similarly, Tuerkheimer criticizes the insistence on the discrete event requirement, noting that under the Court's new definition, "'events' have either happened or 'are actually happening.'"[40]

Additionally, a feminist analysis would note the Court's repeated appeal to objectivity. For instance, Justice Scalia wrote for the majority: "The question before us in *Davis*, then, is whether, objectively considered, the interrogation that took place in the course of the 911 call produced testimonial statements."[41] Justice Scalia asserted that the test set out in *Davis* and *Hammond* is "objective and quite 'workable.'"[42] He concluded of the *Hammon* facts: "Objectively viewed, the primary, if not indeed the sole, purpose of the interrogation was to investigate a possible crime – which is, of course, precisely what the officer should have done."[43] Even Justice Thomas in dissent could not help noting and disapproving of the "Court's repeated invocation of the word 'objectiv[e]' to describe its test."[44]

The emphasis on objectivity is a red flag for anyone concerned with the rights and interests of women. Feminist jurisprudence is foundationally skeptical about appeals to neutrality and objectivity, which often unwittingly promote a male archetype as the norm and treat women who do not fit that norm as the irrational other.

39 Deborah Tuerkheimer, *A Relational Approach to the Right of Confrontation and Its Loss*, 15 J.L. & POL'Y 725, 731 (2007). *See, generally*, Aviva Orenstein, *Sex, Threats, and Excited Words: Bedingfield and Its Lessons for Modern Evidence Law*, 79 FORDHAM L. REV. 115 (2010).

40 Tuerkheimer, *supra* note 39, at 734.

41 547 U.S. at 826.

42 *Id.* at 830 n. 5.

43 *Id.* at 830.

44 *Id.* at 839 (Thomas, J., dissenting).

Reliance on self-proclaimed objectivity can serve to ignore the effects of rules on women, often masking deep insensitivity to the actual experiences of women.

Throughout his analysis in *Davis* and *Hammon*, Justice Scalia revealed obliviousness and disinterest in the dynamics of domestic violence. This lack of understanding affects not only the test itself (differentiating a cry for help during an ongoing emergency from a report to police about a completed crime) but also the application of the test. In assessing the facts of *Hammon*, Justice Scalia missed major cues that Ms. Hammon – whose statement he deemed testimonial because, according to him, the emergency is over – was still in danger when she spoke with the police. The facts of the case indicate that the accused repeatedly tried to interrupt Ms. Hammon's conversation with police – trying to coach her answers, interfere with her ability to report, and control her behavior. Ms. Hammon also reported that the accused broke the phone and "[t]ore up my van where I couldn't leave the house."[45] This classic domineering and isolating behavior – without phone or transportation, the victim is stuck at home and cannot escape or seek aid – indicates that Ms. Hammon was still in danger (in some ways much more so than the victim in *Davis*, whose assailant had already run off). Because Ms. Hammon was likely still in danger, she was arguably still experiencing an ongoing emergency, and her statements even using the Court's own categories could be construed as non-testimonial.

The test for testimonial statements has proven disastrous in prosecuting domestic violence cases and confusing in subsequent non-domestic violence cases. In *Bryant v. Michigan*,[46] involving a drug deal gone bad, the "ongoing emergency" test was stretched beyond credulity where, despite the fact that there were five police officers protecting the victim, the victim's description of his assailant was deemed non-testimonial because there was a "shooter on the loose." Justice Scalia, who for the first time lost his majority in the Confrontation Clause line of cases that he was instrumental in shaping, complained that the Court both lied about the facts and botched the confrontation analysis.[47]

No evidence scholar believes that we have landed in a good or even coherent place in fashioning a doctrine of confrontation. What began as a noble effort by Justice Scalia to disentangle confrontation from the vagaries of hearsay has morphed into a silly and sometimes dishonest doctrine. A feminist perspective on the Confrontation Clause cannot justly advocate for whatever rule that will convict the greatest number of offenders (though it is not clear that the current approach accomplishes that goal). Feminism provides an outsider's perspective, and feminists could not

[45] *Id.* at 820 (majority opinion).

[46] 562 U.S. 344 (2011).

[47] *Id.* at 379–80 (Scalia, J., dissenting) ("[The majority's analysis of the facts] is so transparently false that professing to believe it demeans this institution … [the] opinion distorts our Confrontation Clause jurisprudence and leaves it in a shambles. Instead of clarifying the law, the Court makes itself the obfuscator of last resort.").

tolerate the inherent racism and "othering" of rules designed simply to convict more criminal defendants at any costs. The underlying problem is that many women do not feel safe testifying in court, or they have major equivocations about testifying against a former partner (particularly if they do not trust the police or the justice system). The true solution is major reform of police, courts, safety, and social security nets that would encourage and enable victims to testify. The solution is not to use their statements made in desperate and extreme moments when they choose not to testify. That "solution" could even lead to women electing to not ask for help when they most need it, for fear how their words will be later used. It is certainly true that the current dichotomy of reporting verses seeking aid misrepresents and demeans women's complicated experiences as they navigate danger in their home and apathy from the outside world.

V. FORFEITURE BY WRONGDOING: UNDERSTANDING "WRONGDOING" IN A DOMESTIC VIOLENCE CONTEXT

In contrast to the jurisprudence defining testimonial statements discussed above, the case law concerning forfeiture by wrongdoing reflects some genuine insight into the nature of women's experiences. It also, however, reflects and revives old and fraught epistemological debates about whether we trust victims of domestic violence to know their own minds and their best interests.[48]

I present four related points about domestic violence and forfeiture by wrongdoing. First, many courts recognize the dynamics of domestic violence and account for them in determining coercion and intimidation. Second, there is no firm consensus on how to handle cases where no evidence of police reports, upcoming police interviews, or court dates directly supports the conclusion that the accused intended to make the victim unavailable as a witness. Third, a subset of domestic violence cases involving the victim's homicide demonstrates that *Giles* was wrongly decided, at least in cases where the accused is alleged to have killed his partner. Finally, courts struggle with how to treat coercion stemming from emotional manipulation, such as where the accused makes pleas for the victim not to testify couched in declarations of love, offers of marriage, promises to change, visions of rekindling romance, and prospects of financial security. I address each point in turn.

First, the semi-good news: The Supreme Court hinted at, and lower courts have begun to adopt, a jurisprudence of forfeiture that acknowledges and accommodates, at least somewhat, the realities and dynamics of domestic violence. In *Giles v. California*, the accused shot and killed his ex-girlfriend, Brenda Avie.[49] At trial,

48 "Epistemology allows us to interrogate what we know or don't know, who is considered credible, and what information we are willing to accept from another person." Yvette Butler, *Silencing the Sex Worker*, 71 UCLA L. Rev. 726, 728 (2024).

49 554 U.S. 353, 356 (2008). Even though some of the bullets entered through Avie's back while she lay on the ground, Giles asserted self-defense. *Id.*

to rebut Giles's testimony that Avie was the aggressor, prosecutors introduced statements that Avie had made to a police officer three weeks before her death, describing violence and threats by Giles.[50] The Court determined that admitting Avie's prior statement violated the accused's confrontation rights, holding that the forfeiture by wrongdoing exception did not apply because the government did not meet its burden of proving, that Giles *intended* to cause his girlfriend's unavailability. By a vote of six-to-three, the Court held, that to trigger the equitable doctrine of forfeiture, the accused must intend to make the declarant unavailable as a witness rather than just render her unavailable by killing her without proof of his intention to obstruct her testimony. Thus, a murderous partner who kills out of spite, jealousy, anger, or a sense of loss of control can object to the admission of his partner's testimonial out-of-court statements. He killed her because he wanted her dead, not to prevent testimony, so the forfeiture rules do not apply (a conclusion whose soundness I challenge below).

Because interpretation of the Confrontation Clause post-*Crawford* perforce reflected Justice Scalia's novel historical-originalist [not an oxymoron] interpretation of the Sixth Amendment apparently, much of the argument in *Giles* addressed the old common law understanding of forfeiture, going back to merry ol' England centuries ago. (Unsurprisingly, these traditional notions of forfeiture did not address domestic violence contexts.)[51] *Giles* was not, however, exclusively mired in history. The dissent and a concurrence by Souter and Ginsburg affirmatively acknowledged the context of domestic violence.

In concurrence, Justice Souter opined that the criteria for forfeiture "would normally be satisfied by the intent inferred on the part of the domestic abuser in the classic abusive relationship, which is meant to isolate the victim from outside help, including the aid of law enforcement and the judicial process."[52] Given such a violent relationship, "it would make no sense to suggest that the oppressing defendant miraculously abandoned the dynamics of abuse the instant before he killed his victim."[53]

This focus on a modern day understanding of forfeiture inspired both Justice Scalia's rage and a grudging acknowledgment that domestic violence cases might include the seeds of forfeiture. As to the umbrage, Scalia decried the dissent's focus on practical consequences, unfairly reframing the dissent's argument to

[50] *Id.* at 356–7. Tearfully, Avie reported that Giles had accused her of having an affair, grabbed her by the shirt, and lifted her off the floor, choking and punching her. She further reported that he had opened a folding knife and threatened to kill her if she was unfaithful. *Id.* at 357.

[51] *Id.* at 380 (Souter, J., concurring) (questioning the utility of the historical analysis, noting that the historical record was murky and "today's understanding of domestic abuse had no apparent significance at the time of the framing, and there is no early example of the forfeiture rule operating in that circumstance").

[52] *Id.*

[53] *Id.*

be "that a forfeiture rule which ignores *Crawford* would be particularly helpful to women in abusive relationships – or at least particularly helpful in punishing their abusers."[54] In response, Justice Scalia queried: "Is the suggestion that we should have one Confrontation Clause (the one the Framers adopted and *Crawford* described) for all other crimes, but a special, improvised, Confrontation Clause for those crimes that are frequently directed against women?"[55] Although acknowledging that domestic violence "is an intolerable offense," he reminded the dissent that "abridging the constitutional rights of criminal defendants is not in the State's arsenal."[56]

Despite his ferocity and outrage at the prospect of compromising the mandate of confrontation to protect a vulnerable group, Scalia left a path open for applying the equitable doctrine of forfeiture in domestic violence cases. Rejecting any special treatment for domestic violence victims per se, he noted that "[a]cts of domestic violence often are intended to dissuade a victim from resorting to outside help, and include conduct designed to prevent testimony to police officers or cooperation in criminal prosecutions."[57] He acknowledged that "[w]here such an abusive relationship culminates in murder, the evidence may support a finding that the crime expressed the intent to isolate the victim and to stop her from reporting abuse to the authorities or cooperating with a criminal prosecution – rendering her prior statements admissible under the forfeiture doctrine."[58] Scalia acknowledged that "[e]arlier abuse, or threats of abuse, intended to dissuade the victim from resorting to outside help would be highly relevant to this inquiry, as would evidence of ongoing criminal proceedings at which the victim would have been expected to testify."[59]

Since *Giles*, many, but certainly not all, courts have adopted a somewhat sophisticated, psychologically informed application of forfeiture in domestic violence cases. Courts have quoted both Justices Scalia and Souter as they examined the relationship dynamics in a particular case to see if the accused's known past intimate partner violence could serve as proof of wrongdoing sufficient to forfeit the

54 *Id.* at 376 (majority opinion). In a portion of his majority opinion not joined by Justice Ginsburg and Justice Souter, Justice Scalia claimed to be "puzzled by the dissent's decision to devote its peroration to domestic-abuse cases." *Id.*

55 *Id.*

56 *Id.* The acerbity and ferociousness of Scalia's rejection of the dissent's concerns about the practical effects of the Court's ruling mirrors in content and tone Scalia's dissent in Maryland v. Craig, 497 U.S. 836 (1990), where Scalia excoriated the Court's endorsement of special confrontation accommodations through closed circuit television to traumatized victims. In *Craig*, he wrote, "Seldom has this Court failed so conspicuously to sustain a categorical guarantee of the Constitution against the tide of prevailing current opinion." *Id.* at 860 (Scalia, J., dissenting). He argued: "Perhaps that is a procedure today's society desires; perhaps (though I doubt it) it is even a fair procedure; but it is assuredly not a procedure permitted by the Constitution." *Id.* at 861.

57 Giles, 554 U.S. at 377.

58 *Id.*

59 *Id.*

right of confrontation.[60] For instance, in *United States v. Blackshire*, the Ninth Circuit upheld the district court's ruling that a domestic violence victim's out-of-court statements to police and a forensic nurse could be admitted against the accused to prove charges of assault and kidnapping under the forfeiture by wrongdoing doctrine.[61] The government could not locate the victim to testify at trial, so it offered her recorded interviews with tribal police and the forensic nurse.[62] To support forfeiture, the government submitted three jailhouse statements where the accused asked third parties to instruct the victim not to testify.[63] In affirming that the recordings established that the accused intentionally caused the victim-witness's unavailability, the Ninth Circuit noted that forfeiture by wrongdoing does not require criminal wrongdoing, but instead, only that the defendant procured or coerced the witness into not testifying.[64] The Court observed that a background of domestic violence was relevant to determine whether there was "coercion, undue influence, or pressure" and if the conduct was "wrongful."[65]

Second, there is no current, clear consensus on whether courts require a pending case or police report to trigger the forfeiture doctrine, or whether a mere intent to silence the victim is sufficient.[66] For instance, in *People v. Quintanilla*,[67] despite the accused's history of extreme violence,[68] the Court concluded that there was insufficient evidence that he killed her to forbid the admission of her out-of-court statements, given that there was no pending proceeding at the time of the killing where the victim could have testified and the defendant did not threaten to kill her if she went to the authorities or otherwise testified against him.[69] But at least

60 *See, e.g.*, United States v. Becker, 80 M.J. 563 (N-M. Ct. Crim. App. 2020); *cf.* State v. Farrington, 2020-NMSC-022, 476 P.3d 1231 (applying the same standard to admit non-testimonial hearsay).

61 98 F.4th 1146, 1154 (9th Cir. 2024).

62 *Id.* at 1150.

63 *Id.* at 1150–1.

64 *Id.* at 1152.

65 *Id.* According to the Ninth Circuit, against the backdrop of the prior abuse, Blackshire's statements could be interpreted as efforts to coerce, unduly influence, or pressure the victim into not testifying; thus, the forfeiture by wrongdoing exception could apply. *Id.* at 1154. *See also*, People v. Reed, No. E075783, 2022 WL 16757488, at *8–9 (Cal. Ct. App. 2022) (noting that the accused's actions in the context of domestic violence deterred the victim from coming to court) ("[The accused] created an environment that by its very nature was threatening to anyone who challenged his control and authority. Defendant terrorized [the victim] for years by bullying and beating her, retaining possession of her important, personal, family items, and deterring her from talking to the police.").

66 *See, e.g.*, United States v. Becker, 81 M.J. 483, 486 (C.A.A.F. 2021) (noting that "'there were no active … and no anticipated investigations' of Appellant regarding [the victim's] earlier allegations of Appellant's physical and emotional abuse").

67 259 Cal. Rptr. 3d 431 (Cal. Ct. App. 2020).

68 The violence included: several strangulations; tying her in a chair, putting duct tape on her mouth and a bag over her head, and then pouring gasoline on her and lighting a lighter; black eyes; pulled hair; a broken nose; bruises; punching her in the stomach when he knew she was pregnant; sexual violence; and forcing her to use illegal drugs. *Id.* at 436–9.

69 *Id.* at 444.

one court has determined that forfeiture does not require a pending case, only a report to authorities.[70] As the Court succinctly summarized in *State v. Moran*: "Mr. Moran said he was going to kill his wife if she reported him to the police. She reported him; he killed her."[71]

Third, the *Giles* requirement that the accused intended to prevent testimony is particularly questionable in "voices from the grave" cases. Such cases involve victims killed by intimate partners who leave behind notes with neighbors, in safe-deposit boxes, and through other means, to the effect that if they ever disappeared or are suspected of suicide, it was their partner who actually killed them.[72] These accurate predictions of their deaths are poignant and sometimes essential evidence. In cases where the victim simply disappears or refuses to testify, one reason to support *Giles*'s approach to forfeiture is that we may be respecting the victim's wishes, and, by absenting herself she is choosing not to testify. By contrast, with the voices from the grave cases, the women have not chosen to abscond; indeed, they affirmatively chose to report after their deaths when they would finally be beyond the reach of their abusers.

I believe that the solution to these voices from the grave cases lies in rejecting the holding of *Giles* and accepting the notion of equitable forfeiture advocated by the dissent in that case. If an accused made a witness unavailable by killing her, he should not be heard to complain about the inability to confront the person he eliminated from the planet.[73] Rather than relying on the tortured and unknowable history of the English common law of forfeiture, it would have been wiser to rely on basic principles of equity. The result in *Giles* excluded vital evidence in domestic violence homicide cases, in my opinion, mistakenly.

Finally, a more subtle and wrenching problem exists in domestic violence cases where the accused convinces the victim not to testify but his method is not by direct threat. Sometimes the threat is simply implied, and the history of violence

[70] State v. Moran, 218 So.3d 749, 758 (La. Ct. App. 2017).

[71] *Id.*

[72] Obviously, the people who write such notes – and there are scores of them – have no personal knowledge of their cause of death, but their belief that they will be murdered by their intimate partner refutes a theory of suicide and offers a plausible alternative to the accused's defenses of suicide, voluntary disappearance, or self-defense. *Cf.* Shepard v. United States, 290 U.S. 96 (1933) (rejecting the notion that charging her husband with murder was admissible to show that victim was not suicidal when the evidence was offered for its truth as a dying declaration and not for the circumstantial evidence of the state of mind of the speaker).

[73] As a technical matter, this would require the judge to make a preliminary finding that the accused killed the victim, which the court would do using FED R. EVID. 104(a) to determine that preliminary fact by a preponderance of the evidence. This sort of preliminary fact-finding, even when it involves an ultimate issue, is routine in evidence law. For purposes of establishing the preliminary facts to find forfeiture, the court would find the homicide by a preponderance of the evidence (and such evidence need not be admissible); the prosecution would still have to prove whatever degree of homicide beyond a reasonable doubt. Barring any other concerns, the jury could consider the victim's hearsay statements.

is enough to scare the victim into compliance. For instance, *People v. Reneaux*[74] noted that although the criminal defendant's statements from jail professing his love and promising to marry the victim once she recanted were not threatening or explicitly directive, the defendant was still attempting to undermine the judicial process.[75] The Court further explained that in the context of domestic violence and abusive relationships, which generally involve psychological coercion, the victim is susceptible to non-violent coercion.[76]

Cases where the violent threat is unspoken but past violence speaks volumes present difficult interpretive problems, but courts seem able to make the requisite inferences. The truly difficult cases arise, however, where the accused appeals to love and makes offers of marriage and financial support. In these disturbing cases, the accused plays upon the relationship and dependence of the victim to get her to drop the case or refuse to testify. The problem arises when courts must determine whether such beseeching, appeals to love, and even offers of marriage are evidence of wrongdoing by the accused. Essentially, courts must determine whether such "words of love so soft and tender"[77] could qualify as forfeiture by wrongdoing for constitutional purposes. Even if designed to deter testimony, do expressions of love constitute "wrongdoing"? If so, what does this say about the victim who refuses to testify? When the courts determine that perpetrators who offer visions of a bright future, financial security, love, and sometimes even marriage are mere manipulators engaging in wrongdoing, they necessarily conclude that the victims are pathetic dupes of this wrongful behavior. This presents yet another example of debates over epistemology where the victim's understandings of her situation are dismissed as deluded, pathetic, naïve, and wrong. On the one hand, it is maddening to imagine that violent domestic partners can use their psychological power and play on the victim's dependence and love to manipulate the victim into refusing to testify. This is particularly true when the perpetrator mixes violence with professions of love, blames her for "making him do it," and claims to have hit the woman because she "deserved it." On the other hand, it seems highly disrespectful of victims and subversive of their autonomy to insist that they have no agency or insight into their relationship, and their violent partners are merely playing them for fools.

This dilemma is reminiscent of legal and scholarly debates over mandatory prosecution in domestic violence cases where the victim does not wish to press charges.[78] Such prosecutions have been challenged as disrespectful and unwise,

[74] 264 Cal. Rptr. 3d 459 (Cal. App. 2020).

[75] *Id.* at 471.

[76] *Id. See also*, State v. Farrington, 2020-NMSC-022, ¶ 13, 476 P.3d 1231, 1241 (stating in dicta that "a history of abusive conduct coupled with conduct designed to isolate the victim was sufficient to support an inference of intent required under the forfeiture exception").

[77] The Mamas and the Papas, *Words of Love*, *on* THE MAMAS AND THE PAPAS (Geffen Records 1966).

[78] *See* Kimberly D. Bailey, *The Aftermath of Crawford and Davis: Deconstructing the Sound of Silence*, 2009 B.Y.U. L REV 1 (arguing against "victimless" prosecutions because they undermine victim

both because they ignore the victim's assessment of what would keep her safe and ascribe to the victim an inability to rationally choose for herself whether she wishes to testify.[79] The question of how to assess forfeiture by wrongdoing when the pressure on the victim comes in terms of love and marriage proposals mirrors this debate, and I am torn about how to treat such behavior on the part of the accused. On the one hand, it seems a tremendously unfair and *chutzpadik* gambit by a person who has already proven himself to be violent and manipulative with his intimate partner. On the other hand, I am not quite willing to insist that courts can divine true love better than the parties themselves and that a woman might, for reasons that are not pathological, choose to renew a relationship with her abuser and therefore decline to testify against him. Labeling love and marriage "wrongdoing" seems highly problematic, but then again, so does allowing a manipulative abuser to silence his victim once again. This dilemma is slightly easier to figure out if the victim actively refuses to testify, less so when she simply fails to appear.

CONCLUSION

The rules of hearsay and confrontation might at first glance seem highly technical and neutral, so much so that they would not benefit from a feminist analysis. In this chapter, I hope I have demonstrated that feminism has important insights to offer on the rules that regulate whose voices will be heard and whose voices will be silenced. Although the Rules of Evidence have often reduced hearsay and confrontation to formulaic tests, undergirding those tests are major assumptions about trustworthiness and fairness. The highly formal nature of hearsay may be alien to the way that some women and other disempowered groups will tend to communicate. When the rules allow for exceptions to in-court testimony, they may favor certain types of powerful entitled speakers. Furthermore, in applying notions of "testimonial statements" and "forfeiture by wrongdoing," the rules rely on an unspoken epistemology that disrespects women's experiences and ways of knowing.

safety, deny victim autonomy, and effectively silence victims); Douglas E. Beloof and Joel Shapiro, *Let the Truth Be Told: Proposed Hearsay Exceptions to Admit Domestic Violence Victims' Out of Court Statements as Substantive Evidence*, 11 COLUMBIA J. GENDER & L. 31–6 (2002) (summarizing the debate on mandatory ("no drop") prosecution of domestic violence cases irrespective of victim's desires); Sheila James Kuehl, *Forum: Mandatory Prosecution in Domestic Violence Cases*, 7 UCLA WOM. L.J. 169 (1997) (encapsulating arguments pro and contra for mandatory prosecution).

79 There is a robust literature surrounding why women return to their abusers that does more than portray these women as pathetic, ascribing their decision-making to "learned helplessness," and manipulation, and instead focuses on realistic assessment of risk, financial exigency, and child welfare.

Facially Neutral, Quietly Skewed

How Symmetrical Evidentiary Practices Obscure and Exacerbate Power Disparities in Asylum Proceedings

Gabriela Rodriguez

INTRODUCTION

The principle of facial neutrality in evidentiary rules rests on an appealing premise: that equally applicable standards ensure fairness between opposing parties. However, this premise overlooks the enormous power disparities that can exist between parties. This dynamic is uniquely apparent in United States Immigration Courts, which have virtually no rules of evidence and consequently allow the Department of Homeland Security (DHS) to leverage its institutional advantages against asylum seekers.

This chapter takes hearsay as a case study. It examines how the hearsay evidence rule, which prohibits parties from introducing out-of-court statements to prove the truth of what is asserted in those statements, may favor powerful parties when applied symmetrically. Through the specific example of DHS Form I-213, Record of Deportable/Inadmissible Alien, a DHS form that records border interviews, I suggest that the Immigration Court's permissive approach to hearsay evidence, though it applies equally to asylum seekers and the DHS, enables the DHS to introduce unreliable documents produced through coercion while affording those documents presumptive credibility.

One might imagine that this problem could be alleviated if Immigration Court proceedings were to adopt the Federal Rules of Evidence (FRE). After all, the Rules seek to advance the truth-seeking and fairness functions of evidence law by providing safeguards against unreliability. Even under such a schema, however, I-213s would likely gain admission through various hearsay exceptions. This is so because the policy rationales underlying these exceptions fail to account for differences in power and the ways that power interacts with credibility and accountability.

The implications of this analysis extend beyond immigration proceedings. If facially neutral evidentiary rules systematically advantage powerful parties regardless of whether they are permissive or restrictive, we must reconsider fundamental assumptions about how procedural neutrality relates to substantive fairness. The

Immigration Court context provides a particularly stark illustration of this problem, but the underlying dynamic, that facial neutrality can mask and perpetuate power imbalances, challenges us to rethink evidence law more broadly.

THE PROBLEM WITH UNREGULATED HEARSAY

Removal proceedings pose extremely high stakes for respondents.[1] Non-citizens in removal proceedings may be detained for years, permanently torn away from their loved ones and communities, and, in the worst cases, exposed to life-threatening persecution abroad. In other high-stakes legal contexts, the gravity of the proceeding is understood to necessitate stringent evidentiary standards. Criminal proceedings, for example, involve extensive rules constraining what evidence may be introduced against a defendant. Removal proceedings, by contrast, have minimal protections.

In removal proceedings, any evidence is admissible so long as it is relevant, probative, and fundamentally fair.[2] This permissiveness extends to hearsay evidence, which has been expressly found by the Board of Immigration Appeals ("the Board") to be admissible in Immigration Court.[3] Because this standard makes it nearly impossible to contest admissibility, evidentiary disputes in removal proceedings tend to center on how much weight to assign a piece of evidence.[4]

In legal proceedings that use evidentiary rules, hearsay is inadmissible, albeit with significant exceptions. In general, "hearsay" refers to any out-of-court statement offered for the truth of its content.[5] The policy justification for hearsay's inadmissibility is that such evidence generates serious reliability concerns.[6]

In the asylum context, the significant barriers asylum seekers face when gathering evidence have been understood to merit a departure from the strictures of the traditional prohibition on hearsay.[7] Sudden flight from one's country and the prospect of

1 Although the term "deportation" is commonly used in lay-speech to denote exile from the United States for immigration violations, "removal" has been the correct legal term in most cases since the passage of the Illegal Immigration Reform and Immigrant Responsibility Act of 1996, and is thus used hereinafter.

2 8 C.F.R. § 1240.7(a) ("The immigration judge may receive in evidence any oral or written statement that is material and relevant to any issue in the case."); Matter of Y-S-L-C-, 26 I&N Dec. 688, 690 (BIA 2015) ("It is well established that the Federal Rules of Evidence are not binding in immigration proceedings, where the test for admitting evidence is whether it is probative and its admission is fundamentally fair.").

3 Matter of C-C-I-, 26 I&N Dec. 375, 384 (BIA 2014) ([H]earsay evidence is admissible in removal proceedings where … it is probative and its use is not fundamentally unfair.")

4 Cath. Legal Immigr. Network, Practice Advisory: Rules of Evidence in Immigration Court Proceedings 6 (2020).

5 Fed. R. Evid. 801(c).

6 2 Kenneth S. Broun et al., McCormick on Evidence §§ 244–5, at 585–9 (8th ed., West Group 2020). This concern has limitations. *See generally*, David A. Sklansky, *The Neglected Origins of the Hearsay Rule in American Slavery: Recovering Queen v. Hepburn*, 2022 Sup. Ct. Rev. 413, 422 (2022); Aviva Orenstein, "Hearsay and Confrontation from a Feminist Gaze," in this volume.

7 Matter of S-M-J-, 21 I&N Dec. 722, 737–8 (1997) (Rosenburg, concurring).

persecution mean that asylum seekers often enter the United States without documents pertinent to their claims, and render it prohibitively difficult, if not dangerous, to obtain such documents later.

The DHS benefits from this same permissiveness. This may be unsurprising, given the general preference in evidence law for symmetrical rules.[8] Yet, as this chapter will explore, the DHS's 100 billion dollar budget,[9] army of attorneys,[10] and "compendium of biographic, criminal, medical, financial, and immigration information gleaned through a network of cooperating federal, state, and local agencies" create an informational asymmetry so great that it renders this symmetrical approach to hearsay fundamentally unfair.[11] Put simply, the Immigration Court's approach to hearsay evidence disregards the vast differences in power between parties, effectively treating them as equally situated. In doing so, it fails to account for and regulate the DHS's disproportionate power, and this, in turn, has real implications for outcomes in asylum proceedings.

As noted above, asylum applicants are forced to rely on hearsay because they face severe obstacles to obtaining any evidence at all. Many applicants flee their countries in a hurry, leaving behind critical documents.[12] Some applicants come from countries that maintain imprecise records.[13] Others may be reticent to ask friends and family members to help them obtain documents for fear of putting them in danger.[14] Still others may be practically precluded from gathering evidence because they are in detention, where they cannot make international phone calls or undertake other actions needed to obtain documents from abroad.[15] Recalling an experience with a former client, one Board member wrote:

> I recall a time, when I was a lawyer in pro bono practice, when long after I submitted his application, my client finally received information on tissue-thin paper, tucked into a false front of an international air letter which his co-worker had unsealed and re-glued to protect it from being intercepted by the authorities of his country.

8 At the very least, virtually no other policy justifications have been articulated in the case law or authorities. While some courts have justified DHS's use of hearsay by observing that the government cannot fully control witnesses and or guarantee their availability, such explanations do not account for the *categorical* admissibility of hearsay evidence. *E.g.*, Baliza v. I.N.S., 709 F.2d 1231, 1234 (9th Cir. 1983).

9 U.S. Dep't of Homeland Sec., Fiscal Year 2026 Budget in Brief (2025), www.dhs.gov/sites/default/files/2025-07/2025_07_03_ocfo_fy-2026-budget-in-brief.pdf.

10 *About ICE*, U.S. Immigr. & Customs Enf't, www.ice.gov/about-ice (reporting that the Office of the Principal Legal Advisor, the office that prosecutes Immigration Court cases, has roughly 1,700 attorneys and 300 support personnel).

11 Geoffrey Heeren, *Shattering the One-Way Mirror: Discovery in Immigration Court*, 79 Brook. L. Rev. 1569, 1627 (2014).

12 Marisa S. Cianciarulo, *Terrorism and Asylum Seekers: Why the Real ID Act Is a False Promise*, 43 Harv. J. on Legis. 100, 119 (2006).

13 Nicole J. Thomas, *"They Told Me He Said He Would Kill Me." Why Hearsay Should Get Full Weight in Asylum Proceedings*, 37 Cal. W. Int'l L.J. 299, 309 (2007).

14 Cianciarulo, *supra* note 12, at 119.

15 S-M-J-, 21 I&N at 737–8 (Rosenburg, concurring).

> *We must be careful to consider when impediments attendant to the asylum applicant's situation have prevented the orderly or even the timely presentation of evidence that would corroborate the material facts which may be central to a specific claim.*[16]

In light of these unique considerations, respondents' ability to use hearsay evidence in removal proceedings eliminates what would otherwise be a cruel barrier to relief, to deny an applicant precisely because the "impediments attendant to [his] situation" hinder evidence gathering.

This policy rationale resonates with scholarly concerns that the hearsay prohibition "tends to pose a bigger problem for disempowered litigants, who have less access to admissible written records and are less able to track down live witnesses and bring them to court."[17] The Immigration Court's approach mitigates that issue in the asylum context by allowing applicants to lean heavily on their own written and verbal testimony to prove the elements of their claims, among other forms of hearsay evidence.

For example, an asylum applicant represented by competent counsel will virtually always draft and submit a lengthy declaration or affidavit describing the events underlying her claim. This document is typically the single most important piece of evidence in her case.[18] The applicant may reiterate much of this testimony orally at her hearing. Asylum applicants also often submit evidence such as written testimony by experts on their countries of origin, relevant news articles, letters or affidavits from foreign witnesses, police reports, medical records, and psychological evaluations. Much of this evidence qualifies as hearsay under traditional rules of evidence, as it is being offered to prove the truth of what the applicant, expert, foreign witness, or letters say.

The DHS also routinely introduces hearsay evidence in these proceedings, such as ex parte affidavits and witness statements offered to prove the truth of the matters they assert, typically damaging facts about respondents. One particularly problematic form of hearsay is DHS Form I-213.[19] The DHS routinely uses the contents of this form, which contains summaries of statements made by non-citizens during border encounters, to undermine asylum applicants' claims and credibility.

After stopping a non-citizen, officers from Customs and Border Patrol (CBP), a DHS subsidiary agency, will typically interview the non-citizen and record the notes of the interview in its Form I-213.[20] The substance of this document typically

16 *Id.* at 738 (emphasis added).

17 Sklansky, *supra* note 6, at 442.

18 Stacy Caplow, *Putting the "I" in Wr*t*ng: Drafting an A/Effective Personal Statement to Tell a Winning Refugee Story*, 14 J. Legal Writing Inst. 249, 249 (2008).

19 For reference, a sample Form I-213 can be accessed at the Catholic Legal Immigration Network's website. Sample Form I-213, Cath. Legal Immigr. Network, www.cliniclegal.org/sites/default/files/2019-12/Sample%20Form%20I-213-Michelle%20Mendez.pdf.

20 Aruna Sury, Practice Advisory: What to Do When ICE Submits an I-213 in Immigration Court 2 (Immigr. Legal Res. Ctr. 2022).

includes information such as the non-citizen's biographic data, the circumstances of his entry into the United States, the circumstances of his apprehension, any past criminal convictions, and any health or humanitarian considerations.[21] These documents contain a CBP officer's summary of a non-citizen's out-of-court statements and they are hearsay when used for the truth of the matter asserted.[22]

Notably, immigration judges give I-213s a high degree of deference. Both the IJ Benchbook, which gives guidance to immigration judges adjudicating Immigration Court matters, and the Board of Immigration Appeals note that I-213s are "inherently trustworthy" absent evidence that the information was incorrect or obtained by coercion or duress.[23] This echoes justifications for certain hearsay exceptions available in Article III courts, like the public records and business records exceptions.[24] This framing is misguided, however, because I-213s are filled out in coercive situations virtually by default. Although hearsay's admissibility in Immigration Courts ameliorates the significant disadvantages faced by asylum applicants, its "party-blind" nature fails to take into account the enormous power differences between respondents and the DHS, resulting in structurally biased outcomes.

While both the DHS and respondents can introduce hearsay evidence, only the DHS can create self-serving evidence through coercive encounters with its opposing party. Surveys,[25] international watchdog reporting,[26] journalistic reporting,[27] and photographic evidence[28] suggest that encounters at the border

[21] Dree K. Collopy et. al, Immigration Practice Pointers: Challenges and Strategies Beyond Relief 523–4 (Am. Immigr. Law. Ass'n 2015); Sample Form I-213, *supra* note 19; John Washington, *Bad Information: Border Patrol Arrest Reports Are Full of Lies That Can Sabotage Asylum Claims*, The Intercept (Aug. 11, 2019), https://theintercept.com/2019/08/11/border-patrol-asylum-claim/.

[22] This is, of course, barring admissibility through an exception to hearsay, which I discuss below.

[23] Matter of Barcenas, 19 I&N Dec. 609, 611 (BIA 1988); Executive Office for Immigration Review, IJ Benchbook: Form I-213 Outline.

[24] Notably, in a still earlier decision, the Board made a similar claim about trustworthiness, but added that Form I-213 would be admissible under the public records exception to the hearsay rule in any event. Matter of Mejia, 16 I&N Dec. 6, 8 (BIA 1976). I turn to a fuller discussion of these comparisons below.

[25] Guillermo Cantor, Hieleras (Iceboxes) in the Rio Grande Valley Sector 9–10 (Am. Immigration Council 2015), www.americanimmigrationcouncil.org/wp-content/uploads/2025/01/hieleras_iceboxes_in_the_rio_grande_valley_sector.pdf; Mercedes P. Palacios et al., "*Estuvimos en una Hielera*": *Migration Trauma and Detainment among Newcomer Latinx Adolescents*, 16 Psych. Trauma: Theory, Rsch., Prac., & Pol'y S 330, S334 (2024).

[26] Hum. Rts. Watch, In the Freezer: Abusive Conditions for Women and Children in U.S. Immigration Holding Cells (2018), www.hrw.org/sites/default/files/report_pdf/uscrd0218_web.pdf.

[27] Washington, *supra* note 21; Simon Romero et. al, *Hungry, Scared and Sick: Inside the Migrant Detention Center in Clint, Texas*, N.Y. Times (July 9, 2019) www.nytimes.com/interactive/2019/07/06/us/migrants-border-patrol-clint.html; Hannah Jiang and Robin Lindsay, *How Mylar Blankets Went from Space Tech to a Symbol of the US-Mexico Border Crisis*, Bus. Insider (Apr. 17, 2020), www.businessinsider.com/mylar-space-blanket-border-migrants-space-2020-4.

[28] Camila Domonoske, *Surveillance Stills from Border Patrol Facilities Show Crowded, Trash-Filled Cells*, Nat'l Pub. Radio (Aug. 19, 2016), www.npr.org/sections/thetwo-way/2016/08/19/490624225/surveillance-stills-from-border-patrol-facilities-show-crowded-trash-filled-cell.

are regularly accompanied by physical abuse. For example, there is significant evidence that the CBP routinely places migrants in freezing cold cells known as *hieleras*, or "iceboxes." In a survey of nearly 400 former CBP detainees, 78 percent reported that they had been exposed to extreme temperatures while in holding.[29] Migrants have reported to international watchdogs that their cells are kept so cold that "[d]etainees' fingers and toes turn blue and their lips chap and split due to the cold."[30]

In one CBP sector, all but one of the 143 individuals surveyed reported that cells were so overcrowded they could neither lie down nor sit.[31] Stills from the CBP's own surveillance footage show rooms filled with migrants crowded together, wrapped in Mylar blankets, and surrounded by trash.[32] In addition to being crowded, these facilities are often dirty, a condition that is exacerbated by migrants often having no means to bathe or engage in other hygiene tasks. Of one facility, the *New York Times* reported:

> Outbreaks of scabies, shingles and chickenpox were spreading among the hundreds of children and adults who were being held in cramped cells, agents said. The stench of the children's dirty clothing was so strong it spread to the agents' own clothing – people in town would scrunch their noses when they left work.[33]

Also, while in holding, migrants have reported that the lights are left on for twenty-four hours a day, disorienting them and making it difficult to sleep.[34]

These harsh conditions do not merely precede the I-213; they directly shape its content. In the conditions just described, migrants may be jostled awake in the middle of the night, if they have been able to sleep at all, interviewed by CBP officers, and pressured into signing immigration documents, sometimes without translation.[35] During these interviews, CBP officers may demean and disbelieve migrants.[36] One migrant reported that a CBP agent filled out portions of her I-213 without even giving her the opportunity to speak:

> One asylum-seeker interviewed by Human Rights Watch said that the CBP agent who interviewed her never asked her about fearing return. "He just looked me up and down and said, 'You're here to work, I'm writing that you're here to work. I don't want to hear anything about you saying you're afraid.'"[37]

[29] CANTOR, *supra* note 25, at 9–10.
[30] HUM. RTS. WATCH, *supra* note 26; Washington, *supra* note 21.
[31] CANTOR, *supra* note 25, at 12.
[32] Domonoske, *supra* note 28.
[33] Romero et al., *supra* note 27.
[34] HUM. RTS. WATCH, *supra* note 26; CANTOR, *supra* note 25, at 12.
[35] HUM. RTS. WATCH, *supra* note 26.
[36] *Id.* ("He said, 'I don't believe you. I don't believe what you're telling me, because many women have come here saying the same thing.'")
[37] Washington, *supra* note 21.

Even absent officer misrepresentations, the power that officers wield over migrants in these encounters puts little pressure on officers to fill out forms carefully, and may chill migrants from demanding as much. The nature of these encounters, in which agents are entitled to use physical force to secure the border, creates an implicit threat of violence. For an immigrant held in the conditions just described, this threat may be all the more apparent. Other factors, such as officer misconduct, may make the threat of violence still more apparent.[38] Those who have fled authoritarian countries and countries rife with police abuse may be particularly attune to the risks that attend interactions with law enforcement.[39] As a result of these facts, an immigrant may "fall in line" to avoid harm, simplifying processing and absolving immigration officials of the need to gather a reliable and complete account of his story.[40]

The reliability concerns created by these circumstances are not merely theoretical. Journalists, practitioners, and former detainees themselves have alleged that I-213s commonly contain statements that are implausible or, in some instances, demonstrably false.[41] For example, there are numerous reports of toddlers and babies purportedly claiming they entered the United States to work.[42] Additionally, a New Jersey attorney recounted that a client's I-213 incorrectly stated that the client had a criminal conviction, when those charges had in fact been dismissed.[43] The attorney provided the immigration judge with his client's certified disposition, confirming the charges had been dismissed, but the judge nonetheless could not be convinced that the I-213 was inaccurate, determined the client was ineligible for bond, and held him in detention for at least two years.[44] Investigative journalists[45] and experienced practitioners[46] alike report that I-213s regularly contain "erroneous, fabricated, and downright bogus information."[47]

[38] There are many recorded incidents of CBP officers physically abusing immigrants at the border. WASHINGTON OFF. ON LATIN AM., BORDER OVERSIGHT, https://borderoversight.org/ (a database of alleged abuses by immigration officials at the U.S. border, containing hundreds of allegations from 2020–2024).

[39] Ramsameachire v. Ashcroft, 357 F.3d 169, 179 (2d Cir. 2004).

[40] For a more detailed discussion on how the threat of violence absolves state actors of the need to accurately gather information, *see generally*, David Graeber, *Dead Zones of the Imagination*, *in* DAVID GRAEBER, THE UTOPIA OF RULES (2015).

[41] SURY, *supra* note 20, at 2; Washington, *supra* note 21.

[42] Washington, *supra* note 21. See also, Michael Kagan, *Mass Surrender in Immigration Court*, 14 U.C. IRVINE L. REV. 163, 198 (2024) ("Over the years we have seen I-213s reporting a six-year-old girl's occupation as a "laborer," describing men as women and vice versa, identifying Guatemalans as Salvadorans, and so on."); DALIA CASTILLO-GRANADOS ET. AL, QUICK GUIDE: DEFENDING SIJS CLIENTS IN REMOVAL PROCEEDINGS (Immigr. Legal Res. Ctr. 2025) ("For example, sometimes CBP officers will copy and paste the details and narrative from someone else's I-213 and will accidentally leave details in the I-213 that do not apply to the client.").

[43] *Id.*

[44] *Id.*

[45] Washington, *supra* note 21.

[46] *Id.*; SURY, *supra* note 20; Kagan, *supra* note 42; CASTILLO-GRANADOS ET. AL, *supra* note 42.

[47] Washington, *supra* note 21.

The Immigration Court's permissive approach to hearsay leaves a migrant with no effective means of excluding evidence created under coercion by her opposing party. The coercive production of I-213s at the border would be troubling enough if these documents remained internal to the CBP. Instead, the agency responsible for collecting evidence under abusive and coercive conditions also introduces that evidence in Immigration Court to undermine asylum claims and attack immigrants' credibility. The non-citizen must somehow disprove statements recorded and controlled by armed officers during encounters that may have taken place several years earlier, and courts treat these documents as presumptively trustworthy.

These dynamics reveal a fundamental flaw in the Immigration Court's symmetrically permissive approach to evidence. In the absence of evidence rules, there are few structural mechanisms preventing powerful parties from exploiting the system's permissiveness. The DHS can coercively manufacture self-serving documentation and introduce it with a presumption of credibility, all while asylum seekers struggle to obtain any evidence at all. Moreover, the DHS's access to information and resources, combined with the coercive authority of the state, is wildly disproportionate to that of asylum seekers, enabling the DHS to derive far greater benefit from the wide admissibility of hearsay. In this way, a symmetrical, permissive approach to hearsay becomes a tool for perpetuating power imbalances. Yet, as the next section will demonstrate, this dynamic would likely persist even under traditional evidentiary rules.

EXISTING HEARSAY RULES: REPRODUCING THE PROBLEM

This account of the disparate effect of the Immigration Court's laissez-faire approach to hearsay raises an obvious question: Would existing evidence rules solve the problems identified above? What would it look like if the Immigration Court were bound by the FRE? The answer is, perhaps surprisingly, that things would not look much different. While the FRE are nowhere near as permissive as the Immigration Court with regards to hearsay, I-213s would nonetheless likely be admitted under Rules 801(d)(2) (opposing party statements), 803(6) (business records exception), and/or 803(8) (public records exception).[48] The policy rationales for these exclusions and exceptions have historically centered on fairness, reliability, and necessity. As this section will show, however, most of these policy rationales break down in the Immigration Court context, because they fail to account for situations where vast power differences exist between parties.[49]

[48] Fed. R. Evid. 801(d)(2)(A), 803(6)(B), 803(8)(A)(ii).

[49] I am not the first to analyze Form I-213 through the lens of the policy rationales underlying these exceptions. Marie S. Celentino, *In Government We Trust: Judicial Deference to Government Evidence in Removal Proceedings*, 78 Vanderbilt L. Rev. 375, 421–6 (2025) (arguing that the policy rationales underlying the public records and business records exceptions ought to render I-213s

As a result of this oversight, I-213s, documents that are empirically unreliable and produced through coercion and the threat of violence, could still potentially be admitted under existing hearsay rules, compromising fair adjudication.

The Opposing Party Statement Exception

The typical rationale for excluding opposing party statements from the hearsay definition is that opposing party statements do not prevent a party from questioning the witness against him, because he can simply explain his past statements on the stand.[50] However, this rationale fails in the Immigration Court context because it ignores the interplay between power and who is viewed as credible.

Scholars have observed that, when hearing witness testimony, adjudicators likely use race and other characteristics as shortcuts to determine credibility.[51] For example, Professor Gonzales Rose has noted that fact finders unfairly attribute low credibility to those belonging to racial and ethnic minority groups, and unfairly attribute high credibility to those belonging to dominant racial and ethnic groups.[52] The diminished credibility of one party tends to bolster the credibility of the other, and vice versa.[53] This dynamic produces unfair trial outcomes, particularly in adversarial proceedings, where credibility is a finite resource.[54]

Undocumented immigrants are disproportionately likely to belong to ethnic and/or racial minority groups.[55] Being an undocumented immigrant is also heavily racialized in popular discourse.[56] Derogatory terms commonly applied to undocumented immigrants, such as "illegals," commonly imply that individuals hail from "undesirable" ethnic, racial, and religious groups, such as Central America, the

inadmissible). I depart from this literature in that I critique these rationales for failing to account for power differences between parties.

50 Broun et al., *supra* note 6, at 620; Edmund M. Morgan, Basic Problems of Evidence 266 (1961); 5 Jack B. Weinstein and Margaret A. Berger, Weinstein's Federal Evidence § 801.30 (Joseph M. McLaughlin ed., 2d ed., Westlaw 2025).

51 *See generally*, Julia Simon-Kerr, *Credibility by Proxy*, 85 Geo. Wash. L. Rev. 152 (2017) (observing that status-markers such as prior convictions can determine how one's credibility is perceived, which in turn disproportionately harms specific demographics); Jasmine B. Gonzales Rose, *A Critical Perspective on Testimonial Injustice: Interrogating Witnesses' Credibility Excess in Criminal Trials*, 7 Quaestio Facti: Revista Internacional Sobre Razonamiento Probatorio 173 (2024) (observing that not only are some given unfairly low credibility on the stand, but that others are given unfairly high credibility, and that these two tendencies are highly interdependent).

52 Gonzales Rose, *supra* note 51, at 175.

53 *Id.* at 181.

54 *Id.* at 174–5.

55 Jeffrey S. Passel and Jens Manuel Krogstad, *What We Know about Unauthorized Immigrants Living in the U.S.*, Pew Rsch. Ctr. (July 22, 2024), www.pewresearch.org/short-reads/2024/07/22/what-we-know-about-unauthorized-immigrants-living-in-the-us/.

56 *E.g.*, Leo R. Chavez, *Fear of White Replacement: Latina Fertility, White Demographic Decline, and Immigration Reform*, *in* A Field Guide to White Supremacy (Kathleen Belew and Ramón A. Gutiérrez eds., University of California Press 2021).

Caribbean, Asia, the Middle East, and so on.[57] To be an "illegal" also triggers connections with poverty,[58] criminality,[59] and in some cases, terrorism,[60] concepts that are in and of themselves heavily racialized.[61]

By contrast, the DHS is a state entity, a status that in and of itself confers a significant credibility benefit.[62] Furthermore, immigration agencies like the CBP may "reify[] societal prejudice … and racial hierarchy" through acts such as racial profiling, physically and verbally abusing racial and ethnic minorities, and disseminating rhetoric that paints racial and ethnic minorities as violent criminals.[63] Professor Gonzales Rose has noted that parties can further inflate their credibility by advancing racial hierarchies, such as through facilitating the prosecution of racial minorities.[64] Moreover, both the agency's staff[65] and attorneys at large[66] are majority non-Hispanic white, meaning that whenever an immigration judge interacts with the agency, the judge is more likely to interact with a white DHS attorney – something that may further inflate the agency's credibility.

In sum, the perceived and actual racial identities of undocumented immigrants, the DHS's status as a state entity, its racially subordinating practices, and its demographic makeup, create a very real possibility that respondents in removal proceedings systematically have unfairly diminished credibility attributed to them, while the DHS's credibility is more likely to be systematically inflated.

Turning to Form I-213, as noted earlier, both the IJ Benchbook and the Board of Immigration Appeals describe I-213s as "inherently trustworthy" absent evidence that the information was incorrect or obtained by coercion or duress.[67] Given the compelling, publicized evidence of widespread coercion surrounding these documents, one might anticipate that I-213s are commonly suppressed or accorded reduced probative value under this standard. In practice, however, immigration practitioners report that "the court is not properly scrutinizing these documents" and that

57 Kevin R. Johnson, *Exclusion and Deportation of Racial Minorities*, *in* Kevin Johnson, The Huddled Masses Myth: Immigration and Civil Rights 13–54 (Temple University Press 2004); Daniel Kanstroom, *From Chinese Exclusion to Post-Entry Social Control: The Early Formation of the Modern Deportation System*, *in* Daniel Kanstroom, Deportation Nation: Outsiders in American History 91–130 (Harvard University Press 2007).

58 *E.g.*, Johnson, *supra* note 57, at 91–108; Kanstroom, *supra* note 57, at 131–2.

59 *E.g.*, Johnson, *supra* note 57, at 109–23; Kanstroom, *supra* note 57, at 133–5.

60 Johnson, *supra* note 57, at 13–54.

61 *Id.*

62 Irving Younger, *The Perjury Routine*, The Nation, May 3, 1967. *See also*, Michael Lipsky, Street-Level Bureaucracy 129–31 (Russell Sage Foundation 2010).

63 Katy Murdza and Walter Ewing, The Legacy of Racism in the U.S. Border Patrol (Am. Immigr. Council 2021).

64 Gonzales Rose, *supra* note 51, at 181.

65 *Equal Employment Opportunity Management Section*, U.S. Dep't of Homeland Sec., www.dhs.gov/eeo-management-section (last updated Aug. 13, 2025).

66 *Demographics, Profile of the Legal Profession*, Am. Bar Ass'n (Jan. 1, 2024), www.americanbar.org/news/profile-legal-profession/demographics/.

67 Barcenas, 19 I&N at 611; IJ Benchbook: Form I-213 Outline, *supra* note 23.

"suppressing evidence presented by Border Patrol or ICE is nearly impossible."[68] One journalist described this legal and practical landscape exceptionally well:

> A 1988 Board of Immigration Appeals case, Matter of Barcenas, made it such that an immigrant had to "come forward with proof" before immigration officers would need to defend their recorded version of events. How an immigrant might obtain proof of a conversation that took place months or sometimes years previously while they were in custody is unclear. But the court basically ruled that if it's one person's word against another, the Border Patrol wins.[69]

Contrast the Immigration Court's deference to the CBP against its treatment of asylum seekers. Scholars have shown that many immigration judges approach asylum seekers' claims from a default position of incredulity and issue credibility determinations based on empirically questionable assumptions about how "genuine victims" should behave rather than evidence-based indicators of truthfulness.[70] In the political arena, the Trump Administration recently released a memo alleging that immigration practitioners "frequently coach clients to conceal their past or lie about their circumstances when asserting their asylum claims, all in an attempt to circumvent immigration policies enacted to protect our national security and deceive the immigration authorities and courts into granting them undeserved relief."[71]

The skepticism asylum seekers face is mirrored in the U.S. Code. The REAL ID Act states that asylum seekers, unlike the DHS, do not benefit from a default presumption of credibility.[72] It permits immigration judges to make adverse credibility findings based on factors that have been widely discredited in the social sciences, such as a judge's subjective impression of an applicant's demeanor.[73] Moreover, the statute permits immigration judges to make adverse credibility findings based on inconsistencies unrelated to the substance of an asylum claim.[74]

68 Washington, *supra* note 21.

69 *Id.*

70 *E.g.*, Michael Kagan, *Believable Victims: Asylum Credibility and the Struggle for Objectivity*, 16 GEO. J. INT'L AFF. (2014); Smita Misra-Latty, *Physician Advocacy in a "Culture of Disbelief": A Critical-Interpretive Study of Asylum Medicine*, 19 INT'L J. COMMC'N 2616 (2025). *See* JESSICA ANDERSON ET. AL, THE CULTURE OF DISBELIEF (Refugee Studies Centre 2014) (discussing similar tendencies in the United Kingdom, which also utilizes an adversarial asylum system).

71 Kristi Noem, *Preventing Abuses of the Legal System and the Federal Court*, WHITE HOUSE: PRESIDENTIAL MEMORANDUM (Mar. 22, 2025), www.whitehouse.gov/presidential-actions/preventing-abuses-of-the-legal-system-and-the-federal-court/.

72 8 U.S.C. § 1158(b)(1)(B)(iii).

73 8 U.S.C. § 1158(b)(1)(B)(iii) (permitting demeanor evidence in credibility determinations); Kiel Brennan-Marquez and Julia Simon-Kerr, *Judging Demeanor*, 109 Minn. L. Rev. 1503 (2025) (showing through social science literature that demeanor is not a reliable means of determining credibility).

74 8 U.S.C. § 1158(b)(1)(B)(iii) (permitting "any inaccuracies or falsehoods in such statements, without regard to whether an inconsistency, inaccuracy, or falsehood goes to the heart of the applicant's claim … ").

This suggests that the policy rationale behind the opposing party statement exclusion to hearsay breaks down in the Immigration Court context. The assumption is that admitting an opposing party's statement is fair because the party can explain himself on the stand. However, if one party enters proceedings with a legal and cultural presumption of trustworthiness, and another enters proceedings with presumptions of untrustworthiness, the latter does not truly have a fair opportunity to explain or deny the accuracy of her past statements on the stand. This, in turn, is one example of how "neutral" evidentiary rules can entrench rather than correct power disparities.

The Business Records and Public Records Exceptions

The business records and public records exceptions to hearsay share similar policy rationales, namely, reliability and necessity. My focus here is the indicia of reliability rationale.

Typical justifications for the business records and public records exceptions include the following:

1. Recordkeepers have an incentive to be honest because organizations typically rely on the accuracy of records.[75]
2. The fact that a record is kept in the regular course of business suggests that it may be checked for accuracy.[76]
3. Public records are likely to come to light, which incentivizes accuracy.[77]

These justifications overlap. An assumption underlying all three is that incorrect recordkeeping produces negative consequences for the recordkeeper. This assumption must underlie those policy rationales because the incentives they describe – organizational reliance, review, public scrutiny – only promote accuracy if errors actually harm the recordkeeper's interests, whether through damage to his organization, professional consequences, or loss of reputation. Via this assumption, the policy rationales for the business records and public records exceptions fail to account for the disparities in power between Respondents and the DHS, much like the opposing party statement exclusion, and much like the Immigration Court's equally permissive approach to both parties.

The DHS's power and undocumented immigrants' accompanying disempowerment insulate the DHS from consequences for inaccurate recordkeeping. One reason for this is that the agency does not need accurate I-213s to function. On the contrary, the more immigrants claim to be migrating for economic reasons, the

75 Paul F. Rothstein, Federal Rules of Evidence § 803 (3d ed., Westlaw 2024).

76 Broun et al., *supra* note 6, at 672 (stating as much with regards to the business records exception); *Id.* at 685–6 (stating as much with regards to the public records exception).

77 *Id.* at 685–6.

more smoothly the DHS can carry out its day-to-day functions. In other words, the reliance discussed in policy rationale 1 does not actually exist in this context.

If a non-citizen without valid entry documents is apprehended by a CBP officer near the border, the officer typically does not have to refer the non-citizen for full removal proceedings before removing him.[78] Rather, CBP officers can quickly remove those individuals from the United States without an opportunity for a hearing or a chance to apply for immigration relief, in a process known as expedited removal.[79]

Arguably, expedited removal is more desirable for the DHS than traditional removal proceedings. Expedited removal allows the DHS to remove an individual without the expenditures associated with detaining the non-citizen, monitoring the non-citizen's location if he is released, or sending a trial attorney to prosecute the non-citizen's removal case before the Immigration Court. Accordingly, over the last three decades, the use of expedited removal has steadily increased.[80] In Fiscal Year 2024, expedited removal comprised nearly 60 percent of all removals.[81]

The expedited removal statutes provide for an important caveat. If a non-citizen claims that she fears returning to her country of origin or that she intends to apply for asylum, she must be taken out of the expedited removal process and referred for what is known as a "credible fear" interview before a separate DHS subsidiary agency.[82] In this way, asylum seekers can slow down the DHS's operations and strain its resources. For these reasons, when a CBP officer incorrectly writes in an I-213 that a non-citizen does not fear harm, it does not bring about negative consequences for the agency. On the contrary, this practice streamlines the agency's operations.

If the DHS were prejudiced by its incorrect recordkeeping at removal proceedings, such as by immigration judges deeming suspect I-213s inadmissible, this would create an accountability mechanism that would incentivize the DHS to reform its recordkeeping practices. As discussed above, however, certain characteristics of the DHS afford it an unfair credibility boost in removal proceedings, which is reinforced by the presumption of credibility for Form I-213.[83] For

[78] 8 U.S.C. § 1225(b)(1)(A)(i).

[79] *Id.* For an accessible explanation of expedited removal, *see*, Immigr. Legal Res. Ctr., Toolkit to Assist People Facing Expanded Expedited Removal (2025), www.ilrc.org/sites/default/files/2025-02/Toolkit%20to%20Assist%20People%20Facing%20Expanded%20Expedited%20Removal_0.pdf.

[80] Am. Immigr. Council, Expedited Removal Explainer (2025), www.americanimmigrationcouncil.org/fact-sheet/expedited-removal (last visited Aug. 9, 2025).

[81] Total removals in FY 2024 were 329,990. *Immigration Enforcement and Legal Processes Monthly Tables*, U.S. Dep't Homeland Sec'y: Off. Homeland Sec'y Stat., https://ohss.dhs.gov/topics/immigration/immigration-enforcement/monthly-tables (last visited Aug. 9, 2025). Total expedited removals in the same period were 193,520. Am. Immigr. Council, *supra* note 80. The proportion of total removals that were expedited is therefore 58.6%.

[82] 8 U.S.C. § 1225(b)(1)(A)(ii).

[83] *See generally*, *supra*.

these reasons, immigration judges give significant deference to Form I-213, to the detriment of asylum seekers.[84] The widespread deference immigration judges show to I-213s forecloses a potential institutional incentive for more careful recordkeeping practices.

Furthermore, formal accountability mechanisms notwithstanding, evidence suggests that CBP officers are rarely held accountable for misconduct. From fiscal years 2014 through 2016, the CBP opened and then closed roughly 7,000 cases per year.[85] These cases primarily involved general misconduct, such as failing to follow procedures.[86] In the majority of these cases, the agency found that no action against the employee was warranted, and closed the case.[87] Note that this outcome is distinct from a finding that the allegation was unsubstantiated, which occurred in only 9 percent of cases.[88]

Accountability is lacking even when more serious allegations are made against CBP officers. In 2014, through a Freedom of Information Act (FOIA) request, the American Immigration Council obtained data on 809 allegations of abuse filed against CBP officers by non-citizens between 2009 and 2012.[89] These reports included allegations of physical abuse, excessive use of force, racial profiling, and sexual abuse, among other harms.[90] At the time the FOIA response was issued, 40 percent of cases were still pending, and had done so for an average of more than one year.[91] Of the cases that had reached outcomes, 97 percent resulted in no action.[92] While there is no way to know what percentage of these cases had merit, the near-total absence of accountability, together with the lengthy delays in adjudication, suggests a systemic failure to take complainants' allegations seriously.

When even physical abuse results in inaction, never mind more mundane misconduct such as failing to follow rules, CBP officers have little incentive to improve their recordkeeping practices. Thus, the rationales for the business records and public records exceptions fail to take into account the kind of power differences between parties that exist in the immigration context. These policy rationales presume that faulty recordkeeping produces negative consequences that incentivize accuracy. In the DHS's case, however, the incentives run in the opposite direction. Inaccurate I-213s that facilitate expedited removal serve the agency's interests better than accurate I-213s. Without robust accountability mechanisms, those incentives may prevail over any contrasting accuracy imperative.

84 *Id.*
85 U.S. Gov't Accountability Off., *Department of Homeland Security: Components Could Improve Monitoring of the Employee Misconduct Process*, GAO-18-405 (2018) (Reissued Sept. 4, 2018).
86 *Id.*
87 *Id.* at 23–5.
88 *Id.*
89 Daniel E. Martínez et. al, No Action Taken 4 (Am. Immigr. Council 2014).
90 *Id.*
91 *Id.* at 8.
92 *Id.*

Trustworthiness

Under the FRE, business and public records can still be excluded if the opponent can show that they lack trustworthiness.[93] Business records created for the purpose of litigation, for instance, face a heavy presumption of unreliability under 803(6)(E).[94] As for public records, their trustworthiness hinges on a host of factors, including, among others, the motivation of the investigator and the procedures followed in the preparation of the record.[95] Whether a hearsay document was created for the purposes of litigation can also impact the admissibility of public records, such as when the document sets out a matter observed by law enforcement in a criminal case.[96]

In an Immigration Court subject to the FRE, this trustworthiness inquiry may open a path for exclusion of I-213s. This inquiry is facially similar to the one set out in *Barcenas* and the IJ Benchbook, but Rule 803's trustworthiness inquiries call for far less extreme showings than coercion or duress, offering a more robust check on the admissibility of I-213s.

While the business records and public records trustworthiness inquiries are a step in the right direction, they suffer from troubling flaws that could undermine their ability to protect disempowered parties. First, like other rules and practices discussed in this chapter, these trustworthiness inquiries start from a presumption that the recordkeeper is reliable and put the burden on the opponent to demonstrate otherwise. This default rule returns us to one of the problematic cycles described above. It again puts the onus on the respondent in an asylum proceeding to demonstrate the unreliability of the DHS's documents. And this, again, places credibility at the center of the inquiry. As discussed above, there are reasons to believe that such credibility contests will favor the DHS at the expense of immigration respondents. For this reason, a default rule that favors admissibility of DHS-produced documents may create an insurmountable burden for those seeking to question their reliability.

CONCLUSION

The Immigration Court's treatment of Form I-213 reveals a fundamental problem with how the law conceptualizes fairness. Whether operating under permissive standards that allow virtually any relevant evidence, or under rules designed to

[93] Fed. R. Evid. 803(6)(E), 803(8)(B).

[94] Palmer v. Hoffman, 318 U.S. 109, 113–14 (1943).

[95] Fed. R. Evid. 803(8) advisory committee's note.

[96] *E.g.*, United States v. Torralba-Mendia, 784 F.3d 652 (9th Cir. 2015) (finding that the biographical portions of an I-213 were admissible in a criminal proceeding under the public records exception, because while the matter was observed by law enforcement, gathering non-citizen's biographical information is routine and ministerial, and is not done with an eye towards future criminal proceedings).

safeguard against unreliable testimony, evidentiary frameworks consistently fail to account for how power shapes the production, presentation, and perception of evidence. The result is that facial neutrality becomes a mechanism through which existing power imbalances are reinforced rather than remedied.

The stakes of this conversation are particularly high in the immigration context, where case outcomes routinely result in individuals being torn away from their families, locked in cages, and exiled to faraway places. That said, the dynamics identified here are likely at play in other parts of the system. Both rules of equal applicability and a largely rule-less approach fail in this context to account for the distorting influence of power on evidence itself. For evidence law to promote truth-seeking and fairness, it may need to embrace asymmetrical checks on that power.

SECTION 6

Experts

INTRODUCTION

Expert testimony is one area where there has been an abundance of Critical Evidence scholarship. From questioning the distinction between lay and expert testimony, to calling attention to the empirical evidence that judges use to assess the reliability of expert testimony differently, depending on who is offering it, to noting the way expert testimony has been used to further marginalize members of the LGBT community, Critical Evidence scholars have found the rules governing lay and expert testimony fertile ground for asking why.

This section reflects this interest in critiquing the admissibility of expert testimony as governed by Rules 702 through 706, and also by the Supreme Court's rulings in a trilogy of cases: *Daubert v. Merrell Dow Pharmaceuticals, Inc.*, 509 U.S. 579 (1993) (rejecting an earlier "general acceptance" test); *General Electric Company v. Joiner*, 522 U.S. 136 (1997) (holding, among other things, that a trial judge's rulings on admitting expert testimony should be reviewed only for abuse of discretion); and *Kumho Tire Company v. Carmichael*, 526 U.S. 137 (1999) (extending *Daubert* to all expert testimony).

This section begins with a critique of the role of medical expert testimony. The excerpt from Deirdre Smith's "Who Says You're Disabled? The Role of Medical Evidence in the ADA Definition of Disability" argues that the requirement of medical expert testimony to establish who is disabled for the purposes of the American with Disabilities Act not only undermines the ADA's purpose, but wrongly allows physicians to serve as gatekeepers of access to disability rights, thereby usurping the role of the jury as proper fact finder. Next, Valena Beety and Jennifer Oliva use their chapter to focus on the LGBT community. In "Beyond the Binary: Expert Evidence and the Civil-Criminal Divide," they offer nothing short of a "queering" of expert testimony, but in ways that can benefit us all. This section also includes chapters that call attention to the ease with which courts deem police officers experts (from Alexis Hoag-Fordjour), a proposal for party-blind review to reduce judicial bias in determining whether to admit expert testimony (from Rebecca Wexler), and a call for the admissibility of lay and expert testimony on racism (from Jasmine Gonzales Rose).

Who Says You're Disabled? The Role of Medical Evidence in the ADA Definition of Disability

Deirdre M. Smith[1]

I. INTRODUCTION

The Americans with Disabilities Act (ADA), enacted by Congress seventeen years ago, offered disabled people a hope of equality and access that has not been fulfilled. Court decisions halt an overwhelming majority of claims, particularly in the employment context, at the summary judgment stage. A key mechanism for fencing out disabled people's claims is the pernicious requirement, based upon the very construction of disability that the ADA's proponents aimed to dispel, that medical evidence is required as a threshold matter to demonstrate that the plaintiff is entitled to seek protection under the statute. The medical evidence requirement embodies and applies a model of disability that pathologizes disabled people and undermines the statute's effectiveness as a tool to advance civil rights.

The *stated* rationales applied to the medical evidence requirement, such as the need for "corroborating" evidence, "objective" evidence, or evidence to assist juries in assessing disabilities that are not "obvious," in fact reflect a common unstated rationale: a deep-seated skepticism of those "claiming disability" generally and ADA plaintiffs specifically. As a result, judges disregard the proper analysis to be applied to summary judgment motions and instead impose hypertechnical, heightened evidentiary burden on plaintiffs in an effort to foreclose potential malingerers' claims from reaching the trial stage. This skepticism, however, is itself another form of entrenched, invidious discrimination against people with disabilities, and the continued reliance on physicians to identify "true" disability unreasonably limits the ADA's reach.

Moreover, judges' reliance on medical evidence to screen out claims brought by people faking or exaggerating disability is misplaced. The determination of whether a person is truly disabled or merely exaggerating her condition to achieve some secondary gain through ADA litigation is one more properly left to jurors than to doctors. Doctors themselves do not profess to be able to ascertain disability or

[1] Excerpted from Deirdre M. Smith, *Who Says You're Disabled? The Role of Medical Evidence in the ADA Definition of Disability*, 82 Tul. L. Rev. 1 (2007).

malingering or to accurately assess limitations on major life activities to any degree of accuracy. A plaintiff's testimony is sufficient to establish a prima facie claim of disability. Whether such evidence, standing alone, is ultimately persuasive in proving disability is a question for the fact finder.

This Article argues that many courts improperly require plaintiffs to produce expert medical evidence to establish that they meet the statute's definition of an individual with a disability. …

VI. EVIDENTIARY CONSIDERATIONS AND QUESTIONS

…

A. *The Evolving Role of the Medical Expert and the Prima Facie Case*

The ADA is not the only context in which some courts require a party to introduce expert testimony to establish a prima facie case. In certain other settings, courts require a party to offer expert testimony, including expert medical evidence, to establish a particular fact "where more than common knowledge and experience are needed to understand the issues and to form an opinion."…

This rule is a contemporary manifestation of the evolving notions of the respective roles of the jury and the expert witness. At one time, the pretrial controversy was almost exclusively over whether to permit the introduction of expert testimony. Courts viewed such "experts" with suspicion, as overeducated hired guns who would confuse the jury or who would usurp the role of the jury or judge. Thus, under the common law rule, such testimony was admissible only where a necessity for such evidence had been demonstrated. …

Many of these notions regarding the limitation on expert opinion evidence were eventually codified in courts' rules of evidence, including those applied to the federal courts. However, during the second half of the twentieth century, courts moved away from notions of necessity and towards analyses of whether such evidence would be "helpful" to the jury. What is remarkable is that in some jurisdictions, the standard for whether expert testimony was admissible has been transformed, in some cases, into the standard for whether such testimony is required … . Although the language mirrors the common law approach to the admissibility of expert testimony, this requirement is not an evidentiary rule at all but, rather, a requisite of the substantive law underlying a plaintiff's claim for relief. Thus, the absence of such testimony necessarily results in the failure to establish each of the elements of such claim.

To a certain degree, [one] line of cases reflects the notion that there are certain medical conditions – those that are "obvious" – regarding which a jury need not receive medical testimony to evaluate and consider. But for certain other claimed impairments, these courts hold, a physician's opinion is an indispensable prerequisite to establishing disability. Under this approach, conditions calling for expert testimony include: a heart condition, deep vein thrombosis, fibromyalgia, a learning disorder, anxiety disorders, and agoraphobia. Although the courts in the Second Circuit follow a *sine qua non* rule of medical evidence, the district court in *Sussle v. Sirina Protection Systems Corp.*, which sets forth the most detailed analysis of the issue, specifically noted that the claimed disability at issue in that case, Hepatitis C, would not be understood by the jury. By comparison, those conditions found to be sufficiently "obvious" and therefore not requiring expert testimony include: arm and neck pain, back and abdominal pain, and hearing loss.

[T]hese ADA cases demonstrate how, in modern case law, the relevant inquiry for allowing the admission of expert evidence has morphed into a nearly identical inquiry for whether such testimony is required as a matter of substantive law. However, as discussed above, there is no basis in the text or regulations of the ADA to conclude that expert testimony is required to establish a prima facie claim of disability.

This conclusion is reaffirmed by examining and contrasting contexts other than the ADA definition of disability in which courts require a plaintiff to offer expert medical evidence to support not simply a given fact, but a prima facie case. One such context is medical malpractice litigation, where a common law rule (codified by some states) evolved requiring the use of expert medical testimony to establish a prima facie case. There, the requirement is not based on the use of a physician's testimony to disclose, explain, or validate the plaintiff's own experience, but to provide competent evidence of one of the elements of claim. Only a physician (with the appropriate training and experience) can testify to the standard of professional medical care in a given context. The same requirement applies equally in other professional malpractice cases: expert testimony by a member of the profession must be presented (or an expert on the profession must testify) as to the profession's standards of care. Thus, in these contexts, the focus of the expert testimony is, to a great extent, on the defendant's actions or inaction, rather than the plaintiff's condition. Indeed, in some medical malpractice cases, where the breach-of-duty issue to be determined in a case is one within the common knowledge of jurors, such as the failure to remove a foreign object or instrument (e.g., "the overlooked sponge") used in surgery or a failure to provide informed consent, no such testimony is required; courts rule that a jury is competent to determine the standard of care without the aid of a medical expert.

Another example of the potential need for medical evidence in a tort claim is where a plaintiff is alleging a complex causation fact, such as the effect of exposure to certain toxins, the development of cancer, or other illnesses. In the absence of such evidence, jurors would be asked to engage in pure speculation about the existence of a causal link between an exposure and an illness. Thus, while there are at least some contexts in which courts appropriately require expert medical testimony before submitting a case to a jury, in no context is the medical evidence required to provide corroboration of a plaintiff's claims.

Moreover, if we broaden the question to the requirement of medical evidence in personal injury cases generally, such as to prove the harm to the plaintiff, courts have little basis to preclude a plaintiff from going to trial without an expert. There are few reported cases in which a plaintiff's failure to provide expert testimony on the issue of injuries resulting from a defendant's negligence was the sole basis to preclude her from going to trial. There can be little question that the testimony of a well-qualified expert to explain the nature and extent of a plaintiff's injury enhances a plaintiff's credibility and therefore the likelihood of her recovery, but this is an issue distinct from whether such testimony is necessary to establish[] the elements of a plaintiff's claim. Indeed, one of the central tactics of defending a personal injury claim is to expose exaggerated levels of injury through the use of discovery tools or cross-examination. A plaintiff who proceeds to trial without some medical evidence to support her claims of harm does so at her own peril, but, of course, courts allow imperiled claims to go to trial all the time. …

Thus, judges evaluating ADA claims appear to be alone in requiring expert medical testimony to corroborate a plaintiff's assertions of a medical condition to establish a prima facie case. Courts have not articulated a reason why ADA claims should receive such additional scrutiny. In both ADA and tort claims, a plaintiff must disclose and discuss the details of the impact of an impairment on her daily life. Certainly, there are important differences between offering evidence to quantify and explicate the specific harm resulting from a tortious act so that a fact finder may attach a numeric value to such harm and establishing that one belongs to a class of individuals which is disadvantaged by a combination of personal physical characteristics and a physical environment structured by society in such a way as to render one disabled. But such differences do not support imposing an additional burden on ADA plaintiffs. Indeed, one could argue that the opposite should be the case because an ADA plaintiff is not asking that a monetary value be placed on her medical condition.

B. *Evidentiary Limitations on a Layperson's Testimony of Disability*

A companion question to whether expert medical testimony is required in ADA, tort, or other cases is whether such evidence is required, even as a purely practical matter, because testimony regarding certain elements of a claim cannot be offered by the plaintiff herself. In other words, can a plaintiff describe to a jury her medical condition and the resulting impairments without running afoul of evidentiary limitations on such testimony? If the answer is "no," it suggests that medical evidence would be needed to prove the existence of the disability.

There are two closely related evidentiary rules that may be implicated with testimony of one's disability. First, a witness is limited to testifying to facts within her personal knowledge. This requirement restricts testimony to those facts that can be perceived and were in fact directly perceived by the witness. A second distinct rule is that against the admission of hearsay statements, or assertions of fact told to the witness out-of-court. Thus, if a witness testifies to a fact as told to her by another, this is hearsay, which is generally inadmissible unless a particular exception applies. If she testifies to a fact for which no foundation for her knowledge has been established (and, indeed, the context indicates that she could be aware of such fact only as a result of being the recipient of a hearsay statement rather than perceiving such fact for herself), such evidence should be excluded because of a lack of personal knowledge, not because her only basis of knowledge is likely to be hearsay, although practitioners and courts frequently confuse the two rules.

However, it is not always apparent what facts are based solely upon a witness's personal knowledge. ... Indeed, a witness cannot testify as to what she has perceived without relating it, consciously or unconsciously, to her own past experience and existing foundation of knowledge and understanding. As the modern editors of *McCormick on Evidence* observed: "When the witness ... bases his testimony partly upon firsthand knowledge and partly upon the account of others, the problem calls for practical compromise." Specifically, such testimony should be admitted (or excluded) based upon the court's determination of the overall reliability of the evidence. The oft-cited example of such knowledge is an individual's age or date of birth. Since no person recalls the actual events surrounding one's own birth, one is necessarily relying upon, to some degree, reports from others regarding the date of that event. The same is true regarding kinship (how can you know someone is your brother, aunt, grandfather, etc. but from what others have told you?), and, as with a witness's age, courts generally permit testimony of such facts.

How do these evidentiary principles apply when a witness offers testimony regarding a medical condition? The general rule stated by courts in reported opinions has been essentially unchanged for years. A plaintiff may testify as to her "general condition" and describe symptoms and their impact on her daily life, but she may not testify as to her medical diagnoses and prognosis.

In practice, the line between what a plaintiff can testify to and what is reserved for the province of medical expertise is unsettled. Some courts may permit use of a diagnostic term by a plaintiff in her testimony, but most will rule that anything "medical" beyond the diagnosis itself is necessarily outside the expertise of the plaintiff or is based upon out-of-court statements made by a treating physician. There is little question that a person can describe subjective experiences of pain and other symptoms or that he or she is in a state of general good health. One may also testify as to what actions may lead (based upon reasonable inference) to an exacerbation of symptoms ("My back hurts when I lift my infant daughter" or "My medication makes me sleepy"). Courts generally permit one to testify as to the impact of a medical condition on one's ability to perform work or other tasks as compared with the time before the onset of the condition.

To the extent that a plaintiff is deemed to be offering an opinion of her own condition, her testimony must fall within the requirements of "Opinion Testimony by Lay Witnesses" in Federal Rule of Evidence 701:

> If the witness is not testifying as an expert, the witness' testimony in the form of opinions or inferences is limited to those opinions or inferences which are (a) rationally based on the perception of the witness, (b) helpful to a clear understanding of the witness' testimony or the determination of a fact in issue, and (c) not based on scientific, technical, or other specialized knowledge within the scope of Rule 702.

More specifically then, the question can be phrased as whether a plaintiff's opinion about her own condition is "rationally based" upon her own perception of the condition rather than upon "scientific, technical, or other specialized knowledge."

The reported opinions indicate that few courts permit one to testify that she has a particular disease or condition, or the permanency of a condition. It would seem, however, that a diagnosis or condition is the sort of fact, noted by the McCormick on Evidence editors, that a plaintiff would offer based upon both reports of others (specifically, her health care provider's diagnosis, for example, of a "spastic colon") and her own perception of the condition (her experience of frequent and painful bowel movements). Thus, courts should not exclude such testimony out of hand, but, as is done with the fact of a person's age, should consider the overall reliability of such evidence given the circumstances in which it is offered, perhaps in light of facts appropriate for judicial notice. Indeed, in practice, courts and opposing counsel will likely raise few barriers to an individual stating a diagnosis unless the fact of the diagnosis is truly a central dispute in the case.

In the ADA context, only a few courts have specifically acknowledged the potential evidentiary limitations on a plaintiff's ability to testify as to her medical condition in the context of proving that she is disabled under the statute. In *Cruz Carrillo v. AMR Eagle, Inc.*, a court noted that the plaintiff was not competent to testify as to the impact of HIV infection on his ability to reproduce, and his failure to produce medical evidence on the issue, in contrast to the plaintiff in *Bragdon v. Abbott*, was fatal to his claim. In *Holt v. Olmsted Township Board of Trustees*, the United States District Court for the Northern District of Ohio ruled that the plaintiff could not testify to her diagnoses of cytomegalovirus, chronic fatigue syndrome, and fibromyalgia, but she could generally describe her "condition."

In *Mehta v. Council for Jewish Elderly*, the United States District Court for the Northern District of Illinois denied a defendant's motion to exclude the plaintiff's testimony regarding her medical condition (patchy bulbar duodentis). The court noted that the plaintiff may testify as to her own perceptions and opinions of her medical condition and that it was up to the jury whether to credit her testimony. This approach was followed in the same district several years later in *Denson v. Northeast Illinois Regional Commuter Railroad Corp.*, which held that a plaintiff may testify as to her own experience of her condition (an arm and shoulder injury) but not what her doctors have told her.

In the ADA context, where issues of causation, prognosis or the adequacy of medical treatment play no role, rules regarding the competency of an individual to testify to her own medical condition need not be so strictly applied as in cases in which such issues are in dispute. Indeed, as described above with respect to testimony about birth and kinship, it is not logical or practical to push the personal knowledge or hearsay rules to an absurd point. There is something inherently odd about not permitting a person with cancer to utter the words "I have cancer" or likewise for an individual to testify "I have a broken leg" or "I have diabetes" if she has such conditions. Of course, in the most literal sense, she does not really "know" she has a tumor, and that is something that her physicians could not themselves discern until they ran a scan, X-ray, or blood tests. She can certainly testify that she has pain, fatigue, and physician-imposed restrictions on her activities, but why should she not state the reason for such pain, fatigue, and restrictions? She can testify that she goes to the hospital once a week and has an intravenous drip; she should not be precluded from testifying that such treatment is "chemotherapy." Similarly, statements such as "They removed a lobe of my lung last March" need not be excluded. There is unquestionably a point at which a person's subjective experience of her illness becomes melded with her personal knowledge and awareness based upon information from reliable sources. In other words, does not one gain personal knowledge of one's own body at some point such that one is no longer merely parroting the words of a physician? To at least some degree, courts' overly technical division of "knowledge" of medical conditions is a further reflection of the role we expect physicians to play in society; that to the exclusion of the patients themselves, physicians are the sole guardians of the knowledge and understanding of their patients' illnesses and physical limitations.

Moreover, since the regulations and case law dictate an individualized case-by-case review of the impact of an alleged impairment on the individual, the central facts in an ADA disability determination analysis must be the plaintiff's individual experience of her disability, particularly as they impact her major life activities. As discussed above, no witness can provide more direct and competent personal knowledge of such facts than the plaintiff herself. For this reason as well, it seems that courts must take a more reasonable approach to the admissibility of such evidence in ADA claims.

VII. CONCLUSION: THE BROADER IMPLICATIONS FOR DISABILITY AS A POLITICAL CATEGORY

This discussion leads us to a final question: Why should we care if courts impose a requirement of producing corroborating medical evidence to establish that one is disabled under the ADA? The answer goes to the fulfillment (or not) of the ADA's mandate to eradicate discrimination on the basis of disability. The continued hegemony of medicine in notions of disability, with a focus on personal impairment and malingering, serves as an impediment to reframing notions of disability as urged by disability scholars and activists. A requirement of "proof" of disability from a medical provider impedes the class of disability from emerging as a truly protected status, approaching that of race, gender, religion, and age. It serves to perpetuate the central role of medicine in notions of disability, preventing a broader, more powerful conceptualization of the term.

The continued association of disability with medicine – and therefore with sickness, tragedy, dependence, and other stigmatizing notions of powerlessness and victimhood – undermines the very paradigm shift that many advocates sought to bring about with the ADA's enactment. By making the plaintiff's role as "patient" the preliminary question – before considering her role as employee, patron, or citizen – judges immediately place a plaintiff in a position of being pathologized, pitied and therefore disempowered. If a plaintiff declines to put forth a construct of herself as "patient," as is the case where a plaintiff offers only her own narrative of her disability, she is precluded entirely from presenting her account of discrimination to the fact finder.

Imposing a requirement of expert medical testimony that goes beyond diagnosis also places many plaintiffs in the position of having to disclose information to attorneys, judges, and perhaps the general public that is deeply personal, private, and perhaps humiliating in the prosecution of her ADA claims. No other category of employment discrimination forces a plaintiff to do so. Thus, the medical evidence requirement itself may serve as a powerful deterrent to those seeking to vindicate their rights under the ADA.

Overreliance on medical evidence similarly reinforces false notions of the objectivity and certainty of medicine, most importantly that of a medical diagnosis. There is no objective basis in science for the discrete and judgmental categories of "normal" and "abnormal" as distinct from the statistically more or less numerous. Moreover, the act of diagnosis and classification is not free from elements of social control, stigma, and political labeling. An ADA plaintiff therefore is compelled to adopt and promote the labels assigned by the medical profession (with accompanying connotations of being disordered or defective) even where such labels may conflict with her self-identity, including her political identity as a citizen entitled to obtain and maintain employment and to have full access to public accommodations and services. …

This Article has argued that in view of the current language of the ADA, and more generally, contemporary approaches to evidence and summary judgment, courts are wrong to grant summary judgment to defendants based solely on an absence of corroborating expert medical evidence to support a finding of disability …

It is important to emphasize that the instant discussion is about establishing a prima facie case, what is required to get to a fact finder's determination, and not about what is ultimately persuasive for a fact finder. The court system is, of course, always and appropriately concerned with issues of deception and fakery by litigants for personal (or corporate) gain. However, warnings about the specter of "abuse" in the disability context fail to recognize that the "system" we worry about protecting from liars and manipulators already has a guardian – the fact finder – and an adversarial process designed to permit parties to test the sufficiency of others' allegations.

This Article is not calling for a legal mandate preventing any plaintiff from losing in court as the result of an absence of expert medical testimony. That is not warranted, practical or appropriate, or consistent with the ADA as presently drafted. But courts should not dismiss claims before trial on the basis that jurors will not likely find the plaintiff to be disabled in the absence of corroborating testimony. It is the job of the defendant's attorney at trial to raise the issue of the sufficiency and quality of the plaintiff's evidence. It is perfectly valid for a defendant's attorney to cross-examine a plaintiff on the extent of a plaintiff's limitations. It is also appropriate for a defense attorney to argue in closing, as would be true in any kind of case, that the plaintiff's testimony should be disbelieved and to point out the dearth of other evidence, whether lay observation or expert opinion, to support such testimony. A defense attorney may or may not succeed with such an approach. A jury may decide that even in the absence of other "corroborating" evidence, the plaintiff's own account of her limitations is credible and sufficient. Courts, then, must step aside to allow fact finders to do their job.

Beyond the Binary

Expert Evidence and the Civil-Criminal Divide

Valena E. Beety and Jennifer D. Oliva

INTRODUCTION

This chapter dives beneath the performatively egalitarian surface of Federal Rule of Evidence 702 (Testimony by Expert Witnesses), explores disparities in the rule's application in civil and criminal cases, and applies queer theory to disrupt these norms and "forg[e] a social justice politics of change."[1] Queer theory is an interdisciplinary approach that dismantles traditional assumptions about gender and sexual identities in furtherance of social justice. Queering the law is not only about the use of gender and sexuality, it also aims to recognize and challenge traditional binaries and seek new possibilities.[2] As Black queer author bell hooks remarked, "'queer' [is] about the self that is at odds with everything around it and that has to invent and create and find a place to speak and to thrive and to live."[3]

For legal scholars, queer theory offers a critical framework for rethinking and reinterpreting ideas and actions in our rigid adversarial process, particularly in standardized criminal courtrooms. "Queering" the law involves expanding these adversarial binaries to discover new avenues of viewing the courtroom, courtroom players, and evidence.

In an effort to queer the law of expert evidence, this chapter includes experiential knowledge from both lawyer and non-lawyer legal system participants. We share various lived experiences from frontline litigants with the aim of drawing legal meaning from these interviews and juxtaposing them with pertinent case law.

Expert evidence is an example of admissibility or non-admissibility based on the binaries of civil or criminal, prosecutor or defense. Empirical studies demonstrate that judges are more likely to admit proffered expert evidence from prosecutors than similar

1 Davina Cooper, Everyday Utopias: The Conceptual Life of Promising Spaces 11 (Duke University Press 2014).

2 *Introduction to Queer Theory*, IU Bloomington Libraries: Philosophy Collection, https://guides.libraries.indiana.edu/c.php?g=995240&p=8361766#:~:text=Queer%20Theory%20is%20an%20interdisciplinary,and%20fights%20against%20social%20inequality (last updated Oct. 10, 2025).

3 The New School, *bell hooks – Are You Still a Slave? Liberating the Black Female Body*, YouTube (May 6, 2014), www.youtube.com/watch?v=rJkohNROvzs&t=5226s.

evidence from either defense attorneys or plaintiffs in torts cases.[4] This chapter adds a substantive analysis approach, applying a largely untapped epistemology (queer theory) to evidence law and Rule 702. The resulting suggestions for recalibrating Rule 702 and reconsidering expert testimony are a starting point to stimulate creative thinking about avenues for change and ensure reliable and accurate evidence in the courtroom. This chapter concludes with a proposed revision of Rule 702, based on the lived experiences of lawyers and non-lawyers alike in the legal system.

THE EVOLVING LAW OF EXPERT EVIDENCE

> When I started, there were literally no decisions [excluding forensic experts and evidence] on the criminal side. And I wasn't getting support on my bench for writing opinions. In fact, one judge told me that I was just putting a target on my back. If I wrote an opinion, the government would appeal.
>
> But that wasn't going to work for me. And besides, I didn't want to be vulnerable to when the government chose to appeal.
>
> It wasn't until after I left the bench that I understood the impact of my opinions. To tell you the truth, I really didn't. When I left the bench, I began to look in casebooks and see my cases. Teaching evidence changed that.
>
> Retired Federal District Court Judge Nancy Gertner[5]

The inherent problem that plagues Rule 702 is systemic: expert evidence that would never be admitted in a civil case due to its lack of reliability and accuracy is routinely relied upon by prosecutors and admitted by criminal courts. Unlike in civil cases, criminal court judges often automatically accept, rather than thoroughly vet, forensic testimony offered by the government, irrespective of its scientific reliability and validity.[6]

The criminal case expert witness system is entrenched with systemic bias that favors the government and disfavors defendants. Prosecution experts are often salaried government employees, who serve as repeat players in similar proceedings. Defense experts, on the other hand, appear less often before criminal courts because many defendants are indigent, and experts must be compensated by the defendant or, uncommonly and more reluctantly, by the courts.[7] These familiarity and funding

4 *See* Rebecca Wexler, "Party-Blind Review: A Proposal to Reduce Judicial Bias in Expert Evidence Admissibility Rulings," in this volume.

5 Valena Beety interview with Judge Nancy Gertner at Seton Hall Law School, Newark, NJ (Feb. 14, 2020) (copy on file with authors). When Judge Gertner retired and left the federal bench, she became a Harvard University Law School professor and continued to educate new lawyers on forensic evidence. *See id.*

6 *See generally*, Jennifer L. Groscup et al., *The Effects of* Daubert *on the Admissibility of Expert Testimony in State and Federal Criminal Cases*, 8 PSYCHOL. PUB. POL'Y & L. 339 (2002); *see also*, United States v. Sherwood, 98 F.3d 402, 408 (9th Cir. 1996) (admitting fingerprint comparison evidence without conducting a *Daubert* hearing). In United States v. Havvard, the court described *Sherwood* as an opinion "asserting that *the reliability of fingerprint comparisons cannot be questioned.*" 260 F.3d 597, 600 (7th Cir. 2001) (emphasis added).

7 But *see* Valena E. Beety and Jennifer D. Oliva, *Policing Pregnancy "Crimes,"* 98 N.Y.U. L. REV. ONLINE 29, 51–2 (2023) (discussing Hinton v. Alabama, 571 U.S. 263 (2014) and the

disparities can lead to the attenuated assumption that defense expert "findings" are simply "bought" in criminal cases. In civil cases, litigants screen experts more intensively, particularly through *Daubert* hearings, and neither party has an institutionalized financial advantage in presenting experts.

As noted by Professor Rebecca Wexler in her chapter proposing party-blind judicial review of expert evidence to reduce judicial bias in admission decisions, judges are more likely to admit forensic evidence proffered by prosecutors than by defense attorneys or even by plaintiffs in mass tort civil lawsuits.[8] Wexler's chapter acknowledges the disparity between civil and criminal evidence admissibility, citing empirical work by Julie Seaman that demonstrates "criminal defendants' expert testimony, when offered, is less likely to be admitted than similar prosecution expert testimony."[9]

Consistent with the prevailing thrust of the Federal Rules of Evidence (FREs), the Article VII rules that apply to expert admissibility, qualifications, and testimony are procedurally neutral on their face.[10] The FREs command the courts to apply the rules that pertain to experts identically in civil and criminal proceedings, and for prosecution and defense experts.[11] The fiction that the expert evidence rules must be applied trans-substantively also holds true in the state codes of evidence.

Core Assumptions of the Federal Rules of Evidence

As critical theories posit, much like the rules of criminal and civil procedure, the rules of evidence are not neutral.[12] The evidence rule drafters constituted an exclusive group of elite White men, all of whom were judges and legal professionals, intent on drafting trans-substantive, clear rules.[13] Neither men of color nor women had any prominent involvement in drafting the rules.[14]

State evidence code committees have mirrored the composition of the Federal Rules Committee.[15] Scholars have critiqued how the rules include biased assumptions and fail to take seriously their as-applied implications. Rule 702, in particular and as taught by Professor Bennett Capers, subjugates lived experience by

requirement for defense counsel to request expert funds from the court if an expert is necessary for the defense theory).

8 Wexler, *supra* note 4.

9 Julie A. Seaman, *A Tale of Two Dauberts*, 47 GA. L. REV. 889, 897 (2013).

10 David A. Sklansky and Stephen C. Yeazell, *Comparative Law Without Leaving Home: What Civil Procedure Can Teach Criminal Procedure, and Vice Versa*, 94 GEO. L.J. 683, 728 (2006).

11 Jennifer D. Oliva and Valena Beety, *Discovering Forensic Fraud*, 112 NW. L. REV. 121, 126–7, 129 (2017).

12 Julia Simon-Kerr, *Relevance Through a Feminist Lens*, in PHILOSOPHICAL FOUNDATIONS OF EVIDENCE LAW 364, 366 (Christian Dahlman, Alex Stein, and Giovanni Tuznet, eds., Oxford University Press 2021).

13 Julia Simon-Kerr, *A New Baseline for Character Evidence*, 76 VAND. L. REV. 1827, 1831 n. 19 (2023).

14 Mae C. Quinn, *Childist Objections, Youthful Relevance, and Evidence Reconceived*, 127 DICK. L. REV. 535, 541–3 (2023).

15 *Id.*

primarily limiting its scope to scholarly and academic expertise.[16] Professor Kit Kinports further points out that expert evidence doctrine often excludes testimony "of importance to women … on the ground that it is not sufficiently reliable."[17] Indeed, and as explained by Professor Julia Simon-Kerr, the requirement that expert evidence be "relevant" is likewise imbued with bias and often discounts the lived reality for many women in court proceedings.[18] The legal system's discriminatory application of the rules of evidence is often dismissed or even ignored, in favor of bolstering the simple narrative that the FREs are neutral and equally applied to all litigants.

Daubert's *Test for Admissibility of Expert Evidence, and Pro-Prosecutor Bias*

The Supreme Court decided the seminal case regarding the standards for admitting expert evidence, *Daubert v. Merrell Dow Pharmaceuticals, Inc.*, in 1993. The petitioner, Joyce Daubert, was prescribed Bendectin early in her pregnancy. Bendectin was manufactured by Merrell Dow and was the only available anti-nausea drug on the market for pregnant people at the time. Joyce's son, Jason, was born without a bone in his forearm and with only three fingers and he suffered additional health challenges.

Daubert was a *civil* case alleging pregnancy harm by a company's product. The case ultimately stands for the proposition that it is the role of courts, as gatekeepers, to rigorously vet expert evidence to ensure that parties present relevant and reliable scientific evidence. *Daubert* requires trial judges in both civil and criminal proceedings to determine "whether the reasoning or methodology underlying the testimony is scientifically valid … ."[19]

Daubert, however, is also an example of the heightened standards courts apply to expert evidence offered by plaintiffs in civil cases relative to prosecutorial expert evidence offered in criminal cases. On remand, Merrell Dow succeeded in *excluding* Joyce Daubert's expert scientific evidence linking Bendectin to severe health problems in newborn children on the theory that such evidence failed to satisfy *Daubert*'s rigorous admissibility test.

By contrast, in *criminal* pregnancy harm cases, prosecutorial expert evidence faces far more lenient review and is overwhelmingly admitted.[20] Nor is this disparity

16 Bennett Capers, *Race, Gatekeeping, Magical Words, and the Rules of Evidence*, 76 Vand. L. Rev. 1855 (2023).

17 Kit Kinports, *Evidence Engendered*, 1991 U. Ill. L. Rev. 413.

18 Simon-Kerr, *supra* note 12, at 366.

19 Daubert v. Merrell Dow Pharm., Inc., 509 U.S. 579, 592–3 (1993).

20 Catherine Grosso, *Female Exonerees Data*, The National Registry of Exonerations (Apr. 11, 2022) (unpublished data) (on file with author). Pregnancy Justice recently reported that, of the 210 fetal harm arrests that have occurred in the United States since *Dobbs v. Jackson's Women's Health Organization* was decided, 191 failed to require any "proof" of harm to the fetus or newborn.

limited to criminal cases alleging pregnancy harm. Nearly 75 percent of exonerated women were wrongly convicted of a crime that never occurred.[21] For many of these women, an accident – a health crisis, a fall, a fire – was misinterpreted and charged as a willful and violent act, and the government's faulty forensic testimony and evidence led to their convictions.[22] Gender stereotypes often influence these no-crime wrongful convictions of women, and queer women are condemned for the alleged harm as well as for violating gender norms.[23]

As the relevant research reveals, judges have been much more willing to rigorously fulfill their *Daubert* gatekeeping roles and exclude questionable expert evidence in civil cases than in criminal proceedings.[24]

The Adversarial Nature of Criminal Proceedings Is No Remedy to Faulty Expert Testimony

Courts rely almost entirely on the adversarial nature of criminal proceedings to mitigate the problem of inaccurate expert opinions. This is because judges make the biased and faulty assumption that the defense will expose any flawed scientific evidence offered by prosecutors. As made clear in the examples below, that is not always the case.

American courtrooms and the rules of evidence rely heavily on an idealized adversarial process, where two co-equal litigants spar to uncover the truth. Instead of performing this theorized truth-seeking function, however, juries and criminal judges are usually presented with two competing stories and choose the tale that holds the most sway often for non-scientific reasons. Moreover, in this story-creating (and not truth-producing) environment, prosecutors usually have the upper hand. They have generous access to police and crime lab resources, they decide whether to offer or press plea bargains, and they largely dictate the defendant's sentence. It is entirely left to prosecutorial discretion whether to charge a defendant.

Post-Dobbs Pregnancy Criminal Cases, PREGNANCY JUSTICE, www.pregnancyjusticeus.org/post-dobbs-pregnancy-criminalization/ (last visited June 4, 2025). Instead, state prosecutors invoked criminal child endangerment laws, which only demand evidence of a "potential risk" of harm to the fetus. Women often are arrested, prosecuted, and convicted of fetal harm based on nothing more than pregnancy and a positive (and typically unconfirmed) drug test due to the inaccurate assumption that any drug exposure creates a risk of harm. Asees Bhasin's chapter ("Relevance, Reconsidered") in this volume presents more information on how prejudicial and irrelevant evidence is admitted in pregnancy prosecutions.

21 Grosso, *supra* note 20.

22 Valena E. Beety, *"Unfit": Gender, Ableism, and Reproductive Wrongful Convictions*, 73 UCLA L. REV. 3 (2026).

23 *Id.*; *see also*, Valena Beety, MANIFESTING JUSTICE: WRONGLY CONVICTED WOMEN RECLAIM THEIR RIGHTS (Citadel Press 2022); VALENA BEETY, PINK CRIME: FIGHTING AGAINST THE CRIMINALIZATION OF MOTHERHOOD, PREGNANCY, AND QUEER IDENTITY (The New Press 2026).

24 D. Michael Risinger, *Navigating Expert Reliability: Are Criminal Standards of Certainty Being Left on the Dock?*, 64 ALB. L. REV. 99, 100 (2000).

Over-reliance on the adversarial system ignores that the Rules of Criminal Procedure and discovery are heavily weighted in favor of prosecutors, in contrast to the civil discovery rules. Such over-reliance also ignores the role of racism and sexism in prosecuting crime.[25] The criminal legal system is empirically based more on identity and control than guilt and innocence.[26]

Using Queer Legal Theory to Deconstruct the Civil-Criminal Divide in Admitting Experts

Queer legal theory is a helpful tool in our examination of power, bias, and faulty expert evidence. Queer legal theory examines how the law forces and reinforces "normalcy" by often oppressively regulating, categorizing, subordinating, and even acting to eliminate marginalized genders and marginalized sexualities as outside of norms.[27] The legal system generally accomplishes this oppression by maintaining the dominance of a particular sex, gender, and sexuality in binaries.

Queer theory is anti-essentialist and fluid, which may be at odds with the rigid status quo nature of law.[28] Queer theory is a useful legal analytical tool, however, precisely because it is *de*constructive and problematizes legal binaries.[29] The crux of queer theory is that sexuality and gender are actively created by society in everyday reinforced interactions and do not arise from nature or a natural order of things.[30] Finally, queer legal theory can be a rights-based prism, criticizing legal rights as "rewards" for normalcy and advancing the general critical legal analysis that law is not an objective and neutral practice.

As discussed below, queer theory disrupts the normalcy of Rule 702's pro-prosecution bent and challenges the divide between expert admissibility in civil and criminal cases.

25 Ion Meyn, *The Creation of Separate and Unequal Courtrooms*, 63 ARIZ. L. REV. 1 (2021).

26 Issa Kohler-Hausmann, *Managerial Justice and Mass Misdemeanors*, 66 STAN. L. REV. 611, 611–39 (2014).

27 "Queer … does not designate a class of already objectified pathologies or perversions … [R]ather, it describes a horizon of possibility whose precise extent and heterogeneous scope cannot in principle be limited in advance." DAVID HALPERIN, SAINT FOUCAULT: TOWARDS A GAY HAGIOGRAPHY 62 (Oxford University Press 1995).

28 Queer J. Thomas, *Constructing Queer Theory in Political Science and Public Law: Sexual Citizenship, Outspeech and Queer Narrative*, 39 NEW POL. SCI. 568, 574 (2017).

29 LIBBY ADLER, GAY PRIORI: A QUEER CRITICAL LEGAL STUDIES APPROACH TO LAW REFORM (Duke University Press 2018).

30 JUDITH BUTLER, GENDER TROUBLE: FEMINISM AND THE SUBVERSION OF IDENTITY (2d ed., Routledge 1999); JUDITH BUTLER, BODIES THAT MATTER: ON THE DISCURSIVE LIMITS OF "SEX" (Routledge 1993); Gayle Rubin, *Thinking Sex: Notes for a Radical Theory of the Politics of Sexuality*, in PLEASURE AND DANGER: EXPLORING FEMALE SEXUALITY (Carole S. Vance ed., Thorsons 1984); EVE SEDGEWICK, EPISTEMOLOGY OF THE CLOSET (University of California Press 1990).

Queering the Law to Recognize Pro-Prosecution and Anti-LGBTQ+ Bias in Rule 702

Professor Francisco Valdes's seminal original work on how to queer the law is particularly applicable to evidentiary expert rule reform: (1) bridge social science and legal knowledge; (2) use narrative and experiential examples to create knowledge; and (3) debunk false rationales for binaries and segregation.[31] Lambda Legal and Black & Pink National's 2022 report, *Protected and Served?*, provides the opportunity to use narrative and experiential knowledge to queer the law.[32]

Protected and Served? is a national survey of LGBTQ+ and HIV+ individuals that centers their experiences with the carceral and criminal legal system. Perhaps unsurprisingly, LGBTQ+ defendants shared that they routinely suffer negative court experiences. The report documents how queer people are misnamed, addressed with the wrong pronouns, and outed by courtroom actors who inappropriately reveal their sexual orientation or transgender status. As one White, transfeminine participant shared, "I had to correct the prosecutor at least three (3) times in open court and ask the court to order the State to use correct pronouns (she, her, Miss.). The prosecutor argued that since I was housed in a male prison, I should be deemed male even though my name and gender marker had been updated to gender-affirming already."[33]

Scholars have identified epistemic erasure as the phenomenon that occurs when a court limits a litigant's ability to share their experience and identity, resulting in epistemic injustice. The state creates knowledge in the courtroom and holds fast to such creation, even when a defendant openly challenges prosecutors with their lived experiences and self-identity. Defendants are frequently advised by their own counsel not to share their identity, knowledge, and experience. As an Indigenous transgender participant shared in the survey: "I revealed my gender identity to my public defenders, and they told me to keep my mouth shut and to keep that info to myself."[34]

Professor Rachel Lopez argues that non-lawyer individuals with legal system experience are organic legal theorists who "generate knowledge and liberatory theory through critical reflection on their lived experience."[35] Such personal legal experiential knowledge is necessary to challenge pervasive queer criminal archetypes in criminal cases. The system weaponizes archetypes of danger, degeneracy, sexual predation, and violence against queer defendants because of their gender non-conformity.[36]

31 Francisco Valdes, *Afterward and Prologue: Queer Legal Theory*, 83 Cal. L. Rev. 343 (1995).

32 Somjen Frazer et al., Protected & Served?: 2022 Community Survey of LGBTQ+ People and People Living with HIV's Experience with the Criminal Legal System (2022).

33 *Id.* at 40.

34 *Id.* at 40.

35 Rachel Lopez, *Participatory Law Scholarship*, 123 Colum. L. Rev. 6 (2023).

36 Joey L. Mogul et. al., Queer (In)Justice: The Criminalization of LGBT People in the United States (Beacon Press 2012).

NON-NEUTRAL SCIENTIFIC AND OTHER EXPERTISE

> [W]hat passes for knowledge and expertise is often a proxy for power
>
> Bennett Capers[37]

> I have a good friend, a criminal county judge, who told me he never saw forensics in his courtroom.
> I said, "you don't have DWIs (Driving While Intoxicated)?"
> "Well, yeah, we have DWIs."
> "Oh, so that blood evidence or those machines, all that stuff. What are you calling that?"
> "Oh, that's just the normal part of the trial."
> "Oh, okay ..."
> He's a smart guy, so this is very much a concern.[38]

The harmful intersection of bias, power, and "scientific" evidence presents most prominently in criminal cases. Criminal judges may assume that evidence presented by the prosecution is reliable, just as they may assume charges are valid, because of the interconnected system in which judicial gatekeepers are predominantly former prosecutors. This reinforces the binary of trusted state power and untrusted civilian defendant, most dramatically exposed in wrongful convictions.

Before exploring certain such examples, it is important to highlight, as Professor Jasmine E. Harris has, that the tendency in legal scholarship and civil rights movements to treat identity markers as separate and biologically based categories has led to the marginalization of people at the intersections. Professor Harris emphasizes the particular impact of that practice on disabled people of color.[39] Her insights draw from critical intersectional analyses and the groundbreaking work of Professor Kimberlé Crenshaw, which depicts identity biases as co-constitutive, rather than simply overlapping forces of subordination.[40] Acknowledging that these biases are co-constitutive promotes understanding how they are formed, perpetuated, and rooted in centuries of structural subordination and resists reproducing existing hierarchies of power.[41]

Consequently, while this chapter addresses only sexual orientation, the authors recognize that biased expert testimony is a greater risk for defendants at the intersection of marginalized identities and that biased testimony presented against such defendants is simultaneously less likely to be acknowledged by courts and opposed

[37] Bennett Capers, *Race, Gatekeeping, Magical Words, and the Rules of Evidence*, 76 VAND. L. REV. 1855, 1869 (2023).

[38] Valena Beety interview with Judge Barbara Hervey at Texas Court of Criminal Appeals, Austin, TX (Sept. 23, 2019) (copy on file with authors).

[39] Jasmine E. Harris, *Reckoning with Race and Disability*, 130 YALE L.J. F. 916, 937 (2021).

[40] *Id.*; Kimberlé Crenshaw, *Demarginalizing the Intersection of Race and Sex*, U. CHI. L.F. 139 (1989).

[41] *Id.*

by defense counsel. The chapter is not intended to divide and label.[42] Applying queer theory aims to identify parallel experiences to further substantiate and challenge the overarching admission of faulty expert evidence based on bias in court proceedings.

Case Examples of Biased Expert Evidence Against Lesbian Defendants

LGBTQ+ identities are criminalized, medicalized, and pathologized, despite decades of research proving that LGBTQ+ people are not intrinsically predatory or pathological.[43] Queer women are criminalized and suffer violence because of their gender performance and sexual behavior, which is labeled "deviant." These case examples demonstrate how courts allow experts to present homophobic and gendered evidence.

The San Antonio Four

Anna Vasquez is a wrongly convicted and now exonerated Latina lesbian who has served as the President of the national Innocence Network. Vasquez shared her courtroom experience of epistemic erasure, and her concern that it contributed to her wrongful conviction. When she went to trial in the early 1990s, she said, "The way they looked at gay people, I even got shit from my attorney. 'You're going to have to put on a dress and you're going to have to curl your hair.'"[44] As a result, Vasquez changed her appearance. "Of course I did, because I'm looking up to this man – who was a complete idiot. I felt I was so fake. That's not me … ." With regard to her deliberating jury, she remarked, "you should at least know the person before you hate them."[45] The jury, mistrusting Vasquez, wrongly convicted her.

In Vasquez's case, she was one of four lesbians, later known as "The San Antonio Four," who faced allegations that they had molested two young girls in a gang satanic ritual. The accused women, Kristie Mayhugh, Cassandra Rivera, Elizabeth Ramirez, and Vasquez, had recently come out as gay to their families. Three of the women were Latina, and Ramirez was an aunt to the two girls. The details of the purported assault were wildly inconsistent, and one of the girls recanted years later, admitting she was coached by her father, who had made sexual advances toward Ramirez. Reporters investigated the case, the medical examiner recanted her expert testimony, and an award-winning documentary, *Southwest of Salem*, captured the new findings on film. Ultimately, the women were exonerated.

42 Simon-Kerr, *supra* note 12, at 364.
43 *Id.*
44 Valena Beety interview with Anna Vazquez (2020) (on file with authors).
45 *Id.*

The government's expert testimony against The San Antonio Four was influenced by bias. During the trials, a pediatrician testified that a scar on one of the girls' hymen was physical evidence of sexual molestation and speculated that the alleged acts by the four women were "satanic related."[46] The notion that LGBTQ+ adults are sexual threats to children has a long and disgraced history as a myth that was debunked decades ago;[47] gay men and lesbians are actually less likely than straight people to sexually abuse children.[48] Fifteen years after the wrongful convictions of The San Antonio Four, the pediatrician recanted her testimony, explaining that had she known then what she subsequently learned about sexual abuse forensics, she would not have testified to physical signs of molestation of the girls.

When Ramirez took the stand at her trial, the prosecutor asked the following irrelevant but bias-stoking series of questions to support the gang sexual assault allegation:

ATTORNEY: Did you have a gay relationship with Anna?
RAMIREZ: No.
ATTORNEY: Did you have a gay relationship with Cassie?
RAMIREZ: No.
ATTORNEY: Well, you were gay, and they were gay –
RAMIREZ: That doesn't mean you have to be together.[49]

The prosecutor in closing told the jury that Elizabeth Ramirez' identity as a lesbian was "important in the sense that that activity is generally consistent with the activity alleged in the indictment."[50] In other words, he argued that the sexual deviance of lesbianism correlated with being a violent rapist. The prosecutor also told the jury: "[W]e're going to ask you to believe a 9-year-old girl who was sacrificed on the altar of lust."[51]

Leigh Stubbs and Tami Vance

The case of Leigh Stubbs and Tami Vance also demonstrates the melding of dangerous stereotypes and "scientific" expert testimony in trials involving queer

[46] At the height of the 1980s/1990s HIV crisis, queer people were wrongly convicted of crimes that did not occur amid a national hysteria over alleged "ritualistic abuse" of children by day care providers and caretakers. Debbie Nathan and Mike Snedekar, Satan's Silence: Ritual Abuse and the Making of a Modern American Witch Hunt (Basic Books 1995).

[47] *See, e.g.*, Gregory M. Herek, *Myths about Sexual Orientation: A Lawyer's Guide to Social Science Research*, 1 Law & Sexuality 133, 152–6 (1991).

[48] Sean Cahill and Sarah Tobias, Policy Issues Affecting Lesbian, Gay, Bisexual, and Transgender Families 107 (University of Michigan Press 2006).

[49] Maurice Chammah, *The Mystery of the San Antonio Four*, Tex. Observer (Jan. 7, 2014), www.texasobserver.org/mystery-san-antonio-four/.

[50] Michelle Mondo, *Did These Women Molest Two Girls?* San Antonio Express-News (Dec. 21, 2010), www.mysanantonio.com/news/local_news/article/Did-these-women-molest-two-girls-908873.php.

[51] *Id.*

defendants. Leigh and Tami were wrongly convicted of assault due to false forensic evidence and a trial infused with homophobia. The state of Mississippi's primary expert witness against Leigh and Tami was Dr. Michael West, an infamous dentist from Hattiesburg who was admitted by the court to provide expert bite mark evidence for the prosecution. His findings – purported bite marks on the victim, whom Dr. West claimed may have had half of her labia bitten off by her assailant – were the only evidence the state presented against the defendants. During the trial, Dr. West explained to the jury that he had "analyzed over three hundred bite marks."[52] He did *not* tell them, however, that bite mark identification and comparison, otherwise known as forensic odontology, is fundamentally invalid, or that numerous people have been wrongly convicted due to faulty bite mark evidence.[53]

Forensic odontology entails examining marks left on skin or an object to determine if they are human bite marks and then comparing those human bite marks to a suspect's dental impressions.[54] Not only has the discipline proved incapable of reliably individuating an alleged bite mark – that is, establishing that a bite mark belongs to a specific individual – it cannot even reliably identify whether various skin marks are human bite marks.[55]

Shockingly, courts continue to admit "scientific" bite mark evidence in criminal trials and do so virtually exclusively based on precedent. Indeed, admitting courts mistakenly rely on prosecutorial arguments that a sister court has ruled that bite mark science is a valid and accepted methodology, rather than engaging in their gatekeeping function by conducting an independent and rigorous *Daubert* analysis.[56]

At Leigh and Tami's trial, the court readily admitted the state's bite mark evidence and expert testimony. Dr. West opined that the victim's right labia was "missing," and may have been "bitten off" during an episode of "intense" oral sex.[57] No other evidence corroborated his theory that the defendants – or anyone, for that matter – had bitten or chewed off the victim's labia. Worse yet, Dr. West, a dentist and not a medical doctor, was entirely unqualified to make any such determination about the victim's genitalia.

That stated, it was the expert trial testimony concerning homosexual sexual assaults that was particularly damning to Leigh and Tami's defense. Dr. West

52 Transcript of Proceedings at 456–7, Stubbs v. State, 845 So. 2d 656 (Miss. 2003) (No. 00-362-MS) [hereinafter Stubbs Trial Transcript].

53 Radley Balko, *Incredibly, Prosecutors Are Still Defending Bite Mark Evidence*, WASH. POST (Jan. 30, 2017), www.washingtonpost.com/news/the-watch/wp/2017/01/30/incredibly-prosecutors-are-still-defending-bite-mark-evidence/.

54 *See* Jennifer Oliva and Valena Beety, *Regulating Bite Mark Evidence: Lesbian Vampires and Other Myths of Forensic Odontology*, 94 WASH. L. REV. 1769 (2019).

55 *See, e.g.*, Michael J. Saks et al., *Forensic Bitemark Identification: Weak Foundations, Exaggerated Claims*, 3 J.L. & BIOSCI. 538, 562–3 (2016).

56 *Id.* at 546.

57 Stubbs Trial Transcript, *supra* note 52, at 513.

testified that the victim's labia was bitten off as part of "a combative or a sexual orientation phenomenon."[58] He then went on to opine that it is "almost expected" that bite marks would be present in a homosexual rape case.[59] "In those cases of violence," he pronounced, "there seems to be a much greater propensity of bite marks."[60] This testimony was never challenged as beyond the scope of his expertise, inflammatory, or inaccurate.

Instead, defense expert and forensic pathologist Dr. Rodrigo Galvez testified about the alleged connection between "lesbian rape" and bite marks. Dr. Galvez, like Dr. West, opined that biting is consistent with lesbian rape, and went on to explain that "homosexual crimes … are very sadistic. The more violent crimes I've seen in my experience are homosexual to homosexual. They do what we call overkill. They do tremendous damage, tremendous damage."[61] Dr. Galvez further added, "they're more gory, the more repulsive crimes I've ever seen were homosexual to homosexual."[62]

Based on this amalgamation of so-called expert evidence and testimony, the prosecutor, in his closing argument, contended that "homosexual assault is the most brutal, it involves torture,"[63] and told the jury that "the bite marks are important because it indicates a homosexual assault, it indicates a sexual assault."[64] Unsurprisingly, given this evidence, the two lesbian defendants were swiftly convicted. They each spent nearly eleven years incarcerated before their wrongful convictions were finally reversed.

Even a cursory examination regarding the depiction of sexuality and sexual orientation in criminal courtrooms demonstrates how expert evidentiary bias against defendants operates to support and elicit said bias in jury members through a veneer of scientific support. This unscientific, prejudicial expert evidence is so detrimental to a defendant that it can instigate a jury to convict the accused even where no crime occurred.

EMANCIPATING EVIDENTIARY EXPERTISE

Recreating Rule 702 and Reconsidering Expert Testimony

Rule 702, which determines who qualifies as an expert and, therefore, whose testimony is admissible and reliable, operates to the detriment of defendants and, thereby, entrenches epistemic erasure of marginalized individuals. As a result, it is

58 *Id.* at 558.
59 *Id.* at 559.
60 *Id.*
61 *Id.* at 777.
62 *Id.*
63 *Id.* at 851.
64 *Id.* at 854.

important for the legal community to be equally active in creating evidentiary standards that *reduce* injustice, even when imperfect.

This chapter details the significant problems with Rule 702 and its real-world implementation in criminal courtrooms. The current structure normalizes the lived experience of the primary repeat courtroom players: straight, White men representing the state against the alleged criminal "other." The question that remains is whether it is possible to create an expert evidentiary standard that reduces injustice by elevating pertinent lived experiences or by challenging the norm that prosecutorial expert evidence is admitted by default while defense expert evidence is viewed with inherent skepticism.

Countering Defendants' Epistemic Erasure

As Professor Bennett Capers explained, one incrementalist reform would be to eliminate the rules' reification of the hierarchy of expertise. The current rules bolster the power structure, particularly in concert with the Rules of Criminal Procedure, such as limited discovery of evidence for criminal defendants. Criminal defendants regularly face epistemic erasure. To counter this reality, defense counsel should listen to their clients' expertise and experience rather than rely exclusively on experts. When defense counsel defers only to experts, they risk denying a client's lived experience, authenticity, and personal narrative before even exploring the ability to share that perspective in court.

Educating and Training Law Students, Lawyers, and Judges

Judges are not inherently courageous. Indeed, judges may snatch defeat from the jaws of victory in cases where prosecutors and defense counsel agree to reverse a wrongful conviction by insisting on a further adversarial process. In this limited perspective, where the prosecutor chooses not to defend an unreliable conviction, the judge steps into those (often familiar) shoes. CIU Director Sunny Eaton experienced this maneuver firsthand.[65] Discussing the judicial denial of Russell Maze's joint motion for post-conviction relief, Eaton said: "[t]he judge was penalizing them because everyone – the state, the defense, the witnesses – agreed that the Mazes committed no crime."[66] Even when there is no battle of the experts because they all agree with the defense, judges sometimes concoct a fight due to their strict adherence to defense adversaries and an established binary.

65 Pamela Colloff, *He Was Convicted of Killing His Baby. The DA's Office Says He's Innocent, but That Might Not Be Enough*, ProPublica (July 11, 2024), www.propublica.org/article/nashville-conviction-review-russell-maze-shaken-baby-syndrome.

66 *Id.*

As Judges Gertner and Hervey teach, law school education and attorney and judge training on forensic evidence matter. Without such education, there is no questioning of, for example, Georgia's no-repeal rule of evidence that mandated the automatic admission of all experts in criminal, but not civil, cases.[67] Training may empower judges to appoint independent experts under FRE 706. Training also may encourage judges to question their willingness to proceed where experts are only presented by the prosecution, and their resistance to proceed when experts are only presented by the defense.

Finally, as noted in Professor Ngozi Okidegbe's chapter, a re-examining of the rules by a special Advisory Committee, composed of representative individuals who have lived experience with the criminal legal system and social bias, would provide insights into how to reshape expert evidence so that it is not simply a captive tool for reinforcing stigma and stereotypes, particularly for parties who lack financial resources in both civil and criminal cases.[68]

Proposed Rule 702-2: Pretrial Discovery and Countering Pro-Prosecutor Bias

The above good ideas noted, we propose a new Rule 702 subsection specifically for criminal cases to address the disparity in the admissibility of expert evidence:

> Rule 702. Testimony by Expert Witnesses
>
> 2. In criminal cases, the court may admit expert witness testimony offered by the prosecution only where the prosecution demonstrates the requirements of Rule 702-1(a)–1(d) by clear and convincing evidence. To further facilitate reliable expert testimony in criminal cases, crime laboratories shall disclose to the defense pre-plea all scientific evidence such laboratories disclose to the prosecution.

This proposed new subsection, Rule 702-2, adds two requirements. First, crime labs would be required to release lab findings directly to both prosecutors and defense attorneys pretrial through their online portals. This suggestion is a direct result of queering the law and nullifying the prosecutor/defendant binary with regard to scientific evidence. Cutting out the prosecutor as the middleman to relay scientific findings diminishes *Brady* problems, the failure of prosecutors to disclose material and exculpatory evidence to defendants. It also provides time for both the prosecution and the defense to meet with relevant experts and enhances the reliability of evidence ultimately presented in court.

Second, we add a provision that requires more rigorous vetting of expert evidence for government experts while retaining the current preponderance standard for defense experts. As research has established, the pro-prosecution bias is often deeply raced. This chapter argues the pro-prosecution bias also works against queer defendants and female defendants.

[67] Ga. Code Ann. § 24-7-707 (2025) ("[T]he opinions of experts on any question of science, skill, trade, or like questions shall always be admissible …").

[68] Ngozi Okidegbe, "Evidence Rulemaking and Community Participation," in this volume.

Rule 702 operates in the shadow of another set of rules: pretrial discovery. Evidentiary rules should require that scientific evidence be disclosed pretrial in both civil and criminal cases, queering the law to break down the detrimental binary between discovery in civil and criminal cases. This would support the more even application of Rules 702 in both criminal and civil cases and among litigants regardless of minoritized or marginalized status. The creation of the Rules of Criminal Procedure diverged from the Rules of Civil Procedure in the hands of White Southern prosecutors in the 1930s' Jim Crow South, to eliminate equality of disclosing evidence.[69] Our Rule 702 amendment aims to address the Jim-Crow-based failings of the Rules of Criminal Procedure that specifically impact expert evidence and the applicability of the rules of evidence equally across criminal and civil courtrooms.

The purpose of our proposed amendment to Rule 702 is to neutralize the ongoing prosecutorial harm against marginalized defendants, which includes overcharging, harsh plea offers, and the admissibility of unreliable expert evidence that can be tainted by bias. While the government, including prosecutors and police, has a long history of creating and presenting forensic evidence, such action does not equate to reliability. Our Rule 702 amendment would encourage greater scrutiny of government-offered expert evidence. As one commentator shared, police and prosecutors have been admitting the same evidence for decades – evidence such as fingerprint evidence, arson evidence, or bite marks – and it should not be admissible simply because it was when the judge was a prosecutor.

CONCLUSION

This chapter is an effort to uncover epistemic silencing, upset the normalized regime of the standard criminal courtroom, and provide opportunities to emancipate expert evidence. By listening to the experiences of diverse courtroom actors and acknowledging the reality of biased expert testimony in criminal cases, the chapter aims to provide a deeper understanding of – and provoke critical thinking about – the rules of expert evidence and their application in the real world.

69 Ion Meyn, *The Creation of Separate and Unequal Courtrooms*, 63 ARIZONA L. REV. 1 (2021).

Presumed Expertise

Police Officer Opinion Testimony

Alexis Hoag-Fordjour

A defendant was facing several charges related to armed robbery and murder. In correspondence on social media with his alleged co-conspirators, the defendant used the slang terms "lick" and "sweet lick."[1] *The state called the investigating law enforcement officer as a lay witness, asking the officer to define the two terms. The defendant objected and claimed the state was improperly attempting to admit an expert opinion. The judge overruled the objection. The officer proceeded, testifying that based on his experience in the robbery unit of the police department, the term "lick" meant robbery and the term "sweet lick" meant an easy robbery or someone easy to rob. The jury convicted the defendant.*

In another case, the government charged a defendant with multiple drug-related counts involving cocaine possession. During recorded phone conversations with his alleged co-conspirators, the defendant used several words that the government alleged were code.[2] *At trial, the government sought to qualify the investigating detective as an expert to ask his opinion about the defendant's use of code words and their meaning. The defendant objected, arguing that the detective was not an expert. The judge overruled the objection. The detective referenced his experience listening to hundreds of recorded calls involving drug traffickers using code language and serving undercover in drug trafficking organizations. Based on his knowledge, the detective testified that drug traffickers use such code words and translated the "coded" words the defendant and his co-conspirators used. The jury returned a conviction.*

Testifying police officers carry a presumption of expertise that is unlike other witnesses.[3] This presumption exists whether the officer's opinion is categorized as lay opinion testimony, as in the first example, or as expert opinion testimony, as in the second example. Judges, who serve a gatekeeping role deciding whether evidence is admissible and the permissible bounds of a witness's testimony, are not immune

1 Based on facts from Freeman v. State, 318 A.3d 1241 (Md. 2024).

2 Based on facts from United States v. Plunk, 153 F.3d 1011 (9th Cir. 1998), overruled on other grounds by United States v. Hankey, 203 F.3d 1160, n. 7 (9th Cir. 2000).

3 *See* Anna Lvovsky, *The Judicial Presumption of Police Expertise*, 130 HARV. L. REV. 1995, 2015–16 (2017).

from this presumption.[4] When applying the rules, judges tend to err on the side of approving an officer's unwarranted expertise or admitting an officer's lay opinion that crosses the line into expertise. Likewise, jurors, who decide issues of fact, assign excess credibility to law enforcement witnesses based solely on their status as law enforcement.[5] At the same time that officer credibility and expertise are assumed, jurors assign a presumption of culpability to defendants based solely on the defendant's status as an accused person.[6] The presumption of guilt is stronger when the defendant is Black.[7]

The presumed credibility and expertise that officers carry harms defendants in two interrelated ways. First, it impacts the way judges receive police officers as potential witnesses, affecting their decisions about expertise and the admissibility of the officers' testimony. The rules of evidence exist to help courts administer criminal trials fairly,[8] including the rules that provide guidance to judges on determining whether a witness can offer lay or expert testimony,[9] and prohibiting experts from testifying about the ultimate issue.[10] These are consequential determinations as they impact pretrial disclosure requirements and the scope of witness testimony. However, when considering officer-witnesses, trial judges routinely misapply the evidentiary rules. The court's misapplication allows officers to testify about matters that surpass their professional knowledge,[11] improperly assess the defendant's mental state,[12] or usurp the jury's role as fact finder.[13] This is where the second harm arises. Absent sufficient scrutiny, jurors then receive police officer testimony through their own lens of trumped-up credibility and expertise. The result is that when police officers testify, it further tips the scale in favor of the prosecution.

This chapter applies a critical lens to the presumption of credibility and expertise that courts and jurors assign police officers who testify in criminal cases. It examines

4 *Id.*

5 *See* Vida B. Johnson, *Bias in Blue: Instructing Jurors to Consider the Testimony of Police Officer Witnesses with Caution*, 44 Pepp. L. Rev. 245 (2017).

6 *See* Bennett Capers, *Evidence Without Rules*, 94 Notre Dame L. Rev. 867 (2018). *See also*, Neil Vidmar and Valerie P. Hans, American Juries: The Verdict 83–106 (2007) (discussing jurors' assumption that people who are arrested and charged are likely guilty).

7 *See* Bryan Stevenson, A *Presumption of Guilt: The Legacy of America's History of Racial Injustice*, in Policing the Black Man: Arrest Prosecution and Imprisonment 12 (Angela J. Davis ed., Alfred A. Knopf 2017); *see also*, Justin D. Levinson, Huajian Cai, and Danielle Young, *Guilty by Implicit Racial Bias: The Guilty/Not Guilty Implicit Association Test*, 8 Ohio St. J. Crim L. 187, 207 (2010) (finding that mock jurors harbored "strong associations between Black and Guilty, relative to White and Guilty").

8 *See* Fed. R. Evid. 102 (describing purpose of evidentiary rules).

9 *See* Fed. R. Evid. 701 and 702 (establishing the criteria for lay and witness testimony).

10 *See* Fed. R. Evid. 704.

11 *See* State v. Daly, 775 N.W.2d 47 (Neb. 2009) (affirming conviction for driving under the influence where officer testified as drug recognition expert opining about the type of narcotic defendant used).

12 *See* Fed. R. Evid. 704 (prohibiting expert witnesses from opining about whether criminal defendants had or did not have the requisite mens rea).

13 *See* People v. Mosley, 239 N.E.3d 928 (N.Y. 2024) (reversing conviction where police officer identified defendant in surveillance video because jurors could make that assessment).

the evidentiary rules that guide whether such witnesses can provide lay or expert opinions, and it demonstrates how courts misapply them. With this critical awareness, this chapter suggests that defendants must do more to protect themselves against law enforcement witnesses and offers two potential interventions. First, defendants can insist on instructions that urge jurors to receive such witnesses with increased scrutiny, and second, they can utilize the opinions of experts from their own communities to even the scales between the parties.

CHANGING NOTIONS OF POLICE OFFICER-WITNESSES

Police officer-witnesses stand in a league of their own. Armed with excess credibility and presumed expertise, their testimony can be detrimental to a defendant's case. Defense questions about whether the state paid the officer to appear in court fail to land with the same zing as with other "hired guns" because officers' time in court is part of their compensated duties as an officer. That an officer has testified in countless other criminal trials, and exclusively on behalf of one side, does not cast doubt on their testimony the way it would other experts. Depending on the jurisdiction, some officer-witnesses may be allowed to remain in the courtroom, listening to the proceedings and potentially altering their testimony to best support the state's case.[14] In contrast, non-officer-witnesses are subject to mandatory sequestration.[15]

In the latter half of the twentieth century, judges began to "identif[y] police officers as stewards of professional insight worthy of deference in court."[16] Law enforcement witnesses became fixtures in criminal trials, routinely supplying testimonial evidence about their investigative roles in cases, opining about matters regardless of whether the court approved them as experts, and offering conclusory opinions about how the defendant's conduct conformed with the criminal acts in question. Although investigating officers are intimately involved in building the case against a defendant, the court often presents them to jurors as a disinterested witness merely reporting the facts. In effect, a wolf in sheep's clothing.

To be clear, this was a departure from prior practice. It developed with courts' increasing reliance on expert witnesses and the professionalization of law enforcement, both of which occurred in the 1970s.[17] Legal historian Ana Lvovsky details this

14 *See* United States v. Escalante-Melgar, 2020 WL 968091 (D.N.J. Feb. 28, 2020) (recognizing that FRE 615 "plainly exempts Government's case agent from sequestration … The Third Circuit permits government agents to remain in the courtroom even if they will later testify.") (citing United States v. Gonzalez, 918 F.2d 1129, 1138 (3d Cir. 1990)).

15 *See* Fed. R. Evid. 615 (describing witness sequestration).

16 Lvovsky, *supra* note 3, at 2015–16.

17 *See* Mason Ladd, *Expert Testimony*, 5 Vand. L. Rev. 414, 417–18 (1952) (describing the increasing use of expert opinion testimony, particularly in criminal cases involving "scientific methods of proof") and Lvovsky, *supra* note 3, at 2003–15 (describing professionalization of policing in the latter half of the twentieth century).

transformation, pointing to the Supreme Court's decision in *Terry v. Ohio* as one turning point.[18] There, the Court encouraged lower courts to rely on the expertise of policemen "in light of [their] experience" when applying constitutional scrutiny to law enforcement and to the actions of people accused of crime.[19] This marked a change from the skepticism that some courts had expressed about officers. In *United States v. Sette*, for example, decided just a few years before *Terry*, the Second Circuit Court of Appeals criticized the practice of police officers serving as expert participant witnesses.[20]

In the *Sette* case, the government charged the defendant with crimes related to gambling and produced two investigating agents as expert witnesses. The officer-experts testified that based on "their observations" and "their general knowledge of the gambling business" that the defendant "might well have been" engaged in the criminal conduct in question.[21] Writing for the Second Circuit, then Judge Thurgood Marshall wrote, "[w]e are cited to no case, and have found none, that remotely justifies this highly unusual method of establishing a prima facie case in a criminal prosecution of this type."[22] Given that the prosecution failed to submit other evidence to support the charges, the court reversed the conviction.[23]

Despite the *Sette* court's description of the government's use of officer-experts as "highly unusual,"[24] it has now become commonplace and permissible. Other federal courts have recognized that "[l]aw enforcement officers may testify concerning the techniques and methods used by criminals."[25] And all of this has consequences, regardless of whether a case proceeds to trial. For starters, a defendant's decision to plead guilty is often based on the prosecution's admissible evidence, including potential witnesses, and on how a defendant believes jurors will receive the defendant's version of events.[26] Sensing that a discriminatorily selected jury, viewing a police officer witness with excess credibility and viewing the accused as guilty, leads many defendants to waive their right to a trial.

Regardless of whether a case goes to trial, police officers frequently participate in criminal prosecutions.[27] Officers routinely testify at pretrial hearings, enabling the court to rule on the admissibility of contested evidence.[28] These proceedings

[18] *See* Lvovsky, *supra* note 3, at 1997–8 (quoting Terry v. Ohio, 392 U.S. 1 (1968)).

[19] *Id.*

[20] United States v. Sette, 334 F.2d 267 (2d Cir. 1964).

[21] *Id.* at 269.

[22] *Id.*

[23] *Id.*

[24] *Id.*

[25] United States v. Rogers, 769 F.2d 1418, 1425 (9th Cir. 1985).

[26] *See* Daniel Harawa, *Trials Without Justice*, INQUEST (Sep. 21, 2021), https://inquest.org/trials-without-justice/.

[27] *See* Joseph Goldstein, *"Testilying" by Police: A Stubborn Problem*, N.Y. TIMES (Mar. 18, 2018), www.nytimes.com/2018/03/18/nyregion/testilying-police-perjury-new-york.html (describing police involvement in criminal prosecutions).

[28] *Id.*

often involve the most critical issues in a case, searches and witness interrogations.[29] The court's pretrial ruling against the defendant on these matters can incentivize the defendant to plead guilty. If the case proceeds to trial and the complainant is unwilling to testify, an officer might be the only testifying witness. This occurs in "evidence-based prosecutions," a term used to describe prosecutions that do not rely on in-court testimony from complaining victims.[30] In those instances, prosecutors rely on alternative evidence, such as testimony from the responding police officer.[31] Whether pretrial or during trial, officers have multiple incentives to lie, including "to further the prosecution of a citizen by adding inculpatory 'evidence' to better secure the conviction, to gild the lily of police conduct, or merely to sanitize the record of uncomfortable facts."[32]

THE RULES FAIL TO CONSTRAIN POLICE OPINION TESTIMONY

Courts have difficulty navigating whether law enforcement testimony constitutes a lay or expert opinion. One federal court conceded that "[t]he line between expert testimony under Fed R. Evid. 702 … and lay opinion testimony under Fed. R. Evid. 701 … is not easy to draw… ."[33] The opening scenarios illustrate this morass. Both officer-witnesses based their opinions on specialized knowledge and experience as police officers. Both witnesses investigated the crimes at issue and their testimony helped secure the defendants' convictions. However, only the trial court in the first example, where the officer testified about the meaning of slang terms, considered that a lay opinion.[34] Conversely, the trial court in the second example about code language and the conduct of drug traffickers, considered that an expert opinion.[35] The one consistency is that courts seem to err on the side of admission whenever a police officer offers an opinion, regardless of whether the state offers the witness as an expert.

Opinion testimony is based on a witness's belief rather than on firsthand knowledge of the facts at issue in the case. Depending on what the proponent seeks to elicit from a witness, courts classify opinion testimony as either lay or expert. The main difference between the two is that a lay opinion, at least in theory, is supposedly based on reasoning familiar in everyday life,[36] whereas an expert opinion is based on

29 *Id.*

30 *See* Tom Lininger, *Prosecuting Batterers after Crawford*, 91 Va. L. Rev. 747, 751–2 (2005) (describing and defining "evidence-based prosecutions").

31 *Id.*

32 David N. Dorfman, *Proving the Lie: Litigating Police Credibility*, 26 Am. J. Crim. L. 455, 461 (1999) and *id.* (identifying police motives to lie).

33 United States v. Colón Osorio, 360 F.3d 48, 52–3 (1st Cir. 2004).

34 Freeman v. State, 318 A.3d 1241 (Md. 2024).

35 United States v. Plunk, 153 F.3d 1011 (9th Cir. 1998), *overruled by* United States v. Hankey, 203 F.3d 1160, n. 7 (9th Cir. 2000).

36 Fed. R. Evid. 701.

reasoning from a specialized knowledge base.[37] Rules 701 and 702 guide the court's determination on these matters.[38] Rule 701 identifies the limits of lay opinion testimony and Rule 702 describes the requirements for expert opinion testimony.[39]

In theory, the distinction between lay and expert opinion testimony should matter given the rule-based differences between how expert and lay witnesses are permitted to testify. Lay opinions are supposed to be limited to what the witness has observed through their senses, such as through sight, smell, feel, taste, hearing.[40] The law allows for some leeway if the opinion is based on an inference, such as the appearance of something. For example, a lay witness can offer their opinion that a person "seemed tall." However, a lay witness must not base their opinion "on scientific, technical or other specialized knowledge."[41] Conversely, if the court deems a witness an expert, the witness can offer an opinion based on their specialized knowledge, skill, experience, training, or education.[42] The expert witness's proponent must also disclose to the opposing party a summary of the expert's proposed testimony, describe the expert's opinions and the basis on which they rely, and the expert's qualifications prior to trial.[43]

The rules contemplate that expert testimony will receive greater scrutiny from the court and opposing counsel to ensure that the expert's opinions are based on sufficient facts or data, and on reliable principles and methodology.[44] Applying such scrutiny is important given the relative freedom, including from hearsay restrictions, expert witnesses have to opine about matters.[45] Thus, a judge's decision on these matters can impact the entire proceeding, from the proponent's pretrial disclosure obligations,[46] to the substance of the witness's opinion,[47] to the court's scrutiny of the witness's opinion,[48] and to the amount of credit jurors' assign to the witness's opinion.[49]

37 Fed. R. Evid. 702.

38 In addition to the ones listed herein, Fed. R. Evid. 703 identifies the permissible information on which a witness can base their testimony, Fed. R. Evid. 704 establishes the parameters for witnesses offering opinions about an ultimate issue, Fed. R. Evid. 705 and 706 directly address experts, and Fed. R. Evid. 401 and 403 help establish relevancy and weigh relevancy against potential prejudice.

39 *See* Fed. R. Evid. 701 and 702.

40 *See* Fed. R. Evid. 701(a).

41 *See* Fed. R. Evid. 701(c).

42 *See* Fed. R. Evid. 702.

43 *See* Fed. R. Crim. Pro. 16.

44 *See* Fed. R. Evid. 702.

45 *See* Fed. R. Evid. 703.

46 *See* Fed. R. Civ. Pro. 26 and Fed. R. Crim. Pro. 16.

47 *See* Fed. R. Evid. 602 (limiting lay testimony to subjects of which the witness has personal knowledge) and Fed. R. Evid. 703 (allowing experts to rely on facts and data beyond what they personally observed).

48 *See* Fed. R. Evid. 702(c) and (d) (requiring the court to assess the reliability of the principles and methods on which expert witnesses rely).

49 *See* United States v. Rodriguez-Berrios, 573 F.3d 55, 72 (1st Cir. 2009) (recognizing "jurors' possible tendency to give undue weight to expert testimony" due to witness's designation as an expert).

Yet, officers' excess credibility and presumed expertise affect these determinations, resulting in courts approving police witnesses as experts with insufficient scrutiny or allowing officers to opine about matters that go beyond the bounds of a lay opinion. Relying on the court's mismanagement of law enforcement witnesses, some prosecutors proffer officers "ostensibly as mere fact witnesses" and then elicit expert-like opinion testimony, enabling the state to avoid evidentiary scrutiny of the witness and disclosure requirements.[50] This background on the murkiness of the lay/expert witness distinction provides helpful context from which to consider examples of courts' inability to coherently apply these rules in cases involving police officer-witnesses.

Judges are charged with deciding issues of law and ensuring that the parties present only relevant, reliable, and admissible evidence to the jury. The jury is then responsible for deciding issues of fact. An officer's excess credibility and presumed expertise can throw off this precarious balance. In *United States v. Colón Osorio*, the government charged Luis Colón Osorio, an indigent defendant, with being a felon in possession of a firearm and carrying an explosive.[51] To address the explosives charge, Colón Osorio sought to present expert testimony, and given his indigency, he requested funding from the court. The court denied Colón Osorio's pretrial funding motion, claiming it was "untimely" and that granting the motion would delay the proceedings.[52] At trial, the government then presented lay opinion testimony from an agent in the Bureau of Alcohol, Tobacco, and Firearms (ATF).[53] The agent opined that the firearm in question had moved in interstate commerce, a necessary element of the charge, and that the gun's color had been altered.[54] The jury convicted Colón Osorio.[55]

On appeal, Colón Osorio argued that the agent's testimony was improper because it constituted an expert opinion and that the government failed to provide proper notice.[56] In denying Colón Osorio's claim, the reviewing court concluded that the witness's testimony constituted a proper lay opinion "because it was based on information gleaned from [the witness's] personal experience" and was based on "reasoning familiar in everyday life."[57] However, the agent's opinion about the firearm – how it traveled and gun's altered appearance – was based on specialized knowledge as an ATF agent. Agents are "[h]ighly trained" and "responsible for investigating violations of Federal law relating to firearms, explosives, arson, and

[50] *See* Christoper Lau, *Shadow Forensics: Uncovering 911 Call Analysis*, 111 CORNELL L. REV. __, at *24 (forthcoming 2026) (describing this phenomenon as part of a larger trend of "shadow forensics").

[51] *See* United States v. Colón Osorio, 360 F.3d 48, 50 (1st Cir. 2004).

[52] Colón Osorio, 360 F.3d at 50.

[53] Raphael Uribe, misspelled as Rafael Uribe, Colón Oscorio, 360 F.3d at 52–3, was an agent in the Bureau of Alcohol, Tobacco, and Firearms. *See* United States v. Lake, 500 F.3d 629, 631 (7th Cir. 2007).

[54] Colón Osorio, 360 F.3d at 52.

[55] *Id.* at 50.

[56] *Id.* (citing FED. R. CRIM. P. 16(a)(1)(G)).

[57] *Id.* at 53 (citing FED. R. EVID. 701).

alcohol and tobacco diversion."[58] An opinion based on such training, experience, and knowledge is beyond the everyday reasoning of a lay person.[59] This is a distinction that Rule 701 makes clear.[60]

Colón Osorio's experience demonstrates the harm that an officer's excess credibility and presumed expertise can render. Jurors tend to assign greater credibility and expertise to testifying law enforcement officers, even when the officer is not formally recognized as an expert.[61] Indeed, the harm to Colón Osorio was compounded when the trial court denied his pretrial motion for funding to hire his own expert.[62] Not only did the trial court enable the officer to improperly opine about Colón Osorio's conduct, but it also used its discretion to curtail Colón Osorio's attempt to present a complete defense.

The trial court in *United States v. Figueroa-Lopez* also enabled a police officer to give opinion testimony without requiring the government to offer the officer as an expert.[63] There, the government charged Figueroa-Lopez with cocaine possession with the intent to distribute.[64] At trial, the arresting officer testified that he observed Figueroa-Lopez drive in circles around the meeting location before parking his car and engaging in a drug transaction with an informant. The government then asked for the officer's opinion about what, if anything, the defendant's conduct indicated. In essence, the government asked the officer to opine about whether the defendant was engaging in the criminal conduct in question.

Figueroa-Lopez objected, arguing that the government was improperly eliciting expert opinion testimony and had failed to offer the officer as an expert. The court overruled the objection, allowing the officer to opine that Figueroa-Lopez's driving indicated that he was engaging in countersurveillance, which was common practice for narcotics dealers, and that Figueroa-Lopez's driving combined with his use of a rental car was indicative of an experienced drug trafficker.[65] The jury convicted Figueroa-Lopez. On appeal, the reviewing court conceded that the trial court erred in categorizing the officer's testimony as lay testimony and allowing the police officer to opine about what Figueroa-Lopez's driving indicated.[66] However, the appellate court deemed the error harmless and denied Figueroa-Lopez relief.[67]

58 Special Agent Informational Packet, Want To Be a Special Agent?, www.atf.gov/file/22196/download.

59 *See* Fed. R. Evid. 701 advisory committee's note to 2000 Amendment.

60 Fed. R. Evid. 701(c) (prohibiting lay witnesses from testifying based off scientific, technical, or other specialized knowledge that is reserved for expert witnesses).

61 *See* Johnson, *supra* note 5 and Capers, *supra* note 6.

62 *Id.* at 50.

63 United States v. Figueroa-Lopez, 125 F.3d 1241 (9th Cir. 1997).

64 *Id.*

65 Figueroa-Lopez, 125 F.3d at 1241.

66 *Id.*

67 *Id. See also*, Fed. R. Crim. P. 52(a) ("Any error, defect, irregularity, or variance that does not affect substantial rights must be disregarded.").

The rulings in both examples illustrate the absurdity of it all. The court in *Figueroa-Lopez* likely deemed the officer's opinion testimony harmless because the government could have easily qualified the officer as an expert. In other words, the evidence would have been admissible under Rule 702 anyway. Herein lies the real problem, the evidentiary rules, as interpreted and applied by the courts, fail to hold officer-witnesses to the same level of scrutiny as other witnesses when making determinations about lay and expert opinion testimony.

EMPOWERING DEFENDANTS TO ADDRESS THESE ISSUES

The way courts apply the evidentiary rules to police officer-witnesses leaves defendants in a bind. Courts, like society, assign a presumption of expertise to police officers. Regardless of whether prosecutors offer law enforcement witnesses as experts, courts seem willing to allow officers to testify in ways traditionally reserved for experts, which includes allowing opinion testimony based on specialized knowledge, skill, experience, training, or education.[68] Nothing in the rules permits courts to assume the credibility or expertise of police officers. Thus, urging courts to rely on the rules to apply greater scrutiny to law enforcement witnesses seems futile.

To address these issues, defendants need to focus on the way jurors receive officer testimony and on countering law enforcement evidence with their own experts. To that end, first, defendants should request courts to instruct jurors to apply greater scrutiny to law enforcement witnesses to prevent jurors from assigning officers undue credit based on their status as law enforcement. Second, defendants should use the evidentiary rules to elevate the opinions of experts from their own communities to provide a counternarrative to law enforcement opinion testimony. Each intervention is detailed below.

Courts should instruct the jury to receive lay law enforcement officer testimony with caution.[69] Given the presumption of credibility and expertise that society assigns law enforcement, combined with the presumption of criminality jurors tend to give to defendants, more scrutiny is warranted. The prevailing practice is for courts to instruct jurors to treat law enforcement witnesses like any other witness.[70] However, this would be inaccurate; law enforcement witnesses are unlike other witnesses.[71] Criminal law scholar Vida Johnson argues that police officer-witnesses are unique given the nature of law enforcement work that can imbue their testimony with

68 *See* Fed. R. Evid. 702.

69 *See* Johnson, *supra* note 5.

70 *See* United States v. Martinez, 981 F.2d 867, 870–1 (6th Cir. 1992) ("People who are involved in law enforcement ... are not automatically entitled ... to be believed simply ... because they are engaged in law enforcement ... [t]hey are to be ... judged by the same standards as anyone else, any other witness ... .").

71 *See* Johnson, *supra* note 5, at 248–9.

unacknowledged bias.[72] Johnson explains that law enforcement officers "are prone to group polarization" and exposed to "limited viewpoints" that result in "more extreme ... views of those they are policing."[73] Further, police officers have an incentive to lie and they do lie, even when providing sworn testimony under oath.[74]

For these reasons, defendants should request instructions similar to what courts provide when an interested party testifies, like an informant or a cooperating witness.[75] For example, one federal court instructs the jury to consider testimony from a cooperating witness "with caution and great care."[76] Defendants should be requesting instructions like these whenever law enforcement officials testify for the prosecution. There is precedent for defendants relying on jury instructions to help balance the scales between the parties. Some jurisdictions allow defendants to request special jury instructions about the fallibility of eyewitness identification.[77] As with eyewitness identification, which counterintuitively has a high rate of inaccuracy, viewing law enforcement witnesses with added scrutiny can be counterintuitive. Most people view law enforcement officials with added credibility. It is for this very reason that a jury instruction cautioning jurors to receive testimony from police officers with caution and great care is crucial.

Secondly, defendants can proffer their own expert to level the playing field. Community experts, someone from the defendant's community or someone with experiential familiarity to the defendant's background, can provide a counternarrative to the expert and lay opinions of law enforcement witnesses.[78] Community experts can offer a more nuanced and accurate view of the same issues about which police officers testify.[79] To be clear, it can be difficult for indigent defendants to marshal the resources necessary to work with experts. In theory, fundamental fairness and due process protect every defendant's right to present a full defense, including state-funded experts for indigent defendants.[80] However, the state is not required to "purchase for the indigent defendant all the assistance that his wealthier counterpart might buy."[81] Indigent defendants do "not have an absolute right"[82] to a state-funded

72 *Id.* at 292.

73 *Id.*

74 *See* Dorfman, *supra* note 32, at 461 and Goldstein, *supra* note 27.

75 *See* Peter A. Joy, *Constructing Systemic Safeguards Against Informant Perjury*, 7 Ohio St. J. Crim. L. 677, 683 (2010) (recommending that jurors receive special instructions when informants testify to help jurors "determine credibility effectively").

76 *See* United States v. Austin, 215 F.3d 750, 752 (7th Cir. 2000) (describing jury instructions).

77 *See* State v. Gilbert, 49 A.3d 705, 726–8 (Conn. 2012) (discussing jury instructions on fallibility of eyewitness identification).

78 Raj Jayadev, Protect Your People 54–5 (The New Press 2024) (defining community experts as people who live in a community and who can provide their real-world expertise in criminal trials).

79 *See id.* at 54–5; *see also*, *Independent Forensic Gang Expert College* (IFGEC), Loyala Law School (LLS), www.lls.edu/academics/centers/centerforjuvenilelawpolicy/ifgec.

80 Ake v. Oklahoma, 470 U.S. 68 (1985).

81 *Id.* at 77.

82 Commonwealth v. Serge, 896 A.2d 1170, 1184 (Pa. 2006).

expert, to receive such funding, they must demonstrate that expert assistance is "necessary for an adequate defense."[83] Courts then have discretion in determining whether to approve funding for expert assistance.[84] In Michele Gilman's chapter, "The Relevance and Prejudice of Poverty Evidence," she exposes the fact that some courts refuse to provide funds to indigent defendants to retain exports.[85]

For defendants who are able, community experts have been quite effective in cases involving gang offenses. Gang offenses and/or gang enhancements result in lengthier sentences upon conviction in several jurisdictions.[86] To support these allegations, prosecutors often rely on police officers to provide opinion testimony that the defendant is a gang member or committed an act that was gang-related.[87] When testifying as an expert, officers base their opinions on their experience investigating alleged gang members and gang conduct.[88] Such testimony deserves special scrutiny for all the reasons stated above.

To challenge this "expert" testimony, defendants should be permitted to proffer expert testimony of their own. In some jurisdictions, defendants are already challenging these one-sided narratives with opinion testimony from community experts, people from the defendant's community or with an intimate knowledge of the defendant's community who can offer an opinion about the defendant, the circumstances related to the defendant's criminal charge, and about whether the defendant is a member of a gang. Defendants working with community experts in California have effectively challenged alleged gang involvement, reducing people's prison sentences and in some cases, securing acquittals.[89] Two California-based organizations that help harness the power of community experts to challenge prosecutor allegations of gang involvement are the Independent Forensic Gang Expert College (IFGEC) in Los Angeles and Silicon Valley De-Bug in the Bay Area. IFGEC trains people who have been involved with gangs, some of whom while incarcerated, to serve as experts in criminal cases.[90] De-Bug is an advocacy and storytelling organization engaged in dynamic community-based justice work.[91]

83 *Id.* at 79–80.

84 *See* United States v. Nicols, 21 F.3d 1016, 1018 (10th Cir. 1994).

85 *See* Michelle Gilman, "The Relevance and Prejudice of Poverty Evidence," in this volume.

86 *See* Cal. Penal Code § 186.22 (Deering 2025) (proving penalty enhancement in state court). *See also*, 18 U.S.C. § 521 (2018) (proving penalty enhancement in federal court).

87 *See* Castillo v. Lewis, 2015 WL 10401594, at *2 (N.D. Cal. May 18, 2015) (identifying prosecution's gang expert as a gang detective with the Los Angeles Police Department and testifying that in his opinion, defendant was "an active member" of a gang).

88 *See* People v. Gamez, 235 Cal.App.3d 957, 966 (Cal. App. 1991) (finding that police officer gang experts can base their opinion testimony on "personal observations of and discussions with gang members as well as information from fellow officers and the department files").

89 Jayadev, *supra* note 78, at 57.

90 IFGEC, *supra* note 79.

91 *See* Silicon Valley De-Bug, *About*, www.siliconvalleydebug.org/about.

Instead of an incomplete, one-sided view from a police officer, community experts are able "to contextualize a [defendant's] gang involvement, explain how it happens, why it happens, and show the limits of it."[92] Moreover, such testimony pushes back against the criteria used to permit police expert testimony. If courts allow police officers to testify as experts based on their experiences, it would be hypocritical to prevent members of the community from testifying as experts based on *their* experiences.

CONCLUSION

The presumption of credibility that testifying law enforcement officers carry should require more from the witness's proponent. However, as currently applied, the evidentiary rules guiding courts in differentiating between lay and expert opinion testimony are not doing enough to protect defendants from the harms police officer-witnesses render. Under the current regime, courts privilege the opinions of those who already hold power: law enforcement, whether as experts or lay witnesses. Given the leeway courts provide law enforcement officers offering opinion testimony, defendants must be vigilant about shaping the way jurors receive such testimony. Jurors should apply exceptional scrutiny to police officer-witnesses because they are exceptional witnesses, unlike traditional fact-based or expert witnesses. Defendants must insist on courts instructing jurors on how to receive police officer testimony. In addition, defendants can utilize the evidentiary rules in their favor to elevate the voices of marginalized people and even the scales of justice. Together, these measures can help fact finders to receive a fuller story and perhaps view the defendant with less culpability and more humanity.

[92] *Id.*

Party-Blind Review

A Proposal to Reduce Judicial Bias in Expert Evidence Admissibility Rulings

Rebecca Wexler

Equal means getting the same thing, at the same time, and in the same place.
Thurgood Marshall[1]

INTRODUCTION

As readers of this volume will be well aware, Federal Rule of Evidence (FRE) 702 and the Supreme Court's famous 1993 opinion in *Daubert v. Merrell Dow Pharmaceuticals* require courts to assess the reliability of expert evidence before admitting it to the jury.[2] Most states impose similar rules.[3] These rules are commonly understood to require courts to perform a gatekeeping function to keep unreliable expert evidence away from the jury.

Thank you to Valena Beety, Erin Murphy, and Julia Simon-Kerr for excellent editorial feedback on prior drafts. This chapter is dedicated to my father, Bruce Wexler, who used a two-stage process to help establish the reliability of a scientific study in a highly contested political context. The study examined how Palestinian and Israeli schoolbooks presented the Israeli-Palestinian conflict, the Self, and the Other. My father and his collaborators put together an international scientific advisory board of experts from across the political spectrum that first evaluated and approved the study methods before any data were collected, i.e. while "blind" to whether the results favored one side or the other. Only in a second stage did the advisory board review the results and analysis. *See* Sami Adwan, Daniel Bar-Tal, and Bruce E. Wexler, *Portrayal of the Other in Palestinian and Israeli Schoolbooks: A Comparative Study*, 37 Pol. Psych. 201, 203 (2016), https://israelipalestinianschoolbooks.blogspot.com. While the board was not blinded in precisely the same way that this chapter proposes for courts, the two-stage process nonetheless helped to mitigate potential bias in judging the reliability of my father's study and inspired my proposal here.

1 Linda Greenhouse, *Thurgood Marshall, Civil Rights Hero, Dies at 84*, The N.Y. Times (Jan. 25, 1993).

2 509 U.S. 579 (1993).

3 While some states have kept the earlier *Frye* standard for the admissibility of expert evidence, it is not clear that the alternate rule makes much difference in admissibility outcomes. *See* Edward K. Cheng and Albert H. Yoon, *Does Frye or Daubert Matter? A Study of Scientific Admissibility Standards*, 91 Va. L. Rev. 471 (2005).

Concerningly, both empirical studies and anecdotal accounts suggest that judges apply this expert gatekeeping function differently to different types of litigants. Judges appear to require more reliability to admit evidence proffered by civil mass tort plaintiffs or criminal defendants and less reliability to admit evidence proffered by prosecutors.[4] Put another way, litigants offering expert evidence do not get "the same thing, at the same time, and in the same place."[5]

This chapter makes two main contributions to our understanding of judicial bias in the application of the expert evidence rules. The first is diagnostic: While the expert evidence rules appear, superficially, to bind judicial discretion, in practice they do nothing of the kind. Contrary to the prevailing view, I contend that the *Daubert* standard as embodied in the Federal Rules of Evidence does not actually set a threshold reliability requirement for expert evidence. Instead, it creates a bureaucratic necessity for judges to assess reliability without dictating how much reliability should be required for admissibility. The rule masquerades as a duty that constrains judges by requiring them to keep junk science out of the courtroom. In reality, it does the opposite: it expands judicial discretion by creating a new rationale for exclusion without a mandate either to admit or to exclude in any given circumstance. Discretion, in turn, invites bias.

My second intervention is prescriptive. To reduce judicial bias in the application of expert evidence admissibility rules, I propose that courts should undertake party-blind review. This would require a two-stage process. Initially, parties would submit expert methods for review without revealing the results of applying those methods to case-specific facts. All party identifications would be redacted from these initial submissions and any opposing briefs. The judge would then rule party-blind on the admissibility of the expert method. Only if the judge decides that the method is sufficiently reliable to satisfy FRE 702 would the proffering party reveal its identity and submit the case-specific results for review.

I. THE PROBLEM OF JUDICIAL BIAS IN THE ADMISSIBILITY OF EXPERT EVIDENCE

Both anecdotal accounts and empirical studies indicate that judges apply their expert evidence gatekeeping function differently to different types of litigants.[6]

For instance, the authors of the *Modern Scientific Evidence* treatise note "that courts tend to be more searching with regard to admissibility in civil rather than criminal cases."[7] Valena Beety and Jennifer Oliva studied admissibility rulings regarding forensic arson evidence and found "that while civil courts closely scrutinize and

4 *See infra* citations and text accompanying notes 6 to 13.

5 Greenhouse, *supra* note 1 (quoting Thurgood Marshall).

6 *See, e.g.*, Déirdre Dwyer, *(Why) Are Civil and Criminal Expert Evidence Different?*, 43 Tulsa L. Rev. 381 (2013).

7 5 Mod. Sci. Evidence, Introduction § 37:1 (2024–2025 ed.).

often exclude unreliable fire science evidence, criminal courts routinely allow it to go to the jury."[8] Judge Nancy Gertner has admonished fellow judges for failing to keep junk science out of criminal cases, stating: "We, the courts, can do better. In fact, we already do, albeit in civil, not criminal, cases."[9] A study by Julie Seaman offers empirical support for these observations. Seaman's study of admissibility decisions regarding forensic handwriting analysis showed that courts admitted evidence from prosecutors in criminal cases while using FRE 702/*Daubert* to discredit and exclude similar evidence from plaintiffs in class action mass tort civil lawsuits.[10]

Nor is the civil versus criminal divide the only site of apparent disparities. Seaman also concluded that, "at least in some areas, criminal defendants' expert testimony, when offered, is less likely to be admitted than similar prosecution expert testimony."[11] Meanwhile, another empirical study by Michael Cicchini produced similar results. Cicchini found that, of all the *Daubert* cases that had reached the Wisconsin appellate courts during the prior decade, prosecutors won every decision across all levels of the court system.[12] He concluded that, "in practice, *Daubert* does nothing to protect defendants from pseudo-science experts [acting as prosecution witnesses] and instead makes it more difficult for defendants to call their own legitimate experts."[13]

Biased application of the expert evidence rules is harmful for a variety of reasons. To start, the accuracy costs cannot be overstated. If judges assess expert methods differently in criminal versus civil cases, or for prosecutorial versus defense evidence, it means that judges are either admitting unreliable evidence or excluding reliable evidence in some cases. That has serious consequences. For one example among many, a recent study estimated that in 491 out of 732 exonerations, "a forensic error contributed to the balance of evidence in a wrongful conviction."[14] Erroneous expert evidence rulings lead to erroneous case outcomes.

Beyond accuracy, biased application of the expert evidence rules undermines two other overarching goals of the rules of evidence: fairness and justice.[15] The accuracy

[8] Valena E. Beety and Jennifer D. Oliva, *Evidence on Fire*, 97 N. Carolina L. Rev. 483, 487 (2019). *See also*, Jennifer D. Oliva and Valena E. Beety, *Discovering Forensic Fraud*, 112 Nw. U. L. Rev. 121 (2017) (positing that structural differences in discovery rules between civil and criminal cases contribute to poor judicial gatekeeping of unreliable expert evidence proffered by prosecutors).

[9] Nancy Gertner, *National Academy of Sciences Report: A Challenge to the Courts*, 27 Crim. Just. Mag. 8 (2012), www.americanbar.org/content/dam/aba/publications/criminal_justice_magazine/sp12_report.pdf. Note that sometimes the very same judges will preside over both criminal and civil cases and may treat the same type of evidence differently in the two situations.

[10] Julie A. Seaman, *A Tale of Two Dauberts*, 47 Ga. L. Rev. 889, 898–9 (2013). Notably, Seaman did *not* find the same disparity with regards to forensic arson evidence, which other commentators have alleged is treated differently by civil and criminal courts. *Cf.* 5 Mod. Sci. Evidence, Introduction § 37:1, *supra* note 7.

[11] Seaman, *supra* note 10, at 897.

[12] Michael Cicchini, *The Daubert Double Standard*, 2021 Mich. St. L. Rev. 705, 706 (2021).

[13] *Id.* at 705.

[14] John Morgan, *Wrongful Convictions and Claims of False or Misleading Forensic Evidence*, 68 J. Forensic Sci. 908, 919 (2023).

[15] *See* Fed. R. Evid. 102.

costs layer onto and risk exacerbating race, class, and other disparities that independently affect who brings civil tort suits and who is charged with crimes. For instance, an empirical study by Andrew Jurs and Scott DeVito concluded that adopting a strict FRE 702/*Daubert* standard for expert evidence from civil plaintiffs disproportionately suppresses filings from Black tort plaintiffs when applied in the context of racial wealth disparities.[16] Meanwhile, race and class disparities in the criminal legal system are notorious. The Bureau of Justice Statistics estimated that "over 80% of felony defendants charged with a violent crime in the country's largest counties and 66% in U.S. district courts had publicly financed attorneys," meaning that they were indigent.[17] Black men account for 35 percent of the incarcerated male population but only 13 percent of the general male population.[18] As long as a disproportionate percentage of criminal defendants come from poor communities of color, the accuracy harms from erroneous judicial gatekeeping of forensic evidence will fall disproportionately on those communities. In short, biased application of the expert evidence rules can produce disparate impacts when applied in the context of other wealth and race disparities.[19]

Finally, biased expert evidence rulings threaten the legitimacy of courts' truth-seeking function. As exceptionally well articulated by the authors of the *Modern Scientific Evidence* treatise, "it is a disservice to the principle of legality, and to the integrity of the system, that the same methods ruled unreliable in one courtroom should be deemed reliable in the courtroom down the hall."[20]

II. HOW THE EXPERT EVIDENCE RULES ENABLE BIASED GATEKEEPING

Critical Evidence scholarship has made a persuasive case that evidence rules can invite biased decision-making through what they do *not* regulate as much as through what they do regulate. For instance, Julia Simon-Kerr has argued that courts apply the

[16] Andrew W. Jurs and Scott DeVito, *A Tale of Two* Dauberts: *Discriminatory Effects of Scientific Reliability Screening*, 79 Ohio St. L.J. 1107, 1110, 1141 (2018) (finding that stricter gatekeeping for civil expert evidence correlated with a disproportionate reduction in filing rates by Black tort plaintiffs and hypothesizing that the gatekeeping suppressed tort claims with lower economic valuation, which disproportionately affected claimants of color because a higher proportion of these claimants live in poverty).

[17] Caroline Wolf Harlow, Defense Counsel in Criminal Cases, Bureau of Justice Statistics Special Report 1 (Nov. 2000), https://bjs.ojp.gov/content/pub/pdf/dccc.pdf.

[18] Elizabeth Hinton, LeShae Henderson, and Cindy Reed, *An Unjust Burden: The Disparate Treatment of Black Americans in the Criminal Justice System*, Vera Evidence Brief (May 2018), https://vera-institute.files.svdcdn.com/production/downloads/publications/for-the-record-unjust-burden-racial-disparities.pdf.

[19] *Cf.*, Bennett Capers, *Race, Gatekeeping, Magical Words, and the Rules of Evidence*, 76 Vand. L. Rev. 1855, 1867 (2023) (arguing that even FRE 702's facially neutral rules for qualifying expert witnesses produce foreseeable racial disparate impacts based on "the history of unequal access to education; the unequal distribution of scientific, technical, or other specialized knowledge; or the unequal distribution of advanced degrees").

[20] 5 Mod. Sci. Evidence, Introduction § 37.1, *supra* note 7.

ban on character-propensity evidence differently to different individuals depending on whether the individual matches or diverges from an unstated yet presumed baseline "middle class, cisgender white man."[21] She identifies this as "part of a broader difficulty for any evidentiary system: the problem of preconceptions,"[22] and she seeks to "identify when the rules themselves amplify problematic preconceptions or ignore others."[23] Anna Roberts warns that implicit biases, and in particular "implicit stereotypes connecting African Americans with violence, weaponry, hostility, aggression, and immorality," risk filling a void in jury decision-making when the rules of evidence chill criminal defendants from testifying and countering such stereotypes through "individuation."[24] Bennett Capers contends that juries consider parties' and witnesses' race, class, ethnicity, gender, and other perceptible characteristics as facts alongside other items of evidence, yet the rules of evidence fail to acknowledge this "unregulated evidence."[25] Relatedly, Ngozi Okidegbe has argued that the pretrial bail algorithms for predicting recidivism ignore, and implicitly discredit, certain categories of information or evidence that she terms "non-carceral knowledge sources."[26]

An overarching lesson from the work of these and other Critical Evidence scholars is that the unstated presumptions, omissions, and silences in evidence law can be as powerful as what the rules say on their face. The rules for expert evidence admissibility are no exception.

Despite the rules' seemingly strict language, I argue that FRE 702 and the *Daubert* doctrine are nearly meaningless constraints on trial court discretion. The rules neither require courts to exclude expert methods that are barely more reliable than chance nor require them to admit expert methods that are highly reliable. In short, FRE 702 and the *Daubert* doctrine create a discretionary gatekeeping option for trial courts, not a gatekeeping duty. As with other forms of judicial discretion and combined with evidence law's standard of abuse of discretion review on appeal, discretionary gatekeeping invites bias in its application.

Of course, the rules do require *something*. FRE 702 states, in relevant part, that the proponent of expert testimony must "demonstrate[] to the court that it is more likely than not that … the testimony is based on sufficient facts or data; the testimony is the product of reliable principles and methods; and the expert's opinion reflects a reliable application of the principles and methods to the facts of the case."[27] This rule clearly compels trial courts to make *some* assessment of reliability. Moreover, a 2023 amendment to this rule clarified that the preponderance standard applies to

21 Julia Simon-Kerr, *A New Baseline for Character Evidence*, 76 VAND. L. REV. 1827, 1828 (2023).

22 *Id.* at 1852.

23 *Id.* at 1853.

24 Anna Roberts, *Reclaiming the Importance of the Defendant's Testimony: Prior Conviction Impeachment and the Fight Against Implicit Stereotyping*, 83 U. CHI. L. REV. 835, 864, 873 (2016).

25 Bennett Capers, *Evidence Without Rules*, 94 NOTRE DAME L. REV. 867, 867 (2018).

26 *See generally*, Ngozi Okidegbe, *Discredited Data*, 107 CORNELL L. REV. 2007 (2022).

27 FED. R. EVID. 702.

the court's analysis.[28] And appellate courts have found error when trial courts fail to conduct a reliability assessment or fail to record any findings as to reliability.[29]

However, despite appearing quite rigorous at first glance, FRE 702's required assessment of reliability is essentially a bureaucratic exercise of magic words that imposes no outcome-determinative restraints on a judge's admissibility ruling. In implementation, the rule is extremely malleable because it sets no threshold for *how reliable or unreliable* expert evidence must be to be admitted or excluded. Reliability is a spectrum, not a binary. Without a set threshold, nothing stops judges from admitting evidence with exceedingly low reliability so long as they label it sufficiently reliable. And nothing stops them from excluding evidence with exceedingly high reliability so long as they label it insufficiently so. Nor does the rule offer courts any guidance as to how they should determine the threshold amount of reliability to require for admission, or of unreliability to require for exclusion. Instead, the rule is silent on the matter, failing even to acknowledge that setting a threshold is an outcome-determinative issue that every court must reach.

The Supreme Court has done little to remedy this gap. Considered together, the Supreme Court's *Daubert* precedents set an extraordinarily low bar for mandatory reliability to surpass. *Daubert* states that expert testimony must be "more than subjective belief of unsupported speculation."[30] *Joiner* held that the basis of an expert's testimony must be connected to the expert's conclusions by more than only "the ipse dixit of the expert."[31] In *Kumho Tire*, the Court emphasized the trial judge's "broad latitude … in respect to its ultimate reliability determination."[32] Finally, in a lesser known precedent, *Weisgram v. Marley*, the Court affirmed an Eighth Circuit ruling that it was abuse of discretion to admit expert evidence.[33] The Eighth Circuit had found that the evidence "was patent speculation" based on "unsubstantiated theories" and "inferences that have absolutely no record support."[34] Each of these opinions characterizes unreliability with such extreme rhetoric that they barely set a substantive floor. As observed by the authors of the *Modern Scientific Evidence* treatise:

> [The rule] still does not answer the question of how much error is too much error to be admissible. For example, would expert predictions that are shown by all of the available evidence to be correct only 51% of the time be sufficiently "reliable" to be admissible? Would expert predictions that are wrong more often than they are right be admissible?[35]

[28] *See, e.g.*, FED. R. EVID. 702 advisory comm. notes on 2023 Amendment.
[29] *See, e.g.*, United States v. Valencia-Lopez, 971 F.3d 891, 898–9 (9th Cir. 2020); Elsayed Mukhtar v. California State Univ., Hayward, 299 F.3d 1053, 1065–6 (9th Cir. 2002).
[30] Daubert v. Merrell Dow Pharmaceuticals, Inc., 509 U.S. 579, 590 (1993).
[31] General Electric v. Joiner, 522 U.S. 143, 146 (1997).
[32] Kumho Tire Co. v. Carmichael, 526 U.S. 137, 142 (1999).
[33] Wesigram v. Marley Co., 538 U.S. 440, 442 (2000).
[34] Weisgram v. Marley Co., 169 F.3d 514, 519 (8th Cir. 1999).
[35] 1 MOD. SCI. EVIDENCE § 1:9 (2023–2024 ed.) (applying *Daubert*).

Without answers to these questions, FRE 702's mandatory reliability inquiry amounts to nothing more than a bureaucratic requirement that judges make a finding one way or the other.[36] They can find whichever way they want to if it is explicit. Actual gatekeeping is optional – judges can choose to do it or not.

As a result, the expert evidence rules merely increase judges' discretion by creating an additional avenue to exclude expert testimony beyond finding it to be irrelevant or unduly prejudicial. As with a FRE 403 analysis, this additional avenue is optional for judges. The gatekeeping "option" allows courts to choose when to axe an expert and when not. And, as with all forms of discretion, bias flourishes in that leeway to swing the axe.

III. A PROPOSAL TO BLIND JUDICIAL REVIEW OF EXPERT METHODS

So, what should be done? This section proposes a means to curtail judicial bias in the application of the expert evidence rules: party-blind review of expert methods. If judges had to review an expert's foundational methods without knowing whether that expert was being proffered by the plaintiff or defense in a mass tort case, or by the prosecution or defendant in a criminal case, then they would be more likely to give the same treatment, at the same time, in the same place to evidence from each type of litigant. Of course, it is likely that certain details about the expert's application of the method to case-specific facts could not be adjudicated without exposing the results. Those details could be addressed in a second round of unredacted briefing.

Blinding is hardly a novel response to bias. In a famous field study from 2000, Claudia Goldin and Cecilia Rouse showed that when orchestra directors conducted auditions behind a screen that concealed the musician's gender, female musicians had a greater likelihood of passing the initial rounds and ultimately getting hired.[37] Years later, the statistics for that study were questioned.[38] Yet its motivating intuition remains compelling: stopping decision-makers from learning a protected

[36] One possible reason that the FRE fail to set a uniform reliability threshold for expert evidence is that doing so would be exceedingly difficult. To start, it is difficult to quantify reliability. A wide array of measurements can be relevant, including precision, specificity, reproducibility, accuracy, and error rates, many of which may be unavailable in any given case. And even in a world of perfect measurement, setting a precise numerical threshold, or even a more general state-of-the-art requirement, could cause parties and courts to miss out on lesser evidence that might still form a robust basis of decision when considered in conjunction with other corroborating information. For a more detailed analysis of the limitations and drawbacks of setting uniform *ex ante* performance thresholds for expert witness methods, *see generally*, Rebecca Wexler, *Metrics Not Thresholds: How to Regulate AI and Other Expert Methods for Use in Criminal Investigations and Proceedings*, 8 U. PA. J. L. & INNOVATION 82 (2026).

[37] Claudia Goldin and Cecilia Rouse, *Orchestrating Impartiality: The Impact of "Blind" Auditions on Female Musicians*, 90 AM. ECON. REV. 715, 715–16 (2000).

[38] *See, e.g.*, Andrew Gelman, *Did Blind Orchestra Auditions Really Benefit Women?* BLOGPOST (May 11, 2019), https://statmodeling.stat.columbia.edu/2019/05/11/did-blind-orchestra-auditions-really-benefit-women/.

characteristic can help to prevent them from discriminating based on that characteristic. Indeed, this is an intuition that motivates multiple areas of law. As Ignacio Cofone has observed, "[l]aw often blocks personal information from human decision-makers in many areas (including employment, health care, and banking) to prevent discrimination."[39] Some parts of criminal procedure have applied these insights as well. Research has shown that adopting blind lineup procedures improves the accuracy of eyewitness identifications, and best practice policy recommendations for police departments is to use such procedures.[40] Likewise, beyond law, best practices for scientific journals is to use double-blind peer review to, in the words of Maneka Sinha, "prevent bias from infecting the review process and to encourage honest review of the work."[41] In all these different areas, blinding is thought to mitigate bias.

Some of the FRE also already adopt a similar approach. Rules 411 and 412 limit whether or how juries may learn certain facts about a party – specifically that they purchased liability insurance or engaged in prior sexual activity – at least in part to prevent juries from discriminating against people based on that information.[42] Similarly, Rule 610 prevents lawyers from using "a witness's religious beliefs or opinions" to attack or bolster their testimony.[43] The idea behind these rules is to blind jurors to certain characteristics to prevent them from drawing biased inferences.

Yet, it is generally not feasible for the rules of evidence to blind decision-makers to the very identity of the party submitting the evidence. For instance, in most cases, it will be obvious that it is the prosecution rather than the defense introducing an item of evidence because that evidence will clearly support the narrative of guilt, or vice versa. The substance of the evidence will reveal the party it favors. Moreover, it is the role of the lawyer to characterize the evidence to emphasize its narrative polarization.

Expert evidence is the exception in this regard because it *is* possible to divorce consideration of the foundational methodology from its application in any given case. Indeed, the idea of separating judicial review of expert methods from judicial review of expert results is not new. David Faigman, Christopher Slobogin, and John Monahan observed nearly a decade ago that "expert testimony describing basic science, 'framework' science, and the scientific methods an expert uses to reach conclusions transcend the case at hand," whereas disputes over whether an expert properly applied that method to the facts are case-specific.[44] Faigman, Slobogin,

39 Ignacio Cofone, *Algorithmic Discrimination Is an Information Problem*, 70 HASTINGS L.J. 1389, 1406 (2019).

40 *See, e.g.*, Brandon L. Garrett, *Eyewitness Identifications and Police Practices in Virginia*, 2 VA. J. CRIMINAL L. 1, 3 (2014).

41 Maneka Sinha, *Radically Reimagining Forensic Evidence*, 73 ALA. L. REV. 879, 899 (2022).

42 FED. R. EVID. 411 and 412.

43 FED. R. EVID. 610.

44 David Faigman, Christopher Slobogin, and John Monahan, *Gatekeeping Science: Using the Structure of Scientific Research to Distinguish Between Admissibility and Weight in Expert Testimony*, 110 NW. U. L. REV. 859, 859 (2016).

and Monahan used that division to argue that different standards of review should apply to expert methods and expert conclusions, both in the trial court (preponderance versus sufficiency) and in the appellate court (de novo versus abuse of discretion).[45]

More recently, Edith Beerdsen has argued convincingly that evidence law should exploit the division between expert methods and their application by requiring, or at least permitting, parties to pre-commit to the methods before an expert deploys them.[46] Inspired by the rise of preregistration requirements in the social sciences as a means to constrain "Analytical Flexibility" and *p*-hacking,[47] Beerdsen proposed early admissibility proceedings on pre-deployment expert methods as a "commitment device," "requiring an expert to describe her intended study in detail, including every variable she intends to collect, every envisioned analytical step, and the criteria she is going to use in excluding data and in interpreting the results," all before the expert applies the methods to the facts of the case.[48] There would be another admissibility hearing "after all data have been gathered and analyzed" to assess the expert's application of the methods.[49] Moreover, as Beerdsen points out, some courts have already adopted a two-stage admissibility analysis that separates expert methods from their application, albeit motivated by efficiency rather than reliability or fairness.[50] These examples show that a two-stage process is possible.

The same division in the structure of scientific knowledge that Faigman, Slobogin, and Monahan describe, and the same two-stage possibilities for admissibility determinations that Beerdsen lays out, could also enable judges to conduct party-blind review. Specifically, judges could conduct blind review of the foundational methods before they receive briefing on the case-specific application of an expert's proposed testimony. Judges could then decide whether a method's foundational reliability suffices for admissibility before they know which party its application favors.[51]

Blind briefing of expert methods would surely require some administrative overhead work for the courts. To fully redact any party-identifying information, lawyers might have to submit their briefs via a special anonymized channel on the courts' electronic filing system. The judge would have to set deadlines for those briefs without knowing to which party they apply. Requests for extensions would have to be anonymized. Oral argument could not be conducted until after the blind review stage was complete. But these hurdles, while novel, do not seem unsurmountable. Judges could experiment with them in their individual rules, even without a central

45 *Id.*

46 Edith Beerdsen, *Litigation Science after the Knowledge Crisis*, 106 CORNELL L. REV. 529 (2021).

47 *Id.* at 573.

48 *Id.*

49 *Id.* at 575.

50 *Id.* at 576–7.

51 *Cf. id.* at 587 (proposing that "when results of a study are not yet known, the methodology that will produce them may be more capable of being judged on the merits").

shift in the Rules of Evidence. Jurisdictions open to more systemic change could go further and establish specialized courts to review party-blinded expert methods on referral from the presiding judge, adding a double-blind layer that could further reduce bias.[52]

Notably, policies to prevent discrimination by redacting information can be ineffective or even counterproductive if decision-makers "use other information as proxies for such blocked information [such as] zip code as a proxy for race, or height as a proxy for gender."[53] A study by Amanda Agan and Sonja Starr showed that laws intended to prevent employment discrimination against job candidates with criminal records by preventing employers from asking about candidates' criminal history "backfired by fostering discrimination based on race."[54] Cofone therefore observes that, to be successful at preventing discrimination through privacy or information redaction, laws must also succeed at "identifying and blocking data points that are proxies for categories that the law protects."[55]

Party-blind review of expert testimony about foundational methods could fail, then, if expert reports contain proxies for the party that submits them to review. Yet the possible proxies appear to be neither numerous nor insurmountable. Perhaps the quality or style of writing could be a tell, particularly in cases where one party is litigating *pro se*. However, the likelihood of a *pro se* litigant having access to expert evidence is low (a problem in and of itself, but of a different vein). Alternately, perhaps judges serving over many years could become familiar with repeat experts and learn that certain individuals tend to testify on behalf of certain types of litigants. This possibility might be especially acute when the field of experts in a particular discipline is relatively small. Perhaps, then, the expert's name should also be redacted from the party-blind submission materials.

Here is another possible proxy. Perhaps certain methods will be used by some types of litigants more often than others. For instance, most forensic evidence in criminal cases is introduced by the prosecution. Hence, a judge who is biased in favor of prosecutors might adopt a more lenient approach to expert admissibility in criminal cases across the board than they do in civil disputes. The result would be more equalized treatment of prosecution and criminal defense evidence, but not a full elimination of bias. Still, it would contain judicial bias to some degree and improve over the status quo.

A final caveat is in order. Blind briefing is a targeted solution for judicial *bias* in the application of the expert evidence rules. It would not solve the great epistemic challenge of tasking non-expert judges with evaluating the quality of expert

52 Thank you to Bennett Capers for suggesting this "double-blind" extension of my blind-review proposal to a specialized, alternate court.

53 Cofone, *supra* note 39, at 1408.

54 Ignacio N. Cofone, *Antidiscriminatory Privacy*, 72 SMU L. REV. 139, 143–4 (2019).

55 Cofone, *supra* note 39, at 1408.

methods.[56] Nor would it necessarily increase overall accuracy. After all, judges could eliminate the bias in their decisions by leveling down, wrongly admitting exceedingly unreliable evidence from all types of litigants rather than just from some. Yet party-blind review could chip away at this broader epistemic problem to the extent that bias contributes to it. For instance, party identity might be distracting judges from focusing on the substance of a proposed expert's method. Regardless of how one thinks judges should undertake the epistemic task of evaluating expert methods, judging based on the identity of the proffering party should not be part of the process.

CONCLUSION

This chapter has been motivated by empirical and anecdotal evidence indicating that judges require more rigorous showings of reliability to admit expert evidence from civil mass tort plaintiffs and criminal defendants than they require to admit similar expert evidence from prosecutors. This bias in the application of the expert evidence rules threatens accuracy, fairness, justice, and judicial legitimacy. Moreover, when layered on top of preexisting disparities in the legal system and beyond, including disparities regarding wealth and race, biased application of the expert evidence rules is almost certain to disproportionately harm groups of people who are already comparatively disadvantaged.

To attempt to curtail this bias, the chapter has made both diagnostic and prescriptive contributions. Diagnostically, the chapter challenged the prevailing view that the expert evidence rules embodied in FRE 702 and the *Daubert* doctrine constrain judges by imposing a gatekeeping duty to exclude evidence that falls below some minimum threshold of reliability. On the contrary, the rules fail to set such a threshold and, as a result, merely expand judicial discretion regarding expert evidence admissibility rulings. That expanded discretion invites bias.

Prescriptively, the chapter has proposed that judges should review expert evidence for admissibility without knowing which party has proffered the expert. This would require two stages of review. The first stage should focus on the expert's foundational methods and should be blind to both the identity of the party seeking to introduce the expert's testimony and the expert's as-applied conclusions. If the judge deems the methods sufficiently reliable to admit, then the results of applying the method in the given case should be disclosed and reviewed in the second stage. This approach would curtail bias in expert admissibility determinations, helping to move the law of evidence towards improved accuracy, fairness, justice, and integrity.

56 *See, e.g.*, Edward K. Cheng, *The Consensus Rule: A New Approach to Scientific Evidence*, 75 Vand. L. Rev. 407 (2022); Ronald J. Allen and Joseph S. Miller, *The Common Law Theory of Experts: Deference or Education?*, 87 Nw. U. L. Rev. 1131 (1993).

Unequal Burdens of Proof

Racism, Legal Epistemic Injustice, and Opinion Testimony

Jasmine B. Gonzales Rose

INTRODUCTION

The poet Maya Angelou once said that there is "no greater agony than bearing an untold story inside you."[1] The agony of an untold story seems particularly acute when a person is unheard or disbelieved in a courtroom. When one cannot testify or have their testimony believed, the facts of their story – their truth – for all practical purposes, do not exist in the determination of their case. When a person's story relates to racism and they have been silenced or not fully believed due to structural bias in evidence rules, attorneys' evidentiary practices, the judge's gatekeeping of evidence, or fact finders' conclusions, it constitutes a profound legal epistemic injustice that warrants evidentiary intervention. This chapter examines the historical and contemporary silencing of evidence of racism as a form of legal epistemic injustice and explores the potential role of lay and expert opinion testimony in addressing this injustice.

This chapter adds to the growing scholarly project of interrogating evidence law as a site of racial subordination and racial advantage by exemplifying how evidentiary rules and practices perpetuate racial inequities in terms of whose racialized experiences are known, considered, and believed. Racialized patterns of credibility excess and deficit – where the testimony and lived experiences of white individuals are more readily believed, and those of people of color are more often disbelieved – contribute to disproportionate evidentiary burdens for people of color. This reflects deep epistemic distortions embedded within evidence law itself. These epistemic and evidentiary harms should be affirmatively remedied through evidentiary mechanisms designed to bolster belief and knowledge of racism. One way to do this is to employ Federal Rules of Evidence 701 and 702, and their state counterparts, to introduce lay and expert opinion testimony to help judges and juries better understand racism and minoritized racial experiences. What follows seeks to expose the persistence of unequal evidentiary burdens in proving racism – echoes of evidence

[1] Maya Angelou, I Know Why the Caged Bird Sings (Random House 1969).

law's overtly racist past – and to prompt more liberal admission and widespread use of anti-racist lay and expert opinion testimony, while noting its limitations.

HISTORICAL SILENCING OF EVIDENCE OF RACISM

Historically and currently, people of color have not been able to be fully heard in court concerning their experiences of racism. Race-based witness competency laws – statutes and judicial decrees – existed in the majority of U.S. jurisdictions through the late nineteenth century.[2] Some of these laws barred people of color from testifying altogether, while others prohibited people of color from testifying in cases involving or against a white person.[3] For example, the California Crimes and Punishments Act of 1850 stated: "no black or mulatto person, or Indian, shall be permitted to give evidence in favor of or against any white person."[4] The California Civil Practice Act of 1850 similarly provided that "[n]o Indian or Negro shall be allowed to testify as a witness in any action in which a White person is a party."[5] Such racial testimony restrictions explicitly gave white litigants an evidentiary advantage and put litigants of color at an evidentiary disadvantage. This harm was not merely epistemic or dignitary; it undermined access to justice. People of color could not obtain legal redress for racial violence and other wrongs against them, as they were often unable to present evidence.

While race-based witness competency rules explicitly excluded Black people, and to a lesser degree Indigenous people, they were interpreted to apply broadly to people of color. For instance, while the California statutes only named Black and American Indian people, in the 1854 case of *People v. Hall*, the California Supreme Court held that Chinese eyewitnesses to the murder of a Chinese victim by a white perpetrator should not have been allowed to testify.[6] The *Hall* court held that California's Crime and Punishment Act excludes all races other than white people from testifying.[7] Additionally, Mexican Americans were deemed incompetent to testify because they were mestizos – people with a mix of Native American and Spanish ancestry.[8] In addition to the western states, several northern and almost all

2 Alfred Avins, *The Right to Be a Witness and the Fourteenth Amendment*, 31 Mo. L. Rev. 471, 473 (1966) (referencing Senator Charles Sumner's report *To Secure Equality before the Law in the Courts of the United States*, S. Rep. No. 38–25, at 2–6 (1864)).

3 *Id.* at 474–5.

4 Crimes and Punishments Act, ch. 99, § 14, 1850 Cal. Stat. 229, 231.

5 Civil Practice Act, ch. 142, § 394, 1850 Cal. Stat. 428, 447.

6 People v. Hall, 4 Cal. 399, 404 (1854); *see* Gabriel J. Chin, *"A Chinaman's Chance" in Court: Asian Pacific Americans and Racial Rules of Evidence*, 3 U.C. Irvine L. Rev. 965 (2013).

7 Hall, 4 Cal. at 405.

8 *See* Ian F. Haney López, Racism on Trial: The Chicano Fight for Justice 66 (Harvard University Press 2009) (discussing Manuel Domínguez's case); Juan F. Perea et al., Race and Races: Cases and Resources for a Diverse America 296 (3d ed., West 2015) (same).

southern states barred people of color from testifying.[9] Race-based witness competency laws were pervasive, far-reaching, and even enforced by the Supreme Court.[10]

Race-based witness competency rules were not the only legal provisions used to deny people of color the opportunity to testify. The Fugitive Slave Act of 1850, notorious for its summary proceedings overseen by commissioners who had a financial incentive to find that Black people were enslaved, also imposed racial testimony restrictions.[11] The Act explicitly silenced Black people accused of escape, stating that "in no trial or hearing under this act shall the testimony of such alleged fugitive be admitted in evidence," thereby making a ruling in the targeted person's favor effectively impossible.[12] The Act had a formal but meaningless opportunity for appeal. People could appeal these summary rulings in the state they were removed to, but southern states had evidentiary presumptions that Black people were enslaved,[13] which were nearly impossible to refute without the ability to present evidence.

While alleged fugitives could not testify on their own behalf, white enslavers could testify and call white expert witnesses. These experts testified based on pseudoscience that the alleged fugitive's skull shape, voice, hair, or other features showed they were Black and accordingly enslaved.[14] These trials also admitted character and opinion evidence testimony to prove the accused was Black and therefore enslaved. This character and opinion evidence related to whether the person was accepted in white society, had exercised political rights, or had moral qualities seen as characteristic of whiteness, such as "worth, honesty, industry and respectability."[15] Race-based witness competency rules, summary proceedings under the Fugitive Slave Act of 1850, and the use of character and opinion witnesses to establish racial classification reveal how the assumptions that white people are inherently trustworthy and

[9] I. Bennett Capers, *The Unintentional Rapist*, 87 WASH. U. L. REV. 1345, 1377 (2010) (citing THOMAS D. MORRIS, SOUTHERN SLAVERY AND THE LAW, 1619–860, at 239–48 (University of North Carolina Press 1996); Paul Finkelman, *Prelude to the Fourteenth Amendment: Black Legal Rights in the Antebellum North*, 17 RUTGERS L.J. 415, 424–5 (1986); Sheri Lynn Johnson, *The Color of Truth: Race and the Assessment of Credibility*, 1 MICH. J. RACE & L. 261, 267 (1996)).

[10] *See* Blyew v. United States, 80 U.S. 581, 593 (1871).

[11] *See* DON E. FEHRENBACHER AND WARD M. MCAFEE, THE SLAVEHOLDING REPUBLIC: AN ACCOUNT OF THE UNITED STATES GOVERNMENT'S RELATIONS TO SLAVERY 252 (Oxford University Press 2002) (discussing $10 fee paid for commissioners determining a Black person was an escaped slave, but $5 fee paid for determining they were not an escaped slave).

[12] *Id.*

[13] Robert Westley, *Restitution Claims for Wrongful Enslavement and the Doctrine of the Master's Good Faith*, 3 BRIT J. OF AM. LEGAL STUD. 287, 289 (2014).

[14] Ariela Gross, *Litigating Whiteness: Trials of Racial Determination in the Nineteenth-Century South*, 108 YALE L.J. 109, 124–37 (1998) (observing some southern states allowed white guardians to re-enslave free Black people, excluding their testimony from the process). Jasmine E. Harris, *The Political Economy of Conservatorship*, 71 UCLA L. REV. 1364, 1431–2 (2024) (citing An Act Permitting Free Negroes to Select a Master and Become Slaves § 2, 1860 Ala. Laws 63; Alexis Cathcart, *A Black Woman's Story of Sacrifice and Survival*, AFR. AM. INTELL. HIST. SOC'Y (Mar. 21, 2024), https://perma.cc/99AD-5GMB).

[15] Gross, *supra* note 14, at 164 (citing State v. Casey, 20 S.C.L. (2 Hill) 615 (1845)).

non-white people are inherently untrustworthy were foundational to determining who could testify and whose testimony was believed.[16] Evidence law and practices controlled which races could tell their truth and be believed and, consequently, receive or be denied legal protection. While these overt exclusions are no longer codified, their epistemic impacts remain entrenched.

CONTEMPORARY SILENCING OF EVIDENCE OF RACISM

Vestiges of the aforementioned historical evidentiary rules and practices, which centered notions of white veracity and non-white unbelievability, endure. Once people of color were no longer explicitly barred from testifying as witnesses on the basis of race, their credibility was attacked and diminished in other ways. For instance, prosecutors argued that Black witnesses were inherently unreliable or should not be trusted because they lie to protect other Black people.[17] This sort of problematic racial logic is consistent with immigration rules that required Chinese individuals to present white witnesses to prove residence,[18] and with Second World War policies that presumed Japanese Americans were disloyal, regardless of individual evidence.[19] When overt racial attacks on witness believability became frowned upon, the epistemic diminishment became more subtle. Today, there are at least three interconnected ways in which the believability of witnesses of color is diminished: (1) racial character evidence; (2) prior conviction impeachment; and (3) the interaction of white normativity with the differing treatment of evidence related to the racialized realities of white people versus people of color.

As Montré Carodine,[20] Mikah Thompson,[21] and Julia Simon-Kerr[22] have elucidated, racial character evidence – the use of a person's race and associated racial stereotypes, to infer their character traits or conduct – is surreptitiously presented to

[16] *See, e.g.*, Kenneth S. Greenberg, *The Nose, the Lie, and the Duel in the Antebellum South*, 95 AM. HIST. REV. 57, 65 (1990) (discussing how enslavers believed their words must be accepted as true "simply because they were the words of a man of honor" and believed that "slaves lied all the time – and that their lies were intimately connected to their position as slaves").

[17] Johnson, *supra* note 9, at 267 (discussing cases where prosecutors argued Black people were inherently untrustworthy and where prosecutors argued Black people willingly lie for each other in early twentieth century).

[18] Fong Yue Ting v. United States, 149 U.S. 698 (1893).

[19] Korematsu v. United States, 323 U.S. 214 (1944).

[20] Montré D. Carodine, *"The Mis-Characterization of the Negro": A Race Critique of the Prior Conviction Impeachment Rule*, 84 IND. L.J. 521, 527 (2009); Montré D. Carodine, *Contemporary Issues in Critical Race Theory: The Implications of Race as Character Evidence in Recent High-Profile Cases*, 75 U. PITT. L. REV. 679, 687 (2014).

[21] Mikah K. Thompson, *Blackness as Character Evidence*, 29 MICH. J. RACE & L. 321, 335–40 (2015); Mikah K. Thompson, *Bias on Trial: Toward an Open Discussion of Racial Stereotypes in the Courtroom*, 2018 MICH. ST. L. REV. 1243 (2019).

[22] Julia Simon-Kerr, *Credibility by Proxy*, 85 GEO. WASH. L. REV. 152 (2017).

and considered by juries to assess witnesses' credibility and knowledge.[23] Jurors too often rely on this de facto evidence without prompting, or opportunistic attorneys employ "stereotype emphasis evidence" to enflame racial stereotypes about a group, thus portraying the witness as less credible, less knowledgeable, or more likely to be a wrongdoer.[24] This could entail highlighting a witness's grooming, attire, interests, manner of speech, or activities to suggest they fit a stereotype of a racial minority deemed untrustworthy or unknowledgeable. An example of this is the treatment of Rachel Jeantel, a key fact witness in the George Zimmerman trial for his vigilante killing of teenager Trayvon Martin.[25] Defense counsel highlighted and amplified racial stereotypes by expressing skepticism, impatience, feigned confusion, and condescension in response to Ms. Jeantel's use of African American Vernacular English, appearance, demeanor, and inability to read cursive[26] – markers that were deliberately emphasized to invoke racist and classist stereotypes portraying her as inherently unknowledgeable and untrustworthy.

Inherent and provoked implicit racial bias among jurors leads to Black, Latine, Indigenous, and other racially minoritized witnesses, especially those who do not perform whiteness in the courtroom, being viewed as less credible and believable than white witnesses.[27] At the same time, racial character evidence works in the reverse to bolster the character of white (or comparatively racially privileged) witnesses who are seen as more impartial, accurate, knowledgeable, and honest.[28] Because racial character evidence operates below the evidentiary admission radar, it escapes the evidentiary scrutiny applied to character evidence. This allows bias to replace legitimate evidential reasoning. Consequently, racial character evidence boosts white witnesses' believability and diminishes the believability of witnesses of color.[29]

Prior conviction impeachment is another evidentiary mechanism that undermines the believability of witnesses of color. Under prior conviction impeachment

[23] *See* Jasmine B. Gonzales Rose, *Toward a Critical Race Theory of Evidence*, 101 MINN. L. REV. 2243, 2262–3 (2017); *see also*, Chris Chambers Goodman, *The Color of Our Character: Confronting the Racial Character of Rule 404(b) Evidence*, 25 L. & INEQ. 1, 3 (2007).

[24] *See* Jasmine B. Gonzales Rose, *Racial Character Evidence in Police Killing Cases*, 2018 WIS. L. REV. 369, 405–8 (2018).

[25] *See George Zimmerman Trial: Friend's Full Testimony*, CBS NEWS (Jun. 26, 2013), www.cbsnews.com/video/george-zimmerman-trial-friends-full-testimony/.

[26] *George Zimmerman Murder Trial*, CNN: TRANSCRIPTS (June 27, 2013), https://transcripts.cnn.com/show/ng/date/2013-06-27/segment/01; *see also*, John R. Rickford and Sharese King, *Language and Linguistics on Trial: Hearing Rachel Jeantel (and Other Vernacular Speakers) in the Courtroom and Beyond*, 92 LINGUISTIC SOC'Y OF AM. 948, 978–9 (2016).

[27] *See* Johnson, *supra* note 9, at 276–303 (analyzing four modern (post-1970) cases to show how juror bias influences Black witness credibility); Amanda Carlin, *The Courtroom as White Space: Racial Performance as Noncredibility*, 63 UCLA L. REV. 450, 471, 477–84 (2016) (noting juror credibility in George Zimmerman trial more negative when minority witnesses do not "perform whiteness").

[28] Johnson, *supra* note 9, at 306.

[29] *See* I. Bennett Capers, *Evidence Without Rules*, 94 NOTRE DAME L. REV. 867, 885–95 (2019).

rules, like Federal Rule of Evidence 609 and state equivalents, a witness's prior criminal conviction can be introduced to challenge their credibility for truthfulness. George Fisher has articulated the historical connection between race-based witness competency rules that precluded Black witnesses and the development of Rule 609.[30] Structural racism – both systemic and institutional – leads to people of color being more policed, stopped, searched, arrested, charged, coerced into pleas, found guilty, and subjected to harsher sentencing than white people.[31] As a result, people of color are more likely to have felony convictions, which can then be introduced after they testify, undermining their believability. If the would-be witness with a prior conviction is a criminal defendant, they may opt not to testify out of fear that their prior conviction will lead to a guilty verdict once the jury learns of their criminal record.[32] When the defendant is a person of color, this risk is amplified because stereotypes linking criminality to Black, Brown, and Indigenous people are emphasized and confirmed through the introduction of their prior convictions. As Anna Roberts, Julia Simon-Kerr, Montré Carodine, Bennett Capers, and Marsha Griggs have illuminated, prior conviction impeachment thus serves as a mechanism that gives evidentiary weight to the products of structural racism, disproportionately diminishes the testimonial capacity of people of color, and serves to limit protection under the law.[33]

The believability of witnesses of color is further diminished through the interaction of white normativity with differential treatment of majoritized versus minoritized racialized reality evidence. White normativity is the idea that white experiences are the natural, normal baseline.[34] Racialized reality evidence refers to proof of how one experiences race, racialization, and racism.[35] Put together, a white racialized reality is one where race, racialization, and preferential racial treatment might go unnoticed because whiteness and the treatment associated with it are perceived as the norm. On the other hand, the racialized reality of a person of color is one where race, racialization, and disfavored racial treatment are ever-present but not fully captured or acknowledged in the legal system.

30 George Fisher, *The Jury's Rise as a Lie Detector*, 107 YALE L.J. 575 (1997).

31 *See generally*, MICHELLE ALEXANDER, THE NEW JIM CROW: MASS INCARCERATION IN THE AGE OF COLORBLINDNESS (The New Press 2010).

32 Valerie P. Hans and Theodore Eisenberg, *Taking a Stand on Taking the Stand: The Effect of a Prior Criminal Record on the Decision to Testify and on Trial Outcomes*, 94 CORNELL L. REV. 1353, 1370 (2009); Jeffrey Bellin, *The Silence Penalty*, 103 IOWA L. REV. 395, 397–9 (2018).

33 Jasmine B. Gonzales Rose, *Race, Evidence, and Epistemic Injustice*, *in* PHILOSOPHICAL FOUNDATION OF EVIDENCE LAW (Christian Dahlman, Alex Stein, and Giovanni Tuzet eds., Oxford University Press 2021); Carodine, *supra* note 20, at 527; Capers, *supra* note 29, at 890–2; *see generally*, Anna Roberts, *Reclaiming the Importance of the Defendant's Testimony: Prior Conviction Impeachment and the Fight Against Implicit Stereotyping*, 83 U. CHI. L. REV. 835 (2016); Anna Roberts and Julia Simon-Kerr, *Reforming Prior Conviction Impeachment*, 50 FORDHAM URB. L.J. 377, 392–5 (2023); Marsha Griggs, *Race, Rules, and Disregarded Reality*, 82 OHIO ST. L.J. 931 (2021).

34 *See* PATRICIA WILLIAMS, SEEING A COLOR-BLIND FUTURE: THE PARADOX OF RACE 6 (Virago 1997).

35 Gonzales Rose, *supra* note 23, at 2244.

A tangible example is the different racialized experiences presented by the presence of an armed police officer in an alley. The officer's presence might influence whether a white person or a person of color feels more or less safe walking down that alley. If a person of color's avoidance of the alley was introduced to prove their consciousness of guilt, this would be an example of white racialized reality evidence. Here, the dominant white racialized experience – where police officers are perceived to increase safety – is the norm, accepted without proof. However, the racialized reality of Black, Latine, and Indigenous people – that taking a different route is prudent to avoid racial profiling or brutality and to increase personal safety – is not automatically considered.

Three additional examples of common white racialized reality evidence follow: (1) violent lyrics in white-associated genres of music (like country music) are fictitious; but violent lyrics in genres of music associated with people of color (like rap and reggaeton) are viewed as autobiographical;[36] (2) clothing and accessories associated with white people are not affiliated with crime, but styles associated with Black and Brown communities are indicative of criminal lifestyles, including gang affiliation;[37] (3) socializing occurs in private spaces with community members who have not been over-policed, racially profiled, or unfairly placed in gang databases; and thus those who interact with people or areas identified with gangs must be gang affiliated themselves.[38] In each of these instances, white racialized experiences are presumed true, while people of color's racialized experiences – fictional music, common clothing, everyday socializing – are disbelieved because they diverge from the dominant norm.

Since fact finders are disproportionately white, evidence reinforcing a white racialized worldview is often fast-tracked to the jury, with minimal formal evidence or scrutiny to challenge its relevance or potential unfair prejudice.[39] The perceived dangerousness and criminality of flight, rap, style, and proximity to individuals identified as gang members or within gang territory are introduced through commonsense reasoning, implicit judicial notice, or collective understanding.[40] White racialized reality is accepted as fact, while the racialized reality of people of color is neither known nor believed. In this way, white normativity, white privileged experience, and negative perceptions associated with Blackness, Brownness, and Indigeneity receive preferential evidentiary treatment.

Conversely, witnesses of color must obtain and introduce evidence that refutes white norms, proves Black, Latine, and Indigenous racialized realities, or demonstrates the

[36] Erik Nielson and Andrea L. Dennis, Rap on Trial: Race, Lyrics, and Guilt in America (The New Press 2019); Carrie B. Fried, *Who's Afraid of Rap: Differential Reactions to Music Lyrics*, 29 J. Applied Soc. Psych. 705, 709–11 (1999).

[37] Jasmine B. Gonzales Rose, Asees Bhasin, and Spencer Piston, *Antiracist Expert Evidence*, 134 Yale L.J. 2362, 2377 (2025).

[38] *Id.* at 2376–7.

[39] Gonzales Rose, *supra* note 23, at 2245.

[40] *Id.* at 2299.

existence and operation of racism. When people of color want to refute such white racialized reality evidence or prove their racialized reality – how racism operates and impacts their daily lives – they have to secure and introduce evidence which is subject to the full rigors of evidentiary scrutiny.[41] A litigant of color has to produce formal evidence if they want to prove that avoidance of law enforcement was not evidence of guilt but rather a response to racial profiling and brutality; that rap and reggaeton music employ metaphor and fantasy rather than reflecting the actual lawlessness of the artist; that popular styles are not gang garb; and that living in one's neighborhood is not demonstrative of gang affiliation.[42] Evidence of racism or racialized reality of people of color could be proven in a variety of ways: judicial notice, factual witness testimony, lay opinion testimony,[43] and expert opinion testimony. However, producing evidence takes significant resources, time, and evidentiary effort.

Similar to how witnesses of color are disbelieved due to racial bias or credibility reduction through prior conviction impeachment, evidence of the racialized experiences of people of color are also disbelieved. This leads to disproportionate belief and unequal evidentiary scrutiny along racial lines. Evidence that validates whiteness and the white racialized reality of how systems, institutions, and society operate is privileged in evidentiary terms, while the counter-perspective of people of color is relatively subordinated. Instead of believing the racialized lived experiences of people of color – just as white racialized experiences are believed – litigants of color are required to prove them. When litigants of color must prove their racialized reality through tangible, formal evidence – while white litigants do not – it amounts to comparative disbelief, where racially privileged people are seen as full, credible knowers, and racially minoritized people are not. Not believing people on the basis of race and the higher evidentiary burden placed on people of color to prove their racialized experiences of racism constitute epistemic injustice, and more specifically legal epistemic injustice.

EPISTEMIC INJUSTICE

Miranda Fricker introduced the concept of "epistemic injustice," describing it as "a wrong against someone in their capacity as a knower,"[44] and identifying two forms: "testimonial injustice" and "hermeneutical injustice."[45] Testimonial injustice arises

41 *Id.* at 2365.

42 *Id.*

43 Bohannon v. Pegelow, 652 F.2d 729, 732–3 (7th Cir. 1981) (holding lay opinion testimony from an eyewitness suggesting that the arrest was motivated by racial bias permissible); Hogan v. American Tel. & Tel. Co., 812 F.2d 409, 411–12 (8th Cir. 1987) (holding lay-opinion testimony in race discrimination case allowed to reach ultimate issue on discrimination permissible).

44 Miranda Fricker, Epistemic Injustice: Power and the Ethics of Knowing 1 (Oxford University Press 2007).

45 *Id.*

where a speaker's credibility is unfairly diminished due to the hearer's prejudice.[46] Hermeneutical injustice is "the injustice of having some significant area of one's social experience obscured from collective understanding owing to a structural identity prejudice in the collective hermeneutical resource."[47] Legal epistemic injustice is particularly concerning because it produces real consequences for litigants, witnesses, and those who would seek legal recourse if it were available.

Legal epistemic injustice harms individuals as legal subjects by impairing their capacity to contribute knowledge within the legal system.[48] This can take the form of testimonial injustice, such as when a witness's account is unjustly discounted due to bias by a fact finder or advocate acting as a hearer.[49] Such injustice is exacerbated when a more privileged individual receives undue credibility by contrast, deepening the inequity. Hermeneutical injustice arises when gaps in the law's shared interpretive framework render marginalized or minoritized individuals – such as litigants or would-be claimants – unable to effectively articulate their experiences in legally cognizable terms, leaving them at a structural disadvantage.[50] The inequitable evidentiary practices – both historical and contemporary – described above exemplify legal epistemic injustice in both its testimonial and hermeneutical forms.

Pre-Reconstruction statutes, rules, and practices barring people of color from testifying exemplify blatant testimonial injustice. During this period, people of color were categorically deemed too unreliable to testify due to their race, regardless of their knowledge or character. Today, implicit racial biases of fact finders – who rely on stereotypes to assess credibility and knowledge – and the actions of attorneys who exacerbate these biases through the use of racially charged evidence perpetuate testimonial injustice. In these instances, fact finders' racially biased assumptions overshadow the legitimate factual content of the witness's testimony, undermining fair and rightful belief in the witness as a reliable knower. Further, prior conviction impeachment rules disproportionately prevent defendants of color from testifying in their own defense.

While Fricker emphasized "credibility deficit," testimonial injustice also encompasses the epistemic wrong of "credibility excess," particularly in adversarial court proceedings[51] where white witnesses receive undue presumptions of knowledge,

46 *Id.* at 17.

47 *Id.* at 155.

48 Jasmine B. Gonzales Rose, *Critical Race Theory as Legal Epistemic Justice*, 104 B.U. L. Rev. 1295, 1308 (2024).

49 *Id.*

50 *Id.* at 1308–9.

51 Jasmine Gonzales Rose, *A Critical Perspective on Testimonial Injustice: Interrogating Witnesses' Credibility Excess in Criminal Trials*, 7 Quaestio Facti Int'l J. Evidential Reasoning 173, 173–85 (2024) (citing Emmalon Davis, *Typecasts, Tokens, and Spokespersons: A Case for Credibility Excess as Testimonial Injustice*, 31 Hypatia 3 (2016); Sarah Lackey, Criminal Testimonial Injustice 32 (Oxford University Press 2023); Jose Medina, *The Relevance of Credibility Excess in a Proportional View of Epistemic Injustice: Differential Epistemic Authority and the Social Imaginary*, 25 Soc. Epistemology 1, 17–19 (2011)).

impartiality, honesty, and reliability while witnesses of color are presumed the opposite. These epistemic asymmetries diminish the weight of testimony from witnesses of color and entrench systemic inequality in the evidentiary legal system. As a result, witnesses of color must overcome greater evidentiary hurdles to establish credibility, particularly when testifying about racism or other racialized experiences.

The heightened evidentiary burden placed on people of color to prove racism reflects a distinct layer of testimonial injustice. Courts and jurors often discount these firsthand accounts, treating them as less reliable than dominant interpretive frameworks, thereby reinforcing the legal system's devaluation of racially minoritized knowledge. In contrast, white racialized perspectives are rarely scrutinized and often treated as commonsense, even when not explicitly introduced as evidence.

As José Medina observes, testimonial justice cannot exist without hermeneutical justice.[52] Hermeneutical injustice – structural marginalization in collective meaning-making – exacerbates testimonial injustice by obstructing fair understanding and placing marginalized individuals at a conceptual disadvantage.[53] It arises when the social experiences of marginalized groups are hidden or misrecognized due to interpretive gaps.[54] The evidentiary practices above exemplify this: dominant interpretive frameworks privilege white perspectives and experiences, particularly in defining what counts as everyday, innocent life and in recognizing how racism operates.

When people of color cannot fully testify and have their experiences of racism and racialized realities believed, the legal system's collective epistemic resources on racism remain narrow and rooted in a dominant racial experience. This exclusion reinforces a status quo where the knowledge and experiences of racially privileged groups dominate, leaving little room for the voices of those who experience racism firsthand. The systematic devaluation of testimony about racism from people of color contributes to hermeneutical injustice: people of color's lived experiences are inadequately represented and the law fails to evolve to address racism effectively. In turn, fewer racially minoritized people have access to legal justice.

Historically, evidence law imposed testimonial silencing that barred people of color from testifying about racial violence or challenging their enslavement status. Today, evidentiary law and practices continue to limit whose knowledge is heard and credited in court, often discrediting witnesses of color and privileging dominant racial perspectives over minoritized experiences. Applying an epistemic injustice lens to this enduring problem exposes how people of color are hindered in contributing knowledge about racialized experiences, including racism. This framework clarifies the need for targeted evidentiary reform to increase more equitable

[52] Medina, *supra* note 51, at 20.

[53] FRICKER, *supra* note 44, at 155.

[54] *Id.* at 1.

pathways to introduce racialized knowledge. Permitting lay and expert opinion testimony on racism offers a concrete way to address the systemic exclusion of knowledge of racism and minoritized racial experiences.

OPINION TESTIMONY

One under-utilized intervention within the existing evidence framework to address this legal epistemic injustice is the more liberal admission of anti-racist opinion testimony from both lay and expert witnesses.[55] Opinion testimony on racism could be helpful in some[56] cases where parties need to prove racism or minoritized racialized reality. This does not mean that anti-racist opinion witnesses – particularly those who are people of color – will ultimately be believed. But it is an evidence intervention that could facilitate knowledge on minoritized racial experiences and racism to mitigate some ignorance or disbelief of racism and the lived experiences of people of color.

Anti-racist opinion testimony could come in the form of lay opinion or expert opinion testimony, which are governed by Federal Rules of Evidence 701 and 702 respectively. Rule 701 applies to lay opinion testimony, providing a framework for admitting testimony from non-expert witnesses who offer opinions based on their personal knowledge and experience. Rule 701 permits such testimony if it satisfies three specific criteria. First, the opinion must be "rationally based on the witness's perception."[57] A lay opinion witness could testify about acts and expressions of racism that they have observed and provide an opinion that these actions were indeed racist. Unlike a fact witness, whose testimony is confined to direct observations of specific events at issue, an opinion witness may offer insights informed by patterns, context, or lived experience that extend beyond the discrete incidents being litigated. Such testimony allows the witness to offer an informed opinion on the racist nature of the conduct of actors or its impact on a community, drawing on their firsthand experience with similar incidents or other direct observations that shape their understanding of racial bias or subordination, short of specialized knowledge.

Second, lay opinion testimony must be "helpful to clearly understanding the witness's testimony or to determining a fact in issue."[58] This requirement centers on whether the opinion assists the fact finder in comprehending facts that may not be adequately conveyed through factual descriptions. For instance, a lay opinion witness's testimony about repeatedly observing acts of racial profiling by local law enforcement could shed light on broader behavioral patterns, directly aiding the jury in understanding evidence of racial profiling or brutality. Racism, especially in

55 *See* Gonzales Rose et al., *supra* note 37, at 2367.
56 *Id.*
57 FED. R. EVID. 701(a).
58 FED. R. EVID. 701(b).

its subtler or ostensibly "colorblind" forms, can be challenging for jurors to grasp, especially those who are racially privileged. Given that white Americans are disproportionately represented on juries, many jurors may lack firsthand experiences with racism.

Finally, lay opinion testimony must "not [be] based on scientific, technical, or other specialized knowledge within the scope of Rule 702."[59] This limitation distinguishes lay from expert testimony, which requires specialized qualifications. A lay witness may testify about their personal experiences and observations of racism, but they cannot provide sociological, psychological, anthropological, or other scientific analyses, statistical insights, or conclusions rooted in academic frameworks of structural racism unless they are properly qualified as an expert. When applied to evidence of racism in a community, Rule 701 provides a pathway for individuals to testify about observed racially discriminatory, biased, and subordinating behaviors or practices, as well as the ways in which these actions affect the community.

When opinion testimony is based on specialized knowledge, it can be introduced under Rule 702, which governs expert witness testimony. Rule 702 provides that a person must be "qualified as an expert by knowledge, skill, experience, training, or education"[60] to offer opinion testimony, provided their knowledge is scientific, technical, or specialized. The 1972 Advisory Committee on Proposed Rules, noted that the term "expertise" is broad and includes not only learned professionals, but also skilled individuals with practical experience in their fields.[61] In the context of anti-racism expertise, qualified experts could include scholars, researchers, physicians, data scientists, and organizers or social service providers who work directly with impacted communities of color.

Rule 702 permits a qualified witness to testify in the form of an opinion if their expertise, derived from knowledge, skill, experience, training, or education, can assist the trier of fact in understanding the evidence or determining a fact in issue.[62] Rule 702 provides a framework that ensures the testimony is both relevant and reliable, enabling experts to offer insights on the complex and nuanced dynamics of racial bias, discrimination, and subordination.

Under Rule 702, expert testimony must meet four core criteria. First, the testimony must be relevant and helpful to the trier of fact.[63] There are many factual scenarios that may arise in cases where evidence of racial bias, racial subordination, racial disparities, or race-based animus might be relevant. As racism may be unknown, not understood, demonstrated by statistical disparities, inconspicuous, or obscured, an expert's knowledge might assist the fact finder in understanding the

59 Fed. R. Evid. 701(c).
60 Fed. R. Evid. 702.
61 *Id.* advisory committee's note to 1972 proposed rules.
62 *Id.*
63 Fed. R. Evid. 702(a).

evidence or in resolving an issue in the case. For instance, an expert could analyze and explain racial profiling, targeting, and trauma that leads to Black and Brown flight from police; rap as a musical genre and its use of fantasy and metaphor; over-policing in certain communities; errors and racial bias in gang registries; the meaning of racist terminology or images; as well as other instances where the impact of discriminatory and biased practices and policies on communities or individuals may be relevant.[64]

Second, the expert's testimony must be based on sufficient facts or data.[65] This criterion ensures that the expert's conclusions are grounded in reliable and adequate information. In anti-racist expert testimony, this might include empirical research, historical data, case studies, or fieldwork that provides evidence of racial disparities, discrimination, or the effects of racial prejudice. Experts are expected to draw upon this learned or specialized body of knowledge to substantiate their opinions on the existence or impact of racism.

Third, the expert's testimony must be derived from reliable principles and methods,[66] and their "opinion must reflect a reliable application of the[se] principles."[67] Rule 702 mandates that the methods used by the expert to form their opinion are trustworthy and generally accepted in the field. In the context of anti-racist work, this could involve using established scientific, including quantitative and qualitative, methodologies across the social sciences, health sciences, and humanities to establish the existence of racial bias or to assess the impact of racism in a particular context. For instance, a musicologist might be called to explain the metaphor and fantasy in rap lyrics when they are introduced as autobiographical evidence of criminal behavior; a sociolinguist could clarify the meaning and intent behind racist language or correct the misinterpretation of African American Vernacular English; a criminologist or clinical psychologist specializing in trauma could contextualize a defendant of color's flight from police as a response to racial profiling rather than consciousness of guilt; and a sociologist or criminologist with expertise in racialized policing could challenge the assumption that socializing in over-policed neighborhoods or wearing certain clothing signifies gang affiliation.

From 1923 until the late twentieth century, the admissibility of expert testimony was largely governed by the *Frye* standard, derived from *Frye v. United States*.[68] Under this test, expert evidence was admissible only if the underlying scientific technique or principle was "generally accepted" within the relevant scientific community. The enactment of Rule 702 of the Federal Rules of Evidence in 1975 introduced a new framework for expert testimony, requiring that such testimony be

64 *See* Gonzales Rose et al., *supra* note 37, at 2376 (discussing use of expert witnesses in each of these contexts).

65 Fed. R. Evid. 702(b).

66 Fed. R. Evid. 702(c).

67 Fed. R. Evid. 702(d).

68 Frye v. United States, 293 F. 1013 (D.C. Cir. 1923).

based on scientific, technical, or specialized knowledge and emphasizing reliability as a key factor. However, subsequent concerns about the proliferation of unreliable "junk science" in trials prompted the Supreme Court's landmark decision in *Daubert v. Merrell Dow Pharmaceuticals*, in 1993.[69]

To assist judges in evaluating reliability, the *Daubert* Court outlined five non-exhaustive factors: (1) whether the theory or technique has been tested; (2) whether it has been subjected to peer review and publication; (3) its known or potential error rate; (4) the existence and maintenance of standards controlling its operation; and (5) whether it has gained general acceptance within the relevant scientific community.[70] Later, in *Kumho Tire Co. v. Carmichael*, the Supreme Court extended the *Daubert* standard to non-scientific expert testimony, underscoring the flexibility of the inquiry and recognizing that not all factors apply in every case.[71] The *Daubert-Kumho* standard now governs the admissibility of expert evidence in federal courts and has been adopted by most states, although some variations exist and New York, Pennsylvania, and California continue to use the *Frye* standard.[72]

The *Daubert* standard was originally developed with the so-called "hard" sciences in mind, making it less directly applicable to some recognized methodologies in the social sciences, humanities, and ethnic studies – which are fields that study racism. Despite the *Kumho Tire* Court's emphasis that not all *Daubert* factors must apply, some judges still apply overly rigid interpretations of the standard. This unnecessarily leads to the exclusion of qualified anti-racist expert witnesses whose testimony could provide critical insights into how racism operates or influences a particular case. Such restrictive applications are problematic, as they can prevent fact finders from fully understanding a litigant's experiences with racism. It is crucial to recognize that the *Kumho* standard emphasizes flexibility when evaluating non-scientific expert testimony. Further, evidence rules "should be construed so as to administer every proceeding fairly, eliminate unjustifiable expense and delay, and promote the development of evidence law, to the end of ascertaining the truth and securing a just determination."[73] Thus, Rules 701 and 702 should be read to allow liberal admission of opinion testimony on racism.

Expert and lay opinion testimony on racism can serve as an important evidentiary intervention to educate fact finders about minoritized racial realities, challenge white normativity, and confront the unequal evidentiary burdens imposed along racial lines. However, as Bennett Capers has observed, there is still epistemic injustice in having to call a witness to explain people of color's lived reality of

[69] Daubert v. Merrell Dow Pharms., Inc., 509 U.S. 579 (1993).

[70] *Id.*

[71] Kumho Tire Co. v. Carmichael, 526 U.S. 137, 158 (1998).

[72] *See* Christine Funk, Daubert *Versus* Frye: *A National Look at Expert Evidentiary Standards*, Expert Inst., www.expertinstitute.com/resources/insights/daubert-versus-frye-a-national-look-at-expert-evidentiary-standards/ (last visited July 10, 2024).

[73] Fed. R. Evid. 102.

racism[74] and in having to secure and introduce witnesses in contrast to being able to simply ask or rely on fact finders using their "common sense." Epistemic injustice remains when parties of color have to put on this additional evidence, and is particularly unjust for criminal defendants who have limited litigation budgets and struggle to find anti-racist witnesses – especially expensive experts who may not represent their demographic identities in terms of race, gender, or class.[75] In these ways, while attempting to address epistemic injustice, opinion evidence – particularly expert opinion – continues to perpetuate epistemic injustice and the problem of unequal evidentiary burdens.

Accordingly, while lay and expert opinion testimony on racism is a crucial evidentiary intervention, it is only one part of the reform needed. Courts must also hold parties advancing racially privileged perspectives to the same evidentiary standards as minoritized parties, not to mention equalizing financial and other access to evidence. Instead of accepting white normative assumptions as proof, courts should require proponents to submit actual admissible evidence. For example, when introducing evidence of a defendant of color's flight from law enforcement to establish guilt, the proponent must prove the full chain of inferences – the behavior constitutes flight, the flight indicates consciousness of guilt, the guilt concerns the crime charged, and this guilt points to actual culpability[76] – without relying on white normative assumptions. The proponent should demonstrate, with admissible evidence, that avoidance of the police is not normal, reasonable, justified, or explained by non-guilt factors such as fear of racial profiling, immigration enforcement, or police violence, rather than shifting the burden onto the defendant to disprove the assumption that only the guilty avoid police. Judges must therefore fulfill their gatekeeping role and ensure that all parties are held to equal evidentiary standards. Thus, while opinion testimony on racism is important, it represents only one among several necessary evidentiary interventions to redress epistemic injustice and rectify the unequal evidentiary burdens imposed along racial lines.

CONCLUSION

The legal epistemic injustice that results in litigants of color being disbelieved or silenced about their experiences of racism is not a historical footnote – it is a present and ongoing harm that demands sustained evidentiary intervention. Legal epistemic *justice* requires recognizing all individuals as knowledgeable legal agents capable of contributing meaningful insights. This justice necessitates expanded opportunities to testify – both as lay and expert opinion witnesses – about racism and minoritized

[74] I. Bennett Capers, *Race, Gatekeeping, Magical Words, and the Rules of Evidence*, 76 VAND. L. REV. 1855, 1867 (2023).

[75] *See* Gonzales Rose, *supra* note 23, at 2416–23.

[76] United States v. Myers, 550 F.2d 1035, 1049 (5th Cir. 1977).

racialized realities. Ultimately, anti-racist opinion testimony, while important, is only one intervention among the many needed to confront the discrediting and exclusion of evidence of racism and the marginalization of minoritized racialized perspectives, along with their resulting unequal evidentiary burdens. Courts must become more attuned to racially unequal evidentiary assumptions and apply evidentiary standards more rigorously and equally across all racialized identities. Legal epistemic justice thus requires a comprehensive approach – combining evidentiary innovations, such as opinion testimony, with procedural fairness, and firm judicial commitments to equal evidentiary enforcement that actively work to correct racialized knowledge inequities. This chapter has been an invitation to imagine a legal system where previously unheard stories of racial injustice are no longer silenced, but told and believed.

SECTION 7

Privileges

INTRODUCTION

It is "a fundamental maxim that the public … has the right to every man's evidence."[1] But there is one prominent exception. Even when evidence satisfies the rules associated with relevancy and reliability, that evidence may still be excludable. That is because we deem certain communications privileged, and thus inadmissible in court. Everyone, or almost everyone, has heard of the attorney-client privilege. But in fact, there are a number of federally recognized privileges, running the gamut from the attorney-client privilege to the patient-therapist privilege to the clergy-penitent privilege to marital communications privileges (yes, married couples have two) to the state secrets privilege. Even more privileges exist under state law. In theory, what undergirds all of these privileges is a policy choice: that permitting some communications to remain private and confidential, on balance, can benefit society as a whole. In other words, keeping some communications confidential, however relevant and trustworthy, can further a "public good transcending the normally predominant principle of utilizing all rational means for ascertaining the truth."[2] Interestingly, most of the federal privileges exist not in rules, but in caselaw. This is because in the end, rather than promulgating specific privileges, Congress instead passed Rule 501 of the Federal Rules of Evidence, providing that "common

[1] United States v. Bryan, 339 U.S. 323, 331 (1950) quoting 8 J. WIGMORE, EVIDENCE § 2192, p. 64 (3d ed., 1940).

[2] Trammel v. United States, 445 U.S. 40, 50 (1980).

law – as interpreted by United States courts in the light of reason and experience" will generally govern privileges.

But are the privileges we have "really a public good" for everyone? Or do they benefit some groups at the expense of others? And what might happen if we extended privileges to others beyond the current carveouts? These are the questions taken up in this section. In "Underprivileged: A ClassCrit Perspective on Evidentiary Privileges," Thomas Lininger methodically shows the class-bias inherent in the privileges courts have recognized and explores how to make privileges fairer for everyone. In "Parent-Child Privilege as Resistance," Nila Bala focuses on the lack of privilege for parent-child communications. Bala argues that creating such a privilege is both consistent with Rule 501 and has the potential to provide "refuge, a means of resistance against increasingly punitive systems."

Underprivileged

A ClassCrit Perspective on Evidentiary Privileges

Tom Lininger

INTRODUCTION

In evidence law, a privilege can prevent the discovery or evidentiary use of certain sensitive information. Many privileges apply to communication with specified persons such as lawyers, doctors, psychologists, accountants, clergy, or spouses. A major shortcoming of current privilege law is that it tends to protect relationships that are more common in higher economic strata. Low-income people do not benefit equally from privileges because their relationships are less likely to meet the requirements set forth in statutes and case law.[1] The time has come to level the playing field and extend the valuable protections of evidentiary privileges more uniformly throughout society. Evidentiary privilege should not depend on economic privilege.

WHAT IS A CLASSCRIT PERSPECTIVE?

The author is a member of the ClassCrits scholarly network. This group resolves to "foreground economic injustice" in theorizing a "jurisprudence of law, economic inequality, and class."[2] ClassCrit scholars recognize that inequalities of race, gender, and sexuality intertwine with economic inequality. By focusing on disparate economic impacts, ClassCrit scholars intend to shed light on, rather than distract from, inquiries into racial and other categories of inequality. The law of evidentiary privilege seems particularly deserving of a ClassCrit analysis because in many respects, this law conditions its protections on the ability of the privilege holder to afford expensive professional services.

The author is grateful for helpful suggestions by participants in a colloquium at Fordham Law School on March 28, 2025.

1 *E.g.*, Rebecca Wexler, *Ignorance of the Rules of Omission: An Essay on Privilege Law*, 76 VAND. L. REV. 1609, 1618 (2023) ("Those wealthy enough to hire attorneys and psychiatrists can shield their confidences from compulsory legal process; those who can afford to confide solely in friends and family generally cannot.").

2 *Call for Papers and Participation, ClassCrits XIV*, CLASSCRITS, https://classcrits.org/2024CFP (last visited Feb. 16, 2025).

WHY ARE EVIDENTIARY PRIVILEGES IMPORTANT?

Evidentiary privileges are valuable in litigation. They prevent the questioning of witnesses about certain matters, particularly confidential communications within privileged relationships. Evidentiary privileges also thwart the opposing party's attempt to obtain documents or other information through the discovery process. So great is the protection of an evidentiary privilege that the court itself may not consider privileged information at any time, even though the court may consider most other categories of inadmissible evidence when the court is addressing pretrial questions.[3] There can be no doubt that parties with robust privileges have better odds of winning litigation than do parties with weak privileges: the latter are more vulnerable because they must "show their cards" more frequently to their opponents.

Privilege law reflects the policy judgment that fostering candid, forthright communication in a privileged relationship is worth the cost of excluding evidence.[4] Society benefits when there is repose in privileged relationships – such as the spousal relationship, the doctor-patient relationship, or the clergy-penitent relationship – so that people in those relationships can share secrets without inhibition. Privileged relationships provide refuge and solace, and give the privilege holders freedom to discuss sensitive topics without fear. The strong connections that privileges facilitate can strengthen society as a whole.

An evidentiary privilege protects the liberty and dignity of the privilege holder.[5] Individual rights – such as the right against self-incrimination, the right to religious freedom, and the right to reproductive freedom – are more secure when evidentiary privileges are strong and outsiders cannot extract information that might lead to infringement of these rights. Evidentiary privilege law reflects the deontological notion that the privilege holder is an autonomous moral agent who cannot be a means to some other end.

Law enforcement agencies are less likely to conduct surveillance of communication within privileged relationships, such as communication between lawyers and their clients. Under certain circumstances, courts could determine that a search or seizure of privileged information is unreasonable under the Fourth Amendment.[6]

[3] FED. R. EVID. 104(a) (indicating that when a court makes rulings on preliminary questions, "the court is not bound by evidence rules, except those on privilege").

[4] For a general discussion of the utilitarian case in favor of evidentiary privileges, *see* 8 JOHN HENRY WIGMORE, WIGMORE ON EVIDENCE § 2285, at 527 (McNaughton rev. 1961) (laying out instrumentalist rationale for privileges); but *see* JEREMEY BENTHAM, THE WORKS OF JEREMY BENTHAM, 441, 473–5 (John Bowring ed. 1843) (deploring social costs of attorney-client privilege because it helps the guilty to go free, while the innocent have nothing to hide).

[5] For a general discussion of the humanistic case in favor of evidentiary privileges, *see* Edward Imwinkelried, *The New Wigmore: An Essay on Rethinking the Foundation of Evidentiary Privileges*, 83 B.U. L. REV. 315, 325–42 (2003) (discussing various rationales under rubric of "humanistic theory, based on autonomy or decisional privacy").

[6] To be sure, police surveillance or seizure of information subject to the attorney-client privilege is not automatically a violation of the Fourth Amendment, but some scholars have pointed out that the

Even when police do not foresee constitutional problems with particular evidence, they may be reluctant to collect it if they expect that prosecutors would be unable to use it due to privilege objections.[7] Furthermore, to the extent that prosecutors must direct or supervise certain categories of surveillance, prosecutors must operate under rules that limit the gathering of privileged information.[8] Prosecutors also must refrain from calling lawyers to be grand jury witnesses concerning communication with their clients and other privileged matters.[9] These rules create, to varying degrees, zones of privacy in which people can be free from spying by the government. People who lack such privacy are more vulnerable to police investigations and prosecution.

WHY IS CURRENT PRIVILEGE LAW UNFAIR TO LOW-INCOME COMMUNITIES?

A review of several evidentiary privileges shows that these privileges are of greater benefit to well-off people. The application of a privilege to a particular communication often turns on the credentials of the audience. Low-income people sometimes cannot afford to hire the professionals with whom communications would qualify for protection. Other privileged relationships, such as spousal relationships and traditional clergy-penitent relationships, are less common at the lower end of the economic spectrum.[10] The privileges listed below are elitist in the sense that they are more likely to apply to higher-income parties.

applicability of the privilege bears on the "reasonable expectation of privacy" test relevant to certain Fourth Amendment protections. *E.g.*, Eric McArthur, Note, *The Search and Seizure of Privileged Attorney-Client Communications*, 72 U. CHI. L. REV. 729, 740–6 (2005) (collecting judicial opinions in which "judges assume that privileged attorney-client communications cannot be searched and seized"); *see* Mihailis Diamantis, *Privileging Privacy: Confidentiality as a Source of Fourth Amendment Protection*, 21 U. PA. J. CONST. L. 485, 521–41 (2018) (recognizing complexity of issue and urging that courts should consider applicability of attorney-client privilege when considering reasonable expectation of privacy under Fourth Amendment).

7 Tom Lininger, *Abortion, the Underground Railroad, and Evidentiary Privilege*, 80 WASH. & LEE L. REV. 663, 706 (2023) ("While privileges do not apply directly to law enforcement personnel, the inability to use evidence in court has an indirect effect on investigative strategies: police generally do not gather evidence that prosecutors cannot use later in court.").

8 *See generally*, MODEL RULES OF PRO. CONDUCT r. 3.8 & 4.4(a) (AM. BAR ASS'N 2020) (imposing special duties on prosecutors and requiring all attorneys to refrain from "methods of obtaining evidence that violate the legal rights" of others); *see* ABA Standards for Crim. Just.: Prosecutorial Investigations std. 2.2(c)(ix), 2.3(d)(vi), 2.4(c)(vi), 2.5(j), 2.7(d)(i), 2.8(h), 2.12(e)(ii) (AM. BAR. ASS'N 2008) (directing prosecutors to avoid infringing privilege when conducting various types of investigations); JUSTICE MANUAL § 9-13.000 "Obtaining Evidence" (U.S. DEP'T OF JUSTICE 2020) (setting forth several procedures to prevent criminal investigations from intercepting privileged information).

9 MODEL RULES OF PRO. CONDUCT r. 3.8(e) (AM. BAR. ASS'N 2020) (prohibiting prosecutors from subpoenaing lawyers to grand jury proceedings when the purpose is to inquire about the lawyers' clients and obtain information "protected from disclosure by any applicable privilege").

10 *Infra* notes 26–33 and accompanying text.

Attorney-Client Privilege

The attorney-client privilege protects against disclosure of confidential communication between an attorney and a client when the purpose of the communication is to give or receive legal services.[11] Studies have consistently shown that low-income people with legal problems are only able to secure the services of counsel about 20 percent of the time.[12] When low-income people do obtain lawyers, they interact less frequently with these lawyers than do wealthier clients.[13] Without adequate access to counsel, low-income people might choose to confer with non-lawyers – for example, a friend or family member, a paralegal or law secretary who lives in the neighborhood – for advice about how to proceed. However, such communication with non-lawyers will be outside the scope of the attorney-client privilege. When unrepresented people decide to proceed pro se (i.e., representing themselves instead of relying on legal counsel), they cannot invoke the attorney-client privilege.[14] They may still avail themselves of the work product doctrine, which applies to information that parties collect in preparation for litigation, but this protection breaks down when opponents demonstrate a "substantial need" for that information.[15] In sum, parties who can afford lawyers are able to buy more secrecy than parties who lack lawyers.

Doctor-Patient Privilege

Communication with doctors, nurses, and other medical personnel is subject to statutory privileges in most states (although not in the federal court system).[16] These privileges are of little avail to low-income people who lack access, or who have only infrequent

[11] Edward Imwinkelried, The New Wigmore: Evidentiary Privileges § 6.2.4 (Aspen 2022) (summarizing attorney-client privilege).

[12] Deborah Rhode, *Access to Justice: An Agenda for Legal Education and Research*, 62 J. Legal Ed. 531, 531 (2013) ("For decades, bar studies have consistently estimated that more than four-fifths of the individual legal needs of the poor … remain unmet"); *see Measuring the Unmet Civil Legal Needs of Low-Income Americans*, Legal Services Corporation (Jun. 2017), www.lsc.gov/our-impact/publications/other-publications-and-reports/2017-justice-gap-report (estimating, based on survey data, that 85% to 97% of civil legal problems experienced by low-income Americans do not receive adequate attention from lawyers).

[13] *E.g.*, Christopher Campbell and Kelsey Henderson, *Bridging the Gap between Clients and Public Defenders: A Structured Shadow Method to Examine Attorney Communication*, 43 Just. Sys. J. 26, 26 (2021) (noting infrequency of meetings between public defenders and clients).

[14] J. Vincent Aprile II, *The Pro Se Litigant and the Work Product Doctrine*, 31 Crim. Just. 35 (2016) ("The attorney-client privilege does not come into play when the accused proceeds pro se as the client and the client's legal representative are one and the same.").

[15] Fed. R. Civ. Proc. 26(b)(3)(A) (setting forth exception to work product doctrine when opponent has "substantial need"); *see* Aprile, *supra* note 14, at 36 (arguing that work product doctrine should apply to a pro se defendant in a criminal case, and expressing concern that without the protection of the work product doctrine, "a pro se litigant is defenseless against intrusion into his or her files").

[16] Iwinkelried, *supra* note 11, at §§ 6.2.7–6.2.8 (discussing medical privileges); Abdullah Azkalay, *A Comparative Examination of the Doctor-Patient Privilege in Federal and State Courts in Iowa*, 67 Drake L. Rev. 495, 500–5 (2019) (summarizing federal law).

access, to medical care.[17] Low-income people might talk with relatives, friends, and neighbors about the best way to deal with health issues, but these communications are not secret, no matter how sensitive. For example, in the wake of the Supreme Court's decision in *Dobbs v. Jackson Women's Health Organization*,[18] low-income people who become pregnant sometimes need to make difficult decisions about whether and how to seek abortions. Whereas a well-off patient contemplating an abortion might discuss options with medical personnel in whom the patient can repose confidence, a low-income person might need to have these discussions with friends and relatives, even strangers online, who are outside the scope of medical privileges – a hazard that could lead to criminal prosecution or civil liability in certain states.[19]

Psychotherapist-Patient Privilege

At both the state and federal levels, there are privileges for certain categories of communication between psychotherapists and their clients.[20] Mental health care is often out of reach for low-income populations, however.[21] The vast majority of psychotherapists are serving wealthy patients.[22] The U.S. Supreme Court has extended the federal psychotherapist-patient privilege to cover certain conversations with social workers,[23] but that approach does not apply uniformly at the state level.[24] Given that

[17] Lilian Witting, *Limited Access: Poverty and Barriers to Accessible Health Care*, Nat'l Health Council (Jan. 20, 2023), https://nationalhealthcouncil.org/blog/limited-access-poverty-and-barriers-to-accessible-health-care/ (citing evidence indicating that "the availability and quality of health care resources are heavily dependent on a patient's financial situation").

[18] 597 U.S. 215 (2022).

[19] Lininger, *supra* note 7, at 673–94, 706–16 (explaining the civil and criminal liability that could befall abortion seekers, abortion providers, and third parties facilitating abortion; arguing that existing privilege law is insufficient to protect low-income people from this potential liability).

[20] Jaffee v. Redmond, 518 U.S. 1, 12–15 (1996) (recognizing federal psychotherapist privilege, and observing that all states have enacted a version of this privilege).

[21] Christi A. Grimm, U.S. Dep't. of Health & Human Servs.: Office of Inspector General, A Lack of Behavioral Health Providers in Medicare and Medicaid Impedes Enrollees' Access to Care (2024), https://oig.hhs.gov/documents/evaluation/9844/OEI-02-22-00050.pdf (reporting that Medicaid and Medicare enrollees have very limited access to mental health care providers).

[22] Shalina Chatlani, *Here's How Psychologists Are Serving Patients with Lower Incomes*, American Psychological Association: Monitor on Psychology (Mar. 1, 2023), www.apa.org/monitor/2023/03/serving-low-income-patients ("Almost two thirds of psychologists rarely serve those earning the lowest incomes, and most have never worked with people facing housing instability.").

[23] Jaffee, 518 U.S. at 15.

[24] *Id.* at 35 (Scalia, J., dissenting) (noting that states vary considerably in their treatment of social workers under the psychotherapist-patient privilege: some states have restricted the privilege for social workers, and some states have rejected that privilege entirely); Robert Aronson, *The Mental Health Provider Privilege in the Wake of Jaffee v. Redmond*, 54 Okla. L. Rev. 591, 609 (2001) (surveying state privilege rules after Jaffee and finding a wide range of exceptions); *see* Jared Sunshine, *Secrets Clutched in a Dead Hand: Rethinking Posthumous Psychotherapist-Patient Privilege in Light of Reason and Experience with Other Privileges*, 37 J. L. Health 249, 324 (2024) (indicating that the notion of uniformity in the state social worker privilege was a "mirage").

the protection of the psychotherapist privilege is strongest with a traditionally pedigreed professional, and more speculative with a social worker, low-income people are again at a disadvantage.

Accountant-Client Privilege

A substantial number of states have created privileges for communications with accountants.[25] These privileges favor the wealthy. Low-income people rarely have the means to hire accountants. While the accountant-client privilege usually does not apply in criminal cases, it does shield communication from discovery and evidentiary use in civil cases. Well-heeled parties facing lawsuits for abusive financial practices will enjoy significant protection from opponents' discovery of accounting records, whereas low-income people lacking accountants are vulnerable to creditors' discovery of wide-ranging financial records.

Clergy-Penitent Privilege

The clergy-penitent privilege applies to communication between religious leaders and members of their congregations.[26] This privilege disproportionately benefits high-income communities. Courts are more likely to apply the clergy-penitent privilege to traditional religious institutions.[27] Such institutions are less common in low-income communities,[28] where many residents attend to religious matters privately or informally[29] rather than in settings that are familiar to the judges interpreting the clergy-penitent privilege (especially in communities that include immigrants from countries with religious practices differing from those of the U.S.).

[25] 23A Kenneth W. Graham, Jr. and Ann Murphy, Federal Practice and Procedure § 5427 (1st ed., Wright & Miller 2025) (reporting that "a substantial number" of states have adopted the accountant privilege, and reproducing the relevant statutes in those states).

[26] Imwinkelried, *supra* note 11, at § 6.2.3 (reviewing basics of clergy-penitent privilege).

[27] Ronald Colombo, *Forgive Us Our Sins: The Inadequacies of the Clergy-Penitent Privilege*, 73 N.Y.U. L. Rev. 225, 232–3, 243–6 (1998) (indicating that conservative states have used narrow, traditional definitions of "clergy" and have excluded non-traditional spiritual advisors); *see* Nathan Ristuccia, *The Priesthood of All Citizens: On the Pseudo-Theology of Penitent Privilege*, 93 Miss. L.J. 291, 298, 304 (2023) (noting that there are thousands of denominations in the U.S., and courts sometimes "manipulate facts to rationalize admitting evidence" rather than apply the privilege broadly).

[28] Patton Dodds, *Low-Income Communities Are Struggling to Support Churches*, The Atlantic (Jan. 11, 2018), www.theatlantic.com/politics/archive/2018/01/low-income-communities-churches/549677/ (discussing economic and social considerations that have led to declining numbers of churches in low-income neighborhoods).

[29] Pamela Joshi, et al., U.S. Dep't. of Health & Human Servs.: Office of the Assistant Secretary for Planning & Evaluation, Role of Religiosity in the Lives of Low-Income People: A Comprehensive Review of the Evidence (2009), https://aspe.hhs.gov/reports/role-religiosity-lives-low-income-population-comprehensive-review-evidence-0 ("Lower-income adults, as well as youths, have higher levels of religious beliefs and adherence to doctrine but lower participation in organizational religiosity.").

Marital Privileges

The marital communication privilege protects against evidentiary use of confidential communication between spouses.[30] A related privilege, the spousal testimonial privilege, allows one spouse to avoid testifying against the other spouse.[31] Wealthy communities have higher marriage rates than do low-income communities,[32] so the spousal privileges give greater protection to wealthy communities. To be sure, there are strong marriage-like relationships in low-income communities – including couples who cohabitate or raise children together – but absent state-recognized marriage, these relationships do not meet the requirements for the current spousal privileges.

Reasons for Persistence of Elitist Privilege Law

It may seem surprising that judges and legislators tolerate current privilege law when it plainly disadvantages low-income people. One possible explanation is that judges prefer bright lines in privilege law.[33] When privileges are limited to familiar professional and personal relationships, judges find privilege law to be more easily administrable, because the boundaries of privilege law are clear. For their part, professional groups are content with the current restrictive approach,[34] and they lobby zealously to protect their evidentiary privileges.[35] These professionals recognize that evidentiary privileges make their services more highly compensable: they can sell secrecy along with their other services.

HOW CAN WE MAKE PRIVILEGE LAW MORE EGALITARIAN?

Privilege law should not be elitist. Privileges should be equally accessible to low-income people. While the complete elimination of disparities may be impossible,

[30] IMWINKELRIED, *supra* note 11, § 6.2.1 (indicating that most states have this privilege).

[31] *Id.* at § 1.3.6 (explaining that the privilege holder may refuse to testify about any subject, not simply about confidential marital communication).

[32] Richard Fry and Kim Parker, *Rising Share of U.S. Adults Are Living Without a Spouse or Partner*, PEW RESEARCH CNTR. (Oct. 5, 2021), www.pewresearch.org/social-trends/2021/10/05/rising-share-of-u-s-adults-are-living-without-a-spouse-or-partner/ (citing census data to show that marriage rates are declining in the U.S., particularly in low-income and minority communities).

[33] Edward Imwinkelried, *Questioning the Behavioral Assumption Underlying Wigmorean Absolutism in the Law of Evidentiary Privileges*, 65 U. PITT. L. REV. 145, 149 (2004) (noting that a bright-line approach to enforcement "simplifies the courts' task in administering privilege rules").

[34] *Id.* at 149 (stating that strict enforcement of privilege rules "is undeniably comforting to the members of the professions that enjoy the privileges").

[35] Wexler, *supra* note 1 (observing that the "benefits of privileges may track special interest lobbying"); Kenneth Broun, *Giving Codification a Second Chance: Testimonial Privileges and the Federal Rules of Evidence*, 53 HASTINGS L.J. 769, 778 (2002) (discussing lobbying by "particular interest groups which see a privilege as protecting their self-interests," and suggesting that legislatures are politically sensitive to such lobbying).

the need to narrow the gap is urgent. Litigants are more likely to lose in court if they lack the benefit of evidentiary privilege law, so fairness demands a more equitable approach.[36]

Broadening Availability of Professional Services

One possible solution would be to improve access to the professional services covered by traditional privileges. For example, if more low-income people had attorneys and doctors, the protection of the attorney-client privilege and the doctor-patient privilege would apply more evenly throughout society. There is little reason, however, to be optimistic that public funding is forthcoming to pay for greater legal representation or more extensive medical care for low-income people. While some academics and progressive politicians have expressed enthusiasm for a "civil Gideon" or "health care for all," the political reality suggests bleak prospects for both of these proposals.[37] Indeed, many U.S. states do not even allocate sufficient funding for legal representation of indigent defendants in felony prosecutions, though the Constitution requires such representation.[38]

Widening Eligibility under Current Privilege Law

Another possible avenue for reform would be to extend privilege law to practitioners who do not have the same pedigree as traditional professionals. In *Jaffee v. Redmond*,[39] which involved the issue of whether courts should recognize a psychotherapist privilege, the U.S. Supreme Court acknowledged that by its terms, Rule 501 "did not freeze the law governing the privileges of witnesses … at a particular point in our

[36] *See generally*, FED. R. EVID. 102 ("These rules should be construed so as to administer every proceeding fairly …"); MODEL RULES OF PRO. CONDUCT Preamble 12 (AM. BAR ASS'N 1983) (stating that the legal profession "has a responsibility to assure that its regulations are conceived in the public interest and not in furtherance of parochial or self-interested concerns … "); *see* Jayne Reardon, *As Lawyers, We Must Further the Public Interest*, ABA GP SOLO MAG., Aug. 13, 2021 (interpreting Preamble of ABA Model Rules to require that lawyers prioritize concerns of low-income people); *cf.* JOHN RAWLS, A THEORY OF JUSTICE: 65 (revised ed., Harvard University Press 1999) (contending that the concerns of the worst-off subgroup within society deserve higher priority in determining the justice of a particular policy or proposal).

[37] Benjamin Barton, *Against Civil Gideon (and for Pro Se Court Reform)*, 62 FLA. L. REV. 1227, 1237 (2010 (opining that a civil Gideon, i.e., a mandate for legal aid to the indigent in civil cases, "is very unlikely to occur"); Katharine Seelye, *Medicare for All? "Crazy," "Socialized" and "Unlikely,"* N.Y. TIMES (Sept. 19, 2009), https://archive.nytimes.com/prescriptions.blogs.nytimes.com/2009/09/19/medicare-for-all-crazy-socialized-and-unlikely/ (discussing political impediments to extending Medicare eligibility to the entire U.S. population).

[38] Andrew Engelson, *Defenseless: The Lack of Public Defenders Creates a Crisis for Indigent Clients and Increased Caseloads for Lawyers*, 110 ABA J. 52, 52–3 (2024) (reporting that many states are "facing a crisis in public defense").

[39] 518 U.S. 1 (1996).

history, but rather directed federal courts to 'continue the evolutionary development of testimonial privileges.'"[40] Indeed, relying on Rule 501's directive that courts should interpret privileges "in the light of reason and experience,"[41] the *Jaffee* Court not only recognized a psychotherapist privilege. It did so with a class-conscious bent, noting privilege law should recognize a wider range of eligible practitioners in order to avoid undue burdens on the poor.[42] Thus, the *Jaffee* majority ruled that the federal psychotherapist-patient privilege should also apply to communications with licensed social workers providing therapeutic services.[43] The Court noted that social workers often treat low-income people "who could not afford the assistance of a psychiatrist or psychologist, ... but whose counseling sessions serve the same public goals" that the psychotherapist-patient privilege seeks to advance.[44]

This reasoning and Rule 501's flexibility could potentially support the extension of other privileges to a wider range of practitioners. Perhaps a revamped version of the attorney-client privilege, renamed the "legal advisor privilege," could apply to a broader group of people who assist with litigation, even those people who are not under the supervision of an attorney. For example, immigrants seeking asylum in the U.S. sometimes rely on non-lawyers to help with preparation of their cases, and incarcerated litigants sometimes rely on lay "jailhouse lawyers" to assist with filings, but the current attorney-client privilege does not apply to such assistance.[45] An expanded privilege could potentially provide better protection for information collected by pro se parties,[46] rather than relegating such information to the porous work product doctrine.[47] *Jaffee*'s reasoning could also support the extension of the

[40] *Id.* at 9 (quoting Trammel v. United States, 445 U.S. 40, 47 (1980)).

[41] FED. R. EVID. 501.

[42] Jaffee, 518 U.S. at 15–16.

[43] *Id.* at 15.

[44] *Id.* at 16.

[45] Ann Naffier, Note, *Attorney-Client Privilege for Nonlawyers? A Study of Board of Immigration Appeals-Accredited Representatives, Privilege, and Confidentiality*, 59 DRAKE L. REV. 583, 584–6 (2011) (focusing on a subset of non-lawyers who assist in immigration cases – BIA-accredited non-lawyer representatives – and concluding that the application of the attorney-client privilege to these non-lawyers is unclear, although they can offer a form of confidentiality); Julie Nobel, Note, *Ensuring Meaningful Jailhouse Legal Assistance: The Need for a Jailhouse Lawyer-Inmate Privilege*, 18 CARDOZO L. REV. 1569, 1577–2 (1997) (indicating that inmates' communications with laypeople serving as "jailhouse lawyers" are outside the scope of the attorney-client privilege); see Justin Van Orsdol, *Crying Wolves, Paper Tigers, and Busy Beavers – Oh My!: A New Approach to Pro Se Prisoner Litigation*, 75 ARK. L. REV. 607, 630 (2022) (mentioning that, due to courts' inconsistent treatment, "pro se prisoners seeking the aid of jailhouse lawyers fall victim to saying too much (without a privilege shield) or saying too little out of fear of not having privilege").

[46] A pro se litigant's consultation of a third-party legal advisor should not be treated as a confidentiality breach that defeats the application of the privilege. *Cf.* Washington v. Babb, 104 Wash.2d 515, 525 (1987) (indicating that pro se defendant in a criminal case may invoke attorney-client privilege to shield communications with court-appointed standby counsel).

[47] FED. R. CIV. PROC. 26(b)(3) (providing that work product doctrine falls away when an opponent has "substantial need" for the information at issue); *see* Aprile, *supra* note 14 (discussing application of doctrine to pro se litigants).

medical privilege to a wider range of workers in the health care system,[48] or the extension of the clergy-penitent privilege to spiritual counselors not presently covered by that privilege.

Establishing Additional Categories of Privileges

Legislatures should also consider creating entirely new privileges. Examples might include privileges for communication with domestic violence counselors, shelter workers, debt counselors, union organizers, and participants in recovery groups for substance abusers.[49] Legislatures should also consider whether to create a new parent-child privilege,[50] or perhaps a more general "affectional privilege" for communication with a longer list of relatives,[51] including siblings,[52] or even friends.[53] In determining whether a relationship merits a new privilege, legislatures should consider whether that relationship is socially valuable and whether the protection of confidentiality would help to strengthen the relationship. There is no principled reason to limit privileges to communication with high-priced professionals such as lawyers, doctors, and accountants when

48 *E.g.*, Rebecca Pierce, *Statutory Solutions for a Common Law Defect: Advancing the Nurse Practitioner Patient Privilege*, 47 J. Marshall L. Rev. 1077, 1078–9, 1097–8 (2014) (arguing that the medical privileges do not sufficiently protect communication with nurses, who provide a high percentage of the overall medical care in the U.S.; proposing a nurse-patient privilege that would not depend on a nurse's role as an agent for a doctor).

49 *E.g.*, Legal Momentum: The Women's Legal Defense and Education Fund, State Confidentiality Statutes 3–49, https://perma.cc/3VS7-DZ8A (last visited Dec. 17, 2024) (providing a state-by-state breakdown of privilege statutes for communications with DV counselors and communications with shelter workers); Nicole Hallett, *From the Picket Line to the Courtroom: A Labor Organizing Privilege to Protect Workers*, 39 N.Y.U. Rev. L. Soc. Change 475, 494–511 (2015) (advocating for privilege covering communication with union organizers); Phyllis Coleman, *Privilege and Confidentiality in 12-Step Self-Help Programs*, 26 J. Legal Med. 435, 471–4 (2005) (arguing for a privilege protecting communications made at meetings of Alcoholics Anonymous and Narcotics Anonymous).

50 Nila Bala, *Parent-Child Privilege as Resistance*, 65 B.C. L. Rev. 2629, 2668–82 (2024) (proposing a parent-child privilege).

51 Graham and Murphy, *supra* note 25, at § 5572 (quoting proposal for affectional privilege in Canadian courts: "A person has a privilege against disclosure of any confidential communication between himself and a person who is related to him by family or similar ties if, having regard to the nature of the relationship, the probable probative value of the evidence and the importance of the question in issue, the need for the person's testimony is outweighed by the public interest in privacy, the possible disruption of the relationship or the harshness of compelling disclosure of the communication.").

52 Michael Moberly, *Am I My Brother's Secret-Keeper? Contemplating the Recognition of a Sibling Testimonial Privilege*, 41 Am. J. Trial Advoc. 239, 248 (2017) (proposing a privilege for communication among siblings).

53 *See* Ethan J. Leib, Friend v. Friend: The Transformation of Friendship – and What the Law Has to Do with It 100–4 (2011) (arguing for extending privileges to designated friends).

communication with other categories of third parties could offer comparable social benefits.[54] Indeed, the greater vulnerability at the low end of the economic spectrum makes the case for new privileges even stronger than is the case for traditional privileges that disproportionately benefit the rich.

Requiring Symmetrical Application of Privileges in Each Case

An alternative approach would be to adopt new procedural rules requiring some degree of symmetry in the application of privilege law within a particular court case. There are many "David v. Goliath cases" in which a party with limited resources must oppose a party assisted by several categories of professionals. In such a case, perhaps a court should inquire whether the well-resourced party intends to invoke the protection of privilege law, and if so, the court could invoke Rules 102 and 403[55] to extend comparable subject-matter protection to the other side, even if the other side has not hired the same sort of professionals. If a certain category of information is off-limits to use by one side, that same category of information should be off-limits to the other side. The rules of evidence show a concern for symmetry in many contexts,[56] so there is some precedent for the even-handed application of confidentiality rules.

[54] The exclusivity of a privilege undermines the utilitarian argument for that privilege. Steven Lubet, *Professionalism Revisited*, 42 EMORY L.J. 197, 202–3 (1993) (indicating that "if counsel were only available to the wealthy few, there would be less social basis for the attorney-client privilege and all of the accompanying entitlements that make lawyers' services so valuable"); *see* Hallett, *supra* note 49, at 500–1 (urging extension of current privilege to categories of professionals "with whom low-income people are more likely to come into contact").

[55] As Judge Weinstein noted in United States v. Jackson, "Rule 403, read in the light of Rule 102, contemplates a flexible scheme of discretionary judgments by trial courts designed to minimize the evidentiary costs of protecting parties from unfair prejudice." United States v. Jackson, 405 F. Supp. 938, 945 (E.D.N.Y. 1975).

[56] One example is permissive symmetry, ensuring that if one side introduces a certain category of evidence, the other side may also offer the same or similar evidence, notwithstanding preclusions that would normally apply if the opponent had not "opened the door." *E.g.*, FED. R. EVID. 106, 404(a), 408(b), and 410(b) (setting forth categories of evidence that both sides can introduce if one side "opens the door," even though the other side might otherwise be unable to introduce such evidence); Harris v. New York, 401 U.S. 222, 226 (1971) (adopting similar rule allowing prosecution to use an unmirandized custodial confession for impeachment of a defendant whose trial testimony contradicted that confession); *cf.* MODEL RULES OF PRO. CONDUCT r. 3.6(c) (AM. BAR ASS'N 2002) (providing that a lawyer may make an extrajudicial statement of the sort normally prohibited by Rule 3.6(a) if the other side has made such a statement). Another example is restrictive symmetry, imposing limits or costs on a litigant that has made witnesses or information inaccessible to the other side. *See* Wexler, *supra* note 1, at 1624–5 (citing examples of "cost sharing" when the prosecution invokes privileges that burden the accused); FED. R. CRIM. PROC. 16(b) (conditioning prosecutorial discovery rights on full compliance with discovery requests by defense); FED. R. EVID. 804(a) and 804(b)(6) (providing that once a party has purposefully and wrongfully procured the absence of a potential trial witness, that party may not benefit from rules admitting or excluding the statements of the absent declarant).

Reorienting Privilege Law to Focus on Topic Rather Than Identity of Audience

A more basic, but logistically challenging, approach would be to shift privilege law from protecting *communication with specified audiences* to protecting *information about specified topics*. At the present time, privilege law usually applies to communication within certain relationships (which tend to be less common in low-income communities). A reorientation of privilege law could change the focus from relationships to topics. In other words, information about certain topics could be privileged, whether or not that information were communicated to the third parties enumerated in current privilege statutes. Examples of such topical privileges in current law include privileges for trade secrets, political votes, and attorneys' mental impressions in preparation for litigation.[57] Perhaps this list should include additional topical privileges that would be valuable to low-income people. For example, given the unique vulnerability of low-income people to the fallout from the *Dobbs* decision, the topics of pregnancy and abortion should be covered by topical privileges.[58] The applicability of a topical privilege would require that the privilege holder has only shared the information with people who are reasonably likely to keep it confidential.[59]

Updating Ethical Rules for Judges and Lawyers

Another important aspect of reform should be to change the ethical rules for judges and lawyers. Ethical codes for judges should include explicit language requiring admonitions to unrepresented parties or witnesses about their opportunity to invoke privileges, including the privilege against self-incrimination, and should even require judges to appoint counsel for unrepresented parties or witnesses when necessary to assert privileges effectively in urgent circumstances. Ethical rules for attorneys, particularly prosecutors, should include more explicit duties to refrain from seeking information protected by privilege. These prohibitions should apply whether the attorneys are seeking information from opponents or third parties.

Advocating for New Common Law Privilege Rules

When Congress adopted Federal Rule of Evidence 501[60] instead of more precise privilege rules, one purpose was to leave space for the innovation of privilege law on

57 IMWINKELRIED, *supra* note 11, at §§ 9.2, 9.3 (discussing topical privileges); FED. R. CIV. PROC. 26(b)(3) (providing protection for evidence reflecting attorneys' mental impressions).

58 Lininger, *supra* note 7, at 721–2 (setting forth model privilege statute).

59 *Id.*

60 FED. R. EVID. 501 (providing that common law governs privileges except in a diversity case, when the state supplying the rule of decision with respect to a claim or defense also supplies the privilege rule).

a case-by-case basis.[61] As noted earlier, the Supreme Court has recognized the need for "courts to continue the evolutionary development of testimonial privileges."[62] A new privilege "may be justified … by a public good transcending the normally predominant principle of using all rational methods for ascertaining truth."[63] While a few federal cases have expanded or contracted existing privileges, some state courts have gone further. At the state level, some courts have shown a willingness to change privilege law abruptly. For example, the New Mexico Supreme Court transformed its spousal privilege rule repeatedly over the course of a few years, abolishing it in 2019, reinstating it partially in 2020, and settling on a more comprehensive rule over the following years.[64] Attorneys should challenge courts to consider extending privilege rules on a case-by-case basis when current rules would create hardships for low-income clients, and advocating for new privileges entirely. Failing that, attorneys could argue as a last resort that the admission of the information in question would be unduly prejudicial under Federal Rule of Evidence 403 or its state analogs.[65]

Shrinking Protections for Rich and Powerful Litigants

While the primary purpose of this chapter is to strengthen privileges for low-income people, it is important to consider the other side of the equation. Has the time come to curtail the privileges for well-resourced parties? Arguably the scope of the privilege for corporate attorneys should shrink so that a wider range of internal communications would be accessible to plaintiffs suing corporations.[66] The government's deliberative process privilege, which shields public officials' discussions preceding a final decision, sweeps too broadly and may thwart discovery of information that is vital for public interest litigation.[67] The government's excessive power is most stark in criminal cases. Privileges shielding informants, and confidentiality rules shielding members of police unions from accountability for misconduct, need

[61] S. Rep. No. 93-1277, at 13 (1974), quoted in *Jaffee*, 518 U.S. at 8 (stating that Rule 501 "should be understood as reflecting the view that the recognition of a privilege based on a confidential relationship … should be determined on a case-by-case basis").

[62] Jaffee, 518 U.S. at 9 (quoting Trammell v. United States, 445 U.S. 40, 47 (1980)).

[63] *Id.* at 9.

[64] State v. Gutierrez, 482 P.3d 700, 703 (N.M. 2019) (abolishing spousal testimonial privilege), *vacated on rehearing*, State v. Gutierrez, 2020 N.M. LEXIS 36*, at *1–4 (N.M. Nov. 5, 2020). The rule evolved further in subsequent years. N.M. R. Evid. 11-505 (reflecting that New Mexico Supreme Court approved a more comprehensive version of the spousal testimonial privilege after the Gutierrez case).

[65] Fed. R. Evid. 403 (authorizing exclusion of evidence when prejudice substantially outweighs probative value).

[66] Elise Bernlohr Maizel, *The Case for Downsizing the Corporate Attorney-Client Privilege*, 75 U.C. L. Rev. 373, 401 (2024) (offering proposals that "would dramatically narrow the scope of a corporation's attorney-client privilege").

[67] *See generally*, Michael Ray Harris, *Standing in the Way of Judicial Review: Assertion of the Deliberative Process Privilege in APA Cases*, 53 St. Louis U. L.J. 349, 349 (2020) ("As a basic principle, secrecy in government is contrary to the notion of democracy held by most Americans.").

careful reevaluation.[68] Another way to improve balance in criminal cases would be to recalibrate the rule admitting statements by party opponents: the rule should extend to police, but should not cover alleged co-conspirators unless they are actually agents of the accused.[69] The hearsay exception for government records should apply to police reports offered by the accused, because such use of hearsay presents no problems under the Confrontation Clause.[70] In sum, powerful parties such as corporations and the government do not deserve so much help in hiding evidence.

WHAT ARE THE LIKELY OBJECTIONS TO BROADER PRIVILEGES FOR LOW-INCOME LITIGANTS?

This chapter's proposals to expand privileges for low-income people will probably draw several objections. One foreseeable concern is that the proposals could hinder the administrability of privilege law. The Federal Rules of Evidence seek to "eliminate unjustifiable expense and delay" in the administration of court proceedings.[71] At the present time, the scope of privilege law is fairly well settled, and judges usually do not need to spend a lot of time interpreting privilege law. The expansion of privilege law to cover new relationships, or to cover certain categories of information that are not presently privileged, might slow down judicial proceedings. These concerns do not justify perpetuating the status quo, however. The Supreme Court in *Jaffee* determined that expanding the coverage of a privilege was worth whatever sacrifice in judicial efficiency might be necessary.[72] While topic-based privileges are somewhat harder to interpret than relation-based privileges, the courts have somehow managed to administer the topic-based privileges in current law. More important, efficiency concerns cannot trump concerns about procedural fairness to low-income parties.

Another potential objection to any expansion of privilege law is that it would undermine the truth-seeking goal.[73] Whenever a new privilege applies, it risks the

[68] *See* Stephen Saltzburg, *Informant Privilege*, 30 CRIM. JUST. 60 (2015) (explaining case law relating to scope of informant privilege); Katherin Bies, *Let the Sunshine in: Illuminating the Powerful Role Police Unions Play in Shielding Officer Misconduct*, 28 STAN. L. & POL'Y REV. 109, 117–20 (2017) (arguing that union confidentiality laws thwart police accountability for misconduct).

[69] FED. R. EVID. 801(d)(2) (classifying statements by party opponents as non-hearsay); Jared Kelson, *Note, Government Admissions and Federal Rule of Evidence 801(D)(2)*, 103 VA. L. REV. 355, 356–68 (2017) (discussing difficulty faced by defendants in criminal cases when they try to introduce statements by law enforcement officers as agent admissions under Rule 801(d)(2)).

[70] FED. R. EVID. 803(8)(A)(ii) excludes police reports offered by the defense against the government in a criminal case, even though the Confrontation Clause does not require such exclusion. Crawford v. Washington, 541 U.S. 36, 51–3 (2004) (explaining scope of modern confrontation right).

[71] FED. R. EVID. 102.

[72] Jaffee, 518 U.S. at 15.

[73] *See generally*, United States v. Nixon, 418 U.S. 683, 710 (1974) (expressing concerns about the cost of privileges: "these exceptions to the demand for every man's evidence are not lightly created nor expansively construed, for they are in derogation of the search for truth").

possibility of denying relevant evidence to the fact finder. This concern is not unique to privilege law, however. In other contexts such as search and seizure law under the Fourth Amendment, suppression is sometimes necessary even if it would impair truth-seeking. Further, it is important to bear in mind that privileged information might not exist but for the privilege: confidentiality emboldens the privilege holder to communicate with a third party as to whom the privilege applies, and if the privilege were not available, the privilege holder would be less likely to engage in such communication. Therefore, the privilege has little effect on the availability of evidence.[74] In any event, the tradeoff between truth-seeking and confidentiality must be interpreted uniformly. There should not be a different cost calculation for privileges benefiting the wealthy. It is somewhat disingenuous to insist on stasis in privilege law because a more egalitarian set of privileges might undermine truth-seeking.

Finally, critics might argue that the best way to promote economic equality would be to "level down" evidentiary privilege law. In other words, if privilege law afforded little protection to anyone, then the class-based disparity would shrink. Several scholars have argued against the strict enforcement of privilege law, although these scholars usually have not grounded their critique in egalitarian theory.[75] In any event, an across-the-board reduction of evidentiary privileges would hardly be an optimal way to promote the interests of low-income people. A litigant who lacks privileges is vulnerable to aggressive lawyering by the opponent. In the absence of privileges, opposing counsel could extract sensitive information through discovery and through questioning at trial. There already exists a significant class-based disparity in both access to counsel and effectiveness of legal representation (given that attorneys for the indigent have little time to devote to each client). The unavailability of evidentiary privileges would exacerbate this disparity. Imagine a medieval battle in which one side has much more effective weapons: The denial of shields to both sides would actually reduce, not increase, parity. The imbalance of power is particularly worrisome in criminal prosecutions, and any erosion of privilege law in that context would greatly benefit the government, significantly weakening the accused.

CONCLUSION: CHECK YOUR PRIVILEGE!

Over the last decade, the phrase "check your privilege" has gained currency as an exhortation for self-assessment to consider whether one is benefiting from unearned societal advantages, and whether one is insufficiently sensitive to the plight of others

[74] 3 Jack Weinstein and Margaret Berger, Weinstein's Federal Evidence § 504.03[4][a] (Joseph McLaughlin ed., 2d ed. 1997) ("The recognition of the privilege has little cost to the judicial system, because … if the privilege were not recognized, many of the confidential disclosures would never be made.").

[75] *E.g.*, Imwinkelried, *supra* note 33, at 149 (arguing against strict enforcement of evidentiary privileges, suggesting that absolutism sacrifices potentially valuable information and is not necessary to accomplish goals of privileges).

who lack such advantages. This chapter has issued the same challenge to the judicial system. Evidentiary privilege law is elitist.[76] Its inequities harm low-income people. Reforms are possible that could expand the eligibility for evidentiary privilege, change procedure to protect privilege holders, and impose ethical duties on judges and lawyers to make sure that they respect privileges. Some of these reforms could be challenging to implement, but they would make progress toward the goal of a more egalitarian judicial system. When evidentiary privilege is coextensive with economic privilege, low-income people do not have equal access to justice.

[76] Graham and Murphy, *supra* note 25, at § 5421 ("The bottom line is that privilege law favors the wealthy, by and large.") (citing scholars).

Parent-Child Privilege as Resistance

Nila Bala

Privileges are generally disfavored as impeding the truth. But in this chapter, I propose a novel way to think of privilege altogether: privilege as a means of *resistance*, a tool to oppose unjust systems and laws. Current privilege scholarship essentially assumes faith in the adversarial legal system and the interest in soliciting, collecting, and admitting all available evidence. This assumption implicitly accepts that (1) the adversarial system is valid, and (2) the substantive law that privilege limits is also valid. However, if we question the legitimacy of the adversarial system and the substantive laws it upholds, the cost-benefit analysis shifts. Privilege could serve as an instrument of resistance by prioritizing the preservation of relationships over the legal system's pursuit of truth.

In this chapter, I use the case study of a parent-child privilege to explore how privilege as resistance could work. I critique the prioritization of the carceral system's search for "truth" over the parent-child relationship. In addition, I consider the power of privilege as resistance because of *Dobbs v. Jackson Women's Health Organization*, given that parent-child conversations now carry criminal implications.[1]

BACKGROUND ON PARENT-CHILD PRIVILEGE

Modern American law recognizes several types of privileged communications: attorney-client, marital, clergy-penitent, physician-patient, and most recently,

The author would like to thank the UC Davis faculty, attendees of the Harvard/Yale/Stanford Junior Faculty forum, Decarceration Law Professors Workshop, AALS Family Law WIP, Crimfest, as well as my wonderful research assistants, Sasha Gordon, Simone Montgomery, Sinporion Phuong, Madeline Reed, and Seton Talty. Special thanks to Ellie Citron and Kamran King. The author is also grateful for the assistance of George Fisher, Kellen Funk, Cynthia Godsoe, Jasmine E. Harris, Esther Hong, Edward Imwinkelried, Laurie Kohn, Evelyn Malave, Jamelia Morgan, Sarah Polcz, David Sklansky, Lisa Washington, and Rebecca Wexler. This chapter is adapted from this Article, Nila Bala, *Parent-Child Privilege as Resistance*, 65 B.C. L. Rev. 2629 (2024).

[1] Dobbs v. Jackson Women's Health Organization, 597 U.S. 215 (2022).

psychotherapist-patient.[2] Privileges provide a special status to these communications. They exclude these relevant conversations from the judicial process in order to protect interests that are seen as more important than revealing the truth. Unlike almost every other evidence rule, privileges do not originate from an interest in safeguarding the quality or reliability of evidence.[3] Rather, the evidence withheld because of privilege is often relevant and reliable.[4] Thus, privileges are disfavored.

Almost all recognized privileges are professional in nature.[5] The exception is the spousal privilege, a domestic privilege that parallels the parent-child privilege in certain respects. Despite few domestic privileges, there is nothing explicitly preventing the development of a parent-child privilege.[6] Federal Rule of Evidence Rule 501 empowers courts to interpret and create privileges governed by common law and "in light of reason and experience." Privilege can and has adjusted to changing social norms, and in the past, the court has used the phrase "experience and reason" in Rule 501 to support these changes.

Most states do not have a parent-child privilege, though it is the first relationship to exist and is often where children turn for guidance. Given the evolution of families and relationships in the twenty-first century, re-evaluating evidentiary privileges is a worthwhile endeavor to ensure these legal protections reflect the value society currently places on certain bonds. Feminist scholars and others have argued that privilege rules have historically only sheltered those relationships traditionally valued by men.[7] In contrast, caregiving relationships – such as the parent-child one – have not been afforded the same protections, perhaps because they are implicitly devalued as they are associated with the women's role in the family.[8] Additionally, prioritizing the marital relationship over others is a particular Western conception. In other cultures, the parent-child relationship is seen as a closer, more important relationship.[9] Even in the West, parents and children are more likely to be self-defined as "immediate family" than spouses.[10] Recognizing a parent-child privilege

[2] *See* Ronald L. Carlson et al., Evidence: Teaching Materials for an Age of Science and Statutes (with Federal Rules of Evidence Appendix) 755–56 (9th ed., Carolina Academic Press 2023).

[3] For example, Rule 702, which governs testimony by expert witnesses, places a strong emphasis on reliability to ensure that expert evidence is both credible and relevant.

[4] *See, e.g.*, People v. Hall, 194 Ill.2d 305, 336 (2000).

[5] Fed. R. Evid. 501 (further explanation in the advisory committee's note to 1974 enactment).

[6] Catherine J. Ross, *Implementing Constitutional Rights for Juveniles: The Parent-Child Privilege in Context*, 14 Stan. L. & Pol'y Rev. 85, 86 (2003).

[7] Kit Kinports, *Evidence Engendered*, 1991 U. Ill. L. Rev. 413, 425 (1991).

[8] *Id.*

[9] *See generally*, Tsui-Feng Wu et al., *Choosing Your Mother or Your Spouse: Close Relationship Dilemmas in Taiwan and the United States*, 47 Cal J. Cross-Cultural Psych. 558 (2016).

[10] Taylor Orth, *All on the Family: Ties, Proximity, and Estrangement*, YouGov (Dec. 20, 2022, 12:11 PM GMT-8), https://today.yougov.com/topics/society/articles-reports/2022/12/20/poll-family-ties-proximity-and-estrangement.

might be the first step to recognizing the importance of privacy within a relationship that is as significant (if not more so) than the marital one.[11]

Instrumental justifications for privilege have been criticized since individuals may be unaware of privileges or it may not shift their behavior in obvious ways.[12] Children may be especially unlikely to be aware of evidentiary privilege. But privilege can be supported through a non-instrumental approach. This perspective focuses on the inherent value of privilege and asserts that privacy in the relationship is valuable in itself.

Privacy is often conceptualized as a purely individual right; the right to be free from interference from all others and the right to solitude. This is the way Samuel D. Warren II and Louis Brandeis conceived of it in their seminal article, *The Right to Privacy*, defining privacy primarily as a right to be let alone.[13] But a second conception of privacy is just as important to young people. The process of establishing a sense of self does not occur in total isolation. While the Western liberal tradition historically situated privacy as a zone of solitude, free of interference, this notion has been critiqued by many, including feminist philosophers.[14] In reality, family members often share a collective sense that there is a "we" to protect.[15] Relational privacy is particularly relevant to how we think of children's privacy.[16] Children, as

[11] Full description of relational privacy below.

[12] See, e.g., Edward J. Imwinkelried, *State v. Gutierrez Abolishing the Spousal Communications Privilege: An Opinion Raising Profound Questions about the Future of Evidentiary Privileges in the United States*, 53 N.M. L. REV. 71, 82–3 (2023) ("If the spouses do not realize that there is a privilege, they cannot rely on it; and even if they have some awareness of the privilege, in most instances, it will be far in the back of their minds."); 25 CHARLES A. WRIGHT AND KENNETH W. GRAHAM, JR., FEDERAL PRACTICE AND PROCEDURE: EVIDENCE § 5574 (Supp. 2003) ("[I]f the privileges are ever to be extended to nonmarital relationships, it seems likely that this will be the result of either greater emphasis on the noninstrumental justifications for the privileges or of legislative enactment."); Mikah K. Story, *Twenty-First Century Pillow-Talk: Applicability of the Marital Communications Privilege to Electronic Mail*, 58 S.C. L. REV. 275, 308 (2006) ("Indeed, Wigmore … questioned whether the instrumental model would support the case for a spousal privilege.").

[13] *See generally*, Samuel D. Warren and Louis D. Brandeis, *The Right to Privacy*, 4 HARV. L. REV. 193 (1890). *See also*, Ken Gormley, *One Hundred Years of Privacy*, 1992 WIS. L. REV. 1335, 1345 (1992) (articulating this as the accepted position on privacy); Sarah A. Seo, *The New Public*, 125 YALE L.J. 1616, 1619 (2016) (that free men (and they were *men*) enjoyed the presumption of the right to be left alone and do as they pleased).

[14] ALAN F. WESTIN, PRIVACY AND FREEDOM 32–37 (Atheneum 1967) (for a traditional, Western notion of privacy). For relational privacy theories, *see generally*, Julie E. Cohen, *What Privacy Is For*, 126 HARV. L. REV. 1904, 1905 (2013) ("[F]reedom from surveillance, whether public or private, is foundational to the practice of informed and reflective citizenship."); JULIE E. COHEN, CONFIGURING THE NETWORKED SELF: LAW, CODE, AND THE PLAY OF EVERYDAY PRACTICE (Yale University Press 2012); Alice E. Marwick and Danah Boyd, *Networked Privacy: How Teenagers Negotiate Context in Social Media*, 16 NEW MED. & SOC'Y 1051 (2014); Laurent Sacharoff, *The Relational Nature of Privacy*, 16 LEWIS & CLARK L. REV. 1249 (2012).

[15] Kenneth L. Karst, *The Freedom of Intimate Association*, 89 YALE L.J. 624, 629 (1980).

[16] To be clear, I am not arguing that children do not also need the more separate sense of privacy, both from third parties and parents. But there is this second relational sense of privacy that children also need. This also has conceptual meaning in areas like disability law. Jasmine E. Harris, *The Privacy*

compared to adults, live in relation to others. While they are active agents with their own interests, they are not legally autonomous. Relationships, built upon the trust that information disclosed will not be shared with others, are central to children's growth.[17] While there are domains and activities we wish complete privacy for, much of our lives are richer through sharing it with those we love.[18] This relational privacy "sees emotional well-being arise not from the ability to drop our masks, but from acts of co-creating selves through networks."[19]

Relational privacy is increasingly relevant in the digital age. In this new era, it is less productive to focus on the mere fact that information was disclosed to someone else. Rather, each privacy-related behavior should be understood in the specific context and relationship in which the information is released. Privilege mirrors other legal structures that recognize information shared can still be considered private.[20] Privacy takes on additional importance when we consider how intimate relationships – particularly familial bonds – can become sites of oppression and state control.

PRIVILEGE AS RESISTANCE

Privilege is not merely an evidentiary rule; it stands as a potential bulwark against oppressive regimes. Compelled testimony from parents and children recalls surveillance states that encouraged, rewarded, and even required families to turn against each other.[21] During the Cultural Revolution in Communist China, the Red Guards "encouraged and even compelled parents and children to denounce each other at

Problem in Disability Antidiscrimination Law, *in* DISABILITY, HEALTH, LAW, AND BIOETHICS 159–70 (I. Glenn Cohen, Carmel Shachar, Anita Silvers, and Michael Ashley Stein eds., Cambridge University Press 2020).

17 For the seminal work on this subject, *see* JOSEPH GOLDSTEIN, ANNA FREUD, AND ALBERT J. SOLNIT, BEYOND THE BEST INTERESTS OF THE CHILD 9–16, 31–35 (Free Press 1973) (a "[c]ontinuity of relationships, surroundings, and environmental influence are essential for a child's normal development"); Anne C. Dailey, *Children's Constitutional Rights*, 95 MINN. L. REV. 2099, 2155–61 (2011) (discussing the child's psychological need for relationships, particularly one's parents); Pamela Laufer-Ukeles, *The Relational Rights of Children*, 48 CONN. L. REV. 741, 783 (2016).

18 Sacharoff provides examples of bodily functions, certain secrets, and time alone to think and relax as examples. Laurent Sacharoff, *The Relational Nature of Privacy*, 16 LEWIS & CLARK L. REV. 1249, 1270 (2012).

19 Sara Bannerman, *Relational Privacy and the Networked Governance of the Self*, 22 INFO. COMMC'N & SOC'Y 2187, 2187–202 (2019).

20 Information disclosed that was confidential may be subject to suits under a breach of confidentiality or fiduciary duty theory. E.g., RESTATEMENT (SECOND) OF TORTS § 874 (1979); Horne v. Patton, 291 Ala. 701, 708–9 (1973). There are also laws to keep health information private and protect some digital information. *See, e.g.*, Health Insurance Portability and Accountability Act of 1996, Pub. L. No. 104-191, 110 Stat. 1936; The Electronic Communications Privacy Act of 1986, Pub. L. No. 99-508, 100 Stat. 1848. These are all laws that recognize that even though information might be shared, there is still a sense of privacy over it.

21 *Id.* at 890.

the extrajudicial mass accusation and condemnation rallies."[22] In 1933, the Nazis issued a decree requiring Germans to turn in anyone who spoke out against the party. Parents, children, and other family members were mandated to report one another.[23] Similarly, the Soviet criminal system considered non-reporting of criminal activities, including by family members, as aiding and abetting the criminal, with a term of imprisonment up to fifteen years.[24] In reaction to such oppressive histories, many nations have recognized familial privileges as a crucial component to safeguard against state abuses and overreach.[25]

In the United States, surveillance, policing, and disruption of Black and Brown parents and their children has long been used as a method of control.[26] Black families, both during slavery and after abolition, were intensely scrutinized and surveilled.[27] Black families were split apart and their children sold. Enslaved individuals were often denied the freedom of intimate association and the ability to care for and communicate with their own children.[28] Thus, family life – taking care of one's children, teaching children to communicate and read, and passing down traditions – became a form of agency and resistance for enslaved individuals.[29] Similarly, the government removed Native children from their families at high rates, placing them in white homes and boarding schools.[30] By the 1970s, close to a third of Native children had been removed and placed in adoptive homes.[31] This chapter is centered on evidentiary privilege, but another meaning of *privilege* is also relevant: the

[22] Tao-tai Hsia, Child-Parent Privilege in Criminal Proceedings 3 (L. Libr. Cong. 1999), www.loc.gov/item/2019669608.

[23] *Shaping the Future: Indoctrinating Youth*, U.S. Holocaust Mem'l Museum, https://encyclopedia.ushmm.org/content/en/article/indoctrinating-youth (last visited Jan. 25, 2024).

[24] Peter Roudik, *Russian Federation*, *in* Child-Parent Privilege in Criminal Proceedings (Tao-tai Hsia ed., L. Libr. Cong. 1999).

[25] The parent-child privilege is also recognized in France, Sweden, Australia, Germany, Yugoslavia, Israel, the Netherlands, Russia, Japan, Czechoslovakia, and others. *See* Catherine Chiantella Stern, *Note, Don't Tell Mom the Babysitter's Dead: Arguments for a Federal Parent-Child Privilege and a Proposal to Amend Article V*, 99 Geo. L.J. 605, 609 (2011) for full list.

[26] Anita Sinha, *A Lineage of Family Separation*, 87 Brook. L. Rev. 445, 449–59 (2022).

[27] *Id.*

[28] Equal Just. Initiative, The Transatlantic Slave Trade, ch. 12 (2022), https://perma.cc/734L-PGLC ("Enslaved women were sometimes punished for attempting to care for their children.").

[29] *See generally*, Emily West, Family or Freedom: People of Color in the Antebellum South (University Press of Kentucky 2012); Phyllis Jane Hicks Brown, *Narratives of Enslaved People: Lifting the Veil, Resisting the Peculiar Institution* (Master's thesis, California State University, Fresno); Sarah L. H. Gronningsater, The Rising Generation: Gradual Abolition, Black Legal Culture, and the Making of National Freedom (University of Pennsylvania Press 2024).

[30] Christie Renick, *The Nation's First Family Separation Policy*, Imprint News (Oct. 9, 2018, 5:05 AM), https://imprintnews.org/child-welfare-2/nations-first-family-separation-policy-indian-child-welfare-act/32431.

[31] *Id.*

privilege of having private spaces, a privilege that has been systematically denied to marginalized people throughout history.[32]

In contrast, evidentiary privilege could be a form of resistance, to seek relief from a state prioritizing unjust laws over the parent-child relationship. Privilege as resistance can align with libertarian and progressive visions, recognizing the need to divest from and minimize the impact of an unjust criminal legal system. Thanks largely to the Innocence Movement, which has "revealed the troubling reality and ... causes of erroneous convictions," many question the fairness and accuracy of the criminal legal system's outcomes.[33] And individuals across the political spectrum share concerns about state intrusion on the privacy rights of individuals and families through its police power.[34]

This vision of privilege also has echoes in early American understandings of privilege, namely of the attorney-client privilege. Norman Spaulding's survey of attorney-client privilege cases from the nineteenth century demonstrates that privilege was originally not about compliance with the law, but instead about the individual's right to know and understand their legal decisions. As Spaulding writes, "Counseling resistance to law [through the attorney-client privilege] is a core function of law practice in a pluralistic society committed to decentralized, participatory legal decision-making."[35]

While Spaulding writes of a professional privilege rather than a familial one, the same proposition is possible here – that privilege can be justified based on a right of resistance to law.[36] This notion stands in opposition to most previous privilege scholarship, which has implicitly accepted the notion that privileges should be disfavored because they are impediments to justice and obstruct the factual inquiry.[37] Privilege is seen as a bug – an aberration in an evidentiary code that bends towards

[32] Mary Anne Franks, *Democratic Surveillance*, 30 Harv. J.L. & Tech. 425, 441 (2017) ("slavery is less often described in terms of its destructive effects on human privacy, but the description is no less true for that"). *See generally*, Khiara M. Bridges, The Poverty of Privacy Rights (Stanford Law Books 2017) (arguing poor mothers do not actually have real privacy rights).

[33] Jenny Roberts, *The Innocence Movement and Misdemeanors*, 98 B. U. L. Rev. 779, 780 (2018). 71 percent say it is important to reduce the prison population in America. The same percent agree that incarceration is often counterproductive to public safety, with two-thirds recognizing racial bias in the criminal legal system. Press Release, ACLU, *91 Percent of Americans Support Criminal Justice Reform, ACLU Polling Finds* (Nov. 16, 2017 10:15 AM), www.aclu.org/press-releases/91-percent-americans-support-criminal-justice-reform-aclu-polling-finds.

[34] Morris Lipson and Peter Vallentyne, *Libertarianism, Autonomy, and Children*, 5 Pub. Affs. Q. 333, 333 (1991).

[35] Norman W. Spaulding, *Compliance, Creative Deviance, and Resistance to Law: A Theory of the Attorney-Client Privilege*, 2013 J. Prof. Law. 135, 136 (2013). *See also*, Norman W. Spaulding, *The Privilege of Probity: Forgotten Foundations of the Attorney-Client Privilege*, 26 Geo. J. Legal Ethics 301 (2013).

[36] Spaulding, *Compliance*, *supra* note 35, at 154.

[37] *See* Ronald L. Carlson et al., Evidence: Teaching Materials for an Age of Science and Statutes(with Federal Rules of Evidence Appendix) 755–6 (9th ed., Carolina Academic Press 2023).

truth-seeking.[38] Implicit in this judgment, however, are the assumptions that the legal system itself is valid, and that the substantive law privilege would impede is just. But if that system *and* the evidence it is collecting are suspect, or at least worth deprioritizing over family relationships, then adopting privilege merits serious consideration.[39] Specifically, privilege could function as an instrument of resistance in the context of two legal contexts: the juvenile legal system, and the post-*Dobbs* landscape of health care rights.

PRIVILEGE AND THE JUSTICE SYSTEM

In the words of Nancy Dowd, "the current juvenile justice system is a failure for virtually all who come in contact with it."[40] Children in the system experience high rates of reoffending (both as minors, and later, as adults), separation from their families and communities, negative effects to their physical and mental health, and diminished educational and employment outcomes.[41] But the truth is that the juvenile legal system, like the adult criminal system, is harmful and ineffective.

At least part of the system's failure is promoting rules and procedures that undermine the parent-child relationship and rank professional privileges above relational ones.[42] The child's attorney will likely advise the child client not to discuss their case with their parents, and will not include parents in client discussions, partly because of the lack of privilege.[43] Parents can and have been subpoenaed as witnesses in criminal and juvenile proceedings, and so lawyers must

[38] *Id.* (describing "substantial judicial hostility to the recognition of new privilege," and the prevailing sentiment of most American courts that "[e]videntiary privileges in litigation are not favored … ").

[39] A purest view of abolitionism might argue that attempts to work within the system continues to support and legitimize that very system. However, even abolitionist thinkers have acknowledged the need for "non-reformist reforms," measures that actually contest the underlying logic of those systems and provide relief. In contrast, a reformist reform would strengthen existing systems. *See generally*, Ruth Wilson Gilmore, Golden Gulag: Prisons, Surplus, Crisis, and Opposition in Globalizing California 28 (University of California Press 2007); Angela Davis, Are Prisons Obsolete? (Seven Stories Press 2003). Privilege here would be an iterative step that invests in family relationships rather than the adversarial system.

[40] Nancy E. Dowd, *Black Lives Matter: Trayvon Martin, the Abolition of Juvenile Justice and #BlackYouthMatter*, 31 U. Fla. J.L. & Pub. Pol'y 43, 45 (2020).

[41] *Id.*

[42] Hillary Farber, *To Testify or Not to Testify: A Comparative Analysis of Australian and American Approaches to a Parent-Child Testimonial Exemption*, 46 Tex. Int'l. L.J. 109, 141 (2010).

[43] The protections of parental communications are not covered under the narrower (attorney-client) evidentiary privilege. Nancy J. Moore, *Conflicts of Interests in the Representation of Children*, 64 Fordham L. Rev. 1819, 1856 (1996). However, ethical standards may seek to "hold parents' secrets confidential to the extent they can [be] consistent with rules of law and the primary responsibility to their clients' interests." Juv. Just. Standards: Standards Relating to Couns. for Private Parties Standard § 3.3(c) & commentary (IJA-ABA Joint Comm. on Juv. Just. Standards, 1980) (*cited by* Moore, at 1833).

advise children not to discuss the facts and circumstances of their case with their parents.[44] But parents (often lacking in information) continue to advise their children throughout the court process. How can they not? Children inevitably rely on their parents, a role that does not suddenly end because of justice system involvement.

While shutting parents out of involvement with their children's case, the system paradoxically sees a parent's participation, if not consent, as a legitimizing force. The American juvenile legal system wants parents to serve vital roles as an "interested adult" throughout proceedings, with a number of states opting for requiring parental consultation before waiving Miranda rights.[45] Additionally, the justice system leans on the parent throughout the court process so that children can access other constitutional rights. Catherine Ross writes, "many of the constitutional rights afforded to children cannot be exercised meaningfully absent free and open communications with their parents … In light of children's vulnerabilities and dependency, parents may be the intermediaries through which children can best assert their rights."[46] Yet parent-child conversations are not protected by privilege, and parents can be subpoenaed, undermining any benefit these conversations could have.

Protecting the communication can have significant benefits. Recognizing a parent-child privilege may help further goals of rehabilitation and family preservation, particularly if the child is justice-involved, a term referring to youth who have had contact with the justice system. For these young people especially, privilege can facilitate unencumbered conversations between children and their parents. Structures that have explicitly made parent participation a focus have led to better outcomes for youth.[47] In Australia, for example, recognition of the parent-child privilege allows for added opportunities to consider diversion from the legal system, through a restorative process called "conferencing."[48] The Australian legal system places the emphasis on a restorative process, dialogue between the parties, and family involvement, rather than formal adjudication and a process that shames and

44 Kristin Henning, *It Takes a Lawyer to Raise a Child?: Allocating Responsibilities among Parents, Children, and Lawyers in Delinquency Cases*, 6 Nev. L.J. 836, 865 (2006).

45 Some studies have shown children are more likely to waive Miranda after a parent consultation. Thomas Grisso, *Juveniles' Capacities to Waive Miranda Rights: An Empirical Analysis*, 68 Cal. L. Rev. 1134, 1151–2, 1160–1 (1980).

46 Catherine J. Ross, *Implementing Constitutional Rights for Juveniles: The Parent-Child Privilege in Context*, 14 Stan. L. & Pol'y Rev. 85, 86 (2003) (arguing privilege is key to a meaningful exercise of Fifth and Sixth Amendment rights).

47 Neelum Arya describes long-standing family-based practices such as Functional Family Therapy, but only 5% of youth in the juvenile justice system have the opportunity to take advantage of these types of programs. Neelum Arya, *Family-Driven Justice*, 56 Ariz. L. Rev. 623, 645 (2014). However, some young people (for example those who enter the system on domestic violence charges) may need special accommodations to a parent-integrated strategy. *Id.* at 663.

48 Hillary Farber, *To Testify or Not to Testify: A Comparative Analysis of Australian and American Approaches to a Parent-Child Testimonial Exemption*, 46 Tex. Int'l L.J. 109, 140 (2010).

stigmatizes the young person.[49] In sum, if the family holds responsibility for helping young people succeed and "keeping them out of trouble," then the system should support that goal.

We ask both too much and too little of parents. A parent-child privilege responds to both issues – it facilitates needed communications in youth proceedings while protecting conversations. Recognizing a parent-child privilege redistributes power away from the system back to parents and their children, one step among many to address a fundamentally broken system.

PARENT-CHILD PRIVILEGE IN THE HEALTH CARE CONTEXT

Children depend on their parents, especially within medical settings. It is a relationship that is generally not chosen, unlike the spousal relationship. Historically, most young people have involved a parent before an abortion.[50] One reason is that thirty-six states mandate minors get parental consent or notification for abortions, laws that are unchanged post-*Dobbs*.[51] In addition, parental support is essential for transgender and gender-non-conforming youth, functioning as a key protective factor in preventing depression, anxiety and suicide.[52] Yet, there is no widely recognized parent-child or intrafamilial privilege to protect these conversations. Contemporary issues necessitate a renewed focus on the parent-child privilege.

Conversations around reproductive access and gender affirming care, traditionally tough, now carry a greater risk of generating evidence and creating potential criminal or civil liability because of the *Dobbs* decision.

49 *Id.* at 111.

50 Some minors seek support due to the barriers to obtaining an abortion; but for many, it is because they have a meaningful relationship with their parent. *See* Lee A. Hasselbacher et al., *Factors Influencing Parental Involvement among Minors Seeking an Abortion: A Qualitative Study*, AM. J. PUB. HEALTH (Nov. 2014).

51 *Parental Involvement in Minor's Abortions*, GUTTMACHER INST. (Sept. 1, 2023), https://perma.cc/3Y2Y-GLP5. The process can be incredibly complicated: in Indiana, for example, consent requires a notarized parental form, in-person counseling, an ultrasound, and an 18-hour waiting period. *See* Tracey Wilkinson, Julie Maslowsky, and Laura Lindberg, *A Major Problem for Minors: Post-Roe Access to Abortion*, STAT NEWS (June 26, 2022), www.statnews.com/2022/06/26/a-major-problem-for-minors-post-roe-access-to-abortion/. An alternative to parent involvement is judicial bypass – a process where a judge approves an abortion without parental consent, a topic taken up by other scholars. *See generally*, Jessica Quinter and Caroline Markowitz, *Judicial Bypass and Parental Rights after Dobbs*, 132 YALE L.J. 1908 (2023).

52 Amanda Doyle, *For Kids and Teens Exploring Gender Identity, Family Engagement in Care is Critical*, HEALTHCITY (Aug. 22, 2019), https://healthcity.bmc.org/population-health/family-engagement-should-be-integral-part-gender-care; Amy Hillier and Elisabeth Torg, *Parent Participation in a Support Group for Families with Transgender and Gender-Nonconforming Children: "Being in the Company of Others Who Do Not Question the Reality of Our Experience,"* TRANSGENDER HEALTH (Aug. 12, 2019), www.ncbi.nlm.nih.gov/pmc/articles/PMC6689185/.

Advocates and scholars are forecasting progressively intensifying prosecutions in a post-*Roe* landscape, including actions targeting parents and pregnant minors.[53] And like the disproportionality already present in the juvenile legal system, law enforcement activities against pregnant people are more likely to burden and harm marginalized communities, such as Black and Indigenous people, immigrants, those with disabilities, and those with the fewest resources.[54] These are not theoretical concerns: Prosecutors have already weaponized parent-minor conversations to criminalize pregnancy, targeting both pregnant minors and their parents.[55]

Parent-child privilege can be part of an arsenal of protective laws, but its efficacy faces constraints within the current legal framework. Any privilege would likely be passed at the state level, and as privilege law currently stands, a parent-child privilege enacted in a progressive state has limits on what it can achieve when parents and minors are prosecuted in restrictionist states. A privilege from a progressive state is unlikely to be extended in other states due to interstate laws governing privilege.

However, there are ways to fashion privileges so that it still has significant benefits for those traveling to other states. The privilege can include a subsection making clear that the privilege provides a basis to obtain a court order quashing a subpoena, warrant, or discovery request served by an out-of-state party seeking potentially privileged information.[56]

Nevertheless, the most effective parent-child privilege would be one adopted by restrictionist states themselves. The current states that have recognized a parent-child privilege lean Democrat, but not all are (e.g., Idaho), and there is nothing inherently partisan about a general parent-child privilege. While this chapter examines parent-child privilege through the lens of resistance to adversarial systems, the privilege itself aligns with multiple political values. A general parent-child privilege fits within the rhetoric of the parents' rights movement and holds libertarian appeal by safeguarding the private realm of the family from government intrusion.[57] Crafted intelligently, a parent-child privilege could garner support from both parties, while providing minors with increasing control over their bodies.

[53] David Dayen, *The Inevitable Prosecutions of Women Who Obtain Abortions*, The American Prospect (Jan. 16, 2023), https://prospect.org/health/2023-01-16-prosecution-women-mifepristone-abortion-alabama/.

[54] Liza Fuentes, *Inequity in US Abortion Rights and Access: The End of Roe is Deepening Existing Divides*, Guttmacher Inst. (Jan. 17, 2023), www.guttmacher.org/2023/01/inequity-us-abortion-rights-and-access-end-roe-deepening-existing-divides.

[55] A recent Nebraska case involving a third-trimester abortion demonstrates how parent-child communications can produce incriminating evidence, even though the abortion timing itself falls outside the scope of this piece. Shaila Dewan and Sheera Frenkel, *A Mother, a Daughter and an Unusual Abortion Prosecution in Nebraska*, N.Y. Times (Aug. 18, 2022), https://perma.cc/YM3T-LZEK.

[56] In his abortion-specific evidentiary privilege proposal, Lininger makes this very suggestion (but specific to communications concerning abortion). Tom Lininger, *Abortion, the Underground Railroad, and Evidentiary Privilege*, 80 Wash. & Lee L. Rev. 663, 722 (2023).

[57] *See* Morris Lipson and Peter Vallentyne, *Libertarianism, Autonomy, and Children*, 5 Pub. Affs. Q. 333, 333 (1991).

SHAPING THE PARENT-CHILD PRIVILEGE AS RESISTANCE

Not all parent-child privileges are created alike.[58] The "essential privilege," applies where the minor child holds the interests at stake, the parent serves as the witness, and the source of the parent's knowledge stems from confidential communications with their child.[59] The other three variations include: (1) minors testifying against parents; (2) parents testifying against adult offspring; and (3) adult offspring testifying against parents.[60] One likely reason most courts have declined to find any parent-child privilege is because these distinct variations have been lumped together and treated as doctrinally identical, when each is quite different.[61]

Six states have some version of a parent-child privilege – Idaho, Minnesota, New York, Connecticut, Washington, and Massachusetts. Most have enacted a version of the "essential" parent-child privilege to protect confidential communications from a minor to a parent, though they vary in terms of duration of the privilege and exceptions. Reflecting on these existing privileges can provide insight into three critical dimensions of privilege: its conceptual scope, the definition of parent, and the necessary exceptions to protections.

A. *Scope of the Privilege*

For the parent-child privilege to function as resistance, it must, at the very least, protect the child's communications to the parent (the "essential" parent-child privilege). Additionally, the length of the privilege matters, and should exist both before and during court proceedings. A privilege that starts only when an individual is taken into custody will not protect those conversations that occur when minors need help deciding what to do before legal system involvement.[62] These are exactly the sorts of conversations the system should protect and incentivize.

An additional consideration regarding scope is that a parent-child privilege should encompass both testimony and communications. The American Bar Association Model Statute contemplates protecting both a testimonial and communication privilege for the parent-child relationship.[63] Under the "adverse testimonial privilege," a parent cannot be compelled to provide adverse testimony about the child in a grand

[58] Ross, *supra* note 46, at 94.
[59] *Id.*
[60] *Id.*
[61] *Id.*
[62] Washington State and Connecticut have privilege that only starts after the judicial process has commenced. *See* CONN. GEN. STAT. § 46b-138a (1979); WASH. REV. CODE § 5.60.060 (2023).
[63] *See* David A. Schlueter, *The Parent-Child Privilege: A Response to Calls for Adoption*, 19 ST. MARY'S L.J. 35, 37–8 (1987). Note the ABA contemplates a reciprocal privilege (one that protects parent to child and child to parent communication). A child forced to testify against their parent may undergo great psychological stress, which could irreparably damage their relationship. Thus, the framework of privilege as resistance also supports creating a reciprocal privilege – though I do not fully take up a

jury proceeding or when the child is a defendant in a criminal proceeding or the subject of a juvenile proceeding. The witness holds the privilege. Under the "confidential communications privilege," a parent cannot be compelled to testify about confidential communications between them. Both the parent and the child hold the privilege and either may prevent the other from testifying, with exceptions for intrafamilial violence.[64] In the context of reproductive and health decision-making, structuring the privilege in this way will ensure that even when a young person is unsure of their parent's position regarding choice, a young person is protected from their parent sharing confidential communications.

B. *Defining Parent*

Conceptions of family and parent have changed across history. More than ever before, children are parented by those who are not biological parents, but are a source of love, affection, and guidance.[65] These individuals are increasingly recognized by courts as "functional parents."[66] Privilege demands an expansive definition of parenthood that reflects our nation's diverse family structures. As scholars have explained, caregiving itself can be transgressive and liberating for non-traditional families – a form of political expression.[67] Framing caregiving in this way not only means extending support and acknowledgment to these parental figures, but "provides a conceptual basis for limiting unwanted state intervention into their families."[68] Privilege as resistance furthers both aims, shielding a wider array of caregiving relationships.

Relatedly, for children who are "wards of the state," the question of privilege is a more complicated one. For these children, the state may be both parent and an adversarial party in court. Practically, the state facilitates the exercise of constitutional rights, arranges for medical treatment and mental health treatment, and provides for schooling while simultaneously amassing meticulous records on vulnerable communications shared by the child. In contexts where the state is functioning as the child's guardian, a parent-child privilege may be able to protect the

privilege protecting minor children from testifying against parents in this book chapter, I hope to do so in future work.

64 The ABA statute lists nine possible exceptions, some of which are overly expansive or would have negative consequences. *Id.* I do not endorse or incorporate all the exceptions here.

65 Christina McClurg Riehl and Tara Shuman, *Children Placed in Kinship Care: Recommended Policy Changes to Provide Adequate Support for Kinship Families*, 39 CHILD.'S LEGAL RTS. J. 101, 103 (2019) ("Kinship care placements are the federally prioritized placements that occur when children are unable to be cared for by their parents and are brought into the child welfare system.").

66 A person standing in loco parentis is one who puts him or herself in the position of a lawful parent by assuming the obligations incident to the parental relation without legally adopting the child. 28 AM. JUR. 2D *Proof of Facts* § 545 (1981).

67 Laura T. Kessler, *Transgressive Caregiving*, 33 FLA. ST. U. L. REV. 1, 2 (2005).

68 *Id.* at 1.

child's privacy expectations and reduce the blurring of boundaries that currently exists when the state exercises power through *parens patriae*. A parent-child privilege could recognize that even when children are separated from their family of origin, the privilege persists.[69] By shielding these exchanges from state intrusion, privilege as resistance pushes back against the unchecked discretion *parens patriae* grants. Though incomplete, privilege represents one avenue to help preserve family connections within the system.

C. *Exceptions*

Most states provide exceptions to the parent-child privilege, yet these exceptions can be overbroad in three key ways. First, they disregard how expansively "abuse and neglect" are defined and fail to consider the reality of family regulation in this country. The family regulation system disproportionately targets communities of color, with nearly one in three children nationwide subjected to child protective services investigations that are often driven by poverty rather than genuine child welfare concerns. As Dorothy Roberts has noted, "by taking away children or weaponizing their children with the threat of removal, the child welfare system imposes intensive surveillance and regulation on families."[70] One potential reform is limiting exceptions to parent-child privilege to cases of intrafamilial violence. Cabining the exception and generally protecting the communications between child and parent may lead to a more harmonious reunification when children are separated from parents.

Second, parent-child privilege should not exclude civil contexts (a current exception in two states where the privilege exists).[71] Critiques of criminal law cut across the criminal/civil divide, as administrative and civil sanctions take on a punitive character. Parent-child privilege is especially valuable in problem-solving courts (where children often find themselves), which operate with relaxed evidentiary rules. The less formalistic nature of these courts actually strengthens the case for explicitly protecting parent-child communications. In sum, the benefits of privilege extend to other civil systems, including implications in family regulation and immigration.

Third, privileges may incorporate a crime/fraud exception that does not account for health care access in our legally altered landscape. This exception, long recognized in common law, negates an evidentiary privilege when the privilege holder has communicated to seek assistance in committing a crime or fraud. If a state were to adopt a parent-child privilege, the legislature may choose to specify that

[69] *See* Lenore M. McWey, Alan Acock, and Breanne Porter, *The Impact of Continued Contact with Biological Parents upon the Mental Health of Children in Foster Care*, 32 CHILD & YOUTH SERVS. REV. 1338, 1342 (2010) (describing the benefits of continued contact with families of origin).

[70] Dorothy Roberts, *The Regulation of Black Families*, THE REGULATORY REV. (Apr. 20, 2022), https://perma.cc/V86Q-WU4Q.

[71] MINN. STAT. § 595.02 (2020); MASS. R. EVID. § 504(c)(2).

"crime" and "fraud" do not include obtaining or providing, attempting to obtain or provide, or assisting someone in obtaining or providing reproductive care or gender affirming care.[72]

CONCLUSION

Privilege serves many roles – it can protect a young person's privacy, help ensure a parent is informed, and safeguard a youth's other protected and privileged relationships. While this chapter examined parent-child privilege as a case study, a privilege as resistance framework can offer broader insights about evidentiary privilege. At its core, privilege provides refuge, a means of resistance against increasingly punitive systems.

[72] *See* Lininger, *supra* note 56, at 671 (proposing federal legislation that would codify an evidentiary privilege for communication with any audience concerning abortion).

PART III

Expanding Evidence

SECTION 1

Decarceration and Abolition

INTRODUCTION

We are living in a country that has one of the highest incarceration rates in the world, with jails that cycle through approximately 10 million people each year, and where on any given day approximately 2 million people are behind bars.[1] Indeed, we are now at the point where one in every three adults in America has an arrest record.[2] And of course, none of this is distributed equally. Our jails and prisons are disproportionately populated with the poor, and disabled people, and with Black and Brown people.[3] As such, it is little surprise that a rallying cry among some criminal justice scholars has been that our criminal system is beyond repair, beyond tinkering, and that the only answer now is abolition: abolishing prisons, abolishing the police, even abolishing prosecutors. And if not full abolition, that we must at least work to reduce the number of people we imprison and reduce our carceral footprint.

It is little surprise too that some Critical Evidence scholars count themselves among the abolitionists, or at least among those who think we incarcerate too many people, and do so too easily. Critical Evidence scholars are beginning to ask whether the Rules of Evidence give the veneer of legitimacy and neutrality

1 *See* Bennett Capers, Roger A. Fairfax, and Eric J. Miller, eds., Criminal Law: A Critical Approach 3–13 (Foundation Press 2023) (and sources cited therein).

2 *Id.*

3 *Id.*

to a system that is deeply flawed and biased. Going a step further, some Critical Evidence scholars are also asking whether the Rules themselves reflect a carceral bent. And if so, what can be done?

As we were putting this book together, we knew early on we wanted it to feature a connection to abolition and decarceration. The chapters that follow do just that. In "Bending Evidence Rules Towards Decarceration," Erin Collins argues it is time, indeed past time, to address the imbalance in power between the state and criminal defendants. Put simply, a criminal trial is not a "fair fight," and never has been. To at least begin to rectify this imbalance, she proposes a limiting principle for judges' evidentiary decision-making: "judges should not bend rules to admit evidence on behalf of the government. In other words, evidentiary rule bending should be allowed only to the extent judges bend the rules towards decarceration."

This section also includes Maneka Sinha's "Reimagining *Daubert v. Merrell Dow Pharmaceuticals, Inc.* as a Non-Reformist Reform," a contribution that could easily have gone in the section on experts, but which we chose to include here to show how so many of these issues are interconnected. Viewing the admission of expert testimony through an abolitionist lens, Sinha calls attention to the ease with which judges admit expert evidence against criminal defendants even as they vigilantly screen the same evidence when offered by defendants or in civil cases. Ultimately, Sinha argues that more is needed than simply stricter application of Federal Rules of Evidence Rule 702, the rule that governs the admissibility of expert testimony. Instead, she argues for other interventions, including taking power to determine the admissibility of scientific evidence away from judges.

Bending Evidence Rules Towards Decarceration

Erin R. Collins

Evidence rules purport to be transubstantive. Therefore, they *should* apply equally and predictably to all cases, both civil and criminal, irrespective of the nature of the charge or claim, the identity of the parties, or the severity of the harm the defendant has allegedly caused. Yet, those who interact with how evidence rules are actually applied – whether in the courtroom or the academy – know this to be false. Sometimes this uneven or inconsistent application results from a judge's mistake about the evidence rules. But other times, judges misapply the rules to admit evidence that the rules technically preclude, but that the judge determines is "in some way essential to the case."[1] In other words, they bend the evidence rules.[2]

One issue with rule bending is that it is, technically, invisible. Bending occurs when judges intentionally admit evidence that the rules would otherwise preclude, but they do so while pretending that they are adhering to those very rules. Professors Cheng, Nunn, and Simon-Kerr have crafted a proposal to help address this concern: the creation of a residual evidence rule that allows bending.[3] This proposed rule would function to admit otherwise excluded evidence and provide a conceptual counterweight to the exclusionary power of Federal Rules of Evidence Rule 403. In so doing, it would bring the practice of rule bending to the surface and provide more transparency – and perhaps grounds for appeal when such bending has gone too far.

This chapter joins the call of Professors Cheng, Nunn, and Simon-Kerr to bring rule bending out of the shadows, where it can be acknowledged and addressed. But any analysis of the operation and future of evidence law, especially in the contemporary

Many thanks to Bennett Capers, Jasmine E. Harris, Anna Roberts, and Julia Simon-Kerr for helpful feedback and commentary. This chapter also benefited greatly from presentations to the Critical Evidence Colloquium and the Critical Evidence classes at Fordham, University of Connecticut, and University of Pennsylvania law schools.

1 Edward K. Cheng, Alexander Nunn, and Julia Simon-Kerr, *Bending the Rules of Evidence*, 118 Northwestern L. Rev. 295, 299 (2023).

2 *Id.* (defining evidence rule bending).

3 *See id.* at 333.

criminal law context, which is the focus of this chapter, must also grapple with the origins and operation of both the evidence rules and the criminal system more generally. It must account for the ways that power operates in the criminal law context, and the way that the criminal law enforcement, prosecution, and punishment practices reify and exacerbate structural inequalities, especially with regard to race. Evidence rules are not neutral nor objective. They have been created by and within existing power structures. They reflect and operate to protect structures of inequality that are deeply gendered and deeply racialized.[4] The operation of the criminal legal system is similarly not neutral or objective – and works to advance many of the same structures of power and privilege. The people who are disproportionately targeted by the criminal system are often the very same people against whom evidence will be admitted when judges bend evidence rules for the prosecution.

In light of these dynamics, this chapter proposes a limiting principle for evidentiary rule bending in criminal prosecutions: judges should not bend rules to admit evidence on behalf of the government. In other words, evidentiary rule bending should be allowed only to the extent judges bend the rules towards decarceration. The remainder of the chapter will offer reasons in support of this limiting principle and some preliminary thoughts on what such one-way bending could look like.

Rule bending for decarceration acknowledges the reality that criminal prosecutions are not a "fair fight" between two adversaries with equal power, authority, and resources. Prosecutors exercise nearly unfettered discretion over charging decisions and are authorized to exercise this discretion with the goal of attaining a guilty plea.[5] Those few people who resist the many structural and individual incentives to plead guilty – including the threat of a "trial penalty" should they exercise their constitutional right to a trial – are then confronted with an adjudicatory process in which the government has the time and capacity to conduct a thorough investigation, methodically gather and prepare evidence, and hire experts as necessary to assist its case. Meanwhile, indigent defendants proceed to trial with defense attorneys who are often juggling crushing caseloads and provided investigatory resources that pale in comparison to the government's.[6] Thus, before a

4 *See, e.g.*, Bennett Capers, *Race, Gatekeeping, Magical Words, and the Rules of Evidence*, 76 VANDERBILT L. REV. 1855, 1855 (2023) ("[T]here is a long history in this country of tying evidence – what is deemed trustworthy – to race."); Jasmine B. Gonzales Rose, *Toward a Critical Race Theory of Evidence*, 101 MINN. L. REV. 2243, 2244 (2017) (applying Critical Race Theory to uncover how evidence law can "insidiously operate to perpetuate racial subordination"); Julia Simon-Kerr, *Unchaste and Incredible: The Use of Gendered Conceptions of Honor in Impeachment*, 117 YALE L.J. 1854 (2008).

5 Bordenkircher v. Hayes, 434 U.S. 357, 364 (1978) ("[B]y tolerating and encouraging the negotiation of pleas, this Court has necessarily accepted as constitutionally legitimate the simple reality that the prosecutor's interest at the bargaining table is to persuade the defendant to forgo his right to plead not guilty.").

6 *See* Nicholas M. Pace, Malia N. Brink, Cynthia G. Lee, and Stephen F. Hanlon, *National Public Defense Workload Study*, RAND (2023), www.rand.org/pubs/research_reports/RRA2559-1.html (last visited March 26, 2026).

criminal trial begins, the scales of justice are already tilted in favor of the government. Rule bending to admit evidence against the criminal defendant exacerbates this imbalance.

The system is, in fact, supposed to offer the opposite orientation; to the extent the processes and procedures favor one party over another, they are supposed to tip in favor of the criminal defendant. As Professor Roberts has argued, within the criminal prosecution context equality of treatment for both parties is not synonymous with fairness.[7] Indeed, there are numerous examples in constitutional criminal procedure that demonstrate that "asymmetry is a central component of the system's design and its attempts to achieve fairness."[8] The Constitution provides a number of rights to criminally charged people – rights that are not equally allocated to the government – such as the right to confront accusers, the right to refuse to be compelled to be a witness against oneself, and the right to disclosure of certain favorable evidence.[9] And sometimes evidence law must give way to an accused person's right to present a defense.[10] This asymmetrical allocation of constitutional criminal procedure rights acknowledges that criminal trials do not occur on an equal playing field and, sometimes, it is necessary to give an apparent advantage to the accused person to advance fairness and justice.[11]

Evidence law itself reflects this need for asymmetry, providing rules that offer more protection to or evidentiary flexibility for defendants in criminal cases than the government. For example, Rule 410 prohibits the government – but not the defendant – from admitting certain evidence regarding plea negotiations, no contest pleas, or pleas that are later withdrawn.[12] The business records hearsay exception does not extend to factual findings from a legally authorized governmental

7 Anna Roberts, *Asymmetry as Fairness: Reversing a Peremptory Trend*, 92 WASH. U. L. REV. 1503, 1539 (2015).

8 *Id.*

9 *See id.* at 1539 (describing these constitutional asymmetries).

10 Chambers v. Mississippi, 410 U.S. 284, 302 (1973) ("[W]here constitutional rights directly affecting the ascertainment of guilt are implicated, the hearsay rule may not be applied mechanistically to defeat the ends of justice."); *see also*, Holmes v. South Carolina, 547 U.S. 319, 324–5 (noting the "broad latitude" given to lawmakers to establish rules that exclude evidence in criminal trials has limits, and does not allow the use of evidence rules that deprive a criminal defendant of a meaningful opportunity to present a complete defense).

11 *See* Tehan v. United States, 382 U.S. 406, 416 (1966) (noting that, although the "basic purpose of a trial is the determination of truth," the "Fifth Amendment's privilege against self-incrimination is not an adjunct to the ascertainment of truth," but nonetheless demands "undiluted respect"); *In re* Winship, 397 U.S. 358, 372 (1970) (Harlan, J., concurring) ("I view the requirement of proof beyond a reasonable doubt in a criminal case as bottomed on a fundamental value determination of our society that it is far worse to convict an innocent man than to let a guilty man go free."). Brady v. Maryland, 373 U.S. 83, 87 (1963) ("Society wins not only when the guilty are convicted but when criminal trials are fair; our system of the administration of justice suffers when any accused is treated unfairly.").

12 FED. R. EVID. 410. Nevertheless, courts sometimes disregard the rule's text and apply this prohibition equally to the defense and the prosecution. *See* GEORGE FISHER, EVIDENCE 143 (3d ed., Foundation Press 2013) (noting that since admitting evidence against prosecutors would frustrate the

investigation – unless such findings are offered by the criminal defendant against the government.[13] Rule 404(a)(2) allows the defense – but not the government – to open the door to evidence regarding the defendant's or victim's pertinent character trait.[14] And Rule 609 provides a more searching balancing test before the government can impeach a criminal defendant with past convictions than that which applies to all other witnesses.[15] Therefore, one-way evidentiary rule bending would not be aberrational; it would be simply another practice that provides "asymmetry in service of fairness."[16] And ensuring fairness and justice are central goals of evidence law.[17]

Some of the most prominent prosecutorial rule-bending practices may seem consistent with these principles of fairness and justice. Evidentiary rule bending often occurs in cases that have historically presented problems of proof for the government. In such cases, judges allow the government to admit evidence that a consistent and correct application of the evidence rules would keep out. For example, judges bend hearsay rules to admit statements of non-testifying child complainants in child abuse cases.[18] And in prosecutions for sexual assault or intimate partner violence, they often admit proof of the defendant's past assaultive acts against the same victim or other people to help support the inference that the defendant committed the charged crime – even when doing so violates Rule 404's prohibition on propensity evidence, and when such prior acts do not faithfully satisfy a non-propensity theory of relevance under Rule 404(b)(2).[19] The judge presiding over the New York state trial of Harvey Weinstein for sexually assaulting two women allowed testimony from three other women that Mr. Weinstein had assaulted them under similar circumstances. As the New York State Court of Appeals clarified in reversing Mr. Weinstein's conviction, a principled application of New York's common law version of Rule 404 prohibited this evidence from being introduced.[20]

It is easy to understand why some judges are willing to bend rules in prosecutions for deeply troubling allegations. Criminal conviction and punishment are popularly

purpose of the rule, "courts generally have ignored the strict language of the rule and have barred the evidence").

13 Fed. R. Evid. 803(8). The rule also allows any party in a civil case to admit such factual findings. *Id.*

14 Fed. R. Evid. 404(a)(2). If the defendant opens the door in this way, the government may respond in kind. Fed. R. Evid. 404(a)(2)(B).

15 As applied, however, this test leaves much to be desired. *See generally*, Anna Roberts and Julia Simon-Kerr, *Reforming Prior Conviction Impeachment*, 50 Fordham Urb. L.J. 377 (2023).

16 Roberts, *supra* note 7, at 1539.

17 *See* Fed. R. Evid. 102 ("These rules should be construed so as to administer every proceeding fairly, eliminate unjustifiable expense and delay, and promote the development of evidence law, to the end of ascertaining the truth and securing a just determination.").

18 Cheng, Nunn, and Simon-Kerr, *supra* note 1, at 312–14.

19 *See generally*, Erin Collins, *The Evidentiary Rules of Engagement in the War Against Domestic Violence*, 90 NYU L. Rev. 397 (2015). In the context of federal prosecutions for sexual assault or child molestation, judges need not bend the rules to admit past acts. *See* Fed. R. Evid. 413 and 414.

20 People v. Weinstein, __ N.E. 3d__, 2024 NY Slip Op 02222 (NY Ct. App., Apr. 25, 2024).

seen as the only apparent avenue for achieving justice and imposing accountability in response to behavior deemed criminal. In the first trial of Bill Cosby for sexual assault, at which the judge severely limited prior act evidence, the jury could not reach a unanimous decision. At the second trial, the judge bent Pennsylvania's version of Rule 404 to admit testimony by five other women detailing how Cosby had assaulted them.[21] The jury convicted him on all counts.[22]

But a conviction achieved as a result of bending is not synonymous with justice, even when done in cases involving particularly noxious allegations. For example, Rule 404's prohibition on propensity evidence is one "not of logic, but of policy."[23] It reflects a judgment by the rule drafters that a just process is one in which the jury is not tempted to convict a person for who they are or what they have done in the past. It is one of a number of evidence rules designed to advance social policy goals that are independent of – and sometimes at odds with – the truth-seeking function of trial.[24] This distinction between a process that advances justice with one that prioritizes accuracy is consistent with the purposes of the Rules themselves[25] and constitutional protections for criminally accused people that keep out evidence that may be quite probative of "the truth" – but the admission of which would undermine overriding societal values and notions of fairness.[26]

That the prosecution, with all its resources and structural advantages, may not be able to successfully convict those accused of deeply troubling allegations without bending evidence rules reveals a persistent problem: despite decades of feminist activism and even after the MeToo movement, jurors still bring gendered biases (among others) to their assessment of evidence. But bending the rules to favor the prosecution does not address this core issue. Certainly, much work remains to be done to achieve true fairness and equality in credibility assessments; but this goal will not be accomplished by selectively and intentionally misapplying evidence rules to facilitate conviction. Indeed, even when evidence rules are changed for the express purpose of redressing entrenched biases, jurors will continue to draw

[21] *See* Cheng, Nunn, and Simon-Kerr, *supra* note 1, at 298–9 (identifying the Cosby decision as an example of rule bending).

[22] Mr. Cosby challenged the admission of other act evidence on appeal. The Pennsylvania Supreme Court reversed his conviction on other grounds without reaching the merits of that argument. Commonwealth v. Cosby, 252 A.3d. 1092 (2021).

[23] People v. Zackowitz, 172 N.E. 466, 468 (N.Y. 1930).

[24] For example, Rule 407's prohibition of evidence of subsequent remedial measures to prove fault "rests on a social policy of encouraging people to take, or at least not discouraging them from taking, steps in furtherance of added safety." FED. R. EVID. 407 advisory committee's notes. *See also*, FED. R. EVID. 408–11.

[25] *See* FED. R. EVID. 102 (requiring that the Rules "should be construed so as to administer every proceeding fairly, eliminate unjustifiable expense and delay, and promote the development of evidence law, to the end of ascertaining the truth and securing a just determination").

[26] *See* Chambers, 410 U.S. 284; Holmes, 547 U.S. 319. Evidence rules defer to these constitutional exclusions. *See* FED. R. EVID. 402 (specifying the relevant evidence is not admissible if the constitution provides otherwise).

on their own stereotypical scripts to make sense of the evidence presented[27] and are influenced by information that is not technically evidence – like the demeanor, dress, and race of witnesses and parties.[28]

Prosecutorial rule bending is even more concerning when it is done to make up for evidentiary gaps left by complainants who choose not to testify for the government in domestic violence prosecutions – or to undermine the credibility of those who choose instead to testify for the defense.[29] Doing so undermines the integrity and authority of the very person the government purports to protect and empower. And it allows the government to ignore the many reasons why people who have experienced harm may decide the traditional criminal system will not bring them safety or meaningful accountability while advancing the myopic pursuit of one conception of justice: justice as conviction.

Moreover, evidentiary rule bending for the government can dissuade people from going to trial – where they can present their defense, have a fact finder decide whether the government has met its burden by fair and sufficient proof of guilt, and where the evidence rules can actually be applied – which then thwarts the further development of evidentiary rules.[30] And when evidence rules are bent in favor of the government, it increases the likelihood of conviction, through a trial or a guilty plea.[31]

Of course, criminal punishment follows a conviction. Contemporary punishment practices cause harm to those who are then subject to violence and deprivation within jails and prisons or invasive surveillance if they are sentenced to community supervision. Meanwhile traditional punishment practices do not advance their utilitarian aims – they do not deter, and they do not rehabilitate.[32] Given what we know

27 For example, Professor Capers has revealed how jurors fill evidentiary gaps created by rape shield laws with stereotypical scripts – to the detriment of women "who, because of race or class or some other trait, do not fit the ideal victim script. In these cases, when a rape shield law conceals evidence of a complainant's sexual history, jurors may fall back on default assumptions diametrically at odds with the rape shield law's expressive message." *See* I. Bennett Capers, *Real Women, Real Rape*, 60 UCLA L. Rev. 826, 830 (2013).

28 *See* I. Bennett Capers, *Evidence Without Rules*, 94 Notre Dame L. Rev. 867 (2018).

29 *See generally*, Collins, *supra* note 19. For example, courts have bent forfeiture by wrongdoing principles to admit hearsay evidence based on a finding that the defendant intentionally caused the complainant's absence – despite the complainant's sworn testimony that she was declining to testify of her own free will. *See id.* at 434–44. And courts routinely bend the medical treatment and diagnosis hearsay exception to admit statements of the alleged victim to their doctor identifying the defendant as the person who caused the injury, despite the exception's clear exclusion of statements of identification. *See id. at* 428–34.

30 *Cf.* Fed. R. Evid. 102 ("These rules should be construed so as to … promote the development of evidence law …").

31 Many criminal cases are, of course, resolved through a guilty plea. As I have argued elsewhere, decisions to plead guilty happen in the shadow of trial – a shadow that is shaped by pre-trial decisions about what evidence will come in if a case goes to trial. *See* Erin R. Collins, *Evidence Rules for Decarceration*, 50 Fordham Urb. L.J. 353, 353 (2023).

32 *See, e.g.*, David Roodman, *The Impacts of Incarceration on Crime*, Open Philanthropy Project, at 7 (2017), www.openphilanthropy.org/wpcontent/uploads/The_impacts_of_incarceration_on_crime_10.

about the humanitarian and fiscal costs of incarceration and other forms of criminal punishment, and amidst the increasingly loud calls to slow the carceral creep of mass incarceration from activists, academics, and communities impacted by punitive policing and punishment systems, we should be wary of any practice that allows system actors to set aside established rules to help facilitate conviction. And those who are working to radically reduce the scope of the carceral state must be mindful of the ways that legal processes and reforms may strengthen the problematic equation of conviction with accountability and incarceration with public safety.

In short: enhancing the power of the prosecution by bending the rules towards conviction is not fair, and it does not advance justice. Perhaps in an ideal world no rule bending would occur; criminal trials would truly be a match between two equally empowered and resourced parties, and judges would apply the evidence rules consistently and fairly to both parties. While work continues to achieve a reality that is closer to this ideal, I suggest one thing judges may do to address this imbalance by unbending the rules towards incarceration and bending instead towards decarceration.

My proposal for decarceratory rule bending is not synonymous with a principle that would entitle defendants to admit any evidence they want. Rather, it is an invitation to judges to think more capaciously about the purpose and principles of evidence rules with particular attention to issues of fairness and justice in both the individual case and the criminal system writ large. It would provide an evidence law-based supplement to a criminal defendant's constitutional right to present a defense[33] and provide an easier pathway to admission than the constitutional right, which requires proof that the application of a particular evidence rule infringes on a "weighty interest of the accused" and is "arbitrary" or "disproportionate to" its designed purpose.[34]

The particular rule or rules that would warrant bending in a specific case would vary. But one rule that may be a primary target of decarceratory rule bending is relevance. Every item of evidence that is admitted at trial must be relevant – it must tend to prove a fact that is "of consequence" to that particular case.[35] A primary purpose of the relevance requirement is to make sure that the factfinder is considering only evidence that is material to the resolution of the case at hand. But a judge's determination of what is material – what matters to a particular case – is hugely consequential; if evidence is not relevant, it is not admissible.[36]

In *Old Chief v. U.S.*, the Supreme Court acknowledged the gravity of the jury's task in a criminal case, noting that jurors have an "obligation to sit in judgment" of

pdf (reviewing studies and concluding "the best estimate of the impact of additional incarceration on crime in the United States today is zero").

33 *See* Chambers, 410 U.S. 284.

34 Holmes v. South Carolina, 547 U.S. 319, 324–5 (2006).

35 FED. R. EVID. 401.

36 FED. R. EVID. 402.

another person, an obligation that carries deep moral significance.[37] Towards that end, the Court reasoned that "the prosecution may fairly seek to place its evidence before the jurors, … to convince the jurors that a guilty verdict would be morally reasonable as much as to point to the discrete elements of a defendant's legal fault."[38] Criminal defendants, however, are deprived of this ability to appeal directly to jurors' sense of morality in coming to judgment. While juries possess the inherent power to nullify – to acquit because doing so is morally justified, even if the evidence supports a conviction – defense attorneys may not tell jurors about this power. Decarceratory rule bending could help counter this imbalance; it would allow the defense to "fairly seek" to present evidence that an acquittal would be morally reasonable, and help the jury see the moral implications and concrete consequences of a finding of guilt.

At its core, relevance is about storytelling; relevance rulings "determine[] whose stories are told and how they are told."[39] In the spirit of decarceratory rule bending, there is much space for judges to push the boundaries of traditional determinations of what issues are "of consequence" to the resolution of a particular case in order to expand what stories the jury hears and how such stories are conveyed. Bending relevance principles could expand the story of a particular criminal prosecution to help fact finders see how the criminal law is applied and understand how structural forces, including structural racism, impact the behavior of individuals who are empowered to enforce the law and those who are targeted by law enforcement. As Judge Bazelon reflected in his dissent in *U.S. v. Alexander*,

> Criminal trials … compel us to explore these problems, and thereby offer some slight hope that we will learn, in the course of deciding individual cases, something about the causes of crime. Not only the defendant but the criminal justice system as a whole has a vital interest in insuring that trials are conducted without significant error and in a manner that guarantees the ventilation of all the pertinent issues and information. We cannot afford to obscure the difficult questions for the sake of speed and efficiency in obtaining convictions, since efficiency of that order yields a specious economy.[40]

In *Alexander*, for example, Judge Bazelon suggested that introducing more evidence about the racially charged atmosphere in which the defendants committed the charged acts could force society to reckon with structural inequality. As Judge Bazelon concluded: "We cannot rationally decry crime and brutality and racial animosity without at the same time struggling to enhance the fairness and integrity of

37 Old Chief v. United States, 519 U.S. 172, 187–8 (1997).

38 *Id.*

39 Julia Simon-Kerr, *Relevance Through a Feminist Lens*, *in* PHILOSOPHICAL FOUNDATIONS OF EVIDENCE LAW (Christian Dahlman, Alex Stein, and Giovanni Tuzet, eds., Oxford University Press 2021).

40 United States v. Alexander, 471 F.2d 923, 926 (D.C. Cir. 1973) (Bazelon, C.J., dissenting).

the criminal justice system. That system has first-line responsibility for probing and coping with these complex problems."[41]

Criminal prosecutions are conducted in the name of "the people." Yet, the very jurors who are asked to sit in moral judgment of their peers may know very little about how the criminal system operates and the consequences of a conviction. For example, issues of race and racism are central to the operation of the criminal system, yet lawyers, judges, and commentators pretend even the most obviously racially charged cases have "nothing to do with race."[42] As a result, many jurors come to a verdict without hearing evidence about how race influences law enforcement. They may not know that law enforcement practices do not reflect actual behavior in society. For example, many jurors likely remain unaware that the rates of drug use and possession are largely consistent across racial groups, while rates of arrest, prosecution, and conviction are disproportionately focused on people of color, and in particular Black men.[43] And such ignorance by criminal jurors is largely by design; people who have had negative experiences with law enforcement are often deemed incapable of being fair and impartial in assessing the government's evidence and struck for cause. And in many jurisdictions people who have themselves been targeted by law enforcement and convicted of a felony are ineligible for jury service. Decarceratory rule bending could allow defendants to introduce evidence about how seemingly neutral enforcement policies are deeply influenced by race, class, gender, ability, and many other axes of difference and inequality. There are valid arguments that such evidence is relevant under traditional principles and does not require bending any rules.[44] But if there are no allegations of racially motivated bias on behalf of the particular police officer, most judges likely would deem such evidence irrelevant.[45]

Perhaps even more controversially, decarceratory rule bending could provide jurors with information about the consequences of conviction. Jurors may not know that conviction of even a seemingly low-level crime can carry a significant term of incarceration – a punishment that not only has extremely deleterious consequences for the convicted individual and their community, but also society writ large. Not only is incarceration incredibly expensive and inherently violent, but people who

41 United States v. Alexander, 471 F.2d 923, 926 (D.C. Cir. 1973) (Bazelon, C.J., dissenting).

42 Capers, *supra* note 28, at 885–6 (providing examples from high-profile prosecutions).

43 *See, e.g.*, Michelle Alexander, The New Jim Crow: Mass Incarceration in the Age of Colorblindness 121–37 (The New Press 2010).

44 *See, e.g.*, Jasmine Gonzales Rose, Asess Bhasin, and Spencer Piston, *Antiracist Expert Evidence*, 134 Yale L.J. 2362, 2449 (arguing that "expert evidence establishing or explaining the existence, effect, or impact of racism can be relevant in many circumstances").

45 *See, e.g.*, *id.* ("A very high proportion (82.67%) of criminal-defense attorneys surveyed identified 'judges['] determin[ations] that such evidence is not relevant' as a barrier to introducing antiracist expert evidence").

are incarcerated often leave prison or jail less able to achieve stability and safety than when they entered.[46]

Information about the consequences of a finding of guilt is technically irrelevant to the jury's resolution of an individual case. Jurors are tasked with assessing the strength of the government's evidence and are instructed that what happens after conviction should not concern them. I suggest that all people in whose name we punish should be informed about and concerned with the consequences of a criminal conviction – especially the very people who are tasked with the grave moral duty to assess legal guilt. Jurors possess the inherent power to nullify a verdict in a criminal case – to say that they do not believe a conviction is appropriate, independent of the strength of the evidence. Decarceratory rule bending would provide them evidence that would help them assess whether or not a conviction is morally justified.[47]

Abolitionist and decarceration-oriented scholars and activists are actively pushing against the scope of the carceral state and creating mechanisms beyond criminal punishment to advance safety, enhance thriving, and reduce harm. And other scholars are engaging in the promising project of re-drafting evidence rules in whole or in part to reflect different experiences, perspectives, and include different voices.[48] Hopefully, these different initiatives will reduce the temptation to bend evidence rules to facilitate the imposition of carceral sanctions. While this crucial work to build a different future is underway, the conventional criminal law apparatus will continue unabated. In the meantime, one way to rebalance the evidentiary scales and give fact finders a more robust understanding of the context in which the criminal law is applied – and the consequences of that application – is to bend evidence rules towards decarceration.

[46] Nazgol Ghandnoosh, Luke Trinka, and Celeste Barry, *One in Five: How Mass Incarceration Deepens Inequality and Harms Public Safety*, The Sentencing Project (Jan. 2024), www.sentencingproject.org/app/uploads/2024/02/One-in-Five-How-Mass-Incarceration-Exacerbates-Inequality-and-Harms-Public-Safety.pdf.

[47] Of course, there is no certainty to what ends a particular jury will put any evidence, including evidence that would be admitted under this proposed rule. Whether to invoke this rule would remain in the discretion of the individual defense attorney.

[48] *See, e.g.*, Roberts and Simon-Kerr, *supra* note 15.

Reimagining *Daubert v. Merrell Dow Pharmaceuticals, Inc.* as a Non-Reformist Reform

Maneka Sinha

INTRODUCTION

In 2011, David Cesar Coronado was charged in Dallas County, Texas with severely injuring his five-month-old child.[1] Critical to the case against him was the testimony of Dr. Robert Williams, a dentist and odontologist who testified that alleged bitemarks found on the child matched Mr. Coronado's teeth.[2] Prior to trial, Mr. Coronado sought to exclude Dr. Williams's testimony arguing that bitemark analysis is unreliable.[3] The judge overseeing the case held a hearing to consider the issue, but denied Mr. Coronado's request.[4]

Dr. Williams testified at trial that he "could not exclude" Mr. Coronado as the source of the bitemarks – essentially telling the jury Mr. Coronado bit his child.[5] The jury convicted.[6]

Appealing his conviction, Mr. Coronado had both the science and the law on his side, at least in theory. Criticism of the reliability of bitemark analysis had been growing for years.[7] And in 2009, an explosive report issued by the National Academy of Sciences decried bitemark analysis as scientifically unsupported.[8] Moreover, DNA testing had revealed numerous wrongful convictions based on false bitemark identifications and controversy surrounding the method was raging.[9]

As for the law, in 1993, the Supreme Court issued the watershed decision, *Daubert v. Merrell Dow Pharmaceuticals, Inc.* Through *Daubert*, the Court fundamentally

[1] Coronado v. State, 384 S.W.3d 919, 921 (Tex. App. 2012).

[2] *Id.* at 922.

[3] *Id.*

[4] *Id.*

[5] *Id.*

[6] *Id.*

[7] *E.g.*, Paul Giannelli, *Bite Mark Analysis*, 43 CRIM. L. BULLETIN 930 (2007).

[8] COMM. ON IDENTIFYING THE NEEDS OF THE FORENSIC SCI. CMTY., NAT'L RSCH. COUNCIL, STRENGTHENING FORENSIC SCIENCE IN THE UNITED STATES: A PATH FORWARD 176 (2009), www.ojp.gov/pdffiles1/nij/grants/228091.pdf (hereinafter NAS REPORT).

[9] Giannelli, *supra* note 7, at 939–40.

altered how lower courts were to determine whether scientific evidence may be considered by a jury in a way seemingly favorable to Mr. Coronado.[10] The decision imposed a new duty on judges, requiring them to assess the relevance and reliability – or, trustworthiness – of proposed scientific evidence before admitting it at trial.[11] The Supreme Court explained that in order for scientific evidence to be found to be reliable under an evidentiary standard, it must be scientifically valid.[12] The Court suggested judges consider five factors to evaluate reliability: whether a theory or technique: (1) can be and has been tested; (2) has been subjected to peer review and publication; (3) has a known or potential error rate; (4) has standards governing its operation; and (5) is generally accepted within the relevant scientific community.[13] It emphasized that whether a method has been tested is "a key question" in determining its validity.[14] Bitemark analysis, however, had hardly undergone meaningful testing.[15]

Notwithstanding Mr. Coronado's advantages, the appellate court's decision was rife with questionable logic. Although Texas had long since required scientific validity as a prerequisite for admissibility of expert evidence,[16] the court's reliability exploration was cursory.[17] It neglected to even evaluate whether Dr. Williams's analysis amounted to valid science.[18] The court's logic was somewhat circular too; it cited to Dr. Williams's own claims about the validity of the discipline to find it reliable.[19] The court also pointed to a pre-*Daubert* case admitting bitemark evidence without putting in the effort to determine whether the case was correctly decided or aligned with good science.[20] The appellate court rounded out its opinion by suggesting that because bitemark analysis is based on "experience and training," "hard science methods" like validation and assessment of error rates are not suitable measures of reliability.[21] It failed to acknowledge that validity testing and error assessment are used to determine the reliability of even experience-based disciplines[22]

[10] 509 U.S. 579, 589–91 (1993).

[11] *Id.* at 589–90.

[12] *Id.*

[13] *Id.* at 593–95.

[14] *Id.* at 593.

[15] NAS Report, *supra* note 8, at 176; Giannelli, *supra* note 7, at 933–4.

[16] Jordan v. State, 928 S.W.2d 550, 554 (Tex. Crim. App. 1996) (describing the *Daubert* standard as "virtually identical to the one [previously] adopted by this Court").

[17] As one body of experts summarized it, "The appellate court engaged in a *Daubert* analysis heavy on description of the expert's experience and education and light on any genuine scientific evaluation ...." David L. Faigman et al., 4 Mod. Sci. Evidence § 35:8 (2024–2025 ed.).

[18] Coronado v. State, 384 S.W.3d 919, 926 (Tex. App. 2012).

[19] *Id.* at 924.

[20] *Id.* at 926.

[21] *Id.* at 924.

[22] President's Council of Advisors on Sci. & Tech., Forensic Science in Criminal Courts: Ensuring Scientific Validity of Feature-Comparison Methods 55 (2016), https://obamawhitehouse.archives.gov/sites/default/files/microsites/ostp/PCAST/pcast_forensic_science_report_final.pdf.

or that the *Daubert* framework applies with equal force to non-scientific expert evidence.[23]

The appellate court denied Mr. Coronado's appeal.[24] Mr. Coronado, who was first convicted at age twenty-six, is serving a life sentence in prison.[25]

***

An outsider without experience with the evidentiary standards at play or the controversy surrounding bitemark analysis might be tempted to think that justice was served. That as a factual matter, Mr. Coronado may well be guilty. They might even think that, since the judge weighed arguments before admitting the evidence, the process was legitimate and justice was done. At least on paper, judges evaluated the bitemark evidence both before and after it was presented at trial. A judge held a pretrial hearing on the reliability question and an appellate court reviewed the trial court's decision. But still, it is worth asking: Did those measures merely create a farce of legitimate process where there was none?

In recent years, scholars have increasingly grappled with questions like this one. Discussion around whether established legal standards entrench carceralism – the deeply rooted prioritization of policing, prosecution, and punishment to resolve societal issues – is mounting.[26] Mr. Coronado's case is far from unique. Bitemark analysis falls within a long line of forensic and technological tools of questionable reliability that have contributed to harms ranging from detention to conviction and even execution,[27] but which have nevertheless survived *Daubert* scrutiny. As scholarly and popular examination of whether traditional reform or more radical transformative steps are necessary to stem carceral harm increases, scholars are recognizing that evidence law's core features require similar evaluation.[28]

Against this backdrop, this chapter considers, through an abolitionist lens, the role of the evidence law governing the admission of scientific, technical, and specialized

23 Kumho Tire Co. v. Carmichael, 526 U.S. 137, 141 (1999) ("We conclude that *Daubert*'s general holding – setting forth the trial judge's general 'gatekeeping' obligation – applies not only to testimony based on 'scientific' knowledge, but also to testimony based on 'technical' and 'other specialized' knowledge.").

24 *Coronado*, 384 S.W.3d at 928.

25 *Id.* at 922; *Inmate Information Search*, TEX. DEP'T OF CRIM. JUST., https://inmate.tdcj.texas.gov/InmateSearch/viewDetail.action?sid=08295222 (last visited Apr. 7, 2025) (search SID number "08295222").

26 *E.g.*, Thomas Ward Frampton, *The Dangerous Few: Taking Seriously Prison Abolition and Its Skeptics*, 135 HARV. L. REV. 2013, 2014–16 (2022).

27 Cameron Todd Willingham was convicted of murder by arson in 1992 after a fire consumed his house, killing his three daughters. The arson investigation that concluded that Mr. Willingham started the fire has since been discredited and he is widely believed to have been wrongfully convicted. He was executed in 2004. David Grann, *Trial by Fire*, NEW YORKER (Aug. 31, 2009), www.newyorker.com/magazine/2009/09/07/trial-by-fire.

28 Anna Roberts, *Models and Limits of Federal Rule of Evidence 609 Reform*, 76 VAND. L. REV. 1879, 1893 (2023).

(STS) evidence in criminal cases.[29] It questions whether *Daubert* was a reform, as many have suggested, or if instead, it allows the criminal legal system to operate under the guise of having meaningful checks for preventing carceral unfairness. It explores how and whether to reduce the power and influence of carceral institutions in governing use of STS evidence. In short, it reimagines *Daubert*. For example, it asks whether it is possible to reduce harm by divesting courts of their power to admit STS evidence and reinvesting that power in ways that better ensure evidence reliability and are consistent with abolition *and* accountability.

Reimagining *Daubert* invites reconsideration of whether evidentiary rules *combat* carceral harm, or if alternatively, they *enable* imposition of carceral harm behind a façade of judicial scrutiny. It thus offers an opportunity to creatively envision how to prevent the harms caused by junk science both from within and outside of evidence law. In tackling these issues, this chapter builds upon the critical approaches to examining evidence law introduced by the editors and contributors to this volume.[30]

STS EVIDENCE AND THE NEED FOR REFORM

The predominant standard governing STS evidence admissibility is Federal Rule of Evidence 702. In its original form, Rule 702 stated:

> If scientific, technical, or other specialized knowledge will assist the trier of fact to understand the evidence or to determine a fact in issue, a witness qualified as an expert by knowledge, skill, experience, training, or education, may testify thereto in the form of an opinion or otherwise.[31]

Notwithstanding this language, before *Daubert* was issued, many courts used a standard set in the 1923 case, *Frye v. United States*, which permits admission of scientific evidence if the underlying methodology has gained "general acceptance" in the scientific community.[32] *Frye* allowed judges to let scientists decide whether scientific evidence was sufficiently reliable rather than require them to conduct a reliability assessment themselves.[33]

[29] I am not the first to contemplate whether abolitionist goals can be achieved through evidence law reform. Anna Roberts, another contributor to this volume, as one example, has considered whether Federal Rule of Evidence 609 can be meaningfully reformed without confronting the Rule's original outgrowth from associations between Blackness and criminality or without reifying the current legal regime. *Id.* at 1896.

[30] *E.g.*, Bennett Capers, *Race, Gatekeeping, Magical Words, and Evidence*, 76 VAND. L. REV. 1855 (2023); Andrea Dennis, *Poetic (In)Justice? Rap Music Lyrics as Art, Life, and Criminal Evidence*, 31 COLUM. J.L. & ARTS 1 (2007); Jasmine B. Gonzalez Rose, *Toward a Critical Race Theory of Evidence*, 101 MINN. L. REV. 2243 (2017); Julia Simon-Kerr, *Unmasking Demeanor*, 88 GEO. WASH. L. REV. ARGUENDO 158 (2024).

[31] FED. R. EVID. 702 (1975).

[32] 293 F. 1013, 1014 (D.C. Cir. 1923).

[33] *Id.*

Moreover, prior to *Daubert*, courts struggled with whether to utilize the *Frye* test or Rule 702 to decide scientific evidence admissibility questions, and with how to interpret and apply the new rule.[34] It was a pressing issue, since unscientific and pseudo-scientific evidence was inundating courts.[35]

Daubert brought clarity to the confusion and held that Rule 702, not *Frye*, governs the admission of scientific evidence. Specifically, the *Daubert* opinion interpreted the rule to require proposed scientific evidence be based on scientifically valid reasoning or methodology and a proper application of the method to the case as conditions of admissibility.[36] The holding was extended beyond scientific evidence to technical and specialized evidence in 1999 in *Kumho Tire Co. v. Carmichael*.[37] The *Daubert* and *Kumho Tire Co.* holdings have since been incorporated into the text of Rule 702.[38]

Daubert was quickly hailed as a positive reform, as "revolutionary"[39] and "one of the more important decisions of the twentieth century."[40] The decision was lauded for imposing on judges a requirement to examine the scientific underpinnings of STS evidence.[41] In criminal cases, which are the focus of this chapter, it is used by judges to decide whether powerful and persuasive evidence purportedly connecting an accused person to a crime, like bitemark, fingerprint, and DNA evidence, can be considered by a jury in deciding guilt. For accused persons, the result of a Rule 702-*Daubert* inquiry can be the difference between freedom and imprisonment.

But as the next section makes clear, *Daubert*, in practice, is more carceral than revolutionary. To make this point, the next section considers the power and danger of STS evidence against the backdrop of abolitionism.

THE POWER AND DANGER OF STS EVIDENCE

Particularly on the criminal side, the excitement over *Daubert* and its focus on scientific validity made sense. Although the standard governing whether expert evidence is admitted at trials may seem like an in-the-weeds debate for legal wonks, *how* STS evidence is evaluated has uniquely concerning implications. STS evidence powers

34 David E. Bernstein and Eric G. Lasker, *Defending* Daubert: *It's Time to Amend Federal Rule of Evidence 702*, 57 Wm. & Mary L. Rev. 1, 4 (2015).

35 David E. Bernstein, *The Misbegotten Judicial Resistance to the* Daubert *Revolution*, 89 Notre Dame L. Rev. 27, 34 (2013).

36 Daubert v. Merrell Dow Pharmaceuticals, Inc., 509 U.S. 579, 592–3 (1993).

37 526 U.S. 137 (1999).

38 Fed. R. Evid. 702 advisory committee's note to 2000 Amendment.

39 David L. Faigman, *The* Daubert *Revolution and the Birth of Modernity: Managing Scientific Evidence in the Age of Science*, 46 U.C. Davis L. Rev. 893, 895 (2013).

40 Christopher B. Mueller, Daubert *Asks the Right Questions: Now Appellate Courts Should Help Find the Right Answers*, 33 Seton Hall L. Rev. 987, 987 (2003).

41 Faigman, *supra* note 39, at 907–8. The Rule 702-*Daubert* framework for determining the admissibility of STS evidence applies in all federal courts and the vast majority of state courts.

the criminal legal system. By purporting to connect perpetrators to crimes, STS methods facilitate the essential functions of the carceral state – surveillance, policing, prosecution, and punishment.[42] STS evidence "can be both powerful and quite misleading because of the difficulty in evaluating it."[43] Juries are easily persuaded by expertise – real or feigned. Indeed, juries perceive even unreliable STS evidence as more persuasive than other evidence.[44]

These problems are exacerbated by the commonly held belief that forensic and technological methods are accurate, objective, and neutral.[45] This gives STS evidence a little-discussed cleansing effect that makes prosecutions that would otherwise seem unsavory appear legitimate.[46] Where "science" suggests guilt, STS evidence can have the effect of laundering away the stains of police violence and misconduct, bias and rights violations, withholding of evidence, overcharging, coercive plea practices, and harsh punishments and allow juries to feel good about convicting.[47] How we decide what STS evidence juries hear, accordingly, has significant consequences for accused persons and for the criminal legal system as a whole. These consequences come into even sharper relief when viewed against the goals of abolition.

For the uninitiated, abolitionism is a theoretical and practical agenda for dismantling carceral institutions and eradicating the harm they cause to individuals and communities.[48] It rejects the idea that carceral institutions are necessary for preserving public safety or solving societal problems. Abolitionism focuses on confronting the origins of today's racialized carceral system in its more overtly oppressive antecedents, like chattel slavery and Jim Crow.[49] An underlying premise of abolitionism is that carceral institutions maintain racial hierarchy in modern society.[50]

Abolitionists seek to strengthen communities by replacing the carceral apparatus with systems that promote safety, care, and wellbeing without traditional

42 In addition to traditional forensic identification methods, law enforcement agencies routinely employ high-tech surveillance systems, computer vision, and biometric and other databases among other tools for wide-ranging tasks from street investigation to producing courtroom evidence. Maneka Sinha, *Radically Reimagining Forensic Evidence*, 73 ALA. L. REV. 879, 892 (2022).

43 Daubert v. Merrell Dow Pharmaceuticals, Inc., 509 U.S. 579, 595 (1993) (quoting Jack B. Weinstein, *Rule 702 of the Federal Rules of Evidence Is Sound; It Should Not Be Amended*, 138 F.R.D. 631, 632 (1991)).

44 Mark Joseph Stern, *Forensic Science Isn't Science*, SLATE (June 11, 2014 at 7:11 ET), https://slate.com/technology/2014/06/forensic-science-is-biased-and-inaccurate-but-juries-believe-it-and-convict-the-innocent.html.

45 *E.g.*, Chaz Arnett, *Black Lives Monitored*, 69 UCLA L. REV. 1384, 1411 (2023).

46 Maneka Sinha, *The Entrenched Carceralism of Forensics*, INQUEST (July 26, 2021), https://inquest.org/entrenched-carceralism-of-forensics/.

47 *Id.*

48 Angela Y. Davis, ARE PRISONS OBSOLETE? 43–45 (Seven Stories Press 2003).

49 *E.g.*, Marbre Stahly-Butts and Amna A. Akbar, *Reforms for Radicals? An Abolitionist Framework*, 68 UCLA L. REV. 1544, 1563 (2022).

50 Alexis Hoag, *Abolition as the Solution: Redress for Victims of Excessive Police Force*, 48 FORDHAM URB. L.J. 721, 737 (2021).

punishment.[51] Abolitionists also seek to empower communities impacted by carceral harm to make their own decisions about how to promote safety and justice.[52] Abolitionists advocate for "non-reformist" reforms that seek to shrink and delegitimize the carceral state and reduce harm to individuals and communities affected by them until abolition can be fully realized.[53] Non-reformism aims to reduce the control and influence of carceral institutions by divesting them of power and returning it to communities while exposing the oppression such institutions impose.[54] Non-reformist reforms, in short, aim to support communities through care, without "accommodat[ing] the current system."[55]

Traditional reform advocacy, by contrast, generally accepts carceral institutions as fundamentally legitimate, but seeks to improve them and reduce abuses through modest reforms.[56] Abolitionists respond that conventional reform advocacy increases harm by treating the carceral apparatus as though it can be "fixed." They urge that conventional approaches cement carceralism through expansion and legitimization of the current system without contending with its roots.[57] Critically, because abolitionists recognize their origins in oppression, they reject actions that invest in, expand, or legitimize carceral institutions.[58]

Legitimization of the carceral state may occur when there is an appearance of checks to ensure justice, but those checks are merely superficial. For example, abolitionists decry conventional reforms like police training (e.g., on proper methods for conducting vehicle stops) or transparency measures (e.g., requiring patrol officers to wear body cameras) as inadequate because they take for granted the carceral system as inherently valuable and seek only to mitigate or deflect from abuse. Such traditional reforms may require additional funding and investment to implement and end up equipping police with even more tools to pursue carceral goals.[59] Modest actions like these, thus, create an appearance of reform, while doing little in reality to upend the status quo.

[51] Patrisse Cullors, An Abolitionist's Handbook: 12 Steps to Changing Yourself and the World 8 (Own It! 2021) ("Abolitionist practice is also about establishing a system that is rooted in dignity and care for all people. A system that does not rely on punishment as accountability.").

[52] Alex Vitale, The End of Policing 224–5 (Verso 2017).

[53] Amna A. Akbar, *Demands for a Democratic Political Economy*, 134 Harv. L. Rev. F. 90, 101–4 (2020).

[54] *Id.* at 104–6.

[55] Mark Engler and Paul Engler, *Andre Gorz's Non-Reformist Reforms Show How We Can Transform the World Today*, Jacobin (July 22, 2021), https://jacobinmag.com/2021/07/andre-gorz-non-reformist-reforms-revolution-political-theory.

[56] Amna A. Akbar, *An Abolitionist Horizon for (Police) Reform*, 108 Calif. L. Rev. 1781, 1814 (2020).

[57] Allegra M. McLeod, *Prison Abolition and Grounded Justice*, 62 UCLA L. Rev. 1156, 1164 (2015).

[58] Dorothy E. Roberts, *Abolition Constitutionalism*, 133 Harv. L. Rev. 1, 43 (2019); Mariame Kaba, We Do This 'Til We Free Us: Abolitionist Organizing and Transforming Justice 96, 133 (Tamara K. Nopper ed., Haymarket 2021).

[59] *Reformist Reforms vs. Abolitionist Steps in Policing*, Critical Resistance (May 14, 2020), https://criticalresistance.org/resources/reformist-reforms-vs-abolitionist-steps-in-policing/.

Having provided a primer on abolition, the next part applies an abolitionist framework to consider the admissibility of STS evidence.

ABOLITION AND ADMISSIBILITY

Applying an abolitionist frame to admissibility rules has dual purposes. First, it encourages us to re-examine whether evidentiary filters are meaningful. Viewing legal frameworks that uphold the criminal legal system through a lens that forces confrontation with its oppressive origins challenges our understanding of the purposes and function of evidence law. In the case of the law governing the admission of STS evidence, the confrontation challenges us to question whether *Daubert* is a useful reform or merely another feature of the criminal process that enables carceral function and carceral harm. That is, the frame allows evaluation of evidence law's role in governing use of STS evidence and the damage caused by unreliable STS evidence, not with the aim of "improving" the law, but with the aim of understanding its function in legitimizing the carceral apparatus. At the same time, it offers a new vehicle for considering how to prevent carceral harm caused by use of STS evidence consistent with abolitionist goals.[60]

How do *Daubert* and other evidentiary law governing the admission of STS evidence perform when evaluated through an abolitionist lens? As Mr. Coronado's case reveals, despite lofty language about "good grounds" and adherence to the scientific method,[61] misapplication of *Daubert* can allow criminal justice consumers to assume STS evidence reliability is being vetted, when in fact, much admissibility analysis is superficial. As in his case, courts often rely on precedent to admit STS evidence and the *Daubert* factors can facially appear to be satisfied even without rigorous adherence to the reliability requirement.[62] *Daubert* analysis often appears more like a judge is ticking boxes, treating the admissibility requirements like a grocery list, than serious reliability vetting.[63] Mr. Coronado's case is a worrying example of how nominal gesturing towards *Daubert* by judges can give carceral science unwarranted legitimacy by creating an appearance that forensic and technological evidence admitted against accused persons has been scrutinized by a judicial authority.

60 Hoag, *supra* note 50, at 737–8 ("[Abolitionist] reorientation enables us to reimagine systems capable of dismantling white supremacy, redistributing resources to prevent harm, and advancing remedies that do not center on carceral punishment.").

61 Daubert v. Merrell Dow Pharmaceuticals, Inc., 509 U.S. 579, 590 (1993).

62 Brandon L. Garrett and M. Chris Fabricant, *The Myth of the Reliability Test*, 86 FORDHAM L. REV. 1559, 1564 (2018).

63 *E.g.*, United States v. Adams, 444 F. Supp. 3d 1248, 1258 (D. Or. 2020) (explaining, in deciding the admissibility of firearms analysis evidence, that each *Daubert* factor can "at a superficial level" be "check[ed]" off, but that "problems with … [the] methodology begin to emerge" "when you look beneath the surface …").

Bitemark analysis is not an aberration among STS methods that are too often assumed to be reliable. Traditional forensic methods like comparative bullet lead analysis, hair comparison analysis, shoeprint analysis, firearms analysis, as well as newer technologies like automated gunshot detection systems and facial recognition technology have all been either wholly discredited or seriously questioned over reliability.[64] Even so, with few exceptions, they have repeatedly been used to produce evidence against accused persons. Each has been analyzed under *Daubert*'s multi-factor test and been found sufficiently reliable to be admitted as evidence against accused persons. Jurors hearing evidence produced by them, accordingly, would have little reason to question their reliability.

Daubert's most significant role may be upholding the carceral function of the criminal system. Discrepancies between how strictly *Daubert* is applied, depending on whether the defense or prosecution seeks to introduce or exclude STS evidence, corroborate what many long suspected. More than thirty years of research since *Daubert*'s issuance confirms that courts are far more lenient in admitting prosecution experts – even dubious ones – than defense experts.[65] Prosecution challenges to defense experts under *Daubert*, likewise, are drastically more successful than defense challenges to prosecution experts, which research suggests succeed in fewer than 10 percent of cases.[66]

In fact, when accused persons seek to challenge the admissibility of prosecution-proffered STS evidence, judges routinely decline to even hold hearings on why evidence law should preclude the admission of unreliable STS evidence against them.[67] Commentators have noted that the across-the-aisle divergence in admission rates of STS evidence are not due to differences in evidence quality.[68]

What is the source of these discrepancies? Some have pointed to the disparity of resources between the defense and the state. Most accused persons are indigent and represented by court-appointed counsel who are unable to bring the robust

64 E.g., Maneka Sinha, *The Automated Fourth Amendment*, 73 Emory L.J. 590, 613–14 (2024).

65 D. Michael Risinger, *Navigating Expert Reliability: Are Criminal Standards of Certainty Being Left on the Dock?*, 64 Alb. L. Rev. 99, 104–12 (2000).

66 Faigman et al., *supra* note 17, at § 1:35; Jed S. Rakoff and Goodwin Liu, *Forensic Science: A Judicial Perspective*, 120 Proc. Nat'l Acad. Scis. (2023), www.pnas.org/doi/10.1073/pnas.2301838120 (describing survey of 300 federal civil and criminal cases finding that "in the criminal cases, less than 10% of the Daubert challenges made by defendants were successful (although those made by prosecutors typically succeeded)").

67 E.g., Johnson v. Commonwealth, 12 S.W.3d 258, 260–61 (Ky. 2000) (describing trial court's refusal to hold a hearing on accused's request to exclude microscopic hair analysis evidence despite evidence of unreliability).

68 Faigman et al., *supra* note 17, at § 1:35. Differences in how *Daubert* is applied in civil versus criminal cases also support understanding *Daubert* as upholding the carceral status quo. Courts apply *Daubert* more strictly in civil cases than in criminal cases where STS evidence is being offered against an accused person, even when the *same type* of evidence is being offered. Julie A. Seaman, *A Tale of Two* Dauberts, 47 Ga. L. Rev. 889, 896–7, 908 (2013).

litigation that results in serious scrutiny of STS methods.[69] Prosecutors, on the other hand, have access to police and state crime labs, along with the examiners who work in them.[70]

But this resource imbalance cannot be the only explanation for these significant – and enduring – disparities. Although resource constraints do plague defenders,[71] a number of defenders do bring robust challenges to prosecution STS evidence and defend vigorously against challenges to their own evidence. They still lose.

Some scholars are more blunt in offering a reason for the disparities: Judges simply "disfavor" criminal defendants.[72] For starters, judges may be biased against those charged with a crime. In addition, criminally accused persons are predominantly poor. Black, Latine, Indigenous, and transgender people, along with members of other minoritized and marginalized communities, are overrepresented among the accused population.[73] All of the communities just named have been "disfavored" throughout our nation's history.

As others have explained, evidence law cannot be understood outside of this intersectional context.[74] The disparities in how STS evidence is filtered may seem inexplicable without situating them against who comprises the accused population. With the added context, the disparities become understandable. More importantly, they render visible evidence law's role in upholding the current state of the criminal legal system.

Where do these revelations leave us? If they do serve to uphold carceralism, do we abolish the rules of evidence governing STS admissibility? Maybe, but that is unlikely to happen anytime soon. Abolitionists generally acknowledge that carceral institutions are not easily eliminated and cannot be quickly eradicated.[75] Major changes to the existing legal apparatus are rare. There is little reason to believe the rules of evidence will be abandoned in the near future and modifying even

69 Michael J. Saks, *Judging Admissibility*, 35 J. CORP. L. 135, 145 (2009).

70 Keith A. Findley, *Innocents at Risk: Adversary Imbalance, Forensic Science, and the Search for Truth*, 38 SETON HALL L. REV. 893, 929–30 (2008).

71 BRYAN FURST, A FAIR FIGHT: ACHIEVING INDIGENT DEFENSE RESOURCE PARITY, BRENNAN CENTER FOR JUST. 1–3 (Sept. 9, 2019), www.brennancenter.org/our-work/research-reports/fair-fight.

72 Michael J. Saks and David L. Faigman, *Expert Evidence after Daubert*, 1 ANN. REV. L. & SOC. SCI. 105, 122 (2005). The authors also include civil plaintiffs among those judges disfavor. *Id.*

73 *E.g.*, Nazgol Ghandnoosh and Celeste Barry, *One in Five: Disparities in Crime and Policing*, SENT'G PROJECT (Nov, 2023), www.sentencingproject.org/reports/one-in-five-disparities-in-crime-and-policing/; Valerie Jenness and Alexis Rowland, *The Structure and Operation of the Transgender Criminal Legal System Nexus in the United States: Inequalities, Administrative Violence, and Injustice at Every Turn*, 7 ANN. REV. CRIMINOLOGY 283, 284 (2023).

74 *E.g.*, Jasmine B. Gonzales Rose, *Racial Character Evidence in Police Killing Cases*, 2018 WIS. L. REV. 369, 375 (2018) ("Most … assume that since evidence law is facially race-neutral, it applies equally to all persons irrespective of race and is immune from racially disparate application and impact. However, … evidence rules – and perhaps, even more importantly, the principles and values behind these rules – are not applied or enforced equally along racial lines.").

75 KABA, *supra* note 58, at 72.

single rules is a sluggish process that typically yields only modest results.[76] Perhaps, however, the underlying principles of *Daubert* connecting scientific validity to evidentiary reliability can be used to construct a non-reformist agenda focused on harm reduction for constraining use of STS evidence. This possibility is taken up next.

CONCEPTUALIZING NON-REFORMIST ADMISSIBILITY REFORM

It is important to set out why it is worth retaining any reliability vetting of STS evidence at all. Conventional STS evidence is used primarily to connect crimes to individuals, suggesting that at least some STS evidence is important for non-carceral purposes, like identifying those who cause harm to others and fully understanding the harms caused. Both those who believe in the carceral state as it exists and those who seek its abolition agree that those responsible for causing harm should be identified accurately.[77] Abolitionists recognize that people will harm each other regardless of whether the system regulating their actions is carceral or a reimagined one in a post-abolition future. Holding those who cause harm accountable is not inconsistent with abolitionism; rather, abolitionists oppose the oppression, punitive punishment, and social hierarchy the current system imposes.[78] Reliability of STS evidence, thus, will remain important even under a non-carceral system for regulating harm.

The threshold question, then, becomes whether reform to evidence law governing admissibility of STS evidence consistent with a non-reformist agenda is possible. Professor Bennett Capers, one of the co-editors of this volume, posits that perhaps we should abandon Rule 702, which, as described, codifies the principles embedded in *Daubert*, and with it evidence law's distinction between expert and lay witnesses.[79] He persuasively argues that Rule 702 "reifies and entrenches a racial status quo" by favoring expertise that white people are more likely to have because of historical inequality in access to education generally and technical education and advanced degrees more specifically.[80] Professor Capers argues that Rules 401 and 403, by focusing on whether testimony will assist the trier of fact and have probative value not substantially outweighed by prejudice, can do the work Rule 702 currently claims to do, while simultaneously eradicating the "hierarchy of expertise" it embeds.[81]

[76] Mark A. Behrens and Andrew J. Trask, *Federal Rule of Evidence 702: A History and Guide to the 2023 Amendments Governing Expert Evidence*, 12 TEX. A&M L. REV. 43, 48–65 (2024) (summarizing the yearslong lead-up to amendments to Rule 702 in 2023).

[77] Sinha, *supra* note 42, at 941.

[78] Allegra M. McLeod, *Envisioning Abolition Democracy*, 132 HARV. L. REV. 1613, 1616 (2019).

[79] Capers, *supra* note 30, at 1875.

[80] *Id.* at 1866–8.

[81] *Id.* at 1874–5.

In many cases, Rule 403 could indeed make Rule 702 superfluous. That, however, is because whether STS evidence is probative will usually turn on whether it is reliable. Unvalidated, untrustworthy STS evidence hardly tends to prove a fact in controversy. The problem that follows is that even if Rule 702 is eradicated, evidence law will require some means of vetting reliability. Eliminating Rule 702 may simply result in Rule 702's reliability prongs being subsumed – whether explicitly or not – by Rule 403.

By removing STS from how evidence law defines expertise, jettisoning Rule 702 may also go some distance in expanding who qualifies as an expert. Still, the Rule 403 inquiry is highly subjective. Meaning, shifting the STS admissibility decision fulcrum from Rule 702 to Rule 403 and eliminating the reliability inquiry embedded in Rule 702 would allow judges to shield admissibility determinations behind the subjective – and amorphous – question of whether proffered evidence is "probative," which STS will usually appear to be unless method or application flaws are exposed.

There may be other ways to reform evidence law governing how STS evidence is vetted. Scholars have argued for a more rigid filtration mechanism to be adopted in criminal cases. Others have argued that a more stringent standard should be adopted specifically for evaluating reliability of traditional forensic methods[82] because they were largely developed in police labs rather than for scientific purposes[83] and have long contributed to wrongful convictions. Dean David Faigman recommends a different reform that essentially seeks to bring a cornerstone of scientific evaluation – peer review – into courtrooms, whereby judges could employ neutral experts to evaluate expert reports submitted by parties to litigation.[84]

The standard of review of STS admissibility decisions could also be reconsidered. Judges' admissibility decisions are currently reviewed under an "abuse of discretion" standard, which requires appellate courts to accord lower court decisions significant deference.[85] Perhaps *de novo* review, which would allow admissibility decisions to be reviewed afresh without providing the same deference to the underlying ruling, would create an incentive for lower courts to act with greater diligence in making STS admissibility determinations.

Evidence law reforms like these might indeed result in greater scrutiny of STS methods in some cases. Even so, it is not hard to imagine why locating solutions within evidence law may be inconsistent with non-reformist principles. Current STS admissibility standards are already strict – at least on paper. Nevertheless, they are applied strictly against defendants, and laxly against prosecutors, in ways that

82 *E.g.*, Daniel J. Capra, *Foreword: Symposium on Forensic Expert Testimony, Daubert, and Rule 702*, 86 Fordham L. Rev. 1459, 1460 (2018).

83 NAS Report, *supra* note 8, at 42.

84 David L. Faigman, *Overcoming Judicial Innumeracy: A Proposal to Bring the Venerable Process of Peer Review to the Enduring Problem of Courts' Scientific Illiteracy*, 26 Colum. Sci. & Tech. L. Rev. 76, 106–9 (2025).

85 Gen. Elec. Co. v. Joiner, 522 U.S. 136, 146 (1997).

allow – if not perpetuate – harm to people being churned through the criminal legal system. There is little reason to believe that more stringent standards could not be subverted in the same ways.

Again, judges apply STS admissibility rules in ways that systematically disfavor accused persons. This suggests that carceral logic, or a punitive orientation towards the admissibility evaluation, infects judicial decision-making.[86] This raises concerns about the potential for evidence law reform proposals to allow greater imposition of harm through the criminal legal system, particularly those that might result in strengthening judges' power to gatekeep. Underneath a patina of law "reform," modifications to evidence law like those sketched out above may ultimately have the consequence of condoning carceral governance of how STS evidence is used against accused persons without unsettling the underlying carceral logic that permeates the criminal legal system.

While *Daubert* has been ineffective at preventing admission of unreliable STS evidence, the issue is not that the fundamental premises underlying the case are unsound. In essence, the opinion requires that, in order to be admissible, evidence that claims to be scientific should be grounded in good science.[87] This is hardly a controvertible principle. The issue, rather, is that courts have largely employed the *Daubert* framework in ways that create an appearance of serious vetting even where no actual vetting is being conducted. Who decides the question may matter more than the standard being applied.

Given the above, this chapter argues for something different: transferring the power over determining admissibility of STS evidence from the judiciary to outside the courtroom. Judges play an essential role in ensuring that the criminal legal system functions pursuant to its original design. In doing so, they reinforce the appearance of carceral legitimacy. Accordingly, locating interventions outside of the judiciary may be a starting point for non-reformist reform of how STS evidence is handled in the criminal legal system. And it is consistent with nascent efforts to shift power from the state to communities, including those most impacted by policing.[88]

In addition, legislative action requiring reliability before forensic methods and technology may be used by police and/or introduced by the state can also help to reallocate the power to determine whether and how STS evidence can be used in courtrooms.[89] Particularly at the local level, where municipality governments may be small and nimble enough to take community goals and concerns into account,

86 Christy E. Lopez, *Abolish Carceral Logic*, 17 Stan. J. C.R. & C.L. 379, 386 (2022) (defining "carceral logic" as "a punishment mindset that views retribution and control, including by physical constraint (e.g. imprisonment), surveillance (e.g. electronic monitoring via ankle bracelet), or violence, as central components of a public safety system").

87 Daubert v. Merrell Dow Pharmaceuticals, Inc., 509 U.S. 579, 590 (1993).

88 Jocelyn Simonson, *Police Reform Through a Power Lens*, 130 Yale L.J. 778 (2021).

89 Sinha, *supra* note 64, at 653–4.

legislatures can take steps to ensure the reliability of STS evidence and reduce harm to affected community members.

In this way, Dean Faigman's proposal of bringing a panel of peer review experts to assist the court in Rule 702/*Daubert* evaluations might be adapted to more radical goals. For example, community organizations or legislatures might seek to form their own neutral, expert panels to vet STS methods prior to their use by law enforcement or admission in court. Such panels could incorporate the perspectives of individuals subject to harm by STS evidence.[90] This may have the added benefit of beginning the process of dissolving the existing hierarchy of expertise rooted in today's legal system.

Reforms aimed at moving STS evidence vetting outside of the courtroom could even be extended to non-trial phases of criminal prosecutions. Evidentiary rules only apply to trials.[91] STS methods used prior to trial (for example, for policing) or after trial (for example, at sentencing) do not require analysis under *Daubert* or Rule 702. Expanding STS vetting beyond the trial phase may have the significant benefit of reducing the harms imposed by policing technology used to surveil and monitor communities in clandestine ways with little oversight. The same may be true for unvetted STS evidence used at sentencing to secure harsh punishments.

It is critical, however, to acknowledge that the *Daubert* framework cannot be cleanly disentangled from the carceral system it operates within. The carceral logic underpinning judicial decision-making is not confined to courtrooms or even to the criminal legal system broadly. It extends outward, taking hold in and pervading social structures. Meaning, efforts to divest judicial power and transfer it externally without puncturing the permeating logic will encounter challenges and may not satisfy non-reformist aims. *Daubert*'s emphasis on and Rule 702's elevation of science in its framing of what types of knowledge justify opinion testimony has facilitated favoritism of supposed scientific evidence[92] and exclusion of other forms of expertise such as anti-racist or community experts.[93] Developing non-carceral means of vetting STS methods would face substantial hurdles, not least of which is a deficiency of truly neutral experts.[94]

To be sure, none of this will be easy. Scholars have described how power imbalances between legislatures and community members can impede meaningful

90 *See* McLeod, *supra* note 78, at 1646–7 (explaining that the abolitionist conception of justice requires "paying careful attention to experienced harm and its aftermath ...").

91 FED. R. EVID. 101, 1104.

92 Erin Collins, *Abolishing the Evidence-Based Paradigm*, 48 B.Y.U. L. REV. 403, 459 (2022) (highlighting "privileging [of] quantitative methodologies" over "other kinds of expertise" including "the insights of people who are most impacted by criminal legal policies").

93 *See* Jasmine B. Gonzales Rose, Asees Bhasin, and Spencer Piston, *Antiracist Expert Evidence*, 134 YALE L.J. 2362, 2439–40 (2025) (contrasting one court's narrow interpretation of Rule 702 and rejection of expert culture evidence with courts' routine admission of prosecution police experts with equivalent knowledge bases).

94 Sinha, *supra* note 42, at 898 (describing entrenched carceral culture within forensics).

community involvement in controlling use of STS methods.[95] Others have noted that policy solutions can also appear as meaningful progress when in fact they do little to disrupt the current carceral system. Professor Cynthia Godsoe acknowledges the inherent difficulty in balancing harm reduction and "inadvertently strengthening or prolonging the system[,]" given that both reducing harm and ending the current system are critical steps under a non-reformist agenda.[96] It is thus critical that the non-evidence law proposals described above are designed with careful adherence to non-reformist principles.

CONCLUSION

Evidence is the currency of the courtroom. It fuels operation of the criminal legal system. In criminal cases, where the government bears the burden of proving its case, prosecutors put on most of the evidence and, as a result, evidence flows mostly in the direction of convictions. Evaluation of evidence law through an abolitionist lens should not end with this chapter's examination of STS admissibility frameworks. Applying an abolitionist frame to evidentiary rules and frameworks invites novel and creative exploration by legal scholars, abolitionists, and community members of evidence law's role in enabling and mitigating carceral harm. As critical approaches to interrogating evidence law grow, that exploration should continue in earnest.

ACKNOWLEDGMENTS

I am grateful to Nina Chernoff, Amanda David, Lula Hagos, Ieshaah Murphy, and Amanda Rogers for the thoughtful comments they provided during the development of this chapter and to Susannah Gilmore, Corinne Noonan, and Jared Wiese for excellent research assistance. Finally, I thank the editors, Bennett Capers, Jasmine E. Harris, and Julia Simon-Kerr, for their improvements to this chapter and for the vision and labor that went into producing this volume.

95 Vincent M. Southerland, *The Master's Tools and A Mission: Using Community Control and Oversight Laws to Resist and Abolish Police Surveillance Technologies*, 70 UCLA L. Rev. 2, 61 (2023).

96 Cynthia Godsoe, *Disrupting Carceral Logic in Family Policing*, 121 Mich. L. Rev. 939, 961 (2023).

SECTION 2

And Beyond

INTRODUCTION

We hope this volume serves both as an introduction and an invitation: An introduction for those unfamiliar with the field of Critical Evidence, and an invitation to all to engage in future investigation of the themes and questions raised. To that end, this final section offers some additional food for thought. First, in the excerpt from Alex Nunn's article, "The Incoherence of Evidence Law," he poses two central, yet underexplored questions: Why do rules of evidence exist? and "how do the goals of modern evidence law cohere?" To this, we would add a third: Is coherence of purpose necessary in an evidentiary regime? Whatever the answer to these questions, they deserve a place in evidence scholarship. The Critical Evidence project, in particular, makes this clear by questioning our default assumption that rules should aim for "accuracy," and by centering other values, such as justice, that should and must matter to evidence.

At the same time, we should not overlook what existing rules can offer. In "The Anti-Transgender Medical Expert Industry," Alejandra Caraballo describes a problem with medical experts on gender affirming care. In contrast to many chapters in this volume, Caraballo argues that attention to the proper application of expert rules, with the support of the *Daubert* trilogy, offers a way to combat less rigorous scientific claims of expertise regarding gender affirming care. Caraballo's excerpt suggests another important perspective on the rules of evidence – that, in some instances, application of the rules themselves can be prescriptive.

Montré Carodine's contribution to the volume pushes us to expand our scholarly vision in a different way. She asks not what a critical race lens can tell us about evidence rules, but what evidence rules can tell us about racism. We invite readers to accept her invitation to sit with the many questions her chapter raises:

> What would our evidentiary regime look like if it had been created and developed in an equitable society? What if there had been no competency rules excluding people of color from testifying against white people, for example? What if people of color and women had been equally free as white males to become lawyers and judges at the founding (and prior to the founding) of our nation? What crucial jurisprudential developments have we missed because of racism and racial exclusion?

Carodine pushes us to be creative and fearless as scholars and students of evidence. Rather than arguing the bias in the rules, why not use the rules' framework to look outward and illuminate our society and its problems? Who should bear the burden of proving racism, those who say it is there or those who say it is not? These questions are only the beginning of what may be a new turn in Critical Evidence scholarship. We look forward to seeing where they lead.

The Incoherence of Evidence Law

G. Alexander Nunn[1]

INTRODUCTION

At the root of evidence law's current troubles is, in a literal sense, an existential crisis; an inability to provide a coherent answer to a seemingly simple question – what is the purpose of evidence law? …

[E]vidence law is rife with junctures that demand a normative hierarchy. In outlining the purpose of evidence law, it is insufficient to merely present a facile laundry list of policy goals. Rather, identifying the purpose of evidence law requires pinpointing precisely how the different objectives underlying our evidentiary regime *cohere*. Do accuracy, legitimacy, and efficiency truly work together on equal footing, such that the goal of evidence law is to maximize each policy goal to the extent possible? Or, alternatively, does one of evidence law's normative objectives – such as verdict accuracy or procedural legitimacy – take precedence over the others? But if one normative goal is prioritized, how should we conceptualize the role of the subordinate policy aims?

These questions are far more than mere academic fancy. They establish order for our evidentiary regime and serve as the North Star for its substantive contents. As the pages below demonstrate, an evidentiary code that seeks to jointly maximize accuracy, legitimacy, and efficiency would contain many provisions that might be omitted entirely from a code that more forcefully prioritizes the search for truth. So too would a code centrally focused on procedural justice depart radically from a regime that chiefly aims to minimize costs. In a real sense, then, determining evidence law's normative equilibrium sets the course for the entire field. …

[G]iven the absence of a coherent vision for evidence law, rule makers have met the Federal Rules' growing dilapidation with apathy rather than the desire to vindicate a normative ideal. Consider, for instance, all the fruitless policy tradeoffs that remain entrenched in the code. Contemporary studies have revealed that the hearsay

[1] Excerpted from G. Alexander Nunn, *The Incoherence of Evidence Law*, 99 Notre Dame L. Rev. 1255 (2024).

exceptions contained within Rules 803(1), 803(2), and 804(b)(2) undercut accuracy and yield no normative recompense in return. Rule 609 delegitimizes trials while neither aiding the search for truth nor streamlining proceedings. Rule 702's *Daubert* doctrine hoists unnecessary inefficiencies on judges while failing to most effectively safeguard the accuracy of scientific evidence. Put simply, the incoherence among the Federal Rules' policy pursuits has led evidence law into suboptimality. With no investment in a clear policy hierarchy, normative ineffectuality ensues.

The path ahead for evidence law thus demands a more robust existential framework. After all, it's easy enough to declare that the Federal Rules of Evidence should be *better*; it's another thing entirely to actually define what "better" means. Why do the Federal Rules of Evidence exist? How do the policy goals of modern evidence law cohere?

Responding to these questions is, contrary to intuition, no simple task. Identifying evidence law's normative equilibrium requires careful and complex balancing that deftly calibrates the relationship among evidentiary policy goals. …

EVIDENCE LAW'S FAULTY FOUNDATION

…

Defining evidence law's purpose is a deceptively complex task. In fact, at first glance, it seems a truly elementary endeavor.

Consider, for instance, how simple intuition provides a number of credible explanations for the purpose of our evidentiary regime. For one, evidence law exists to help fact finders determine *what happened* in a particular case. Left to their own devices, fact finders would struggle with this responsibility, potentially falling prey to any number of epistemological shortcomings and biases. For example, fact finders might yield to the strong temptation to engage in character or propensity reasoning. They might fixate on some extraneous, prejudicial information at trial, decoupling their verdict from the salient evidence at issue. They might overly defer to an out-of-court declarant whose testimonial capacities have gone wholly unchecked. Evidence law prevents these pitfalls by stepping into the breach and regulating the flow of information in the courtroom, thereby facilitating the discovery of truth.

Of course, intuition points to additional explanations as well. Most notably, evidence law also plays a role in legitimizing proceedings, ensuring trials are considered fair and just by all relevant stakeholders. History is full of infamous tribunals that enjoy notoriety due to their procedural inadequacies; the Star Chamber, for example, has become synonymous with adjudicatory injustice. Evidence law therefore serves as a bulwark against trial illegitimacy. That is, the purpose of evidence law is to delineate the informational boundaries of what can fairly come to bear against a defendant in the courtroom. By regulating certain types of evidence, the juridical system ensures procedural fairness for litigants and, by extension, safeguards external societal benefits.

Though perhaps less obvious, intuition dictates that evidence law also serves an efficiency function. Were there no restrictions limiting the material that a party could present in the courtroom, the potential for abuse would be substantial. A party could run up the cost of proceedings simply by presenting needlessly cumulative evidence, thereby dragging trials on for weeks. Likewise, a party might seek to disrupt proceedings by surprising her opponent with previously concealed material evidence. Evidence law prevents these excesses, streamlining trials and ensuring the expediency of our adjudicatory system.

Thus, although a more granular examination might further subdivide these policy goals, the intuitive responses above ably show that evidence law exists to bolster accuracy, legitimacy, and efficiency. The tripartite focus accords with instinct and provides a desirable framework for how evidence law can provide a host of valuable policy benefits during adjuration.

It's no surprise, then, that the Federal Rules of Evidence turn the implicit explicit. … [W]hen defining the purpose of our controlling evidentiary code, Rule 102 merely enshrines intuition, dictating that the Federal Rules "should be construed so as to administer every proceeding fairly, eliminate unjustifiable expense and delay, and promote the development of evidence law, to the end of ascertaining the truth and securing a just determination." Moreover, rule makers clearly felt that the reasoning underlying Rule 102 was obvious to the point of banality, warranting no further explanation. Unlike many rules, which contain Advisory Committee notes that serve as an aid for deciphering the vagaries of an evidentiary restriction, Rule 102's advisory Committee note contains no substantive clarification or supplement. Rather, Rule 102 was, for rule makers, self-explanatory. No addendum necessary.

But Rule 102 – and the instinctive reasoning that underlies it – is facile. Despite its intuitive appeal, Rule 102 proves reductive in its insistence that evidence law exists to concurrently maximize accuracy, legitimacy, and efficiency. Most pressingly, that account ignores the inescapability of normative tradeoffs in any evidentiary code.

But why do normative tradeoffs matter? To be sure, were it possible to craft an evidentiary regime that maximized the likelihood of verdict accuracy, fully legitimized proceedings, and drove costs to an absolute minimum, few would argue against aligning our evidentiary regime's purpose toward the simultaneous achievement of those objectives. In fact, any other course would be nonsensical. Unfortunately, however, the reality of evidence law undercuts that quixotic ideal. The concurrent maximization of accuracy, legitimacy, and efficiency ultimately proves impossible precisely because unavoidable normative tradeoffs force mutually exclusive choices between evidence law's policy focuses.

Consider, for example, a staple of evidence law – privileges. Generally stated, an evidentiary privilege is an exclusionary rule that prevents a party from introducing a statement that was made in the course and scope of a protected status relationship. Thus, many communications between marital partners, or attorneys and their clients, or doctors and their patients, are wholly excluded from the courtroom. The justification for the ironclad protection of privileges rests in a legitimacy rationale. The weaponization of statements made within the confines of a trust relationship would certainly undermine perceptions of adjudicatory fairness. Moreover, the absence of evidentiary privileges could potentially destabilize those trust relationships altogether. But privileges come at a cost. Often, privileges conceal incredibly probative information. A candid statement made between marital partners or a client and her attorney might constitute the most effective piece of evidence for determining what actually happened in a particular case. Yet privileges forgo that probative evidence in the name of procedural justice and societal good. Privileges therefore constitute one of the starkest policy tradeoffs in evidence law, sacrificing verdict accuracy for greater levels of procedural legitimacy. And this normative tradeoff is inescapable. Were an evidentiary regime not to enshrine privileges, verdict accuracy might increase, but legitimacy would suffer. A policy choice is inevitable.

Another example is found in Rules 408 and 410. Rule 408 dictates, inter alia, that statements made during settlement negotiations are inadmissible at a later trial if offered to impeach a witness or provide insight into the validity of a claim. Rule 410 extends the principle to the criminal context, dictating that statements made during plea negotiations are inadmissible against the defendant who participated. In normative terms, then, Rules 408 and 410 are quite clearly grounded in efficiency and legitimacy rationales. Regarding efficiency, the protection of settlement and plea negotiations facilitates the expedient disposition of cases, as parties can engage in open, transparent negotiations without fear of later recourse. Regarding legitimacy, Rules 408 and 410 also safeguard procedural fairness, as they prevent a party from facing a trial penalty for engaging in settlement or plea negotiations in good faith. But Rules 408 and 410 also come at a cost. Of course, immensely probative evidence often comes to light during settlement and plea negotiations, whether it be a party's inadvertent admission or an implicit concession regarding the strength of a party's case. Allowing for the admission of statements made during pretrial negotiations could therefore occasionally improve the accuracy of verdicts. Thus, Rules 408 and 410, too, constitute a juncture requiring stark policy compromises, yielding a moderate potential accuracy gain in exchange for improved procedural efficiency and legitimacy.

So too does Rule 401's permissive definition of relevance constitute a tradeoff between legitimacy and efficiency. Under Rule 401, evidence is relevant – and therefore generally admissible – if it has "*any* tendency to make a fact more or less probable than it would be without the evidence." Evidence scholars have rightly recognized that "[i]t would be hard to devise a more lenient test of probativeness than Rule 401's 'any tendency' standard." Of course, Rule 401's liberal relevancy standard promises significant legitimacy gains for evidence law, as it affords a party substantial leeway to present her case in the manner she sees fit. At the same time, however, Rule 401 undercuts, to some degree, efficiency. A more exacting relevancy bar could certainly streamline proceedings and simplify the issues presented; for instance, if probativeness was instead defined as having a "*strong* tendency to make a fact more or less probable," a wide range of relatively unimportant evidence could be discarded at trial. Thus, once more in Rule 401, we see a clear normative tradeoff. …

These are the existential questions that define evidence law. An evidentiary regime that places the pursuits of accuracy, legitimacy, and efficiency on equal footing would contain many provisions that might be omitted entirely from a code that forcefully prioritizes the search for truth. For example, … if verdict accuracy is held out as the core purpose of evidence law, privileges, the character evidence rules, and even the hearsay rule itself could face a dramatic narrowing in scope. Yet each of these rules are mainstays in a regime that adjoins the pursuit of accuracy with an equal emphasis on legitimacy and efficiency. So too would a code that prioritizes adjudicatory legitimacy vary wildly in substance from a regime that primarily pursues efficiency. The former would of course emphasize evidentiary rules, like the hearsay rule, that help foster fair and just proceedings; the latter would prefer provisions, like Rule 606(b)'s no-impeachment rule, that minimize costs and streamline proceedings.

The Anti-Transgender Medical Expert Industry

Alejandra Caraballo[1]

I. INTRODUCTION

Medical and scientific expertise are often essential for factual development in the American legal system. When used as intended, medical and scientific experts are able to provide context and expertise to discern difficult issues of fact and to establish a common baseline for the court. However, given the adversarial system, each party to a lawsuit seeks to use witnesses that will support their perspective and will discredit the opposition's experts. To ensure a minimum baseline of scientific rigor and professional credentials, the *Daubert* standard is used by federal courts to measure the admissibility of expert witness testimony. While this standard may often keep the unqualified cranks and quacks out of the legal system, it is not a difficult standard to meet, and many contrarian medical and scientific experts are often allowed to testify in court despite lacking the consensus of the relevant scientific community. This often presents a quandary where incongruous opinions held by otherwise qualified experts are admitted into court along with the opinions of more reputable experts explaining the scientific consensus view. This has often been the case in LGBTQ civil rights litigation for decades, but it has taken more urgency in the recent years as transgender rights cases have become increasingly litigated.

This comment will focus on the role of incongruent outlier experts and their use in civil rights litigation, particularly in the context of transgender civil rights.

I will use my experience litigating several major trans rights cases in federal court to provide context to this issue. The first part will discuss the history and structure of the *Daubert* standard in evidence. The second part will discuss anti-transgender experts and their roles. The third part will analyze how anti-transgender parties in litigation are able to establish a veneer of professional credibility through the use of a limited number of incongruent experts who share similar views and appear to make a living solely out of their role as a scientific expert in litigation. Finally, the

[1] Excerpted from Alejandra Caraballo, *The Anti-Transgender Medical Expert Industry*, 50 J.L. MED. & ETHICS 687 (2022).

conclusion will make a normative argument against the use of these experts in court and the admissibility of their testimony and a legal argument that courts should rigorously apply the standard set by Rule 702.

II. TESTIMONY BY EXPERT WITNESSES

Rule 702 of Federal Rules of Evidence sets the standard for which witnesses may qualify as an expert and the requirements they must demonstrate to be permitted to testify as such. Expert witness testimony gives an opportunity for the trier of fact to hear from experts in the relevant field who are able to provide the context for questions of scientific and medical facts. The relevant factors under Rule 702 are:

(a) the expert's scientific, technical, or other specialized knowledge will help the trier of fact to understand the evidence or to determine a fact in issue;
(b) the testimony is based on sufficient facts or data;
(c) the testimony is the product of reliable principles and methods; and
(d) the expert has reliably applied the principles and methods to the facts of the case.

The judge is the ultimate arbiter and serves as the "gatekeeper" of what constitutes sufficient qualifications to meet expert testimony under Rule 702. The current standard under Rule 702 enumerated in *Daubert*, sets a highly flexible standard that looks to several factors. This flexible standard gives courts wide leeway into what is admissible which can lead to disparate outcomes if counsel does not sufficiently challenge expert testimony that does not meet the requirements of rule 702.

The relative flexibility of these standards can often lead to pseudo-science or outlier experts providing testimony if they are not vigorously challenged by opposing counsel. There is often a hesitation to challenge these experts by opposing counsel because blatantly bad expert testimony can be viewed as beneficial to their client's case. However, this is a mistake since those bad foundations can serve as a basis for a hostile appellate judiciary to decide in favor of the anti-trans side as was the case in *Doe v. Snyder*. On the contrary, the plaintiffs in *Kadel* zealously challenged the defendant's expert testimony and was successful in striking the vast majority of it from the record. Nothing less than vigorous challenging of pseudo-science in the context of gender affirming care is required to push back against the concerted effort to launder misinformation, pseudo-science, and bias into the courtroom through "experts." The effort in *Kadel* to use *Daubert* motions to challenge the admission of testimony from defendant's testimony serve as an effective model.

III. THE ANTI-TRANSGENDER EXPERTS: THE USUAL SUSPECTS

There are so few medical experts willing testify against the well-established and accepted standards of care for gender dysphoria that most trans rights litigator can name them from memory. Some of these experts are Dr. Stephen B. Levine, Dr. Paul McHugh, and Dr. Michael Laidlaw. Combined, they have served as experts on dozens of cases, often appearing together. This is not an exhaustive list but consists of some the most prolific and notable. Additionally, several anti-trans organizations have recently sprung up to provide a veneer of legitimacy to the transphobic views of these experts. These orgs include the Society for Evidence Based Medicine, Genspect, and the Pediatric and Adolescent Gender Dysphoria Working Group. These groups do not publish peer-reviewed original research and simply amplify research that aligns with their views such as work published by Lisa Littman and Kenneth Zucker.

A. *The "Experts"*

Dr. Steven B. Levine is a Clinical Professor of Psychiatry at Case Western Reserve University School of Medicine and one of the most prolific anti-transgender medical expert in the country. Dr. Levine is involved in nearly every single major trans rights case in the country as a medical expert for the party opposed to transgender rights. Dr. Levine is able to maintain a veneer of expertise on transgender issues as he was a former committee chair of the Harry Benjamin International Gender Dysphoria Association, the predecessor of the World Professional Association for Transgender Health (WPATH) and he created and practiced at a gender identity clinic at Case Western Reserve in 1974 that later became independent from the university in 1993.

However, much of his work around "gender exploratory therapy" is considered by some to be conversion therapy since it presumes that patients suffering gender dysphoria have underlying causes other than being transgender. Similar practices in the context of sexual orientation conversion therapy have been found to be ineffective and fraudulent. Levine got his initial start serving as an expert to deny medical care to trans people in the case of Michelle Kosilek, an incarcerated transgender woman in Massachusetts seeking gender affirming surgery. From there, Levine rapidly expanded his work as a state expert to deny trans people in prison gender affirming care. His background as a previous committee chair for WPATH and practice with "gender exploratory therapy" for decades bolsters his credibility before the courts despite being out of sync with the medical consensus that supports the affirmative model. Despite claims to the contrary, Stephen Levine has not published peer-reviewed research in the relevant field and he relies solely on anecdotal data from his own books and prior work with patients with gender dysphoria. These idiosyncratic views have resulted in multiple courts diminishing the value of his expert opinions on their decisions.

Dr. Paul R. McHugh is a psychiatrist infamous for his role in opposing the treatment of gender dysphoria in the United States. In the 1960s Johns Hopkins had established a world leading center to treat gender dysphoria. Similar clinics started to appear around the country and a growing acceptance of gender affirming medicine began to become more prevalent. However, Dr. McHugh was serving as Johns Hopkins Hospital's head of psychiatry, and used his influence to shut down the clinic in 1979. Two years later in 1981, Dr. McHugh lobbied the Centers for Medicaid and Medicare services along with the anti-trans feminist Janice Raymond to declare gender affirming procedures as experimental. This lobbying effort succeeded. Within a short time, nearly all gender clinics in the country shut down and transgender medicine was set back for nearly three decades. Since that time, Dr. McHugh served as an expert in several gay rights cases stating that gay relationships were harmful to children and that homosexuality was a result of childhood trauma. He famously supported California's Prop 8. Since the major win of same-sex marriage in *Obergefell* in 2015, Dr. McHugh has shifted his role as medical expert in trans rights cases. This is despite being over 90 years old, retired, and not actively practicing medicine.

Dr. Michael Laidlaw is an endocrinologist who has participated in multiple amicus efforts to deny access to gender affirming care, including a brief in the *Brandt v. Rutledge* case in the 8th Circuit submitted by the Southern Poverty Law Center designated anti- LGBTQ hate group, Alliance Defending Freedom. Dr. Laidlaw has no specific training, board certification, or personal experience working with pediatric or transgender patient populations. This would be a clear indicator that he is insufficient to provide expert opinions within the rule 702 and *Daubert* framework. Dr. Laidlaw is a contributing member of the Pediatric and Adolescent Gender Dysphoria Working Group, a pseudo-medical group with anti-trans medical experts that have an "interest" in the treatment of gender dysphoria in children but advocates for conversion therapy. Despite his lack of experience in treating youth with gender dysphoria, Dr. Laidlaw served as an expert witness in a case in Arizona challenging the exclusion of coverage for gender affirming care in minors. As noted in the reply expert report, Dr. Laidlaw's expert report "made errors that would not have been made by a medical provider that regularly treats transgender patients." This is another clear violation of rule 702.

B. *The "Medical Orgs"*

Anti-LGBTQ movements are no stranger to creating entire medical organizations to back their discredited and unscientific views on LGBTQ people. For instance, in 2002 opponents of marriage equality created the American College of Pediatricians as a form of protest against the acceptance of LGBTQ families by the American Academy of Pediatricians. The fundamental belief driving these orgs is that being transgender is in of itself, a bad thing that should be avoided at all costs. These organizations are defined by a singular purpose, to disseminate outlier contrarian views to manufacture a controversy that is then used to undermine access to care. These tactics are not novel, they have been employed in other contexts to stall public health efforts around smoking and government action in addressing climate change.

The most prominent of the pseudo-scientific organizations in the anti-trans space is the Society for Evidence Based Gender Medicine (SEGM). SEGM posits that the level of medical evidence for the treatment of gender dysphoria in youth is of "low quality" and as a result treatments for gender dysphoria should be barred by law, such as the *Doe v. Snyder* case in Arizona in which it submitted an amicus brief seeking to affirm the denial of a preliminary injunction. They cite to the results of their own advocacy efforts in the UK NHS, and the Swedish Karolinska Hospital[,] which has been subject to substantial public pressure to restrict access to gender affirming care. In a snowball effect, the small successes in their efforts are built up to create momentum to further restrict care for trans youth around the world. Unfortunately, the veneer and "teach the controversy" tactics are beginning to gain traction in the courts. The 9th Circuit cited amici briefs['] discredited desistance theories as a reason to affirm the denial of preliminary injunction by trans youth in Arizona seeking "top surgery." This rested on a basis of expert testimony at the trial court that was insufficiently challenged and a trial court judge that was partial to the anti-trans side.

IV. THE OUROBOROS OF ANTI-TRANS EXPERTS AND ORGANIZATIONS

At a basic level, the citations and minimal scientific evidence reported by anti-trans experts resemble that of the ouroboros. Research is constantly self-referenced and recycled among many of the anti-trans experts and organizations to create an insular and incestuous self-reinforcing body of work to provide backing for their anti-trans views.

One prominent example is the 2019 study on the widely panned and precarious concept of rapid onset gender dysphoria ("ROGD") conducted by Lisa Littman, which required a correction, has been a catalyst for the anti-trans movement. Every major medical professional organization that deals with psychological and psychiatric health in the United States signed a statement opposing any use of the term ROGD in any clinical or medical setting citing the lack of any rigorous empirical support for its existence. Despite this, several groups, activists, and authors have continued to push the ROGD concept as a means to undermine access to gender affirming care for trans youth. For example, a group calling itself the Parents of ROGD Kids quickly popped up with a flashy website citing an "epidemic" of young girls identifying as trans. The research was quickly cited in a brief before the Supreme Court in *Bostock v. Clayton County* in 2019. SEGM cited Littman's research in their amicus brief in *Doe v. Snyder*. The ROGD concept was then picked up by Dr. Stephen Levine[,] who cited it in his expert declaration in *Kadel v. Folwell* on January 19, 2022.

Perhaps the most notorious example of Littman's research breaking through to the mainstream was inspiring the basis for the book *Irreversible Damage: The Transgender Craze Seducing Our Daughters* by Abigail Shrier, a freelance journalist with no medical training or expertise. Despite the lack of medical expertise or rigorous empirical evidence bolstering Shrier's claims, her book has been cited repeatedly in several briefs from the Supreme Court to multiple circuit courts urging to restrict access to gender affirming care for trans youth and oppose bans on conversion therapy.

It becomes quickly evident to any reasonable observer that a house of cards was built on a single highly criticized and flawed ROGD study, but it has not stopped anti-trans experts and organizations from citing it. Rather than rigorous empirical peer-reviewed research, these experts rely on dubious conjectures reinforced through popular media written by lay authors with no medical expertise. Attorneys and advocates for trans youth are left combating medical misinformation and intentionally manufactured controversy to impede access to gender affirming care.

V. A PATH FORWARD

It should not take the amicus of every major medical organization in court to validate and support access to gender affirming care while the opposition simply relies on pseudo-scientific theories and manufactured controversy. The ethics of testifying outside of one's expertise to opine on the validity of treatment of transgender youth should be disfavored by professional medical organizations. Greater care should be taken to ensure that medical experts are not using their qualifications to testify outside of their experience. An expert should not testify under these circumstances due to ethical considerations; however, when they try, the legal standards should keep their testimony out of court. It should be considered unethical for doctors such as Paul R. McHugh and Michael Laidlaw, who have absolutely no experience treating transgender youth, to opine on the appropriateness of the treatment in other contexts. Similarly, Dr. Levine, whose conversion therapy practice contradicts mainstream medical opinion should not be used by states in court to justify anti-trans policies. While endocrinologists, psychiatrists, and other relevant medical professionals may be able to competently interpret the medical evidence, their personal opinions on treatments they do not have any experience in providing should not be given admitted in the courts under FRCE 702(a).

Attorneys facing these anti-trans experts should not hesitate to challenge their testimony's admissibility in court under the *Daubert* standard as was done in *Kadel v. Folwell.* Additionally, efforts to challenge the weight of expert testimony should be taken as well, which was done to great effect against James Cantor in the challenge against Alabama's felony ban on gender affirming care. Those efforts succeeded and severely limited the testimony of the defendant's expert witnesses as a result of their lack of relevant expertise. Much as the anti-trans side has been able to use their efforts in Europe for persuasive authority, getting anti-trans experts disqualified in a federal district court provides greater persuasive authority in other courts to exclude their testimony. Once an expert is found to lack the proper expertise at the trial court level, it is likely that other courts will adopt similar conclusions. Oftentimes, litigators face strategic questions around the use of *Daubert* motions to exclude witness testimony. These issues can be anything from a prickly judge to a concern about frivolous motions to exclude filed in retaliation. However, pseudoscience needs to be met with vigorous opposition as they have no place in our courts. Courts should be more scrupulous of expert testimony in civil rights litigation, especially when suspect classes are involved in the case.

Finally, professional medical organizations should strongly discourage experts from testifying outside of their experience and expertise in litigation involving civil rights. Without providing pushback within each profession's community, we will continue to see a growing cottage industry of anti-trans experts used to roll back the access of transgender people to gender affirming care, restrooms, appropriate identification documents, and the ability to participate in sports. Without an intervention, medical misinformation will continue to spread, and the courts will continue to begin accepting pseudo-scientific opinions and theories. This will ultimately undermine the reliability of medical experts across the country and harm equal access to justice.

Race Is Evidence/Evidence Is Race

Flipping the Script on the "Racial Lens"

Montré D. Carodine

INTRODUCTION

This chapter posits that evidence law is best understood, developed, and advanced by examining it through the prism of race. By the same token, our understanding of race and racial hierarchies can be greatly enhanced by considering race through the prism of evidence law. Race informs evidence, and evidence informs race. The bulk of this chapter is devoted to the latter premise.

Previously, I have written about race as evidence in the context of racially biased rules of evidence and racially biased actions by state actors, such as the police and prosecutors.[1] This chapter goes well beyond my previous work in the sense that I am freeing myself from the confines of the courtroom and the activities by state actors and others that might lead to courtroom processes. I am freeing myself to think beyond how individual rules of evidence operate in a racially biased manner. I am freeing myself from operating only within the evidentiary framework that the writers of the rules of evidence presented – the same rules that developed historically without making any attempt to consider the impact or, frankly, the collective expertise of people of color.

THE RELEVANCE OF THE TIMES

These are hostile, and challenging times for people of color in America and for anyone who has traditionally been "othered" by American society. Of course, this truth has always been evident – since this country's inception and before. There is a uniqueness, perhaps, to the current times because many thought that we had progressed to a point of post racialism only to be rudely awakened by the election and now reelection of Donald Trump, who has openly appealed to racialized and

[1] Montré Carodine, *Contemporary Issues in Critical Race Theory: The Implications of Race as Character Evidence in Recent High Profile Cases*, 75 U. Pitt. L. Rev. 679 (2014); Montré Carodine, *The Mis-Characterizaton of the Negro: A Race Critique of the Prior Conviction Impeachment Rule*, 84 Ind. L.J. 521 (2009).

irrational fears of white people angered by the idea that they are losing "their country" to people of color.[2]

As I write this chapter, Donald Trump is transitioning into his second presidential term and making good on his vows to brutalize immigrant communities, deporting people in large numbers, spearheading the continued assault on Diversity, Equity, and Inclusion initiatives, and pardoning criminals (many of them known racists) who committed acts of violence in the January 6, 2021, insurrection on the U.S. Capitol.[3] And while these are indeed dark times for people of color in the U.S., the reality is that in one way or another, the times for us have always been dark. Sure, we have had bright spots in the midst of the darkness, but the times have always been dark. Some times have been darker than others.

THE PRESUMPTION OF RACIALLY BIASED RULES

As is the American legal system, the development of American evidentiary law is deeply flawed, from the foundational level to the present. Consider the fact that huge swaths of the American population, whose lives were regulated and impacted by courtroom decisions, were completely shut out of the courtroom and trial process.[4] What would our evidentiary regime look like if it had been created and developed in an equitable society? What if there had been no competency rules excluding people of color from testifying against white people, for example?[5] What if people of color[6] and women[7] had been equally free as white males to become lawyers and judges at the founding (and prior to the founding) of our nation? What

2 *See, e.g.*, Maxine Eichner, *Free Market Family Policy and the New Parental Rights Laws*, 101 N.C. LAW. REV. 1305, 1345 (2023). Professor Eichner aptly states that "[m]ost of the critical threats to democracy the U.S. faces – including restrictions on the right to vote, the undermining of confidence in voting and refusal to accept the results of valid elections, and the rise of political violence – are linked to white citizens' perceptions that they are in danger of losing their country as the nation becomes more diverse. Further, ample evidence shows that support for former President Donald Trump, who has brought many of these threats to a head, is deeply associated with racist beliefs."

3 Chris Cameron, *What Trump Did on Day 1: Tracking His Biggest Moves*, N.Y. TIMES (Jan. 21, 2025).

4 *See* Marsha Griggs, *Race, Rules, and Disregarded Reality*, 82 OHIO STATE L.J. 931, 942 (2021) (noting the historical existence of competency rules that "prevented Black people, Chinese immigrants, Native Americans, and people of mixed race from giving testimony against a white person").

5 *See* Bennett Capers, *Evidence Without Rules*, 94 NOTRE DAME L. REV. 867, 889 (2018) (discussing "our [country's] long history of tying race to credibility, beginning with laws and customs that prohibited nonwhites, including Latinos and Asians, from testifying against whites").

6 Athena D. Mutua, et al., *Who Gets In? The Quest for Diversity after* Grutter, 52 BUFF. L. REV. 531, 540 (2004) ("For more than a century, the profession was largely comprised of white, Anglo-Saxon males. Women, ethnic immigrants, and people of color were consciously excluded and/or marginalized in the legal profession by law, regulation, and custom.").

7 Jalene S. Fenwick, *See Her, Hear Her: The Historical Evolution of Women in Law and Advocacy for the Path Ahead*, A.B.A. (Nov. 15, 2023), www.americanbar.org/groups/business_law/resources/business-law-today/2023-november/see-her-hear-her-historical-evolution-women-in-law/ (last visited Mar. 4, 2026) (noting that "[t]he legal system, renowned for its rigorous traditions, has historically been a bastion of male dominance" and outlining the history of women in the profession).

crucial jurisprudential developments have we missed because of racism and racial exclusion? What progress and innovation in our legal system, including our rules of evidence, simply never occurred because of sexism and the intersection of racism and sexism, and because of who had a seat at the table in fashioning laws, and who did not? How has the growth of evidence law been stunted or warped because so many in our society did not have a representative seat at the table?[8] These are questions that we do not spend enough time pondering, but we need to sit with them for a while.

So often we expend our energy researching and documenting affirmative evidence of discrimination that we fail to acknowledge and give due attention to the glaring omissions in our judicial system that are a direct result of racism and white male dominance. We must think systemically about the ways in which racism and white male privilege shaped our entire legal system, affirmatively *and* by omission and exclusion, including our evidentiary framework.

It is simply not enough to look at individual rules and apply a racial critique to them. To be clear, we certainly should do that work, but it is a mere starting place. And if we stop there, or operate as though we are *required* to demonstrate or affirmatively prove the racial bias in each rule, we fall into the trap of always carrying the burden of proving racism, which is exhausting, unfair, and often inefficient. Indeed, this heavy burden that our legal system and larger society so often places on people of color is a cruel silencing tactic. What I have found is that to those who choose to deny what is so obviously a part of our history and what still haunts us today, no amount of evidence that you show them will ever be enough.

And, given this history of racial exclusion, why should we have to affirmatively prove that racism is embedded in the American legal system, including the rules of evidence? When has our justice system ever affirmatively proven its fairness to people of color? When has it ever established that it is unbiased and metes out justice equitably? The short answer is never. The legal system – again, founded on exclusion – simply presumes its own objectivity and fairness. The system simply presumes the racially neutral operation of the rules of evidence. But why should there be such a presumption? Simply enacting rules with race-neutral language or even adopting rules that reference fairness and justice (as Federal Rule of Evidence 102 does[9]) is not enough. References to equality[10] and justice[11] in founding documents

8 As but one example, in his excerpted chapter in this volume, David A. Sklansky makes a compelling argument that the strictness of our hearsay rules owes much to the reluctance of courts to disturb the institution of slavery. *See* David A. Sklansky, "The Neglected Origins of the Hearsay Rule in American Slavery: Recovering *Queen v. Hepburn*," in this volume.

9 FED. R. EVID. 102 provides: "These rules should be construed so as to administer every proceeding fairly, eliminate unjustifiable expense and delay, and promote the development of evidence law, to the end of ascertaining the truth and securing a just determination."

10 *See* THE DECLARATION OF INDEPENDENCE para. 2 (U.S. 1776).

11 *See* U.S. CONST. pmbl.

of our nation prove that point. Our nation at its inception was neither equal nor just. Simply saying it was did not make it so.

Despite current efforts to silence Critical Race Theory scholars and whitewash history,[12] the reality is that our country was birthed out of and founded on racism. As Professor Robert Parkinson has noted, "[w]e have been reluctant to admit just how thoroughly the Founding Fathers thought about, talked about, and wrote about race at the moment of American independence."[13] But "[s]lavery and arguments about race were not only at the heart of the American founding; *it was what united the states in the first place*."[14] Indeed, "Founding Fathers" helped to unite groups of white men who did not even particularly like each other. They did so by sowing racists fears, "publicizing stories to make Americans afraid of British-sponsored slave 'insurrections' and Native 'massacres.'"[15]

All of this leads inexorably to my first argument: Groups who have been brutalized, subjugated, and marginalized in this country since its beginning and well before should not be forced to prove racial bias in the operations of its legal system's rules. To the contrary, I would argue that in a system created by racists, for racists, and to further racist agendas, there should be a *presumption* that *all* of our rules operate in a racially biased manner. The system should work to overcome the presumption of racial bias, prove that it does not exist or eradicate the bias when it does, and I would argue that it almost always does. In a sense our legal system, and our rules of evidence in particular, have their own reparations[16] work to do.

Our system should do its own work and not force this labor on people of color and our allies. Applying my "flip the script" method will result in more just evidentiary frameworks. A consideration of the Supreme Court's recent case on Colorado's version of Federal Rule of Evidence 606(b) – sometimes called the no-impeachment rule, because it bars juror testimony to impeach a verdict – underscores my point. In *Peña-Rodriguez v. Colorado*, the Supreme Court found that Colorado's version of Rule 606(b) cannot keep jurors from testifying post-verdict about racially bias statements made by another juror during deliberations.[17] Specifically, the Court stated that "where a juror makes a clear statement that indicates he or she relied on racial stereotypes or animus to convict a criminal defendant, the Sixth Amendment requires that the no-impeachment rule give way in order to permit the trial court to

12 *See* Jennifer Harison Macon, *Critical Race Theory: Another Casualty in the Attack on Facts*, 69 UCLA L. R. Discourse (2022) (discussing the attack on Critical Race Theory and the efforts to strip race and racism from history).

13 *See* Robert G. Parkinson, *You Can't Tell the Story of 1776 Without Talking about Race and Slavery*, Time (July 4, 2021 at 07:00 ET), https://time.com/6077468/united-states-1776-racism-slavery/.

14 *Id.* (emphasis added).

15 *Id.*

16 For a recent article discussing the need for monetary reparations to Black people for the devastating harms caused by slavery and ideas for funding such reparations, *see* Jeremy Bearer-Friend, *Paying for Reparations*, 67 How. L.J. 1, 11 (2023–2024).

17 580 U.S. 206, 225 (2017).

consider the evidence of the juror's statement and any resulting denial of the jury trial guarantee."[18]

The Court previously had been quite protective with respect to jurors when attorneys sought to call them as witnesses in post-conviction proceedings to impeach their verdicts. For example, in *Tanner v. United States*, the Court read Rule 606(b) as barring juror testimony to impeach a verdict, even when there was substantial proof (from statements by jurors seeking to clear their consciences) that several jurors had consumed alcohol and illegal drugs during trial.[19] The Court in *Tanner* elevated the protection of our jury system over justice and fairness for criminal defendants. But it saw *Peña-Rodriguez* differently. Affirmative evidence of racism by a juror was not to be tolerated or protected.

The Court's stand against racial bias seems laudable, but it does not go far enough, as Daniel Harawa points out in his chapter.[20] My concern here is slightly different. The problem, for me, is that holdings like the one in *Peña-Rodriguez* keep litigants ensnared in the trap of always having to demonstrate racial bias. This harm is compounded by the high hurdle the Court sets: The *Peña-Rodriguez* Court insisted, "Not every offhand comment indicating racial bias or hostility will justify setting aside the no-impeachment bar to allow further judicial inquiry."[21] Rather, there must "be a showing that one or more jurors made statements exhibiting overt racial bias that cast serious doubt on the fairness and impartiality of the jury's deliberations and resulting verdict."[22] So there are some levels of racial bias that we are willing to accept without requiring further investigation through post-verdict juror testimony? The Court's willingness to look away when racial bias is not deemed severe enough is troubling. Or it suggests that what really troubles the Court is the appearance of bias, rather than the fact of bias. As long as it is not too obvious or too visible, the Court seems indifferent.

Furthermore, the Court's no-impeachment rule jurisprudence is troubling because the outrageous behavior that it permitted to stand in *Tanner* is potentially just as harmful to defendants of color (and all criminal defendants for that matter) as what it found intolerable in *Peña-Rodriguez*. And to be sure the almost impenetrable no-impeachment Rule of 606(b) stands to harm defendants of color disproportionately. Focusing only on instances where jurors are openly racist allows the courts to ignore egregious situations, as in *Tanner*, in a criminal justice system where people of color are overpoliced and prosecuted. Courts should address all situations of egregious behavior by jurors, including by allowing evidence of jurors' racial bias, and should not be limited to situations of overt juror racism.

18 *Id.*
19 483 U.S. 107, 125–7 (1987).
20 *See* Daniel Harawa, "*Peña-Rodriguez v. Colorado,* Jury Secrecy, and the Performance of Racial Justice," in this volume.
21 Peña-Rodriguez, 580 U.S. at 225.
22 *Id.*

Similarly, as Critical Evidence scholars, we should move beyond the confines of our existing approaches, which typically identify isolated rules and demonstrate their racial bias. The reality is that the entire American legal system, including the rules of evidence that govern our trial process, was conceived and developed to reinforce a brutal racial caste system. We have to move beyond the idea of race *and* the law, to an understanding that race *is in* the law. Indeed race *is* the law.

MOVING FROM A RACE THEORY OF EVIDENCE TO AN EVIDENCE THEORY OF RACE

In many ways, I view the *entire life* of a person of color, particularly Black people in America, as one extensive and relentless trial, within which are a series of major trials (sometimes categorized as macroaggressions) and mini-trials (often characterized as microaggressions). My interest in the remainder of this chapter is not so much to demonstrate the racially biased operation of the rules of evidence – though, as I have shown previously and have others after me have shown, they certainly do and always have operated that way. My goal is higher. It is to contribute to the theoretical framework of the modern civil rights movement that we are witnessing right now. I want people of color and those who sympathize with our plight to have a new way to think about our struggle.

By bringing my work on race and evidence out of the confines of the courtroom, freeing my own self intellectually, my goal also is to add to the language and theories of the new civil rights movement. Because much of the movement involves critiquing and transforming legal institutions (such as the criminal justice system), it makes sense to look to those institutions and use their very language to critique their hypocrisies and expose the fallacies of their assumptions.

In the context of evidence law, race can and should inform the development and advancement of evidence law and has more power to do so than any other framework. In other words, the race critique offers the most thorough and encompassing critique, the best critique. Professor Jasmine Gonzales Rose's recent work applying Critical Race Theory to evidence underscores this point. The best critique of rules and policies comes from those situated at the bottom.

In "Towards a Critical Race Theory of Evidence," Professor Gonzales Rose masterfully establishes a Critical Race Theory framework for critiquing evidence law.[23] Specifically, she turns a critical eye towards stand your ground defenses, flight evidence, and cross-racial identification.[24] Her analysis is guided by what she dubs the seven "Ps" of critical race inquiry: the power behind racialization, the purpose of

[23] Jasmine Gonzales Rose, *Toward a Critical Race Theory of Evidence*, 101 MINN. L. REV. 2243 (2017).
[24] *Id.* at 2260.

racism, privilege, property of whiteness, the pervasiveness of racism, the permanence of racism, and the perspectives of people of color.[25]

The last "P" in Professor Gonazales Rose's seven "Ps" (the perspectives of people of color) recalls the Critical Race Theory tenet of looking to the bottom. As Professor Cummings has noted, "From its inception," the U.S. legal system "has been developed and refined by the privileged and the powerful, or those individuals who have little to no experience or realistic understanding of poverty, despair, voicelessness, or victimization. Critical Race Theory argues and advocates for a legal system that can and should be developed from the bottom-up."[26]

For those of us who have taken up the previously uncharted territory of critiquing individual rules of evidence on the basis of race, I suggest our next challenges. We must bring race to the forefront of evidence thought. Evidence scholars should look to race not just to see how individual rules operate in a biased manner. We should look to race as a way of understanding, developing, and advancing evidence law, which is currently underdeveloped because it has largely ignored race and pretended to be race-neutral.

My main argument, however, is broader. Inasmuch as race can and should be used as a prism through which to view evidence law, evidentiary principles can and should be used to inform, and question, ideas about race. Racism, which is an illness,[27] is deeply embedded in the DNA of the nation. And it continues to be passed down from generation to generation. In one of his most profound statements, the late Professor Derrick Bell, one of the founding fathers of the Critical Race Theory movement, discussed what he called the "permanence of racism" in his book *Faces at the Bottom of the Well*:[28]

> Black people will never gain full equality in this country. Even those Herculean efforts we hail as successful will produce no more than temporary peaks of progress, short-lived victories that slide into irrelevance as racial patterns adapt in ways that maintain white dominance. This is a hard-to-accept fact that all history verifies. We must acknowledge it, not as a sign of submission, *but as an act of ultimate defiance*.[29]

I agree with Professor Bell. So, my goal is not to offer solutions to this country's incurable cancer of racism. My goal is not to submit, but to defy. My goal is to take

25 *Id.* at 2249.

26 André Douglas Pond Cummings, *A Furious Kinship: Critical Race Theory and the Hip Hop Nation*, 48 U. LOUISVILLE L. REV. 499, 502–3 (2010).

27 FRED JEROME AND ROGER TAYLOR, EINSTEIN ON RACE AND RACISM (Rutgers University Press 2006) (noting that Albert Einstein said, during a visit to Lincoln University, that racism is a "disease of the white man").

28 DERRICK BELL, FACES AT THE BOTTOM OF THE WELL: THE PERMANENCE OF RACISM (Basic Books 1993).

29 *Id.* at 373–4 (emphasis added).

the master's tools, in this chapter the rules of evidence, to demonstrate the master's suppression – even if only to achieve temporary progress.[30] I have found, through my years of studying, writing about, and simply appreciating the rules of evidence, that evidentiary principles are far more valuable outside the courtroom than inside it. If the life of a person of color is viewed as one extensive trial, then we need to know the rules of engagement to successfully navigate it. Conceptualizing race as evidence will aid us significantly in doing just that.

RACE AS CHARACTER EVIDENCE: A CRITICAL RACE THEORY CONCEPT

Whenever I teach a class on Critical Race Theory, one of the first topics we cover centers on the question of what exactly is race. Students typically offer a variety of answers, ranging from race as an "experience" to race as simply "color." Students quickly realize that the concept of race is in many ways vague, amorphous, indeterminant. Yet, race has very real consequences and has shaped all of our lives, so it most certainly is real. We can conceptualize race as many things, and all of those things can be accurate descriptions at the same time.

I believe that one of the most effective and encompassing ways to view race is *as* character evidence. Character in evidence law is generally prohibited. Though there are a few exceptions, Rule 404 generally prohibits evidence offered to show that someone acted in conformity with their character on a particular occasion. The idea is that we should judge people on the basis of *what* they did, not *who* they are.

Evidence law purports to disaggregate alleged actions at issue in a particular case from the character of the person alleged to have acted. The problem is that we never have been able to do that. Hence, our rules of evidence are rife with ways to get around the character-propensity ban, as there are numerous ways to get character-propensity evidence admitted by simply labeling it something else. And there are also outright exceptions to the character-propensity ban.

The best way to truly understand the dangers of character evidence and why it is crucial to have a character evidence ban that is not rife with exceptions and workarounds is by looking at race as character evidence. In my article, "The Mis-Characterization of the Negro: A Race Critique of the Prior Conviction Impeachment Rule," I demonstrated that race is character evidence.[31] Historically and today – in routine day-to-day interactions, in the media, and in the legal system – too many in our society instinctively equate whiteness with innocence

[30] As the great Black feminist Audre Lorde observed: "[T]he master's tools will never dismantle the master's house. They may allow us temporarily to beat him at his own game, but they will never enable us to bring about genuine change." Audre Lorde, *The Master's Tools Will Never Dismantle the Master's House*, in THE SECOND SEX: WOMEN'S STUDIES CONFERENCE PAPERS 98 (1979).

[31] *See* Carodine, *supra* note 1.

and Blackness with guilt. Race is equated with character – good for white people, bad for people of color.

In addition, in the "Mis-Characterization of the Negro," I demonstrated that one of the most controversial and oft-utilized rules of evidence, Rule 609, implicitly uses race as evidence and operates in a racially biased manner.[32] Rule 609 provides for the admissibility of a witness's criminal record, most often felonies, though certain misdemeanors might be admissible as well, as evidence of untruthfulness. The theory underlying Rule 609 is that someone who has been convicted of a crime is less credible as a witness. In other words, the person's criminal record can be used to argue that they are less worthy of belief on the stand.

In the "Mis-Characterization of the Negro," I extensively and painstakingly outlined the history of Rule 609's development and its current application. The rule was developed as a "compromise" which abolished the old competency rules, such as those that kept Black and Brown people off the witness stand in many cases as well as criminal defendants generally, but permitted the impeachment of all witnesses with their criminal records. Moreover, this rule was developed at a time when people of color were disproportionately targeted by police and prosecutors for the main source of Rule 609 evidence, i.e., felony convictions, a targeting that continues today. I also argued that Rule 609 evidence is essentially hearsay – hence, the need for Rule 803(22), a hearsay exception for judgments of conviction – with the racially biased criminal justice system being the hearsay declarant. But the system, because of its targeting, is an unreliable declarant, undeserving of an exception. Put differently, a prior conviction – already racially inflected – is not only character evidence, but it is *unreliable* character evidence.[33]

Since I wrote the "Mis-Characterization of the Negro," others have written on race and Rule 609, including Professor Anna Roberts, who has focused on Rule 609 and implicit bias.[34] Scholars before us had critiqued Rule 609 and the fallacies underlying its assumptions, but in my view, none of those critiques exposed the profound fallacies of Rule 609 as effectively as those of us who have critiqued it on the basis of race. And how could they when they ignore the groups that are most impacted by Rule 609 – racial minorities?

If I were writing the "Mis-Characterization of the Negro" today, it would be a much shorter piece. I would spend much less time trying to convince and persuade readers that Rule 609 operates in a racially biased manner. I would start with the presumption that this rule, with its roots in English common law colonial America, was at its inception harmful and racially biased toward Black and Brown people,

[32] *Id.*

[33] *Id.*

[34] Anna Roberts, *Reclaiming the Importance of the Defendant's Testimony: Prior Conviction Impeachment and the Fight Against Implicit Stereotyping*, 83 U. Chi. L. Rev. 835 (2016). In this volume, Professor Roberts adds to her critique by turning to the traditional way scholars teach Rule 609, which reifies carceral logics. See Anna Roberts, "Teaching Impeachment," in this volume.

and continues to be so today. As I alluded to at the beginning of this chapter, utilizing presumptions is a perfectly legitimate means by which to proceed in our legal system generally and in evidence law in particular. As with any other presumption, this presumption of racial harm and bias can be overcome in individual cases, but I will never (again) take on the burden of proving to the privileged majority the racial demons permeating this rule, or any other rule. Those who would deny that Rule 609 and the common law prior conviction impeachment rule are and always were racially biased should have the burden of proving that it operates in a race-neutral manner. Not me.

Evidence law focuses on what is admissible in the courtroom. But using evidence law to think about what is "admissible" and "relevant" outside the courtroom may be even more important. Were I writing my earlier piece today, I would (and in future work will) spend more time exploring how what I call "609-ing" occurs with arguably more far-reaching consequences *outside* the courtroom. First, there is the matter of language. There is a need for a collective way of describing – and I believe that "609-ing" is an apt description – what happens to Black and Brown people who are targeted and criminalized in our justice system when they attempt to function in a society that sees them as forever tarnished with the stain of their criminal records. The vast majority of those subjected to 609-ing will not have the privilege of having society look the other way and reward them at the highest levels, as millions of Americans have done for Donald Trump, the first convicted felon sworn in as President of the United States. Instead many of those with criminal records will not be able to vote, will be turned down for jobs and housing, and will face other discriminatory practices and the social stigma of having "a record." They will be 609'd.

More broadly, given that one of my aims is also to use evidentiary concepts to contribute to a larger discussion on race, I believe that conceptualizing race as character evidence is quite useful for Critical Race Theory. In the past, Critical Race Theory scholars have devoted scholarly inquiry to exploring "race as" metaphors. Professor Cheryl Harris's classic piece on "Whiteness as Property"[35] comes to mind, as does the Blackness as a tax metaphor used by many in the legal academy[36] and beyond.[37]

Interestingly, understanding race as character evidence helps to explain why whiteness is property (with positive value) and Blackness is a tax (negative value). The centuries' old lie about Black people in this country is that our character is poor. Harkening back to the slave era, we have been called dishonest,[38]

35 *See* Cheryl Harris, *Whiteness as Property*, 106 HARV. L. REV. 1709 (1993).

36 *See, e.g.*, JODY DAVID ARMOUR, NEGROPHOBIA AND REASONABLE RACISM: THE HIDDEN COSTS OF BEING BLACK IN AMERICA 13 (New York University Press 1997).

37 *See, e.g.*, SHAWN D. ROCHESTER, THE BLACK TAX: THE COST OF BEING BLACK IN AMERICA (self-published 2018).

38 Mikah K. Thompson, *Just Another Fast Girl: Exploring Slavery's Continued Impact on the Loss of Black Girlhood*, 44 HARV. J.L. & GENDER 57, 72 (2021).

lazy,[39] immoral,[40] and violent,[41] among other negative traits.[42] Indeed, "[w]hen slavery first began in the American colonies, its proponents explained that God had created different 'types of mankind' and that Black people were 'cursed by God.'"[43] To justify slavery, Black people were portrayed as "deserving of enslavement, and White slave owners as advancing God's plan."[44] These lies have been and continue to be used to justify our subjugation. But they are lies. And if race is character evidence, then race, at least the American concept of race, is a lie. And we should not allow a lie to dictate who is able to reap value and who should be required to pay penalties.

Professor Ian Haney Lopez, a Critical Race Theorist, has written about the "confounding problem" of defining race. In "The Social Construction of Race: Some Observations on Illusion, Fabrication, and Choice," Professor Lopez observed that:

> critical race theorists, those legal scholars whose work seems most closely bound together by their emphasis on the centrality of race, follow the same approach when they powerfully decry the permanence of racism and persuasively argue for race consciousness, yet do so without explicitly suggesting what race might be. Race may be America's single most confounding problem, but the confounding problem of race is that few people seem to know what race is.[45]

He goes on to describe race as a social construct but acknowledges that many people of color will be uncomfortable with that description.[46] His anticipation of resistance calls to mind some of the intense resistance from Black students to the idea of race as a social construct during a discussion in my Major Race Trials course. For people of color in American society, race is real. It is also a way that we identify with each other, form community with shared culture, and organize our resistance to white supremacy. But the positive actions that we have taken to make sense of race in this country distract us from the socially constructed nature of race. Analyzing race as character evidence, almost invariably based on and "proved" through hearsay, can add to Critical Race Theory's approach to the "confounding problem" of defining

[39] *See* Andrea Freeman, *You Better Work*, 53 U.C. Davis L. Rev. 1531, 1556 ("The trope that Blacks were naturally lazy and therefore needed Whites to force them to be productive supported White brutality and alleviated White guilt. It continues to serve that purpose today for some scholars who argue that Blacks were 'better off' as slaves than they would have been as free people, because slave owners provided them with food and shelter.").

[40] Praatika Prasad, *Implicit Biases in Prosecutorial Summations: Proposing an Integrated Response*, 86 Fordham L. Rev. 3091, 3097 (2018).

[41] *See* William W. Fisher, III, *Ideology and Imagery in the Law of Slavery*, 68 Chi.-Kent. L. Rev. 1051, 1057–64 (1993).

[42] *Id.*

[43] Prasad, *supra* note 40, at 3096.

[44] *Id.*

[45] Ian Haney Lopez, *The Social Construction of Race: Some Observations on Illusion, Fabrication, and Choice*, 29 Harv. C.R.-C.L. L. Rev. 1, 5–6 (1994).

[46] *Id.* at 9.

race and perhaps ease some of the discomfort among people of color who resist the idea of race as a social construct.

THE INTERPLAY BETWEEN RACE AS CHARACTER EVIDENCE AND HEARSAY PRINCIPLES: WHO TOLD YOU THAT YOU WERE BLACK?

Race quite possibly may best be understood as hearsay, and in the final part of this chapter, I analyze it as such. I understand that race is not unique in being subject to a hearsay analysis, as it is not unique in being subject to the tax and property metaphors. Almost any idea can potentially be hearsay as almost anything can potentially be property or taxed. My goal in analyzing race as hearsay is to offer another way of looking at race that will be useful in the Critical Race Theory discourse.

In evidence parlance, hearsay is an out-of-court statement offered to prove the truth of the matter asserted.[47] In other words, hearsay is a statement other than one made by the declarant while testifying at trial, that is now being offered to prove the truth of what that declarant said.[48] The concern with hearsay is not that it is irrelevant, as there are many out-of-court statements that meet the general relevance standard of the rules of evidence.[49] The problem with hearsay, is a problem of reliability.[50] We are concerned that what is being repeated in court is not as reliable as it would have been had the declarant made the statement in real time before the fact finder and in open court. And the problem with this form of testimony, i.e., the repetition of what someone else said, even with the person repeating the statement, is that we are unable to test the underlying statement by the declarant because the statement was said outside of court.

One of the central problems with hearsay is that we are unable to test the perception of the declarant.[51] If, for example, the declarant stated that he saw a driver (now the defendant in a civil suit) run a red light, how do we know that the declarant did not misperceive what happened? Was there anything obstructing the declarant's view? How sure is the declarant that it was actually the defendant who was driving? How far away from the intersection at issue was the declarant? Was the declarant a driver or passenger in a vehicle, or was the declarant a pedestrian? Does the declarant have any vision impairments that require medical correction, such as glasses or contacts? If so, was the declarant wearing his glasses or contacts at the time that he supposedly saw the driver/defendant run the red light? How is the declarant's

47 *See* FED. R. EVID. 801.
48 *Id.*
49 James McDonald Moorehead, *Compromising the Hearsay Rule: The Fallacy of Res Gestae Reliability*, 29 LOY. L.A. L. REV. 203 (1995) (noting that the "hearsay rule and its exceptions exist in order to add a measure of reliability to adjudicative decisionmaking").
50 *Id.*
51 Laurence Tribe, *Triangulating Hearsay*, 87 HARV. L. REV. 957, 959–61 (1974).

memory? Does the declarant have a grudge against the defendant, or owe a favor to the plaintiff? In short, is the declarant sincere or might he have his own agenda? We cannot answer any of these questions without the declarant.[52] We cannot contemporaneously challenge or test the declarant on inconsistencies, contradictions, or the potential for biases in motivating her to speak.

The hearsay doctrine can help us further address a fundamental question: What is race? More specifically, I believe that hearsay doctrine can assist in further debunking the very idea of race. Applying the principles from hearsay doctrine (substituting the traditional courtroom for the contemporaneous court of public opinion, or the daily trials people of color endure), we can see that race presents to us a classic hearsay issue.

At its most basic, race raises the problem of perception. How does one really know if someone is Black? Homer Plessy, the plaintiff in the infamous Supreme Court case, *Plessy v. Ferguson*,[53] and countless others with similar appearances present a challenge to the perception of the amorphous and elusive declarant who established what it means to look Black in American society. Plessy was said to be an "octoroon" seven-eighths white and one-eighth Black. No doubt many would and did perceive him to be white. Yet, he was considered Black. Because of the hearsay nature of race, and the categorization of Blackness in particular, we are unable to challenge or test the perception of the declarant who established that the Plessys of this country are indeed Black. But it mattered for Plessy and others like him – because it determined his status in society. And so it does today.

And that also raises the question of sincerity. Recall that a significant concern with the hearsay doctrine is the sincerity of the declarant. And that concern is present whether the declarant is a person, or a country, or a law. The admittedly elusive and amorphous declarant in American society that established the racial categories and the characteristics of each must be questioned for sincerity. We cannot do that – the opportunity for such contemporaneous questioning has been lost. But we can consider the historical development of the idea of race in this country. It was intimately tied with the institution of slavery. And the institution of slavery was fundamentally important to the American economy and way of life. To state it quite simply, the creation and articulation of racial categories – "let there be race!" – was anything but neutral and objective. The declaration that there are races is necessarily entangled with the fact that America was built on the backs of slaves.

The determination of who actually was a slave was based on a determination of who was Black, and who was not. So, if a system of categorization has such implications as the determination of who would provide free labor to facilitate the economic development and growth of a nation – think of the one-drop rule – how then could we ever trust those determinations? Would not such a system have a vested interest in placing as many people as possible in captivity and lifetime bondage?

[52] *Id.*

[53] Plessy v. Ferguson, 163 U.S. 537 (1896).

This explains why the law bent over backward to create racial categories and to categorize Black persons as slaves. A person's very appearance created a *presumption* of enslaved status. It explains too why the law broke with the English common law's tradition of determining a child's status on the basis of that of the father: to facilitate the use of Black women as suppliers of the slave market, the law elected to deem a child born to a Black woman and a white master a slave.[54] Given this backdrop, how could we ever trust the sincerity of such a system to create racial categories, and then to determine who should be put into each category?[55]

Looking to hearsay doctrine helps to further establish the great lie of slavery – that there really is a definitive Black race. Slavery racialized people for economic gain. The hearsay nature of race is backed by the social construction theory of race. "There are no genetic characteristics possessed by all Blacks but not by non-Blacks; similarly, there is no gene or cluster of genes common to all Whites but not to non-Whites."[56] Indeed, "[t]he rejection of race in science is almost complete."[57] Race is socially constructed. Race is evidence that is the product of a social construction. And race is hearsay.

If someone is categorized as Black – or white, or Asian, or Hispanic, or anything else – that categorization is an assertion. The problem is that the person who is doing the categorizing is doing so on the basis of statements heard elsewhere – or second-hand knowledge, which is basically what hearsay is.[58] As one scholar has noted, "[i]n everyday conversation, we might refer to hearsay as "second hand information."[59] It is the type of information that is unreliable – and unreliability is the problem that the hearsay rule aims to address. To be more precise, the categorization of a person as Black, or white, or something else rests not just on hearsay, but on multiple layers of hearsay – statements upon statements passed down through the historicity of the American experience, which was conceived on the basis of a racial caste system that enslaved people based on their category.

As scholars and students of evidence law know, however, identifying a statement as hearsay is just the first step to dealing with the hearsay problem. Our hearsay ban in evidence law is rife with exceptions,[60] based either on the so-called reliability of the statement despite its hearsay nature, the necessity of the statement, or both reliability and necessity.[61] I will leave for future work a deeper exploration of race as hearsay

54 *Id.* at 556.

55 As one commentator has noted, "[s]lavery helped change the significance of race, 'investing pigment – both white and black – with a far greater weight in defining status than heretofore.'" *Id.*

56 Lopez, *supra* note 45, at 11.

57 *Id.*

58 *See* Moorehead, *supra* note 49, at 204.

59 *Id.*

60 *See, e.g.*, Fed. R. Evid 803, 804, and 807.

61 George Fisher, Evidence 430 (4th ed., Foundation Press 2023) ("Most of the exceptions to the hearsay rule reflect two values: necessity and trustworthiness. There is said to be some special *need* for the hearsay evidence or some special reason to deem it more *reliable* than run-of-the-mill hearsay – or both." (emphasis added)).

as well as a fuller development of my evidentiary theory of race. I will end here by suggesting that those of us who understand that race is real and have organized our communities and our resistance around race are doing so out of necessity. We did not create the racial caste system, but we must operate within it and find community within it. And in that sense, and under these circumstances – to organize for community and resistance – we can utilize and give credence to race though it is socially constructed and though it is hearsay. It is not acceptable or *exceptable* to use race as character evidence. But as scholars and students of evidence law also know, evidence can be admissible for one purpose and inadmissible for another.[62]

[62] *See* Fed. R. Evid. 105 ("If the court admits evidence that is admissible against a party or for a purpose – but not against another party or for another purpose – the court, on timely request, must restrict the evidence to its proper scope and instruct the jury accordingly.").

Suggested Readings

In addition to the chapters (plus their rich footnotes) and the excerpted articles in this book, we offer this list of further readings, including recommended readings from our contributing authors. We look forward to expanding this list as readers engage with the book and its ideas.

PART I: INTRODUCTION TO THE FIELD AND ITS ACTORS

Section 1: The Rulemakers

Bernstein, Anya and Julia Simon-Kerr, *Keeping Evidence Real*, 111 IOWA L. REV. 589 (2026).

Chutkow, Dawn M. and Michael Heise, *The Rulemakers: An Empirical Analysis of Chief Justice Appointments to the Judicial Conference Rules Committee*, 74 CASE W. RSRV. L. REV. 99 (2024).

Coleman, Brooke D., *#SoWhiteMale: Federal Procedural Rulemaking Committees*, 68 UCLA L. REV. 370 (2020).

Rice, Paul R., *Advisory Committee on the Federal Rules of Evidence: Tending to the Past and Pretending for the Future?*, 53 HASTINGS L.J. 817 (2002).

Section 2: And Jurors

Griffin, Lisa Kern, *Narrative, Truth, and Trial*, 101 GEO. L.J. 281 (2013).

Harawa, Daniel, *The False Promise of Peña-Rodriguez*, 109 CALIF. L. REV. 2121 (2021).

Schauer, Frederick, *On the Supposed Jury-Dependence of Evidence Law*, 155 U. PA. L. REV. 165 (2006).

PART II: THE RULES

Section 1: Relevance and Prejudice

Armour, Jody D., *Race Ipsa Loquitur: Of Reasonable Racists, Intelligent Bayesians, and Involuntary Negrophobes*, 46 STAN. L. REV. 781 (1994).

Brown, Teneille R., *Shifting the Male Gaze of Evidence*, 76 VAND. L. REV. 1903 (2023).

Budzinski, Andrew C., *Overhauling Rules of Evidence in Pro Se Courts*, 56 U. RICH. L. REV. 1075 (2022).
Hunter, Rosemary C., *Gender in Evidence: Masculine Norms vs. Feminist Reforms*, 19 HARV. WOMEN'S L.J. 127 (1996).
Johnson, Sheri L., *Racial Imagery in Criminal Cases*, 67 TUL. L. REV. 1739 (1993).
Kinports, Kit, *Evidence Engendered*, 1991 U. ILL. L. REV. 413.
Quinn, Mae, *Childist Objections, Youthful Relevance, and Evidence Reconceived*, 127 DICK. L. REV. 535 (2023).
Rubinson, Robert, *A Theory of Access to Justice*, 29 J. LEGAL PROF. 89 (2005).
Simon-Kerr, Julia, *Relevance Through a Feminist Lens*, *in* PHILOSOPHICAL FOUNDATIONS OF EVIDENCE LAW (Christian Dahlman, Alex Stein, and Giovanni Tuzet, eds. Oxford University Press 2021).
Taslitz, Andrew E., *What Feminism Has to Offer Evidence Law*, 28 SW. U. L. REV. 171 (1999).
Thompson, Mikah, *Methinks the Lady Doth Protest Too Little: Reassessing the Probative Value of Silence*, 47 U. LOUISVILLE L. REV. 21 (2008).
Walker, L. Alexander III, *Black English for Lawyers: A Primer*, 113 CALIF. L. REV. 81 (2025).

Section 2: Character Evidence

Blinka, Daniel D., *Character, Liberalism, and the Protean Culture of Evidence Law*, 37 SEATTLE U. L. REV. 87 (2013).
Brown, Teneille R., *The Content of Our Character*, 126 PENN ST. L. REV. 1 (2021).
DENNIS, ANDREA ET AL., RAP ON TRIAL: RACE, LYRICS, AND GUILT IN AMERICA (The New Press 2019).
Gonzales Rose, Jasmine B., *Racial Character Evidence in Police Killing Cases*, 2018 WIS. L. REV. 369 (2018).
Hillman, Elizabeth Lutes, *The "Good Soldier" Defense: Character Evidence and Military Rank at Courts-Martial*, 108 YALE L.J. 879 (1999).
Levinson, Laurie L., *Courtroom Demeanor: The Theater of the Courtroom*, 92 MINN. L. REV. 573 (2008).
Stone, James, *Past-Acts Evidence in Excessive Force Litigation*, 100 WASH. U.L. REV. 569 (2022).

Section 3: Credibility

Bellin, Jeffrey, *Eliminating Rule 609 to Provide a Fair Opportunity to Defend Against Criminal Charges: A Proposal to the Advisory Committee on the Federal Rules of Evidence*, 92 FORDHAM L. REV. 2471 (2024).
Capers, I. Bennett, *The Unintentional Rapist*, 87 WASH. U. L. REV. 1345 (2010).
Carlin, Amanda, *The Courtroom as White Space: Racial Performance as Noncredibility*, 63 UCLA L. REV. 450 (2016).
Eisenberg, Theodore and Valerie P. Hans, *Taking a Stand on Taking the Stand: The Effect of a Prior Criminal Record on the Decision to Testify and on Trial Outcomes*, 94 CORNELL L. REV. 1353 (2009).
Roberts, Anna, *Conviction by Prior Impeachment*, 96 B.U. L. REV. 1977 (2016).
Roberts, Anna, *Reclaiming the Importance of the Defendant's Testimony: Prior Conviction Impeachment and the Fight Against Implicit Stereotyping*, 83 U. CHI L. REV. 835 (2016).
Roberts, Anna, *Impeachment by Unreliable Conviction*, 55 B.C. L. REV. 563 (2014).

Rosario-Lebrón, Anibal, *A Wee Bit Racist: What Are the Rules of Evidence, Alex?*, 7 LSU L.J. Soc. Pol'y 7 (2022).
Simon-Kerr, Julia, *Credibility in an Age of Algorithms*, 74 Rutgers L. Rev. 111 (2021).
Simon-Kerr, Julia, *Credibility by Proxy*, 85 G.W. L. Rev. 152 (2017).

Section 4: Sex Trials

Baker, Katharine K., *Once a Rapist? Motivational Evidence and Relevancy in Rape Law*, 110 Harv. L. Rev. 563 (1997).
Bienen, Leigh, *A Question of Credibility: John Henry Wigmore's Use of Scientific Authority in Section 924a of the Treatise on Evidence*, 19 Cal. West. L. Rev. 235 (1983).
Gruber, Aya, The Feminist War on Crime: The Unexpected Role of Women's Liberation in Mass Incarceration (University of California Press 2020).
Lave, Tamara Rice and Aviva Orenstein, *Empirical Fallacies of Evidence Law: A Critical Look at the Admission of Prior Sex Crimes*, 81 U. Cin. L. Rev. 795 (2013).
Orenstein, Aviva, *Deviance, Due Process, and the False Promise of Federal Rule of Evidence, 403*, 90 Cornell L. Rev. 1487 (2005).
Scheppele, Kim Lane, *Just the Facts, Ma'am: Sexualized Violence, Evidentiary Habits, and the Revision of Truth*, 37 N.Y.L. Sch. L. Rev. 123 (1992).

Section 5: Hearsay and Confrontation

Griffin, Lisa Kern, *False Accuracy in Criminal Trials: The Limits and Costs of Cross-Examination*, 102 Tex. L. Rev. 1011 (2024).
Scheppele, Kim Lane, *The Ground-Zero Theory of Evidence*, 49 Hastings L.J. 321 (1998).

Section 6: Experts

Blum, Binyamin, *Silent Witnesses: The Material Turn in Forensic Sciences*, 7 Law, Soc'y, and Culture (2024).
Capers, I. Bennett, *Race, Gatekeeping, Magical Words, and the Rules of Evidence*, 76 Vand. L. Rev. 1855 (2023).
Giannelli, Paul C., *The Supreme Court's "Criminal"* Daubert *Cases*, 33 Seton Hall L. Rev. 1071 (2003).
Gonzales Rose, Jasmine B., Asees Bhasin, and Spencer Piston, *Antiracist Expert Evidence*, 134 Yale L.J. 2249 (2025).
Jayadev, Raj, Protect Your People (New Press 2024).
Lau, Christopher, *Shadow Forensics: Uncovering 911 Call Analysis*, 111 Cornell L. Rev. __ (forthcoming 2026).
Lvovsky, Anna, *Rethinking Police Expertise*, 131 Yale L.J. 370 (2021).
Obasogie, Osagie K., *Excited Delirium, Policing, and the Law of Evidence*, 138 Harv. L. Rev. 1497 (2025).
Seaman, Julie A., *A Tale of Two* Dauberts, 47 Ga. L. Rev. 889 (2013).
Simonson, Jocelyn, *Abolition, Expertise, and the Law*, 105 B.U. L. Rev. 1175 (2025).
Sinha, Maneka, *The Entrenched Carceralism of Forensics*, Inquest (July 26, 2021), https://inquest.org/entrenched-carceralism-of-forensics/.
Smith, Deidre M., *The Disordered and Discredited Plaintiff: Psychiatric Evidence in Civil Litigation*, 31 Cardozo L. Rev. 749 (2009).

Section 7: Privileges

Lininger, Tom, *Abortion, the Underground Railroad, and Evidentiary Privilege*, 80 WASH. & LEE L. REV. 663 (2023).
Ross, Catherine J., *Implementing Constitutional Rights for Juveniles: The Parent-Child Privilege in Context*, 14 STAN. L. & POL'Y REV. 85 (2003).
Smith, Deidre M., *An Uncertain Privilege: Implied Waiver and the Evisceration of the Psychotherapist-Patient Privilege in the Federal Courts*, 58 DEPAUL L. REV. 79 (2008).

PART III: EXPANDING EVIDENCE

Section 1: Decarceration and Abolition

Collins, Erin, *Evidence Rules for Decarceration*, 50 FORDHAM URB. L.J. 353 (2023).
KABA, MARIAME, WE DO THIS 'TIL WE FREE US: ABOLITIONIST ORGANIZING AND TRANSFORMING JUSTICE (Tamara K. Nopper ed., Haymarket 2021).
Sinha, Maneka, *Radically Reimagining Forensic Evidence*, 73 ALA. L. REV. 879 (2022).

Section 2: And Beyond

ADLER, LIBBY, GAY PRIORI: A QUEER CRITICAL LEGAL STUDIES APPROACH TO LAW REFORM (Duke University Press 2018).
Crenshaw, Kimberlé, *Demarginalizing the Intersection of Race and Sex*, 1989 U. CHI. LEGAL F. 139.
Harris, Jasmine E., *The Aesthetics of Disability*, 119 COLUM. L. REV. 895 (2019).
Lopez, Rachel, *Participatory Law Scholarship*, 123 COLUM. L. REV. 6 (2023).
Macleod, James A., *Evidence Law's Blind Spots*, 109 IOWA L. REV. 189 (2023).
Meyn, Ion, *The Creation of Separate and Unequal Courtrooms*, 63 ARIZ. L. REV. 1 (2021).
Nicolson, Donald, *Truth, Reason and Justice: Epistemology and Politics in Evidence Discourse*, 57 MOD. L. REV. 726 (1994).
Orenstein, Aviva, *The Religion of Evidence*, 25 J.L. & SOC'Y 181 (2025).

For EU product safety concerns, contact us at Calle de José Abascal, 56–1°,
28003 Madrid, Spain or eugpsr@cambridge.org.

www.ingramcontent.com/pod-product-compliance
Ingram Content Group UK Ltd.
Pitfield, Milton Keynes, MK11 3LW, UK
UKHW051048151026
476588UK00021B/50

* 9 7 8 1 0 0 9 8 5 1 5 5 8 *